Veranstalter *Organizer*
Industrie Forum Design Hannover, Messegelände, D-30521 Hannover

Vorstand *Board*
Ernst Raue, Prof. Herbert Lindinger, Erich Schaaf, Herbert H. Schultes, Rudolf Stilcken

Geschäftsführer *Managing Director*
Ralph Wiegmann

VORSTAND iF BOARD iF:
Ernst Raue, Hannover (1. Vorsitzender Chairman)
Prof. Herbert Lindinger, Hannover, Erich Schaaf, Lemgo,
Herbert H. Schultes, München, Rudolf Stilcken, Hamburg

GESCHÄFTSFÜHRUNG MANAGING DIRECTOR:
Ralph Wiegmann Hannover

ORDENTLICHE MITGLIEDER FULL MEMBERS:
Knut Bliesener, Hannover, Sepp D. Heckmann, Hannover, Prof. Dr. Stefan Lengyel, Essen
Alexander Neumeister, München, Carl-August Sautier, Bad Münder
Dr. Martin Riemer-Streicher, Hannover, Prof. Volker Weinert, Braunschweig.

EHRENMITGLIEDER HONORARY MEMBERS:
Ernst Josef Auer, Überlingen, Fritz Hahne, Hannover, Karl-Heinz Krug, Leverkusen
Edwin A. Schricker, Rodach, German A. Voment, Hirschbach

FÖRDERNDE MITGLIEDER INLAND GERMAN ASSOCIATE MEMBERS:

AEG Aktiengesellschaft, Frankfurt/Main.
Aesculap AG, Tuttlingen.
Jürgen Aha, Frankfurt/Main.
Artemide GmbH, Hilden.
Bang & Olufsen Deutschland, GmbH, Gilching bei München.
BAUFA Werke GmbH, Menden.
Baumüller Nürnberg GmbH, Nürnberg
BEGA Gantenbrink-Leuchten, oHG, Menden.
Benzing Zeit+Daten GmbH, Villingen-Schwenningen.
Bizerba-Werke, GmbH & Co.KG, Balingen.
Braun AG, Kronberg, Taunus.
Crecon Design Consulting, Crown Gabelstapler GmbH, München.

design praxis diener, Ulm.
DLW Büroeinrichtungen GmbH, Röder, Frankfurt/Main.
Drabert GmbH, Minden, Westfalen.
DZ Licht GmbH & Co.KG, Menden.
EBA Maschinenfabrik, Adolf Ehinger GmbH, Balingen.
design studio hartmut s. engel, Freiberg, Neckar.
erfi, Ernst Fischer GmbH & Co., Freudenstadt.
Geha-Werke GmbH, Hannover
GIRA Giersiepen GmbH & Co., KG, Radevormwald.
Druckerei Josef Grütter, GmbH & Co.KG, Ronnenberg, Empelde.
Grundig AG, Fürth.
Heidelberger Druckmaschinen AG, Heidelberg.

helit Innovative Büroprodukte GmbH, Kierspe.
IBM Deutschland GmbH, Stuttgart.
Köttermann GmbH & Co., Uetze-Hänigsen.
LOEWE-OPTA GmbH, Kronach
Mensch & Büro Verlags GmbH, Baden-Baden.
Pressebüro Hans H. Mertens, Hannover.
Meyer-Hayoz Design Engineering GmbH, Konstanz.
OCTANORM Vertriebs GmbH, Filderstadt.
Odenwälder Kunststoffwerke GmbH & Co.KG Buchen/Odw.
Philips GmbH, Consumer Electronics, Hamburg.
Rowenta Werke GmbH, Offenbach/Main.

Sartorius Werke GmbH, Göttingen.
Georg Schlegel GmbH & Co., Dürmentingen.
Siemens AG, München.
Staff GmbH & Co.KG, Lemgo.
Rudolf Stilcken & Partner, Hamburg.
Tandem Computers GmbH, Frankfurt/Main.
Viessmann Werke GmbH & Co., Allendorf, Eder.
Vorwerk & Co. Teppichwerke KG, Hameln.
VSF-Arch. Völker-Schwedux-Filipschack, Hannover.
C.A. Weidmüller GmbH & Co., Detmold.
WILA Leuchten GmbH, Iserlohn
Wilkhahn GmbH & Co., Bad Münder.

FÖRDERNDE MITGLIEDER AUSLAND ASSOCIATE MEMBERS FROM OUTSIDE GERMANY:

Ascom Holding AG
Bern, Schweiz.

Grass AG
Höchst, Österreich.

Philips
Corporate Industrial Design
Eindhoven, Niederlande.

Zumtobel AG
Dornbirn, Österreich.

iF Jahrbuch 1996

IMPRESSUM *IMPRINT*

Herausgeber/Editor:
Industrie Forum Design Hannover
Messegelände, D-30521 Hannover
Phone +49-511-8932400, Fax +49-511-8932401

Konzept, Redaktion, Gesamtmanagement/Concept, Editorial work:
Ringe International Design Promotion
Brun Ringe
Bodenstedtstraße 12, D-30173 Hannover
Phone +49-511 8093287, Fax +49-511 809389

Gesamtherstellung und Verleger des Katalogs/
Overall production and publisher of the catalogue:
bangert verlag, München/Schopfheim
Art Direction:
grafikdesign margot bangert, Schopfheim
Koordination Katalog/Catalogue Coordination:
Barbara Lange, bangert verlag
PrePress consulting:
Jörg Drees, Nordenham

Texte/Editorial Top Ten:
Klaus Thomas Edelmann, Hamburg/Frankfurt (exkl. BMW)
Lektorat der englischen Texte/Editing of English texts:
Jeremy Gaines, Frankfurt
Lektorat der deutschen Texte/Editing of German texts:
Klaus Binder-Poensgen, Textkontor, Frankfurt
Recherchen/Research:
Sabine Foraita, Braunschweig
Datenmanagement/Data management:
Alexander Strebel, econnect, München
Fotos/Photos:
Herstellerfotos, Manufacturers material
Dokumentation/Documentation:
Erhard Heidenreich, Hannover
Thomas Deutschmann Fotodesign, Hannover

iF-Logo: Mendell & Oberer, München

Gedruckt auf/Printed on: MEDIAPRINT SEIDENMATT
Stora Papyrus Deutschland GmbH,
100% chlorfrei gebleichter Zellstoff/
100% chlorine-free, bleached pulp

Stora Papyrus Deutschland GmbH,
Feldmühlplatz 1 D-40545 Düsseldorf, Germany

Keine Haftung für die Vollständigkeit und Richtigkeit der Angaben
No liability for the completeness and correctness of entries

ISBN 3-925560-53-X

Printed and bound in Italy by Printer Trento s.r.l.

INHALT CONTENTS

- 6 EINLEITUNG *INTRODUCTION*
- 16 10 BESTE DES JAHRES *TOP TEN OF THE YEAR*
- 56 BÜRO *OFFICE*
- 140 WOHNUNG *HOME*
- 170 HAUSHALT *HOUSEHOLD*
- 298 BELEUCHTUNG *LIGHTING*
- 232 HAUSTECHNIK *HOUSE TECHNOLOGY*
- 256 FREIZEIT *LEISURE*
- 304 INDUSTRIE *INDUSTRY*
- 362 TRANSPORT+VERKEHR *TRANSPORTATION*
- 386 MEDIZIN *MEDICAL*
- 410 INTERFACE
- 422 JUROREN *JURORS*
- 428 HERSTELLER INDEX *INDEX OF MANUFACTURERS*
- 440 DESIGNER INDEX *INDEX OF DESIGNERS*

GRUSSWORT

Der Wandel bestimmt das Handeln. Wer heute weltweit mitreden will, muß sich dieser Herausforderung stellen und ganz vorn an zukunftsträchtigen Innovationen arbeiten. Zwischen den großen Wirtschaftsblöcken findet ein andauerndes Wettrennen um technologische Führerschaft statt. Wirtschaftskraft ist gefordert, um in diesem Wettrennen einen ertragreichen Platz zu bekommen. Es ist ein Kopf-an-Kopf-Rennen, und wenn ein Unternehmen oder gar eine ganze Region zu spät kommt, sind die Marktanteile schon verteilt.

Mit den heute zur Verfügung stehenden Maschinen ist nahezu an jedem Ort der Welt ein vergleichbares Produkt zu erzeugen. Bei unterschiedlichen Lohnkostenstrukturen hat das zur Folge, daß qualitativ vergleichbare Produkte zu unterschiedlichen Preisen angeboten werden können. Das geht natürlich für die alten Industrienationen schlecht aus. Rationalisierung und Verschlankung sind unsere Antworten. Wenn aber beispielsweise die »Tigerstaaten« ebenso reagieren werden, geht die Spirale von vorn los. Also der Wandel bleibt uns erhalten. Wer glaubt, nur Großunternehmen sind diesem Wettbewerb ausgesetzt, der irrt. Der internationale Wettbewerb trifft schon längst den Mittelstand voll. Denn seine Produkte können ebenfalls überall in der Welt hergestellt werden, wie das Beispiel Textilindustrie zeigt.

Ich will kein düsteres Szenario zeichnen, aber die Globalisierung der Wirtschaft führt zu rasanten Veränderungen. Sie haben große Auswirkungen auf Deutschland und Europa. Technische Innovationen und Strukturveränderungen sind Antworten. Es gibt aber mehr, auf das wir uns besinnen können, z. B. unsere Kultur, unser Wissen über Menschen und Märkte.

Ich wundere mich, daß in einem derart harten Wettbewerb nur wenige Unternehmen mit Design-Management und Design-Produkten an den Markt gehen. Man spricht von weniger als 15 % der Unternehmen, die in Deutschland diese Chancen nutzen. Dabei hat Design als Produkteigenschaft unbestreitbare Vorteile: Profilierung, geringere Bedeutung von Preiskämpfen und klarere Zielgruppenansprache sind einige Stichworte, die die Vorteile am Markt beschreiben. Darüber hinaus ist eine Designorientierung gegenüber anderen Profilierungsstrategien relativ risikolos, vor allem, wenn man technologische Führerschaft und Designführerschaft vergleicht. Design ist also nicht nur ein zusätzlicher Wettbewerbsvorteil, sondern möglicherweise der entscheidende Wettbewerbsvorteil.

Die meisten großen Unternehmen haben schon längst Designstrategien entwickelt und in ihre Organisation integriert. Ebenso gibt es ein festes und erfolgreiches designorientiertes Klientel mittelständischer Unternehmen. Mich würde es freuen, wenn noch mehr Unternehmen die Chance Design für sich prüfen und nutzen. In Deutschland gibt es ein hochwertiges Potential an Ausbildung und Dienstleistungen, das dieses im Grunde leicht macht.

Richtig ist, daß man Design nicht einfach auf Produkte kleben kann. Es ist mehr. Es fängt bei der Idee an und ist nicht nur etwas für Schöngeister. Wenn man bedenkt, daß große Unternehmen in ihrem F- und E-Budget einen festen Prozentsatz für Designleistungen einplanen, wird deutlich, daß Design sehr viel mit Technologie zu tun hat. Lange vor dem Prototyp wird gestritten über Produzierbarkeit und Kosten auf der einen Seite sowie Kundennutzen, Servicefreundlichkeit und Ökologie auf der anderen Seite. Wenn man so arbeitet, kommen bessere Produkte heraus. Sie sind eben nicht vergleichbar. Wichtig ist, daß diese Produkte vom Kunden identifiziert werden können. Damit eröffnen sich für Unternehmen völlig neue Marktchancen.

Die Veränderung der Gesellschaft zu einer sehr pluralistischen, zumindest was die Lebensstile betrifft, ist eine exzellente Voraussetzung, um gerade für mittelständische Unternehmen Marktsegmente gezielt mit designorientierten Produkten für sich zu gewinnen.

Die Herausforderung ist da!

Bester Beleg dafür, wie man sie annehmen kann, sind die Ergebnisse der Designwettbewerbe beim Industrie Forum Design Hannover. Hier werden Erfolgsbeispiele ausgezeichnet. Zurecht nutzen diese Produkte ihre Auszeichnung für ihre eigene Vermarktung. Gleichzeitig sind sie beispielgebend. Sie regen Unternehmen und Designer an, sich dem Wettbewerb zu stellen. Tausende von Entscheidern der Industrie aus aller Welt nehmen während der internationalen Messen in Hannover die Gelegenheit wahr, die Ausstellung der Wettbewerbssieger im Industrie Forum Design zu besuchen. Die Verbindung von Business und Design macht die Ausstellung zu einem Multiplikator und Botschafter der Idee. Das dazugehörende Jahrbuch für Industrie Design ist Dokumentation, Lehrbuch und ein Stück Industriekultur. Ich wünsche dem Jahrbuch für Industrie Design 1996 eine große und aufmerksame Leserschaft.

Hannover,
im März 1996
Gerhard Schröder
Ministerpräsident
des Landes Niedersachsen

PREFACE

It is change which prompts action. Today, anyone who wants to have a say on the international scene must face up to this challenge and work up front on innovations geared to the future. The large economic blocs are constantly racing to take the lead in technology. Countries require economic muscle in order to secure a place among the winners. It is a neck-and-neck race and if a company, not to mention an entire region, should come too late, then they will find that the market has already been divided up.

Thanks to the modern machinery available today, it is now possible to manufacture a comparable product virtually anywhere in the world. In view of the different wage and cost structures, this means that products of comparable quality can be made available on the market at different prices. The old industrialized nations certainly have a difficult time holding their own in this situation. Rationalization and lean production are our answers. But if the »Tigers«, for example, decide to fight fire with fire, then the whole spiral will start again from the beginning. The only thing we can count on remaining the same is change itself. Anyone who believes that only large corporations are subject to competition is sadly mistaken. Competition on an international scale has already taken medium-sized businesses by storm. The products manufactured by these businesses can also be manufactured anywhere in the world, as the textile industry has clearly illustrated. I do not want to paint a bleak picture, but the globalization of industry is leading to rapid changes and they are having a significant impact on Germany and all of Europe. Technological innovations and structural changes are the answers here. But there is more for us to remember, things such as our culture and our knowledge of humans and the markets.

I am surprised that, in the face of such stiff competition, only few companies approach their markets using design management and design products. It has been estimated that less than 15 percent of all companies in Germany take advantage of this opportunity, even though design has indisputable advantages as a product characteristic: a distinctive image, unmistakable form, decreasing importance of price wars and direct appeal to the target group are but a few of these market advantages. In addition to this, an orientation towards design harbors considerably less risk than other image strategies, particularly if technological leadership and design leadership are compared with one another. Design is not merely just another competitive advantage, it could be the decisive one.

Most large companies developed design strategies and integrated them into their organizations long ago. But there is also a firmly-based, successful design-oriented clientele in the medium-sized business sector. I would be pleased to see even more companies exploring and tapping the advantages of design. In Germany, there is a high-quality potential of training and services available to facilitate these effects.

It is true that it is not possible to merely stick design onto products. Design involves more than that. It starts out with the idea and it is not limited to an intellectual elite. Considering the fact that large companies set aside a fixed percentage of their R&D budgets for design services, it becomes clear that design has a great deal to do with technology. Long before the prototype is created, discussions focus on potential production problems and costs on the one hand, as well as customer benefits, serviceability and the effects on the environment on the other. Working according to this method, it is possible to create completely different products. They simply cannot be compared with one another. It is important that the customer is able to identify these products, possibly creating entirely new market opportunities for the companies.

The gradual transition of our society into a highly pluralistic society, at least as far as lifestyles are concerned, is an excellent prerequisite, especially for medium-sized businesses. For it makes it possible for them to secure specific market segments for themselves by producing design-oriented products.

The challenge is there! The best example of how to deal with it are the winners of the design competition at Industrieforum Design in Hannover. Prizes have been awarded to the successful entries. And the winning products are proud to be able to use their awards in their own marketing campaigns. At the same time, they serve as model examples. They encourage both companies and creative spirits to take up the challenge. Thousands of decision-makers in industry from all four corners of the globe avail themselves of the opportunity to visit the exhibition of the winning entries in the Industrie Forum Design competition during their visits to the international trade fairs in Hanover. The combination of business and design makes this exhibition a multiplier and an ambassador for the idea of design. The accompanying Yearbook for Industrial Design is documentation, textbook and a piece of industrial culture. I wish the Hanover Yearbook for Industrial Design 1996 a large and attentive audience of readers.

Hannover, March 1996
Gerhard Schröder
Minister President
of Lower Saxony

GRUSSWORT *PREFACE*

Unternehmerischer Erfolg wird neben technischem Know-how und dem betriebswirtschaftlichen Können heute auch wesentlich von der Design-Kultur des Unternehmens geprägt. Der Stellenwert des Designs wächst in der Öffentlichkeit und wird damit zu einem wichtigen Faktor der Vermarktung. Aber was in der breiten Öffentlichkeit bekannt ist, zielt im wesentlichen auf Produkte, die im häuslichen Bereich Anwendung finden. Daß Maschinen, Komponenten ebenso von Designern benutzerfreundlich wie auch ergonomisch gestaltet werden können, zeigt das Industrie Forum Design Hannover. Während der Messe haben die Besucher aus aller Welt die Möglichkeit, den aktuellen Stand des Industrie-Designs kennenzulernen. Daß es sich hierbei um das Beste vom Besten handelt, dafür garantiert eine fachkundige Jury, die die Einsendung zum iF-Design-Wettbewerb beurteilt und auswählt.

Diese fundierte Beurteilung von Design hat in den letzten Jahren nicht nur bei Herstellern und Designern, sondern auch beim Handel und - nicht zu vergessen - bei den Medien dazu geführt, daß der Stellenwert eines iF-ausgezeichneten Produkts beachtet und geachtet wird. Deshalb leistet das Industrie Forum Design Hannover eine wirksame Förderung des Industrie-Designs und damit auch der wirtschaftlichen Entwicklung insgesamt. Nehmen Sie sich deshalb trotz eines prall gefüllten Terminkalenders eine Stunde Zeit und informieren Sie sich über die Highlights des Industrie-Designs. Vielleicht erhalten Sie auch Ideen und Anregungen, um sich in Ihrem Unternehmen verstärkt dem Design zu wirdmen.

Professor
Dr. Klaus E. Goehrmann
Vorsitzender
des Vorstandes der
Deutschen Messe AG
Hannover

Today, corporate success is determined not just by technological know-how and business acumen but also in large parts by a company's design culture. The public status of design is growing and is therefore becoming an important factor in marketing. However, the public awareness of design trends to focus essentially on products used within the home. The Industrie Forum Design Hannover exhibition, by contrast, shows how designers often ensure that machines and components are more user-friendly and ergonomic. During the Hannover Trade Fair, visitors from all around the globe will have the opportunity to familiarize themselves with the current state of industrial design. And an expert jury has carefully scrutinized the entries submitted to the iF Design Competition and selected the absolutely top design, so that only the very best designs are on display.

This knowledgeable assessment of design has led in recent years among manufacturers and designers, not to mention the trade and the media, to a considerable attention and the recognition of an iF awarded product. Thus, iF is playing a strong role in promoting industrial design in particular and, of course, economic growth in general.

Although I am sure you have very busy schedules, I would encourage you to take an hour's time and cast a glance over the highlights of industrial design. They can perhaps serve as a source of ideas and inspiration, causing your company to devote itself more strongly to design.

Professor
Dr. Klaus E. Goehrmann
CEO of
Deutsche Messe AG
Hannover

DER iF DESIGNWETTBEWERB *THE iF DESIGN COMPETITION 1996*

Für den iF Design Wettbewerb 1996 reichten Hersteller und Designer insgesamt 1.212 Produkte zur Bewertung ein. Von diesen Einreichungen kamen aus Deutschland 775 Produkte. Das Ausland beteiligte sich mit 437 Einsendungen am diesjährigen Wettbewerb. Für die ausgeschriebene Auszeichnung Ökologie und Design bewarben sich Hersteller und Designer mit der Anmeldung von 311 Produkten. Eine internationale Jury zeichnete innerhalb von drei Tagen 332 Produkte mit dem iF-Award aus, darunter 195 deutsche und 137 ausländische Beiträge. Darüber hinaus erhielten 24 Einreichungen die Auszeichnung »Beste der Branche« und zehn wurden wegen ihrer überragenden Designqualität in die Gruppe der Top Ten aufgenommen. Auszeichnungen für eine richtungsweisende Ökologie- und Design-Qualität wurden insgesamt 27 Produkten zuerkannt.
Manufacturers and designers submitted a total of 1.212 products to the 1996 iF Design Competition. Of these entries, 775 from Germany and a further 437 from outside Germany. All in all, manufacturers and designers entered some 311 products for the special »Ecology and Design« division of the competition, which was held for the first time. After three days work an international jury granted the iF design award on 332 products; of this figure, 195 came from Germany, and 137 from foreign countries. 24 products has been awarded as »best of group«. In addition exhibiting absolutely outstanding design were specially premiated as the Top Ten of the year. 27 products won the award for pioneering ecological and design qualities.

VORSITZENDER DER JURY *CHAIRMAN OF THE JURY*
Prof. Herbert Lindinger, Institut für Indstrial Design, Hannover, Germany

10 BESTE DES JAHRES *TOP TEN OF THE YEAR*
BESTE DER BRANCHE *BEST OF GROUP*
Norbert Haugg, Präsident des Deutschen Patentamts *President of the German Patent Office*, München, Germany
Andrée Putman, Innenarchitektin *Interior designer*, Paris, France
Ernst Raue, 1. Vorsitzender iF *Chairman iF*, Deutsche Messe AG, Hannover, Germany
Horst Diener, Designer, Ulm, Germany (Vorsitzender der Gruppe 1 *Chairman of jury group1*)
Bob Blaich, Designer, Aspen, USA (Vorsitzender der Gruppe 2 *Chairman of group 2*)

GRUPPE *GROUP* 1
1 Büro *office*, 2 Wohnung *home*, 3 Haushalt *household*, 6 Freizeit *leisure*
Horst Diener (Vorsitzender der Gruppe 1 *Chairman of jury group 1*) Designer, Ulm, Germany
Christoph Böninger, Designer, Siemens AG, München, Germany
Isao Hosoe, Designer, Mailand, Italy
Martin Iseli, Designer Ascom Corporate Industrial Design, Solothurn, Switzerland

GRUPPE *GROUP* 2
4 Beleuchtung *lighting*, 5 Haustechnik *house technology*, 7 Industrie *industry*
8 Tranport+Verkehr *transportation*, 9 Medizin *medical*
Bob Blaich (Vorsitzender der Gruppe 2 *Chairman of jury group 2*), Designer, Aspen, USA
Hartmut S. Engel, Designer, Ludwigsburg, Germany
Andreas Haug, Designer, Phoenix Product Design, Stuttgart, Germany
Hartmut Warkuß, Designer, VW Design, Wolfsburg, Germany

GRUPPE *GROUP* 3
10 Interface
Prof. Burghardt Schmitz, Designer, HDK Berlin, Berlin, Germany
Joannes Vandermeulen, Designer, Using It, Brüssel, Belgium
Frank Zebner, Designer, Siemens AG, München, Germany

GRUPPE *GROUP* 4
Ökology *ecology*
Jens Clausen, IÖW, Hannover, Germany
Caroline van Hemel, Technical University of Delft, Delft, The Netherlands
Carl August Sautier, Wilkhahn, Bad Münder, Germany

iF JURY 1996 AT WORK

KRITERIEN FÜR EINE DESIGNAUSZEICHNUNG VON INDUSTRIEPRODUKTEN

PRODUKTE ODER PRODUKTSYSTEME VON ÜBERRAGENDER DESIGNQUALITÄT ZEICHNEN SICH DURCH EINE REIHE VON EIGENSCHAFTEN AUS:

1. Praktischer Nutzen
Hohe Gebrauchstauglichkeit und einwandfreies Funktionieren.

2. Ausreichende Sicherheit
Erfüllung einschlägiger Sicherheitsvorschriften und bestehender Leistungsnormen sowie Berücksichtigung von flüchtigem und unachtsamem Gebrauch (Narrensicherheit). Eliminierung von Verletzungsgefahren beim Bedienen.

3. Lebensdauer und Gültigkeit
Übereinstimmung von ästhetischer und physisch angemessener Lebensdauer.

4. Ergonomische Anpassung
Anpassung des Gegenstandes an die physischen Gegebenheiten der Benutzer (leichte Bedien- und Ablesbarkeit, geeignete Arbeitshöhen, Greifweiten, Komfort, Vermeidung von unnötiger und belastender Ermüdung). Visuelle Störungsfreiheit (Vermeidung von Irritationen, Blendung und visueller Fehlinformation).

5. Technische und formale Eigenständigkeit
Vermeidung von Nachahmungen (Plagiat).

6. Umfeld-Beziehungen
Der Gegenstand soll in Funktion und Gestalt nicht nur für sich, sondern auch in zwischengegenständlicher Beziehung, d. h. in seiner späteren Produkt-Nachbarschaft, sinnvoll sein. Angemessenheit des Aufwands an Formen, Farben, Materialqualitäten in Bezug auf Gebrauch und Stellenwert des Produktes.

7. Umweltfreundlichkeit
Energie- und ressourcenschonend in Herstellung und Gebrauch, abfallarm und recyclinggerecht.

8. Gebrauchsvisualisierung
Die Form des Produktes soll nach Möglichkeit informieren über Funktion oder Nutzung des Objektes und seiner Teile, um seine Handhabung zu erleichtern oder um seinem Sinn Ausdruck zu verleihen.

9. Hohe Gestaltungsqualität
Überzeugender struktureller Aufbau, Erkennbarkeit des beabsichtigten Gestaltungsprinzips, z. B. bewußte Schalen- oder Skelettbauweise u. ä. Augenscheinliche Beziehung des Ganzen zu seinen Teilen hinsichtlich Formen, Volumen, Massen, Farben, Materialqualitäten, Produktgrafik, Durchgängigkeit von einmal gewählten Konstruktions- bzw. Gestaltungsprinzipien (formale Konsequenz). Prägnanz und Eindeutigkeit der Gestaltungselemente, z. B. Formübergänge, Kontraste von Formen, Farben und Schriften, Proportionen. Ästhetisch sinnvolle Gliederung im Einklang mit Herstellung, Montage, Nutzung und Wartung der Teile. Logik der Form hinsichtlich des verwendeten Materials, des jeweiligen Herstellungsverfahrens und Gebrauchs.

10. Eine sinnlich-geistige Stimulanz
Eine Gesamtwirkung, die den Nutzer animiert, erfreut, seine Sinne stimuliert, dort, wo es sinnvoll ist, seine Neugierde weckt, zum Spielen oder eigenem Gestalten anregt, die Lust an Witz, Ironie oder Verfremdung anspricht. Kurzum eine Form, die zu einer Identifikation führen kann.
Je nach Objekt und Branche werden diese Kriterien meist von produktspezifischen ergänzt. Auch ihre Bedeutung bzw. Gewichtung hängt von der Funktion der Objekte ab. Sie wird z. B. bei einer Blumenvase oder einem Möbelstück anders ausfallen als bei der Einrichtung einer Intensivstation. Zudem sollte betont werden, daß diese Wertmaßstäbe einer langsamen, aber stetigen Veränderung unterliegen. Industrieprodukte entstehen in einem Spannungsfeld zwischen technischem Fortschritt, sozialem Wandel, ökonomischen Gegebenheiten und den Entwicklungen in Künsten, Architektur und Design.

Prof. Herbert Lindinger
Dipl. Industrial Designer
Institut für Industrial Design
Universität Hannover

CRITERIA FOR DESIGN AWARDING OF INDUSTRIAL PRODUCTS

PRODUCTS OR PRODUCT SYSTEMS USUALLY HAVE A RANGE OF DESIRABLE FEATURES SUCH AS:

1. Practicability
Fitness for the intended purpose and faultless functioning.

2. Safety and security
Compliance with all relevant safety regulations and performance standards as well as being proof against misuse and carelessness (foolproof); avoidance of potential sources of injury during operation.

3. Useful life and effectiveness
Conformity of aesthetic and physical durability.

4. Compliance with ergonomic requirements
The article accords with the physical requirements of the user, including ease of operation, good readability, convenient working heigh; controls, etc. within easy reach; avoidance of features that cause tiring (avoidance of irritation; dazzle, wrong visual information).

5. Originality of technique and design
Avoidance of imitation (plagiarism).

6. Harmony with surroundings
The article should be meaningful in function and form not only in itself but also in relation to other objects in its neighbourhood. The effort expended on form, colour, material qualities to be in keeping with the use and importance of the product.

7. Environmental aspects
The product to be sparing of energy and resources in manufacture and use, minimal waste and conducive to recycling.

8. Visualization of use or function
The form or shape of the product should give an indication of its use or function of the object and that of its parts, to allow easy handling or to visualize its purpose.

9. High quality of design
Convincing structural arrangement; recognition of the intended design principle, e. g. shell or frame construction, etc. Obvious relationship of the whole to its parts in respect of form, volume, dimensions, colour, material qualities, product graphics. Adherence to a once chosen design or styling principle (design consistency). Exactitude and clarity of the design elements; e. g. form transitions, contrasts in shape, colour and lettering, proportions. Aesthetically meaningful, arrangement in harmony with manufacture, user, assembly and maintenance of the parts. No visual disturbance. Logical design with respect to the materials used, the manufacturing process and the purpose or application.

10. Stimulation of sense and intellect
An overall effect which animates and pleases the user, which stimulates his senses, awakes his curiosity where this is meaningful, encourages play or one's own creativity, appeals to the inclination to wit, irony or incongruity. A form which can lead to an identification.

Depending on article and sector, these criteria may be supplemented by productspecific considerations. Also their importance or weighting will depend on the article's function. For example, they will be different depending on wether it is a crystal vase, c furniture or an intensive care unit that is being assessed. It should also be emphasized that the criteria are subject to a gradual but constant change. Industrial products come into being in a field of interaction between the technical progress, social change, economic circumstances and developments in the arts, architecture and design.

Prof. Herbert Lindinger
Dipl. Industrial Designer
Institute of Industrial Design
University of Hannover

ÖKOLOGIE UND DESIGN
von Jens Clausen, Carolien van Hemel und Carl-August Sautier

Gutes Design ist ökologisch verantwortliches Design. Unter diesem Leitsatz steht der auf fünf Jahre angelegte Wettbewerb Ökologie und Design des iF Industrie Forum Design Hannover. Mit wechselnden Schwerpunkten soll die Aufmerksamkeit im Wettbewerb auf jeweils ein wichtiges Problemfeld des ökologischen Designs gelenkt werden. Dabei verfolgt die Jury »Ökologie und Design« das Ziel, Beispiele zu präsentieren, die für einzelne (oder mehrere) Kriterien ökologisch verantwortlicher Produktgestaltung vorbildlich sind. Im Rahmen des Wettbewerbes wurden ausschließlich Produkte ausgezeichnet, die auch von der Designjury für auszeichnungswürdig gehalten wurden. Einige gute Ideen zum Ökodesign, die die grundlegenden, designbezogenen Bewertungskriterien nicht erfüllten, konnten daher im Wettbewerb Ökologie und Design nicht ausgezeichnet werden.

Die im Wettbewerb Ökologie und Design ausgezeichneten Produkte werden in der iF-Ausstellung und im iF-Katalog präsentiert. Wir hoffen, daß so Designerinnen und Designer auf vorbildliche Lösungen zu Ökologie und Design aufmerksam werden und sich bei ihrer eigenen Arbeit von ihnen inspirieren lassen.

DER WETTBEWERB 1996
Die im Sonderwettbewerb ausgezeichneten Produkte geben unabhängig von den Produktgruppen einen Überblick über die vorbildliche Realisierung von Ökodesign-Anforderungen. 1996 standen neben den Grundanforderungen an die Produkt-Leitidee auch die Anforderungen an Gestaltung und Konstruktion im Mittelpunkt.

Einfachheit von Produkten als Grundanforderung an gutes Design kann, z. B. durch die Beschränkung auf nur wenige Bauteile oder Materialien, erreicht werden, wie dies beim Formholzstuhl von Lang Produkt Design (S. 115) oder dem Tisch von Arco (S. 144) gegeben ist. Aber auch mechanische Geräte können durch manuellen Antrieb z. B. der Wandseilwinde von Hartmann & Selic (S. 380) oder dem Wasserantrieb des Badlifts vom Designprojekt Dresden (S. 402) besonders einfach gestaltet werden. Der geringe Wirkungsgrad von Wasserantrieben wurde hier in Anbetracht der geringen Nutzungshäufigkeit in Kauf genommen. Eindeutigkeit und Transparenz können in der Materialwahl demonstriert werden. Dies gelingt naturgemäß eher bei einfachen Produkten. Vorbildliche Lösungen sind z. B. die Tische von Arco (S. 144) und Thonet (S. 143), aber auch die Leuchten von BEGA (S. 203, 204 und 206).

Langfristige Gültigkeit drückt sich zum einen in einer Gestaltung aus, die Modeströmungen bewußt nicht folgt, in der wirkliches Design stattfindet und nicht Styling. Dabei ist die übliche Lebensdauer des Produktes zu beachten. Langlebige Produkte sollten auch von der Gestaltung her zeitlos sein. Beide Anforderungen werden z. B. durch die BRIGG-Leuchte von Steng Licht (S. 226) vorbildlich erfüllt. Die Hersteller des Schreibgerätes von Messmer Pen (S. 136) und der Duschwanne Rondoplan von Kaldewei (S. 168) drücken dies auch in ihren Garantiefristen aus: Unbegrenzt bei Messmer, 30 Jahre bei Kaldewei.

Sparsamkeit in Material- und Energieverbrauch ist eines der wichtigsten Paradigmen ökologisch verantwortlichen Designs. So findet auch bei einigen im Rahmen des Wettbewerbs »Design und Ökologie« ausgezeichneten Produkten die Effizienzrevolution konkret statt. Hier ist die Rad-Brems-Einheit für Güterwagen der RWTH-Aachen (S. 384) zu nennen, die gegenüber heute üblichen Vergleichsprodukten 80% weniger Material verbraucht. Diese Gewichtsreduktion um den Faktor 5 führt zu enormen Einsparungen auch beim Energieverbrauch der Züge, denn jeder Güterwagen wird um einige Tonnen leichter und diese Masse muß nicht mehr beschleunigt und in Bewegung gehalten werden. Funktionsgerechtigkeit ist in vielen Fällen Grundlage einer umweltgerechten Produktgestaltung. So sollten z. B. Leiterplatten für Elektronikbauteile zur Erfüllung ihrer Funktion zum einen selbst nicht leiten, zum anderen möglichst nicht brennbar sein. Dies wird üblicherweise in Kunststoffleiterplatten durch einen ganzen Zoo an Chemikalien erreicht, der dem Trägermaterial beigemischt wird. Im Loewe Opta Fernsehgerät CS1 (S. 302) werden die Elektronikkomponenten dagegen auf eine Keramik-Stahl-Struktur gelötet. Hier wirkt zum einen die Keramik als perfekter Isolator, zum anderen ist das Material unbrennbar. Konsequent wird auch das Gehäuse aus Stahlblech gebaut, so daß das Fernsehgerät nach Ausbau einiger Komponenten im gut funktionierenden Recyling der Stahlbranche verarbeitet werden kann. Auch der Röhrenkollektor zur Gewinnung solarer Wärme von Viessmann (S. 38-40) zeigt eine vorbildhafte Funktionsgerechtigkeit, indem er die Funktion einer Balkonbrüstung zusätzlich übernimmt. So wird ein Bauelement eingespart.

Als funktionserklärendes Produkt ist die Wandseilwinde von Hartmann & Selic (S. 380) beispielhaft. Die Funktion selber ist durch die große Kurbel sowie durch die sichtbare Doppelsperrklinke klar, die Betätigungsrichtung wird durch Pictogramme deutlich gemacht. Lösbare Verbindungen sind sowohl für die Reparatur als auch für die Demontage beim Recycling unerläßlich. Das Hewlett-Packard Spectralphotometer (S. 307) und der Stollmann ISDN Terminal Adapter (S. 93) zeigen beide Wege zu einer ungewöhnlich einfachen Demontage von Elektronikbauteilen. Der Océ Kopierer 3045 (S. 54) macht die Demontierbarkeit zur Grundlage eines umfangreichen Angebotes von technischer Aufrüstung und Wiederaufarbeitung der Geräte.

THE ECOLOGY AND DESIGN COMPETITION 1996
by Jens Clausen, Carolien van Hemel and Carl-August Sautier

Good design is ecologically responsible design. Taking this as the leitmotif, the Ecology and Design Competition, which will run for five years initially, organized by iF Industrie Forum Design Hannover. The intention is by means of changing focal themes, to bring attention to bear in the competition on a respectively important problematic area of ecological design. In this context, the jury of »Ecology and Design« has the goal of presenting submissions which are exemplary for individual (or several) criteria for ecologically responsible product design. In the framework of the competition, only products received distinctions which were also judged by the design jury to be worthy of such. Some good ideas on eco-design which did not fulfill the fundamental, design-related evaluative criteria therefore did not receive an award in the Ecology and Design Competition.

The products which were named winners in the competition are presented in the iF exhibition and in the catalog. We hope that the attention of designers will thus be drawn to exemplary solutions to ecology and design and that this will inspire their own work.

THE COMPETITION IN 1996

The products which won in the special competition provide an overview of the exemplary implementation of eco-design requirements independent of the specific product groups. In 1996, the focus was on not only the basic requirements of the main underlying idea of each product, but also on design and construction requirements.

The simplicity of products — a basic demand of good design — can, for example, be achieved by limiting it to a few components or materials; this is the case with the molded wooden chair by Lang Produkt Design (see page 115) or the table by Arco (see page 144). But mechanical instruments can also be given a simple but elegant design: for example by means of a manual drive, as with the wall-mounted winch by Hartmann & Selic (see page 380) or the water-driven bath-lift by Designprojekt Dresden (see page 402). The lower efficiency of water drives was acceptable here, given the low frequency of use.

Clarity and transparency can be demonstrated by the choice of materials. This is naturally achieved more easily with simple products. Exemplary solutions are, for example, the tables by Arco (see page 144) and Thonet (see page 143), but also the lighting by BEGA (see pages 203, 204, 206).

Long-term validity is expressed on the one hand by a design which consciously does not follow fashion trends, in which there is real design and not merely styling. The usual service life of the product must be considered here. Durable products should also be timeless in terms of design. Both demands are fulfilled, for example, by the Brigg light (see page 226) by Steng. The makers of the Messmer Pen (see page 136) and Kaldewei, manufacturers of the Rondoplan shower tray (see page 168), also show this with the warranty periods they offer: Unlimited in the case of Messmer, and 30 years in the case of Kaldewei.

Frugality in material and energy consumption is one of the most important paradigms for ecologically responsible design. Thus, design and ecology also takes the shape of a concrete "revolution in efficiency" with some of the award-winning products. Here, the wheel and brake unit for boxcars by RWTH-Aachen (see page 384) bears mentioning, which consumes 80 percent less material then comparable current products. The reduction in weight by a factor of five leads to enormous energy savings by the train, for each boxcar is some tonnes lighter easier and this mass no longer needs to be got rolling and kept rolling. Doing justice to functions often forms the basis for an ecologically-sound product design. Thus, for example, circuit boards for electronic components should not themselves be conductive when fulfilling their function and should also not be inflammable, if possible. This is usually achieved in plastic circuit boards by using a whole morass of chemicals which are added to the basic plate. In the Loewe Opta TV CS1 (see page 302), by contrast, the electronic components are soldered onto a ceramic and steel structure. Here, the ceramics works on one hand as a perfect insulator and, on the other, is non-flammable. Logically, the casing is also made of steel sheet, so that the TV, after extraction of some components, can be integrated into the well functioning recycling processes in the steel industry. Also the tubular solar energy collector by Viessmann (see page 38-40) is exemplary in doing justice to its function, for it can also double up as a balcony balustrade. So one component becomes dispersable.

The winch by Hartmann & Selic (see page 380) is an exemplary case of a product explaining its own function. The function itself is clear, given the long crank and the visible double-locking handle, the direction in which it needs to be turn is clearly shown by the pictograms.

Soluble combinations are imperative both for repair as well as for dismantling for recycling. Both the Hewlett-Packard Spectrophotometer (see page 307) as well as the Stollmann ISDN terminal adapters (see page 93) are perfect examples of unusually simple dismantling of electronic components. The Océ copier 3045 (see page 54) makes disassembly the basis for a comprehensive offer of technological upgrading and reprocessing.

»In früheren iF-Juries hatte ich von Anbeginn ein klares Bild, zumindest von 9 Objekten, die am Schluß unter den 10 Besten landeten. Ich hätte kräftig grübeln müssen, wenn man mich diesmal schon zu Beginn unserer Zusammenkunft nach einer Liste der voraussichtlichen 10 Top-Entwürfe gefragt hätte. Es sprang nichts gleich ins Auge. Vielleicht liegt das am durchgehend hohen Niveau«, antwortete der amerikanische Designmanager Bob Blaich auf die Frage nach dem Niveau des diesjährigen Wettbewerbs. Die Einreichungen für den iF-Design-Wettbewerb 1996 reichten von Gehhilfen im Bereich Medizin, Gabelstaplern, Studien für Nahverkehrszüge, bis zu Kugelschreibern, Hochleistungscomputern und Einrichtungen für den Arbeitsschutz. Ausgezeichnet von einer eigenen Jury wurde die Kategorie Top Ten, unabhängig von den Produktgruppen. Es dominierten letztendlich die Bereiche Office mit insgesamt vier Auszeichnungen. Aus der Kategorie Freizeit, Beleuchtung, Haustechnik, Verkehr, Industrie und Interface ist 1996 jeweils ein Produkt in die 10 Besten des Jahres aufgenommen worden.

"In past iF juries I always had a clear image from the very outset of at least nine objects that then at the end of the day landed among the Top Ten. But I would have had to think hard if at the beginning of this year's jury meeting someone had asked me for a list of the probable Top Ten designs. Nothing immediately caught the eye. Perhaps because overall level of the entries was so high." This was the comment design manager Bob Blaich gave when asked to assess the level of the competition this year. The submissions to the 1996 iF design competition ranged from walking frames in the medical products divisions, via fork-lifts, studies for commuter trains, to ballpoint pens, high-tech computers and work protection facilities. The entries that were considered for the Top Ten were selected by a separate jury from that which evaluated the product groups. In the final analysis, the "office" division dominated here, picking up four awards. One product was selected respectively from the lighting, the household products, the leisure products, the transportation, the industry, and the interface divisions.

10 Beste des Jahres
top ten of the year

Jury: Andrée Putman, Bob Blaich, Horst Diener, Norbert Haugg, Prof. Herbert Lindinger, Ernst Raue

DEUTSCHE TELEKOM/DETEBERKOM MEDIATEL *MULTIMEDIA-DISPLAY*

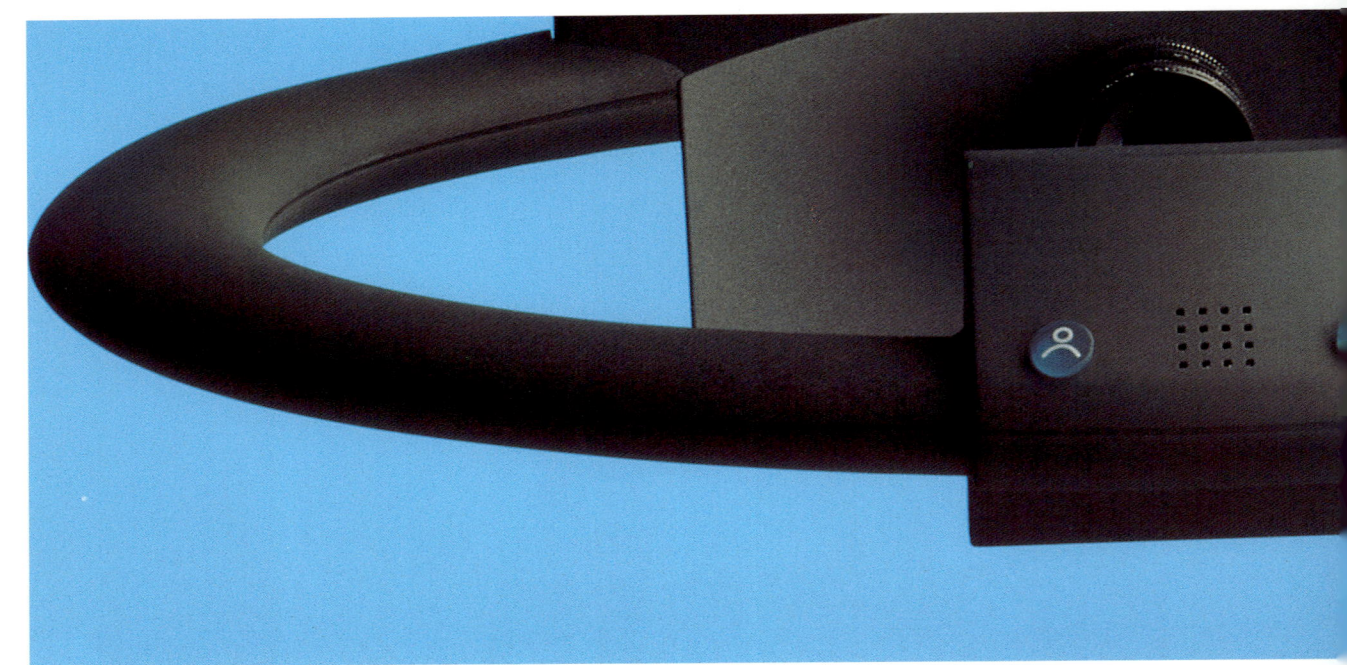

HERSTELLER MANUFACTURER
TRION Präzisionselektronik GmbH & Co KG Berlin, Germany für/for Deutsche Telekom, DeTeBerkom

PRODUKT PRODUCT
MediaTel Multimedia-Display

DESIGN
Franz Lenz, Berlin, Germany

MEDIATEL ist ein neues Multimedia-Display fürs Büro. Der vielfach strapazierte Begriff »Innovation« - hier ist er einmal angebracht. Durch erfreulich klare Gliederung wurde ein technisch sehr komplexes Gerät alltagstauglich. Es unterstützt räumlich entfernte Partner dabei, multimediale Dokumente gemeinsam interaktiv zu bearbeiten. MediaTel, ein Kommunikationssystem, das für die Deutsche Telekom entwickelt wurde, kann durch sein neuartiges Display-Design die bisherigen Systemteile Monitor, Lautsprecher, Mikrofon, Personen- und Objektkamera in einem Gerät integrieren. Und ist dabei kaum komplizierter zu handhaben als ein Telefon.

Die Grundidee, ein patentiertes parallaxefreies Strahlengangsystem, das bei Videokonferenzen den direkten Blickkontakt von Schreibtisch zu Schreibtisch ermöglicht, mit einem rundum beweglichen Schwenkarm zu kombinieren, stammt vom Berliner Art & Com e.V. Später überarbeitete der Designer Frank Lenz zusammen mit der TRION GmbH das Gerät für die Serienproduktion.

Das Konzept ist einfach und überzeugend: Auf einem Ringgriff sitzt ein leichter LCD-Flachbildschirm mit einem halbdurchlässigen Spiegel, darunter eine Videokamera. Außen am Griff ist ein Umlenkspiegel angebracht. Bildschirm, Ring und Kamera sitzen auf einem gasfedergestützten Ausleger, der alle Versorgungs- und Datenleitungen aufnimmt und sich frei über den Tisch bewegen läßt. So nimmt es trotz seiner Größe nur wenig Schreibtischfläche in Anspruch.

Bei Bedarf kann das Gerät in Stehhöhe ausgefahren werden. Die Tischklemme enthält Lautsprecherbox und Infrarotfernbedienung. MediaTel wird in Verbindung mit einem Arbeitsplatzrechner (PC, Apple Macintosh oder Workstation) betrieben.

MEDIATEL is a new multimedia display for the office. The overburdened notion of »innovation« is actually appropriate here. The gratifyingly clear arrangement, a technically very complex instrument becomes accessible in everyday contexts. It supports spatially remote partners when jointly processing multimedia documents interactively. MediaTel: a communications system developed for Deutsche Telekom, has a novel display design which enables the current system components (monitor, loudspeakers, microphone, camera for persons and objects) to be integrated in one instrument. And is hardly more complicated to handle than a telephone.

The basic idea for a patented parallax-free beam system which enables direct visual contact desk-to-desk at videoconferences combined with a fully rotatable swivel arm, originates from the Berlin Art & Com e. V. Later, Frank Lenz revised together with the TRION GmbH the instrument for mass production.

The concept is convincing and simple: a light LCD with a semi-translucent mirror is mounted on a ring grip and below it a video camera. On the outside of the grip is a passive reflector. The monitor, ring handle and camera are placed on an arm supported on pneumatic springs that houses all the supply and data lines and can be moved freely over the table. Thus, despite its size, the unit requires only minimal desk space.

If required, the instrument can be extended at standing height. The table clamp contains the speaker and the IR-remote control. MediaTel is operated together with a PC or Apple Macintosh workstation.

10 BESTE DES JAHRES *TOP TEN OF THE YEAR* 19

HERSTELLER MANUFACTURER
TRION Präzisionselektronik GmbH & Co KG Berlin, Germany für/for Deutsche Telekom, DeTeBerkom

PRODUKT PRODUCT
MediaTel Multimedia-Display

DESIGN
Franz Lenz, Berlin, Germany

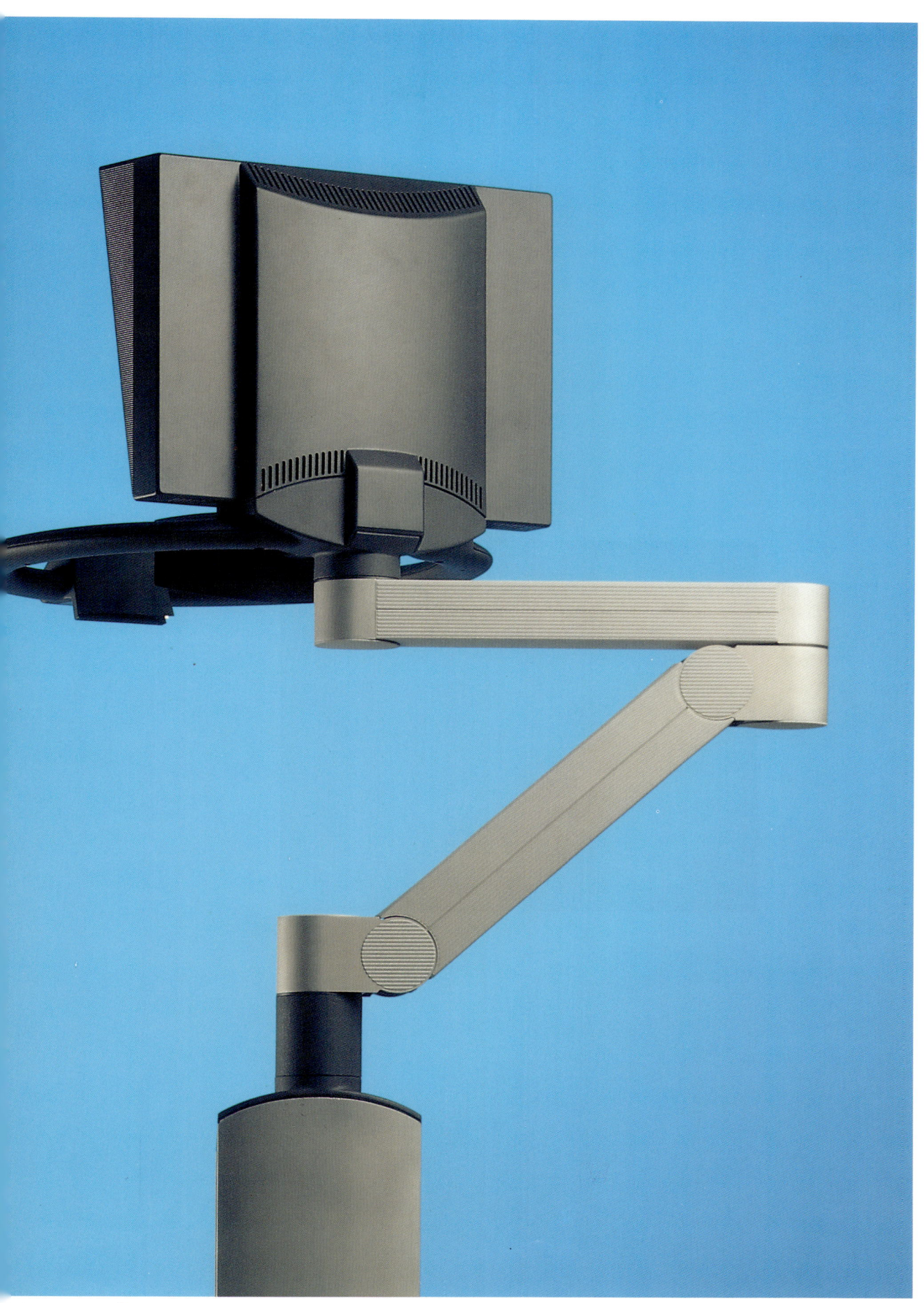

IBM THINKPAD 701 TRAGBARER COMPUTER *PORTABLE COMPUTER*

HERSTELLER *MANUFACTURER*
IBM Corporation, Armonk, USA

PRODUKT *PRODUCT*
IBM ThinkPad 701 Tragbarer Computer, *Portable computer*

DESIGN
IBM Corporation, Samuel Lucente, Robert Tennant, Armonk, USA, Richard Sapper, Milano, Italy

IBM THINKPAD 701 TRAGBARER COMPUTER *PORTABLE COMPUTER*

Sieht man das neue NOTEBOOK von IBM zuerst in aufgeklapptem Zustand, ist man sicher: Das kann nicht gut gehen. Wie um alles in der Welt soll die breite Tastatur, die links und rechts über das Gehäuse des mobilen Rechners ragt, gut geschützt darin verschwinden, wenn das Notebook zugeklappt wird? Keine Frage: Es geht nicht – und es geht doch. TrackWrite nennt sich der Mechanismus, den die Designer Samuel Lucente, Robert Tennant und sicher nicht zuletzt Richard Sapper erdacht haben. Denn Sapper, den Mann, der die »Tizio« und den Alessi-Flötenkessel entwarf, interessieren Dinge, die sich vor den Augen ihrer Nutzer verwandeln. Die sich augenzwinkernd selbst ironisieren. Wie radikal denken Designer, die unumstößliche technische Gegebenheiten ignorieren?

Und wie lange brauchen sie wohl, um Ingenieure und Verkäufer von ihren genialen Ideen zu überzeugen?
Bei dem ThinkPad 701 hält der Überraschungseffekt an. In den Abmessungen eines Subnotebooks steckt ein zeitgemäß ausgestatteter Mobilrechner mit Infrarotschnittstelle und PC-Card-Slots, einem schnellen Chip und Aktivmatrix-Bildschirm sowie einer Festplatte von 360 bis 720 Megabyte. Auch wer aus der Nähe betrachtet, wie sich die Tastatur mit ihren 85 Tasten beim Zuklappen langsam teilt, sich hintereinanderschiebt, um schließlich doch gänzlich in dem kaum 25 mal 20 Zentimeter messenden Kästchen zu verschwinden, der muß immer wieder staunen wie ein Kind. Selbst, wenn es ein Business-Mensch sein wird, der das ThinkPad 701 alle Tage benutzt.

When you first see the IBM NOTEBOOK with the lid open, you think: »That simply won't work. How on earth will the broad keyboard, which towers over the casing on the left and right, fit into the notebook snugly and safely when closed?« No question: It won't work - but it does. Known by its project codename, »Butterfly«, the IBM ThinkPad 701 notebook was created by a small group of engineers working with designers Sam Lucente, Robert Tennant and IBM's Industrial Design consultant Richard Sapper. The surprise is hidden inside the elegant black box until the top cover is lifted. The clever mechanism performs a well choreographed ballet before your eyes as you open and close the unit. Here, innovative technology, expressed in a playful but serious tool, compromised nothing from a users perspective.
With the IBM ThinkPad 701 the unexpected continues. The dimensions of a subnotebook, conceal a modern, mobile PC with an IR interface, PC card slots, a fast processor and a 10,4« active matrix screen, as well as a hard disk capacity up to 720 megabytes. Any anyone who watches how the fullsize keyboard, with its 85 keys, splits into two when shutting slowly, slotting into itself to disappear completely inside a box measuring less than 25 x 20 cm, will marvel at the object again and again like a child.

HERSTELLER MANUFACTURER
IBM Corporation, Armonk, USA

PRODUKT PRODUCT
IBM ThinkPad 701 Tragbarer Computer, Portable computer

DESIGN
IBM Corporation, Samuel Lucente, Robert Tennant, Armonk, USA, Richard Sapper, Milano, Italy

SIEMENS NIXDORF PRIMERGY PC SERVER SERIE *PC SERVER SERIES*

HERSTELLER MANUFACTURER Siemens Nixdorf Informationssysteme AG, Augsburg, Germany
PRODUKT PRODUCT PRIMERGY PC-Server-Serie, PC-Server series
DESIG Siemens Design, Michael Lanz, München, Germany

26 10 BESTE DES JAHRES *TOP TEN OF THE YEAR*

Reduziert gestaltet und trotzdem völlig ungewöhnlich sehen die neuen PRIMERGY SERVER von Siemens Nixdorf aus. Ihre moderne, farbenfrohe Front springt sofort ins Auge. Drei Modelle für unterschiedliche Zwecke wurden entwickelt. Primergy 100/300 ist für den Betrieb in kleinen bis mittleren EDV-Systemen gedacht. Primergy 500 und Primergy 700 bieten ein weitaus höheres Leistungsniveau und kommen überall dort zum Einsatz, wo große Datenmengen verarbeitet werden, etwa in Rechenzentren, Versicherungen und Banken. Primergy 500 und Primergy 700 entsprechen sich in Technik und Leistung weitgehend. Primergy 500 ist als alleinstehendes Gerät, Primergy 700 für den Einbau in 19-Zoll-Schränke konzipiert.

Unterschiedliche Server als Familie erkennbar zu machen, war eine der Intentionen des Siemens Designteams. Zugleich sollte ihre neue, mutige formale Ausprägung ein neues Leitbild schaffen, das vom branchenüblichen PC-Design wegführt.

So reduktiv der Designansatz ist: Alle gestalterischen Elemente sind geboren aus der Funktion. Das Lochblech in den Türen dient als Schirmung, welche die elektromagnetische Verträglichkeit (EMV) der Server weiter erhöht. Zylindrische Durchbrüche dienen als Lüftungsöffnungen, die sich vom Schlitzraster-Einerlei der gängigen PC-Gestaltung deutlich abheben. Vor dem unberechtigtem Zugriff ist das System durch eine abschließbare Tür geschützt. Die Füße aus Aluminumdruckguß sorgen für die notwendige Kippsicherheit.

Auch technisch bietet die neue Server-Systemplattform einige Neuerungen. Alle Systeme sind skalierbar und dank verbesserter EMV auch für kommende Prozessor- und BUS-Generationen mit höherer Taktrate bestens gerüstet. Die beiden Topmodelle Primergy 500 und Primergy 700 besitzen jeweils sechs hot-replacefähige Festplattenlaufwerke. Während des Betriebs können sie mit wenigen Handgriffen gewechselt werden. Nicht die quaderförmigen, anthrazitfarbenen Gehäuse überraschen den Betrachter, sondern die Türen aus transluzentem Terlux. Ein Material, das sich auch im Konsumgüterbereich derzeit großer Beliebtheit erfreut. Designer Michael Lanz war vor einiger Zeit am »Citizen Office«-Projekt beteiligt, bei dem – von Vitra initiiert – Andrea Branzi, Michele De Lucchi und Ettore Sottsass ihre Visionen vom Büro der Zukunft offenbarten, unter Mitwirkung der Siemens-Designer um Herbert Schultes.

Die Primergy-Familie nimmt Impulse aus dem »Citizen Office«-Projekt auf. Und läßt das Design des Büros unerwartet farbiger werden.

Siemens-Nixdorf's new PRIMERGY SERVERS have a no-trimming design and nevertheless look exceptional. Their modern, colorful front is a real eye-catcher. Three models for different purposes have been developed. Primergy 100/300 is meant for small to medium-sized computer systems. Primergy 500 and Primergy 700 offer far greater power and can be used wherever large amounts of data have to be processed — in computer centers, insurances and banks. Primergy 500 and Primergy 700 largely feature the same technology and performance specifications. Primergy 500 is a standalone, Primergy 700 for installation in 19-inch cabinets.

One of the goals of the Siemens design team was to make different servers identifiable as a family. At the same time, their new, courageous formal design had to create a new image that led away from the customary PC design.

However straightforward the design is: All the design elements stem from the functions. The perforated sheet doors serve as screening augmenting the electromagnetic compatibility (EMC) of the server further. The cylindrical openings serve as air vents that clear stand out compared with the usual slats in PCs. A lockable door protects the system from unauthorized access. The cast aluminum footprints ensure the unit does not tilt.

The new server platform also has some technological innovations to offer. All systems are scalable and, owing to the improved EMC are well-equipped to handle the forthcoming processor and bus generations with faster tact rates. The two top models Primergy 500 and Primergy 700 each have six hot-replaceable hard disk drives. During operation, they can be changed with a few movements.

However, it is not the rectangular, charcoal-gray casing which is the surprise, but the doors made of translucent Terlux. A material which is currently very popular in the consumer goods domain. Designer Michael Lanz participated some time ago in the »Citizen Office« project initiated by Vitra and in which Andrea Branzi, Michele De Lucchi and Ettore Sottsass presented their visions for an office of the future, with the assistance of the Siemens designers under Herbert Schultes.

The Primergy line takes its cue from the »Citizen Office« project. And enables office design to become unexpectedly more colorful.

Siemens Nixdorf Informationssysteme AG, Augsburg, Germany   HERSTELLER MANUFACTURER
PRIMERGY PC-Server-Serie, PC-Server-series   PRODUKT PRODUCT
Siemens Design, Michael Lanz, München, Germany   DESIGN

WILKHAHN CONFAIR KONFERENZSYSTEM CONFERENCE SYSTEM

HERSTELLER MANUFACTURER
Wilkhahn, Wilkening+Hahne, GmbH+Co, Bad Münder, Germany
PRODUKT PRODUCT
Wilkhahn Confair, Flexibles Konferenzmobiliar, Flexible conference system
DESIGN
Wiege Wilkhahn Entwicklungsgesellschaft, Bad Münder, Germany

Dynamisch konferieren – wer möchte das nicht?
Ausgangspunkt für die Produktidee des neuen Konferenzsystems Confair war die Absicht, ein flexibles mobiles Mobiliar für neue »aktive« Konferenzformen zu entwickeln. Nicht nur statische Konferenzanlagen, die, einmal arrangiert, weitgehend unverändert bleiben, sondern offene, vielfältig kombinierbare Kleinmöbel, die sich nach Ende eines Workshops platzsparend verstauen lassen, hat Wilkhahn nun im Programm. Variable Ausstattung, gleichermassen für Ad-hoc-Sitzungen, Workshops, Kleingruppen- und Plenumssitzungen geeignet, ist viel gefragt. Oft müssen die Konferenzteilnehmer selbst die Einrichtung von einer Minute auf die andere verändern oder damit umziehen.
Confair will dies erleichtern. Aus einem bequemen leichten Armlehnstuhl und einem mobilen Schreibpult, beide stapelbar, bestehen die minimalistisch konzipierten Kernelemente.
Weitere Bestandteile des Confair-Systems sind der große Falttisch, ein leichtes bewegliches Rednerpult, die Pinwand, das Flipchart und eine ganze Familie von »Servern« sowie kleine bewegliche Tablar- und Boxen-Racks für unterschiedlichste Konferenzzwecke. Letztere erlauben einen effektiveren Zugriff auf Arbeitsmaterial, Projektoren oder Erfrischungen. Ein formales Bindeglied des neuen Konferenzmobiliars ist das elliptische Aluminiumprofil, das als Gestellsäule dient, also ein Detail, das der Devise »Überflüssiges weglassen« folgt. Eine Maxime, die auch manch einer Konferenz gut anstünde.

Who wouldn't opt for dynamic conferencing?
The product idea for the new Confair conference system was based on the wish to develop flexible and mobile furniture for new »active« forms of conferencing. Not just static conference settings, which, once arranged, remain largely unchanged – but also open furniture that can be combined in many ways and stowed at the end of workshops to save space. Wilkhahn now makes precisely such furniture available. The order of the day is variable items suitable for ad hoc meetings and workshops, for small groups and plenary sessions alike. Often conference participants have to change the furniture at the last minute themselves or change location with it. Confair wants to facilitate this. The two core elements, with a minimalist design: A comfortable, lighter chair with armrest and a mobile desk, both stackable. Further Confair system elements include the large folding table, an easily movable speaker's desk, pinboard, flipchart and a whole family of »servers«, small movable table and box racks for a wide range of conference purposes. The latter offer rapid access to work materials, projectors or refreshments. The formal element linking the new conference furniture is the elliptical aluminum profile which serves as the frame's pillar. A detail in keeping with the motto »leave out what is superfluous« - a motto which many a conference could benefit from.

HERSTELLER MANUFACTURER Wilkhahn, Wilkening+Hahne, GmbH+Co, Bad Münder, Germany
PRODUKT PRODUCT Wilkhahn Confair, Flexibles Konferenzmobiliar, Flexible conference system
DESIGN Wiege Wilkhahn Entwicklungsgesellschaft (System), Dipl.Des. Andreas Störiko (Falttisch/Folding table), Bad Münder, Germany

STAFF TELEDANCER STRAHLERSYSTEM *SPOTLIGHT SYSTEM*

STAFF GmbH & Co KG, Lemgo, Germany HERSTELLER MANUFACTURER
TeleDancer Strahlersystem Spotlight system PRODUKT PRODUCT
design studio hartmut s.engel, Ludwigsburg, Germany DESIGN

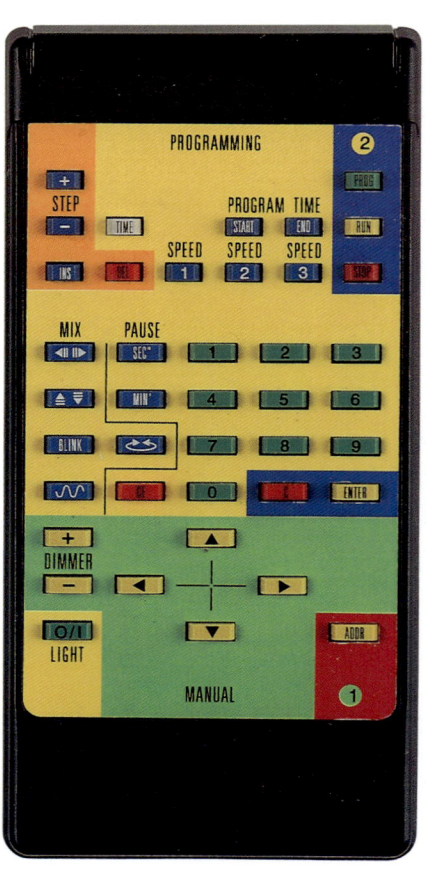

34 10 BESTE DES JAHRES *TOP TEN OF THE YEAR*

TELEDANCER, ein Baustein des Strahlersystems Dancer, ist ein motorisch gesteuertes Strahlersystem, mit dem sich Licht gezielt inszenieren läßt. Ob Messepräsentation oder Schaufenstergestaltung: Gut geplante Lichtspiele sorgen für gesteigerte Aufmerksamkeit.
Der Strahler wird durch Schrittmotore ruckfrei und nahezu geräuschlos angetrieben. Präzise Start- und Endzeiten lassen sich mit TeleDancer frei programmieren. Bewegungen und Lichtfunktionen können gemischt werden. Waagerechte, senkrechte und kreisförmige Bewegungen, Blinken, an- und abschwellendes Licht sind programmierbar oder auch direkt fernsteuerbar.
Bis zu 31 Strahler sind individuell adressierbar und können von einer einzigen Infrarotfernsteuerung angesteuert werden. Drehbewegungen bis zu 360° oder Kippbewegungen um 90° kann der Strahler ausführen.

TELEDANCER, part of the Dancer System', is a spotlight system which allows the dramatic use of light. Be it for trade fair presentations or window decorations: Well-planned lighting constellations enhance attention.
The spot is powered smoothly and next to noiselessly by step motors. TeleDancer lets you program precise scheduling of start and stop times as you want. Movements and light functions can be combined. Horizontal, vertical and circular movements, as well as blinking, growing and fading light are programmable or can be handled by remote control.
Up to 31 spots can be managed by a single Infrared remote control. The spots can rotate up to 360 degrees, and can dip up to 90 degrees.

STAFF GmbH & Co KG, Lemgo, Germany   HERSTELLER MANUFACTURER
TeleDancer Strahlersystem Spotlight system   PRODUKT PRODUCT
design studio hartmut s.engel, Ludwigsburg, Germany   DESIGN

36   10 BESTE DES JAHRES *TOP TEN OF THE YEAR*

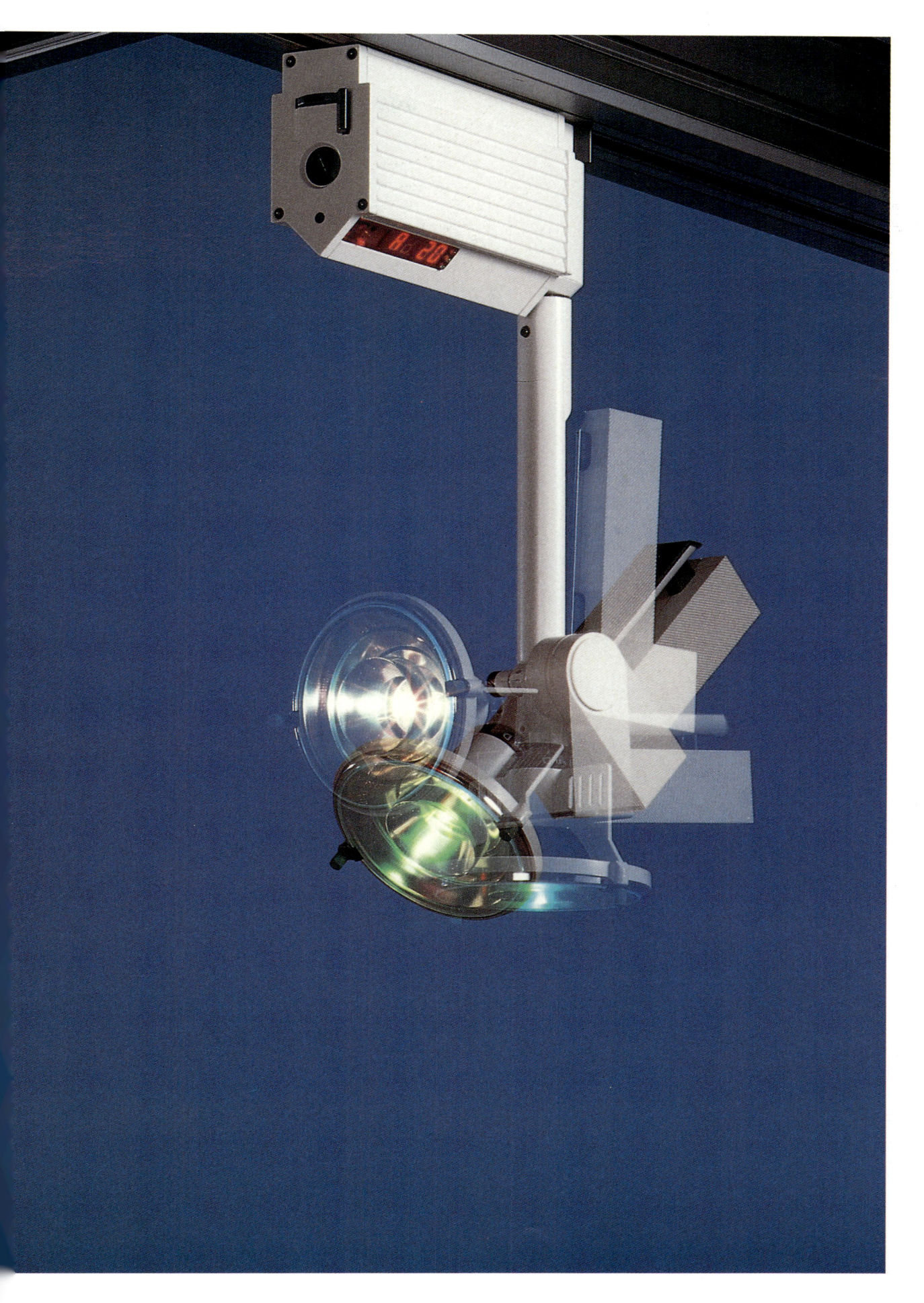

10 BESTE DES JAHRES *TOP TEN OF THE YEAR* 37

VIESSMANN SOLAR-TUBUSOL VAKUUM-RÖHRENKOLLEKTOR
VACUUM TUBULAR COLLECTOR

HERSTELLER MANUFACTURER Viessmann Werke GmbH & Co, Allendorf, Germany
PRODUKT PRODUCT Viessmann Solar-TubuSol Vakuum-Röhrenkollektor Vacuum tubular collector
DESIGN designpraxis diener, Ulm, Germany

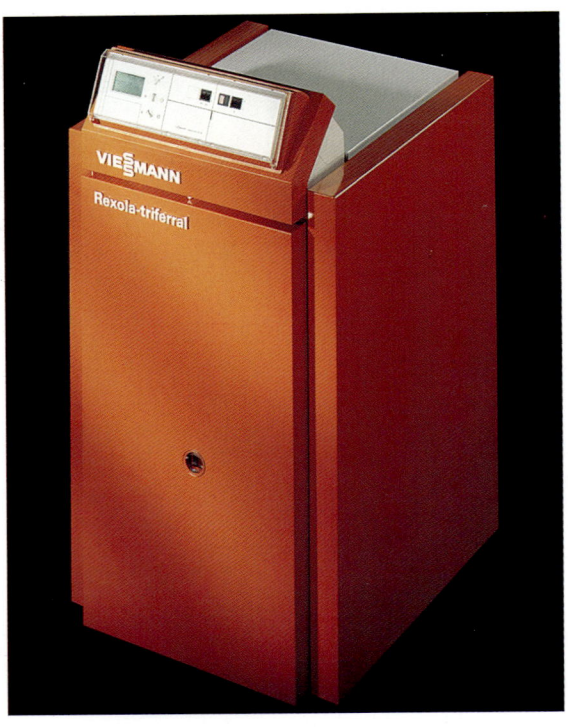

Vorbei die Zeiten, da Ästheten auf die Segnungen der Solarenergie verzichten mußten. Der Solar-TubuSol Vakuum-Röhrenkollektor von Viessmann ist universell dort einsetzbar, wo anspruchsvolle Architektur nicht durch großflächige Solarpaneele leiden soll. Überall, wo senkrechte oder waagerechte Installation gewünscht ist, z. B. auf Schräg- und Flachdächern oder freistehend an Fassaden, läßt sich Solar-TubuSol anbringen. Die einzelnen Röhren können optimal zur Sonne ausgerichtet werden. Dickwandiges Borosilikatglas und eine dauerhafte und vakuumdichte Glas-Metallverbindung garantieren hohe Betriebssicherheit und lange Nutzungsdauer des Solar-TubuSol. Besonders bei diffuser Sonneneinstrahlung ist die Leistung dieses Vakuum-Röhrenkollektors um ca. 30% höher als die von Flachkollektoren. Vorgefertigte Module wie auch ein bewährtes Stecksystem sorgen für einfache schnelle Montage. Der Vakuum-Röhrenkollektor ist Teil eines umfassenden Solarenergie-Systems, das die Ulmer designpraxis diener entwarf. Im berühmt gewordenen Freiburger »Heliotrop«, einem drehbaren Solarwohnturm, setzte Architekt Rolf Disch Solar-TubuSol-Kollektoren als wärmespendende Balkonbrüstung ein.

Gone are the days when aesthetes had to go without the blessings of solar energy. Viessmann's Solar-TubuSol vacuum tubular collector can be deployed wherever discerning architecture would suffer if large solar panels were to be used. Solar-TubuSol can be installed wherever a vertical or horizontal positioning is called for: e. g. on slanting or flat roofs or freestanding in front of facades. The individual tubes can be directed optimally toward the sun. Thick borosilicate glass and a durable vacuum-sealed glass-metal collector ensure optimal safety and a long service life. Particularly given diffuse sun light, the vacuum tubular collector outperforms flat-bed collectors by about 30 percent. Prefabricated modules as well as a proven socketing system afford simple, fast installation. The Solar-TubuSol vacuum tubular collector is part of a comprehensive solar energy system which designpraxis diener, an Ulm design studio, has dreamed up. In the well-known Fribourg »Heliotrop«, a revolving residential solar tower, Rolf Disch used Solar-TubuSol collectors as a heat-providing balcony balustrade.

Ökologie/Design Auszeichnung Awarded for Ecology/Design: Vorbildlich durch Funktionsintegration eines Solarkollektors in eine Balkonbrüstung. Exemplary for its doubling of functions: solar collector and balcony balustrade.

10 BESTE DES JAHRES *TOP TEN OF THE YEAR* 39

HERSTELLER MANUFACTURER Viessmann Werke GmbH & Co, Allendorf, Germany
PRODUKT PRODUCT Viessmann Solar-TubuSol Vakuum-Röhrenkollektor Vacuum tubular collector
DESIGN designpraxis diener, Ulm, Germany

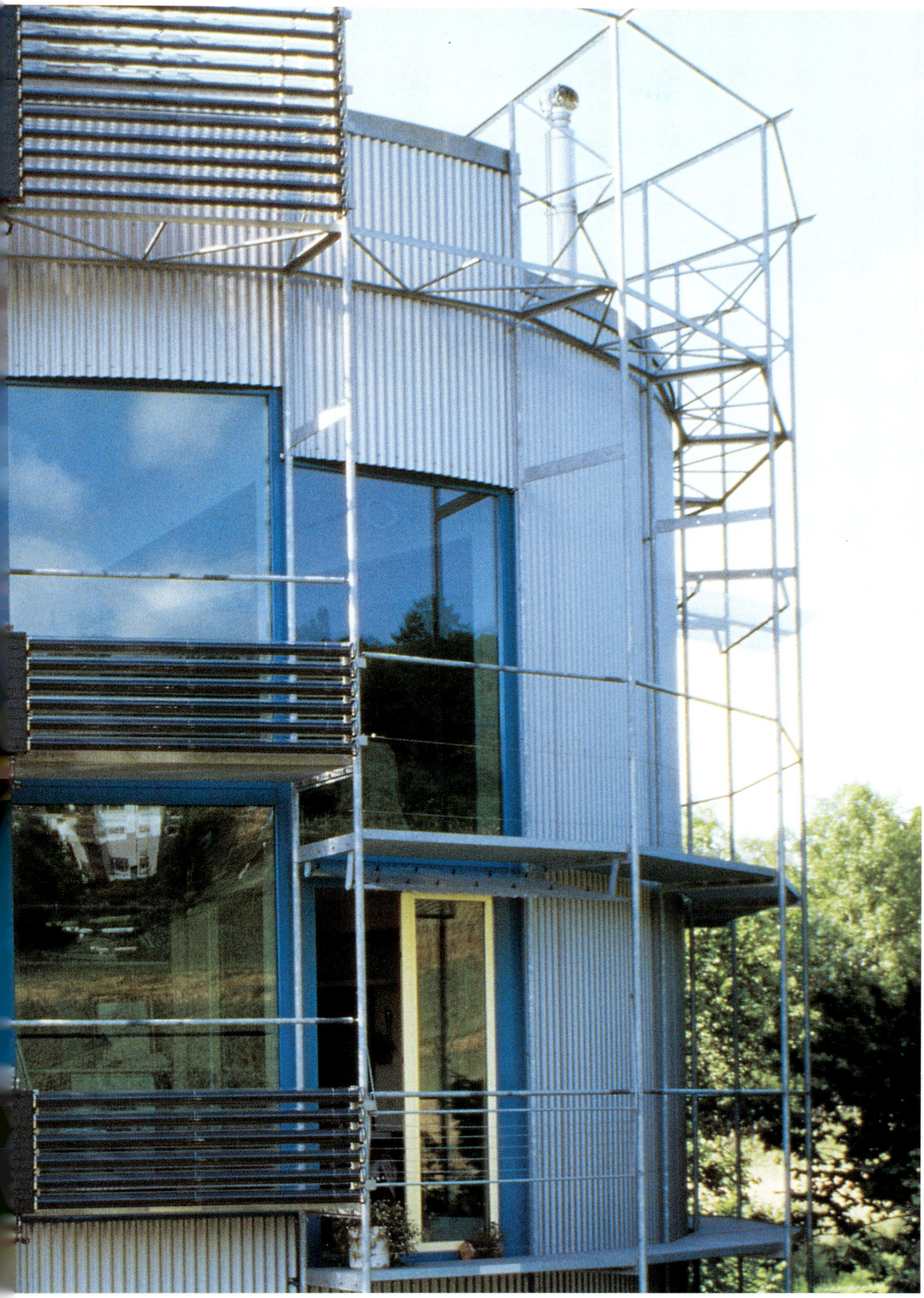

BANG & OLUFSEN VIDEOSYSTEM BEOVISION AVANT *VIDEOSYSTEM*

HERSTELLER MANUFACTURER Bang & Olufsen Technology A/S, Struer, Denmark
PRODUKT PRODUCT Videosystem BeoVision AVANT
DESIGN David Lewis, Copenhagen, Denmark
VERTRIEB DISTRIBUTION Bang & Olufsen Deutschland GmbH, Gilching, Germany

42 10 BESTE DES JAHRES *TOP TEN OF THE YEAR*

BEOVISION AVANT ist ein integriertes Videosystem. Es vereint einen 16:9-Fernseher mit Videorekorder und zwei hochwertigen Aktiv-Lautsprechern. Dabei wurde das Volumen dieser Gerätschaften völlig neu geordnet. Dem Zuschauer springt zunächst eine Wand ins Auge. Sie ist Gehäuse für Bildröhre, Rekorder und Lautsprecher. Zugleich verhilft sie den üblicherweise aufgestapelten Apparaten zu einem einheitlichen Äußeren. Hinter dieser hochragenden Wand aus zweifach lackiertem MDF sind nützliche Anschlüsse und Erweiterungsmodule angebracht. Zum Beispiel die BeoLink-Schnittstelle, die aus dem Fernseher mit Videogerät die Quelle eines vernetzten, raumübergreifenden Audio-/Videosystems macht. Auch die Module für Satellitenempfang, für Dolby Surround Sound und die Bild-in-Bild-Technik, mit denen sich BeoVision Avant erweitern läßt, sind hier untergebracht. Leicht zugänglich, doch so gut wie unsichtbar, verschwinden sie hinter der Gerätewand.

Die strenge Gliederung in augenfällig sichtbare und abgewandte Partien des Geräts konzentriert alle Blicke auf den Bildschirm. Damit das Fernsehvergnügen auch bei ungünstigen Lichtverhältnissen ungetrübt bleibt, läßt sich der motorgesteuerte Drehfuß mittels der individuell programmierbaren Fernsteuerung Beo4 in Idealposition bringen. Schaltet man den Fernseher ein, öffnet sich der Bildschirm langsam wie ein Vorhang. Selbsttätig wird das ideale Bildformat eingestellt, von 16:9 über 14:9 bis 4:3.

Oben am Gehäuse ist dezent ein rotes LED-Display angebracht, das Funktionshinweise übermittelt, ohne das Fernsehbild zu beeinträchtigen. Auf der Rückseite des Displays findet sich eine Drucktastenleiste mit den wichtigsten Steuerelementen. Einzig ein kleines Dreieck markiert das Kasettenfach des Videorekorders – ein funktionales Detail. Selbst den Einschaltknopf hat der Designer David Lewis fast unsichtbar untergebracht, um die betont neutrale Vorderpartie ungestört wirken zu lassen. Den Avant gibt es in den Farben Perlschwarz, Perlgrün, Perlrot und Perlblau.

BEOVISION AVANT is an integrated video system. It unites one 16:9 TV with a video recorder and two high-grade active loudspeakers. The sizes of these devices was completely re-organized. You immediately jump at the sight of a wall. It houses the TV, recorder and loudspeakers. At the same time, it creates a uniform exterior for devices otherwise simply stacked on top of one another. Behind this high wall made of twofold varnished MDF are useful sockets and appropriate extension modules. For example, the BeoLink interface, which networks the television and video set to form the source of a spatial audio-video system. The modules for satellite reception, for Dolby Surround Sound and picture-in-picture technology, with which BeoVision Avant can be expanded can also be housed here. Easily accessible, but invisible to the viewer, they disappear behind the wall. The strict division into clearly visible and hidden sections focuses the gaze on the screen. To ensure that TV enjoyment is upheld even given unfavorable light, the motor-driven swivel base can be rotated to put Beo4 in the ideal position via a programmable remote control. If the TV is switched on, the screen slowly opens like a curtain. The ideal picture format is automatically selected, from 16:9 via 14:9 to the format 4:3. At the top of the housing there is a discreet red LED which indicates functions without distracting from the picture. On the back of the display is a row of push-buttons with the most important controls. A small triangle marks the cassette slot in the video recorder – a functional detail. Designer David Lewis has even made the on/off button largely invisible, in order not to sully the decidedly neutral front. The Avant is available in pearl black, pearl green, pearl red and pearl blue.

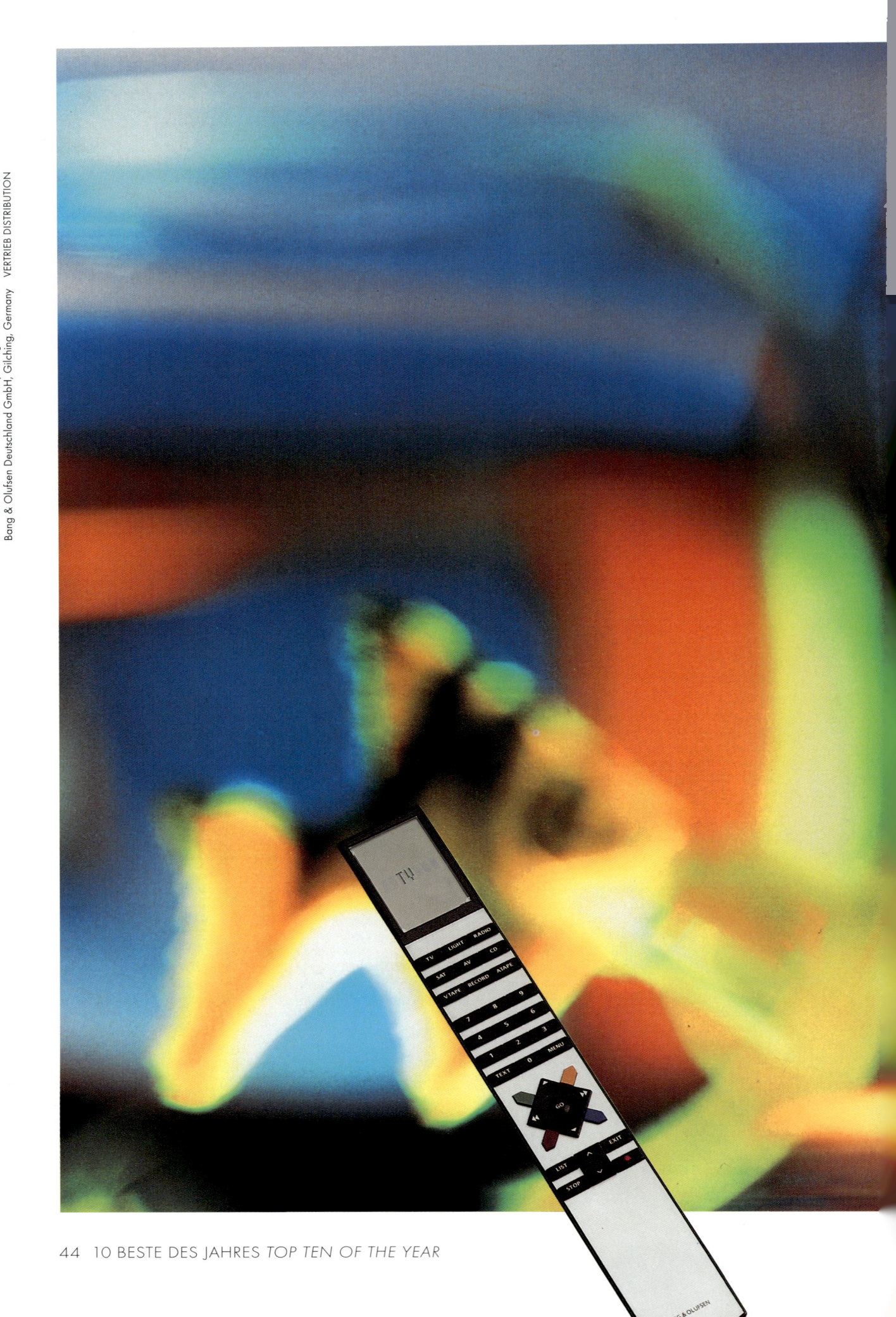

Bang & Olufsen Technology A/S, Struer, Danmark HERSTELLER MANUFACTURER
Videosystem BeoVision AVANT PRODUKT PRODUCT
David Lewis, Copenhagen, Denmark DESIGN
Bang & Olufsen Deutschland GmbH, Gilching, Germany VERTRIEB DISTRIBUTION

44　10 BESTE DES JAHRES *TOP TEN OF THE YEAR*

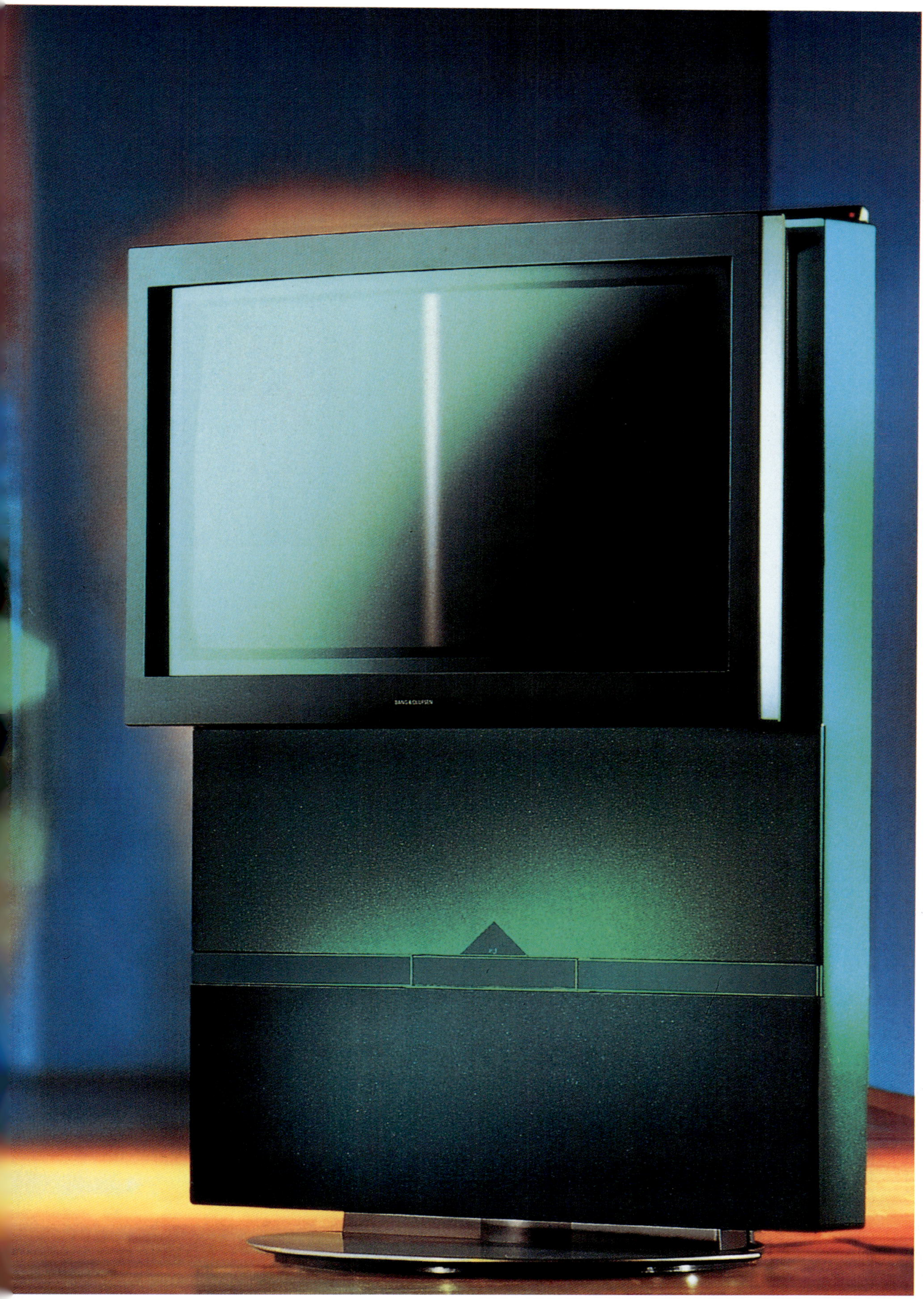

BMW 5ER-REIHE *5 SERIES*

HERSTELLER *MANUFACTURER*
BMW AG, München, Germany

PRODUKT *PRODUCT*
BMW 5er-Reihe *BMW The 5 Series*

DESIGN
BMW Design Team

Freude am Fahren auf allen Plätzen - Innenraum und Ausstattung des neuen 5er:
Der Innenraum des neuen 5er ist ein Maßanzug: Er läßt Freiräume ohne Leere, geht auf Tuchfühlung ohne zu kneifen, kurz, er paßt wie angegossen. Das Resultat ist ein direkter Kontakt zum Fahrzeug und zu seinem Fahrverhalten, eine ideale Verbindung von Komfort und Sicherheit. Im Inneren des neuen 5er setzt sich mit innovativer Konsequenz das dezent sportlich-elegante Konzept fort, das Fahrer und Insassen unter allen Bedingungen möglichst ungetrübte Freude am Fahren ermöglicht. So ist das Cockpit eine Weiterentwicklung des beispielhaften Ergonomiekonzeptes, mit der angewinkelten, fahrerorientierten Instrumententafel. Die formale Einbeziehung der Türverkleidung in die I-Tafel und die optische Öffnung des Fahrerplatzes nach rechts unterstützen das großzügige Raumgefühl. Die vom Fahrerplatz bis zur C-Säule durchgehende Linie schafft die elegante Verbindung von Cockpit und restlichem Innenraum. Das gesamte Ambiente des neuen 5er erscheint nicht von ungefähr vertraut und wie organisch gewachsen. Schon in der Konzeptphase setzten sich Designer, Konstruktions- und Produktionsingenieure zusammen, um für die Insassen die anspruchsvolle Material- und Verarbeitungsqualität zu einem Erlebnis werden zu lassen. Fünf Farbwelten und je drei Stoff- und Ledervarianten erlauben es, dieses Fahrzeug nach individuellen Bedürfnissen auszustatten. Insgesamt ist es die Harmonie des Ganzen und die Stimmigkeit im Detail, welche die für BMW sprichwörtliche »Freude am Fahren« auch im neuen 5er auf eindrucksvolle Weise erlebbar machen.

Sheer driving pleasure whichever seat you occupy - the new 5 Series interior trim and equipment: The interior of the new 5 Series model is like a made-to-measure suit: free movement without superfluous material, a pleasant ambience with no sense of stifling, oppressive restraint. The result is direct contact with the car, awareness of its responses and an ideal blend of comfort and safety. Inside the new 5 Series, restrained sporting style and elegance are taken a stage further, to provide the driver and all the car's occupants with pure driving pleasure in every possible situation. The driver's area and controls feature exemplary ergonomic layout with the fascia angled towards the driver which BMW has steadily developed and refined over the years. The transition from door trim to fascia and the visual opening-up of the driver's area towards the centre of the car emphasise the generous feeling of space. The continuous line leading back to the C-post acts as an elegant link be-ween the driver's area and the remainder of the interior. The new 5 Series creates an ambience that has grown up as an organic entity and seems somehow familiar and welcoming. This is due to its designers', stylists' and production engineers' concerted efforts to ensure material quality and craftsmanship standards that represent a true sensual experience. With five colour environments and three cloth or leather upholstery and trim variants this car caters for the owner's individual needs and wishes. It is this overall harmony and the rightness of every detail which enables the new BMW 5 Series models to communicate the »sheer driving pleasure« for which BMW is renowned in such an immediate, impressive manner.

10 BESTE DES JAHRES *TOP TEN OF THE YEAR* 47

HERSTELLER MANUFACTURER
BMW AG, München, Germany

PRODUKT PRODUCT
BMW 5er-Reihe BMW The 5 Series

DESIGN
BMW Design Team

Elegant und energiesparend, rassig und rücksichtsvoll: Das Exterieurdesign des neuen 5er. Nichts beschreibt den Charakter des neuen 5er besser als seine Formen. Das Design ist kraftvoll und doch leichtfüßig, seine stilistische Raffinesse weckt hohe Emotionen. Nicht der Zeitgeist führte den Designern die Zeichenstifte, sondern der Ehrgeiz, eine zeitgemäße Form zu finden und diese mit historisch gewachsenen Stilelementen wie zum Beispiel Doppelniere und Gegenschwung in der C-Säule harmonisch zu verbinden. Den sportlichen Charakter signalisiert die ansteigende Seitenlinie im Zusammenwirken mit der starken Neigung von Front- und Heckscheibe. Die kurzen Überhänge unterstützen diesen dynamischen Gesamteindruck ebenso wie die typische Sicke in den Seitenwänden, die über die Heckleuchten in die Heckansicht übergeht. Die Heckansicht, die sich durch die Leuchten zu einer klaren Familienähnlichkeit bekennt, ist geprägt durch einen konkaven Gegenzug. Ebenso zitieren die Doppel-Rundscheinwerfer mit ihren schräg angeschnittenen Deckgläsern die bewußte Verwandtschaft zu den anderen Modellreihen. Gelungenes Design ist auch aktiver Partnerschutz. Die glattflächige Gestaltung der Außenkontur, verdeckte Kanten und Teile verringern das Verletzungsrisiko für Fußgänger und Zweiradfahrer. Und gelungenes Design ist auch energiesparend: Der neue 5er bewegt sich mit einem cW-Wert von 0,27 (520i) an der Spitze in seiner Klasse.

Elegant and energy-saving, a tolerant thoroughbred: The new 5 Series body design.

There could be no better way of describing the character of the new 5 Series model than to study its shape. It is a power-ful yet by no means a heavy-footed design, attaining a level of styling refinement that stimulates the emotions. Its designers were inspired less by current fashion than by the urge to achieve a contemporary outline that would harmonise effectively with styling elements of traditional significance for BMW, for example the kidney-shaped radiator grille and the kink formed by the window frame in the C-post. Sporting character is implied by the way in which the waistline rises towards the rear, combined with the steeply raked windscreen and rear window. Short body overhangs confirm this dynamic impression, as does the typical swage-line along the side panels, which extends beyond the rear light clusters and on to the tail panel. Viewed from the rear, the lights create a strong family resemblance, aided by the concave tail panel. Twin circular headlights under angled glass covers are another deliberate echo of other BMW model series. Successful styling can also mean active protection for other road users. Smooth outer panels, concealed edges and the absence of protecting parts reduce the risk of injury to pedestrians and cyclists or motorcyclists. Successful styling saves energy too: the new 5 Series model has a drag coefficient (c_o) of only 0,27 (520i), which puts it among the leaders in its class.

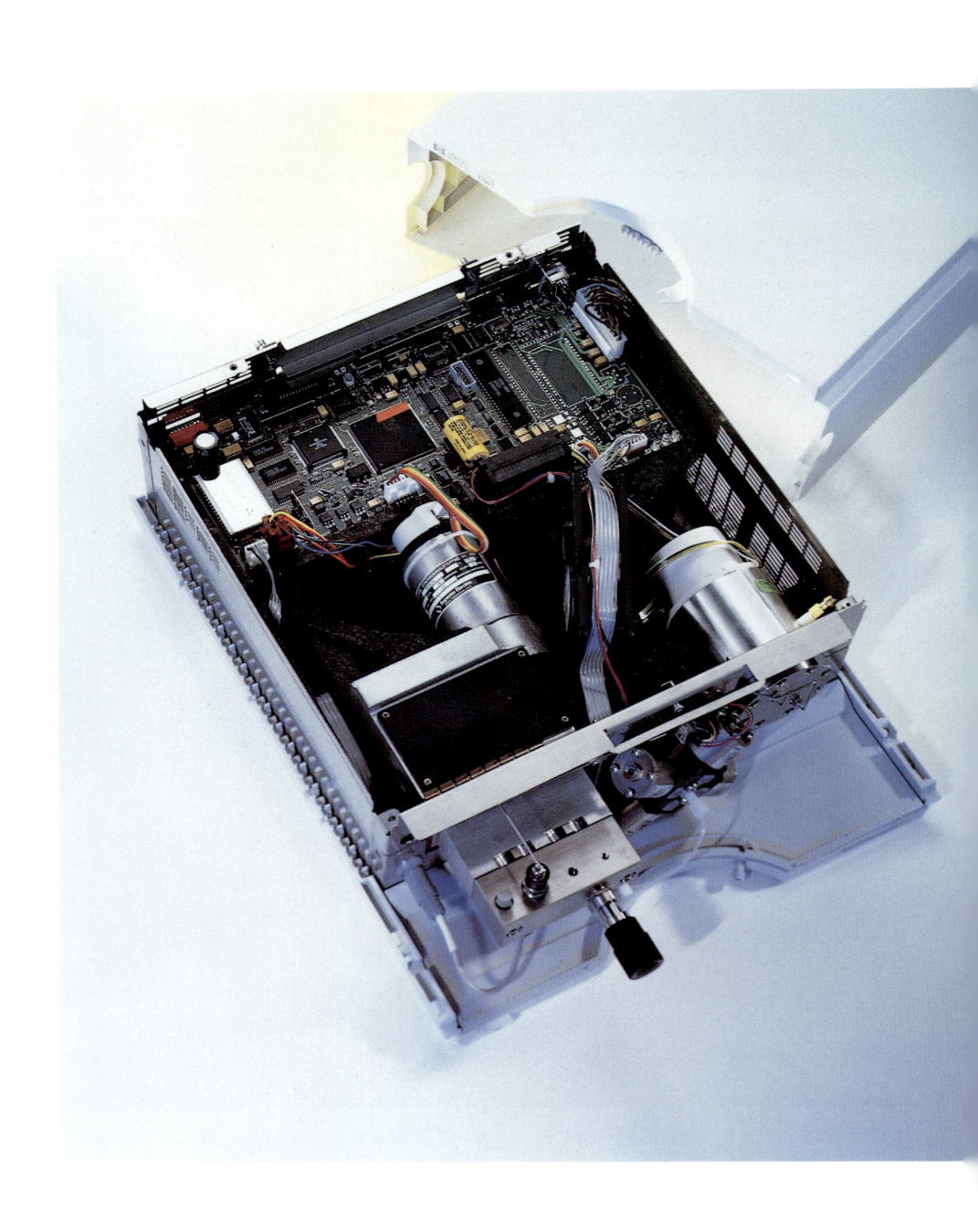

HEWLETT-PACKARD HP SERIE 1100 FLÜSSIGKEITSCHROMATOGRAPH
LIQUID CHROMATOGRAPH

HERSTELLER MANUFACTURER
Hewlett-Packard GmbH, Waldbronn, Germany
PRODUKT PRODUCT
HP Serie 1100 Flüssigkeitschromatograph Liquid chromatograph
DESIGN
Raoul Dinter, Waldbronn, Germany, Consultant: Via 4 Design, Th. Gerlach

FLÜSSIGKEITSCHROMATOGRAPHEN wie die Module der neuen HP Serie 1100 werden zur chemischen Analyse von nicht verdampfbaren Proben, vor allem in der Pharmazie, der Umwelt- und Nahrungsmittelanalytik eingesetzt. Das Gerätesystem läßt sich bei Bedarf automatisieren. Durch Modularität ist es in seiner Leistungsfähigkeit variabel. Gleichermaßen wird das System den Ansprüchen von bestausgebildeten Chemikern und weniger gut trainierten Laboranten gerecht. Mit der Neuentwicklung sollten die Kosten für Erwerb, Betrieb und Unterhalt gegenüber den Vorläufermodellen deutlich verringert werden. Das vereinfachte Gehäusedesign, das mit weniger Bauteilen eine bessere Teileintegration erzielt, hat erheblichen Anteil daran. Raoul Dinter und das Designbüro Via 4 entwarfen ein System, bei dem Baugruppenanordnung, Statik und Schutz der Komponenten und nicht zuletzt das Erscheinungsbild des Systems funktional getrennt sind. Das ermöglicht die Verwendung sortenreiner und wiederverwertbarer Materialien. Auch die Installation wird einfacher. Kürzeste hydraulische Verbindungen hinter leicht zu entfernenden Frontblenden sorgen für simple Wartung. Laborleiter und ausgebildete Laboranten können Abläufe und Analysemethoden auf eine PC-Card programmieren, die von Laborassistenten zur automatisierten Steuerung benutzt werden kann. Die menügesteuerte Eingabeeinheit mit grafischem User-Interface erleichtert die Arbeit und verfügt über erweiterte Selbstdiagnosefähigkeiten.

LIQUID CHROMATOGRAPHS like the modules in the new HP 1100 Series are used for chemical analysis of evaporatable specimens, above all in the pharmaceutical industry, and in environmental and food analysis. The system can, if required, be fully automated. The modules mean that the output can be varied. Yet the system fully meets the requirements of highly-trained chemists and less well-trained lab technicians. The new models were meant to clearly cut purchase, operational and maintenance costs compared with prior models. Largely thanks to a simplified casing design, which ensures better integration of parts with fewer components. Raoul Dinter and the Via 4 design studio drafted a system in which the layout of the modules, stationary qualities and protection of the components and the overall appearance are functionally distinct. This enables materials to be used that can be sorted and recycled. And it makes installation simpler. Shortest hydraulic connections behind easy-to-remove front panels provide for simple maintenance.
Lab managers and trained lab technicians can input the processes and analysis methods on a PC Card program, which can then be used by the lab assistants for automated control. The dialog-based entry unit with a graphic user interface facilitates work and has an expanded self diagnosis capability.

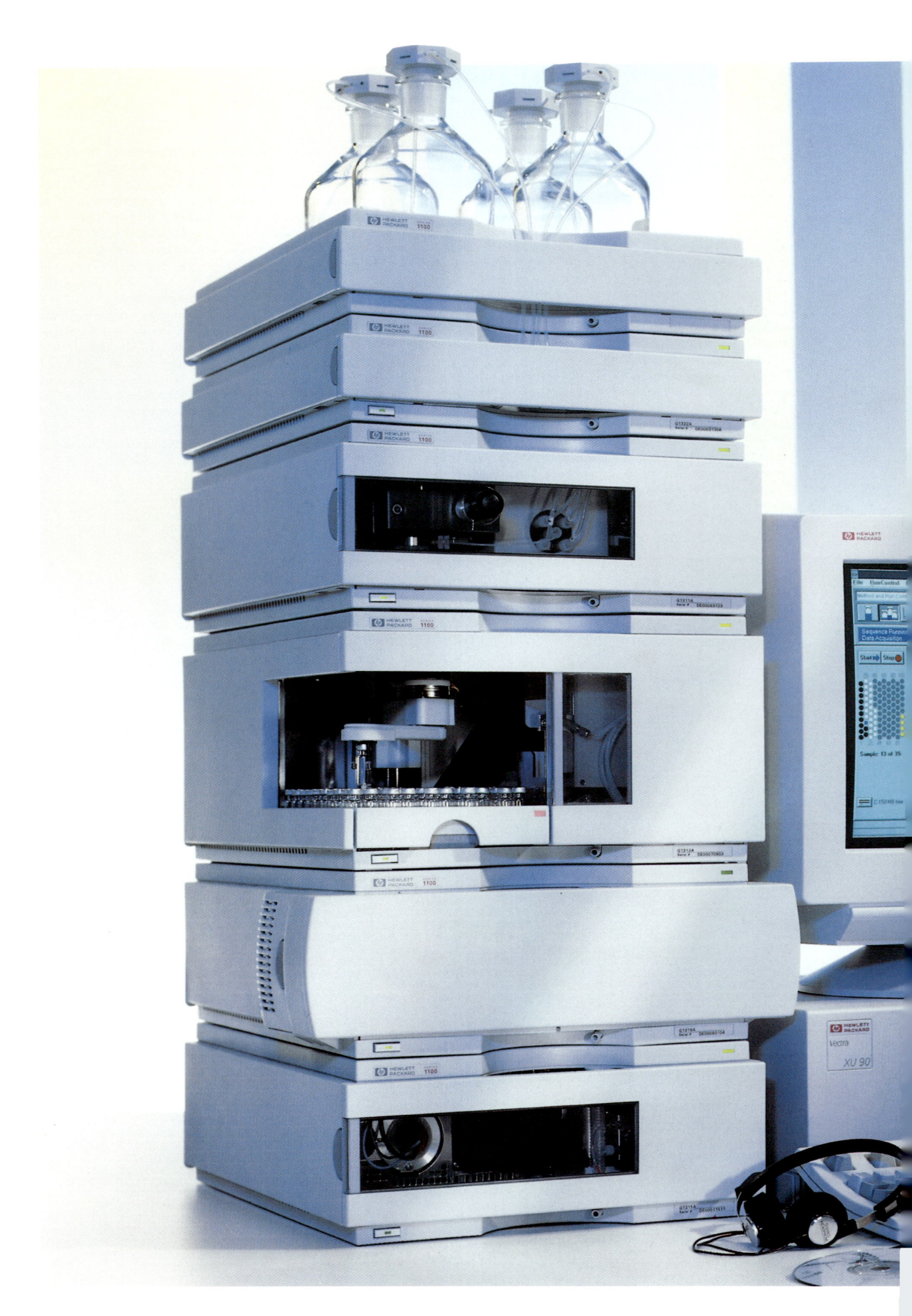

HERSTELLER MANUFACTURER
Hewlett-Packard GmbH, Waldbronn, Germany
PRODUKT PRODUCT
HP Serie 1100 Flüssigkeitschromatograph liquid chromatograph
DESIGN
Raoul Dinter, Waldbronn, Germany, Consultant: Via 4 Design, Th. Gerlach

10 BESTE DES JAHRES *TOP TEN OF THE YEAR* 53

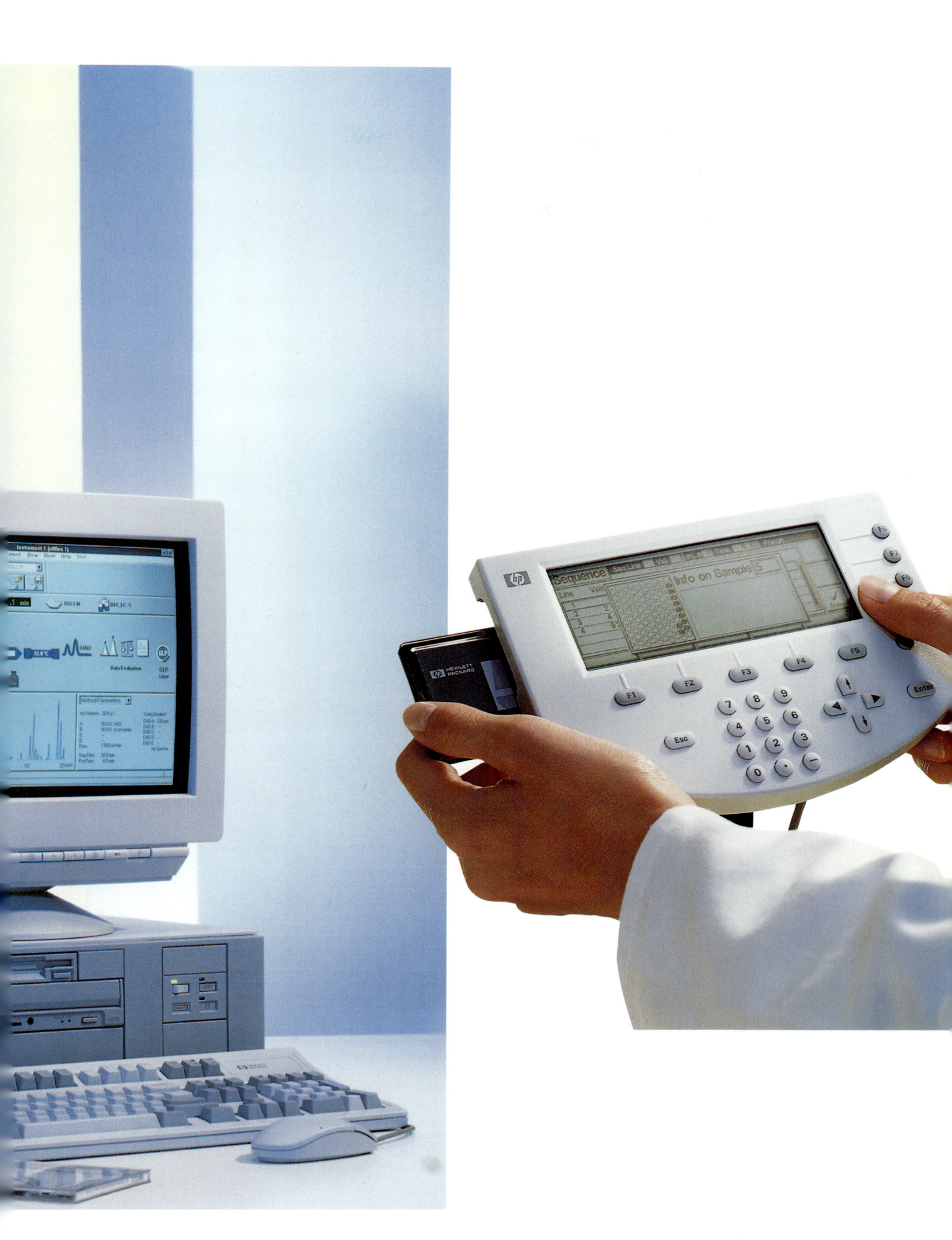

OCÉ 3045 KOPIERGERÄT *PLAIN PAPER COPIER*

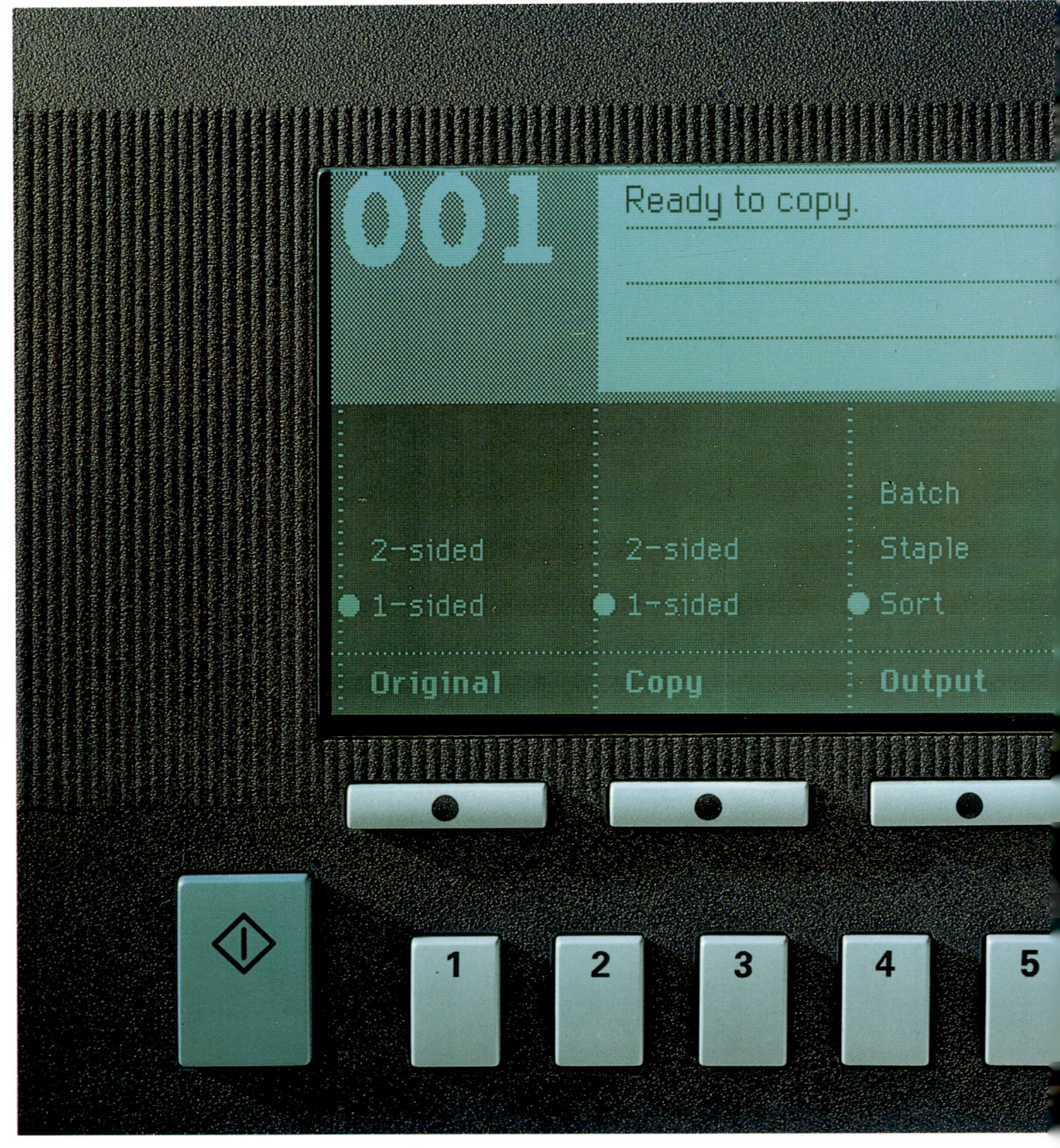

HERSTELLER MANUFACTURER
Océ Nederland B.V., Venlo, The Netherlands
PRODUKT PRODUCT
Océ 3045 Kopiergerät Plain paper copier
DESIGN
Océ Design Team, Venlo, The Netherlands

Ein Kopierer mit der Kapazität von 45 A4-Kopien pro Min. braucht mehr als nur Knöpfchen, nämlich eine intelligente Steuerung. Für den Océ 3045 entwickelte die hauseigene Designabteilung ein grafisches User Interface, das sowohl gelegentlichen wie auch geschulten Nutzern die Arbeit erleichtert. Auf kleinstem Raum eines Vollmatrix-Displays wurden kleinste Pixel derart in Form gebracht, daß sie an Qualitäten holländischer Typographie erinnern. Das Display ist so klein, daß jeder Nutzer sicher sein kann: Hier kann ich nichts falsch machen. Statt auf unverständlichen Symbolen basiert das Interface auf knappen Texten. Nicht nur Programmbefehle, auch Fehlermeldungen sind bewußt einfach und leichtverständlich aufgebaut. Auf Level 1 sind die alltäglichen Kopierfunktionen problemlos einstellbar. Speziellere Funktionen können auf Level 2 programmiert werden. Darüber hinaus kann nur der Systemadministrator bestimmte Einstellungen vornehmen. Ein beispielhaftes Produkt, das beweist: Elektronik kann tatsächlich einen einfacheren Zugang zu den Dingen ermöglichen. Wenn das Interface stimmt.

54 10 BESTE DES JAHRES *TOP TEN OF THE YEAR*

A COPIER that can produce 45 A4 copies in a minute needs more than a few buttons and an intelligent control system. Océ's in-house design department created the graphic user interface for the 3045, facilitating its operation by occasional and trained users rather than confronting them with impossible technical complexity. Within a miniature full matrix display, the minute pixels are designed such that they have the feel of the best Dutch typography. And the display is so small that it convinces any user. Well, I can't go wrong here. Instead of incomprehensible symbols, the interface uses brief texts. All commands and error messages are deliberately easy to understand. At Level 1, every-day copying functions can easily be adjusted. More specialized functions can be programmed at Level 2. And only the system manager can change certain settings. It is an exemplary product and fully proves that electronics can indeed make it easier to use things. With the right interface.

Ökologie/Design Auszeichnung Awarded for Ecology/Design: Vorbildlich durch lange Lebensdauer aufgrund Nachrüstung neuer Funktionen beim Kunden, Aufarbeitung gebrauchter Geräte und Weiterverwendung einzelner Bauteile nach Ende der Gerätelebensdauer. Exemplary long service-life owing to upgrading with new functions on-site, the revamping of used machines and the re-use of individual components after the end of the machine's service life.

büro
office

BÜRO OFFICE

Jury: Christoph Böninger, Horst Diener, Isao Hosoe, Martin Iseli

In welche Richtung sich heute die Bürowelt bewegt, geht exemplarisch aus den Einsendungen zu dieser Kategorie des diesjährigen iF-Design-Wettbewerbs hervor. Abgesehen davon, daß diese Kategorie die umfassendste ist - über 60 Produkte allein wurden ausgezeichnet - spiegelt die Arbeitswelt des Büros und ihr Umfeld das breiteste Designspektrum vom Supercomputer, nicht größer als ein Aktenkoffer auf Rollen, effizient unterm Schreibtisch zu plazieren, genauso wie ein schön gestalteter Bleistiftspitzer für den Schreibtisch, der die mechanisch orientierte, traditionelle Welt des Schreibens in eine optisch wie praktisch gut funktionierende Form bringt. »Elektronik sehen wir im Büro als einen gegebenen Standard«, analysiert Christoph Böninger aus der Jury Office die neuen Trends, »wir drängen die Technik bereits in den Hintergrund und verstärken stattdessen die Designhaltungen«. Als Haltung spielt auch die da und dort bereits sichtbare Recyclingfähigkeit von Produkten der Bürowelt eine Rolle. »Recycling ist vielfach bereits Bestandteil des Produktkonzepts, das semantisch zum Ausdruck gebracht wird.« Office, ob in der Farbgebung, der Produktkommunikation oder Produktdifferenzierung, hat im Designbereich eine Leitfunktion. Der Trend steht auf Transparenz und Leichtigkeit. Der ernste Respekt vor den teuren Maschinen ist einem anmutigen und eher spielerischen Umgang gewichen, der einer weichen Welle der Corporate Culture entspricht. Diesen ungezwungeneren Leitbildern folgt auch die Gestaltung der Büromöbel, die sich ebenfalls weg vom herkömmlichen Schematismus orientieren.

Das hohe Niveau der Leistungen im Office-Bereich und der dort herrschende stimulierende Wettbewerb spiegelt sich auch darin, daß von den Top Ten, den 10 besten des Jahres, die internationale Jury allein vier Produkten aus diesem Bereich die höchste Auszeichnung zuerkannte. Ausgezeichnet wurde, was als repräsentativ für die gesamte Kategorie Büro gewertet werden kann:

1. Ein flexibles Konferenzmöbel, ein Programm stilistisch und semantisch angesiedelt zwischen Schulmilieu und High-Tech,
2. ein Server System, in dem der Designer die sachliche Welt des Computerdesigns mit modischen farb- und material-orientierten Einflüssen aus dem avantgardistischen Möbeldesign zusammenbringt,
3. ein tragbarer Computer mit scherenförmig ausziehbarer Tastatur, ein von Hand nachvollziehbares und mechanisches Wunder und gleichzeitig ein elektronischer Hochleistungs-Fetisch, der sich vor den Augen des Nutzers erst zu einer praktikablen Größe ausziehen läßt,
4. ein Telekommunikationsgerät als Videokamera in einem schwenkbaren Ring, das formschön und bedienerfreundlich zur Videokonferenz einlädt.

The direction in which the office world is moving today is reflected in exemplary manner by the entries submitted under this category to this year's iF design competition. Apart from the fact that this category is by far the most comprehensive - over 60 products received awards, the workaday office world and the office environment reflects the broadest design spectrum, ranging from super computers no larger than an executive briefcase on rollers that fits efficiently under any desk, to a beautifully modeled pencil sharpener for the executive's desk, which gives the mechanically oriented traditional world of writing a striking visual form and a handy practical form, too.

"We consider that electronics is a given standard in any office," explains Christoph Boeninger from the Jury Office with regard to the new trends. "We are already confining technology to the wings and instead fostering the design approach taken." One approach that is playing a role is the recyclability of products for the office world, something already to be seen here and there. "In many areas, recycling is already part of the product concept and is already lent semantic expression." The office, be it with regard to color, product communication or product differentiation, functions as the pace-maker in design. The trend is for greater transparency and lightness. The serious respect shown expensive machines has given way to a graceful and decidedly more playful approach, which corresponds to the softer strategy in corporate culture. The design of office furniture also follows these more unrestrained models as has likewise started to orient itself away from the traditional schematism. The high level of achievements in design in the office area and the stimulating competition that predominates there is also reflected in the fact that the international jury selected four products from this area for the outstanding distinction as Top Ten designs of the year. The award was given for designs that could be considered representative for the category of Office as a whole:

1. A flexible conference furniture system, a program stylistically and semantically positioned halfway between a school environment and high tech;
2. a server system in which the designer had blended the down-to-earth world of computer design with fashionable colors and materials influenced by trends in avant-garde furniture design;
3. a portable computer with a scissors-like pull-out keyboard, a mechanical miracle immediately apparent to the user and simultaneously an electronic high-performance fetish, which first attains its practical size when the user pulls it out;
4. a telecommunications device, namely a video camera in a revolving ring which with its formal beauty and user-friendliness encourages participants to take part in a video conference.

Ums-Pastoe bv, Utrecht, The Netherlands — HERSTELLER MANUFACTURER
Perception, Schranksystem Cupboard system — PRODUKT PRODUCT
ninaber/peters/krouwel industrial design, Leiden, The Netherlands — DESIGN

PERCEPTION, Schranksystem mit einer klaren, offenen Struktur, aufgebaut aus liegenden und schlanken Aluminiumträgern sowie vertikalen Multiplexständern. Diese Grundstruktur läßt sich mit Umklapptüren, diversen Schubladen und Rückwänden verschiedener Ausführung kombinieren. Durch variable Flächen und Umklapptüren läßt sich vor allem die Front einfach umgestalten. Mit elektrischen Anschlüssen und Beleuchtung auszustatten.

PERCEPTION is a cupboard system featuring a clear, open structure and consisting of sleek aluminum shelves and multiplex side panels. These can be fitted with hinged doors, drawers and rear panels in various finishes. With the variety of possible surface finishes and color combinations, the appearance can easily be altered. The unit can also be fitted with electrical equipment and light fittings.

Microsoft Corporation, Redmond, USA — HERSTELLER MANUFACTURER
Microsoft Natural Keyboard — PRODUKT PRODUCT
ZIBA Design, Portland, USA — DESIGN

MICROSOFT NATURAL KEYBOARD, eine preisgünstige ergonomische Tastatur für Haus- und Bürogebrauch, die man einfach anschließt und ohne Übung nutzen kann. Es gibt keine besonderen oder vom Benutzer zu verändernden Einstellungen. Die Ergonomie liegt im Design des Peripheriegeräts, darum hat es z. B. keine entfernbaren Handgelenkstützen.
MICROSOFT NATURAL KEYBOARD is a low-cost ergonomic keyboard for home or office use, simple to connect and needing no special training or adjustments. The design focuses on ergonomic peripherals, making detachable wrist pads unnecessary.

Hagenuk Telecom GmbH, Kiel, Germany   HERSTELLER MANUFACTURER
HomeHandy CD Schnurloses Telefon, Cordless telephone   PRODUKT PRODUCT
Phoenix Product Design, Stuttgart, Germany   DESIGN

HOMEHANDY CD, schnurloses Telefon mit digitaler DECT-Technik für excellente Sprachübertragung. Set besteht aus Mobilteil und Basisstation. 1-zeiliges Display, 10 Speicherplätze für Kurzwahl, 48 Stunden Betriebsbereitschaft.

The HOMEHANDY CD is a cordless phone featuring digital DECT technology guaranteeing exceptional voice quality. The set consists of a mobile unit and a base station. The handset has a 1-line display, 10 destination memory, at 48 hours standby.

HERSTELLER MANUFACTURER
Interflex Datensysteme GmbH, Stuttgart, Germany
PRODUKT PRODUCT
IF 611, Zutrittskontrollterminal, Access control card reader
DESIGN
Neumeister Design, München, Germany

oben: IF 611 Zutrittskontrollterminal, das in Zutrittskontrollsystemen der Erfassung und Dekodierung von Ausweisen dient, wahlweise auch mit zusätzlicher Vorrichtung zur Eingabe eines Pin-Code. Mit der dazugehörigen Standsäule kann das Terminal freistehend im Innen- und Außenbereich eingesetzt werden.

above: The IF 611 card reader terminal is ideally suited for access control systems. The card reader can be used for data capture and ID-recognition with or without an additional Pin code. The special pillar mounting means the card reader can function as a standalone device for either indoor or outdoor applications.

rechte Seite: IF 7000 Zutrittskontrollterminal, ein Kartenleser mit zusätzlichem automatischen Gesichtsvergleich, für Systeme mit hohen Sicherheitsanforderungen. Biometrische Eigenschaften werden auf der Basis neuronaler Netze zur sicheren Verifikation von Ausweisbild und Ausweisinhaber verglichen.

right side: The IF 7000 is an access control card reader with additional automatical face recognition for use in high security applications. Biometric characteristics are compared on the basis of neuronal networks, thus enabling verification that cards are held by the actual cardholders.

62 BÜRO OFFICE

Terminal IF 7000 mit maschinellem Gesichtsvergleich Access control card reader with automated face recognition
Neumeister Design, München, Germany DESIGN

Interflex Datensysteme GmbH, Stuttgart, Germany HERSTELLER MANUFACTURER
PRODUKT PRODUCT

HERSTELLER MANUFACTURER IBM Corporation, Armonk, USA
PRODUKT PRODUCT IBM RISC System/Model E20, Workgroup server
DESIGN IBM Austin Design Center, Karen MacMurtie, Kurtis Sakai; Austin, USA

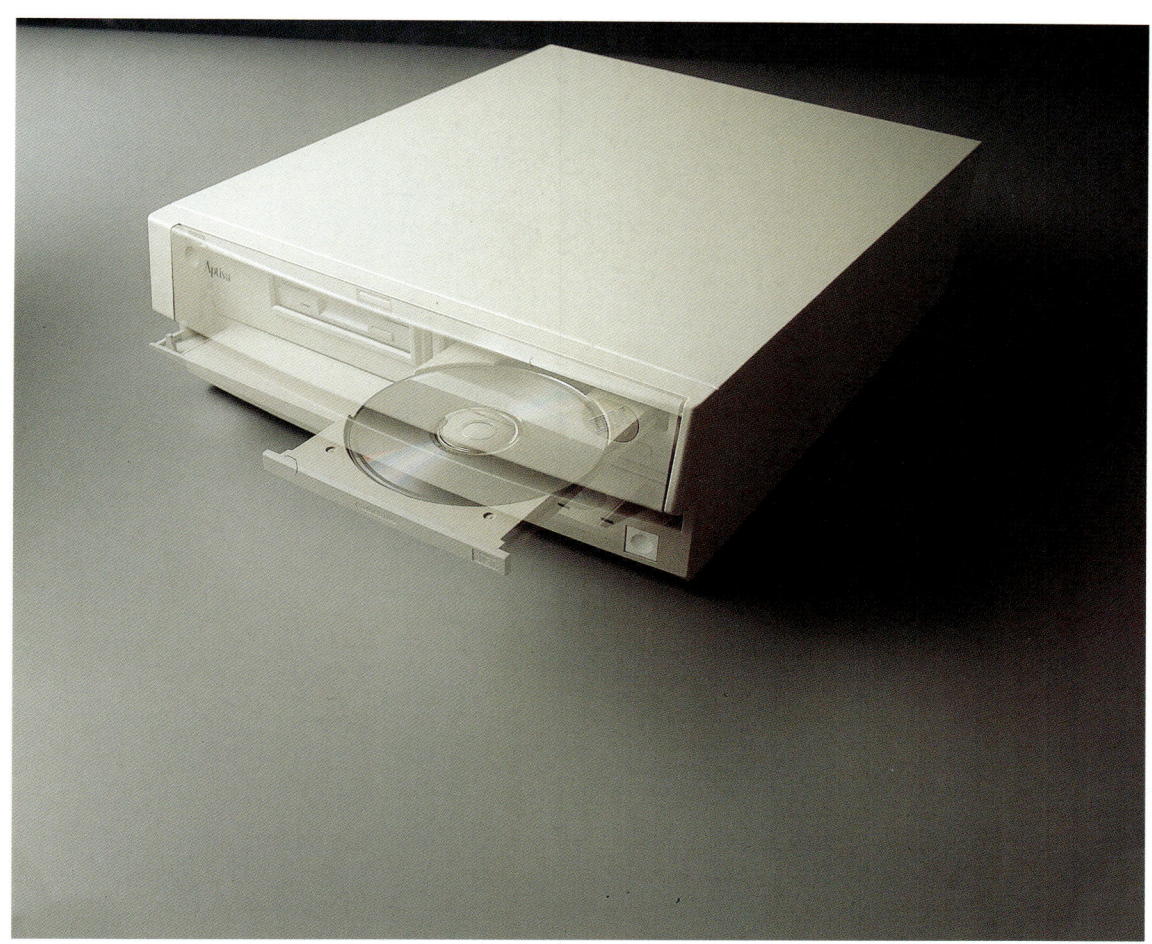

HERSTELLER MANUFACTURER
IBM Corporation, Armonk, USA
PRODUKT PRODUCT
Aptiva M50, Desktop Personal Computer
DESIGN
IBM Design, Armonk, USA

links: E20 WORKGROUP SERVER aus dem IBM RISC System/ 6000, das Einsteigermodell dieser Serie, das auf der leistungsstarken PowerPC-Technik aufbaut. Einfache Inbetriebnahme durch das AIX Betriebssystem, Version 4, von IBM und eine Vielzahl vorinstallierter, konfigurierter Optionen. Modular konzipierte Prozessorkarte kann mit der Weiterentwicklung der PowerPC-Technik bequem Schritt halten. Acht Laufwerke, acht Steckplätze für die gängigsten Zusatzgeräte. Die I/O Steckplätze des E 20 unterstützen den neuesten High Performance PCI Standard sowie den traditionellen ISA Bus.

left: The IBM RISC System/ 6000 Model E20 is an entry-level server based on the powerful and popular PowerPC technology. Initial setup is easier than ever with IBM's AIX version 4 operating system as well as the wide variety of pre-installed and pre-configured options. The modular processor card makes it convenient to upgrade as new PowerPC technology emerges. Eight media bays and eight expansion slots provide adequate internal space for commonly used components. The I/O slots in the E 20 support the emerging high performance PCI standard, as well as the traditional ISA bus.

oben: IBM M 50 Desktop PC aus der Aptiva-Produktfamilie, die speziell für die Anwendung zu Hause oder in kleinen Büros entwickelt wurde. In Funktion und Technik auf den Experten zugeschnitten, dennoch auch für Einsteiger einfach zu installieren und zu bedienen. Vorinstallierte Software mit beliebten Anwendungsprogrammen und Spielen. Die meisten Modelle mit Lautsprechern, Mikrofon etc. für Multimedia eingerichtet. Eine Klappe schützt die Laufwerke, wenn sie nicht genutzt werden.

above: The IBM M 50 Aptiva is a Desktop PC designed specially for the home and small businesses. It is easy for the beginner to set up and use, yet has advanced functions and features suitable for an expert. The Aptiva computers have popular personal productivity and entertainment software installed. Most models have speakers and microphone and multimedia capabilities. A protective cover conceals the disk drives when not in use.

BÜRO OFFICE 65

HERSTELLER MANUFACTURER IBM Corporation, Research Triangle Park, USA
PRODUKT PRODUCT IBM PC Server 320
DESIGN IBM Design Program, PC Server Business Unit, Roland K. Alo, Research Trinagle Park, USA

IBM PC Server 320, ein symmetrisches Multiprozessorsystem (SMP) mit zwei 90 Mhz Pentium Prozessoren. Entwickelt für Datenbankanwendungen in Unternehmensnetzwerken. Unterstützt von 50 bis zu 400 Workstations. Formal attraktive und funktionale Kühlschlitze in der Gerätefront.

The IBM PC SERVER 320 is a symmetric multiprocessing (SMP) system powered by two 90 Mhz Pentium processors. Designed for file and database applications in LANs in companies. The server supports 50 to 400 workstations. Front louvers, attractive as well as functional, provide a path for fresh air to cool the internal components.

66 BÜRO OFFICE

BÜRO OFFICE 67

HERSTELLER MANUFACTURER IBM Corporation, Reasearch Triangle Park, USA
PRODUKT PRODUCT IBM PC Server 720
DESIGN IBM Design Program, PC Server Business Unit Roland K. Alo, Reasearch Triangle Park, USA

IBM PC SERVER 720, ein symmetrisches Multiprozessorsystem (SMP) mit zwei 100 Mhz Pentium Prozessoren. Entwickelt für Datenbankanwendungen in Unternehmen. Unterstützt von 50 bis zu 1000 Workstation Clients. Mit 22 Bays für große Datenmengen ausgerüstet, unterstützt bis zu 18 interne Hot-Swap-Festplatten. Attraktiv gestaltete Kühlschlitze in Front und Rückseite der Geräte. Hinter der halbrunden, leicht zu öffnenden bzw. zu entfernenden Verkleidung an der Rückseite verschwinden die Kabel. Die zurückgesetzten Kühlschlitze ermöglichen die Zirkulation der Kühlluft auch bei direkt an die Wand gerücktem Gerät.

The IBM PC SERVER 720 is a symmetric multiprocessing (SMP) system powered by six 100 Mhz Pentium processors. This commercial, LAN server supports file and database applications for 50 to 1,000 workstations. Designed to provide massive storage, the system has 22 bays and supports up to 18 internal, hot-swap hard disks. This high-performance server supports PCI/EISA and PC I/Micro Channel architectures. Dramatic design incorporates functional front and rear louvers that allow fresh air to cool internal components. The rear bezel, designed with an integrated cylindrical cable cover, can be easily opened or detached. The recessed louvers prevent airflow restriction should the machine be pushed against a wall.

BÜRO OFFICE 69

HERSTELLER MANUFACTURER
Polaroid Corporation, Cambridge, USA
PRODUKT PRODUCT
Polaroid Sprintscan 35, Scanner
DESIGN
IDEO, Scott Stropkay, Mark Nichols, David Weissburg, David Privitera, Lexington, USA

POLAROID SPRINTSCAN 35, ein 35 mm-Bild-Scanner für den Arbeitsplatz von Grafikdesignern, Fotojournalisten und Multimedia-Nutzern. Entwicklungsziele waren die hohe Geschwindigkeit der Bildentwicklung, ein hoher Qualitätsstandard und Bedienerfreundlichkeit. Das kompakte Design ermöglicht einfachen Transport des Geräts zu verschiedenen Einsatzorten »on the road«: so haben Journalisten die Möglichkeit, vor Ort entwickelte Filme zu scannen und sofort über Modem an die Redaktion zu schicken.
The POLAROID SPRINTSCAN 35 is a 35 mm slide scanner for professional use typically by graphic designers, photo-journalists and multimedia users. The goal was to provide high-speed electronic imaging, high quality output and ease of use. The compact design facilitates simple transport to different places »on the road«, enabling journalists for example to scan films developed on site and send them via modem to editorial desks immediately.

rechts: DIGICAD VISION, ein ultraflaches Grafiktablett, mit kabellosem Zubehör zur computergestützten Eingabe von grafischen Daten aller Art.
right: DIGICAD VISION, an ultrathin graphics tablet featuring cordless accessories for computer-assisted input of all kinds of graphics data.

70 BÜRO OFFICE

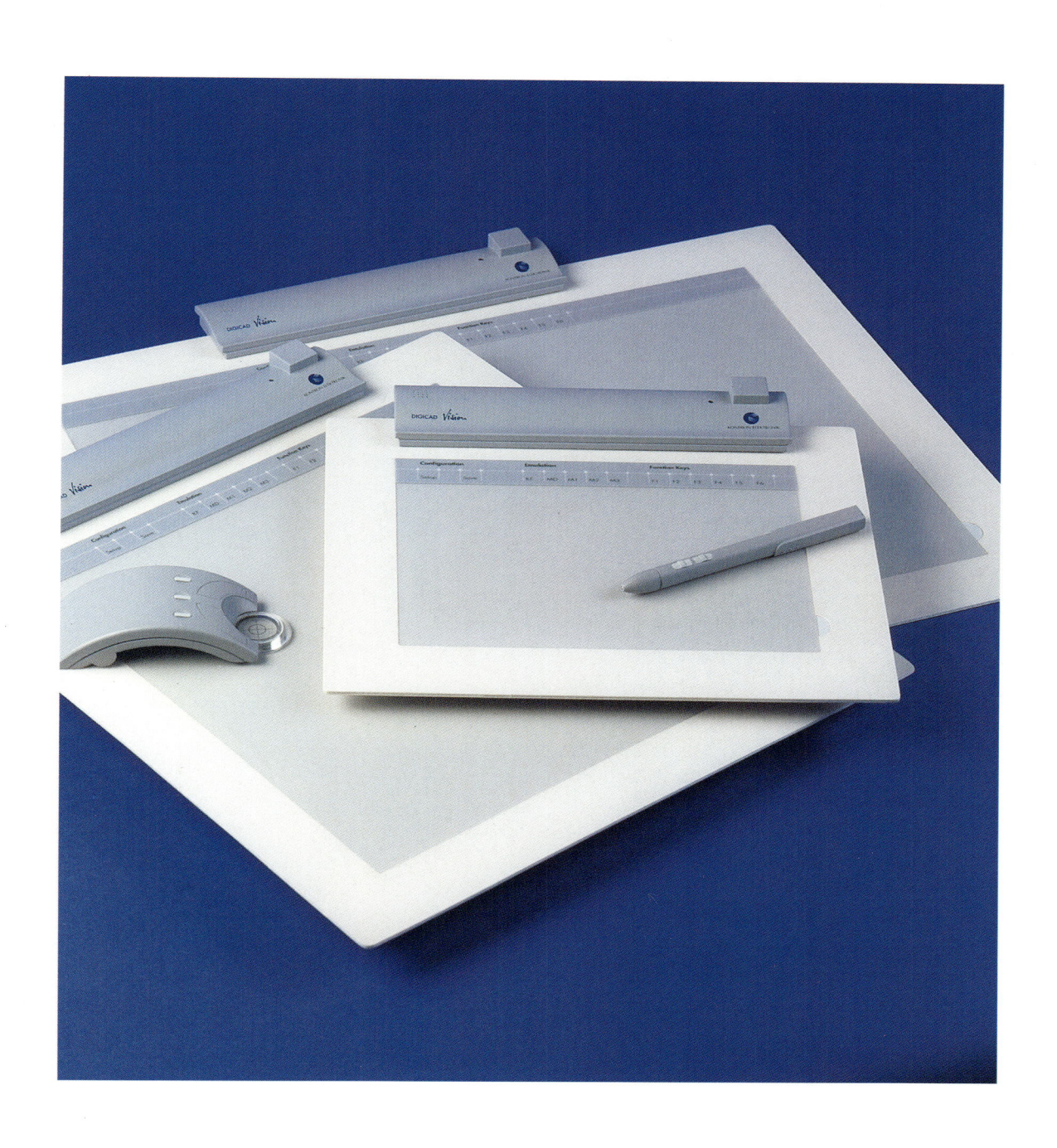

Kontron Elektronik GmbH, Elching, Germany HERSTELLER MANUFACTURER
DCV Digicad Vision Grafiktablett Graphics tablet PRODUKT PRODUCT
Neumeister Design, München, Germany DESIGN

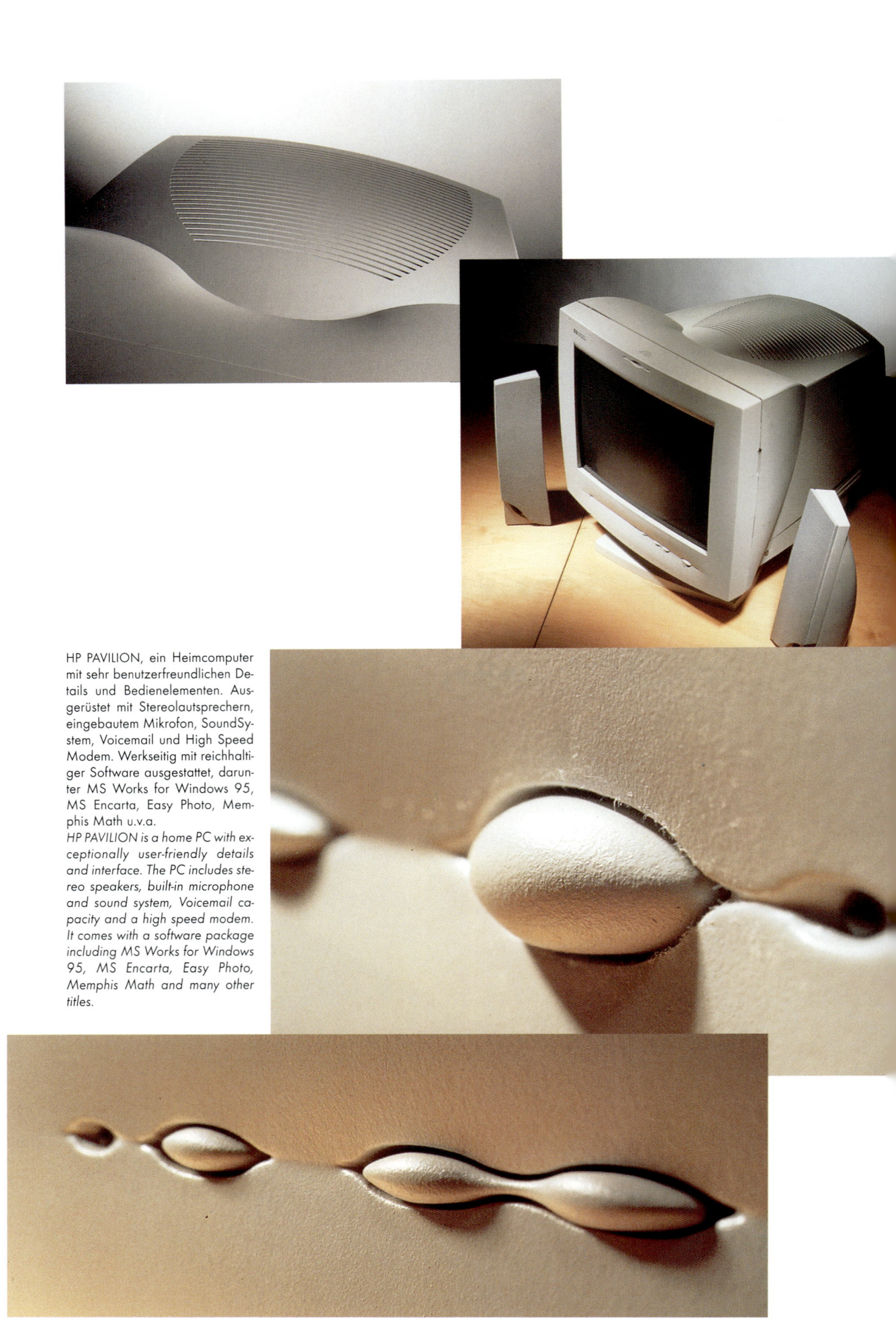

HERSTELLER MANUFACTURER
Hewlett-Packard Company, Santa Clara, USA

PRODUKT PRODUCT
HP PAVILION PC, Heim Computer Home computer

DESIGN
Hewlett-Packard, Peter Lee, Santa Clara, USA, LUNAR Design, Yves Behar, Gil Wong, Palo Alto, USA

HP PAVILION, ein Heimcomputer mit sehr benutzerfreundlichen Details und Bedienelementen. Ausgerüstet mit Stereolautsprechern, eingebautem Mikrofon, SoundSystem, Voicemail und High Speed Modem. Werkseitig mit reichhaltiger Software ausgestattet, darunter MS Works for Windows 95, MS Encarta, Easy Photo, Memphis Math u.v.a.

HP PAVILION is a home PC with exceptionally user-friendly details and interface. The PC includes stereo speakers, built-in microphone and sound system, Voicemail capacity and a high speed modem. It comes with a software package including MS Works for Windows 95, MS Encarta, Easy Photo, Memphis Math and many other titles.

72 BÜRO OFFICE

Hewlett-Packard, Fort Collins Division, Fort Collins, USA   HERSTELLER MANUFACTURER
HP Flachbildschirm Flat panel display   PRODUKT PRODUCT
ZIBA Design, Portland, USA   DESIGN

HP FLAT PANEL DISPLAY ist der erste freistehende Flachbildschirm für Arbeitsplatzrechner. Entwickelt für Finanzmärkte und ähnliche Arbeitsplätze mit beschränktem Raum, in denen es aber auf anspruchsvolle Ästhetik ankommt. Plug and Play-Technik ermöglicht problemlose Installation an der Workstation. Justierbarer Bildschirmwinkel, ergonomisches Design. Geringes Gewicht und ein eingebautes Kabelverwaltungssystem machen den Bildschirm beweglich, dadurch bequemer Informationsaustausch mit dem Kunden.

The HP FLAT PANEL DISPLAY is the first standalone flat panel display for workstations. Designed for the financial markets and similar office scenarios where space is limited and desktop aesthetics are important. The plug and play technology ensures simple connections to workstations. Adjustable screen angle, ergonomic design with ultra-compact footprint. Light weight and integrated cable management system enhance mobility and thus make sharing screen information with clients easy.

BÜRO OFFICE 73

HERSTELLER MANUFACTURER
Hewlett-Packard Company, Greeley, USA
PRODUKT PRODUCT
HP Surestore Optical Library Optisches Datenarchiv
DESIGN
Hewlett-Packard, Jim Dow, Mo Khovaylo, Greeley, USA

SURESTORE OPTICAL LIBRARY, ein virtuelles Archiv zur Sammlung und Verwaltung von Informationen in Bildform. Die Papiervorlagen (Akten, Bücher, Zeitschriften) werden eingescannt, die Daten auf Bildkassetten gespeichert (Kapazität bis zu 100 Gigabyte oder 256 Millionen Buchseiten). Ein interner automatischer Wechsler führt die Kassetten zu Laufwerken, die den Zugriff auf die Daten ermöglichen. Das Archiv ist für Büroumgebungen ausgelegt und über PC-Netzwerkarbeitsplätze aufzurufen. Das virtuelle Archiv spart Papier und Büroraum. Alle über 3 Gramm schweren Plastikteile sind gekennzeichnet und recyclebar; die feuergeschützten Werkstoffe sind ohne Bromierung. Minimierte Verpackung, ungebleichter Karton und Tinten aus organischem Material.

SURESTORE OPTICAL LIBRARY is a virtual archive for collecting and archiving optical digitized data. Such data is scanned in from paper documents such as photos, magazine articles of typewritten and handwritten texts and after then stored on optical cartridges: the cartridge bank has a memory capacity of up to 100 gigabytes, the equivalent of 256 million book pages. An internal robotic changer moves the cartridges from storage slots to optical drives to access the data. The archive is designed for typical offices and can be accessed by networked PC users. The virtual archive saves paper and storage space. All plastic parts weighing more than three grams are tagged with material type IDs and recyclable; no brominated fire-retardant materials are used. Packaging is minimized and utilizes only non-bleached cardboard and organic inks.

HP K-CLASS CLIENT SERVER, ein 1-bis 4-Wege Client Server Computer, geeignet für den Einsatz in einer Mehr-Benutzer-Umgebung im Büro oder im Computerraum. Maßgeblich für das Design war die Bedienungsfreundlichkeit. Die Wartung und Installation des Geräts werden durch einfache Details symbolisch vermittelt. Alle Plastikteile nur durch Steckverbindung mit dem Stahlgehäuse verbunden, dadurch rasche Montage und effektive Demontage im Hinblick auf Wartung und späteres Recycling.

The HP K CLASS CLIENT SERVER is designed for use in a multi-user office or computer room environment. Central priority was attached to user friendliness. Use, servicing, and installation are all indicated with simple intuitive details. The unit features only plastic parts, which snap together over a steel chassis to ensure simple assembly and effective disassembly for servicing and for eventual recycling.

Hewlett-Packard Company, Roseville, CA, USA HERSTELLER MANUFACTURER
HP K-Class Client Server, 1-4 Wege Prozessor Computer 1 to 4-way processing computer PRODUKT PRODUCT
Hewlett-Packard, Bud Mousa, Roseville, CA, USA DESIGN

BÜRO OFFICE 75

HERSTELLER MANUFACTURER
Garny Sicherheitstechnik GmbH, Mörfelden, Germany

PRODUKT PRODUCT
GARNY SAFECONTROL, Bediener- und Kundenterminal, Operator and customer terminal

DESIGN
PATZAK DESIGN, Darmstadt, Germany

GARNY SAFECONTROL, ein Set zur elektronischen Steuerung von Mietfachanlagen in Kreditinstituten: das Bedienerterminal GSC-BT zur Dateneingabe durch das Bankpersonal und Kundenterminal GSC-KTT, ein Tischgerät zur Kundenselbstbedienung z.B. im Schalterraum, eingerichtet zur Benutzung von Magnetkarten und vier- bis achtstelligem PIN. Eine zuverlässige elektronische Überwachung und Steuerung der Schließvorgänge erhöht die Sicherheit und die Wirtschaftlichkeit der Anlage.

GARNY SAFECONTROL is a special electronic terminal set for deposit safebox data inputs in banks. The GSC-BT input terminal is used for data entry by banking staff whereas the GSC-KTT customer terminal is a table-top unit for use by customers: the terminal is operated by magnetic cards and a four to eight digit PIN code. Reliable electronic monitoring and controls for the locking mechanism augment security and cost-effectiveness.

BÜRO OFFICE 77

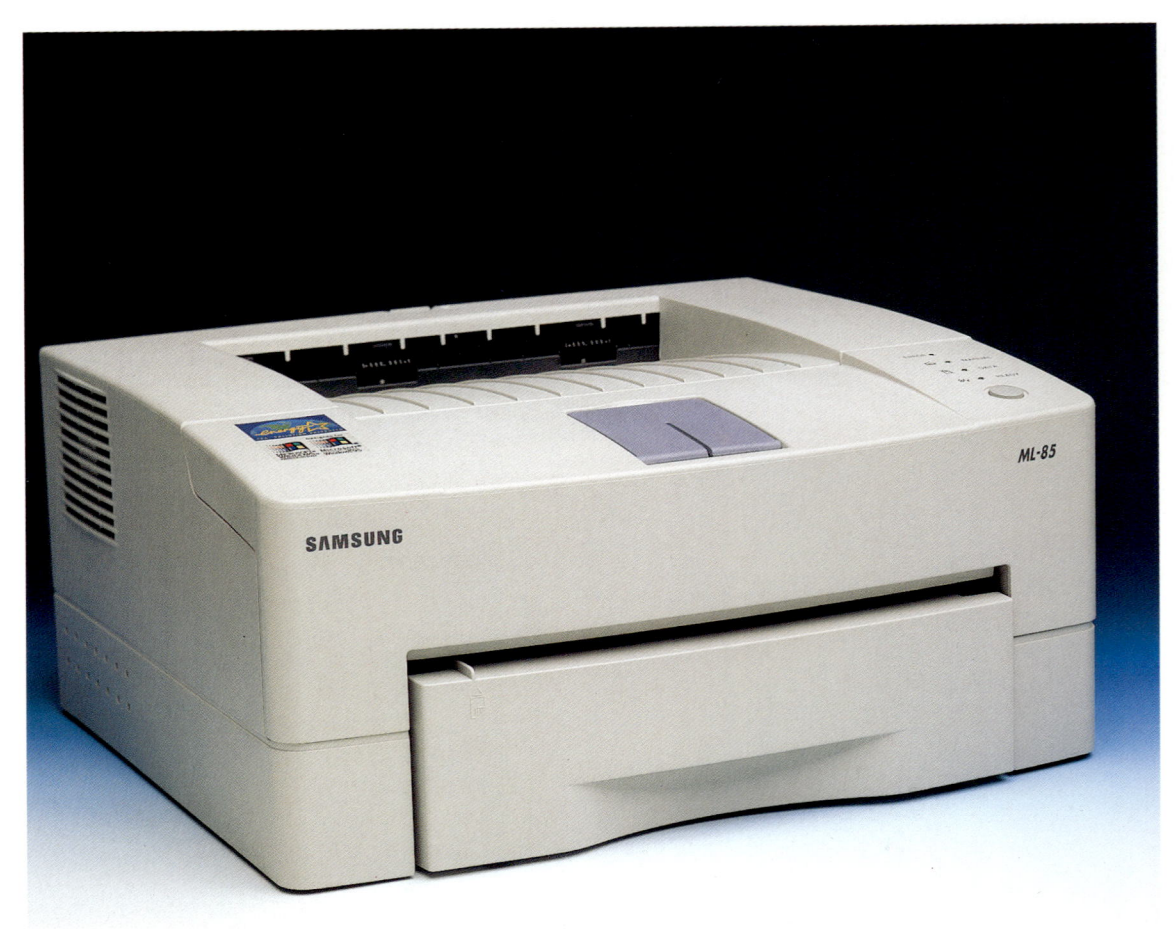

HERSTELLER MANUFACTURER: Samsung Electronics Co., Ltd., Suwon City, Korea
PRODUKT PRODUCT: ML 85 Laserdrucker Laser printer
DESIGN: Samsung Design Center, Seoul, Korea
VERTRIEB DISTRIBUTION: Samsung Electronics GmbH, Sulzbach, Germany

SAMSUNG ML 85, ein Laserdrucker in kompakt strukturiertem Design und umweltfreundlicher Technik. Äußerst schnell, Tonersparmodus, mit 45 installierten Scalable Fonts (darunter 10 True Type Fonts), hoher Auflösung, unterstützt HP-Laser-Jet™- und schnelle MS-Windows™-Druckertreiber. Mit seiner geringen Stellfläche ist der Drucker ohne Probleme in Büro- und häusliche Umgebungen zu integrieren.

The SAMSUNG ML 85: a compact laser printer boasting ecologically-friendly technology. Exceptionally fast print output, toner saving mode and 45 installed scalable fonts (incl. 10 True Type Fonts), high resolution, supporting HP-Laser-Jet™ and fast MS-Windows™ drivers. With its small-size footprint, the printer is perfectly integratable in office and home environments.

LINOTYPE-HELL AG, Eschborn, Germany HERSTELLER MANUFACTURER
DELTA TOWER, Grafikprozessor Graphics processor PRODUKT PRODUCT
MA Design, Kiel, Germany DESIGN

DELTA TOWER, ein Grafikprozessor zur Beschleunigung von Arbeitsprozessen bei der Bildbearbeitung. Die äußere Gestaltung greift die produktübergreifenden Formgebungsprinzipien von Linotype-Hell auf: signalisiert die Funktion als Hardware-Gerät aus dem Computerbereich, visualisiert zugleich hohe technische Leistungsfähigkeit. Markante Kühlschlitze unterstützen die optimale Belüftung. Ein technisches Package in ein inneres Blechgehäuse montiert, das von der Kunststoffummantelung des Geräts völlig unabhängig ist: dadurch unaufwendige Änderungen von Technik oder Design möglich.

DELTA TOWER is a graphics processor to speed up work processes in image designing. The housing is shaped to reflect Linotype-Hell's characteristic corporate design: symbolizing the product's function as computer hardware while also visualizing its high technical capabilities. The striking cooling slits provide optimal ventilation and the technical package as a whole is positioned in an inner thin metal casing surrounded by an additional plastic casing of its own. Consequently, technical changes have no impact on the external appearance which can be varied as desired.

BÜRO OFFICE 79

HERSTELLER MANUFACTURER
Kyushu Matsushita Electric Co., Ltd., Fukuoka-City, Japan

PRODUKT PRODUCT
KX-P6100, Drucker Page printer

DESIGN
Kyushu Matsushita Electric Design Center, Fukuoka-City, Japan

VERTRIEB DISTRIBUTION
Panasonic Deutschland GmbH, Hamburg, Germany

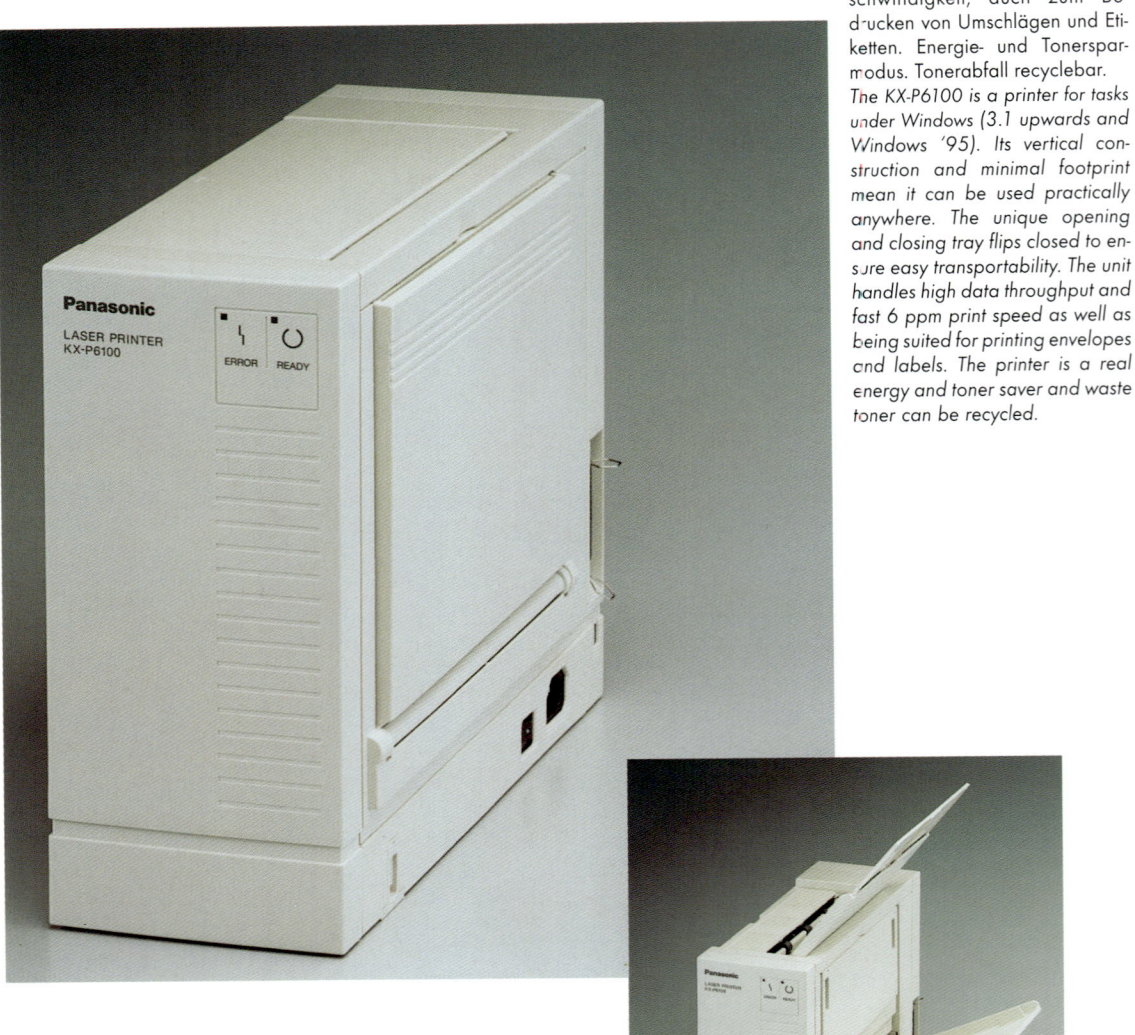

KX-P6100, ein Drucker für Windows (ab 3.1 und Windows 95), der durch seinen vertikalen Aufbau und die geringe Standfläche praktisch überall einzusetzen ist. Zufuhr und Ablageschächte klappbar; mit geschlossenen Schächten leicht transportabel. Hoher Datendurchsatz und hohe Druckgeschwindigkeit, auch zum Bedrucken von Umschlägen und Etiketten. Energie- und Tonersparmodus. Tonerabfall recyclebar.

The KX-P6100 is a printer for tasks under Windows (3.1 upwards and Windows '95). Its vertical construction and minimal footprint mean it can be used practically anywhere. The unique opening and closing tray flips closed to ensure easy transportability. The unit handles high data throughput and fast 6 ppm print speed as well as being suited for printing envelopes and labels. The printer is a real energy and toner saver and waste toner can be recycled.

80 BÜRO OFFICE

Canon Gießen GmbH, Gießen, Germany HERSTELLER MANUFACTURER
Canon NP 6050, Bürokopierer Office copier PRODUKT PRODUCT
Canon Deutschland, Krefeld, Germany DESIGN

CANON NP 6050, ein Hochleistungskopierer mit einer hohen Kopiergeschwindigkeit von ca. 60 DINA4-Kopien pro Minute über die Fast-Feed-Funktion. Einzug für Papiere mit Gewicht von 30-200g. Optimaler Heftsortierer mit drei möglichen Heftpositionen. High-Speed-Modus für doppelseitiges Kopieren von Formaten von DIN A5 bis DIN A3.

The CANON NP 6050 is a high-performance office copier with an operational speed of 60 A4 copies per minute in fast-feed mode. The unit accepts paper ranging from 30-200g per sheet and incorporates a superfast staple sorter offering three stapling positions for professional documents. In high-speed mode, users can opt for double-sided copying of A5 to A3-sized documents.

HERSTELLER MANUFACTURER Supercomputing Systems AG, Zürich, Schweiz
PRODUKT PRODUCT Supercomputer GigaBooster
DESIGN Meyer-Hayoz Design Engineering AG, J. Konaszewski and Team, Winterthur, Switzerland
VERTRIEB DISTRIBUTION Supercomputing Systems Nederland B.V., Rotterdam, The Netherlands

GIGABOOSTER, ein Supercomputer mit einer Rechenleistung von 1,6 Gflops. Um den Faktor 100 kleiner als vergleichbare Rechner (640 x 640 x 190 mm), läßt sich der Gigabooster direkt am Schreibtisch aufstellen. Wegen des geringen Energieverbrauchs (450 Watt Leistungsaufnahme) und der neuartigen »Innenarchitektur« des Ganzmetallgehäuses keine Klimatisierung mehr notwendig. Prozessoren, Laufwerke und Karte nach Aufschwenken einer Tür sofort zugänglich. Innovative Technik und High-End-Performance des Geräts spiegeln sich auch im markanten, nach vorne gepfeilten Design des Gehäuses, das sich dennoch dienend der Funktion unterordnet.

The GIGABOOSTER is a supercomputer with a computing capacity of 1.6 Gflops. 100 times smaller than comparable computers (640 x 640 x 190 mm), the Gigabooster can be installed right at the user's desk. Due to its low energy consumption (450-watt power draw) and the new »interior design« of the all-metal housing, an air conditioned room is no longer required. The processors, drives and cards are easily accessible via a hinged door. Innovative technology and the computer's high-end performance are reflected in the striking, tapered design of the housing, which nonetheless supports the functions rather than eclipsing them.

Ökologie/Design Auszeichnung Awarded for Ecology/Design: Vorbildlich durch Sparsamkeit bei Material- und Energieverbrauch bei extrem hoher Leistung. *Exemplary owing to the sparing use of materials and energy, despite its strong performance.*

82 BÜRO *OFFICE*

BÜRO OFFICE 83

HERSTELLER MANUFACTURER Umax Data System, Inc., Hsinchu, Taiwan
PRODUKT PRODUCT PageOffice Page Scan Device, Einzugsscanner
DESIGN Umax Data Systems, Inc., Tony H. C. Chen, Thomas Chang, Hsinchu, Taiwan

PAGEOFFICE, ein neuartiges Gerät, das als Schnittstelle zwischen dem papierübersäten realen Schreibtisch und dem geordneten virtuellen Schreibtisch fungiert. Besteht aus einem Einzugsscanner (Page Scan Device) und der PageManager-Software. Diese simuliert auf dem Bildschirm ein Büro mit den wichtigsten alltäglichen Funktionen: E-Mail, Faxen, Drucken, Kopieren, Texterkennung, Formular- und Bildbearbeitung, Archivieren. Paßt sich mühelos in die gewohnte Büroumgebung ein. Ziel des Designs ist das papierarme Büro.

PAGEOFFICE is an innovative device which functions as an interface between a real desk covered in papers and a neat-and-tidy virtual desk. It consists of a roller-type scanner and the PageManager software. This simulates an office on-screen with all the most important daily functions, such as e-mail, fax, printer, copier, OCR, form and image processing, and filing. The unit blends harmoniously into the usual office environment, fulfilling the design objective: »paperless office.«

84 BÜRO OFFICE

HERSTELLER MANUFACTURER NEC Technologies, Inc., Wood Dale, USA
PRODUKT PRODUCT MultiSync Graphics Product Line, LCD Projektor LCD projector
DESIGN IDEO Product Development, Naoto Fukasawa, Tim Brown, Sigi Moeslinger, San Francisco, USA
VERTRIEB DISTRIBUTION NEC Corporation, Tokyo, Japan

MULTISYNC GRAPHICS, eine mit jedem PC kompatible Produktreihe aus Farbbildschirmen (15, 17 und 21 Zoll), LCD-Projektor und Lautsprecher. Aufeinander abgestimmt und auslegt für hohe audio-visuelle Qualität, für Büro und Home. Die Software ermöglicht die Feinabstimmung der Geräte direkt am Bildschirm. Der »Multimedia Theater« Projektor läßt sich mit PC oder Fernsehgerät verbinden, ermöglicht Präsentationen mit einer Bilddiagonale bis 380 cm.

MULTISYNC GRAPHICS is a line of peripherals (15, 17 and 21"), multimedia theater LCD-projectors and peripheral speakers — for use with any PC. The products harmonize to provide perfect audio-visual quality, ideal for home or office, private or professional use. The software enables users to adjust the peripherals on-screen. The »Multimedia Theater« projector can be hooked up to a PC or TV video output to present up to 150" pictures.

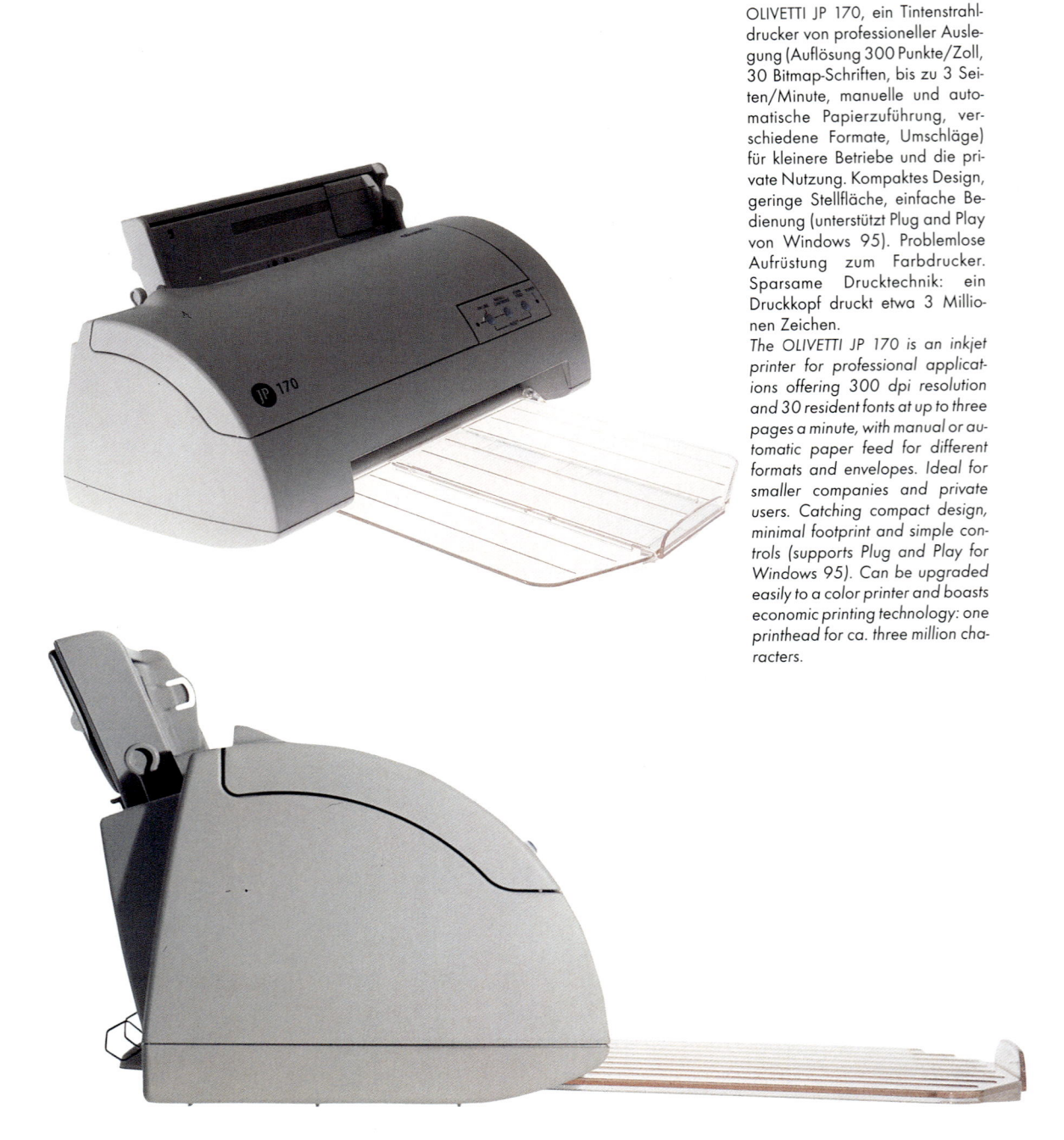

OLIVETTI S.p.A., Ivrea, Italy HERSTELLER MANUFACTURER
JP 170, Tintenstrahldrucker Inkjet printer PRODUKT PRODUCT
Michele De Lucchi, Alessandro Chiarato, Milano, Italy DESIGN

OLIVETTI JP 170, ein Tintenstrahldrucker von professioneller Auslegung (Auflösung 300 Punkte/Zoll, 30 Bitmap-Schriften, bis zu 3 Seiten/Minute, manuelle und automatische Papierzuführung, verschiedene Formate, Umschläge) für kleinere Betriebe und die private Nutzung. Kompaktes Design, geringe Stellfläche, einfache Bedienung (unterstützt Plug and Play von Windows 95). Problemlose Aufrüstung zum Farbdrucker. Sparsame Drucktechnik: ein Druckkopf druckt etwa 3 Millionen Zeichen.

The OLIVETTI JP 170 is an inkjet printer for professional applications offering 300 dpi resolution and 30 resident fonts at up to three pages a minute, with manual or automatic paper feed for different formats and envelopes. Ideal for smaller companies and private users. Catching compact design, minimal footprint and simple controls (supports Plug and Play for Windows 95). Can be upgraded easily to a color printer and boasts economic printing technology: one printhead for ca. three million characters.

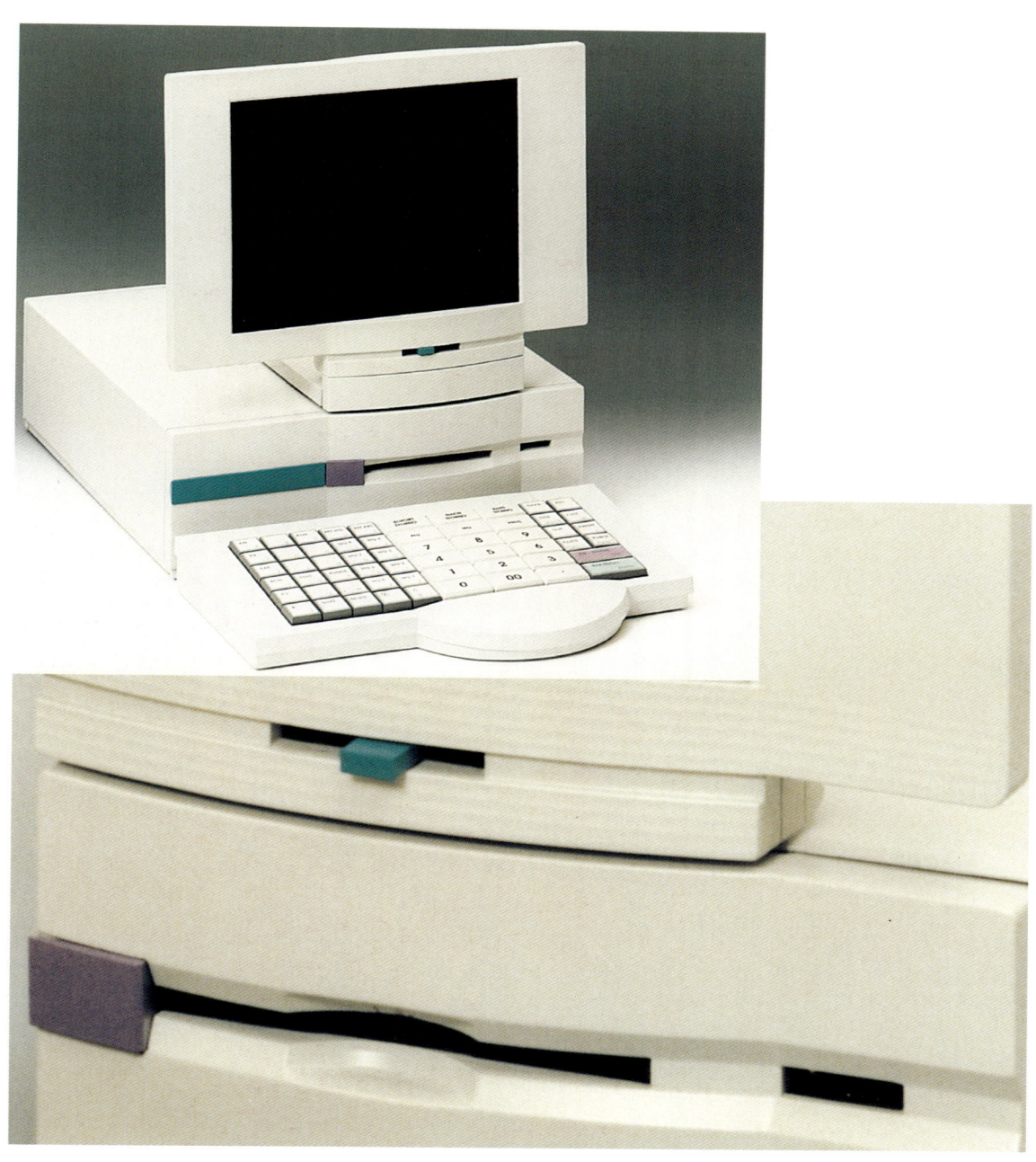

MEONIC Entwicklung und Gerätebau GmbH, Erfurt, Germany   HERSTELLER MANUFACTURER
MDK1-MDK2, Modulare Datenkasse, Modular cash register   PRODUKT PRODUCT
Silvia Mantowski; Erfurt, Germany   DESIGN

MDK 1 und MDK 2 sind modulare Datenkassen. Das Baukastensystem besteht aus Rechner, LCD-Bildschirm (gesteckt und freistehend), Kassentastatur und Kundenanzeige. Diese Module lassen sich beliebig kombinieren und anordnen, ein ergonomisches Formkonzept, das, wie ein Detail der Rückseite zeigt, auch auf Eleganz Wert legt: alle Steckverbindungen verschwinden hinter der Rechnerrückwand.

The MDK 1 and MDK 2 are electronic cash register modules consisting of a computer, an LCD (either integrated with the computer or as a standalone), keyboard and customer display. The modules can be combined and arranged at will. The ergonomic design underscores overall elegance, as the detailing of the rear side shows: all the sockets are concealed behind the rear casing.

BÜRO OFFICE 87

HERSTELLER MANUFACTURER PERTO S.A., Gravataí, Brazil
PRODUKT PRODUCT PERTOCHEK, Zahlstellen-Prüfprozessor Check Processor
DESIGN MHO Design, Oswaldo Mellone, Sao Paulo, Brazil

PERTOCHEK, ein Zahlstellen-Prüfprozessor, ausgestattet mit Tintenstrahldrucker. Liest und codiert, den üblichen Banknormen entsprechend, Dokumente im CMC7- und im E13B-Zeichensatz, liest damit alle international gebräuchlichen Schecks. Lieferbar in zwei Versionen: als »Stand alone« mit verstellbarer Tastatur und als »Connectable« mit einer Schnittstelle zu Zahlstellenterminals, Computern und elektronischen Registrierkassen.

PERTOCHEK is a check processor with an integrated inkjet printer. It can read and encode documents in CMC7 or E13B characters in line with the usual banking norms and can handle the complete range of checks used worldwide. Available in two versions: as a standalone with adjustable keyboard and as a connectable with an interface to POS-terminals, PCs, and retail cash registers.

Der JOULE DRIVE von LaCie, ein flexibles Laufwerkplatzsystem für Macintosh Computer. Einfaches Plug-In ohne Kabel und Stecker: die mechanischen Stifte zur Verbindung der Andockmodule dienen auch als elektronischer Datenweg für den Datenaustausch. Ein kompaktes, turmartiges Design bietet große Speicherkapazität bei äußerst geringer Stellfläche.

LaCie's JOULE DRIVE is a flexible disk array system for Apple Macintosh users featuring a simple plug-in system dispensing with cables and sockets. And it is easy to assemble, with no tools required. The mechanical pins which hold the dock modules together also serve as an electronic pathway for data transfer. The compact tower structure offers exceptional memory capacity in minimized space.

HERSTELLER MANUFACTURER LaCie, Ltd., Beaverton, USA
PRODUKT PRODUCT LaCie Joule Drive, Joule Laufwerk Disk array system
DESIGN ZIBA Design, Portland, USA

HERSTELLER MANUFACTURER
PRODUKT PRODUCT
DESIGN

LOGITECH SA, Romanel, Switzerland
oben/above: TrackMan live! Kabelloser Trackball, Cordless trackball, unten/below: TrackMan Vista Trackball
oben/above: Design Partners, Ireland, unten/below: frog design, USA

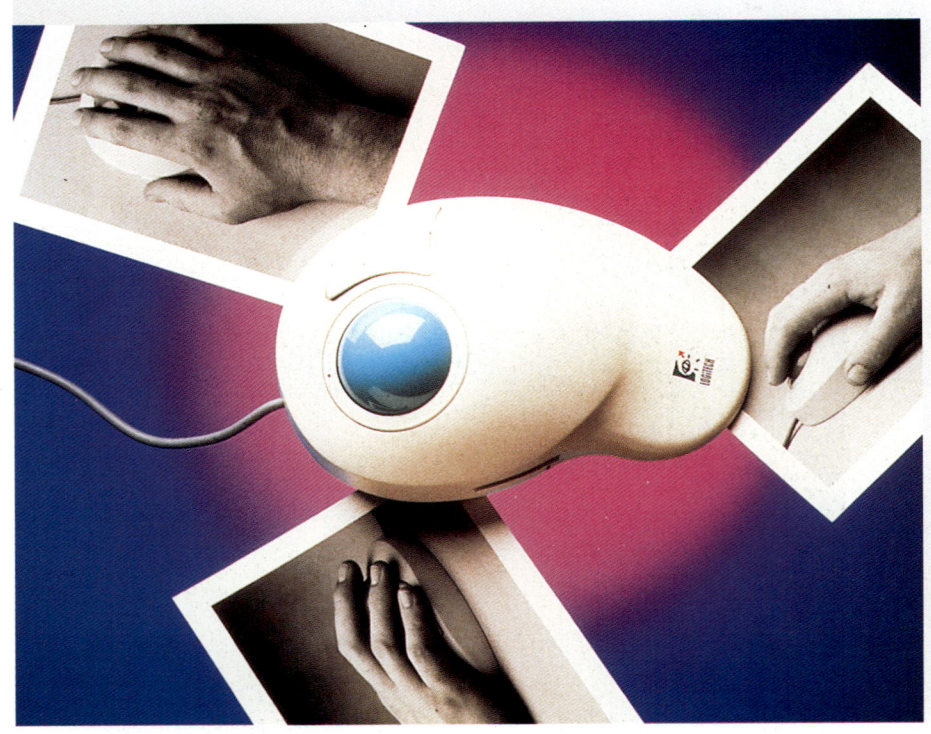

oben: TRACKMAN LIVE!, ein kabelloser Trackman, der speziell für Präsentationen entwickelt wurde und wie eine Fernbedienung des Computers funktioniert. Funkübertragung der Signale mit 10 Meter Reichweite, direkte Sichtverbindung nicht erforderlich. Dreitastengerät mit allen normalen Mausfunktionen, die Tasten sind für die bequeme Bedienung mit dem Daumen konzipiert.
above: TRACKMAN LIVE! is a cordless 3-button trackball developed especially for presentat- ions and that acts like remote controls for your PC. The radio transmitted signals have a range of 10 meters without you having to point the device at the screen. The three buttons provide all the usual mouse functions and are shaped specially for easy use with your thumb.
unten: TRACKMAN VISTA, ein Trackball in ergonomischem Design: abgerundetes Gehäuse stützt die Hand, die erforderlichen Handbewegungen wurden auf ein Minimum reduziert. Der Zeigefinger bedient den Trackball, die übrigen Finger die rechts angeordneten Tasten, der Daumen ruht auf der linken Taste. Unterstützt den Plug and Play-Modus von Windows 95: nach Verbindung mit der seriellen Schnittstelle automatische Installierung des richtigen Treibers. Durch die mitgelieferte MouseWare Software können Tasten mit häufig benutzten Befehlen belegt werden.
below: TRACKMAN VISTA - a trackball with an outstanding ergonomic design featuring a rounded case that gently supports the hand and reduced hand movements to a minimum. The trackball can be moved by your index finger while the others use the two top buttons and your thumb rests on the left button. TrackMan Vista supports plug and play under Windows '95, functioning as a serial port and automatically installing the correct driver. The MouseWare software provided enables user to assign fastkey functions to the buttons.
oben: TRACKMAN MARBLE, ein daumengesteuerter Trackball mit der neuentwickelten Marble

90 BÜRO OFFICE

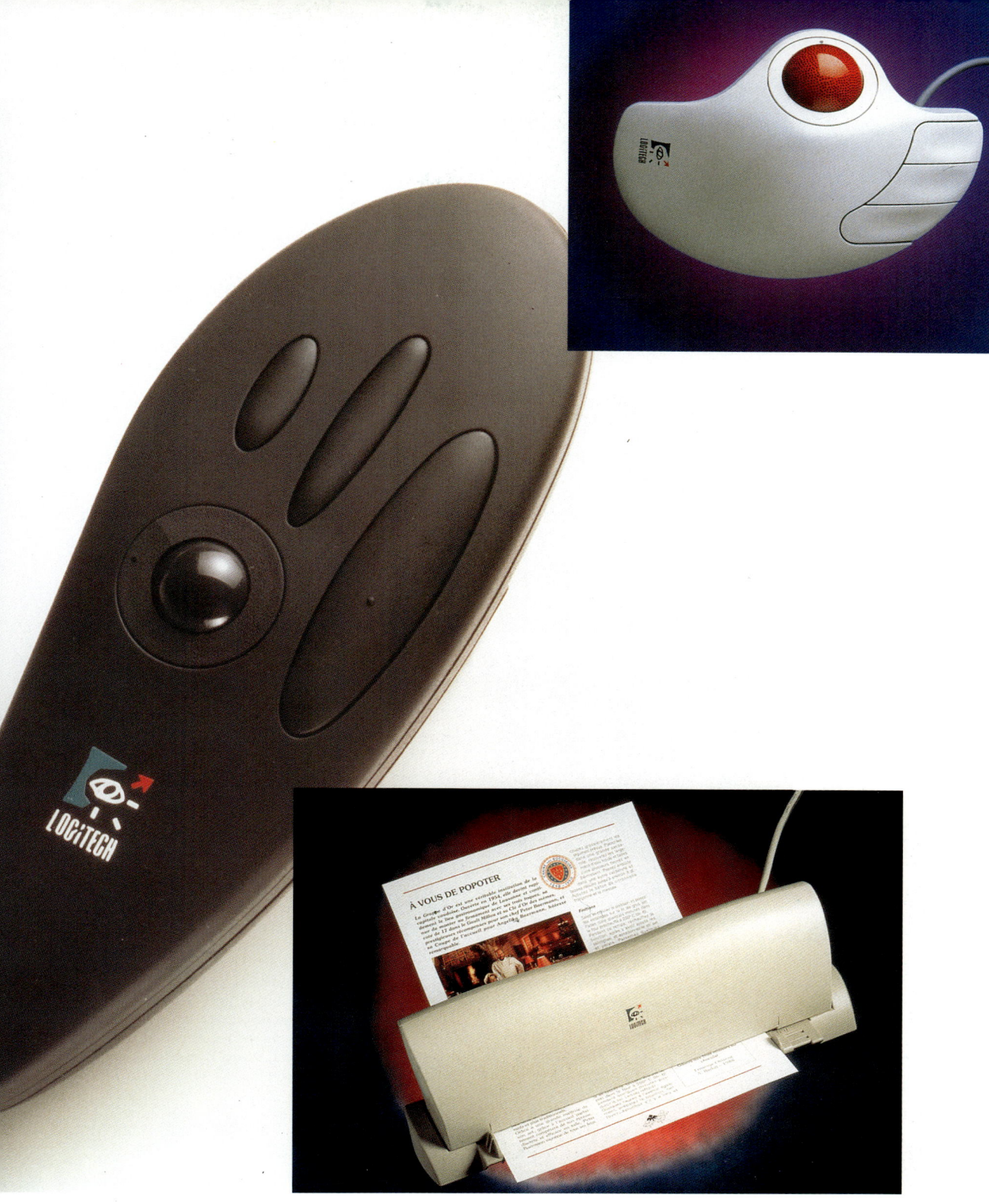

Sensing Technik: Übertragung der Kugelbewegung ohne mechanische Bauteile. Deren Funktion übernimmt ein optisches System mit laserähnlichem Lichtstrahl, der von der Marble-Kugel reflektiert wird. Ein Sensor erzeugt ein elektronisches Abbild der beleuchteten Stelle und setzt dies in Cursorbewegungen um. Keine Verschmutzung mechanischer Teile mehr, darum zuverlässiger in der Funktion als herkömmliche Abtasttechnik.
above: TRACKMAN MARBLE is a trackball featuring the new marble sensing technology and operated by your thumb. The ball's movement is transmitted without any mechanical parts. Instead, an optical system based on a laser-like light beam reflected by the marble ball conveys the necessary data. A sensor then generates an electronic image of the illuminated section and triggers the cursor movements. Wear-and-tear mechanical parts are a thing of the past, so the Marble functions far more reliably than the usual button-based devices.

unten: PAGESCAN COLOR, persönlicher Datenmanager mit umfangreichem Softwarepaket zur elektronischen Verwaltung, Bearbeitung, Archivierung von Dokumenten. Kompaktes Design, geringer Platzbedarf auf dem Schreibtisch, dennoch ein komplettes Dokumentenmanagement mit Ganzseiten-Scannen, Bildbearbeitung, Texterkennung, Archivieren, Kopieren (mit Drukker), und Faxen (mit Faxmodem). Das Gerät wird über den Parallelport mit dem Rechner verbunden.

below: PAGESCAN COLOR is a personal flatbed data manager featuring an extensive software package for electronic data management, processing and archiving of documents. Its compact design saves space and yet offers full-page scans, image processing into files, OCR, archiving, copying capacity (in combination with printer) and faxing (with fax modem). The device is hooked up via the PC's parallel portand therefore requires no extra slot card; it can also be used with a notebook PC.

LOGITECH SA, Romanel, Switzerland HERSTELLER MANUFACTURER
oben: TrackMan Marble Trackball, unten: PageScan Persönlicher Dokumenten Manager Personal document manager PRODUKT PRODUCT
oben/above: Hood Design, Ireland, unten/below: Montgomery-Pfeiffer, USA DESIGN

BÜRO OFFICE 91

HERSTELLER MANUFACTURER
Fast Security AG, München, Germany
PRODUKT PRODUCT
HARDLOCK EYE, Softwareschutz-Adapter Software protection connector
DESIGN
Uwe Spannagel, Köln, Germany

HARDLOCK EYE, programmierbarer Softwareschutz-Adapter. Er verhindert, zwischen PC und Peripheriegerät gesteckt, das unerwünschte Kopieren von Software in beiden Richtungen. Die Gestaltung visualisiert mit Linse und Auge die Wächterfunktion des Geräts. Darstellung des technischen Charakters durch eingeprägte Grafik und die Materialien, gleichzeitig ergonomische Gestaltung für sichere Handhabung. Die unterschiedlichen Verwendungsrichtungen lassen sich an den feinen Rillen »fühlen«. Aus Kunststoffspritzgußteilen zusammengesetzt, Kosten und Material sparende Konstruktion.

HARDLOCK EYE is a programmable software protection connector inserted between the PC and peripherals to prevent undesired copying of software in both directions. The lens and eye in the design visualizes the unit's control function, and the embossed graphics highlight the technological thrust of the unit, an impression borne out by the materials and combined in the ergonomic design for easy use. The direction of use can be »felt« by the fine pointing grooves in the gripping areas. The connector is made of injection-molded plastic, saving costs and material inputs.

Stollmann Entwicklungs- und Vertriebs-GmbH, Hamburg, Germany   HERSTELLER MANUFACTURER
TA + POS , ISDN-Terminaladapter, ISDN terminal adaptor   PRODUKT PRODUCT
Design Planet, José Delhaes, Mühlheim, Germany   DESIGN
OEM   VERTRIEB DISTRIBUTION

STOLLMANN TA+POS, preisgünstiger ISDN-Terminaladapter für alle Geräte, von denen aus über eine V.24-Schnittstelle Daten ins ISDN geschickt werden sollen. Ermöglicht die Nutzung der hohen Übertragungsgeschwindigkeiten, des schnellen Verbindungsaufbaus und der Preisvorteile des ISDN auf dem B-Kanal und im Übergang vom D-Kanal des ISDN in die X.25-Netze.

STOLLMANN TA+POS is a cost-effective ISDN Adapter to link all kinds of terminals with a host via a V.24 basic rate ISDN interface. This ensures fast data transmission speeds, swift connections and ISDN price advantages on B channel connections as well as via the D channel to a X.25 network.

Ökologie/Design Auszeichnung Awarded for Ecology/Design: Vorbildlich durch sparsamen Materialeinsatz und leichte Demontierbarkeit. Exemplary owing to the sparing use of materials and its easy disassembly.

HERSTELLER MANUFACTURER
NEC Corporation, Tokyo, Japan
PRODUKT PRODUCT
VoicePoint + AEC-50, Telekonferenz-Terminal, Teleconferencing terminal
DESIGN
NEC Design, Tokyo, Japan

VOICEPOINT+, Telekonferenz-Terminal, zum Anschluß an jedes analoge Telefonnetz. Duplextechnik und vier Mikrofone ermöglichen die »spontane« Kommunikation der Konferenzteilnehmer ohne störende Rückkopplungen, Hall- und Statikgeräusche. Automatische Akustikregulierung erlaubt den problemlosen Einsatz in unterschiedlichsten Räumen. Ergonomisches Bedienungsfeld zur bequemen Direktwahl. Weitere Features: Stummschaltung und Gesprächstransfer zu anderen Teilnehmern.

VOICEPOINT+ is a teleconferencing terminal for use with any analog telephone network. Featuring duplex technology and four mikes, the device enables spontaneous communication by conference participants without annoying static, echo and acoustic howling. The automatic acoustic modulator offers smooth performance in a wide range of rooms. The design features an ergonomic user interface for direct dialing, a mute function as well as a call transfer facility.

OLYCOM C200, ein schnurloses Telefon des High-End-Bereichs. Set aus Handgerät, Ladeablage und Feststation, die zur Überbrückung von Stromausfällen mit Batterie betrieben werden kann. Kompakte Bauweise. Handgerät mit zweizeiligem Display zur Anzeige von Zustand und Funktion des Geräts, dadurch optimale Benutzerführung. Formgebung der Hörkapsel ermöglicht auch Trägern von Hörgeräten optimale Nutzung. Die gestalterische Entwicklung des Produkts der Olycom-Produktfamilie erfolgte – von der ersten Idee bis zu Gestaltung von Verpackung und Prospekt – rechnergestützt.

The OLYCOM C200 is a high-end cordless phone consisting of a handset, charger and base unit with an integrated battery for operation during power failures. Compact in construction, the handset features a two-line display showing all states and functions for optimal user support. The specially shaped receiver allows for use by people requiring hearing aids. All design development work for the Olycom product line, from the very first idea to execution of packaging and brochures, is computer assisted.

Olympus Optical Co. Europa GmbH, Hamburg, Germany HERSTELLER MANUFACTURER
Olycom C200, Schnurloses Telefon Sendestation, Cordless telephone PRODUKT PRODUCT
MA Design, Kiel, Germany DESIGN

HERSTELLER MANUFACTURER
PRODUKT PRODUCT
DESIGN

unten/below: Österreichische Philips Industrie GmbH, Wien, Austria, oben/above: Philips Dictation Systems, Wien, Austria
unten/below: Philips HFC 10 Kommunikationsgerät Message machine, oben/above: Philips Desktop LFH 730, Diktiersystem Dictation systems, Wien, Austria
unten/below: Philips Corporate Design, Eindhoven, The Netherlands, oben/above: Philips Dictation Systems, Konrad Ellermeier, Wien, Austria

oben: PHILIPS DESKTOP LFH 730, Diktiergerät mit dem innovativen Visual Workflow Display, der blendfrei und ohne störende Reflexe alle wesentlichen Daten zu Betriebszustand und Diktatlänge bietet, daneben Spezialanweisungen, Anweisungen zu Briefen und Priorität anzeigt. Ein markantes Design mit hoher Benutzerfreundlichkeit. Der Tastenblock enthält nur die zum Diktieren laufend notwendigen Funktionstasten; die restlichen Steuertasten liegen unter dem Deckel des Kassettenfachs. Handmikrofon wahlweise links oder rechts am Gerät zu befestigen.

above: The PHILIPS DESKTOP LFH 730 dictation system features the innovative Visual Workflow Display: maximum clarity with minimum reflection while giving you all core data on machine status and length of dictation, including special instructions, letters and priority texts. The striking design offers maximum ease of use. The keypad contains only keys constantly needed in dictation; the remaining control keys are placed under a flap in the cassette compartment. The handheld mike can be attached on the left or right of the device.

unten: PHILIPS HFC 10 mit integriertem Telefon, Faxgerät und Anrufbeantworter für die Nutzung in Büros und im privaten Bereich. Kompaktes Design, nicht viel größer als normale Bürotelefone, wirkt auch eher wie ein Telefon, nicht wie ein Faxgerät, und fügt sich so besser in häusliche Umgebungen. Vielfältige Funktionen, selten genutzte Tasten jedoch hinter einer Klappe verborgen. Automatischer Empfang von Voice und Text Messages: speichert 10 Minuten Sprache und 25 Seiten Text. Weitere Features: Babysitterfunktion, stummer Faxempfang, Fernabfrage.

below: PHILIPS HFC 10 is an integrated phone, fax and ansWerphone for professional and private use. The compact design means the unit is not much larger than the usual office phonesets — so it looks like a phone rather than a fax and thus blends in better with home environments. The device offers a wealth of functions, but seldom used keys are concealed behind a flap. Automatic voice and text message reception: 10 minute voice storage and 25-page text memory. Additional features: babysitter function, silent fax reception, remote control for message playback.

96 BÜRO OFFICE

oben: SHARP LW-1000T, ein Pen-Computer mit elegantem, gefälligen Design für den Einsatz im Empfangsbereich und im Direktverkauf. Das Flüssigkeitskristall-Touchpanel läßt sich auch von Anwendern ohne PC-Kenntnisse nutzen. Wird der LW-1000T per E-Mail mit anderen gleichartigen Geräte verbunden, können die Nutzer per Telefonleitung über die Bildschirmanzeige kommunizieren. Weitere Features: schnelle Handschriftenerkennung, Infrarot I/O-Ports, zwei Kartenslots (PSMCIA Typ II) für vielseitige Erweiterungen. Überkopfdarstellung per Knopfdruck für den gegenüberstehenden Gesprächspartner.

above: SHARP LW-1000T is a pen computer sporting an elegant design for uses in the reception areas and direct sales. The LCD touch panel can easily be used by people without prior PC skills. If the LW-1000T is linked up by e-mail to similar devices, users can communicate via screen displays on-line with each other. Additional features: swift hand-writing recognition, Infra-red I/O ports, two PSMCIA Type II card slots for versatile extensions. Instant top/bottom image reverse: make the images visible to people facing you.

unten: SHARP UX-70, ein Fax-Telefon für den Einsatz in kleinen Büros oder für private Nutzung. Kompaktes Design, platzsparend in jede Umgebung zu integrieren. Funktionale Features: automatische Faxweiche, automatisches Wählen, Abruffunktionen.

below: SHARP UX-70 is a integrated fax-and-phone for private use and small office environments. Featuring a space-saving compact design for any location. And functional characteristics such as an automatic fax/phone switch, automatic dialing, and polling functions.

BÜRO OFFICE 97

HERSTELLER MANUFACTURER
Telekom, Bonn, Germany

PRODUKT PRODUCT
Cyra Telefon Telephone

DESIGN
Design Drei, Hedda Beese, Jan-Michael von Lewinski, Hannover, Germany

CYRA, ein Komforttelefon mit Zielwahltasten, Display und integriertem Lautsprecher. Die markante Formgebung läßt das Gerät sehr leicht, fast schwebend erscheinen. Die Zielwahltasten sind von den übrigen Funktionstasten durch den Handapparat getrennt: eine klare funktionale Gliederung.
CYRA is a telephone with direct dial keys, display and integrated loudspeakers. The striking design gives the unit a very light, almost floating appearance. The direct dial keys are separated from the other keys by the handset to present a clear structure.

Telekom, Bonn, Germany   HERSTELLER MANUFACTURER
AF 385 D Telefaxgerät Fax machine   PRODUKT PRODUCT
Design Drei, Wolfgang Wagner, Hannover, Germany   DESIGN

AF 385 D, ein Faxgerät für Normalpapier. Wesentliche Funktionen wie Papiereinlegen, Service, das Beheben von Papierstaus, sind benutzerfreundlich direkt von vorne möglich. Die gesendeten Vorlagen werden platzsparend direkt hinter dem Papiereinzug gesammelt, fliegen also nicht auf dem Tisch herum. Das TonerJet Direktdruckverfahren ist eine Weltneuheit: das bedeutet keine Wegwerfbauteile und geringere Verbrauchs- und Wartungskosten, darum umweltfreundlicher und weniger aufwendiger Betrieb als beim Laserdruckverfahren. Zudem erleichtern vielfältige Funktionen, durchdachte Benutzerführung über Display und Trackwheel, Ok- und Stoptaste den Einsatz des Geräts.

AF 385 D is a fax machine using normal paper. The main functions such as paper tray, service, and paper jam are easily accessible from the front. Sent documents are collected in a space-saving tray directly behind the paper feed and thus don't lie around the table. The direct TonerJet printer is a first worldwide: no more throwaway components and lower operation and maintenance costs, for more ecological use than with laser printers. Moreover, the wide range of functions, carefully though-out controls via the display and trackwheel, Ok and Stop buttons make the fax simple to use.

BÜRO OFFICE 99

HERSTELLER MANUFACTURER
Alcatel Mobile Phones, Colombes Cedex, France
PRODUKT PRODUCT
HC 400 GSM-Handtelefon Handheld telephone
DESIGN
Alcatel Mobile Phones, Colombes Cedex, France
VERTRIEB DISTRIBUTION
Alcatel Mobile Phones, Stuttgart, Germany

HC 400 GSM, ultraleichtes und formschönes Handtelefon mit ergonomisch durchdachter Gestaltung. One-Touch-Tasten für leichte Bedienung. Sprachübertragung und Sende-/Empfangsempfindlichkeit in Spitzenqualität, lange Betriebsdauer. Die drei am häufigsten genutzten Dienste sind mit einem Tastendruck anzuwählen.
The HC 400 GSM is a slender, light and beautiful handheld telephone based on a consistently ergonomic design. One-touch keys ensure easy use. The unit features outstanding voice transmission and reception quality and a long battery life. Depressing a single key dials the three most frequently used services.

S3 COM, digitales Mobiltelefon für das D-Netz. Handliches und griffiges Kunststoffgehäuse mit Feinstruktur. Einfache dialogorientierte Bedienerführung per mehrzeiligem Display und Tasten. Einbausatz mit Freisprechvorrichtung zur Benutzung beim Autofahren. Bedienzone gegliedert in Display mit zwei Softkeys und zwei Funktionstasten; Tasten für Senden, Beenden, Ein- und Ausschalten; farblich kodiert; Wahlblock mit 12 Tasten. Technische Neuerung: hohe Sprachqualität und Rauschfreiheit. Einfach zu reparieren, recyclebar.

S3 COM, Mobile phone finely structured, synthetic casing with good grip. Simple, dialogue-oriented operating instructions through display area accommodating several lines of text, and large buttons. Built-in unit, loudspeaker allows user to phone while driving. Operating area divided into display with two softkeys and two function buttons; colour coded buttons to transmit, terminate calls, and switch on/off; dialling block with 12 buttons. Technical innovation: high voice quality and low-noise performance. Easy to repair, recyclable.

HERSTELLER MANUFACTURER Siemens Aktiengesellschaft, Berlin - München, Germany
PRODUKT PRODUCT S3 com GSM Mobiltelefon, Mobile telephone for D-Network
DESIGN Siemens Design, Wolfgang Münscher, München, Germany

BÜRO OFFICE 101

HERSTELLER MANUFACTURER Ascom Business Systems AG, Solothurn, Switzerland
PRODUKT PRODUCT Sinus 53, Sinus 53 AB Schnurloses Telefon Cordless telephone
DESIGN Ascom Corporate Industrial Design, Martin Iseli, Susanne Schwarz Raacke, Svend Ona, Solothurn, Switzerland
VERTRIEB Deutsche Telekom AG

SINUS 53 und SINUS 53AB, schnurloses Telefon, wahlweise mit integriertem digitalen Anrufbeantworter. Ein ergonomisch durchdachtes Gestaltungskonzept mit hohem Bedienkomfort und ansprechend unaufdringlicher Formgebung, die auf einem Wechselspiel von konkaven und konvexen Flächen beruht. Typografisch klares Konzept der Bedienungsoberfläche. Konstruktiv wurde bei Telefon und Basisstation konsequent auf minimalen Materialeinsatz, einfache Verbindungstechnik (auch für rasche Demontage) und Trennbarkeit der gekennzeichneten Werkstoffe geachtet. Außer den Akkus schwermetallfreie Elektronik auf einer einzigen Printplatte, die leicht aus dem Gehäuse zu entfernen ist.

The SINUS 53 / SINUS 53AB is a cordless telephone with an optional integrated digital answering machine. The design concept emphasizes ergonomic aspects, high user comfort and an appealing though unobtrusive design based on the interplay of concave and convex surfaces. The user interface is characterized by a clear typographic display. In terms of construction, the telephone and base station consistently use minimal materials, simple connectors (allowing easy disassembly and ensuring labeled materials can be separated for recycling). With the exception of the batteries, no heavy metals are used in the electronics, which are mounted on a single printed circuit board that can easily be removed from the housing.

102 BÜRO OFFICE

BEOCOM 5000, schnurloses Telefon, in dessen Handgerät zusätzlich eine Fernbedienung für entsprechende Audio-Videogeräte des Herstellers integriert ist. Die Gestaltung beruht auf einem spannungsreichen Wechselspiel von streng geometrischer Linienführung der Bedienungselemente und der weichen Flächen von Handapparat und Basisstation. Ein Knopfdruck bringt eine kleine Karte zum Vorschein: Die Notizfläche für gespeicherte Nummern und Kurzbedienungsanleitung. Handgerät wie Basisstation aus jeweils nur zwei von einer Schraube zusammengehaltenen Schalen, dadurch schnelle Montage und effiziente Demontage für den Recyclingprozeß. Mechanische Bauteile aus dem Kunststoff ABS.

The BEOCOM 5000 cordless telephone features a handset with built-in remote controls for AV equipment by the same manufacturer. The design stands out for its exciting combination of clear geometric lines for the user elements and soft surfaces for the handset and base station. At the press of a button, a small card is displayed on the top of the unit – both a notepad for stored numbers and quick-&-easy instructions. The handset and main unit each consist of a two-piece shell fixed together with only one screw, ensuring simple assembly and efficient disassembly for recycling. The mechanical components are made of special ABS plastic.

HERSTELLER MANUFACTURER Bang & Olufsen A/S, Telephone Division, Struer, Denmark
PRODUKT PRODUCT Beocom 5000 Schnurloses Telefon Cordless telephone
DESIGN Ascom Corporate Industrial Design, Martin Iseli, Susanne Schwarz Raacke, Svend Onø, Solothurn, Switzerland

BÜRO OFFICE 103

HERSTELLER MANUFACTURER
Olympus Optical Co., Ltd., Tokyo, Japan
PRODUKT PRODUCT
Olycom FT 100 Fax-Telefon Fax-phone
DESIGN
Olympus Europa, Hamburg, Germany
VERTRIEB DISTRIBUTION
Olympus Optical Co. Europa GmbH, Hamburg, Germany

OLYCOM FT 100, kombiniertes Telefon/Telefaxgerät, kompaktes Design mit einfacher Bedienung für den privaten sowie den semiprofessionellen Telekommunikationsbedarf, gehört technisch und im Design zur Olycom-Produktlinie. Vorlageneinzug für 10 Seiten, zeitversetztes und Senden auf Abruf möglich. Automatische Faxweiche. Zielwahl (Telefon) und Kurzwahl (Fax).

This combined phone and fax is truly compact and stands out for easy controls for both private and also semiprofessional telecommunication requirements. In terms of technology and design it is fully in keeping with the Olycom product family. The fax feed accommodates 10 pages and has a polling facility. The unit switches automatically between fax and phone, offers speed dialing and 20 dial codes for the fax.

104 BÜRO OFFICE

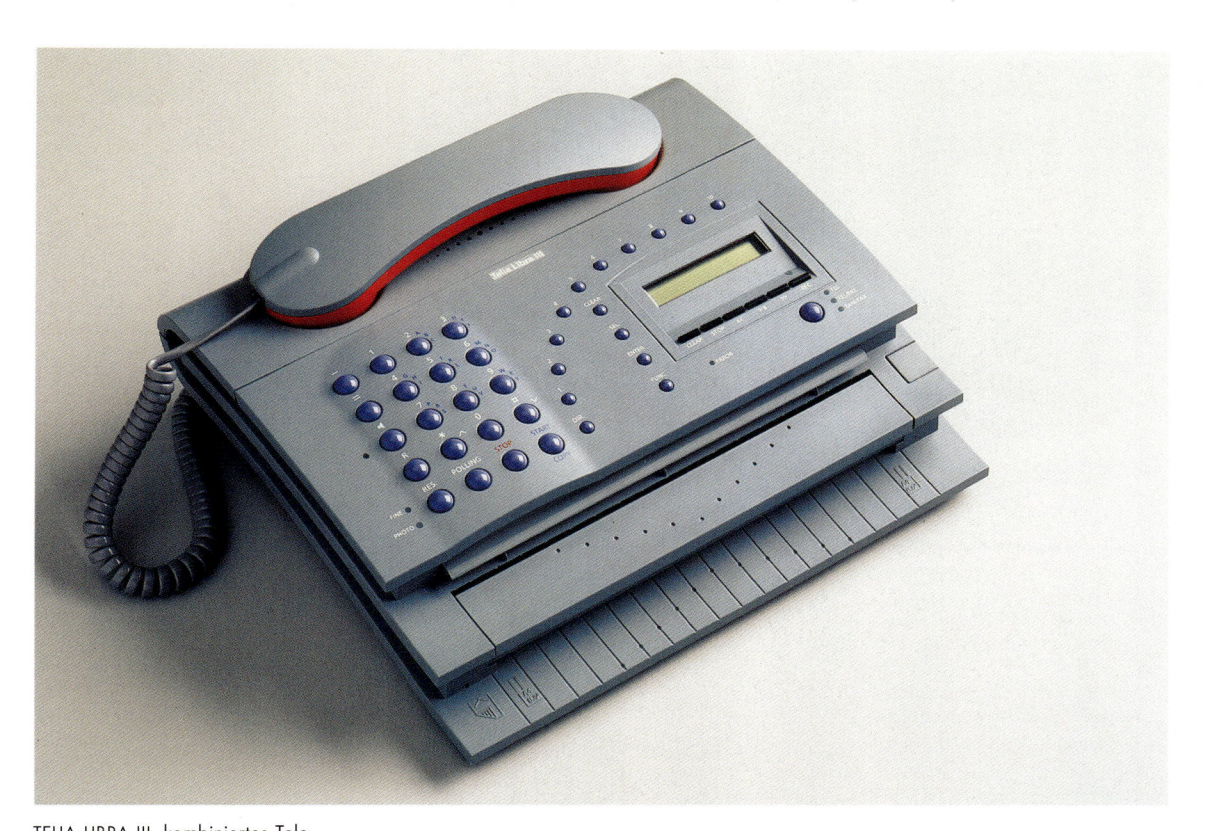

TELIA LIBRA III, kombiniertes Telefax- und Telefongerät mit integriertem Anrufbeantworter. Unkomplizierte Bedienung.
The TELIA LIBRA III is a combined fax and phone, featuring an integrated ansaphone and easy-to-use controls.

HERSTELLER MANUFACTURER Telia AB, Stockholm, Sweden
PRODUKT PRODUCT Telia Libra III Fax-Telefon mit Anrufbeantworter Fax-phone with answering machine
DESIGN Hampf Industrial Design AB, Jan Hampf, Särö, Sweden

HERSTELLER MANUFACTURER
Loewe Binatone GmbH, Langen, Germany
PRODUKT PRODUCT
Loewe Projekt LB 600, Komfort-Telefon Compact phone
DESIGN
Neumeister Design, München, Germany

LB 600, besonders kompaktes Komforttelefon mit integriertem volldigitalem Anrufbeantworter. Klare und einfache Bedienerführung durch die Kombination nur weniger Tasten und Klartext-LCD. Charakteristische Formgebung durch gerundetes Hörerteil. Ablage pultförmig, mit herausgestellem Display.

The LB 600 is an especially easy-to-use compact phone with a fully digital integrated ansaphone. Clear and simple-to-understand user interface is based on a combination of a minimum of keys and alphanumeric LCD. The rounded handset ensures a pronounced design, borne out by the desk-shaped base with tilted display feature.

106 BÜRO OFFICE

GRUNDIG AG, Fürth, Germany   HERSTELLER MANUFACTURER
CP 830 Dect, Schnurloses Telefon Cordless telephone   PRODUKT PRODUCT
GRUNDIG PRODUKT DESIGN, Frank Lamberty, Fürth, Germany   DESIGN

CP 830 DECT, schnurloses Telefon mit bis zu sechs Mobilteilen. Interne und externe Gespräche sind gleichzeitig ohne zusätzliche Nebenstelle möglich. Ergonomische Gestaltung des leicht gewölbten Tastenfelds am handlichen Mobilteil.

The CP 830 DECT is a cordless phone featuring up to six mobile units. In-house and external calls can be made simultaneously without additional extension lines being required. The slightly curved keypad on the mobile units makes them easy to handle and the design is consistent with ergonomic criteria.

BÜRO OFFICE 107

EMAX Architektonische Elemente Architectural components
Exhibitgroup, Inc., Christopher Wendel, Edison, USA

Exhibitgroup, Inc., Roselle, USA   HERSTELLER MANUFACTURER
                                   PRODUKT PRODUCT
                                   DESIGN

EMAX, ein Stellwandsystem für Messen, Präsentationen und Ausstellungen. Extrem leicht durch den Kern aus Styropor-Schaum (49% Gewichtsersparnis). Einfachste Montage, »oben« und »unten« nicht zu beachten, kein falsches Zusammensetzen möglich. »Männlich-weiblich«-Abdeckstifte und Klett-Verschlüsse an den Rändern jedes Wandelements ermöglichen die Verbindung der Stellwände durch Fingerdruck, ohne Werkzeug. Interne Verkabelung. Auf Wiederverwendung und mehrfache Vermietung ausgelegt. Alle Materialien 100% recyclebar. Eine Leuchtkastenwand ist auch lieferbar.

EMAX, Architectural components are for displays and trade fair stands. The extremely lightweight panels are made of polystyrene foam, cutting weight 49%. Foolproof assembly, as there is no top or bottom and parts cannot be put together wrong. »Male-next-to-female« a-lignment of the units (patent pending) and Velcro touch-fastening strips on the edges of the panels enable panels to be connected by hand without tools or loose parts. Internal wiring can be mounted in the ABS extruded plastic troughs around the perimeter of each panel. The unit is specially designed for multiple use. All the materials are 100% recyclable. A rear illuminated light box panel is also available.

HERSTELLER MANUFACTURER ROSSI DI ALBIZZATE SPA, Albizzate, Italy
PRODUKT PRODUCT TUBE Zweisitzer Sofa for two
DESIGN ROSSI DI ALBIZZATE, Carlo+Anna Bartoli, Albizzate, Italy
VERTRIEB DISTRIBUTION SRS Design+Marketing ROSSI DI ALBIZZATE, Leutkirch-Unterzeil, Germany

TUBE, ein zweisitziges Sofa mit einer Tragstruktur aus Metall und elastischen Riemen, Polsterung aus Polyurethanschaum unterschiedlicher Dichte. Die Rohrstützen sind aus eloxiertem Aluminium. Leicht wechselbare Bezüge aus speziellen elastischen Wollstoffen in sechs Farben.

TUBE is a sofa for two with a metal frame featuring elastic belts. The upholstery uses polyurethane foam in different densities, and the tubular supports consist of anodized aluminum. The coverings are simple to remove, and are made of special elastic fabrics: available in six colors.

BÜRO OFFICE 109

HERSTELLER MANUFACTURER van Esch bv, Goirle, The Netherlands
PRODUKT PRODUCT Toro Garderobe Wardrobe
DESIGN Axis Design Europe, London, Great Britain

TORO, ein Garderoben- und Hutständer mit Jackett, für Büros und öffentliche Gebäude ebenso wie für die Wohnung. Eine elegante Konstruktion aus gebogenen und gepreßten Stahlrohren mit blank gelackten Knöpfen aus Buchenholz. Läßt sich mit einem Schirmständer oder einem Papierkorb kombinieren, im Privatbereich mit einer Wandgarderobe zu einer attraktiven Garderobeneineinrichtung zusammenstellen.

The TORO coat rack and hat stand are dual purpose, suited for both public use in offices and administrative facilities and for private use in the home. The coat rack is exceptionally elegant, made of curved and pressed steel tubing with an appealing black epoxy coating, and varnished beech knobs. It can be equipped with a customized umbrella holder and can also feature a jacket-rail for use in working environments. The unit can, if needed, be fitted into domestic wall closets, thus offering horizontal and vertical settings.

RETINO, ein Garderoben- und Raumteilersystem für den Objektbereich. Die Elemente Garderobe, Paravent, Spiegel, Schirmständer, Telefon- oder Ablagetisch etc. sind frei zu kombinieren und werden über drehbare Teile verbunden. Stäbe sind massiv Buche, natur oder schwarz gebeizt; die Metalle einbrennlackiert. Standfüße aus Gußeisen. Garderobenelement mit horizontaler Stange, nach oben weisenden Formholzhaken und darunter angeordneten Metallkleiderhaken: Kleidungsstücke lassen sich aufhängen oder einfach mit Bügel an Haken hängen. Durch die hochwertigen Materialien und ihre Verarbeitung, aber auch durch die Formgebung langlebig. Alle Materialien recyclebar.

RETINO is a coat rack and room divider System for public areas, consisting of a coat rack proper, a wall screen, mirror, umbrella rack, and phone and file stand, etc. The elements can be combined as needed and are linked by swivel parts. The rods are made of solid beechwood, either with a natural finish or stained black; metal parts are annealcoated, and the base is cast iron. The coat rack proper has a horizontal rod, formed wooden hooks sloping upwards and metal coat hooks sloping downwards: Articles of clothing can thus be either hung up or simply thrown over the hooks. High-grade materials, finishing, and design are all timeless. And all materials can be recycled.

BÜRO OFFICE 111

HERSTELLER MANUFACTURER Sedus Stoll AG, Waldshut, Germany
PRODUKT PRODUCT Leggero Tischsystem Desking system
DESIGN Universität Essen, Lehrstuhl für Industrial Design, Prof. Stefan Lengyel, Helge Fedderke, Norbert Geelen, Frank Münter, Stephan Schmitz

SEDUS LEGGERO, ein flexibles Tischsystem aus verschiedenen Plattengrößen und -formen, aus Standgestellen und vielfältigem Zubehör für eine multifunktionale Nutzung. Intelligentes Verbindungssystem ermöglicht leichte Montage ohne Werkzeug, und die Verkettung geschieht unter Einsparung von Standbeinen. Ein klappbares Standgestell gewährleistet besonders hohe Flexibilität und optimale Beinfreiheit. Zubehörangebot umfaßt Knieblenden, Kabelführungen, Ablagen, Medienmöbel, Transportwagen.

The SEDUS LEGGERO is a flexible Desk system offering different tabletop sizes and shapes, frames and a wealth of accessories for multifunctional use. The smart connector system makes it easy to assemble without tools and linking does not require extra legs. The foldaway column frame provides optimal flexibility and leg room. The accessories include knee screens, cable ducts, file trays, media furniture and overhead trolleys.

HERSTELLER MANUFACTURER BULO Kantoormeubelen N.V., Mechelen, Belgium
PRODUKT PRODUCT H$_2$O Arbeitstisch Working surface and desk
DESIGN Claire Bataille & Paul Ibens, Antwerpen, Belgium

H$_2$O, ein Arbeits- und Bürotisch aus der »blauen Periode« von Bulo, dessen Design modernste Funktionalität mit einer Rückbesinnung auf die Grundbedürfnisse verbindet, die ein Tisch erfüllen soll: daher der Name, der an eines der vier Grundelemente erinnern soll. Gestell aus wiederverwertbarem Aluminium, die Platten mit Laminat beschichtet oder mit hellem Holz furniert. Für Büro und Wohnung.

H$_2$O, a remarkable new working surface and desk line from Bulo's »blue period«. The design merges ultra-modern functions and a focus on the basic needs any table must meet: hence the name, which brings to mind the four basic elements of life. The legs and frame are recyclable aluminium, the tops feature a laminate or veneer. Equally well suited for offices or the home.

ASKO Furniture LTD, Lahti, Finland   HERSTELLER MANUFACTURER
POCO Formholzstuhl Plywood chair   PRODUKT PRODUCT
Lang Produkt Design, Wiesbaden, Germany   DESIGN

POCO, ein stapelbarer Formholzstuhl, ganz in Holz, mit konsequent durchgehaltenem, minimalistischem Gestaltungsprinzip. Optisch fließende Verbindung von Sitzschale und Beinen, die ohne Schrauben und zusätzlichen Metallverstärkungen auskommt. Geringes Gewicht von knapp über 4 kg.

POCO, a stackable plywood chair made entirely of wood. The design focuses throughout on a minimalist approach. In optical terms, the seat blends perfectly with the legs, which do not require screws or metal joints. The structure is exceptionally light, weighing in at slightly more than four kilos.

Ökologie/Design Auszeichnung Awarded for Ecology/Design: Vorbildlich durch Einfachheit und extrem sparsamen Materialeinsatz.
Exemplary for its simplicity and extremely sparing use of materials.

BÜRO OFFICE 115

MAGNUS OLESEN A/S, Roslev, Denmark — HERSTELLER MANUFACTURER
PARTOUT Stapelstuhl Stackable chair — PRODUKT PRODUCT
Rud Thygesen, Johnny Soerensen, Copenhagen, Denmark — DESIGN
K. E. Jensen, Hamburg, Germany — VERTRIEB DISTRIBUTION

PARTOUT, ein robuster, leichter und bequemer Stapelstuhl. Gestell aus ofenlackiertem Stahlrohr, mit schichtverleimtem Holzsitz und Rücken aus Buche oder Mahagoni. Wahlweise gepolstert, mit abnehmbarem Polstersitz. Die Konstruktion der Rückenschale gibt sowohl dem Rücken wie den Armen guten Halt. Robuste Metall-Holzkonstruktion mit optimalen Stapeleigenschaften.

PARTOUT is a sturdy, light and comfortable stackable chair. It features a stove-enameled steel tube frame, with a laminated seat and back made of beech or mahogany; an upholstered version with an easily removable seat is optional. The laminated wooden back provides ideal lumbar and arm support and the robust combination of steel and wood provides optimal stacking solutions.

Ökologie/Design Auszeichnung Awarded for Ecology/Design: Vorbildlich leichtes, auf wesentliche Elemente reduziertes Produkt.
Exemplary, light product reduced to the absolutely necessary.

AKQUISA, ein neuartiger Beraterplatz für Geldinsitute, an dem sich der Kunde mit dem Berater »auf gleicher Ebene« befindet und die angebotenen Leistungen bequem auf dem Monitor mitverfolgen kann. Das Design vermeidet die Plazierung des Kunden als »Bittsteller«. Mit Steh- (Kurzberatung) und Sitzplätzen (Intensivberatung) lieferbar.

AKQUISA is a new type of bank consulting unit: client and financial advisor are »on the same level«, and the client can easily follow the offers made on-screen. The design avoids putting the client in the physical position of a »supplicant«. The unit is available either for standing participants or with seating for more intensive advice.

HERSTELLER MANUFACTURER LC-Banktechnik GmbH, Leo Christmann, Aalen, Germany
PRODUKT PRODUCT akquisa, Beraterplatz für Geldinstitute Bank consulting unit
DESIGN Leo Christmann, Bartholomä, Germany

BÜRO OFFICE 117

HERSTELLER MANUFACTURER UNIFOR Spa, Turate, Italy
PRODUKT PRODUCT MOVE Multimedia Trolley
DESIGN Luciano Pagani, Angelo Perversi, Milano, Italy
VERTRIEB DISTRIBUTION UNIFOR Vertrieb Deutschland, Christian Robert GmbH, München, Germany

rechts: FLIPPER, ein stapelbarer Arbeitstisch. Mit seiner soliden Bauweise und dennoch geringem Gewicht ideal für Räume, die häufig umorganisiert werden müssen. Drei Zentimeter dicke Tischplatten mit rundum farbig laminierter Fläche, dazwischen Papierwaben, umlaufende laminierte Leiste und robuste laminierte Ecken. Gestell aus stranggepreßtem Aluminium.
FLIPPER is a stackable work table. A sturdy but light-weight construction, it is ideal for rooms where the furniture constantly has to be rearranged. The table tops are three cm. colored laminates on a paper honeycomb interior with solid laminated edges. The frame is extruded aluminum.
links: MOVE, ein Multimedia trolley für jeden gewünschten Ort. Nach Bedarf in Höhe und Breite verstellbar. Grundkonstruktion des Wagens aus einem Fußteil und zwei Seitenwänden. In diesen sind die Kabel angeordnet. Problemlos zu montierende und höhenverstellbare Böden.

Zusätzlich können Rückwand und Fronttüren angebracht werden.
MOVE goes wherever it is needed. Height and width can be adjusted accordingly. The multimedia trolley consists of a base and two end panels, in which wiring can be arranged. Tops can also be positioned on these panels and adjusted smoothly, without the equipment being removed. A back and doors in the front can be added if required.

HERSTELLER MANUFACTURER UNIFOR Spa, Turate, Italy
PRODUKT PRODUCT FLIPPER Tischsystem Table system
DESIGN Luciano Pagani, Angelo Perversi, Milano, Italy
VERTRIEB DISTRIBUTION UNIFOR Vertrieb Deutschland, Christian Robert GmbH, München, Germany

BÜRO OFFICE 119

HERSTELLER MANUFACTURER VOKO Vertriebsstiftung Büroeinrichtungen KG, Pohlheim, Germany
PRODUKT PRODUCT physio synchro Drehstuhl Swivel chair
DESIGN VOKO Design, Michael Englisch, Pohlheim, Germany

PHYSIO SYNCHRO, ein Drehstuhl mit Armlehnen. Sitz und Rücken haben getrennte Schalen aus verformtem Schichtholz. Polsterung aus FCKW-freiem Polyurethan-Schaum, rundum bezogen. Pneumatische Höhenregulierung. Die Rückenlehne mit Lumbalstütze folgt den Körperbewegungen mit regulierbarem Gegendruck. Das Fünfstern-Drehgestell besteht aus schwarz pulverbeschichtetem Aluminium.

PHYSIO SYNCHRO is a swivel chair with arm-rests. The seat and back are separate units made of formed laminated wood, and the upholstery features CFC-free polyurethane foam covered completely in fabric. Height adjustment is pneumatically regulated and the back-rest offers full lumbar support, matching the seater's movements by providing counter-pressure. The five-star base is made of black epoxy-coated aluminium.

BÜRO OFFICE 121

HERSTELLER MANUFACTURER Fröscher GmbH & Co. KG, Steinheim, Germany
PRODUKT PRODUCT Ego Drehstuhl Swivel chair
DESIGN Prof. Ulrich Böhme, Stuttgart, Germany

EGO, Drehstuhl aus einer Büromöbel-Produktfamilie, der sich jeder individuellen Körperform anpaßt und alle Körperbewegungen mitmacht bzw. Arbeitshaltungen unterstützt. Damit fördert Ego die richtige »dynamische« Haltung für ermüdungsfreies Sitzen. In der »Öko-Version« zusammen mit dem Bundesdeutschen Arbeitskreis für umweltbewußtes Management (B.A.U.M.) entwickelt. FCKW- und PVC- freie Materialien, alle Stahlteile pulverbeschichtet, reparaturfreundliche Konstruktion, leichte Demontage zum Recycling. Werkseitige Rücknahme und Verwertungsgarantie, Lieferung in recyclebarem Verpackungsmaterial.

EGO is a swivel chair from a line of office furniture. The chair adapts itself to suit the shape of the user's body, supporting all movements and adjusting to the seated person's posture. Thus, Ego enhances correct »dynamic« sitting, minimizing user fatigue. The special »Eco Version« was developed with the German Association for Environmentally Friendly Management. The Ego consists only of CFC-free and non-PVC materials as well as epoxy-coated steel components. The chair is easy to repair, and simple to disassemble, fostering recycling. It comes with guaranteed returnability and recycla-bility, and all packaging is recyclable.

Wiesner Hager Möbel GmbH, Altheim, Austria HERSTELLER MANUFACTURER
META Teamarbeitsmöbel, Furniture for teamwork PRODUKT PRODUCT
Design Ballendat, Dipl. Des. Martin Ballendat, Altheim, Austria DESIGN
Wiesner Hager Möbel GmbH, Würzburg, Germany VERTRIEB DISTRIBUTION

META Teamarbeitsmöbel. Das Arbeiten in wechselnden Gruppen verlangt flexible Möbel. META bietet verschiedene, in Größe, Form und Höhe variierende, z. T. rollbare Tische, die sich ohne aufwendige Verkettungen zu den verschiedensten Formen und für verschiedenste Zwecke kombinieren lassen. Ergänzt durch Funktionstische für Medien, EDV, Overheadprojektor und rollbare Flipcharts. Industriebetonte, schlichte Formgebung entspricht der Strapazierfähigkeit der Serie. Multiplexrahmen und Wabenplatten, kein Preßspan. Hell buchenfarben gebeizt. Runde Platten aus lederbespanntem MDF oder Kunststoff massiv (recyclebar). Metallteile pulverbeschichtet. Alle Teile zerlegbar, keine Klebungen.

META furniture for team work, as lean management and quality circles call for flexible furniture. META provides a range of tables that vary in size, form and height, are partly on castors and can be combined without complex connectors to create highly differing forms for different purposes. The line is complemented by functional tables for media, computers, overhead projectors, and castor-based flip charts. The decidedly industrial-looking design is borne out by the units durability. Multiplex frames, honeycomb tops and no chipboard. Stained in light beech. The round tops are made of leather-covered MDF or solid recyclable plastic. The metal components are epoxy-coated. All parts can be disassembled; no glue is used.

BÜRO OFFICE 123

HERSTELLER MANUFACTURER OMK Design Ltd., London, Great Britain
PRODUKT PRODUCT SEVILLE Sitzbank-System Seating system
DESIGN OMK Design, Rodney Kinsman RDI, London, Great Britain

oben: SEVILLE, eine Sitzbank, die ursprünglich für den britischen Pavillon auf der EXPO '92 in Barcelona entworfen wurde. Das gestalterische Konzept wurde entwickelt aus ineinandergreifenden stranggepreßten Aluminiumprofilen für Sitz und Träger. Montage durch Steckverbindung ohne zusätzliche Verschraubung. Befestigung entweder am Boden und an der Wand.
above: SEVILLE seating system designed originally for the British Pavilion at the EXPO '92 in Barcelona. The design concept is based on an inter-locking extruded aluminium seat and beam sections, with the individual components locking together without additional fixings being necessary. Seville can either be fixed to the floor or wall-fastened.

rechts: RADIUS, ein Konferenztisch-System, dessen Design nicht vom Prinzip des »Anbauens«, sondern von dem des »Verkleinerns« ausgeht: Alle Tischelemente sind selbständig, doch verbinden sich die einzelne Tischbeine beim Zusammenfügen zu einem neuen Bein – das Prinzip des »visuellen Magnetismus«. Eine vielseitige Serie zum Aufbau verschiedenster Plattenformen (Rechteck, Dreieck, Sechseck, Rombus sowie runde Tische in drei Größen) für den gestiegenen Bedarf kommunikativer Arbeitsformen in Besprechungen und Arbeitsgruppen. Die Produktserie wird derzeit weiterentwickelt und ausgebaut.
right: RADIUS is a conference desk system with a design that focuses not on »attaching« but on »reducing«. In other words, all desk elements are independent, but the individual desk legs combine on linking to form a new leg – the principle of »visual magnetism«. A multi-application series to create a wide range of desktop shapes (rectangular, hexagonal, rhomboidal, round desks in three different sizes) – to meet the greater need for communicative forms of work for meetings and committees. The product series is currently being advanced and extended further.

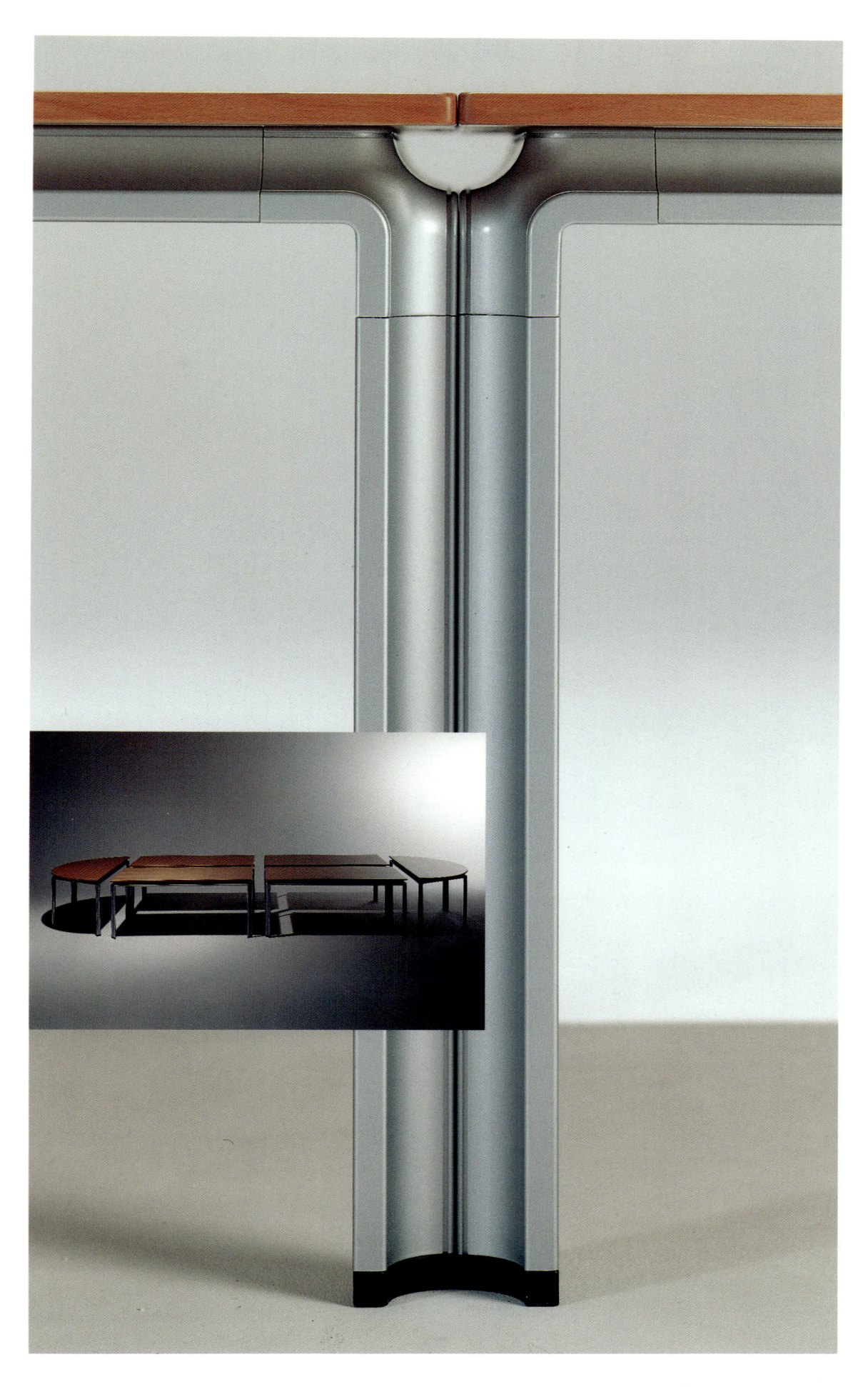

Pohlschröder GmbH & Co. KG, Dortmund, Germany   HERSTELLER MANUFACTURER
RADIUS Konfernenztisch-System Conference-desking   PRODUKT PRODUCT
Siebeneinhalb Biggel + Schmitz, Prof. Franz Biggel, Prof. Burkhard Schmitz, Berlin, Germany   DESIGN

BÜRO OFFICE 125

HERSTELLER MANUFACTURER WINI Büromöbel GmbH & Co., Coppenbrügge, Germany
PRODUKT PRODUCT BRISK Tischsystem Table system
DESIGN WINI Büromöbel, Dipl. Des. Michael Fangmann, Coppenbrügge, Germany

BRISK, Tischsystem für Büros, die mit neuen flexiblen Methoden arbeiten. Ein auf das wesentliche reduziertes statisches Gerüst erlaubt freie Tischformen ohne Rahmen- und Traversenkonstruktion. Ein neuartiger Funktionskopf, variabel in der Höhe, nimmt Tragarme in einem 15°-Raster auf. Jedes Tischbein stützt bis zu vier der multifunktionalen Platten. Daraus ergibt sich bei minimalem Materialeinsatz ein offenes System mit hoher Anordnungsvielfalt. Homogene Materialien, lösbar miteinander verbunden: Stahl, Buche massiv, Buche Multiplex, gekennzeichnetes Aluminium. Austauschbare Bauelemente, so daß nicht das schwächste Element die Gesamtlebensdauer des Systems bestimmt.

BRISK is a desk system for offices with new flexible working methods. The static trestle is stripped down to the essentials, allowing for free choice of desk top shape and no cross-arms. An new profile at the top of legs allows supports to be adjusted in angles of 15° and each of the legs supports up to four multi-functional tops. The result: minimal use of materials for an open and highly flexible system. Homogeneous materials, but connected in such a way that they can be combined at will: steel, solid beechwood, beech multiplex, tagged aluminum. The basic elements can be replaced, so that the system's service life is not defined by the weakest parts it uses.

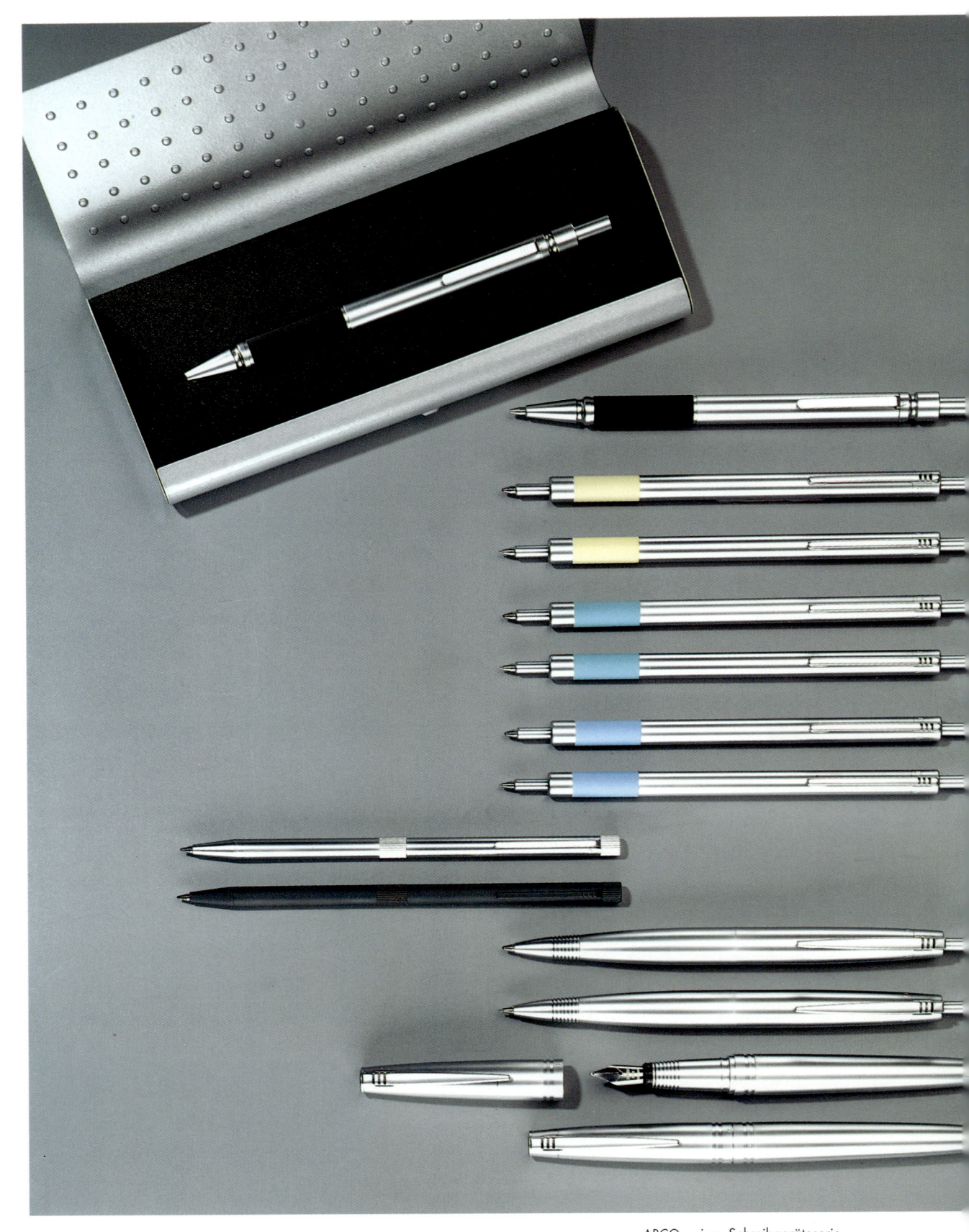

HERSTELLER MANUFACTURER
IMPEX ELECTRONIC Handelsgesellschaft m.b.H., Koblenz, Germany

PRODUKT PRODUCT
ARCO Aston, Iso, Microtec, Startec, Schreibgeräteserie Pen set

DESIGN
Hervé Houplain, Paris, France

ARCO, eine Schreibgeräteserie, die sich durch klare und ergonomische Formgebung und Eleganz auszeichnet.
ARCO pens stand out for their clear forms, ergonomic design and exceptional elegance.

128 BÜRO OFFICE

IBM THINKPAD 701 CARRYING CASES, Tragetaschen für Think-Pad und diverses Zubehör, das in eigens geformten Unterteilungen untergebracht wird. Der in den USA patentierte Safe-Port schützt Laptop und Zubehör vor Stoß und Schlag. Das Laptop und die Zubehörgeräte müssen zur Nutzung nicht aus der Tasche herausgenommen werden, die auch eine Handstütze bietet.

The IBM THINKPAD 701 CARRYING CASES house not only the ThinkPad but also diverse accessories in special compartments. The SafePort suspension system, patented in the United States, protects the laptop and accessories from falls and accidents. Laptop and accessories do not have to be taken out of the carrying case to be used, as the case sports a palm rest.

HERSTELLER MANUFACTURER Port Incorporated, Norwalk, USA
PRODUKT PRODUCT ThinkPad 701 Carrying Cases, Tragetasche für Computer
DESIGN Port Incorporated, W. D. Hollingworth, Samuel Lucente, H.C. Park, Norwalk, USA

BÜRO OFFICE 129

HERSTELLER MANUFACTURER IBICO Portuguesa, Importacao et Exportacao Lda, Arcos de Valdevez, Portugal
PRODUKT PRODUCT Hi Tech Stanz- und Bindemaschine, Binding system
DESIGN Botta Designbüro, Offenbach, Germany
VERTRIEB DISTRIBUTION IBICO Deutschland GmbH, Loitstetten, Germany

HI TECH, ein Bindesystem für Plastikringbindung und stabile Drahtbindung in verschiedenen Formaten bis DIN A 4 mit vielseitigen Anwendungsmöglichkeiten. Zum 2- und 4fach-Locher aufzurüsten. Stanzt bis zu 12 Blatt Papier (80 g) pro Arbeitsgang. Bindestärke: Plastik bis 125 Blatt (14 mm); Draht bis zu 105 Blatt (12,5 mm Binderücken). Bedienungsfreundlichkeit durch ergonomisches Design. Geringes Gewicht ermöglicht mobilen Einsatz.

HI TECH is a new binding system for plastic ring binders as well as offering wire binding capability – for different sizes up to A 4 and a wide range of applications. The 2/4 hole puncher with 12-page (80g) punching is an added extra. The unit provides plastic binding for up to 125 sheets (14 mm) and wire binding for up to 105 sheets (12.5 mm element). The ergonomic design ensures ease of use and the low weight enhances mobility.

Ökologie/Design Auszeichnung Awarded for Ecology/Design: Vorbildlich als langlebiges, funktionsgerechtes und ein sich selbst erklärendes Produkt. Exemplary, self-explanatory product in terms of durability and functions.

130 BÜRO OFFICE

HERSTELLER MANUFACTURER Kratzert & Schrem GmbH, Pfullendorf, Germany
PRODUKT PRODUCT Orga-Schienen Rails to organize files
DESIGN Kratzert & Schrem, Peter Langer, Pfullendorf, Germany

ORGA-SCHIENE, eine Ablagehilfe für Hängeregistraturen, mit Vollsichtreiter für schnellen Zugriff. Zur raschen, problemlosen Aufnahme von Heftern, Mappen, Taschen und Sammlern. Bei Entnahme der Akten bleibt die Orga-Schiene als Platzhalter in der Registratur.

The rails are ideally suited to organize files, cases, folders and collectors. They can be integrated in all the usual suspension files in seconds and are readily accessed with their clear index tabs. After files have been extracted from the organizing rails, the rail stays in place marking where the file belongs.

Ökologie/Design Auszeichnung Awarded for Ecology/Design: Vorbildlich als funktionsgerechtes, einfaches und langlebiges Produkt. Exemplary, simple, durable and functional product.

BÜRO OFFICE 131

HERSTELLER MANUFACTURER Louis Leitz Produktion GmbH & Co., Stuttgart, Germany
PRODUKT PRODUCT Ordnungsmappe Part files
DESIGN TEAMS - SLANY DESIGN, Esslingen, Germany

Eine neue ORDNUNGSMAPPE von Leitz, deren Greifausschnitte den direkten Zugriff auf die Unterlagen ermöglichen. Auch beim Transport rutschsichere Verwahrung der Unterlagen durch Gummibänder. Farbige Kodierung durch Einlageblätter in vier Farben. Wahlweise 7 oder 12 Fächer und drei Einbandfarben. Nach den Bedürfnissen des Nutzers völlig flexibel zu gliedern. Vollständig aus Recyclematerial gefertigt, vollständig recyclebar.

A new Leitz ORGANIZING FOLDER with cut-outs which afford swift and direct access to documents. The elastic strap ensures documents do not slip out during transport. Color coding is possible by means of four insertion sheets, and either seven or 12 sections are available in up to three different binder colors, so the folder system can be customized completely to client needs. The folders are made of recycled material that can be fully recycled.

BÜRO OFFICE 133

HERSTELLER MANUFACTURER
Ranstad Uitzendbureau bv, Diemen, The Netherlands

PRODUKT PRODUCT
Bleistiftspitzer Pencil sharpener

DESIGN
ninaber/peters/krouwel industrial design, Leiden, The Netherlands

Ein BLEISTIFTSPITZER, der die Serie von sechs Büroaccessoires ergänzt, die für das Randstad Uitzendbureau entwickelt wurden. Die Serie, zu der Lineal, Terminkalender, Klebebandabroller gehören, ist als Werbegeschenk konzipiert und zeichnet sich durch einfache, elegante Formgebung aus. Edle Verarbeitung und durchdachte Details signalisieren lange Lebensdauer und hohe Funktionalität und kennzeichnen auch diesen Spitzer.

This PENCIL SHARPENER to complement the series of six office accessories which have been developed for the Randstad Uitzendbureau. The series, including a ruler, desk calendar, tape dispenser, is intended as a giveaway and has a strikingly simple but elegant design. The high-grade workmanship and superb details signal durability and perfect functionality — for this pencil sharpener, too.

MONO TAPE, ein Korrekturband mit Abroller, zur sauberen Fehlerkorrektur auf allen Unterlagen. Das transparente, materialsparend gestaltete Gehäuse läßt erkennen, wieviel unverbrauchtes Band vorhanden ist, und liegt in der Hand wie ein Stift. Einmaliges Abrollen genügt, der dünne, sofort neu zu beschriftende Korrekturfilm haftet ohne Absetzkante und wirft auch beim Fotokopieren keinen Schatten. Das Band läßt sich vor Gebrauch straffen, also gibt es keinen Bandsalat mehr.

MONO TAPE is a correction tape with a dispenser for correcting errors on all kinds of documents. The transparent housing affords a view of remaining fresh tape, and features a compact design that fits comfortably into the hand like a pencil. The thin correction tape removes errors accurately without leaving a mark on the paper or casting a shadow on photocopies. Only a single application is required, and the user need not wait before writing or typing over the correction. The tape can be pulled taut before use, eliminating waste and mess.

HERSTELLER MANUFACTURER Tombow Pencil Co., Ltd, Tokyo, Japan
PRODUKT PRODUCT Mono Correction Tape, Korrekturroller Correction tape
DESIGN Tobow Pencil, Tokyo, Japan
VERTRIEB DISTRIBUTION Tombow Pen & Pencil GmbH, Troisdorf, Germany

HERSTELLER MANUFACTURER Messmer Pen GmbH, Emmendingen, Germany
PRODUKT PRODUCT art 4000 classic/silver, Schreibgerät Pen
DESIGN Jürgen Messmer, Emmendingen, Germany

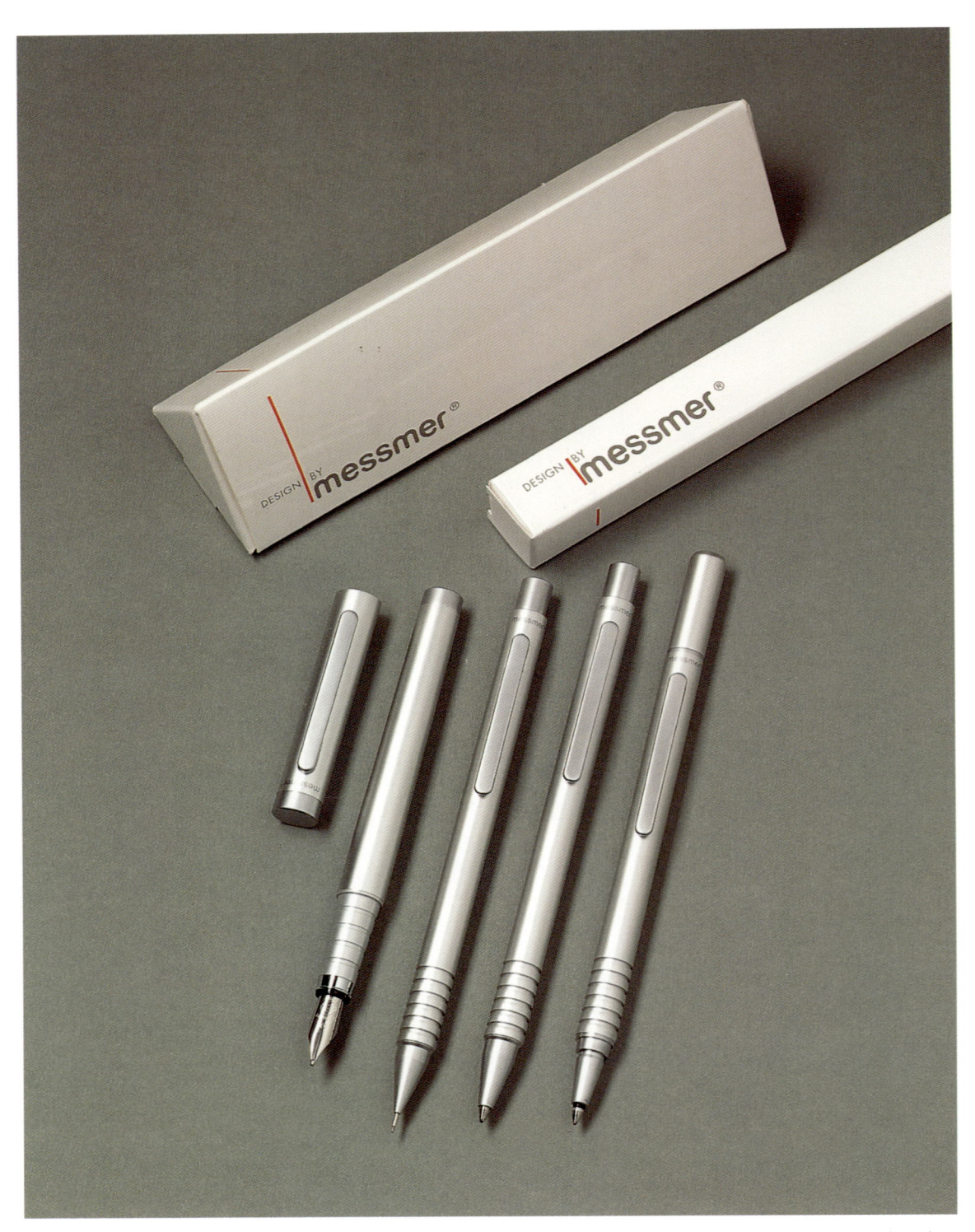

ART 4000, classic oder silver, hochwertige Schreibgeräte aus Aluminium.
ART 4000 in classic or silver is a high-quality pen.

Ökologie/Design Auszeichnung Awarded for Ecology/Design: Vorbildlich durch unbegrenzte Garantie. Exemplary given its unlimited guarantee.

136 BÜRO OFFICE

Schwan STABILOwoody 880/890 kurze Farbstifte mit extradicker Mine und Massivholzstiftende. Kompakte Form unterstützt den »Pfötchengriff« von Kleinkindern, die Formgebung schützt vor »bunter Zunge«. Im Büro- und Industriebereich sind die Stifte als Marker für Flipcharts einzusetzen. Auch in Leuchtfarben lieferbar.

Schwan STABILOwoody 880/890 are short color pencils with extra-thick leads and solid wooden pencil ends. The compact form is easy for children's small hands to grasp, and the design protects against a »colored tongue«. In industry and the office, the pencils can be used as markers for flipcharts. Available also as fluorescent highlighters.

HERSTELLER MANUFACTURER Schwan-STABILO, Schwanhäußer GmbH & Co, Heroldsberg, Germany
PRODUKT PRODUCT Schwan-STABILO woody 880/890, Farbstifte/Leuchtfarbstifte Colored pencils / Fluorescent colored pencils
DESIGN Schwan-STABILO, Marketing und Produktion, Heroldsberg, Germany

HERSTELLER MANUFACTURER STAEDLER MARS GmbH & Co., Schreib- und Zeichengeräte Fabriken, Nürnberg, Germany
PRODUKT PRODUCT Capless Roller Tintenroller Ballpoint
DESIGN STAEDLER MARS, Nürnberg, Germany

CAPLESS ROLLER, Tintenroller mit markantem Design. Spannungsreiche Form durch asymmetrischen Anschnitt, dessen Fläche bei ausgefahrener Mine das Wegrollen des Stifts verhindert.

CAPLESS ROLLER, a Ballpoint with a striking design: The exciting form is an eye-catcher with its asymmetrical cut, that the resulting area functions as an anti-rolling device when the lead is extended.

BASE 410 ist ein Schulfüller mit besonders sorgfältig gestaltetem Griffbereich. Eine formschlüssige Rutschbremse für Daumen und Zeigefinger sowie eine große Anlagefläche für den Mittelfinger ermöglichen ermüdungsfreie Handhabung und wirken einer Verkrampfung der Schreibhand entgegen. Das Material, thermoplastisches Elastomer, reduziert Schweißbildung. Stabiler Federclip, gute Sicht auf beide Patronen, Tintenregler, Feder aus gewalztem, hochglanzpoliertem Stahl mit Iridiumspitze. Auch als »base kid« für den Schreibanfänger und als Modell für Linkshänder lieferbar. Modularer Aufbau, nachkaufbare Ersatzteile.

The BASE 410 is a school fountain pen with a specially designed grip area. The collar and grip ensure the thumb and forefinger do not slip, and there is a large contact area for the middle finger to ensure non-fatiguing use and prevent cramping. The thermoplastic elastomer used reduces sweating. The pen features a stable pen clip, the window showing both cartridges, the ink-feed regulator, and a nib of rolled polished steel with an iridium point. Available also as the »base kid« for beginners and in a left-handed version. Modular construction, with spare parts purchasable.

HERSTELLER MANUFACTURER Schneider GmbH & Co, Produktions- und Vertriebs KG, Wernigerode, Germany
PRODUKT PRODUCT base 410 Schulfüller Fountain pen
DESIGN Atelier für Gestaltung, Dipl.-Des. Andreas Papenfuss, Weimar, Germany

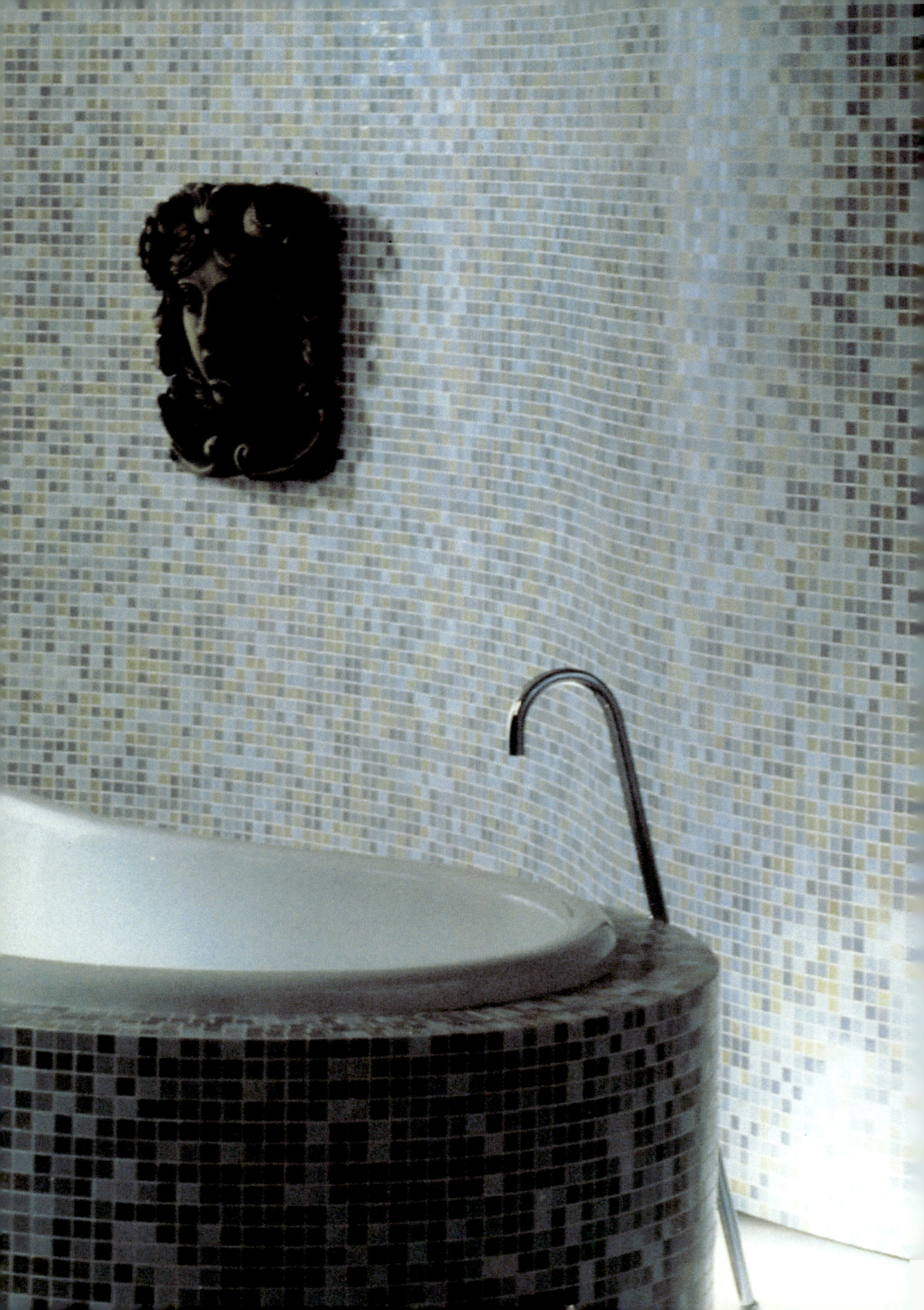

wohnung home

WOHNUNG HOME

Jury: Christoph Böninger, Horst Diener, Isao Hosoe, Martin Iseli

In der Wettbewerbskategorie Wohnung nimmt traditionsgemäß der Sanitär-Sektor die stärkste Position ein. Ein hoher Standard wird repräsentiert, der jedoch nicht ausreichte, daß ein Produkt dieser Kategorie mit in die Top Ten des Wettbewerbs gelangte. »Ich sah kein richtig gutes Bad, keine Dusche, kein überragendes Waschbecken. Alles gab vor, gut und irgendwie clever zu sein. Doch diese Haltung spiegelt das Fehlen eines Traumes. Wenn Designer überragendes auf diesem Gebiet leisten, könnten sie beispielsweise auch genauso gut die Fähigkeit eines Schriftstellers haben, weil sie einen Sinn fürs Leben brauchen und für die Gestaltung des Daseins«, kommentierte die französische Gestalterin Andrée Putman das Fehlen der Visionen in diesem Sektor.

Ein aktueller Trend, der sich gerade im Sanitärbereich abzeichnet, ist das Thema Existenzminimum. Badewannen werden zu Kleinstbädern. Badewannenformen passen sich durch geschickte Asymmetrien dem Grundriß kleinster Räumlichkeiten unter Beibehaltung des Komforts an. Diese auf platzsparende Ökonomie angelegten Kleinstbäder bilden einen Gegenpol zu den Repräsentationsbädern, die ausgezeichnet wurden.

Nicht nur im Sanitärbereich trifft man auf die zeittypische Doppelfunktion vieler Produkte, die sowohl für den privaten wie öffentlichen Bereich konzipiert wurden. Wie handgrifflose Mischer sind es Garderoben, Tischsysteme, Schrankwände, die beim Zusammenwachsen der Bereiche Büro und Wohnung in beiden Welten zuhause sein können.

Waren spirituelle und kulturorientierte Qualitäten nach Meinung der Juroren eher schwach vertreten, wurden ökologisch richtungsweisende Lösungen in dieser Kategorie gleich viermal ausgezeichnet: zwei solide, stark reduzierte Möbelsysteme aus Holz, eine geteilte Taste zur wahlweisen Dosierung des Wasserverbrauchs sowie eine Duschwanne mit extrem hoher Durabilität und 30jähriger Garantie.

Generell kann innerhalb dieses Produktsektors Schlichtheit als Gestaltungstrend angesehen werden: Schlichtheit bei Mobiliar, Schlichtheit bei Möbelbeschlägen, »Low budget«-Design bei Türgriffen. Auf Vereinfachung als Designvorgabe trifft man auch bei einer ausgezeichneten Boden- und Galerieleiste, die das Kabelmanagement in Wohn- wie Arbeitsräumen übernimmt.

In the Home category, traditionally products for the hygiene and sanitation sector occupy the strongest position. The standard this year was exceptionally high, but still did not suffice to place a product of this class among the Top Ten in the competition. "I saw no really good bath, no shower, and no outstanding washbasin. Everything tried very hard to be good and to somehow clever. But such a stance merely reflects the absence of a dream. If designers really create something outstanding in this area, they could, for instance, just as well have the ability of an author, because they need a feel for life and for the design of existence," commented French designer Andrée Putman on the absence of visions in this sector.

A current trend which is emerging precisely in the realm of sanitation is the trend to get by on a minimum. Bathtubs are becoming mini-tubs. Bath tub shapes are adjusted by means of skillful asymmetries to the outlines of the smallest of apartments without relinquishing comfort. These mini-tubs, geared to space-saving economy, form an antipole to the ostentatious representative bathtubs which likewise won awards.

Not only in the realm of sanitation do we encounter a feature many products currently exhibit: namely that they double up functions by being designed for use in both the private and public sectors. Like mixers that require no hand-grips, there are wardrobes, table systems and wall units, which are equally at home in the office or the apartment, given that the latter are growing ever closer together.

Whereas spiritual and culturally-oriented qualities were, in the opinion of the jurors, under-represented, four ecologically pioneering solutions devised in this otherwise small competition category won prizes: two solid, strongly reduced wooden furniture systems, one double-function button to regulate water dosage as well as an extremely durable shower tray complete with 30-year guarantee.

In general, design in this product category can be characterized as straightforward: Plainness in terms of furniture, furniture fixtures, "low budget" designs for door handles. And simplification as the design brief is also to be found in the excellent floor and gallery cable duct for use in residential and professional premises alike.

THONET 737/1737, Tisch mit Stühlen. Aus elementaren geometrischen Formen entwickelt, weicht das schnörkellose Design um eben das Maß ab, das der Körper einem perfekten Sitzmöbel abverlangt. Alle Versionen des Stuhls 737 lassen sich mit dem Tisch kombinieren. Tischplatte aus Buchenholz, Oberfläche gebeizt oder mit Linoleum in den Farben der Thonet-Kollektion belegt. Geschweifte Tischbeine, die in kleinen Rollen enden (an einer Schmalseite beweglich). Tisch 1737 ist mit der eingebauten Verlängerungsplatte von 170 cm auf 225 cm zu verlängern.

THONET 737/1737 is a group of chairs and tables based on elementary geometric forms. The design deviates from them only as far as is necessary to provide the human body with perfect seating. All versions of Chair 737 can be combined with the table. The tabletop comes in beech with a stained surface or in linoleum in the colors of the Thonet Collection. The curved table legs end in small rolls (movable at the narrow end). Table 1737 can be extended from 170 cm to 225 cm using the built-in leaf.

HERSTELLER MANUFACTURER Gebrüder Thonet GmbH, Frankenberg, Germany
PRODUKT PRODUCT Gruppe 737/1737 Tisch und Stuhl Table and chair
DESIGN Design und Innenarchitektur Peter Maly, Hamburg, Germany

Ökologie/Design Auszeichnung Awarded for Ecology/Design: Vorbildlich in Transparenz der Materialien sowie einen sehr leichten und trotzdem stabilen Stuhl. Exemplary for the transparent use of materials as well as the very light and yet sturdy chair.

HERSTELLER MANUFACTURER: arco meubelfabrik bv, Winterswijk, The Netherlands
PRODUKT PRODUCT: CME, CML, CMW Tisch Serie Table series
DESIGN: Charles Marks, Amsterdam, The Netherlands

CM-Tischserie. Das Design wurde aus der Konstruktion entwickelt: die vier L-förmigen Elemente rund um die Tischplatte sorgen für optimale Stabilität und Verwindungssteife bei minimalem Materialeinsatz. Diese technisch identischen Elemente erlauben zudem eine rationelle Produktion der Tische, die in verschiedenen Varianten und Größen geliefert werden. Sie lassen sich einfach zerlegen (auch wenn sie nicht so aussehen), womit das Design ebenfalls den ökologischen Ansprüchen des Herstellers Rechnung trägt. Die Formgebung folgt in allen Details praktischen Erwägungen. So schützt die an der Tischunterseite umlaufende schräge Kante die Platte und die Armlehnen von Stühlen vor wechselseitigen Beschädigungen.

CM is a table series, whereby the design was developed from the construction itself: the four L-shaped elements around the tabletop provide optimal stability and tension with minimum material inputs. These technically identical elements provide for streamlined production of the tables in different versions and sizes. Despite their appearance, they can be easily disassembled and the design meets ecological requirements, too. In all aspects, the details bear practicalities in mind. The chamfer on the underside of the table lessens damage to and by chair armrests.

Ökologie/Design Auszeichnung Awarded for Ecology/Design: Vorbildlich in Transparenz der Materialien und Einfachheit der Konstruktion. *Exemplary for its transparent materials and simple construction.*

CARTESIO, modulares Bücherregal, entworfen von Aldo Rossi. Würfelförmige Container aus Metall können frei zur gewünschten Gesamtgestalt des Regals zusammengefügt werden. Die Front aus furniertem Schichtholz wird dann mit einer numerisch gesteuerten Maschine geschnitten, und zwar Türen und Rahmen aus demselben Stück. Auch mit Glastüren lieferbar.

CARTESIO, a modular book shelf designed by Aldo Rossi. Cubic metal containers can be assembled to create the shape desired. The front, made of veneered plywood, is then cut with a Numeric Control Machine, carving the square doors and frame in one piece. The glazed doors are optional.

HERSTELLER MANUFACTURER UNIFOR Spa, Turate, Italy
PRODUKT PRODUCT CARTESIO Bücherregal Bookshelf
DESIGN Aldo Rossi, Milano, Italy
VERTRIEB DISTRIBUTION UNIFOR Vertrieb Deutschland Christian Robert GmbH, München, Germany

HERSTELLER MANUFACTURER Ress + Sohn Möbelfabrik, Bad Königshofen, Germany
PRODUKT PRODUCT WK 420 ultimo Kastenmöbelprogramm Box furniture line
DESIGN Thomas Althaus, Düsseldorf, Germany
VERTRIEB DISTRIBUTION WK WOHNEN Einrichtungs GmbH, Leinfelden-Echterdingen, Germany

WK 420 ULTIMO Kastenmöbelprogramm für den Wohn- und den Objektbereich. Entwickelt aus der Vorstellung eines einfachen Wandregals im Hinblick auf Flexibilität, schnellen Umbau und neue Nutzungen. Aluminiumprofil, natur oder schwarz eloxiert, als konstruktive Basis für Fachbodenträger, Türen, Leuchten. Schiebetüren (Rasterhöhe), Überblendtüren (2- und 3-fache Rasterhöhe), Podestplatten, U-Winkel für hohe Regale ohne Wandbefestigung, Containerprogramm erlauben die freie Gestaltung von Regalen, Medientürmen, Raumteilern, Sideboards etc., von rollbaren Containern oder Racks. Beleuchtung und interne Kabelführung möglich. Oberflächen in sechs Farben matt lackiert oder in Kirschbaum natur (furniert und massiv).

WK 420 ULTIMO is a furniture line for residential and commercial interiors. It is based on the idea of a simple wall shelf that offers flexibility, can be altered swiftly and used for new purposes. Made of aluminum profiles, available untreated or anodized black, also as the frame for drawers, or with sliding or folding doors, screen doors (in two or three fixed heights), lighting, base and U-shaped corner units for high shelves that are not wall-mounted: allowing you a free hand in shaping your shelves, media towers, room dividers etc. Also available as racks or with castor-based container. Internal cable ducts available. Surface treated with matt varnish in six colors or with a natural cherry finish (as veneer or as solid wood).

HERSTELLER MANUFACTURER ART-LINE Wohndecor GmbH, Kerpen, Germany
PRODUKT PRODUCT FL/GL Fuß- und Galerieleiste Skirting board and gallery rail
DESIGN Jasper Morrison, London, Great Britain, Matthias Dietz, Frankfurt, Germany

ART-LINE aus der Kollektion ALPHA: Fußleiste 7023 und Galerieleiste 8662, aus stranggepreßten Aluminiumprofilen mit diversen Metalloberflächen und speziell entwickelten Eckelementen zur paßgenauen Einfügung in jeden Raum. Problemlose Montage durch einfaches Andrücken auf exzentrisch gebohrte Kunststoffclips, nachträgliches Anpassen und Nivellieren ebenso möglich wie die Kaschierung von Kabeln. Die Galerieleiste ermöglicht die wirkungsvolle Präsentation von Bildern und Objekten, auch in repräsentativen Privaträumen.

ART-LINE, Collection ALPHA: The 7023 skirting board and the 8662 gallery rail made of extruded aluminum profiles with various metal finishes and spec-ially developed corner elements for a snug fit in any angle. Both are easy to assemble by simply pressing together the eccentrically drilled plastic clips, and subsequent adjustment and leveling are possible as is concealment of wiring. The gallery rail enables the effective presentation of pictures and objects - in representative private settings as well.

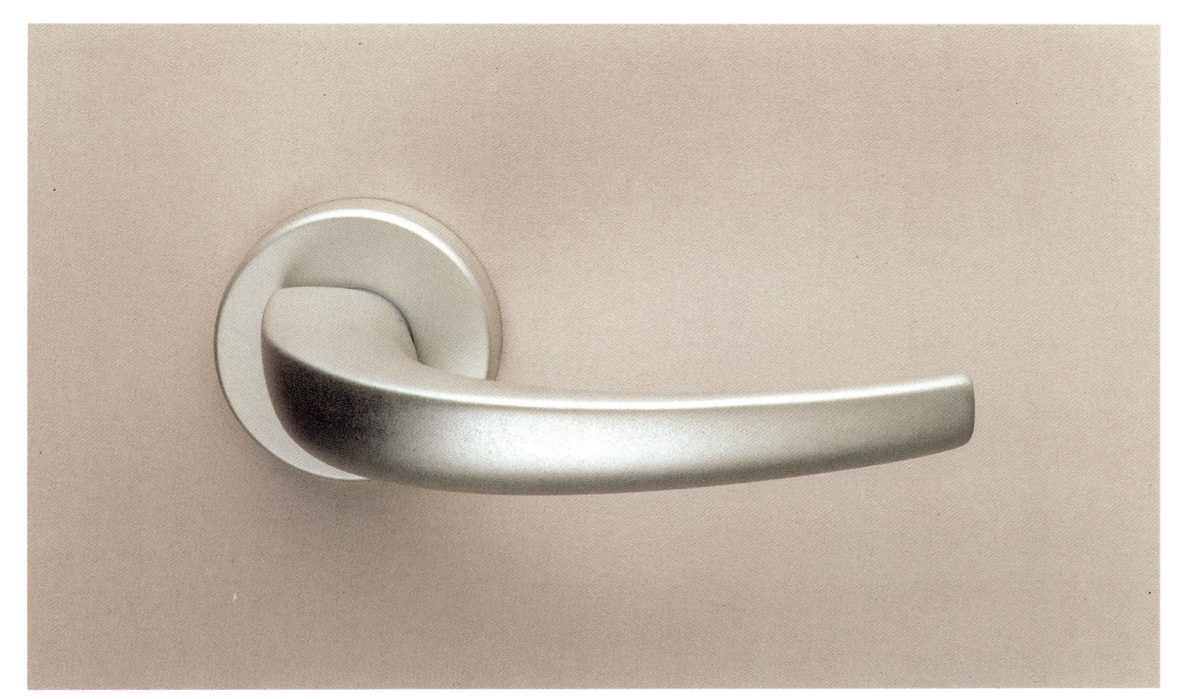

Wilh. Grundmann Schlösser und Beschläge, Rohrbach/Gölsen, Austria HERSTELLER MANUFACTURER
Servus Türbeschlag Door handle PRODUKT PRODUCT
Mag. art. Michael Schaefer, Wien, Austria DESIGN

SERVUS, ein preisgünstiger Design-Beschlag für den modernen Wohnungsbau. Die aus der Entfernung betrachtet radikal moderne Linienführung erweist sich aus der Nähe und beim Anfassen der Klinke als entgegenkommend und griffsympathisch. Der »handliche« Charakter entsteht durch den schräggestellten elliptischen Querschnitt, der aus der Tür herausschwingt und sich dann in einer Drehung verjüngt. Aus silber-eloxiertem und satiniertem Aluminium.

SERVUS is a low-cost handle designed for the modern interior. From a distance it looks radically modern in shape, and close up it feels welcoming and pleasant to touch. Its »handy« character is the product of the slanting elliptical cross-section that swings forward from the door and tapers sharply. Made of silver anodized aluminum with a satin finish.

WOHNUNG HOME 149

Grass AG Möbelbeschläge, Höchst, Austria   HERSTELLER MANUFACTURER
NOVA DELUXE Schubkastenzarge Drawer frame   PRODUKT PRODUCT
Kubus produkt design, Einbeck, Germany   DESIGN

NOVA DELUXE, eine Schubkastenzarge mit verdecktem Führungssystem, in Design und Funktion für das Baukastensystem NOVA entwickelt. Leiselaufender, synchrongesteuerter Vollauszug.
NOVA DELUXE is a drawer frame with concealed runners. It was designed for the Nova furniture system. The drawers are quiet running and can be completely pulled out.

150 WOHNUNG *HOME*

HERSTELLER MANUFACTURER mor'log. Produkte, Darmstadt, Germany
PRODUKT PRODUCT gonio Brief- und Zeitungskasten Letter and newspaper box
DESIGN PULS Design, Darmstadt, Germany

GONIO, ein unverwüstlicher Brief- und Zeitungskasten in zeitgemässer Formgebung, der sogar Päckchen aufnehmen kann. Großer Einwurf, großes Namensschild (auch für Doppelnamen und Wohngemeinschaften). Beim Aufschließen wird die Klappe zum Ablagetablett. Kombination mehrerer Kästen neben- oder übereinander möglich. Aus recyclebarem Stahlblech in vielen Farben und Oberflächengestaltungen.
GONIO is an indestructible letterbox with a decidedly modern design big enough even for parcels. It features a broad entry slit, a large name plate (suited also for lengthier surnames and flat sharers). On being opened, the slit cover functions as a tray. Boxes can be combined next to or on top of each other. Made of recyclable steel sheet in many colors and different finishes.

WOHNUNG HOME 151

HERSTELLER MANUFACTURER
Mayr Schulmöbelgesellschaft mbH, Wilhelm Geisbauer, Scharnstein, Austria
PRODUKT PRODUCT
FIDIBUS Kinderdrehstuhl Children's swivel-chair
DESIGN
Martin Ballendat, Altheim, Austria

FIDIBUS, ergonomischer Kinderdrehstuhl: mit verstellbarer Sitztiefe und Lehnenhöhe sowie allseitig neigbarer Sitzfläche. Für den Wohnbereich entworfen. Zur gleichen Serie gehört ein höhenverstellbarer Kinderarbeitsstisch mit neigbarer Platte und ein Rollcontainer.

FIDIBUS ergonomically designed children's swivel chair with adjustable seat and backrest height and tilt angle. It was conceived for home use. The same series includes a children's work desk, adjust-able in height, with a tilt-able top and a castor-based container.

SELECTOR, Abfalltrennsystem für öffentliche Bereiche. Der Erfolg der Abfalltrennung hängt auch an der Motivation der Nutzer solcher Systeme. Durch eine klare, funktionale und ansprechende Formgebung, durch deutliche Trennung der Abfallbereiche, markante Gestaltung der Einwurföffnungen, Farbgebung, Beschriftung erhöht Selector die Akzeptanz des getrennten Sammelns. Widerstandsfähige Ausführung aus Aluminium (die den besonderen Sicherheitsanforderungen von Flughäfen entspricht). Individuelle Gestaltung und Farbgebung der Oberflächen möglich.

SELECTOR is a public waste separating system. The success of waste separation also depends on motivating the users of such systems. A clear, functional and attractive design: clear segregation of waste areas, designating the input slots, color, labeling enhances the acceptance of waste separation. The system can be expanded at random. The unit is made of durable aluminum, meeting special airport security requirements. Individual design and surface colors are available.

HERSTELLER MANUFACTURER BÜRO CONCEPT, Hannover, Germany
PRODUKT PRODUCT SELECTOR Abfalltrennsystem Waste separating system
DESIGN SYN PRODUCTS DESIGN Gerald Fuhrberg, Hannover, Germany

WOHNUNG HOME 153

HERSTELLER MANUFACTURER Aquis GmbH Wasser-Luft-Systeme Lindau, Rebstein, Switzerland
PRODUKT PRODUCT Iqua Elektronische Armatur Electronic fixtures
DESIGN Via 4 Design GmbH, Nagold, Germany

IQUA, eine sensorgesteuerte Standardarmatur für Waschtische im privaten und öffentlichen Bereich. Berührungslos zu bedienen, dadurch besonders geeignet für hygienisch sensible Bereiche wie z. B. Krankenhäuser. Die Armatur spart bis zu 70 % des normalerweise durchlaufenden Wassers; spart zugleich Energie, denn nicht weglaufendes Wasser muß auch nicht erwärmt werden. Das »intelligente« Sensorauge erfaßt Gegenstände oder Körperteile im Bereich einer »Berührungswolke«; nach spätestens 60 Sekunden permanenter Wasserabgabe schließt das Ventil. Batterie und Netzbetrieb der Armatur möglich. Lebensdauer bei hoher Beanspruchung etwa drei Jahre.

IQUA is a sensor-controlled faucet or fixture for private and commercial applications. Non-touch activation and therefore especially suited for hygienically sensitive areas such as hospitals. The faucet saves up to 70 percent of usual water throughput and saves energy, as water that is saved also does not need to be heated. The »smart« sensor notes objects or parts of the body within a three-dimensional zone; after 60 seconds of uninterrupted water flow the valve shuts. The battery-operated fixture has a service life of three years and can, as an option, be mains powered.

AQUA BUTZKE-WERKE AG, Berlin, Germany   HERSTELLER MANUFACTURER
AQUAMIX Selbstschluß-Eingriffmischer Onetouch autostop faucet   PRODUKT PRODUCT
Büchin Design, Berlin, Germany   DESIGN

AQUAMIX ist ein Selbstschluß-Eingriffmischer für öffentliche Einrichtungen wie Sportzentren oder Autobahnraststätten. Maßgeblich für das Design waren einfache Handhabung und massive Bauweise (Messing verchromt) zur Sicherung der Langlebigkeit und zum Schutz gegen Vandalismus. Bedienfunktionen: Einhandbedienung, Automatic Stop und Regulierung von Wassermenge und -temperatur, wurden nach ergono-mischen und ökologischen Gesichtspunkten entwickelt, die Funktionen in klare ästhetische Formen umgesetzt.

AQUAMIX is a one-touch autostop faucet for public facilities such as sports centers or highway service stations. The design focuses on easy handling and a robust form (chrome-plated brass) to ensure durability and protect against vandalism. User functions: one-hand use, auto-stop and water activation system and temperature regulation. The faucet bears ergonomic and ecological viewpoints in mind and gives them a clear aesthetic form.

WOHNUNG HOME 155

HERSTELLER MANUFACTURER
Hansgrohe, Schiltach, Germany
PRODUKT PRODUCT
Aktiva Caresse Handbrause Hand shower
DESIGN
Phoenix Product Design, Stuttgart, Germany

AKTIVA CARESSE Handbrause. Elegante, futuristisch wirkende Form mit femininem Touch. Ergonomisch in den Handgriff integrierte stufenlose Waterdim-Funktion hilft bei gleichem Duschkomfort bis zu 40 % Wasser zu sparen. Neuartiges Reinigungssystem Turboclean: angetrieben durch die Wasserkraft heben und senken sich abwechselnd Segmente mit Reinigungsstiften und halten so die nierenähnlich angeformten Strahlkanäle kalkfrei. Gleichzeitig entsteht der schmeichelnde, dem Regen nachempfundene Caresse-Strahl.

The AKTIVA CARESSE hand shower has an elegant, somewhat futuristic design with a feminine touch. A water-dimmer function is ergonomically integrated into the hand grip, offering up to 40% water savings without diminishing shower comfort. The new Turboclean cleaning system is powered by the waterflow: different segments with cleaning pins lift up and down, keeping the kidney-shaped spray channels deposit-free. While offering a rain-like spray that caresses the skin.

ORBIS, eine kreisrunde, in sich geschlossene Duschabtrennung. Zylindrischer Korpus mit großzügigen Echtglasscheiben. Markante Profile in allen gängigen Sanitärfarben. Für die platzsparende Eckversion ist eine kreisrunde Duschwanne lieferbar, wahlweise mit und ohne angeformter Schürze.
ORBIS is a circular shower enclosure. The cylindrical body features real glass panels. Striking profiles in all the usual colors. The space-saving corner version is available as a round shower tray with or without integral decorative panel.

HERSTELLER MANUFACTURER Koralle-Sanitärprodukte GmbH, Vlotho, Germany
PRODUKT PRODUCT Orbis Duschabtrennung Shower enclosure
DESIGN Koralle-Sanitärprodukte GmbH, Vlotho, Germany

HERSTELLER MANUFACTURER Duscholux
PRODUKT PRODUCT Piccolo Sky Kleinbadlösung Small bath system
DESIGN Duscholux, Lammel und Kratz, Aachen, Germany
VERTRIEB DISTRIBUTION D+S Sanitärprodukte GmbH, Schriesheim, Germany

PICCOLO SKY, modulares System aus Badewanne, Duschwanne, Waschbecken mit Spiegelfläche, Duschwand; zur Einrichtung auch sehr kleiner Bäder (vier bis sechs Quadratmeter), mit einer getrennten Wanne und Duschwanne. Das erlaubt die raumsparende, dennoch ergonomische Gestaltung der Einzelelemente. Optisch dominieren asymmetrische und elliptische Formen.

PICCOLO SKY is a modular bath tub and shower tray system with glass enclosure and with an optional wash-basin and mirror attachment. It is ideally suited for very small bathrooms of four to six sq m. with separate shower tray and bath tub. The individual elements are designed ergonomically and to save space. The unit has striking asymmetrical and elliptical forms.

ENTRÉE, eine Duschwand, die überall dort pfiffige Lösungen ermöglicht, wo normalerweise Eckeinstieg oder Sonderanfertigungen bestellt werden müßten. Problemlose Gestaltung breiter Eingänge, problemloser Ausgleich schiefer Wände. Hartglas klar, Scharniere in Platinum silber mit »Zoom-Effekt« und neues Griffdesign unterstreichen den innovativen Charakter der Duschwand.

ENTRÉE is a shower enclosure offering ingenious solutions where otherwise corner entry or special-size doors would have been necessary. It affords superb solutions to wide entrances and a simple way of offsetting walls that are not straight. The unit consists of tempered clear glass, hinges in platinum silver with a »zoom effect« and a new handle design: emphasizing the innovative impact of the shower enclosure.

SPRINT, eine Faltduschwand. Wird getragen von zwei Rohrprofilen, die freistehend bis zu einer Höhe von 2,80 Meter zwischen Boden und Decke verspannt werden: damit ist die Duschwand unabhängig von Wannenrand und -höhe. Flügeltüren, die zur Mitte hin geklappt werden; das mittlere feststehende Segment ist mit Ablage und Handtuchhalter ausgestattet und sorgt für Stabilität. Weiße Profile, Sicherheits-Kunststoffglas. Mit mitgelieferten bunten Folien individuell zu gestalten.

SPRINT is a concertina shower enclosure based on two tubular profiles which can be stretched to a height of 2.8 meters between floor and ceiling - so the shower enclosure does not depend on the tub height. The two outer doors swing inwards overlapping the fixed middle section, which features shelves and a towel rail and provides extra stability. The profiles are in white, and the doors are made of acrylic glass, and a foil with decorative designs is included for those who want more color.

HERSTELLER MANUFACTURER: Duscholux
PRODUKT PRODUCT: links/left: Entrée Duschwand Shower enclosure; rechts/right: Sprint Faltduschwand Shower enclosure
DESIGN: Duscholux
VERTRIEB DISTRIBUTION: D+S Sanitärprodukte GmbH, Schriesheim, Germany

WOHNUNG HOME

HERSTELLER MANUFACTURER Villeroy & Boch AG, Mettlach, Germany
PRODUKT PRODUCT VOLANO Waschtisch Washbasin
DESIGN moll design, reiner moll & partner, Schwäbisch Gmünd, Germany

VOLANO Schrankwaschtische, entwickelt von Moll-Design. Klare, elegante Linienführung der umlaufenden Waschtischzargen und weich ausgeformten Beckenränder. Großzügige Ablageflächen. In verschiedenen Grössen lieferbar. Auch als Doppelwaschtisch mit leicht asymmetrisch angeordneten Becken, was gleichzeitige Nutzung beider Becken problemlos macht.

The VOLANO vanity washbasin was developed by Moll Design and boasts clear, elegant lines and a softly contoured rim as well as a spacious countertop. Available in different sizes, also as a double basin with slightly asymmetrical positioning, making use of both at once straightforward.

160 WOHNUNG HOME

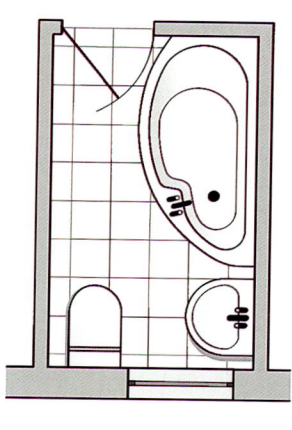

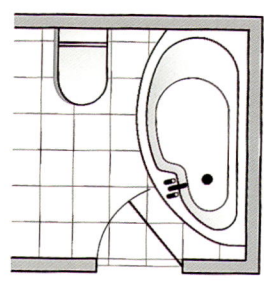

TORNIO, Badewanne. Als Eckwanne mit unterschiedlich langen Schenkeln (1800 und 665 mm, wahlweise linke und rechte Ausführung) besonders geeignet für kleine bzw. schwierig zugeschnittene Räume. Ein Raumsparer, der dennoch genügend Platz für entspanntes Baden bietet. Optional mit 6 Whirl- und/oder 17 Air-Inject-Düsen auszurüsten. Sitzbereich auch als Duschzone geeignet. Am Fußende und auf den breiten Rändern mit den meisten der handelsüblichen Armaturen zu kombinieren.

The TORNIO bathtub is a corner bath with different side lengths (1800 and 665 mm, optionally on the left or right). It is particularly suited for small or sharply angled rooms, saving space but offering a relaxed bath. Option-ally outfitted with 6 whirl or 17 air injection jets. The seating space can double up as a shower zone and the usual faucets can be installed at the foot or on the wide sides.

HOESCH Metall + Kunststoff GmbH & Co., Düren, Germany   HERSTELLER MANUFACTURER
TORNIO Eckbadewanne aus Sanitär-Acryl Corner bathtub   PRODUKT PRODUCT
Babel Design, Adolf Babel, Untergruppenbach, Germany   DESIGN

Eisenwerke Fried. Wilh. Düker GmbH & Co., Karlstadt, Germany HERSTELLER MANUFACTURER
Modula Bad-Kombination Bath system PRODUKT PRODUCT
Artefakt Fiegl/Pohl, Darmstadt, Germany DESIGN

MINIWANNE: System MODULA, eine Serie bestehend aus Badewanne, Waschtisch, Duschabtrennung und Zubehör, mit der sich auch komplexe Einrichtungsprobleme in Bädern lösen lassen. Für ein funktionales und formschönes Bad auf kleinstem Raum.

A MINIATURE TUB: the MODULA system is a series comprising a bath tub, shower encloure, wash basin and accessories specially devised for solving complex bathroom interior design problems. For a functional and beautiful bath using the smallest space.

HÜPPE UNA 1000, Badewannen-Duschabtrennung mit völlig neuem Konzept für das Duschen in der Wanne. Speziell für die Nachrüstung von Bädern in Mietwohnungen entwickelt, wird sie zwischen Decke und Badewannenrand befestigt, bei sehr hohen Decken mit Teleskop-Anbindung an der Wand. Frei drehbare Mittelsäule mit Haltegriff für sicheres Ein- und Aussteigen. Individuelle Einstellung des Duschbereichs durch zwei, um 180° drehbare Flügelelemente. Lieferbar in Echt- und in Kunstglasdekor, in 12 Farben und 2 Farbkombinationen.

The HÜPPE UNA 1000 shower enclosure offers an entirely new concept for showering in bathtubs. Developed especially for bathtubs in rented property, the shower enclosure is mounted between the ceiling and placed on the bathtub side, with a telescopic wall tie for particularly high ceilings. The central profile swivels and features a hand grip for easy entry and exit. Two wing segments to the left and right of the profile can be snapped into various positions and are available in real glass or as design acrylic glass, with 12 different profile colors and two color combinations.

HERSTELLER MANUFACTURER HÜPPE GmbH & Co., Bad Zwischenahn, Germany
PRODUKT PRODUCT Hüppe Una 1000 Duschabtrennung für die Badewanne Shower enclosure for bathtubs
DESIGN Dorian Kurz & Partner, Solingen, Germany, Klaus Bremm, HÜPPE GmbH & Co, Bad Zwischenahn, Germany

WOHNUNG HOME 163

Friatec AG, Mannheim, Germany HERSTELLER MANUFACTURER
Friatec 4000 WC Spülkasten Toilet flush unit PRODUKT PRODUCT
Scholpp Produktgestaltung, Oberriexingen, Germany DESIGN

FRIATEC 4000 WC-Spülkasten mit neuartiger, wassersparender Zwei-Mengen-Spültechnik, die mit einer zweigeteilten Taste sicher zu bedienen ist. Die Formgebung spiegelt die hohe Qualität, die durch verbesserte Herstellungstechnik erreicht wurde.
FRIATEC 4000 is a Toilet flush unit using innovative, water-saving two-volume technology: operated by a bipartite push button. The design reflects the high quality workmanship afforded by improved production technology.

Friatec AG, Mannheim, Germany **HERSTELLER MANUFACTURER**
Friabloc Betätigungsplatte für UP-Spülkasten Wall panel for integrated Toilet flush basin **PRODUKT PRODUCT**
Scholpp Produktgestaltung, Oberriexingen, Germany **DESIGN**

FRIABLOC-Betätigungsplatte für Unterputzspülkästen. Mit neuartiger wassersparender Zwei-Mengen-Spültechnik, die mit der zweigeteilter Funk-tionstaste sicher zu bedienen ist: viel Wasser/wenig Wasser. Dekorleisten in drei Formen und fünf Farben erlauben die Anpassung der Platte an individuelle Badeinrichtungen.

FRIABLOC, a wall panel for integrated Toilet flush units. It features innovative, water-saving two-volume technology operated by a bipartite flush button: the user chooses the amount of water required. Decorative side strips avail-able in three shapes and five colors mean the plate can be adapted to the consumer's exact preferences.

Ökologie/Design Auszeichnung Awarded for Ecology/Design: Vorbildlich durch funktionserklärende Gestaltung. Exemplary for its design, which explains all the funktions.

WOHNUNG HOME 165

HERSTELLER MANUFACTURER Franz Kaldewei GmbH & Co., Ahlen, Germany
PRODUKT PRODUCT Rotonda Bade-/Duschwannenkombination Bathtub/shower tray combination
DESIGN Sottsass Associati Srl, Milano, Italy

ROTONDA, Bade- und Duschwanne in einem. Das ermöglicht die außergewöhnliche Form dieser Wanne, die innen und außen als »Acht« gestaltet ist und deren schlanke Taille die Wanne in Bade- und Duschbereich teilt. Großzügige Abmessungen, Mittelablauf und zwei Rückenschrägen bieten Bequemlichkeit für das Bad zu zweit. Die klassische Linienführung wirkt einladend und körperfreundlich. Großzügig als Wanne (90 cm breit) und Dusche (Durchmesser 56 cm), dennoch raumsparend, weil die übliche Doppellösung entfällt. Stahlwanne mit integriertem Antislip, in Pistazie, Burgund und Softblau lieferbar.

ROTONDA, an unusually shaped combination bath and shower tray, with an interior and exterior designed like a figure eight, with the »cross-over« point dividing the model into a bath and a showering area. Generous proportions, with a central outlet and two backrests, the bath is 90 cm wide and the shower tray has a diameter of 56 cm. Even so, Rotonda saves valuable space, as it does away with the conventional »dual« solution. The integrated anti-slip surface is also available in colours pistachio, burgundy and soft blue.

HERSTELLER MANUFACTURER
Franz Kaldewei GmbH & Co., Ahlen, Germany
PRODUKT PRODUCT
Rondoplan Eckduschwanne Corner shower tray
DESIGN
Phoenix Product Design, Stuttgart, Germany

RONDOPLAN ist eine Eckduschwanne mit halbrunder Ablagefläche, die freitragend über den Innenraum schwingt und den Wasserablauf überdeckt. Dieser hat seinerseits eine flächenbündige, in die Gesamtkontur eingefügte Abdeckung in den Farben chrom, manhattan, alpinweiß, pergamon, edelmessing: nicht nur ein optischer Blickfang, sondern auch Vergrößerung der Fläche zum Stehen. Die im vorderen Bereich zurückgestufte Verkleidung läßt die Wanne besonders flach und elegant wirken. Für den platzsparenden Eckeinbau konzipiert, dennoch wirkt die Wanne, als stünde sie frei und großzügig im Raum.

A typical detail of this shower tray is the half-round shelf that swings over the tray-interior and visually covers the outlet hole. The outlet hole itself is covered by a lid that closes parallel to the shower tray surface. The lid (available in chrome, manhattan, alpine white, emerald and refined brass) is not only an eye-catcher, but enlarges the standing area, too. The bath enclosure is stepped back in the front, giving the tray a clean and elegant appearance. Designed for space-saving, Rondoplan has the feel of a large-scale, standalone shower to it.

168 WOHNUNG HOME

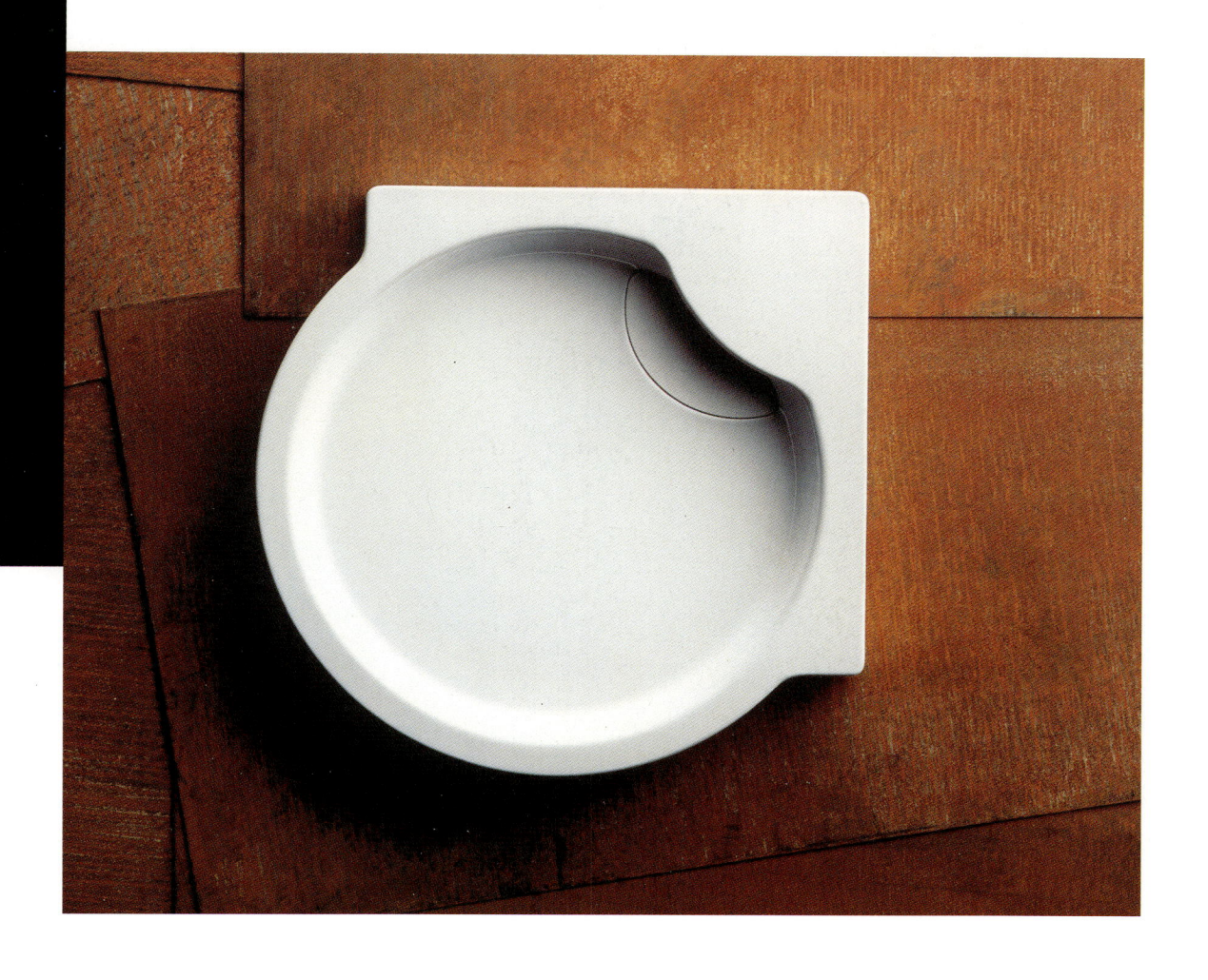

Ökologie/Design Auszeichnung Awarded for Ecology/Design: Vorbildlich durch 30 Jahre Garantie. Exemplary, with its 30 years' guarantee.

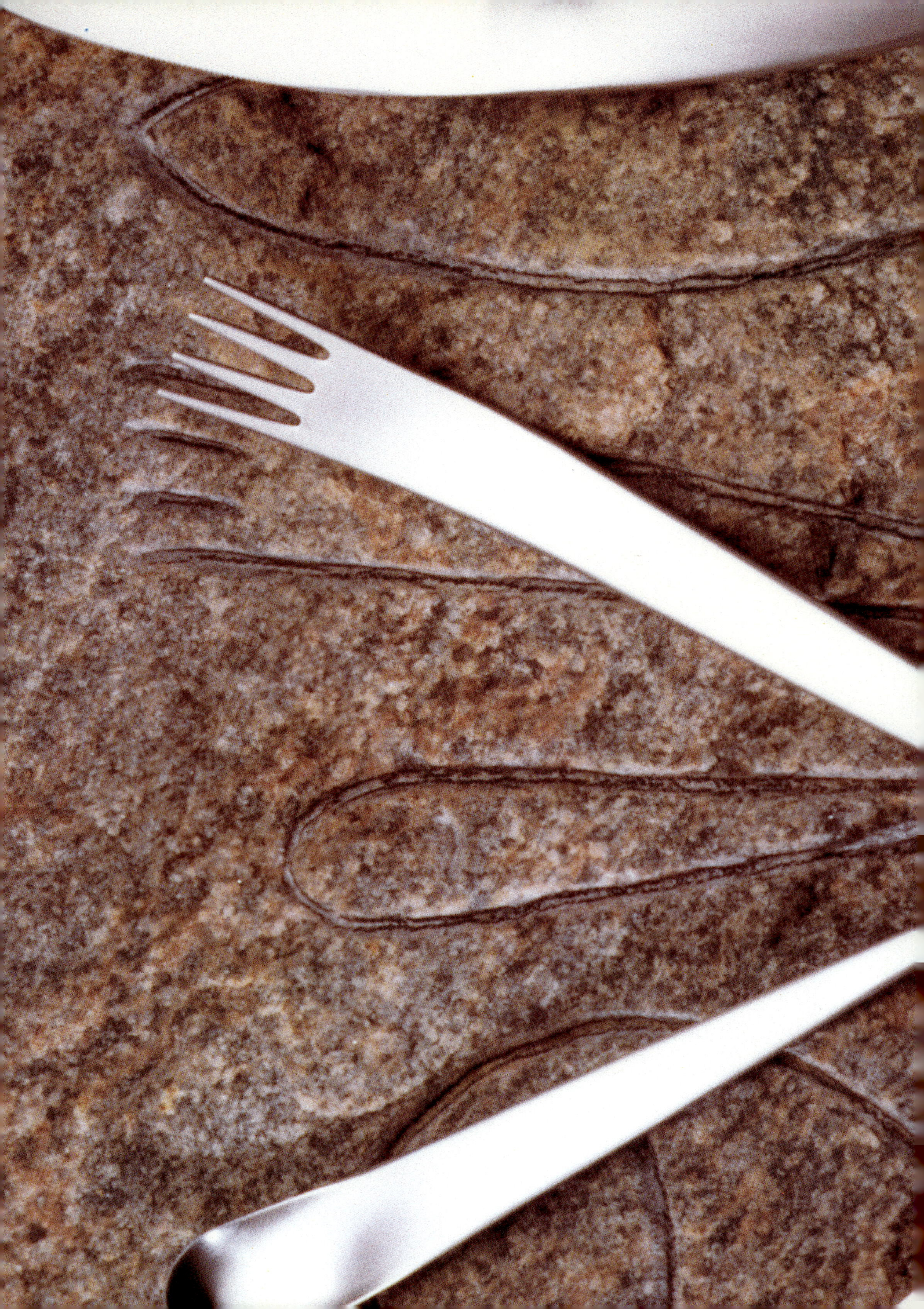

haushalt
household

HAUSHALT *HOUSEHOLD*

Jury: Christoph Böninger, Horst Diener, Isao Hosoe, Martin Iseli

Im Mittelpunkt der Jury-Entscheidungen im Bereich Haushalt stand neben der Frage und Wertung der Schönheit untrennbar die Hauptfrage nach der Funktion, die oft nur einen geringen Gestaltungsspielraum zuläßt. »Im Mittelpunkt steht auch das kleine Stück, schlüssig und logisch, das jedoch in der Gestaltungstiefe nie die Komplexität eines Autos erreichen kann«, kommentiert der Jury-Vorsitzende Horst Diener das Wesen vieler Gebrauchsprodukte, von denen er die willkürlich »niederdesignten« ebenso kategorisch ablehnte wie Design-Editionen, die nach dem Swatch-Prinzip oft funktionslos »Images« auf den Gebrauchsgegenstand applizieren, um ihn für Käufer und Sammler attraktiv zu machen. Produkte wurden hinsichtlich ihrer Brauchbarkeit und Nützlichkeit mindestens ebenso bewertet wie nach formaler Qualität. »Oft behaupten diese Stücke ihre Eigenständigkeit trotz knappem Spielraum für formale Freiheit«, konstatiert der Designpraktiker Diener die knappe Formensprache vieler ausgezeichneter Produkte. Die Jury stellte oft Haptik und Gebrauchstüchtigkeit vor Semantik und forderte »weniger Gerät und mehr Evolution«. Ausgezeichnet wurden originelle und sympathische Beispiele wie das »Urbesteck«, eine ergonomisch reduzierte, formal originelle Lösung, ein stapelbarer Papierkorb aus transparentem farbigen Kunststoff, Kochtöpfe mit intelligent gestalteten, formergänzenden Griffen, praktische Gegenstände wie Wäscheständer und tonnenförmiger Kühlschrank mit als Drehtablett angeordneten Etagen.

Der Ökologiegruppe, die ebenfalls die Kategorie Haushaltsgeräte prüfte, ging es um die »Lebensumständegestaltung«, wie einer ihrer Sprecher, Carl August Sautier, formulierte. »Es geht im richtungsweisenden Design nicht nur um die schöne Oberfläche. Dabei gibt es auch Konflikte, die ausgetragen werden müssen, wenn Form und ökologisches Konzept als gleichrangige Qualität beurteilt werden sollen.« Trotz intensiver Diskussion wurde beispielsweise nach diesen Kriterien eine Waschmaschine mit einem innovativen geschlossenen Wasserkreislauf nicht ausgezeichnet, weil bei ihr auf der formalen Seite »das Gestaltungspotential nicht genützt wurde«.

The jury's decisions in the household category focused above all not only on whether the objects were beautiful, but also, is inseparably connected with this, how the function, which often leaves so little scope for design, had been handled. "Small items were also the center of attention, items which are logical and convincing but will albeit never attain the depth of design to be found, for example, in a complex car design," comments Jury Chairman Horst Diener on the essence of many utility products. Among these, he categorically rejected those arbitrarily reduced to a "lowest design principle" and the design editions which simply apply "functionally meaningless images" to the commodity in line with the Swatching" principle in order to make it attractive for buyers and collectors. Products were rated with regard to their usability and usefulness just as much as for their formal quality. "Often, these pieces assert an independent image of their own, despite the tight scope for formal freedom," affirms Diener, himself a designer, when stressing the rigorous formal idiom of many award-wining products. The jury often judged haptic qualities and utility above semantics and demanded "less device and more evolution".

Original and sympathetic items won the awards, such as the "Ur cutlery", a formally original solution reduced to the ergonomic essentials, a stackable wastepaper basket made of transparent colored plastic, saucepans with intelligently designed handles that contributed to the overall shape, practical objects like a clothes stand, a barrel-shaped refrigerator with racks designed like swivellable trays.

The Ecology Group, which also examined the category of household appliances, investigated the "design of living conditions", as one of its spokespersons, Carl August Sautier, put it. "Pioneering design does not just entail creating beautiful surfaces. There are also conflicts that have to be addressed if the form and ecological concept are to be taken as equivalent criteria in judging the products." Despite intensive debate, applying these criteria, for example, a washing machine with an innovative closed water cycle did not win an award, because in formal terms it did "not exploit the potential for formal design".

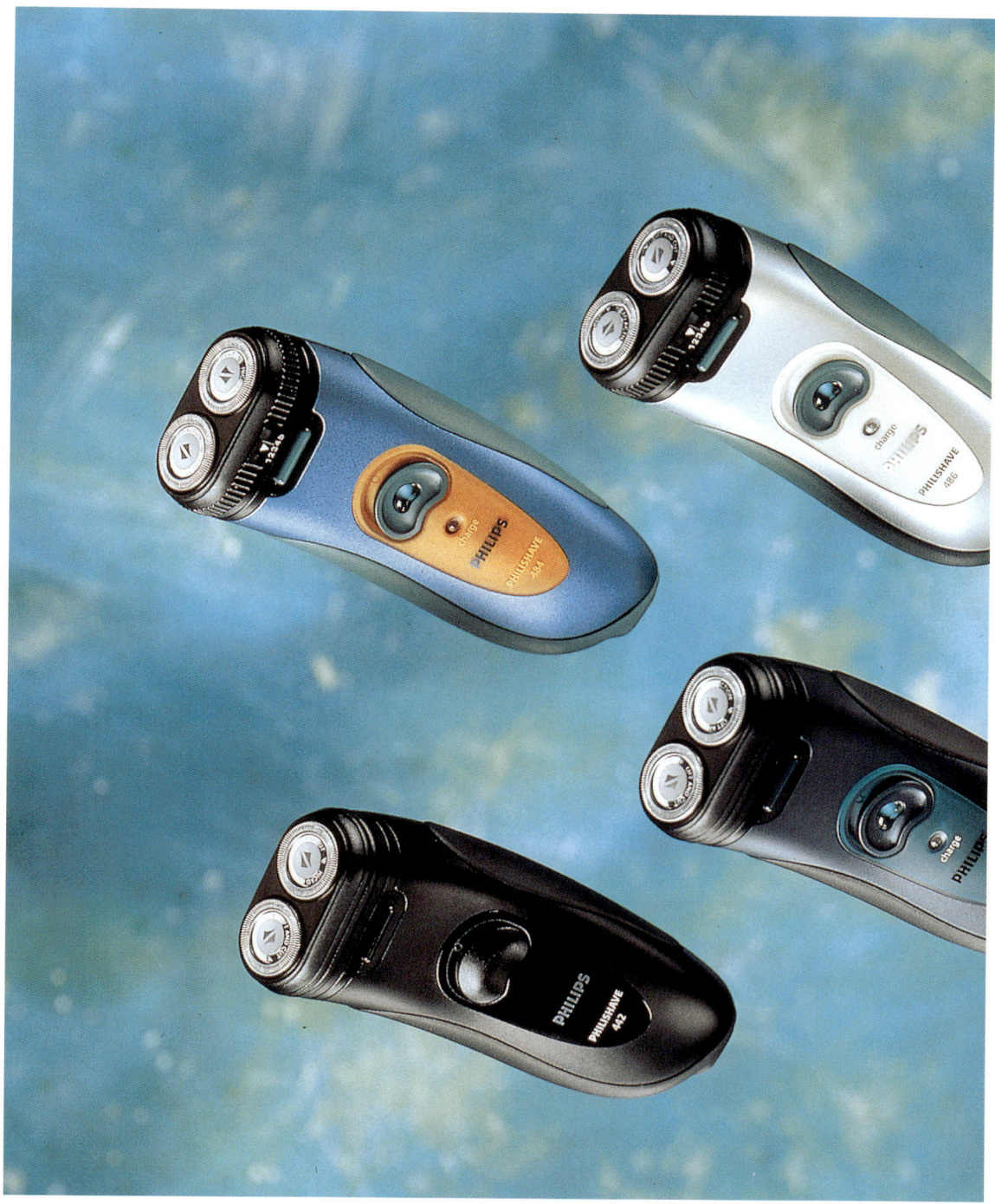

PHILISHAVE 400 micro action, ein elektrischer Rasierer. Die asymmetrische Form des leicht gekrümmten Gehäuses verbindet markante Formgebung mit besten ergonomischen Qualitäten. Die Kombination verschiedener Materialien und Farben unterstützt das Design und die Sicherheit von Bedienung und Führung. Vier Modelle in verschiedener Farbgebung und Ausstattung, Grundmodell nur für Netzbetrieb. Alle mit Philips micro action Scherkopf, leiselaufendem Motor, ausklappbarem Barttrimmer, Halterung und Reisetasche. Ökologisches Designkonzept: schwermetall- und PVC-frei, Trennbarkeit der Werkstoffe, Recyclingpapier für Verpackung und Gebrauchsanweisung.

The PHILISHAVE 400 micro action electric shaver features an asymmetrical shape with a slightly twisted housing: a striking design and superb ergonomic quality. The combination of different materials and colors augments the design and safe usage. Four models in different stylings and with different features, The basic model is for mains use only. They all boast the Philips micro action shaver head, quiet powering, pop-up trimmer, cord and travel pouch. The ecological design concept: no heavy metals or PVC used, materials separable, recycled paper for the packaging and instructions.

HERSTELLER MANUFACTURER
FORON Hausgeräte GmbH, Niederschmiedeberg, Germany
PRODUKT PRODUCT
foron avantgarde kg 4265 R Kühl- und Gefrierkombination Combined refrigerator and freezer
DESIGN
Michael Post, Laupheim

FORON AVANTGARDE KG 4265R, Kühl-/Gefrierkombination in runder Form, eröffnet neue Gestaltungsmöglichkeiten in Küche, Diele oder Speisezimmer. Freistehende und Einbaugeräte, variable Farbgestaltung. Ablageflächen für Kühl- und Gefriergut im zylindrisch runden Innenbehälter drehbar, damit bessere Übersicht, schnelleres Erkennen von Verfalldaten, bequemes Ein- und Ausräumen, leichte Reinigung. Günstiges Verhältnis von Volumen/Geräteoberfläche, dadurch minimierter Energieverbrauch. Fertigungsprozeß und Kühlmittel FCKW- und FKW-frei. Das Kältemittel Isobutan garantiert einen »flüsterleisen« Lauf.

The FORON AVANTGARDE KG 4265 R is a round combined refrigerator and freezer, affording new interior designs in kitchens, hallways or dining rooms. Available as standalone or built-in devices in a variety of colors. Storage shelves for goods in the cooling and freezing compartments are cylindrical and separately rotatable: allowing a close-up view of sell-by dates, easy loading, removal, and cleaning. Favorable ratio of volume to device surface and consequently minimized energy levels. Production process and cooling agents are CFC and FC free. Isobutane is used as a guaranteed »whispering« refrigerant, lowering noise pollution, too.

LEIFHEIT LINOMATIC S 60, Wäscheschirm mit Leinenautomatik: Spart das lästige Abwischen der Leinen vor dem Wäscheaufhängen, denn die Leinen sind in den Tragarmen schmutzgeschützt. Verbesserte Aufspanntechnik. Leinenlänge 60 Meter. Alle eingesetzten Materialien sind witterungs- und UV-beständig. Trotz größerer Leinenlänge wirkt das Gerät deutlich schlanker.

The LEIFHEIT LINOMATIC S 60 is a clothes stand featuring automatic lines: You no longer have to wipe lines prior to hanging washing on them as they are safe away from dirt in the dryer arms. Improved tension technology. Line lengths 60 meter. All materials used are weather and UV-proof. Despite the line length, the unit looks slender.

HERSTELLER MANUFACTURER LEIFHEIT AG, Nassau, Germany
PRODUKT PRODUCT Linomatic 60 Wäscheschirm Clothes stand
DESIGN TEAMS · SLANY DESIGN, Esslingen, Germany

BESTE DER BRANCHE *BEST OF GROUP* HAUSHALT *HOUSEHOLD*

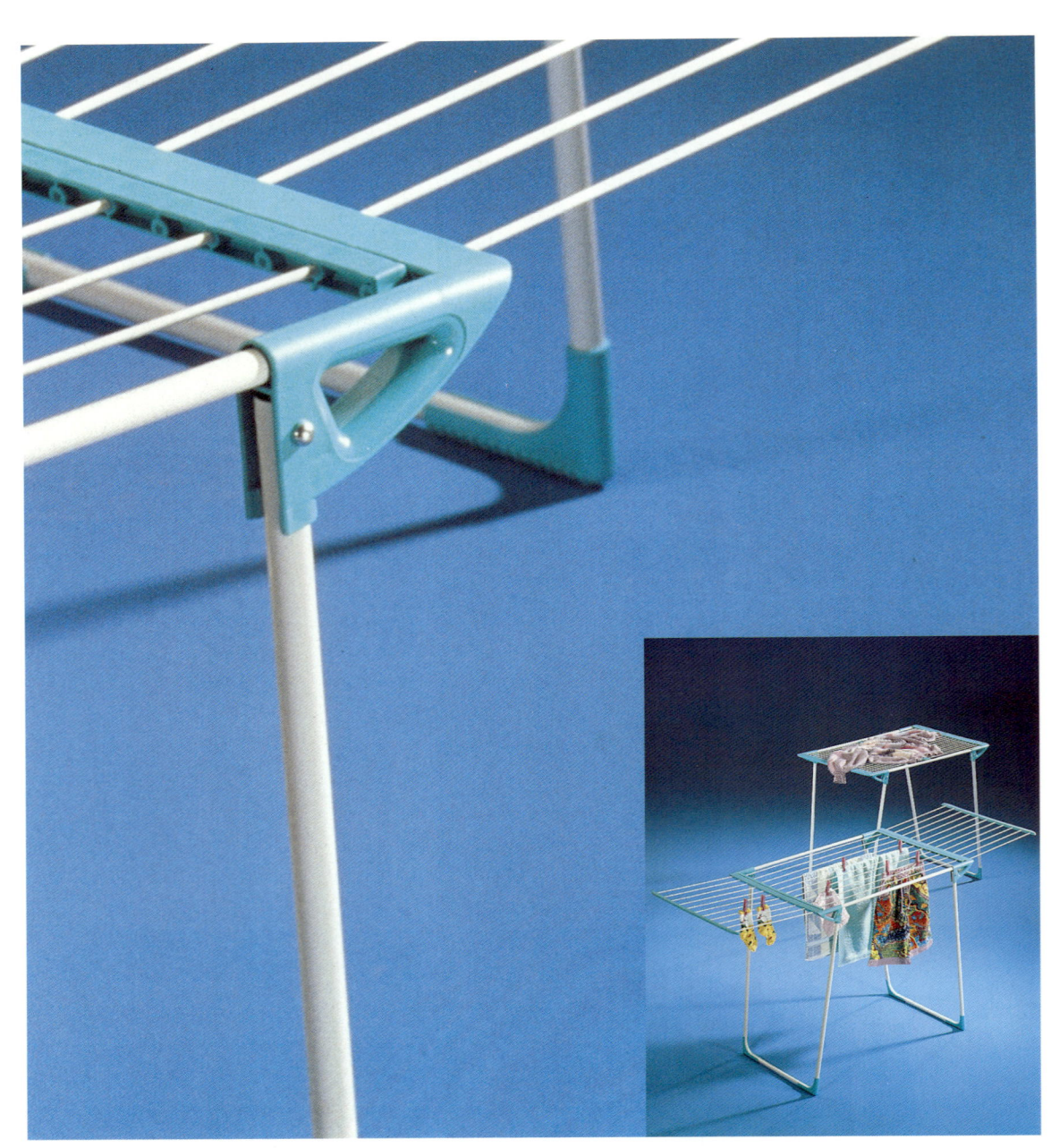

LEIFHEIT AG, Nassau, Germany HERSTELLER MANUFACTURER
Condor Wäscheständer Clothes horse PRODUKT PRODUCT
TEAMS · SLANY DESIGN, Esslingen, Germany DESIGN

CONDOR 200 ist ein Wäscheständer mit einer Trockenlänge von insgesamt 20 Meter. Durch die ausziehbaren Seitenteile ist der Wäscheständer für unterschiedliche Wäschemengen geeignet. Im zusammengeschobenen Zustand idealer Pullovertrockner. Rostfrei, besonders stabil. Farbe: weiß-türkis.

CONDOR 200 is a clothes horse with a total hanging length of 20m. The pull-out wings make the clothes horse ideal for various volumes of washing. Pushed together it is ideal for drying pullovers. Made of stainless steel, it is particularly stable and comes in white and turquoise.

oben/above: SQUARE Papierkorb Waste-paper basket, unten/below: CILINDRICO Thermosflasche Thermosflask   HERSTELLER MANUFACTURER AUTHENTICS artpresent GmbH, Holzgerlingen, Germany   PRODUKT PRODUCT
oben/above: Konstantin Grcic, München, Germany unten/below: Karl Axel Andersson, Malmö, Sweden   DESIGN

oben: SQUARE Papierkorb. Das Erscheinungsbild wird gleichzeitig durch ein Quadrat und die Kreisform definiert. Transluzent und in verschiedenen Farben. Am seitlichen Griffloch kann der Papierkorb auch aufgehängt werden. *above: The SQUARE wastepaper basket is defined visually by both a square and a circle. The basket is translucent and available in several colors, with an oval grip hole from which it can be hung.*
unten: CILINDRICO Thermosflasche. Die Formgebung ist bestimmt durch eine zylindrische Form und das transluzente Material. Form und Durchmesser sind so gewählt, daß auf Griff und Ausgießer verzichtet werden konnte: Das jeweilige Getränk läßt sich über die gesamte konkav ausgebildete Ausgießfläche gießen. *below: The CILINDRICO thermos flask is based on a cylindrical shape and translucent material. Its shape and diameter were designed such as to make a handle and spout unnecessary. The drink can simply be poured out through the pouring surface, which is concave in shape.*

HAUSHALT HOUSEHOLD 177

CLASSIC H 135 MB, Mikrowellen-Kompaktbackofen als Einbaugerät mit Edelstahlfront, großer Backofeneinsicht und elektronischer Steuerung. Neun verschiedene Betriebsarten, mit Betriebsartenanzeige im Klartext, Benutzerführung. Restwärmenutzung, Einschaltsperre und Sicherheitsausschaltung.

CLASSIC H 135 MB is a compact microwave as a build-in with a stainless steel front, a large oven viewing screen and electronic controls. Nine different operational modes with full-text operational display, utilization of residual heat, system lock and safety switch-off.

MIELE H 237 B, Einbau-Backofen mit Edelstahlfront und vergrößerter Backofeneinsicht. Elektronische Steuerung, zehn verschiedene Betriebsarten, Betriebsartenanzeige in Klartext. Neu entwickelt: Halogenbeleuchtung, Restwäremenutzung, Einschaltsperre, Sicherheitsausschaltung.

The MIELE H 237 B is a built-in oven with a stainless steel front and enlarged oven viewing screen. It features electronic controls, ten different operational modes and a full text mode display. Inonvations are the halogen lighting, the utilzation of residual heat and the safety switch-off.

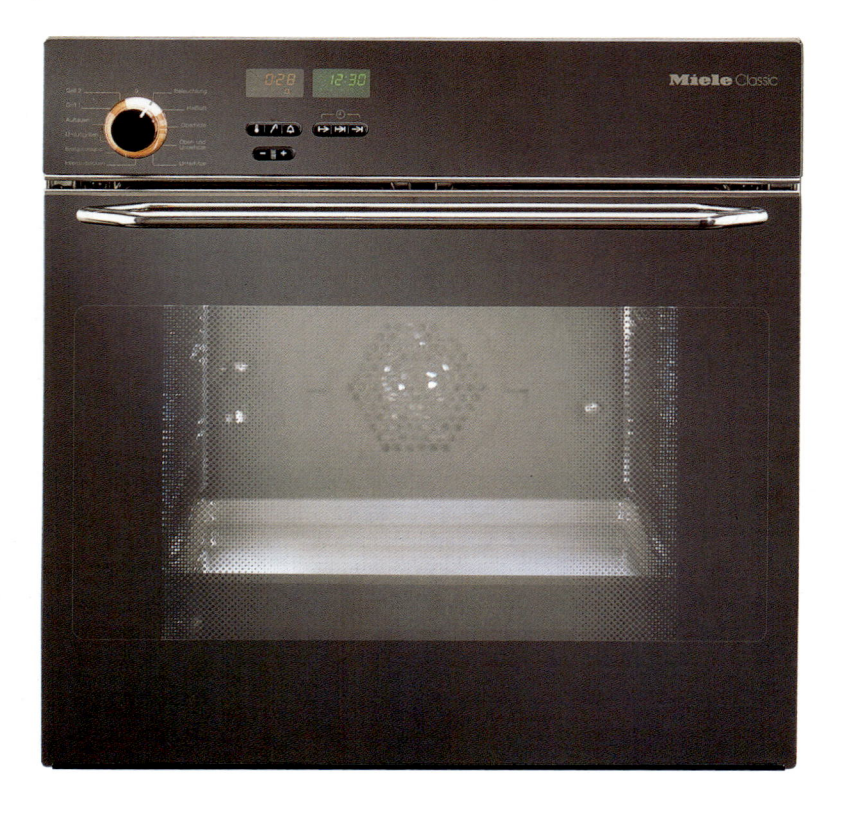

HERSTELLER MANUFACTURER
Miele & Cie. GmbH & Co., Gütersloh, Germany

PRODUKT PRODUCT
H 237 B Einbau-Backofen Built-in oven

DESIGN
Miele & Cie., Gütersloh, Germany

oben/above: H 135 MB Mikrowellen-Kompaktbackofen Compact oven with integrated Microwave, unten/below:

178 HAUSHALT *HOUSEHOLD*

MIELE T 552 C ist ein freistehender Wäschetrockner (90 cm hoch). Technische Merkmale: Kondenstrockner, 5 kg Ladung. Steuerung der Trocknung durch vollelektronische Feuchteabtastung. Durch Pultblende optimale Programmeinsicht und -einstellung.

The MIELE T 552 C is a standalone, 90 cm high tumble dryer. Technical features: Condensor dryer, 5 kg load. Programming for the dryer by fully electronic moisture control. Flat sloping optimal program readability and selection

MIELE W 957, Waschvollautomat als Standgerät (90 cm hoch). Technische Besonderheiten: maximal 1.600 Schleudertouren, 5 kg Ladung, vollelektronische Steuerung. Pultblende erlaubt optimale Programmeinsicht und -einstellung.

The MIELE W 957 is a standalone 90 cm high washing machine. Technical features include: maximal 1,600 rpm, 5 kg full load, full electronic controls. Flat sloping fascia panel facilitates optimal readability and program selection.

HERSTELLER MANUFACTURER Miele & Cie. GmbH & Co., Gütersloh, Germany
PRODUKT PRODUCT links/left: T 552 C Wäschetrockner Tumble dryer, rechts/right: W 957 Waschvollautomat Washing machine
DESIGN Miele & Cie, Gütersloh, Germany

HAUSHALT *HOUSEHOLD* 179

HERSTELLER MANUFACTURER Silit-Werke GmbH & Co. KG, Riedlingen, Germany
PRODUKT PRODUCT Sicomatic-E Silargan 5 Ltr. Schnellkochtopf Pressure cooker
DESIGN TEAMS - SLANY DESIGN, Esslingen, Germany

SICOMATIC E, Schnellkochtopf mit einfacher Handhabung. Seniorengerecht durch den großen Bedienknopf. Betriebssicher durch die große Restdruckanzeige. Ausströmender Dampf wird vom Benutzer weggeleitet. Der geschlossene Bügelgriff bietet eine hohe Abrutschsicherheit und ein Hitzeschild für die Hand. Abnehmbarer Deckelgriff für die leichtere Reinigung.
The SICOMATIC E is a simple-to-use pressure cooker. The extra-large regulator is suited for senior citizens and the larger residual pressure indicator enhances safety. The jet of escaping steam is directed away from users and the stirrup-shaped handle offers protection from slippage and heat. The pot features a removable lid handle for easier cleaning.

HERSTELLER MANUFACTURER Gaggenau-Werke Haus- und Lufttechnik GmbH, Gaggenau, Germany
PRODUKT PRODUCT AH 100 Abzugshaube Cookerhood
DESIGN Jacob Jensen Design, Hoejslev, Denmark

GAGGENAU AH 100 Küchenabzugshaube: besonders flaches Edelstahlgehäuse, freihängend und in die Oberschrankreihe integrierbar. Breiten 60 und 90 cm. Edelstahl-Lüftungskanal, für Räume von 2,20 bis 3,12 m Höhe. Umluftbetrieb mit Aktivkohlefilter oder Abluftbetrieb mit Abluftanschluß. Drei elektronisch gesteuerte Leistungsstufen, leise laufend, auch in der Intensivstufe; Intervall-Lüftung möglich. Fettfilter-Sättigungsanzeige, LED-Funktionsanzeige, Leuchtstoff-Lampe. Gerät mit gesondertem Gebläsebaustein lieferbar, der zur Geräuschvermeidung z. B. an der Außenwand oder auf dem Dach montiert wird.

GAGGENAU AH 100 is a cookerhood with an especially flat stainless casing; free-hanging it can be integrated into the top of a shelf. Available in two widths: 60 and 90 cms. Stainless steel air duct for rooms from 2.2 to 3.12 m in height. Air circulation via an active charcoal filter or air evacuation via a duct. Three electronic speeds, all of them quiet, even at top speed; the unit also boasts an interval setting, a fat filter saturation indicator, LED's, and fluorescent lamp. Also available with a special fan unit that can be mounted in the outside wall or on the roof to minimize noise levels.

HAUSHALT HOUSEHOLD 181

Fissler GmbH, Idar Oberstein, Germany   HERSTELLER MANUFACTURER
Conturo Kochtopfserie Set of cookware   PRODUKT PRODUCT
DESIGN. Mattis, Darmstadt, Germany   DESIGN

CONTURO, eine Kochtopfserie mit kugeliger Form, in Anlehnung an den Archetypus »Kessel über dem offenen Feuer«. Sicherer Verschluß, hohes Volumen und große Standsicherheit. Bügelgriff folgt dem Hauptradius, Deckel entsprechend nach innen gewölbt: dadurch guter Greifraum. Außerdem kann das Kondenswasser gut von der Deckelmitte abtropfen und der Rand bleibt sauber. Ganzmetallgriffe werden auf dem Herd nicht heiß. Alle Töpfe sind backofengeeignet; leicht zu säubern, spülmaschinenfest und stapelbar.

CONTURO is a rounded cookware set creating associations with the »boiling cauldron over an open fire«. The lid closes tightly, and the stable pot has a large volume. The hoop handle follows the main radius, and the lid is correspondingly concave to enhance handle space. Moreover, condensation steam drips into the middle of the food and the edges stay clean. The all-metal handles are ovenproof. All pots in the series are ovenproof, easy to clean, dishwasher-proof and stackable.

HAUSHALT *HOUSEHOLD*

HERSTELLER MANUFACTURER Mono-Metallwarenfabrik Seibel GmbH, Mettmann, Germany
PRODUKT PRODUCT Mono-Zeug Urbesteck Cutlery
DESIGN Michael Schneider, Köln, Germany

MONO-ZEUG, ein Essbesteck. Als »Urbesteck« konzipiert weist es in seiner Formgebung auf den Ursprung des Eßwerkzeugs hin: das Messer = ein Faustkeil, der Löffel = die hohle Hand, die Gabel = ein Span, der kleine Löffel = der Finger.

MONO-ZEUG is a cutlery range. Designed as »primordial cutlery«, its shape alludes to the origins of eating utensils: the knife as handaxe, the spoon as a hollow hand, and the fork as a borer and the small spoon as a finger.

TWINSTAR Messerserie. Das erste Messer mit einer Schneide, die nicht nachgeschärft werden muß: Dafür sorgt die MagnaDur-Beschichtung, die so hart ist wie Keramik und einen Diamantschliff erhält. (Für diese Beschichtung werden bei 2000º C (Hartmetallpartikel) mit einer Geschwindigkeit von Mach 1 auf die Klinge »geschossen«.) Der perfekt proportionierte und ergonomisch geformte Messergriff liegt angenehm und sicher in der Hand.

The TWINSTAR knife set features the first knife with a blade that does not need to be resharpened: It has a special MagnaDur edge, as hard as ceramic and diamond-honed. (Hard metal particles are fired at over 2000º C at Mach 1 onto the edge to achieve such sharpness.) The perfectly proportioned and ergonomically shaped handle fits the hand comfortably and safely.

HERSTELLER MANUFACTURER ZWILLING J.A. HENCKELS AG, Solingen, Germany
PRODUKT PRODUCT TWINSTAR Messerserie Knife set
DESIGN Petra Mangol, Stuttgart, Germany Fraunhofer Institut für Arbeitswissenschaft und Organisation Dipl.-Des.

HERSTELLER MANUFACTURER: WMF Württembergische Metallwarenfabrik AG, Geislingen, Germany
PRODUKT PRODUCT: WMF BISTRO Einzeltassenbrüher Espresso machine
DESIGN: WMF Geislingen, Germany

WMF BISTRO, vollautomatischer Einzeltassenbrüher für die Zubereitung von Espresso und Café Crème. Für jede Tasse wird der Kaffee frisch gemahlen und gebrüht. Milchschäumer für die Zubereitung von Cappuccino. Weitere Funktionen: Display, Mengen- und Tassenvorwahl, Heißwasser für Tee und Dampf für andere Heißgetränke. Zweite Kaffeemühle für unterschiedliche Röstungen und Mahlgrade nachlieferbar.

The WMF BISTRO is a fully automatic Espresso machine for brewing individual cups of espresso und café crème coffee. The coffee is freshly ground for each cup and then brewed. A milk steaming device for cappuccino is an optional extra. Additional features: a display, preselect for amount and number of cups, hot water for tea and steam for other hot drinks. Second coffee grinder for differently roast beans and grinding sizes optional.

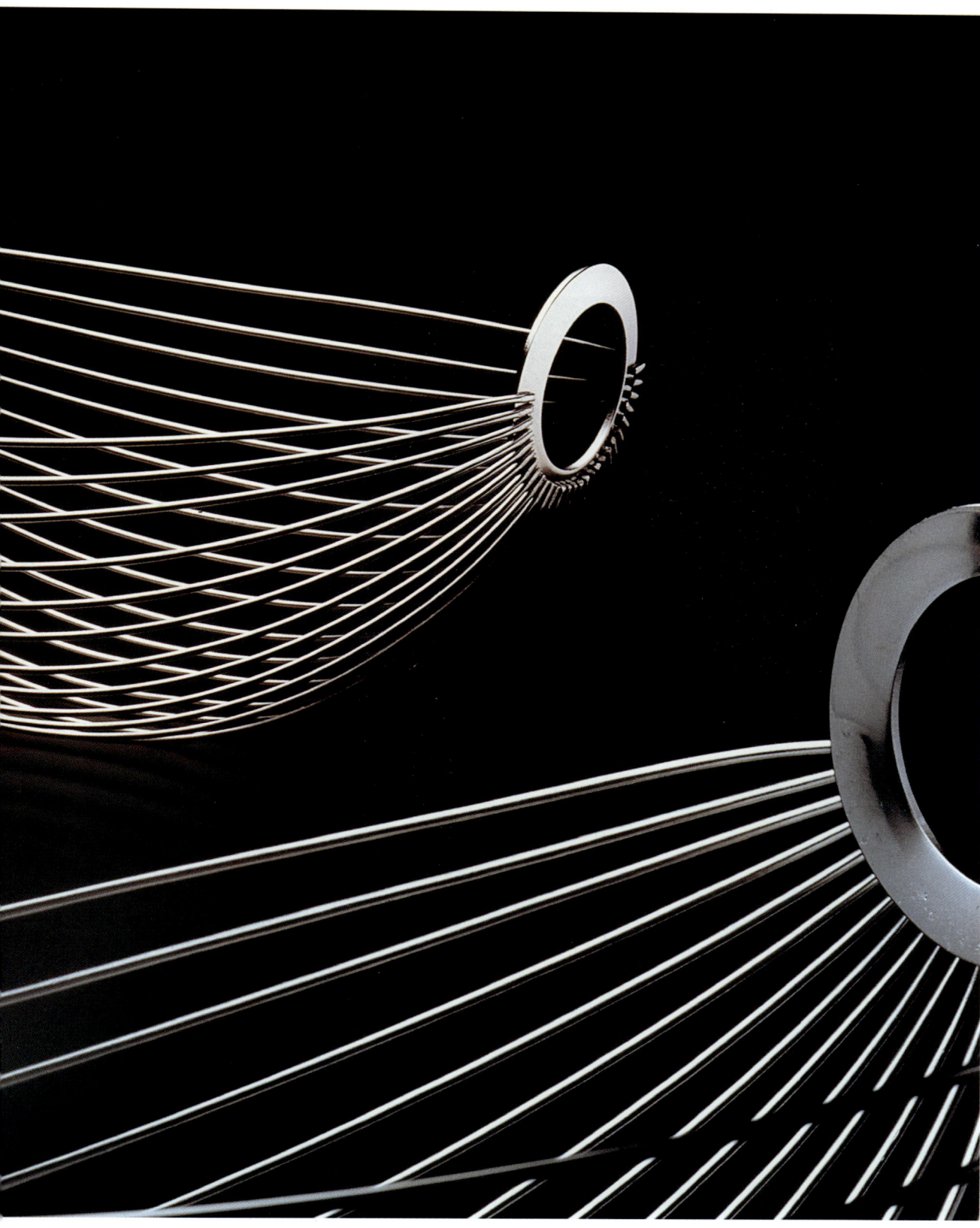

Servierkorb aus der Kollektion »CONCEPT«: eine orginelle Lösung für einen traditionellen Artikel. Dank der ausgeklügelten Konstruktion schwingt der Korb immer in die richtige Lage zurück. Edelstahl rostfrei 18/10.

The »CONCEPT« Collection serving basket offers an original design solution for a traditional item. Thanks to the ingenious construction, the basket always swings back into the right position. Made of 18/10 grade stainless steel.

HERSTELLER MANUFACTURER WMF Württembergische Metallwarenfabrik AG, Geislingen, Germany
PRODUKT PRODUCT Concept Servierkorb Serving basket
DESIGN Ole Palsby, Copenhagen, Denmark

HERSTELLER MANUFACTURER Rosenthal AG, Selb, Germany
PRODUKT PRODUCT Bottiglia Öl- und Essigflaschen Oil- and vinegar flasks
DESIGN Aldo Rossi, Milano, Italy

Links: BOTTIGLIA Öl- und Essigflaschen.
left: BOTTIGLIA *is a range of oil and vinegar bottles.*
rechte Seite: WEIZENBIERGLAS von Schöfferhofer. Maschinell geblasener Becher von hoher Qualität: Absolut schlierenfreies Glas und kalt abgesprengter Mundrand.
right side: *BEER GLASS for Schöfferhofer wheat beer. Machine-blown high-quality glass: Absolutely no flow marks in the glass and lip achieved with cold blow-off.*

188 HAUSHALT *HOUSEHOLD*

Sahm GmbH & Co. KG, Höhr-Grenzhausen, Germany   HERSTELLER MANUFACTURER
Schöfferhofer Weizenbierglas 0,5 l | Wheat beer glass   PRODUKT PRODUCT
Matteo Thun, Milano, Italy   DESIGN

HAUSHALT *HOUSEHOLD* 189

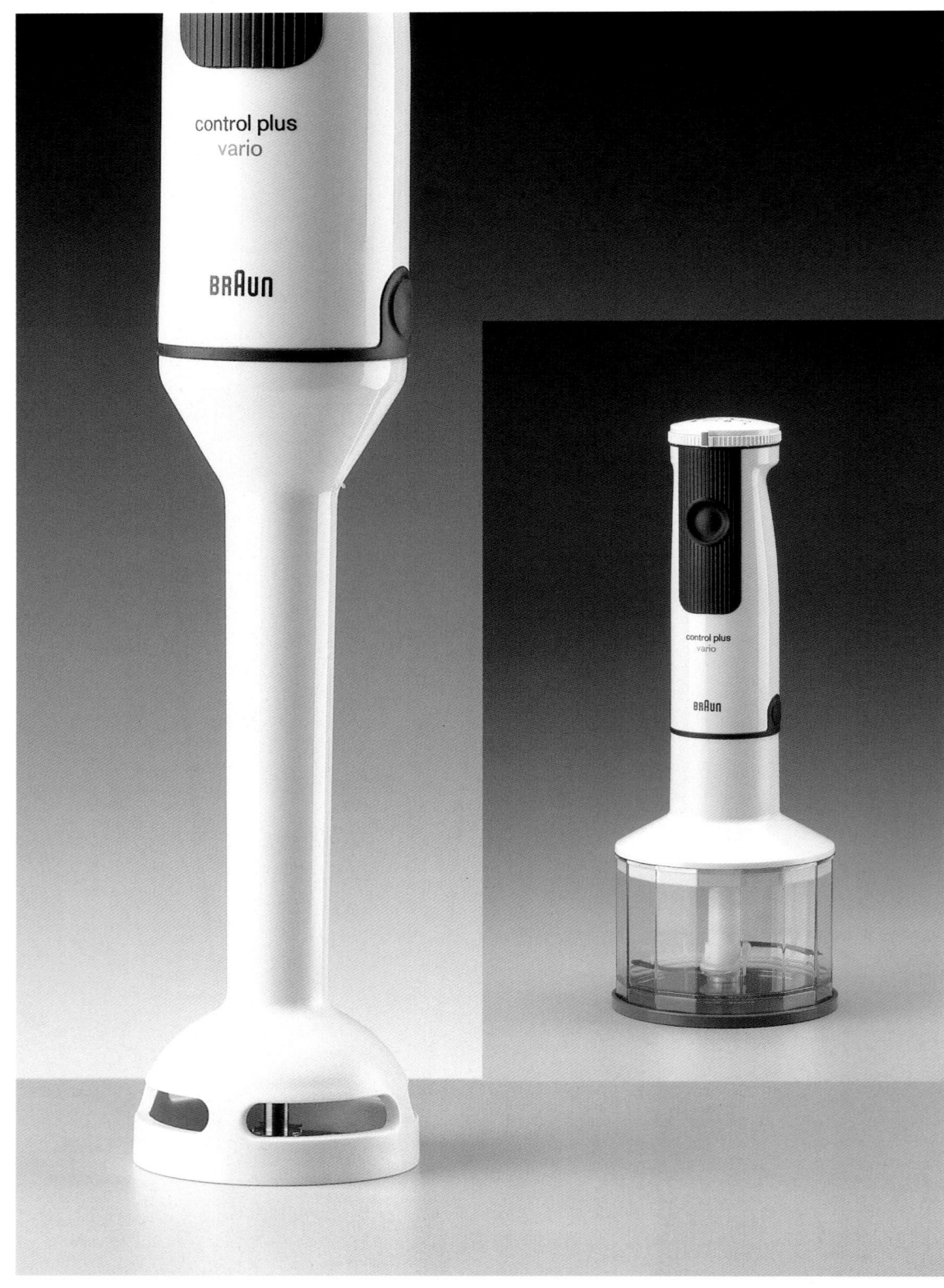

Braun AG, Kronberg, Germany   HERSTELLER MANUFACTURER
Multiquick control plus vario MR 550 CA Stabmixer Mixer   PRODUKT PRODUCT
Braun, Ludwig Littmann, Kronberg, Germany   DESIGN

BRAUN MR 550 CA MULTIQUICK, Stabmixer mit verschiedenen Funktionen: Mischen, Pürieren, Schlagen, Zerkleinern. Motorteil kann direkt auf den Zerkleinerer gekoppelt werden. Das ermöglicht sicheres Arbeiten. Ergonomisch gestaltetes Handstück (=Motorteil) und großflächiger »soft control«-Schalter, sorgen für leichte Führung und Griffsicherheit. Gehäuse von innen wasserdicht versiegelt. Neuer 200-Watt-Motor mit hohem Drehmoment, Arbeitsgeschwindigkeit stufenlos regelbar. Neuartig ausgeformte Messer für gleichmäßige Ergebnisse. Die polygonale Form des Zerkleinerers führt das Gut immer wieder dem Messer zu. Alle Zubehörteile spülmaschinenfest.

BRAUN MR 550 CA MULTIQUICK is a blender featuring various functions: mixing, blending, whipping, and for chopping. The motor part can be attached directly onto the chopper for particularly safe chopping. The grip (motor section) is ergonomically designed and has a large, »soft control« switch for easy use and safe grip. The casing is watertight inside. The new 200W motor offers extra torque at an infinitely variable speed. A new unique blade design ensures even processing. The polygonal shape of the chopper bowl feeds food continually through to the blade. All attachments are dishwasher proof.

190 HAUSHALT HOUSEHOLD

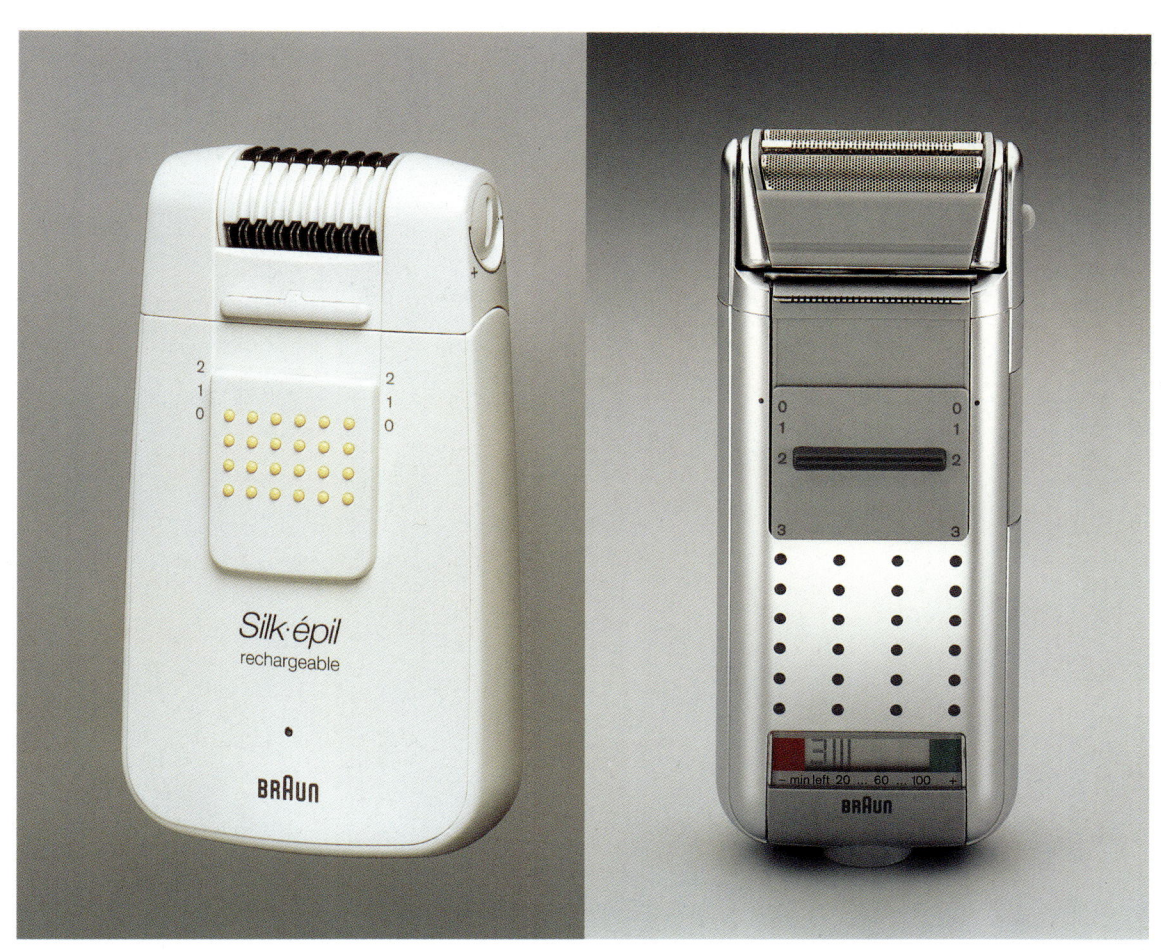

BRAUN SILK-ÉPIL SELECT EE 300, Epiliergerät zur kosmetischen Haarentfernung an den Beinen, das auch sehr kurze Härchen (bis 0,5 mm) an der Wurzel erfaßt, mit einstellbarer Epiliergeschwindigkeit (langsam/schnell) und Pinzettenkraft (stärker/schwächer). Besonders flach und handgerecht, darum gute Führung und Handhabung des Geräts. Der ergonomisch abgerundete Epilierkopf paßt sich den Körperkonturen perfekt an. Das Design realisiert zweierlei: einfache Benutzung und ein feminines Erscheinungsbild des Geräts. Netzbetrieb mit Schnur oder schnurlos über schwermetallfreie, wiederaufladbare Akkus. Mit Ladekontrollanzeige.

BRAUN SILK-ÉPIL SELECT EE 300 is a Epilator for removing leg hair which removes even short hairs (0.5 mm) at the root. It features adjustable speed (slow/ fast) and tweezer grip (stronger/softer). Flat, it fits particularly well in the hand and is thus easy to handle and use. The ergonomically rounded tweezer head follows body contours perfectly. The design fulfills two purposes: simple use and feminine appearance. Can be mains powered or used cordless with rechargable batteries that are free of heavy metals. Includes a charge indicating light.

BRAUN FLEX INTEGRAL 5550, Akkurasierer mit dem neuartigen Dreifach-Schersystem: die erste Scherfolie rasiert kurze Barthaare; der Integral-Schneider richtet längere Haare auf und kürzt sie ein; die zweite Scherfolie rasiert gründlich aus. Scherfolienmagazin zur täglichen Reinigung einfach zu entriegeln. Das griffige Gehäuse ist nicht aus zwei Schalen zusammengesetzt, sondern besteht aus einer Hülse. Dadurch höhere Stabilität, bessere Geräuschdämpfung, keine störenden Kanten. Designelement für die Umwelt: Entsorgungshinweis für Akkus und Elektronik am Geräteboden. Schwermetallfreie Akkus, Ladekontrollanzeigen.

BRAUN FLEX INTEGRAL 5550 is a shaver using a new triple-shaving system: the first shave cuts short hairs, the integrated cutter shaves longer hairs and the second shaving foil ensures a close shave. The foil cartridge is simple to open and clean. The good-grip casing with the rounded sides and soft knobs consist not of two pieces, but of one single shell. The shaver is thus more stable, quieter and has no edges in the way. Designing for the environment: markings for the disposal of the electronic parts and the re- chargeable batteries. Includes charge status indicator.

links/left: Braun Silk-épil select EE 300 Epiliergerät Epilator, rechts/right: Braun Flex Integral 5550 Akkurasierer Shaver   PRODUKT PRODUCT
links/left: Braun, Peter Schneider, Kronberg, Germany, rechts/right: Braun, Roland Ullmann, Kronberg, Germany   DESIGN
Braun AG, Kronberg, Germany   HERSTELLER MANUFACTURER

HAUSHALT *HOUSEHOLD* 191

HERSTELLER MANUFACTURER
Magic Helvetica, La Conversion, Switzerland
PRODUKT PRODUCT
La Base Parfümflacon Perfume flacon
DESIGN
Les Ateliers du Nord, Antoine Cahen, Lausanne, Switzerland

LA BASE Parfümflacon aus einfachen Materialien wie Mattglas und Aluminium. »Für sie« und »Für ihn« bewußt identisch, Unterscheidung nur durch die Farbe des Parfüms und die Pakkungsschleife. Zeitlos minimalistische Formgebung garantiert eine längere Lebenserwartung als topmodisches Design. Auch bei der Verpackung kein Unterschied der Geschlechter: »Für sie« und »für ihn« eine Schachtel aus massivem Lindenholz, die für viele Zwecke weiter- und wiederverwendbar ist.

LA BASE is a small perfume flacon using simple materials such as matt glass and aluminum. Versions for »her« and for »him« are identical, distinguishable only by the color of the perfume and the ribbon on the packag-ing. Timeless, minimalist design guarantees long service life compared with overly fashionable designs. Packaging for men and women is also identical: both involve a solid linden wood casket, which can be used for many other purposes, too.

SYSTEM SMOTHER ES 763 C-S ist ein elektrischer Rasierapparat: Gummiähnliche Lamellen spannen sanft die Haut, lassen so die Barthaare abstehen und führen sie dichter an das Schermesser heran. Zwei Lochscheiben (Netzstruktur) ziehen die Haare in den Rasierer hinein und ermöglichen eine gründliche und schnelle Rasur. Bartschneider (Schlitzstruktur) trimmt lange oder gekräuselte Barthaare. Griffreundliches Gehäuse, verchromt: wirkt hygienisch und kraftvoll.

SYSTEM SMOTHER ES 763 C-S is an electric shaver with a rubberlike fin which stretches the skin softly to raise face hairs and draw them closer to the blade. Two net blades pull and cut the hairs for a smooth, thorough and close shave. The slit blade is suitable for trimming sideburns or longer beard hairs. The casing is easy to grip, chrome-plated, hygienic, and expresses vitality.

HERSTELLER MANUFACTURER Matsushita Electric Works, Ltd., Osaka, Japan
PRODUKT PRODUCT System Smoother ES763C-S Elektrischer Rasierapparat Electric shaver
DESIGN Matsushita Electric Works Ltd. Home Applicance A&I Design Office, Osaka, Japan

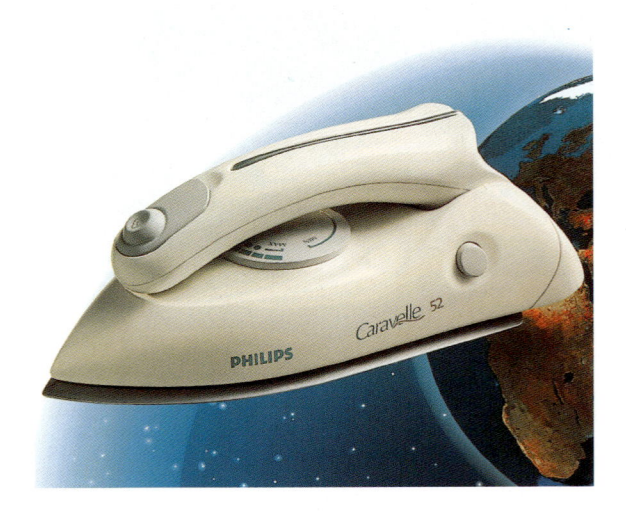

HERSTELLER MANUFACTURER Philips International B.V., Groningen, The Netherlands
PRODUKT PRODUCT Philips Caravelle travel iron Reisebügeleisen Compact travel iron
DESIGN Philips Corporate Design, Eindhoven, The Netherlands

PHILIPS CARAVELLE, ein Reisebügeleisen mit Dampfbügelfunktion. In klarer unverwechselbarer Formgebung. Der markante Griff läßt sich einklappen, damit konnte das Volumen für die Reise, ohne Abstriche an Ergonomie, leichter Handhabung, Robustheit und Sicherheit verringert werden. Der Griff dient zugleich als Wassertank (85 ml). Darunter, leicht erreichbar, der Thermostatschalter. Überhitzungsschutz, Universalstecker mit langer Schnur, Adapter, Spannungswahlschalter.

PHILIPS CARAVELLE is a compact travel iron with a steam iron facility. It has a clear unmistakable shape, a striking foldaway handle to minimize space when traveling: without compromising on ergonomic criteria, ease of use, stability and safety. The handle doubles up as the water tank (85 ml). Under it and easy to reach is the thermostat switch. Manual thermal cut-out, adaptor plug and long cord and voltage selector.

PHILIPS VISION, eine Staubsaugerserie aus vier Grundmodellen der Spitzenklasse. Kräftige Motoren, kompakte Bauweise, und im Design ein Schuß Humor kennzeichnen die Serie insgesamt. Die Modelle unterscheiden sich durch zunehmende Raffinesse der technischen Ausstattung: von einfacher Gleitelektronik zur kompletten Fernbedienung. Die Schalterelemente aller Modelle aus gebürstetem Metall. Die komplex geschwungenen Oberflächen wurden computergestützt entworfen, was den Entwicklungsprozeß beschleunigte. Werkstoffe: ABS, Polypropylen und recyceltes Polypropylen für die inneren Teile.

PHILIPS VISION is a vacuum cleaner range with four basic high-end models. The series is highlighted by real power, compactness and a touch of humour in the design. The models differ in terms of increasing technical outfittings: from simple electronics to complete remote controls. All switches are in brushed metal. The complex curves of the surfaces are the product of CAD to accelerate development time. Materials: ABS plastic, polypropylene and reground polypropylene for the internal parts where possible.

HERSTELLER MANUFACTURER Philips International B.V., Groningen, The Netherlands
PRODUKT PRODUCT Philips Vision Range of Vacuum cleaners Staubsauger Vacuum cleaner
DESIGN Philips Corporate Design, Eindhoven, The Netherlands

oben/above: Rowenta Dentiphant Elektrische Zahnbürste Electrical tooth brush, unten/below: RS007 Bodenstaubsauger Canister vacuum cleaner
oben/above: Rowenta Werke, Franz Alban Stützer, Bernd Figur, Offenbach, Germany, unten/below: Rowenta Werke, Franz Alban Stützer, B. Köhler, Offenbach, Germany
Rowenta Werke GmbH, Offenbach, Germany

HERSTELLER MANUFACTURER
PRODUKT PRODUCT
DESIGN

DENTIPHANT, kleine elektrische Zahnbürste, speziell für Kinderhände. Griffige, bauchige Form, weiche fließende Gesamterscheinung. Borstenkopf organisch gestaltet, Borstenclips auswechselbar. Durch Gegeneinanderdrehen der Gehäusehälften werden die Funktionen Entriegeln/Ein/Aus betätigt, wobei die berührungsfreundlichen Füßchen die Griffigkeit unterstützen. Elektromotor mit Exzenter erzeugt Schwingungen, die sich auf die Borsten übertragen. Oberfläche hochglänzend, leicht zu reinigen.
DENTIPHANT is a small electric toothbrush specially designed to fit children's hands. A handy bulbous form, and soft and fluent overall shape. The bristle head has a soft design and is replaceable. The on/off is activated by turning the two main sections, whereby the small feet help enhance grip. The electrical motor with excenter generates vibrations that are transferred to the brushes. High-polish, easy-to-clean surface.

RS 007, DYMBO Bodenstaubsauger für große Flächen und enge Winkel. Wiegt nur 4 Kilogramm und ist auch an einem Schultergurt zu tragen. Mit 1300 Watt und absolut dichter Luftführung so leistungsstark wie ein großes Gerät. Neues Filter- und Filterwechselsystem garantiert eine staubfreie, hygienische Handhabung. Ein Hygieneknopf schließt den Papierfilter beim Wechseln, das damit auch für Allergiker problemlos wird. Zubehörteile sind fest in den ergonomisch geformten Griff integrierbar. Kompakte Bauweise, Park-System für Zwischendurch und Rohrhalterung erlauben platzsparende Aufbewahrung. Für große und kleine Haushalte.
The RS 007 DYMBO vacuum cleaner for large surfaces and tight corners. It weighs only four kgs and can be shoulder-carried. But its 1300 W and absolutely sealed air circulation make it as efficient as a large cleaner. It features a new filter and filter exchange system, guaranteeing dust-free and hygienic use. A hygiene button closes the paper filter prior to disposal, so allergy-sufferers can also use it. Accessories are integrated in the ergonomically shaped handle. Compact, with a parking system for in-between and a tube mounting: a real space saver ideal for small and large households alike.

VAMPYR 5030, ein Bodenstaubsauger, dessen Gehäuse von nur vier komplexen Kunststoffteilen gebildet und von zwei Schrauben zusammengehalten wird. Neuartige Saugdüse. Erzielt beste Staubaufnahmewerte.

The VAMPYR 5030 vacuum cleaner sports a casing made only of four complex plastic sections held together with just two screws. It features a new suction jet for superior dust suction.

HERSTELLER MANUFACTURER AEG Hausgeräte AG, Nürnberg, Germany
PRODUKT PRODUCT VAMPYR 5030 Bodenstaubsauger Vacuum cleaner
DESIGN AEG Hausgeräte GmbH Industrial Design Center, Hans-Joachim Moll, Nürnberg, Germany

HAUSHALT *HOUSEHOLD* 197

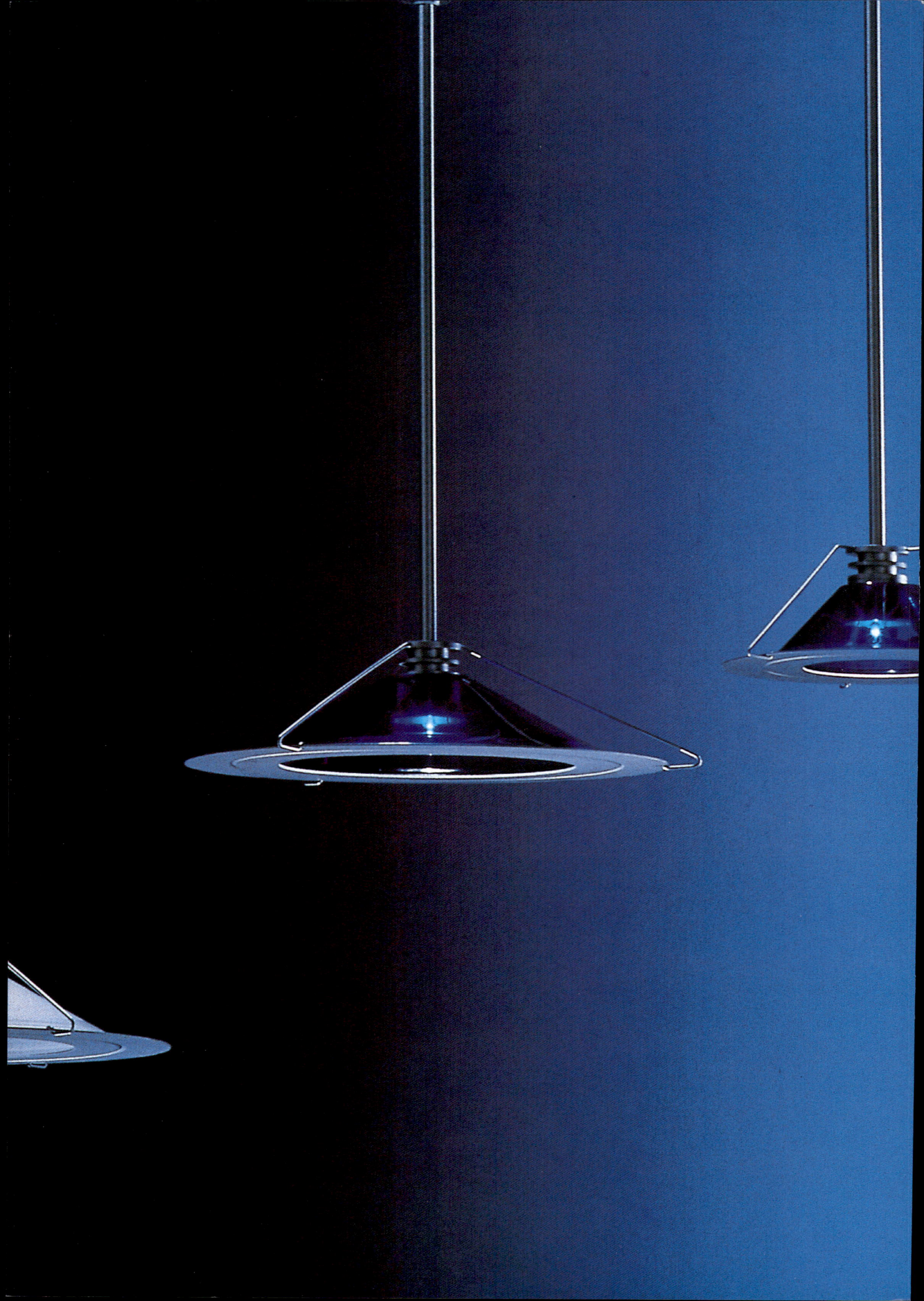

beleuchtung
lighting

BELEUCHTUNG LIGHTING
Jury: Bob Blaich, Hartmut S. Engel, Andreas Haug, Hartmut Warkuß

Die drei »Besten der Branche« im Bereich Licht zeigen bereits repräsentativ das Spektrum, in dem sich die heutige Lichtgestaltung bewegt. Als beispielhaft ausgezeichnet wurde eine dreibeinige Stehleuchte mit einem romantisch anmutenden Stoffschirm. »Solche Objekte versöhnen einen mit Gegenständen, die die Menschen nervös machen, wie technikorientierte Dinge«, begründete Andrée Putman ihr Votum für diesen emotionsgeladenen Gegenstand. Auf der anderen Seite ist die von Philippe Starck entworfene Leuchte trotz aller Emotionalität ein modernes hochwertiges Industrieprodukt, in der Formgebung flüssig, mit minimalem Kunststoffaufwand wie eine Skulptur von Brancusi gestaltet. High-Tech und Imaginationsgabe vereinigen sich zu einem zeittypischen Produkt unseres Fin-de-Siècle.

Im Niedervoltbereich bewegt sich ein abwechslungsreich gestaltetes Lichtsystem, das die Evolutionsfähigkeit der raumumspannenden Niedervolttechnologie deutlich belegt. Die Jury empfand die schlüssige Evolution eines inzwischen gängigen Standards im Niedervoltbereich ebenfalls als auszeichnungswürdig.

Streng in der Tradition des Bauhauses steht der dritte Branchenbeste: moderne Tradition, die die hohe Kultur der Glas- und Metallverarbeitung formal re-interpretatorisch fortschreibt. Solche Formen gehören in die Welt der Industrie und sind Standards, die Kontinuität ausstrahlen.

Alle drei Auszeichnungen vom architekturbezogenen bis zum emotionsbezogenen Licht sind auf höchstem Niveau moderner Technik. Im Leuchtenbereich kommt es nach Ansicht einiger Juroren inzwischen mehr auf die Lichtwirkung als auf die Lichtquelle selber an. Um das zu erzielen, bedarf es der »kreativen Ingenieurleistung - vom Unternehmen und vom Designer«, betont der Designer Hartmut S. Engel als Fachjuror in Sachen Licht. Typisch für die derzeitige Situation und Strategie der Leuchtenindustrie sind evolutionäre Erweiterungen und Ergänzungen zu bestehenden Produktfamilien wie die Erweiterungen des Strahlersystems von Staff zum »TeleDancer«, einer programmierbaren ferngesteuerten Strahlereinheit. Farbige Filterzusätze für Downlights wurden ebenso ausgezeichnet wie neue typologische Varianten eines Entwurfs jetzt als Klemm-, Steh-, Wand-, Decken- oder Tischleuchte.

Wegen ihres materialsparenden Minimalismus hat eine winzigkleine Multipurpose-Steckleuchte sogar eine Ökoauszeichnung erhalten.

The three "Best of Category" in the Lighting category already demonstrate quite clearly the range of current lighting design. A standard lamp with a tripod base and a fabric shade with a romantic feel to it was one of the winners. "Such objects reconcile you with the world of objects that otherwise make people nervous, like many techno-flash things," ascertained Andrée Putman, explaining her vote in favor of this emotionally-charged object. On the other hand, the luminaire designed by Philippe Starck is, for all its emotionality, a modern high-grade industrial product; with a fluent form and a minimal use of plastic, it resembles a Brancusi sculpture. High-tech and a talented imagination blend here to create a product typical for our times, or the fin de siècle.

In the low-voltage class, there was a lighting system with a cheerfully different design, showing just how far room-spanning low voltage technology can advance. The jury felt the logical evolution of a meanwhile current norm in the low-voltage class to also be worthy of a distinction.

The third "Best of Category" is strictly in keeping with the Bauhaus tradition: Modernism as a tradition, which offers a formal re-interpretation of the high culture of glass and metal processing. Such forms have a strong place in the world of the industry and are a standard that exudes continuity.

All three award-winning luminaires, ranging from the architectural to the emotional, exhibited ultra-modern technological workings. In the opinion of some of the jurors, with luminaires, meanwhile more importance must be attached to the effect of the light than to the lighting source proper. Consequently, what is called for is "creative engineering by the company and the designer", emphasizes designer Hartmut S. Engel, one of the specialist jury members in the field of lighting.

Typical for the current situation in and strategy pursued by the lighting industry are evolutionary extensions and additions to existing product lines like the extensions to Staff's spot-light system: it is now a "TeleDancer", a programmable remote controlled spot-light unit. Colored filter attachments for downlighters also won prizes, as did the new typological variants of a design now available as a clamp-on, standalone, wall, ceiling or table-mounted luminaire.

Owing to its material-saving minimalism, a miniature clamp-on luminaire even won a prize for ecological soundness. Congratulations.

HERSTELLER MANUFACTURER FLOS SpA, Bovezzo (Brescia), Italy
PRODUKT PRODUCT ROSY ANGELIS Stehleuchte Floor lamp
DESIGN Philippe Starck, Issy Les Moulineaux, France
VERTRIEB DISTRIBUTION FLOS GmbH, Bonn, Germany

ROSY ANGELIS, Phillipe Starcks Stehleuchte für diffuses Licht. Mit elektronischem Dimmer. Diffusor aus superleichtem Spezialgewebe, Dreifuß aus lackiertem Aluminium. Tragende Teile aus Technopolymer.

ROSY ANGELIS is a standard lamp offering diffuse lighting. It is fitted with an electronic dimmer and a diffuser made of an ultra-light fabric. The base is a painted aluminium tripod and the structural support is made of technopolymer.

HERSTELLER MANUFACTURER Bruck Lichtsysteme GmbH & Co. KG, Herne, Germany
PRODUKT PRODUCT Flex-Line Niedervolt-System Low-voltage luminaire system
DESIGN Achim Bredin, Bochum, Germany

FLEX-LINE, flexibles Niedervolt-Beleuchtungssystem mit zwei Stromkreisen, basiert auf einer neu entwickelten Stromschiene: Vier Kupferlitzen sind mit dem Trägerprofil aus Makrolon® verbunden. Das Profil ist formbeständig und dennoch elastisch, erlaubt kurvenförmige Installationen, ist problemlos von Hand zu kürzen, zu biegen und rückzubiegen: ideal für Messe- und Ladenbau. Die zwei Stromkreise erlauben variable Beleuchtungseffekte. Zur Verfügung stehen die eigens für dies System entwickelten Leuchten »Sail« (Lichtpunkt mit diffundierendem Schirm), »Butterfly« (Decostrahler) und »Bini« (Fluter).

FLEX-LINE is a flexible low voltage luminaire system using two circuits. It utilizes a newly developed power supply rail: four copper conductors are connected to a sectional carrier made of Makrolon®. The profile nevertheless does not go out of shape, despite being elastic and permitting curving installations that can easily be shortened, bent, or bent back by hand: it is ideal for trade fairs and stores. The double circuits generate a variety of lighting effects. Various lamps have been specially developed for the system: »Sail« (emits a point of light diffused through a screen), »Butterfly« (a multi-angle uplighter) and »Bini« (a flood).

BEGA, Menden, Germany HERSTELLER MANUFACTURER
BEGA 6097/6396 Pendelleuchte Pendant luminaires PRODUKT PRODUCT
BEGA DESIGN

BEGA 6097 Pendelleuchte mit Ringöse für alle Beleuchtungszwecke innen und außen: überall dort, wo Leuchten im Raum oder draußen korrosionsbeständig und gegen Feuchtigkeit geschützt sein müssen (Schutzart IP 44): Passagen, Terrassen, Sporthallen, Industriebauten etc. Zur Montage an bauseitigen Rohr- oder Kettenpendeln, Stahlseilen, Deckenhaken; auch an Kragplatten oder Tragekonstruktionen. Neuartige, wartungsfreundliche Konstruktion. Gehäuse, schwarz, aus Aluminiumguß, Aluminium und Edelstahl. Reflektor aus eloxiertem Reinstaluminium, mit Sicherheitsglas. Für energiesparende Leuchtstofflampen und Hochdrucklampen.

The BEGA 6097 is a pendant luminaire with a fixing ring for all indoor and outdoor uses that call for lamps which are anti-corrosive and protected against damp (IP 44 standard) – for shopping centers, terraces, sports halls, industrial buildings, etc. It can be mounted on customers' tubular or chain pendants, steel wires, from ceiling hooks etc., and on cantilever plates or bearing elements. It features a new easy-to-maintain construction. The housing is made of black die-cast aluminum, aluminum and stainless steel. The reflector is anodized pure-grade aluminum and safety glass. It is suited for energy-saving fluorescent lamps and high-pressure bulbs.

Ökologie/Design Auszeichnung Awarded for Ecology/Design: Vorbildlich durch Langlebigkeit, Transparenz der Materialien, zeitlose Gestaltung und energieeffiziente Leuchtmittel. *Exemplary for their longevity, the transparent use of materials, the timeless design and the energy-efficient lamps used.*

HERSTELLER MANUFACTURER BEGA, Menden, Germany
PRODUKT PRODUCT BEGA 6350/6324/6323 Tiefstrahler Ceiling luminaire
DESIGN BEGA

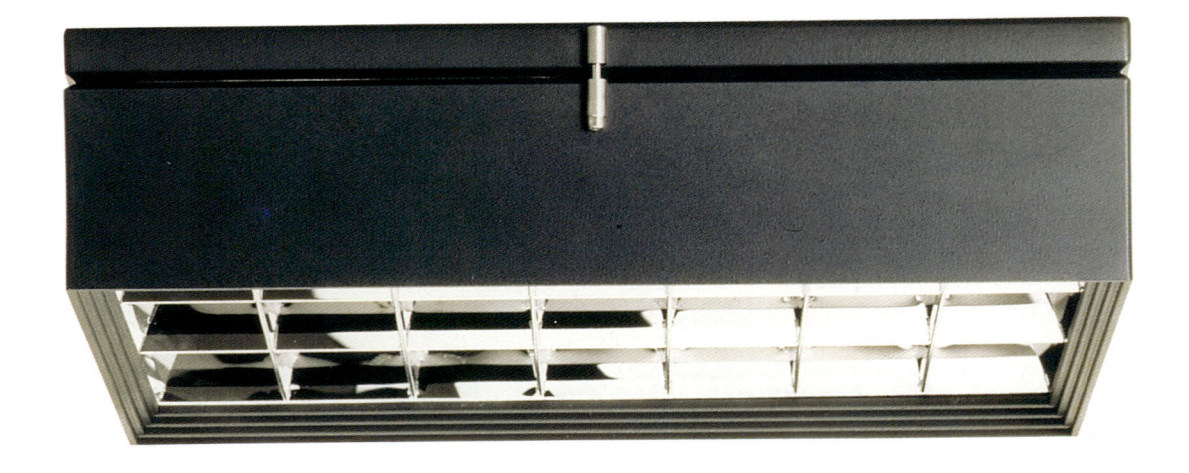

BEGA 6350, 6324, 6323 Tiefstrahler-Deckenaufbauleuchte mit hoher konstruktiver Festigkeit (ballwurfsicher) und hoher Schutzart (IP 54). Aus Aluminiumguß, Aluminium und Edelstahl. Reflektor aus eloxiertem Reinstaluminium. Sicherheitsglas. Geringe Bauhöhe, breitstreuende Lichtverteilung: besonders geeignet für Räume mit niedriger Decke. Hoher Wirkungsgrad, lange Wartungsintervalle und geringe Anschlußwerte, also sehr wirtschaftlich. Für energiesparende Leuchtstofflampen 3 TC-L, je 36 Watt.

BEGA 6350, 6324, 6323 is a ceiling luminaire with a heavy-duty construction (ballproof) and offering high-class protection (IP 54). Made of die-cast aluminium, aluminium and stainless steel; the reflector is pure anodized aluminium. The light features safety glass, is flat, and provides widespread light dis-semination: especially suited for rooms with low ceilings. Wide angle, maintenance friendly, low connection values and very cost effective. Suitable for energy-saving fluorescent 3 TC-L, 36 W bulbs.

Ökologie/Design Auszeichnung Awarded for Ecology/Design: Vorbildlich durch Langlebigkeit, Transparenz der Materialien, zeitlose Gestaltung und energieeffiziente Leuchtmittel. Exemplary for their longevity, the transparent use of materials, the timeless design and the energy-efficient lamps used.

204 BELEUCHTUNG LIGHTING

DECKEN- und WANDLEUCHTEN in vier Größen. Armatur aus Metallguß, poliert; Lampenkörper aus mundgeblasenem Opalglas, seidenmatt. Sorgt für eine gleichmäßige und weiche Verteilung des Lichts. Auch mit weißer Oberfläche lieferbar. Für energiesparende Kompaktleuchtstofflampen, Schutzart IP 44.

CEILING and WALL LUMINAIRES in four sizes. The fittings are in polished die-cast metal; the lamp casings are made of hand-blown opalescent glass with a satin matt finish. The luminaires offer regular and soft light diffusion and are also available with a white surface finish. An energy-saving compact fluorescent lamp affording prime protection.

HERSTELLER MANUFACTURER GLASHÜTTE LIMBURG, Limburg, Germany
PRODUKT PRODUCT Nr. 7434 - 7437 Decken- Wandleuchten Ceiling/wall luminaires
DESIGN GLASHÜTTE LIMBURG, Limburg, Germany

BELEUCHTUNG LIGHTING 205

HERSTELLER MANUFACTURER
PRODUKT PRODUCT
DESIGN

BEGA, Menden, Germany
BEGA 3121, 3231 Wandfluter Wall-mounted luminaire
BEGA

BEGA 3121, 3231 eine Wandleuchte (Wandfluter) mit einer Lichtquelle und zweiseitigem Lichtaustritt, bietet der Lichtarchitektur viele Gestaltungsmöglichkeiten. Dem nach oben und unten weich ausstrahlenden Streulicht dient die Wand als Reflektionsfläche. Aluminiumguß und Edelstahl, schwarz oder weiß; Opalglas. Für Leuchtstofflampen TC-D 13 und 26 Watt (Schutzart IP 44).

BEGA 3121, 3231 a wall-mounted luminaire with two-sided light output and a single light source, offers interior designers numerous possibilities. The diffuse light radiating upwards and downwards uses the wall as a reflecting surface. The luminaire is made of die-cast aluminum and stainless steel, available in black or white, with opaque glass. For fluorescent bulbs TC-D 13W and 26W (IP 44 standard).

Ökologie/Design Auszeichnung Awarded for Ecology/Design: Vorbildlich durch Langlebigkeit, Transparenz der Materialien, zeitlose Gestaltung und energieeffiziente Leuchtmittel. Exemplary for their longevity, the transparent use of materials, the timeless design and the energy-efficient lamps used.

Nr. 4809, 4810, 4812, 4813, 4814 Pendelleuchten Pendant luminaires
GLASHÜTTE LIMBURG, Limburg, Germany   HERSTELLER MANUFACTURER
PRODUKT PRODUCT
GLASHÜTTE LIMBURG, Limburg, Germany   DESIGN

TIEFSTRAHLER-PENDELLEUCHTEN für hohe Lichtleistungen. Gerichtetes und freistrahlendes Licht, blendfrei, mit hohem Wirkungsgrad. Die Lampen sind focussierbar, darum läßt sich die Lichtstärkeverteilung des gerichteten Lichts regulieren. Das Gehäuse ist aus Aluminiumguß, Aluminium und Edelstahl. Mundgeblasenes Opalglas mit Spiegeloptik.

PENDANT LUMINAIRES featuring a pendant mounting for high light efficiency. It offers directed and radiating glare-free light with a prime light output ratio. The lamps can be fo-cused and consequently directed light can be modified. The casing is made of die-cast aluminium, aluminium and stainless steel, and the lamp section consists of mirrored hand-blown tri-ply opalescent glass.

BELEUCHTUNG LIGHTING 207

HERSTELLER MANUFACTURER DZ LICHT AUSSENLEUCHTEN GmbH, Frödenberg, Germany
PRODUKT PRODUCT DZ LICHT Lichtboden Floor luminaire
DESIGN Peter Zegers, Menden, Germany

DZ LICHT LICHTBODEN, Bodeneinbauleuchte für hohe Belastungen. Im Innen- und Aussenbereich niveaugetreu und abstandslos in Geh- oder Fahrwege (bis 16 t Gesamtgewicht belastbar) zu integrieren. Leuchtengehäuse aus Aluminiumguß (Schutzart IP 55). Einscheibensicherheitsglas als Verbundglas. Verbund mittels opalisierender Folien zur gleichmäßigen Ausleuchtung der Glasebene. Glas zu Wartungszwecken mit Saugern abzunehmen.
The DZ LICHT LICHTBODEN is a flush-mounted floor luminaire for high-load areas. It can be flush-mounted both indoors and outdoors in walkways and carriageways (withstands a gross weight of 16 tonnes). The casing is made of die-cast aluminium (IP 55 standard). Triply tempered safety glass. Integrated opalescent foils provide uniform illumination at glass level. The glass can be lifted out by suction cup for maintenance.

HERSTELLER MANUFACTURER
LTS Licht- und Leuchten GmbH, Tettnang, Germany
PRODUKT PRODUCT
CA Downlight Aufbau-Downlight
DESIGN
Schlagheck Design Prof. Norbert Schlagheck, Alfred Brendel, München, Germany

CA AUFBAU-DOWNLIGHTS kommen überall dort zum Einsatz, wo es keine hohlen Decken für den Einbau gibt. Neu entwickelte Stromversorgung von Leuchte zu Leuchte über Kabelrohre mit Deckenabstandhaltern, die beliebige Montageabstände und Konfigurationen erlauben. Kabelrohre werden in einem multifunktionalen Kunststoffring gelagert. Sollbruchstellen, die nach innen aufzubrechen sind und Kabelein- und -ausgang ermöglichen. Durch Verwendung eines vorhandenen Einbaudownlight-Rings nur zwei Werkzeuge, ein Spritzguß und ein Strangpreßwerkzeug, erforderlich. Damit unterschiedliche Rohrlängen möglich, die Leuchtmittel verschiedenster Wattagen verbinden. Resultat der einfachen Montage ist ein Aufbaudownlight von sachlicher Eleganz: »form follows function«.

CA DOWNLIGHT is specially designed for locations where there are no hollow ceilings to take flush-mounted light fittings. The innovative power sourcing from lamp to lamp via wire ducts with ceiling-mounted space holders enables users to select the distance between lights and lighting configurations at will. The wires ducts are mounted in a multifunctional plastic ring. Preset break-off points that double up as wiring entry/exit points are possible. Because the design is based on an existing flush-mounted downlight ring, only two tools are required: an injection mold and an extrusion press. This enables different wiring duct lengths to be made and bulbs of different wattages can be combined: an easy-to-assemble fitted downlighter with graceful elegance that fully meets the motto: »form follows function«.

Baureihe 126K3, eine Serie von Einbau-Downlights, die speziell für den Projektmarkt entwickelt wurde. In Modulbauweise ausgeführt, mit elektronischen Vorschaltgeräten versehen. In drei Größen (Durchmessern), für TC-TEL-Lampen von 16, 26 oder 32 Watt. Gehäuse aus Aluminium-, Magnesium- und Kunststoffspritzgußteilen. Spritzwasserdicht und hitzebeständig. Durch eine neue Steckverbindung leicht zu installieren. Montage in Decken unterschiedlicher Dicke.

The 126K3 is a series of built-in downlights developed specially for the project market. The modular construction features electronic ballast elements. It is available in three different diameters and is suited for use with 16, 26 or 32W TC-TEL lamps. The housing is injection-molded aluminium, magnesium and plastic. It is splashproof, heat-resistant and easy to install thanks to a new connector system. It can be mounted in walls of various thicknesses.

HERSTELLER MANUFACTURER WILA Leuchten GmbH, Iserlohn, Germany
PRODUKT PRODUCT Baureihe 126 K3 Downlights
DESIGN ninaber/peters/krouwel industrial design, Leiden, The Netherlands

RIBAG Licht AG, Muhen, Switzerland — HERSTELLER MANUFACTURER
TRAPEZ Hängeleuchte Fluorescent light — PRODUKT PRODUCT
Erwin Egli, Basel, Switzerland — DESIGN

TRAPEZ, eine Hängeleuchte, die durch ihre Funktionalität überzeugt. Als Pendel-, Wand- und Aufbauleuchte. Vielfältiges Reflektorenprogramm zur Kombination mit den einzelnen Modellen der Serie. Ein klassisch klares Design, fortgeschrittene Technik (für Energiesparleuchten ausgelegt) zur Anwendung im Heim- und im Objektbereich.

TRAPEZ is a fluorescent light offering truly convincing practical features. It can be pendant, ceiling, or flush-mounted. A wide range of reflectors can be combined with the individual models in the series. It features a classical, clear design and advanced technology (designed for energy-saving bulbs) for use in residential and commercial settings.

SIRIUS VITRINE, ein Lichtleitsystem bestehend aus Projektor, den Lichtleitern und Endstrahlern. Geeignet zur Beleuchtung hochwertiger und empfindlicher Exponate z. B. in Vitrinen.

SIRIUS VITRINE is a highlighting system consisting of a projector, optic cables and spotlights. It is ideal for illuminating valuable and sensitive exhibits in showcases and similar display scenario.

Kotzolt Leuchten L. & G. Kotzolt GmbH & Co. KG, Lemgo, Germany HERSTELLER MANUFACTURER
SIRIUS Vitrinen Lichtleitsystem Highlighting system PRODUKT PRODUCT
Helmut Zender, Detmold, Germany DESIGN

BELEUCHTUNG LIGHTING 213

HERSTELLER MANUFACTURER
Lüderitz Licht GmbH, Lübbecke, Germany
PRODUKT PRODUCT
BIRDIE Aufbau- und Einbauleuchten Luminaires
DESIGN
design studio hartmut s. engel, Ludwigsburg, Germany

BIRDIE, Aufbau- und Einbauleuchten (Deckenmontage) für Büro- und Verkaufsräume. Völlig neues Konzept, für weiches und dynamisches Licht. Mattweiße geschwungene Reflektorflügel verteilen das Licht nach einer mathematisch bestimmten Abstrahlcharakteristik. Indirekte Lichtführung. So ergibt sich optimale Verteilung der Helligkeit, zugleich bilden sich weiche Schatten und gut erkennbare Kontraste. Für alle zeitgemäßen Leuchtmittel.

BIRDIE is a flush-mounted or ceiling-mounted luminaiRE for office and sales rooms. The completely new concept generates soft and dynamic light: the curve of the matt-white reflector wings was designed with mathematical precision to radiate light broadly. The indirect light sourcing ensures the optimal spread of brightness, while also creating soft shadows and clear contrasts. Suitable for all modern bulbs.

214 BELEUCHTUNG LIGHTING

BELEUCHTUNG *LIGHTING* 215

HERSTELLER MANUFACTURER
FAGERHULT, Habo, Sweden
PRODUKT PRODUCT
PLEIAD Downlight Serie Downlighters
DESIGN
AB FAGERHULT, Habo, Sweden
VERTRIEB DISTRIBUTION
Fagerhult GmbH, Hamburg, Germany

PLEIAD, Downlight-Serie für vielfältigen Einsatz. Speziell entwickelter Reflektor, geeignet für TC-T Lampen (18–42 Watt), garantiert symmetrische Lichtverteilung bei extrem guter Entblendung. Der schwenkbare Lampenhalter ermöglicht geringe Reflektorabmessungen bei hohem Wirkungsgrad und problemlosen Lampenwechsel. Metallgehäuse, Reflektoren aus Polycarbonat mit Aluminium- oder Messingfinish, mattiert oder hochglänzend.. Eine Vielzahl von Reflektoren (in drei Größen), Abdeckungen und Deko-Rastern steht zur Verfügung. Einfacher, werkzeugloser Anschluß.

PLEIAD, a range of downlighters for numerous uses. It has a specially developed reflector, suitable for TC-T compact bulbs (18–42W), guaranteeing symmetrical light distribution and minimizing glare. The tiltable lampholder ensures minimum reflector diameter without a loss of light output and easy bulb changing. Metal housing, and polycarbonate reflectors with an aluminium and brass finish, ei-ther in matt or high gloss. A number of different reflectors (in three sizes), trim rings and design louvers. Easy to connect without tools.

SOLITÄR, ein Deckenelement zur attraktiven und ergonomischen Lichtgestaltung und zur Lösung akustischer Probleme in großen Räumen ohne abgehängte Decken. Läßt sich mit variabler Neigung aufhängen, erlaubt also flexible Raumgestaltung. Gute Absorbtionseigenschaften des Ausgangsmaterials sorgen für akustische Diskretion, die integrierte Bildschirmarbeitsplatzbeleuchtung garantiert ein angenehmes Arbeitslicht und zugleich mit dem Deckenelement als Reflexionsfläche ein attraktives Raumlicht. Ein neuer Weg im Objektbereich, Konzeptpartner waren Lüderitz Licht, der Akustikspezialist Wilhelmi Werke und das Designbüro Wulf Fiedler.

SOLITÄR is a ceiling unit guaranteeing appealing and ergonomically perfected lighting and solving acoustic problems in large rooms that do not have lowered ceilings. It can be hung at various angles, allowing the interior to be designed flexibly. The absorptive capacity of the material enhances acoustic discretion, and the integrated workstation luminaire provides pleasant working light and, together with the ceiling element as a reflecting surface, affords attractive ambient light. The unit is a new approach to professional lighting: the concept was developed by Lüderitz Licht with Wilhelmi Werke, the acoustic specialists, and the Wulf Fiedler design studio.

HERSTELLER MANUFACTURER Lüderitz Licht GmbH, Lübbecke, Germany, Wilhelmi Werke GmbH & Co. KG, Lahnau, Germany
PRODUKT PRODUCT SOLITÄR Akustik und Licht Acoustic and lighting system
DESIGN Wulf Fiedler, Berlin, Germany

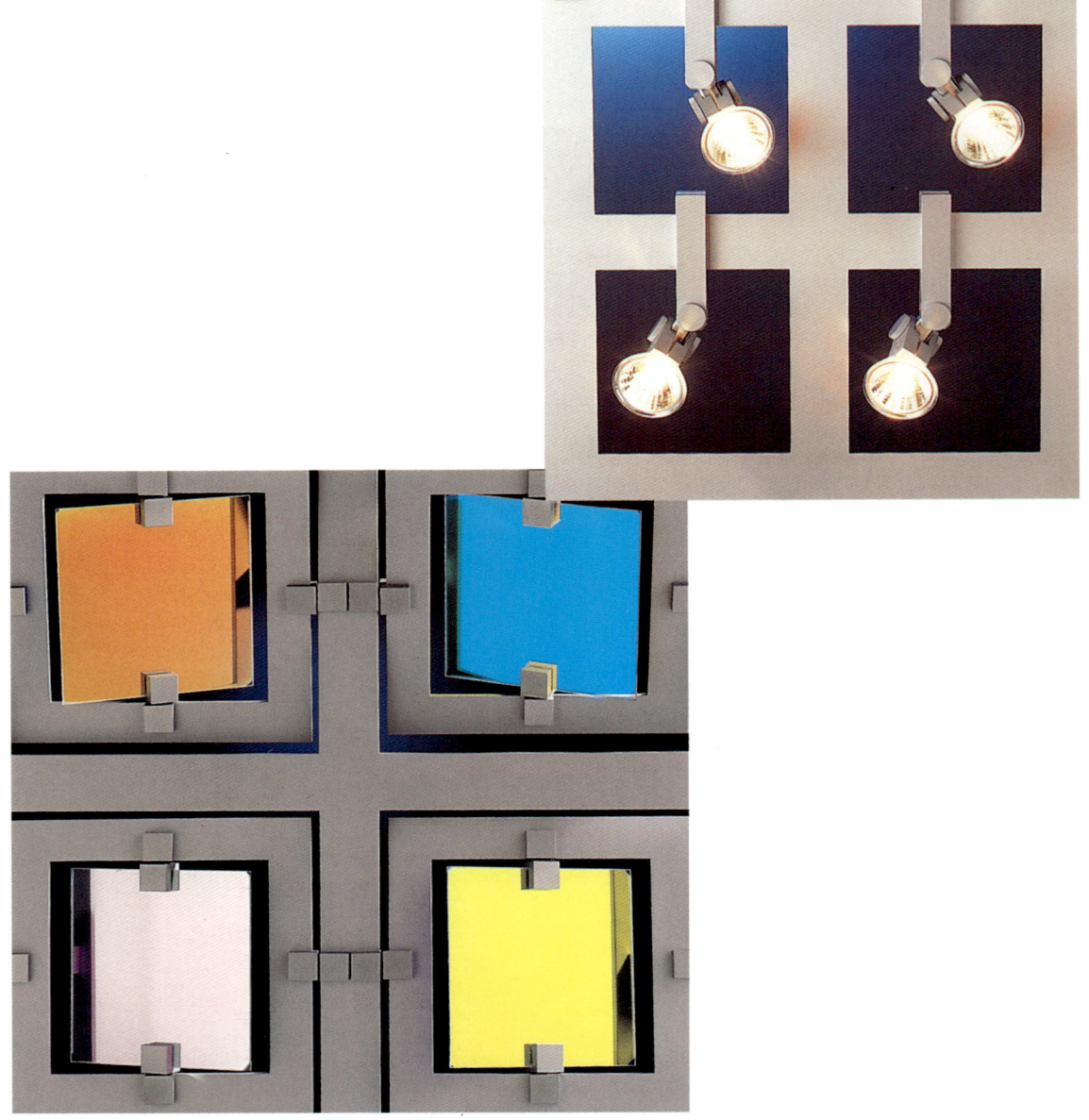

HERSTELLER MANUFACTURER
IDL - Industrie und Design Licht GmbH, Limbach-Oberfrohna, Germany
PRODUKT PRODUCT
Alulite ceiling & wall Serie Wand- und Deckenleuchten Low-voltage luminaires
DESIGN
IDL - Designabteilung, Dominic Sacher, Dietmar Weickert, Limbach-Oberfrohna, Germany

ALULITE ceiling & wall, Alulite mirror, eine Serie aus Niedervolt-Leuchten und Filterhaltern, die sich in ihrer Funktion ergänzen. Alle modular konzipierten Teile lassen sich in Wand- und Deckenmontage kombinieren. Drei verschiedene Strahlertypen und neun dichromatische Filtergläser. Werden diese angestrahlt, ergeben sich effektvolle Farbspiele.

ALULITE ceiling & wall and Alulite mirror are a series of low voltage luminaires including special glass filters in a variety of colors – when illuminated the filters create unique lighting and color effects. All the modular components can be combined and either wall or ceiling-mounted. The Alulite range offers three different spots and nine dichromatic filter glasses.

oben: DROP 2, Wand- und Deckenleuchten für diffuse Beleuchtung im Innen- und Außenbereich. Diffusor aus opalfarbigem Silikon-Elastomer. Wandhalterung aus farbigem und hitzebeständigem Polymer. Staubdicht und spritzwassergeschützt.

above: DROP 2 are wall or ceiling luminaires for the diffuse illumination of indoor and outdoor areas. The diffusers are made of opalescent silicon elastomer. The wall mounting is made of colored heat resistant technopolymer. Lamps are dust and waterproof.

BRERA, Leuchtenserie mit Pendel- Decken-, Wand-, Tisch- und Stehleuchte. Der Ausgangspunkt für das Design war die Pendelleuchte mit Deckenbefestigung, Stahlseil, Lampenfassung (für E 27) und Glaskörper aus geblasenem, geätztem Glas. Dieses Streuelement kann in verschiedenen Positionen befestigt werden und ließ sich darum auch in die anderen Leuchtentypen der Serie integrieren. Die Form des Leuchtkörpers ähnelt dem Ei auf einem Gemälde von Piero della Francesca (»Pala de Montefeltro«), das in der Pinacoteca di Brera, Mailand, gezeigt wird: So ergab sich der Name der Serie.

BRERA is a luminaire line with pendulum, ceiling, and wall mounted lamps, tabletop lamps and standing lamps. The design is based on a suspended steel-wire mounting from the ceiling and a lampholder (for E 27 bulbs) and glass body made of blown and etched glass. The diffusers can be placed in different positions and can therefore also be combined with some other lamps from the series. The diffusers resemble the egg in the painting by Piero della Francesca (»Pala de Montefeltro«) to be seen in the Pinacoteca di Brera in Milan: This is where the series got its name.

HERSTELLER MANUFACTURER FLOS SpA, Bovezzo (Brescia), Italy
PRODUKT PRODUCT links/left: DROP 2 Wandleuchte Wall lamp rechts/right: BRERA Leuchtenserie Luminaire line
DESIGN links/left: Marc Sadler, Asolo, Italy, rechts/right: Achille Castiglioni, Milano, Italy
VERTRIEB DISTRIBUTION FLOS GmbH, Bonn, Germany

HERSTELLER MANUFACTURER STAFF GmbH & Co. KG, Lemgo, Germany
PRODUKT PRODUCT Pendelleuchten Pendant luminaires
DESIGN STAFF DESIGN, Brigitte Esselborn, Lemgo, Germany

GLASPENDELLEUCHTEN für Niedervolt-Halogenglühlampen. Glaskörper aus klarem blauen bzw. mattiertem Silikatglas, Metallteile titanfarben lackiert. Über STAFF NV-Multitec-Steckverbindung erfolgt der Anschluß des elektronischen Anbautransformators, der ebenfalls titanfarben lackiert ist. Das Programm des Herstellers bietet auch andere Anschlußmöglichkeiten.

GLASS PENDANT LUMINAIRES for low voltage halogen bulbs. The glass unit is made of clear blue or frosted silicate glass. The metal elements are enameled in a titanium color. By means of STAFF Multitec plugs and sockets the unit can be connected to a surface-mounted electronic transformer also painted in a titanium hue. The line is also available with different connectors.

T16-FLUTER, ein asymmetrischer Strahler (Fluter) für T16-Lampen unterschiedlicher Leistung und Länge, zur gleichmäßigen Ausleuchtung von Wand- und Deckenflächen. Gehäuse aus Aluminium-Strangpreßprofilen und Aluminiumdruckguß. Der asymmetrische Spiegelreflektor ist aus seidenglanzeloxiertem Rein-Aluminium. Der Lampenraum kann mit Silikatglasscheibe oder mit einem UVA-Sperrfilter aus PMMA abgedeckt werden. Fluter um ±90° aus der Vertikalen zu schwenken. Elektronisches Vorschaltgerät integriert. STAFF-Adaptoren oder Anbau-Armaturen für die Montage gehören zum Lieferumfang.

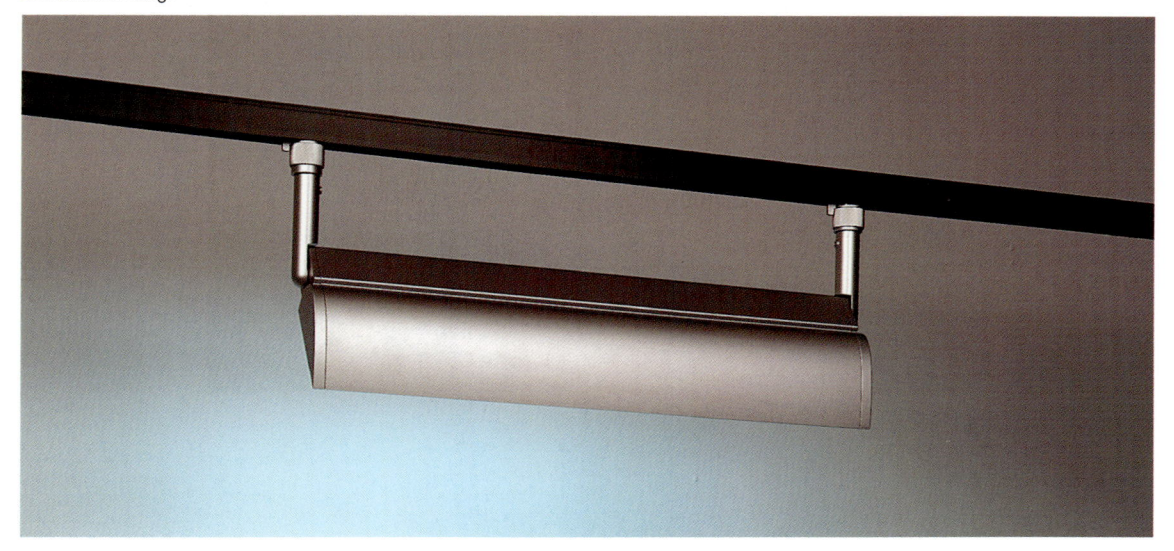

HERSTELLER MANUFACTURER STAFF GmbH & Co. KG, Lemgo, Germany
PRODUKT PRODUCT T16-Fluter Strahler Floodlight
DESIGN STAFF DESIGN, Gerhard Beigel, Lemgo, Germany

The T16 FLOODLIGHT features an asymmetrical flood light for T16 lamps of different wattages and lengths, ensuring uniform illumination of walls and ceilings. The housing is made of extruded aluminium profiles and die-cast aluminium. The asymmetrical mirror reflector consist of satin-matt anodized pure-grade aluminium. The lamp section can be supplied with a silicate protection glass or a UVA reduction filter made of PMMA. The floodlight can be rotated ±90° from the vertical and comes complete with integrated electronic ballast elements. STAFF adapters or mounting plates are available for wall or ceiling mounts.

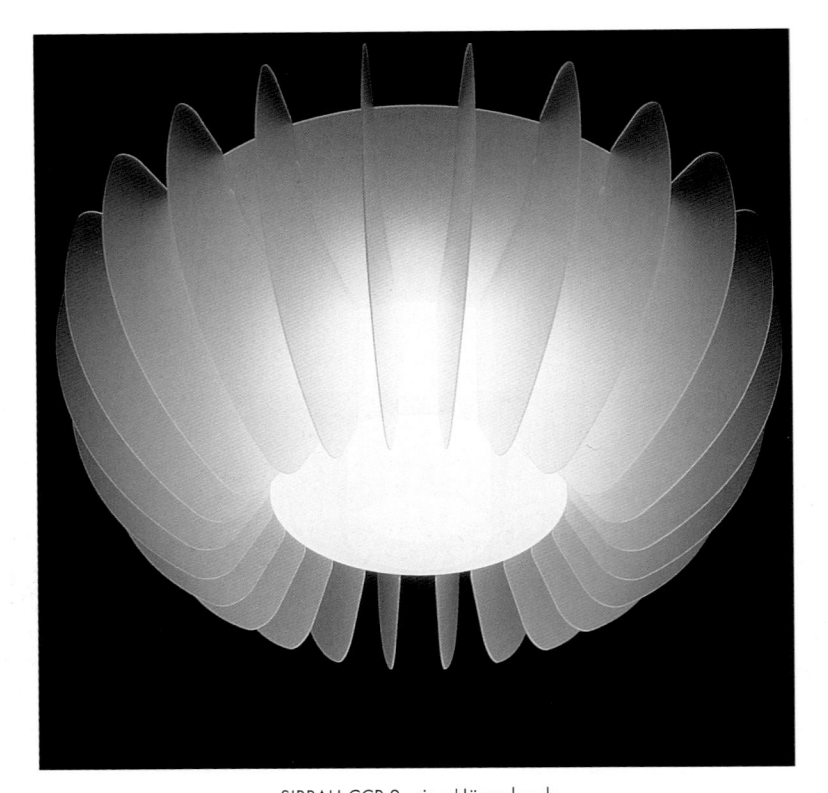

HERSTELLER MANUFACTURER
SIRRAH SRL Gruppo iGuzzini, Imola, Italy
PRODUKT PRODUCT
CCP 2 Hängeleuchte Pole-hung lamp
DESIGN
KING - MIRANDA ASSOCIATI Perry A. King, Santiago Miranda, Milano, Italy
VERTRIEB DISTRIBUTION
iGuzzini Illuminazione Deutschlnad GmbH, München, Germany

SIRRAH CCP 2, eine Hängeleuchte, die aus einem Kernstück und 24 opalinweißen Metacrylatlamellen besteht. Für Glüh- und Leuchtstofflampen (E 27).
SIRRAH CCP 2 is a pole-hung lamp consisting of a central unit and 24 opalescent white metacrylate slats. Can be used with conventional and fluorescent bulbs (E 27).

222 BELEUCHTUNG *LIGHTING*

TITANIA MORSETTO und TERRA, eine Serie aus Klemm- und Stehleuchten, für Wohn- und Arbeitsräume konzipiert. Das Lamellengehäuse aus Aluminium, aufgebaut aus verschiedenen Ellipsen und Rippen, dient zugleich als Abblendschirm, Lichtquellenreflektor und Wärmeableiter. Fünf austauschbare Filterpaare geben dem Lamellengehäuse verschiedene Färbungen. Ausführung in Aluminium natur oder schwarz. Für Halogenlampen 150–200 Watt (E 27).
TITANIA MORSETTO and TERRA is a series of clamp-on and standard lights conceived specially for residential and working inte-riors. The slatted aluminium casing consists of various ellipses and ribs and doubles up as a anti-glare screen, central light source and heat dissipater. Five exchangeable pairs of filters create the different colorings of the casing. Available colors: untreated aluminium or black. For halogen bulbs of 150–200W (E 27).

HERSTELLER MANUFACTURER LUCEPLAN SPA, Milano, Italy
PRODUKT PRODUCT Klemmleuchte/Stehleuchte Clamp-on lamp/floor lamp
DESIGN TITANIA morsetto/terra LUCEPLAN, Alberto Meda, Paolo Rizzatto, Milano, Italy

HERSTELLER MANUFACTURER
Artemide S.p.A., Pregnana Milanese, Italy
PRODUKT PRODUCT
Tolomeo pinza Klemmleuchte Lamp with pincer grip
DESIGN
Michele De Lucchi, Giancarlo Fassina, Artemide S.p.A., Pregnana Milanese, Italy
VERTRIEB DISTRIBUTION
Artemide GmbH, Hilden, Germany

TOLOMEO PINZA, eine neue Leuchte aus der Tolomeo-Familie. Klein, sehr funktional und durch die Klemmvorrichtung universell einzusetzen. Leuchtenkopf aus eloxiertem Aluminium, Klemme aus matt lackiertem Stahl. Lampe: max. 100W (E27).

TOLOMEO PINZA, is a new lamp from the Tolomeo family. It is small, highly functional and its pincer grip means it can be used everywhere. The swivel head is made of anodized aluminium, and the grip out of matt painted steel. Lamp: max. 100W (E27).

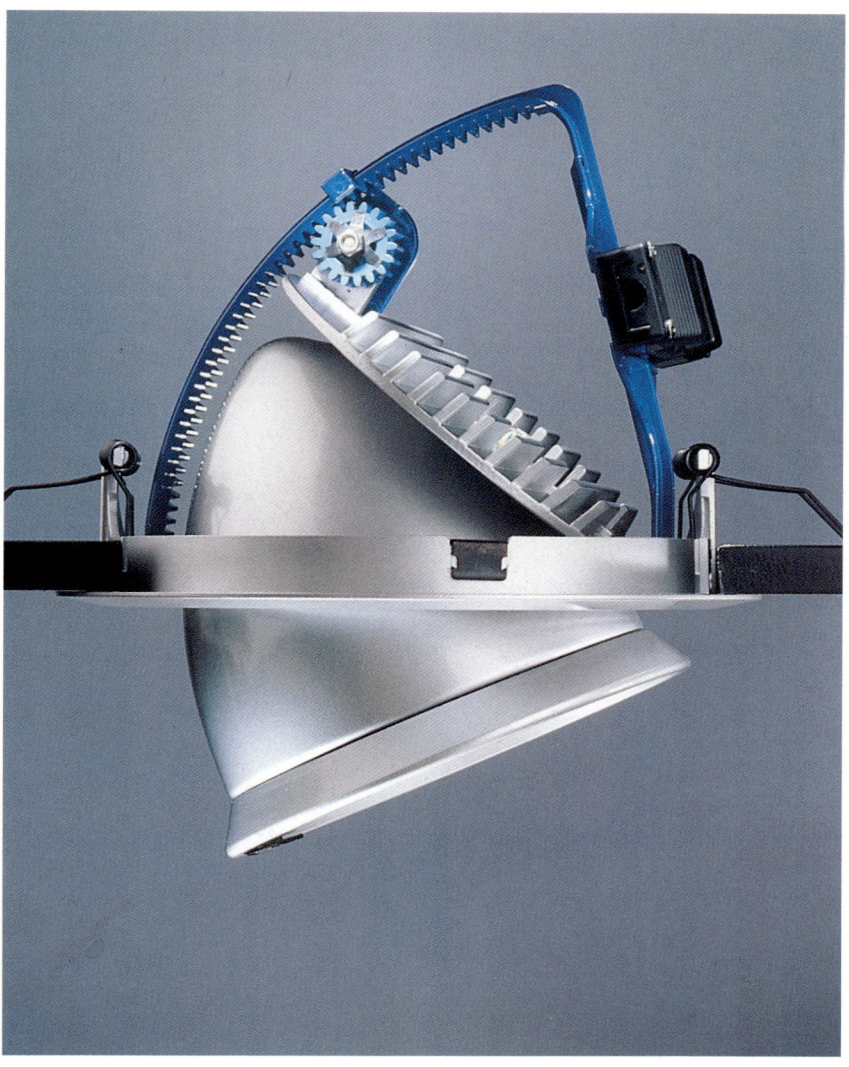

MONDIAL, eine Serie von Niedervolt-Richtstrahlern für den Dekckeneinbau. In Design und Funktion angeregt vom Grand Prix Motorsport: Scheinwerfer mit hochpräzisem Lichtstrahl, für photometrisch perfekte Ausleuchtung. Gehäuse aus pulverbeschichtetem Aluminiumguß, in zwei Größen, 65° schwenkbar und um 360° drehbar, verschwindet plan in der Decke. Komplett mit Schutzglas; wahlweise mit Farb- und UV-Filtern, Diffusionsgläsern und Blendschutzrastern. Auch für Kaltlicht- und Entladungslampen.

MONDIAL, a series of low-voltage directional downlights for ceilings. The design and functions were inspired by motor racing: headlights provide light directed with great precision for photometrically perfect illumination. The housing is epoxy-coated die-cast aluminium, in two sizes, tiltable through 65° and rotatable 360°, disappears flush in the ceiling. Complete with protection glass; available with color or UV filters, diffusion glass and anti-glare louvers. Suitable for cold-light and discharge bulbs.

HERSTELLER MANUFACTURER TARGETTI SANKEY Spa, Firenze, Italy
PRODUKT PRODUCT MONDIAL Serie von NV-Richtstrahlern Precision directional downlights
DESIGN TARGETTI SANKEY, Firenze, Italy
VERTRIEB DISTRIBUTION TARGETTI LICHT Vertriebs-GmbH, Oberhausen, Germany

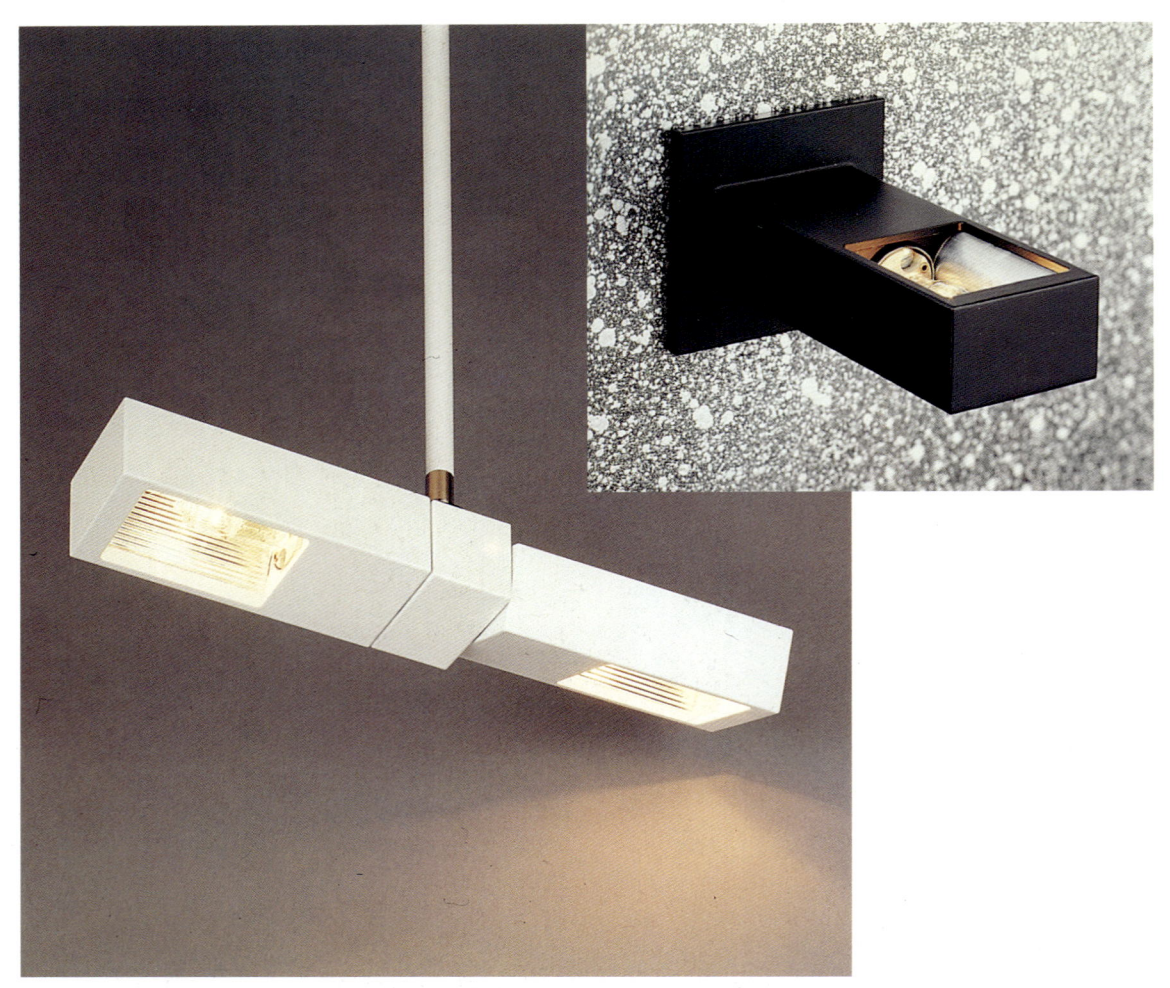

HERSTELLER MANUFACTURER
STENG LICHT STUTTGART GmbH, Stuttgart, Germany
PRODUKT PRODUCT
BRIGG Wand- und Steck-Systemleuchte Wall and system luminaire
DESIGN
Peter Steng, Stuttgart, Germany, Hans Vetter, Stuttgart, Germany

BRIGG, eine Wand- und eine Systemleuchte. Grundelement ist der zylindrische Leuchtenkopf, ein- oder zweiflammig. Als ein flammiger Leuchtenkopf ist er dreh- und schwenkbar. Die Wandleuchte ist konzipiert zur Montage direkt auf die Wand, entweder auf 12V- oder 220V-Anschluß oder auf eine Trafoeinbaudose. Für Niederdruck-Stiftsockellampe (12V) oder für Halogen Röhrenlampe (220V).

Die Systemleuchten mit Steng-Steckkontakt-Systemverbindungen und Verlängerungsstäben bilden eine zweite Funktionsgruppe dieser Lampenserie. Zur Deckenmontage, oder mit entsprechendem Fuß, als Tisch- oder Stehleuchte. Steckkontaktkopf nur für 12V Niederdruck-Stiftsockellampen eingerichtet, seitliche einseitige oder zweiseitige Lichtabstrahlung, dreh- und schwenkbar.

BRIGG is a wall and system luminaire featuring a cylindrical one or dual-side reflector unit. The one-sided reflector unit can be swiveled and tilted. The wall-mounted version can be connected to either a 12V or a 220V power source or to a flush-mounted transformer. Designed for low-pressure pin-based lamps (12V) or for halogen bulbs (220V). The system luminaire uses Steng plug-in system connectors and extension rods: the second modular group in the family: for ceiling mounting or, with a base, for the table top or as a standard uplight. The plug-in contact is suitable only for pin-based 12V low voltage bulbs, offers one-sided or dual-sided light diffusion, and can be swiveled or tilted.

Ökologie/Design Auszeichnung Awarded for Ecology/Design: Vorbildlich durch sparsamen Materialeinsatz, zeitlose Gestaltung und Langlebigkeit. Exemplary for the sparing use of materials, timeless design and durability.

CAMPO, eine Wandleuchte aus der Serie AVANGARDO, die Mastleuchten, Wandleuchten, Lichtpoller, Decken- und Pendelleuchten sowie Bodenstrahler umfaßt. Für Innen- und Außenbereiche. Aufgebaut aus reinen Materialien, mit ungewöhnlicher Formgebung und perfekter Technik.
CAMPO is a wall luminaire in the AVANGARDO family, which includes pole lamps, wall lamps, lighting bollards, ceiling lamps, pendulum lamps and floor uplighters. Campo is ideally suited for both indoor and outdoor use. It is made of high-grade materials, has a striking design and utilizes superior technology.

HERSTELLER MANUFACTURER HESS FORM + LICHT, Villingen-Schwenningen, Germany
PRODUKT PRODUCT AVANGARDO CAMPO, Wandleuchte Wall luminaire
DESIGN Klaus Begasse, Stuttgart, Germany

HERSTELLER MANUFACTURER Siemens AG, Geschäftsgebiet Beleuchtungstechnik, Traunreut, Germany
PRODUKT PRODUCT StATIVE Steh-, Tisch- und Wandleuchtensystem Uplight, table and wall-mounted luminaires
DESIGN Siemens Design, München, Germany

StATIVE, Steh-, Tisch- und Wandleuchten-System, deren gemeinsames Kennzeichen ein Lichtkopf aus Aluminiumstrangpreß-Profilen mit Rillenstruktur ist. Formgebung der Lichtköpfe durch die Konturen der Reflektoren bestimmt. Wahlweise sind die Leuchten mit einem Anteil an dekorativem Direktlicht lieferbar, das durch transluzente Seitenwände fällt. Eine Gabel aus Aluminiumdruckguß dient bei den Stehleuchten als Anbindungselement für den Lichtkopf. Hohe Variabilität, mit der viele Beleuchtungsaufgaben im Innenbereich zu lösen sind.

StATIVE is a line of uplights, table and wall-mounted lights using a striking ribbed extruded aluminium reflector housing. The housing design is defined by the reflector contours. The lights are available as an option as translucent side walls for decorative direct illumination. A two-pronged aluminium fork serves the uplight as a connector for the reflector. The line is suited for all current bulbs, is highly variable and offers solutions for numerous interior lighting questions.

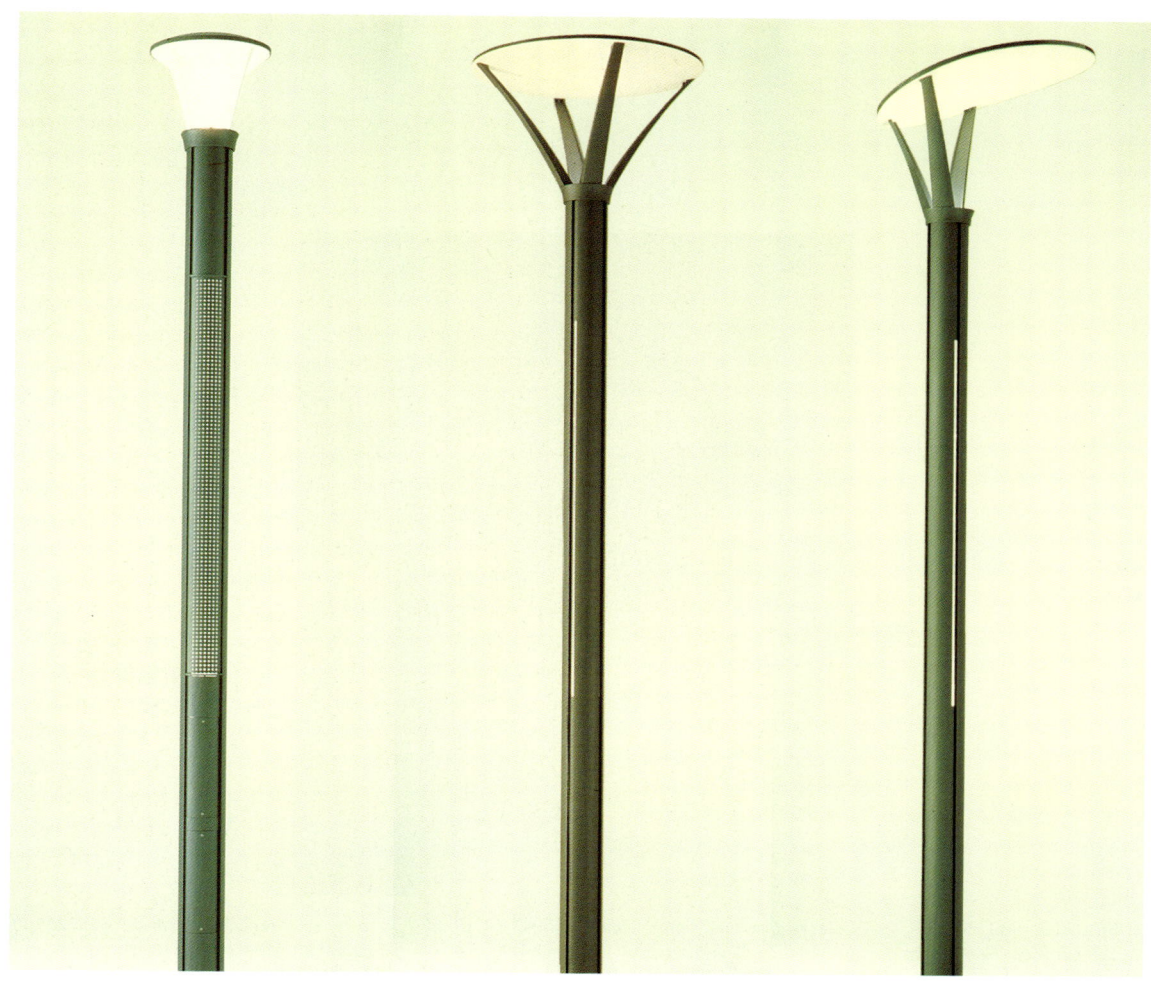

LIGHTCOLUMN, eine Lichtsäule für den Außenbereich. Modular aufgebaut aus Mast und Leuchten. Nach dem Prinzip »verdeckter Lichtquellen« konzipiert: die Lichtquelle befindet sich im unteren Teil des Mastes, das Licht fällt durch verschiedene Öffnungen und Schlitze, die Beleuchtung ist indirekt. Fünf Bauelemente und vier verschiedene Lichtquellen eröffnen viele Wahlmöglichkeiten für Form und Farbe sowie Charakter des Lichts. Ein System für viele architektonische Konzepte.

LIGHTCOLUMN is an outdoor lighting Series: the modular system consists of poles and luminaires. Using the »remote light source« principle, the lamps themselves are positioned in the lower section of the column and light emanates through different openings and slits to provide indirect lighting. The column is made up of five components and four different light sources: offering numerous combinations in terms of form, color, and type of light. A system giving architects' imaginations full rein.

Philips Lightcolumn Lichtsäulen für den Außenbereich Outdoor lighting series
Philips Corporate Design, Eindhoven, The Netherlands
HERSTELLER MANUFACTURER Philips Lighting, Miribel, France
PRODUKT PRODUCT
DESIGN

BELEUCHTUNG LIGHTING 229

HERSTELLER MANUFACTURER AEG Lichttechnik GmbH, Springe, Germany
PRODUKT PRODUCT Stradasole 530 Straßenleuchte Street luminaire
DESIGN Ottenwälder & Ottenwälder, Schwäbisch Gmünd, Germany

STRADASOLE 530, Leuchte für Verkehrsstraßen. Eine formal alternative, in Lichttechnik, Wartung und Montage optimierte technische Leuchte für Straßen und Parkplätze. Gehäuse recyclebar aus glasfaserverstärktem Polyesterharz. Für Ansatz und Aufsatzmontage. Elektrische Komponenten auf werkzeuglos auswechselbarem Elektroblock. Spiegeloptik aus Reinstaluminium, bedampft und klarlackiert. Klare Wanne aus recyclebarem PMMA, schützt vor eindringendem Staub, Feuchtigkeit und Insekten. Zur Bestückung mit Hochdrucklampen, wahlweise mit Leistungsreduzierschaltung. Problemlose Demontage zur Wiederverwertung.

STRADASOLE 530 is a street luminaire. A formal alternative in lighting technology, optimized maintenance and assembly for streets and car parks. The casing is made of recyclable fiberglass-reinforced polyester resin. The supporting structure has a pole plug-in unit and change-over flap. Electrical components on an electric block which can be exchanged without tools. Mirror optics vaporized using high-grade aluminium, and protected by clear varnish. The clear lighting trough is made of recyclable PMMA offers protection against dust, dampness and insects. The unit uses high pressure lamps, optionally with a power reduction switch. Can be easily disassembled for recycling.

BELEUCHTUNG *LIGHTING* 231

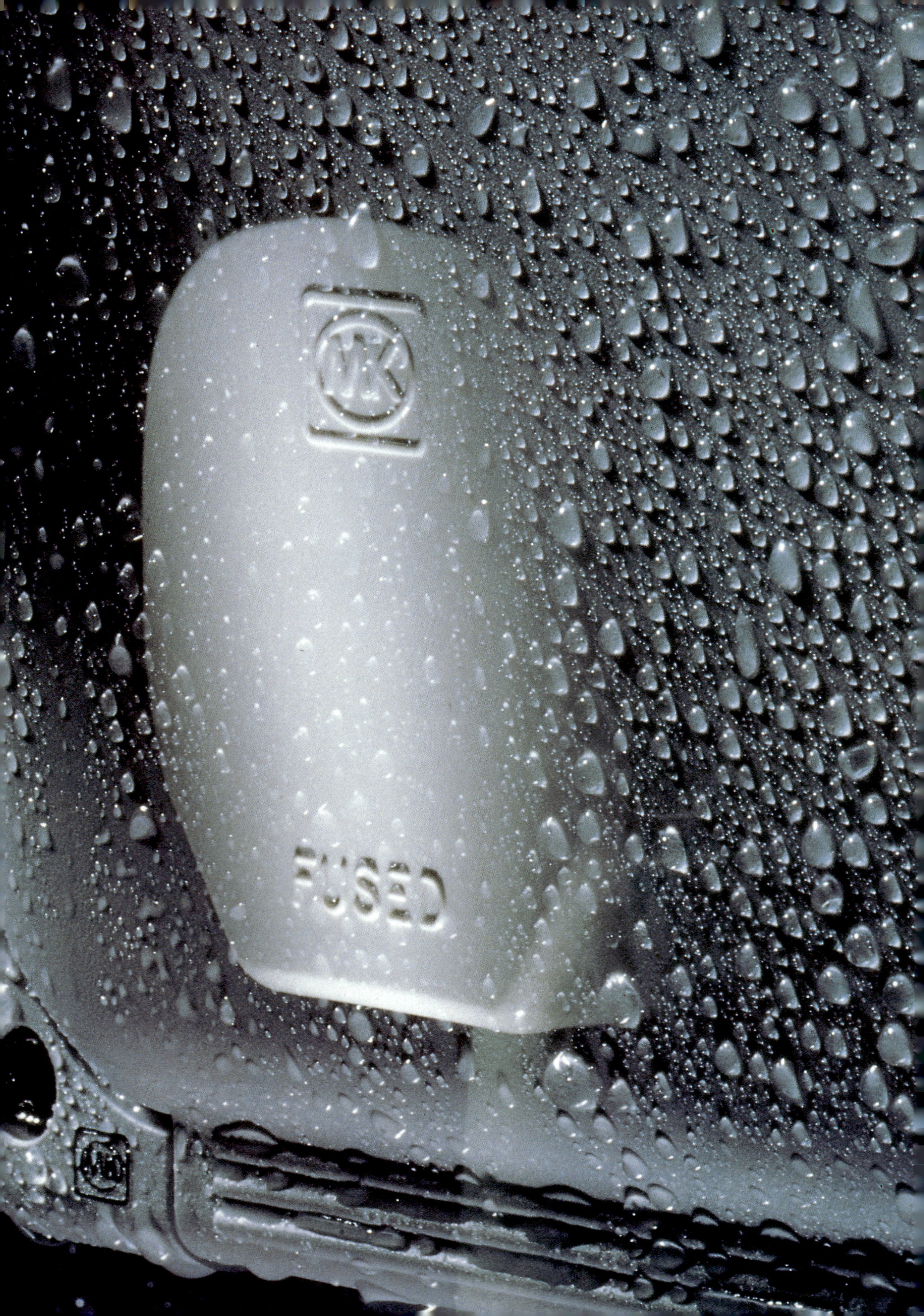
FUSED

haustechnik
house technology

HAUSTECHNIK *HOUSE TECHNOLOGY*

Jury: Christoph Böninger, Horst Diener, Isao Hosoe, Martin Iseli

»An viele Objekte wurde zunächst ein gelber Punkt geklebt, was soviel bedeutet, daß wir die Hintergründe des Produkts erst diskutieren müssen. Mit dem Ökologie-Team haben wir dann viele Aspekte durchgesprochen, viele Ideen diskutiert. Manche Produkte wurden danach grün, manche rot«, berichtet der für die Kategorie Haustechnik zuständige Jury-Leiter Bob Blaich und fährt mit dem generellen Statement fort: »Wir brauchen heute mehr Crossover-Denken zwischen den Leuten«. Haustechnik ist eine ideale Kategorie, wo sich Technologie und Design sinnvoll ergänzen, wenn sie simultan eingesetzt werden. Gleichzeitig ist Haustechnik eine der interessantesten Kategorien, wo sich in dieser Wachstumsbranche Design und technischer Fortschritt hervorragend vereinen.

Ökologiebewußtsein und steigende Energiepreise in Europa machen Einsparungen auf diesem Sektor zum Hauptthema. Steuerungen werden großgeschrieben. Hier sieht man Spitzenleistungen nicht nur in der Technologie, sondern auch parallel in der Formgebung und Interface-Gestaltung.

Intelligente Steuerungen erhalten leicht auswechselbare und ausfahrbare Displays, Heizungs- und Pumpensteuerungen werden gleichzeitig zum Krisenmanagement per Fernbedienung nutzbar, ein neuer Trend, der von der dänischen Firma Grundfos in dieser Auswahl repräsentiert wird. Die Analyse einer Anlage erfolgt einfach über die durch den Einbau einer ferngesteuerten Pumpe erzielbaren Meßwerte. Über eine elektronische, in die Pumpe eingebaute Komponente können Leistungen abgefragt werden, die über den Zustand des gesamten Systems Auskunft geben, eine Qualität, die dann logischerweise wieder in der Kategorie Interface auftaucht und als vorbildliche Lösung Mensch-Maschine-Beziehung ausgezeichnet wurde. Innovationsfähigkeit und Design verbindet auch der Beitrag von Viessmann, der sogar einstimmig in die Spitzenkategorie der Top Ten gewählt wurde. Ausgezeichnet wurde ein Röhrenkollektor, der Sonnenenergie erstmalig über ein architektonisches Brüstungselement speichert.

Generell mutieren ehemals grosse Heizungsanlagen zu kleinen Möbelstücken - reduziert auf die Dimension eines Einbaumöbels. Die Jury legte in diesem, auch produktionstechnisch anspruchsvollen Sektor Wert auf formale Umsetzung und Durchgestaltung bis zur Abkantung eines Bleches. Das Thema Haustechnologie kommuniziert sich in vielfältigen Produkten: Heizstrahlerdecken werden zu architektonischen Elementen, Heizungen für den Badbereich zu dekorativen Schlangen, elektronische Überwachungsanlagen und wohldesignte Service-Stelen zu architektonischen Designelementen, die wie ein Statussymbol zum Einsatz kommen.

»We first stuck a yellow tab on many of the objects, which meant that we needed first to address the background of the respective product. We then discussed many ideas and many aspects with the Ecology Group. After that, some of the products were seen to be green, whereas with others we saw red,« reports Bob Blaich, jury leader responsible for the household technology category. He went on to say somewhat more generally: »Today, we need more crossover thought between different individuals.« House technology is an ideal category in which technology and design complement each other meaningfully if they are only used simultaneously. At the same time, household technology is one of the most interesting categories, as in this growth branch design and technical progress are combining in an excellent way.

The ecological awareness and rising energy prices in Europe have made savings in this sector the main issue. Great attention is given to the right control systems. Here, top achievements have been made not only in technology but also in parallel in design and in interface design.

Intelligent controls are given easily interchangeable and retractable displays, and heating and pump controls can also be used for remote controlled crisis management - a new trend represented in this selection by the Danish firm Grundfos. System analysis can now be readily effected through the measurements outputted by the built-in remote controlled pump. An electronic component installed inside the pump downloads performance data on request, which gives information on the condition of the entire system. This is a feature which logically is also to be found in the Interface category, where it won a prize as an exemplary solution for a human-machine interface. Viessmann's entry also combines a love of innovation with top-notch design: it was unanimously nominated as one of the leading Top Ten. Awards also went to a tubular collector that enabled solar energy to be stored for the first time by means of a balustrade, i.e. part of the building's architecture.

In general, what were once large heating systems have mutated to become small pieces of furniture - reduced to the size of self-assembly furniture. The jury attached great importance in this sector, which is also exacting in terms of production technology, on formal execution and design, right down to the angles of the metal sheeting. The main theme of house technology is communicated by multi-purpose products: ceiling heating radiator elements become architectural components, radiators for the bath area become decorative snakes, electronic surveillance equipment and well-designed service columns become architectural design elements that can be applied almost as status symbols.

arCom TOWER, freistehendes Zugangsterminal als Außenstation, verbindet im Rahmen der Gebäudeautomation Zugangssicherung und audiovisuelle Kommunikation. Enthält Hausklingel, die Kamera zur Videoüberwachung, die Einrichtung zur Audiokommunikation, Steuerungseinrichtung über Tastatur und Zugangskontrolle durch Kartenleser (PIN-Nummer). Kamerabilder können ausgedruckt werden. Für öffentliche und private Gebäude.

The arCom TOWER is an access control system for both indoor and outdoor use in public as well as private buildings. An integral part of building services automation, it combines access control and audiovisual communication. The tower comprises a buzzer, a surveillance camera, an intercom, and a control panel; access is controlled via a card reader and PIN number. The video images can also be printed out.

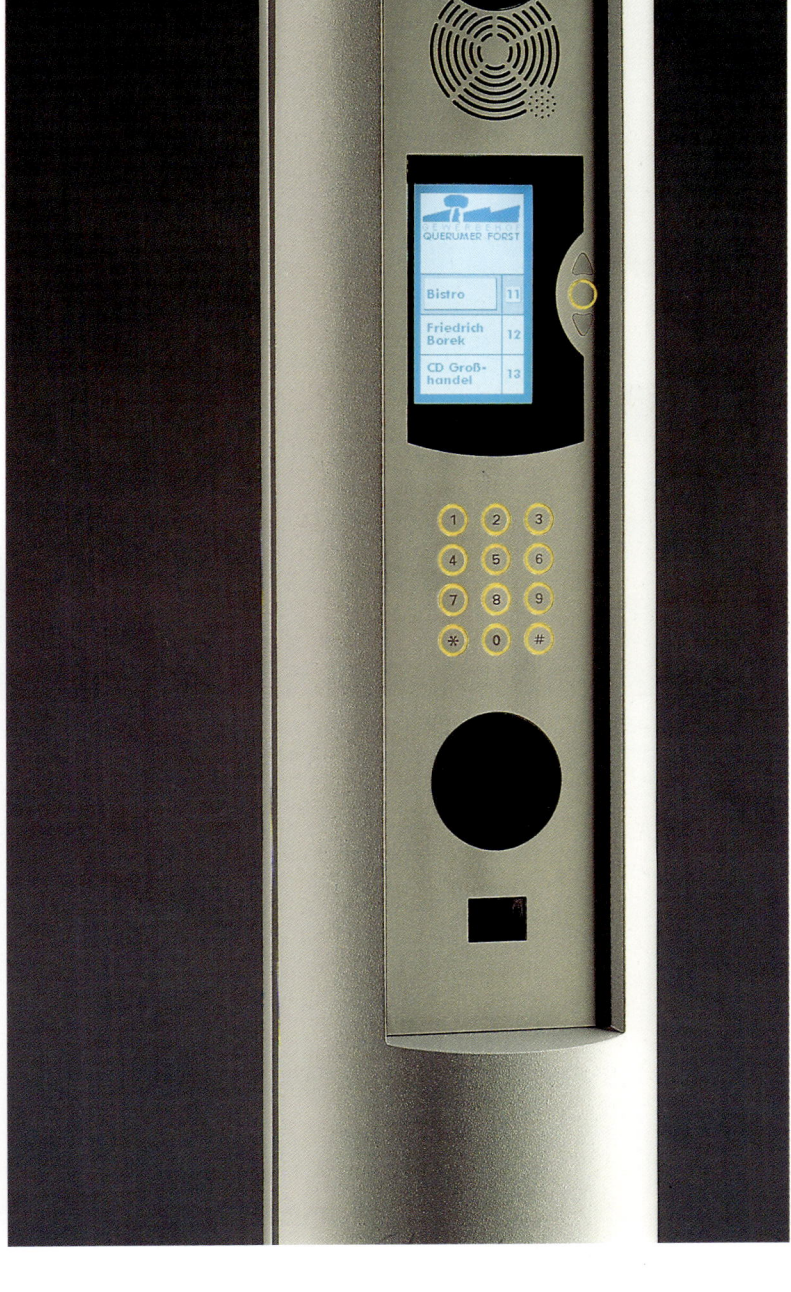

HERSTELLER MANUFACTURER arCom Gesellschaft für Zugangssicherungssysteme mbH, Braunschweig, Germany
PRODUKT PRODUCT arCom tower Zugangssicherungssystem Access control system
DESIGN Prof. Bitsch & Partner, Düsseldorf, Germany

HAUSTECHNIK *HOUSE TECHNOLOGY* 235

HERSTELLER MANUFACTURER Siemens Aktiengesellschaft, Berlin - München, Germany
PRODUKT PRODUCT SIGMASYS Brandmelder Fire detector
DESIGN Siemens Design, Theo Gonser, München, Germany

SIGMASYS, Brandmelder zur Früherkennung von Bränden. Einfache Montage und Wartung. Neuheit: der Anschluß erfolgt mittels Schneidklemmen.

Das reduzierte unauffällige Design ermöglicht eine Verwendung in jedem Raum. Blinkender Alarmindikator. Material: Kunststoff. Farbe: weiß.

The SIGMASYS is a device for advance fire-detection. It is easy to assemble and service, and is now mounted by means of intersecting clamps - a new feature.

The reduced, discreet design means the unit can be installed in any room. The synthetic white casing features a flashing alarm indicator.

F 2000, ein tragbarer Feuerlöscher. Attraktives formschönes Design mit richtungsweisender Technik: der kompakte Behälter aus Kunststoffschalen schützt das Ventil und den Druckkörper für 6 kg umweltverträgliches Löschpulver (Brandklasse A, B, C; entspricht der Norm EN-3). Sicherheitsfach im Standfuß kann Rauchschutzmaske, Löschdecke oder Erste-Hilfe-Set aufnehmen. Hoher Trage- und Bedienkomfort. Optionaler akustischer Rauchmelder. Hohe Lebensdauer, trenn- und recyclebare Bauteile.

F 2000 is a portable fire extinguisher which sports a highly elegant design as well as pioneering technology. The compact container, with its plastic casing, protects the valve and the pressure hull housing 6 kg of environmentally-friendly extinguishing powder (fire classification A, B, and C, which corresponds to the industrial standard EN-3). A safety compartment in the base can be used to store smoke protection masks, a fire-proof blanket, or a first-aid kit; a smoke alarm is optional. The design of the extinguisher provides for comfort during transport and use and a long service life, with components that can be sorted and recycled.

HERSTELLER MANUFACTURER GLORIA-Werke H. Schulte-Frankenfeld GmbH & Co., Wadersloh, Germany
PRODUKT PRODUCT F 2000 Feuerlöscher Fire extinguisher
DESIGN BEST. Büro für Produktplanung, Roland Cölln, Markus Scholemann, Wuppertal, Germany

HAUSTECHNIK HOUSE TECHNOLOGY 237

HERSTELLER MANUFACTURER BTicino S.p.A., Milano, Italy
PRODUKT PRODUCT Light Hausautomationssystem Home automation system
DESIGN Guiseppe Zecca, Milano, Italy
VERTRIEB DISTRIBUTION Seko - BTicino, Freiburg, Germany

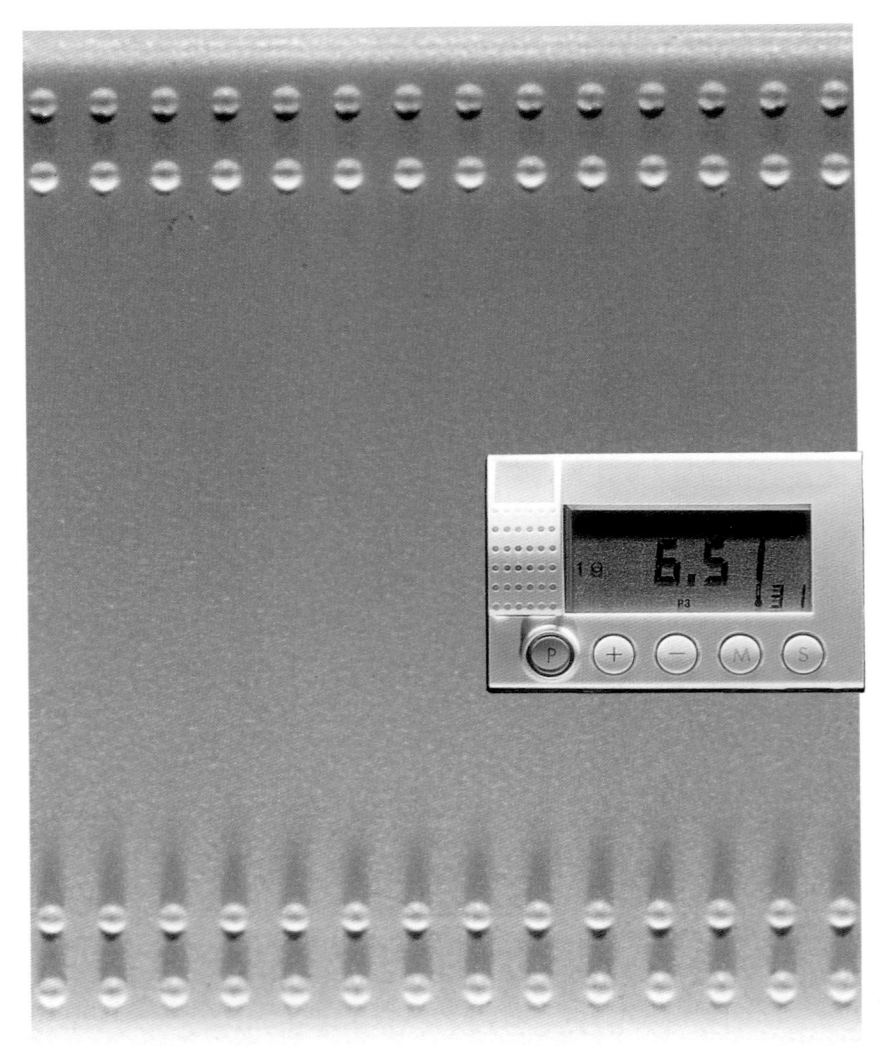

LIGHT ist ein Hausautomationssystem, das mit verschiedenartigen, für jedes Objekt individuell auszuwählenden Komponenten Funktionen wie Schalten, Überwachen, Steuern, Informieren und Kommunizieren erfüllt. In einzelnen Räumen und im ganzen Gebäude einzusetzen.
LIGHT is a home automation system that can perform functions such as turning things on and off, monitoring, operating, informing and communicating based on a wide range of components. The latter can be individually selected for the device at hand. It can be used for single rooms or entire buildings.

ELBIT CTV, ein drahtloses TV-Überwachungssystem für max. vier Kameras. Set besteht aus einer Multifunktionsfernbedienung (schaltet auch die Kameras ein), Trigggereinheit (empfängt die Bedienungssignale und übermittelt sie per Infrarot an die Überwachungskamera), Überwachungskamera mit Bildsender (für Innen- und Außenbereiche), Überwachungsantenne und Watch-TV mit Empfangseinheit. Bei Aktivierung der Kamera erscheint das Überwachungsbild für jeweils 10 Sekunden auf dem Bildschirm und überblendet das eingeschaltete TV-Programm, während der Ton weiterläuft. Drahtlose, einfache Montage. Stromsparfunktion durch das Verfahren der Fernbedienung, bei Batteriebetrieb lange Betriebsdauer (3-6 Monate).

ELBIT CTV is a remote-control TV surveillance system for a maximum of four surveillance cameras. The set features a multifunctional remote control unit, which can also switch on the cameras. It also includes a relay unit, which receives the signal from the remote control device and transmits it to the surveillance cameras using an IR frequency; a surveillance camera with an image transmitter (for indoor and outdoor use); an antenna; and a television with a receiving device. When the camera is activated, an image of the surveillance area appears on the screen for 10 seconds at a time. The current TV program fades into the background while the sound continues. The unit is cordless and can be easily installed. The remote control technology saves electricity, and in battery operation mode, the system can run for three to six months.

HERSTELLER MANUFACTURER ELBIT CTV, Migdal Haemek, Israel
PRODUKT PRODUCT WATCH TV TV-Überwachungssystem Surveillance camera and system
DESIGN Raved Designs, Herzliya Pituach, Isreal

HAUSTECHNIK *HOUSE TECHNOLOGY* 239

HERSTELLER MANUFACTURER Hüppe Form GmbH, Oldenburg, Germany
PRODUKT PRODUCT Sonnenblendschutz Sun blind
DESIGN Hüppe Form, Oldenburg, Germany

SONNENBLENDSCHUTZ, ein neuartiges System für Beschattung und Lichtgestaltung in Büroräumen, insbesondere aber für Bildschirmarbeitsplätze. Ein nachgeführtes Lamellensystem reflektiert das direkt einstrahlende Sonnenlicht wie ein optischer Filter, das diffuse Tageslicht dagegen wird über parabolisch ausgeformte, einseitig verspiegelte Umlenklamellen in die Raumtiefe geleitet. Vereint Hitze- und Blendschutz mit gezielter Lichtlenkung. Schafft leistungsfördernde Arbeitsbedingungen ohne Kunstlicht, spart Energiekosten für Beleuchtung und Klimatisierung. Klares Design unterstreicht die Verbindung von Transparenz und Funktionalität.

SUN BLIND is a new system for handling light and shade in office areas, especially for PC workstations. Solar-tracking prismatic slats reflect direct sunlight like an optical filter, while diffuse daylight is guided further into the room via parabolic deflecting slats with a reflective coating on one side. The system combines heat and dazzle protection with precise light deflection. Creating work-enhancing daylight conditions in the office, saving energy costs for illuminations and air conditioning. The clear design emphasizes the link between transparency and functionality.

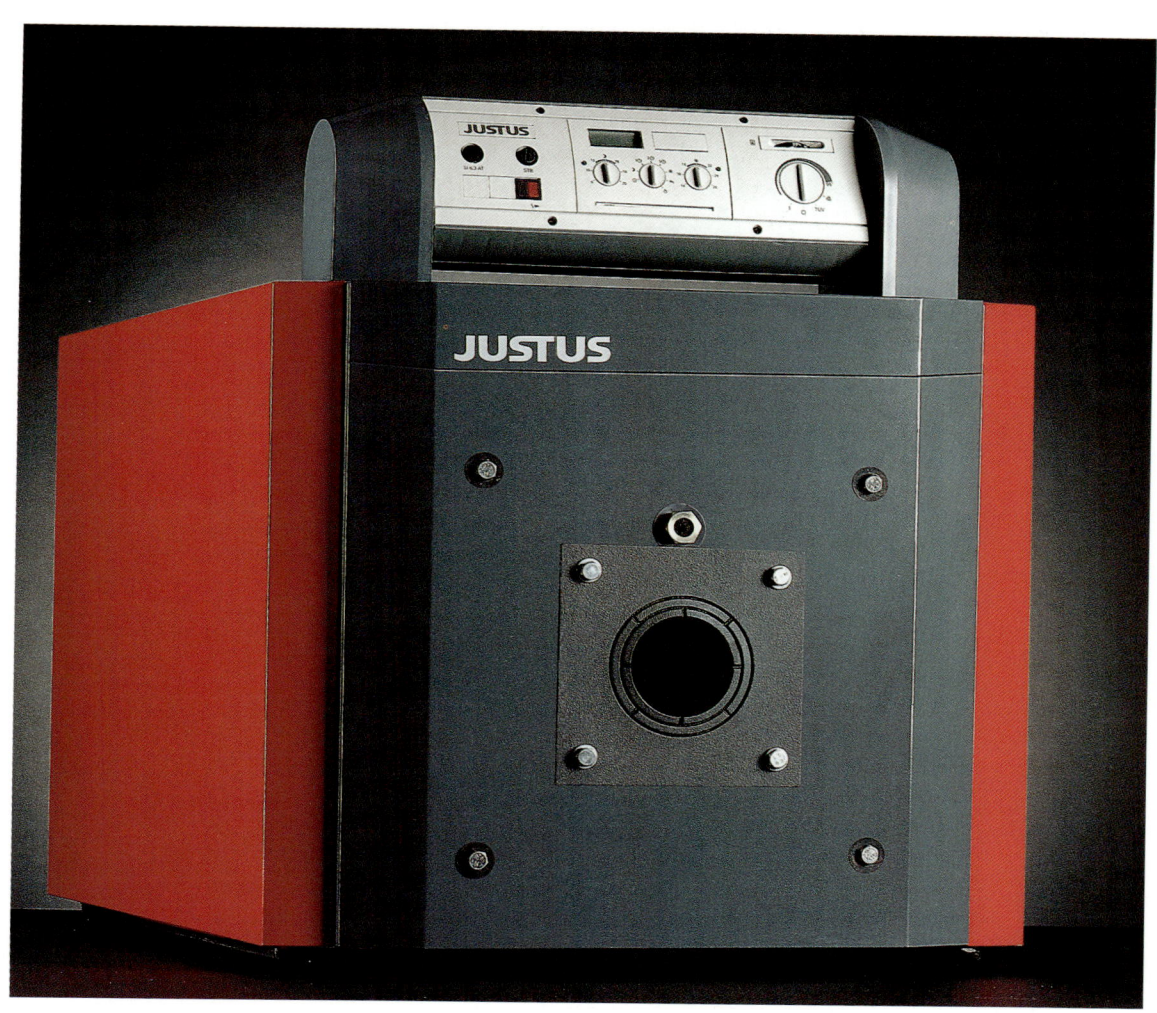

EUTECTOTHERM KN, ein Gußheizkessel für den Niedertemperaturbereich mit bewährtem Dreizug-System. Einfache Handhabung der witterungsgeführten elektronischen Steuerung Justus Control. Energiesparender und umweltschonender Betrieb. Charakteristisch die funktionale Gesamtgestaltung der Justus-Produktreihe.

The EUTECTOTERM KN is a cast-iron boiler for low-temperature applications using the proven three-pass system. The electronic, climate-regulated Justus Control is easy to operate, saves energy and is gentle on the environment. Like the functional overall design of the unit, the controls are characteristic of the Justus product line.

eutectotherm kn   Gußheizkessel für den Niedertemperaturbereich Heating boiler   Justus GmbH, Gladenbach, Germany   HERSTELLER MANUFACTURER
designpraxis diener, Ulm, Germany   PRODUKT PRODUCT
DESIGN

HERSTELLER MANUFACTURER BAUFA-WERKE GmbH, Menden, Germany
PRODUKT PRODUCT BAUFA San Line® Deckenstrahlplatten Ceiling mounted radiators
DESIGN BAUFA-WERKE GmbH; Menden, Germany

BAUFA San Line® Deckenstrahlplatten, die ideale Großraumheizung, zum Beispiel für Sport-, Ausstellungs-, Flugzeug-, Lager oder Fertigungshallen; auch für Kirchen, Garagen etc. Lassen sich auch zum Belüften und, im Sommer, zur Kühlung einsetzen. Mit ihrer klaren, glatten Linienführung und den nicht sichtbaren Aufhängevorrichtungen fügen sich die Strahlplatten in alle Deckenkonstruktionen.

BAUFA San Line® ceiling mounted radiators are ideal for heating large spaces, such as gymnasiums, exhibition halls, hangars, warehouses or production plants, as well as for churches, garages, etc. They can also double up as ventilators and, in summer, as cooling units. With their clear, smooth design and cleverly concealed brackets, the radiators fit in flush with all ceiling constructions.

242 HAUSTECHNIK HOUSE TECHNOLOGY

Ökologie/Design Auszeichnung Awarded for Ecology/Design: Vorbildlich durch funktionsintegriertes Heizen und Kühlen, systembedingte Energieeffizienz und Fertigung aus nur einem Material. Exemplary for its integrated heating and cooling functions, the system-based efficient use of engery and the use of only one material.

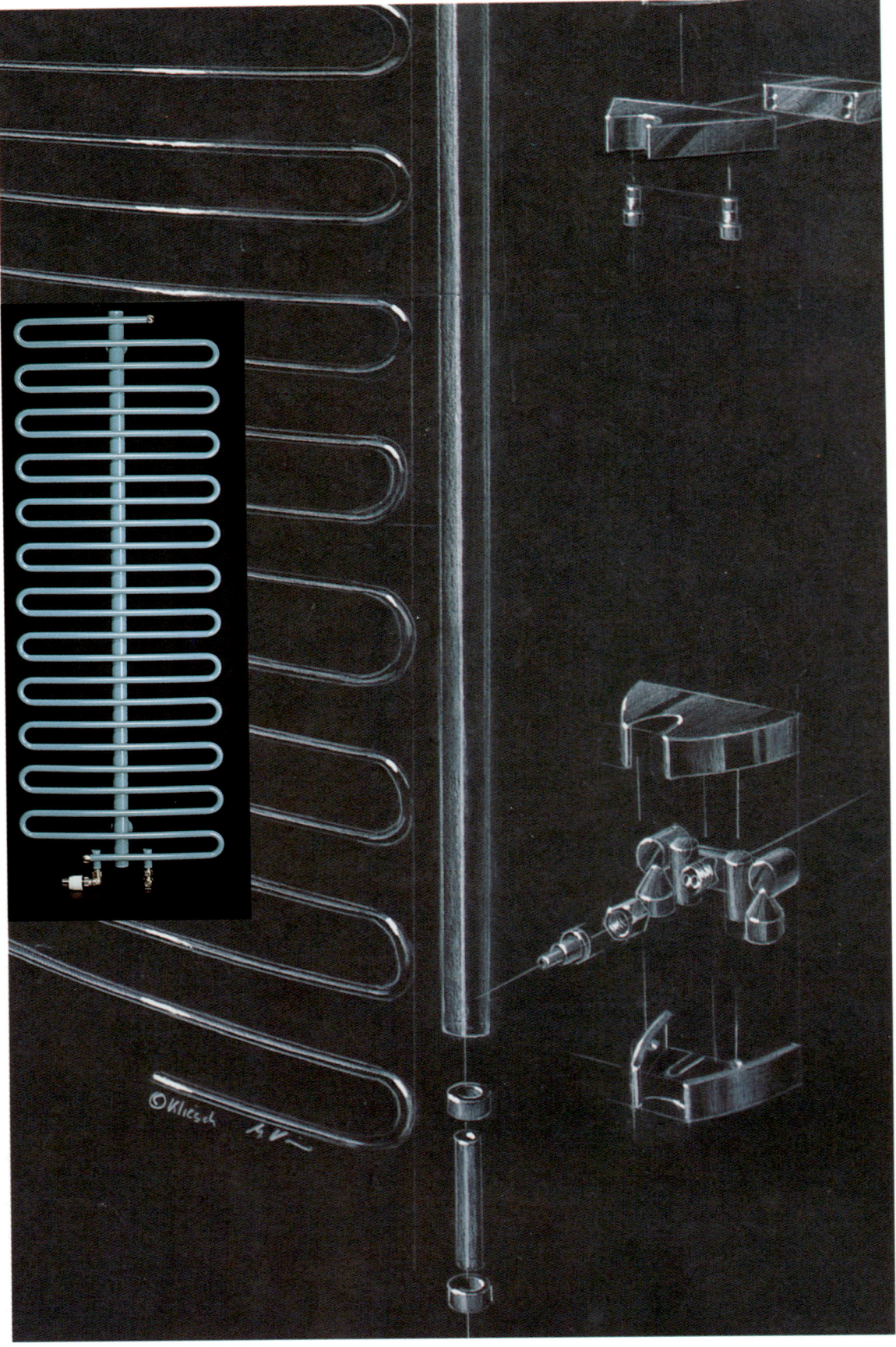

HERSTELLER MANUFACTURER Arbonia AG, Arbon, Switzerland
PRODUKT PRODUCT COBRATHERM R Heizkörper Radiator
DESIGN Arbonia Helmuth Amann, Arbon, Switzerland, Martin Kliesch Industrial Designer, Wuppertal, Germany

COBRATHERM, neuartiger Heizkörper für Badezimmer, auf dem sich auch Handtücher trocknen lassen. Schlangenförmige Heizrohre machen das Einhängen der Handtücher besonders einfach. Betrieb über Zentralheizung oder elektrisch.

COBRATHERM is a novel bathroom radiator which can also be used to dry towels. The open-ended serpentine rail makes towels especially easy to hang. The device can be electrically powered or part of the central heating system.

244 HAUSTECHNIK *HOUSE TECHNOLOGY*

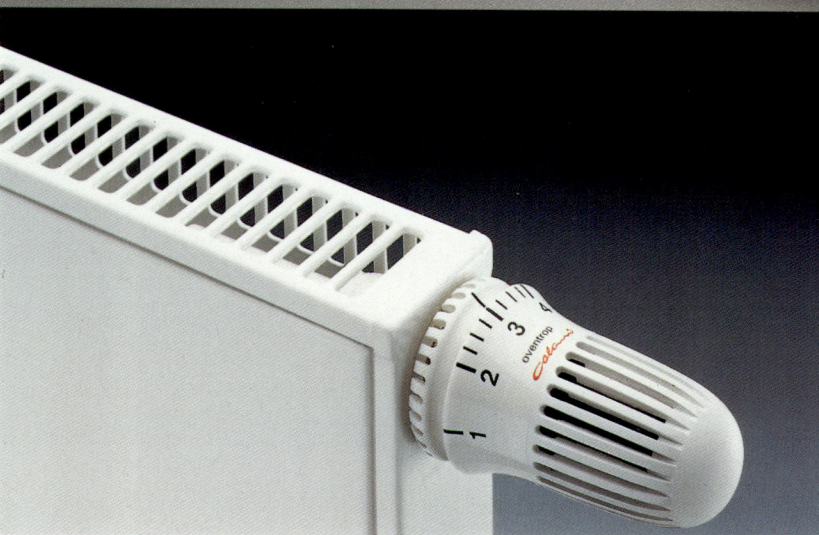

F. W. Oventrop KG, Olsberg, Germany — HERSTELLER MANUFACTURER
Uni C Thermostat zur Temperaturregelung Thermostat for temperature control — PRODUKT PRODUCT
C. D. B. The Agency C. D. G. Prof. Luigi Colani, Köln, Germany — DESIGN

UNI C, Thermostat zur energiesparenden Temperaturregelung von Heizkörpern. Ergonomische Gestaltung, gut ablesbare Einstellwerte. Verwendete Kunststoffe (ASA und Polyamid) gekennzeichnet und recyclebar.

UNI C is an energy-saving thermostat with an ergonomic design as well as settings that are easy to read. The respective parts are labeled with the names of the recyclable plastics used (ASA und polyamide).

HAUSTECHNIK *HOUSE TECHNOLOGY*

HERSTELLER MANUFACTURER NRG Enterprises, Mercer Island, USA
PRODUKT PRODUCT Mistra Frischwasserfilter Fresh water filter
DESIGN ZIBA Design, Portland, USA

MISTRA Frischwasserfilter für den Hausgebrauch. Anders als Filter mit Filterwasserbehälter liefert Mistra gefiltertes Wasser bei Bedarf. Seine Bedienung ist so einfach wie das Betätigen eines Wasserhahns. Werkzeuglose Installation, vertikale und horizontale Wandmontage möglich. Eventuelle Verrohrung kann im Innern des Geräts verschwinden.

Unlike filters with a water container, MISTRA is a household fresh water filter which supplies water as needed. It is as easy to use as turning on a faucet, and can be fixed to the wall without tools either vertically or horizontally. Piping can be concealed inside the device.

HERSTELLER MANUFACTURER Max Weishaupt GmbH, Schwendi, Germany
PRODUKT PRODUCT Weishaupt Thermo Condens Brennwertgerät Heating unit
DESIGN TEAMS · SLANY DESIGN, Esslingen, Germany

WTC, ein Brennwertgerät, entwickelt zur Beheizung von Ein- und Mehrfamilienhäusern. Geringe Abmessungen und schlichtes Design erlauben den Einbau in unterschiedliche Umgebungen. Gehäuse aus pulverbeschichtetem Blech. Mit dem Design anderer Weishaupt-Geräte durch die markante vertikale Nut verbunden. Im unteren Bereich der Frontabdeckung befindet sich ein Kunststoffteil mit integrierter Fingermulde, das die Bedienebene mit grafischer Benutzerführung abdeckt.

The WTC Weishaupt Thermo Condens was developed to heat houses and apartment buildings. With its compact dimensions and straightforward design, it blends in with a variety of surroundings. The housing is made of powder-coated sheet metal, and sports the clearly defined vertical slot characteristic of Weishaupt gas units. The lower part of the front cover features a molded plastic grip for access to the controls, which are labeled with functional symbols for user-friendly operation.

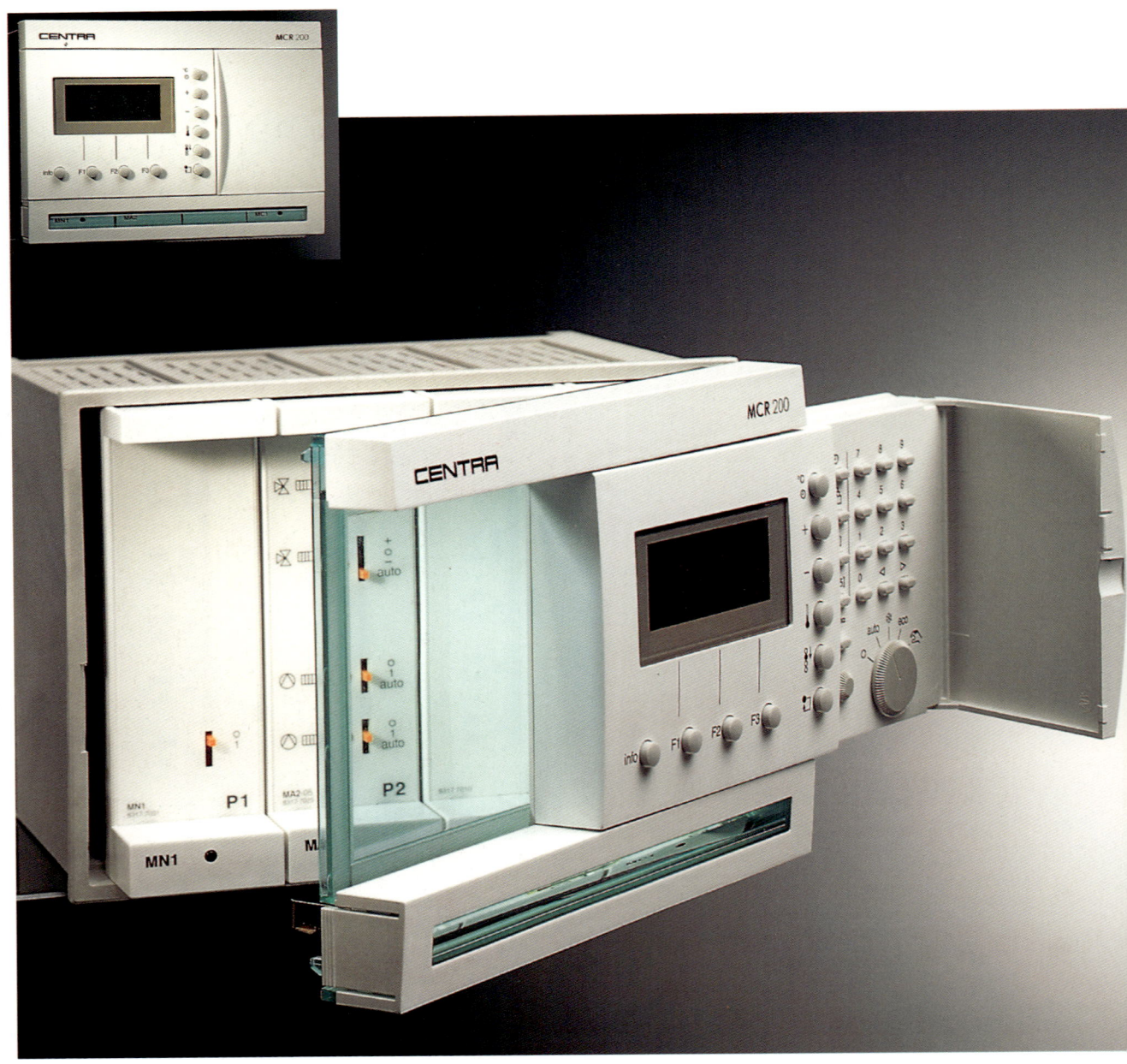

HERSTELLER MANUFACTURER CENTRA-BÜRKLE GmbH, Schönaich, Germany
PRODUKT PRODUCT MCR 200 Regelsystem Control system
DESIGN schroerdesign, Karlsruhe, Germany

MCR 200, ein Regelsystem für Anwendungen in der Heizungs- und Raumlufttechnik in mittelgroßen Gebäuden. Bietet mit der Möglichkeit der Telekommunikation: Informationsübertragung per Telefontastatur und Telefax für die Ferndiagnose, die Voraussetzungen für kostengünstige Wartung. Die Funktionsmodule sind steck- und austauschbar, womit das System für größere Anlagen erweiterungsfähig ist. Das menügeführte Display erlaubt jederzeit den unkomplizierten manuellen Eingriff über nur wenige Tasten.

The MCR 200 is a control system handling heating, ventilation and air-conditioning systems in medium-sized buildings. It features a telecommunications capability, offering data transfer via touch-tone phones and faxes, enabling remote diagnosis and cost-saving maintenance. Function modules fit in slots and can be removed easily, allowing system expansion as required. The interactive display provides constant manual operability by means of a minimum of keys.

Nisko ARDAN GROUP, Holon, Israel — HERSTELLER MANUFACTURER
Flush + Surface Mounting Electrical Enclosure Schaltkasten Fuse and switch box — PRODUKT PRODUCT
Raved Designs, Herzliya Pituach, Isreal — DESIGN

Ein SICHERUNGSKASTEN, der zur Unter- und Aufputzmontage in Wohnhäusern, Bürogebäuden und Industrieanlagen gleichermaßen geeignet ist. Drei Grundtypen, modulare Konzeption, darum geringe Produktionskosten. Abdeckung transparent oder durchsichtig. Schlichte Formgebung paßt sich ohne zusätzliche Abdeckung in verschiedene Umgebungen ein. Montage mit einem eigens entwickelten Kunststoff-Spritzwerkzeug, das so konstruiert ist, daß der Kasten mit und ohne Bund abzuspritzen ist, wenn das Insert gewechselt wird.

This FUSE and SWITCH BOX is equally suitable for flush and surface mounting in residential and office buildings as well as industrial facilities. The three basic types are all modular in design, and thus can be produced at low cost. The doors are transparent or opaque. The straightforward design blends with various surroundings and thus does not need to be concealed. The unit can be mounted with a plastic injection molding die developed expressly for this purpose. The die is constructed so that the peripheral ring needed to flush-mount the unit can be added simply by changing an insert.

HAUSTECHNIK HOUSE TECHNOLOGY 249

HERSTELLER MANUFACTURER Wallace & Tiermann GmbH, Günzburg, Germany
PRODUKT PRODUCT V 10 K Chlordosieranlage Chlorinator
DESIGN TEUFEL DESIGN, Ulm, Germany

V 10 K, Anlage zur Chlordosierung, die unter Verwendung erprobter und zuverlässiger Bauteile völlig neu gestaltet wurde. Die Designaufgabe wurde durch eine sinnvollere Anordnung des Funktionsablaufs im Inneren gelöst, die dann die Neukonzeption des Frontgehäuses ermöglichte. Alle für den Benutzer wichtigen Funktionen wurden gestalterisch hervorgehoben. Sauberes Erscheinungsbild auch bei Reihenschaltung mehrerer Geräte.
V 10 K is a chlorinator which features proven, reliable components in a completely novel design. All functional parts are located inside the device, allowing the casing to be designed in an user-friendly way1. The result is a tidy, attractive appearance, even when a number of chlorinators are used at once.

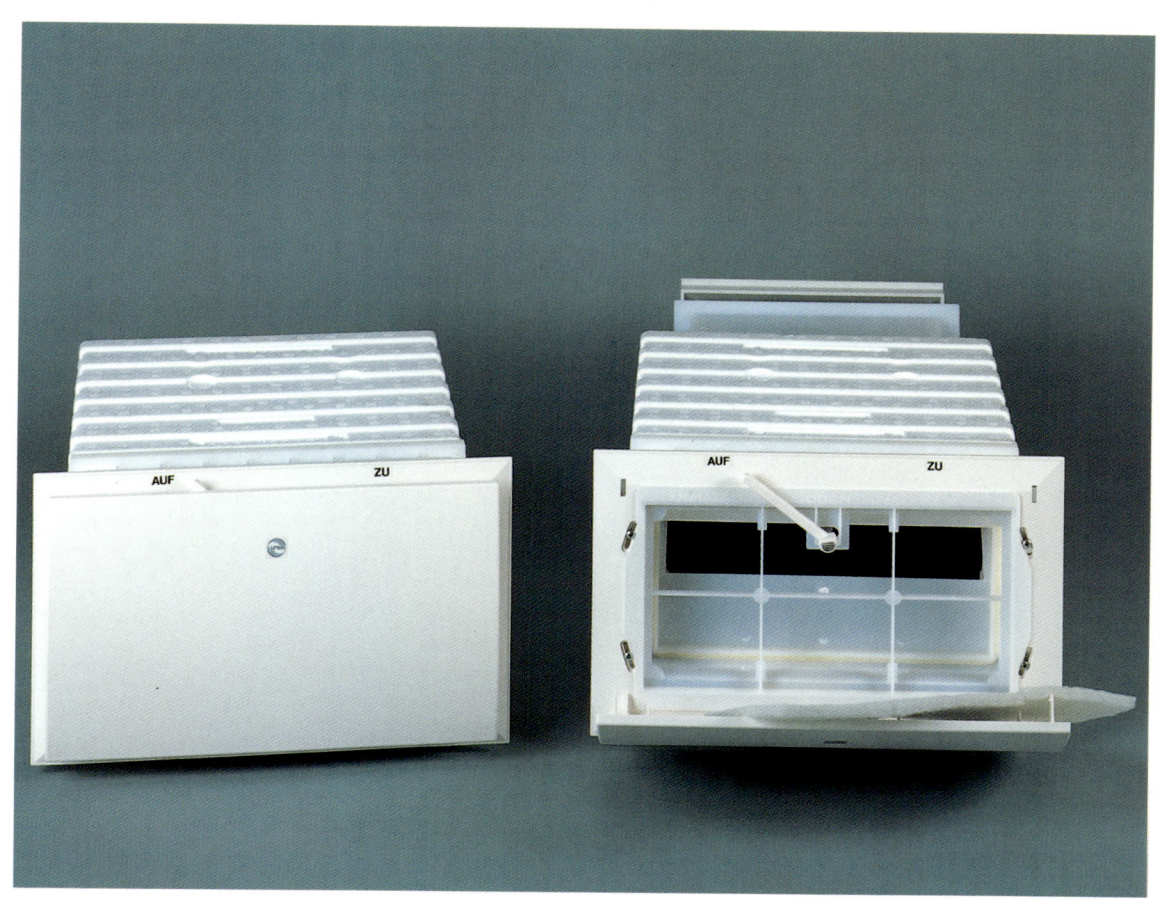

LUNOS-Lüftung GmbH & Co. Ventilatoren KG, Berlin, Germany HERSTELLER MANUFACTURER
ALD Außenwand-Luftdurchlaß Outside wall vent PRODUKT PRODUCT
LUNOS, Berlin, Germany DESIGN

LUNOS ALD, Außenwand-Luftdurchlass zur maschinellen und freien Lüftung von Schlaf- Wohn- und Arbeitsräumen. Einbau im Bereich dichtschließender Fenster. Die wartungsarme, überwiegend aus Kunststoffteilen aufgebaute Konstruktion erlaubt die bedarfsgerechte und zugfreie Zuführung frischer Außenluft bei optimaler Schall- und Wärmedämmung. Attraktive Gestaltung der sichtbaren Teile.

The LUNOS ALD is an outside wall vent which affords machine-generated or natural ventilation for bedrooms, living rooms or workrooms. It can be installed near tightly closing windows. The low-maintenance mainly plastic construction provides fresh air as needed without creating drafts, is optimally insulated against noise and heat loss. The visible parts of the vent sport an attractive design.

HAUSTECHNIK *HOUSE TECHNOLOGY* 251

GRUNDFOS, Bjerringbro, Denmark   HERSTELLER MANUFACTURER
AP 35 Abwasserpumpe Waste water pump   PRODUKT PRODUCT
GRUNDFOS, Bjerringbro, Denmark   DESIGN

252 HAUSTECHNIK *HOUSE TECHNOLOGY*

AP 35, Abwasserpumpe aus rostfreiem Stahl. Geringes Gewicht erlaubt einfaches Verrücken der Pumpe. Glatte Oberflächen zur leichten Reinigung. Details wie die besonders gestaltete Kabeleinführung oder die Montage der Bodenplatte erleichtern den Service.
AP 35 is a stainless steel waste water pump. Its lightweight construction facilitates moving the pump, while smooth surfaces make it easy to clean. Details such as the specially designed cable entry or the way in which the base plate is mounted ensure straightforward servicing.
GRUNDFOS Controller R 100, ein Gerät zur drahtlosen Zwei-Wege-Kommunikation mit der Heizungsanlage. Verbindet Fernbedienung, intelligente Pumpen, Kreiselpumpen, Normmotoren etc. des Grundfos-Systems.
The GRUNDFOS Controller R 100 provides cordless two-way communication between the remote control unit and the heating system. It can be used with smart pumps, Grundfos standard motors, centrifugal pumps etc.

HERSTELLER MANUFACTURER
GRUNDFOS, Bjerringbro, Denmark
PRODUKT PRODUCT
R 100 Kommunikationseinheit Communication unit
DESIGN
GRUNDFOS, Bjerringbro, Denmark

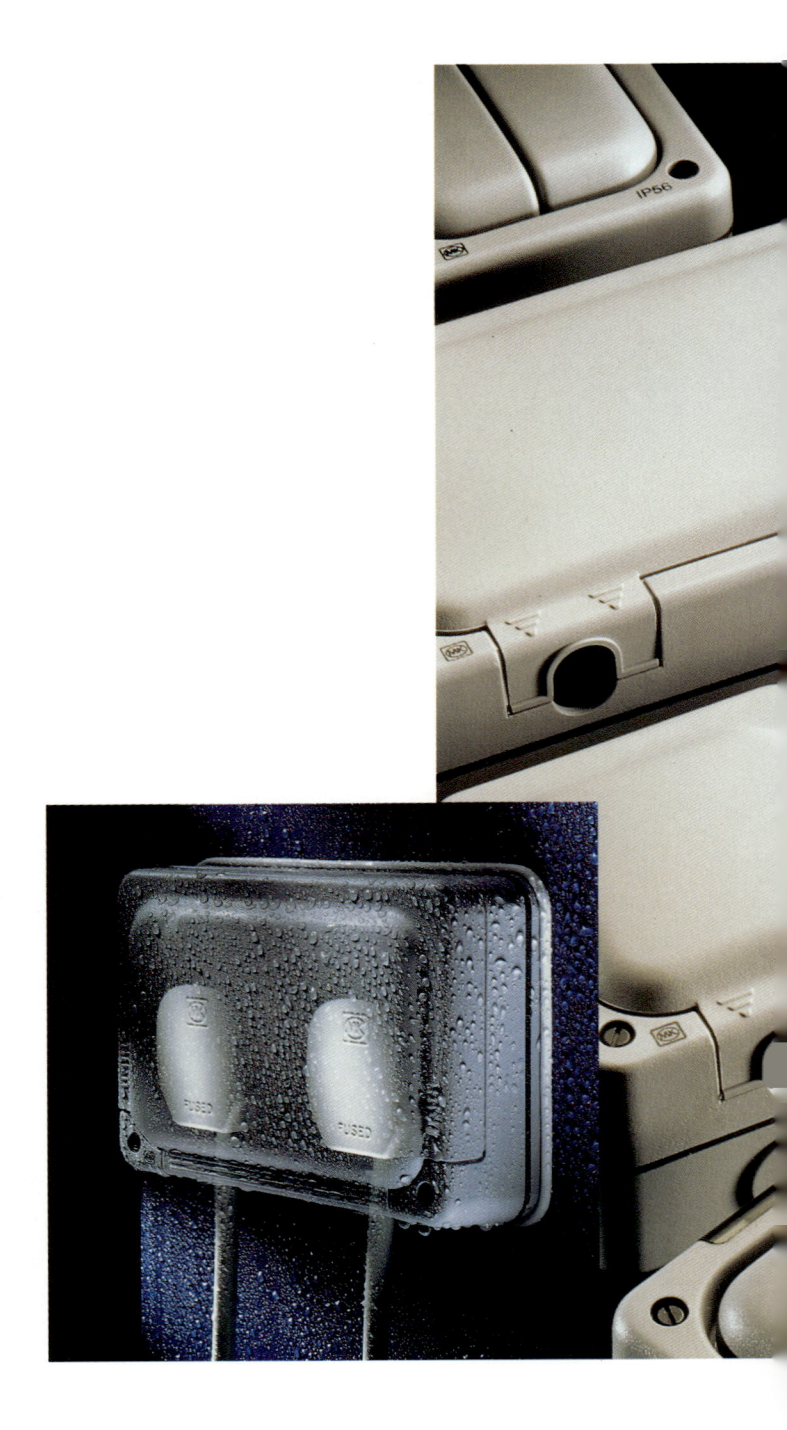

HERSTELLER MANUFACTURER CARADON M.K. ELECTRIC LTD., Basildon, Great Britain
PRODUKT PRODUCT M.K. MASTERSEAL Stecker und Schalter Waterproof switches and sockets
DESIGN APEX PRODUCT DESIGN, London, Great Britain, CARADON M.K. ELECTRIC, Basildon, Great Britain

254 HAUSTECHNIK *HOUSE TECHNOLOGY*

MASTERSEAL, eine Serie von Schaltern und Steckdosen, die eigens für extrem feuchte und staubige Umgebungen entwickelt wurden und entsprechend hohen Schutz (bis IP 55) bieten. Gleichzeitig so konzipiert, daß sie sich mit sämtlichen BS-Steckern und verschiedenen Kabelquerschnitten verbinden lassen.

MASTERSEAL is a series of electrical switches and sockets that were specially developed for use in damp, dusty surroundings and thus offer a correspondingly high degree of protection (up to IP 55). At the same time, they have been designed to take any BS plug as well as a variety of cable sizes.

VIRTUAL i·O
PERSONAL DISPLAY SYSTEMS

freizeit
leisure

FREIZEIT *LEISURE*

Jury: Christoph Böninger, Horst Diener, Isao Hosoe, Martin Iseli

»Im dritten Jahrtausend wird Design ein Ausdruck totaler Lebensqualität sein«, prognostiziert Isao Hosoe, der japanische Wahl-Italiener, Designer und Juror im diesjährigen iF-Wettbewerb. Trotz Dominanz von Technologie und rationalem Wissenschaftsdenken dürften die menschlichen Werte nicht vernachlässigt werden, vor allem müsse sich das Thema Zeit in Zukunft innerhalb der Gesellschaft neu definieren. Damit spricht Isao Hosoe die immer fließender werdenden Übergänge zwischen Arbeitswelt und Freizeit an. Freizeit bildet, wie die Gruppe Büro, schon rein quantitativ einen der größten Sektoren in der diesjährigen Auswahl. Bei einem ebenfalls fliessenden Übergang von professionellem und privatem Nutzen spielt das durch Design erzeugte Qualitätskriterium eine markante Rolle. Professionalisierung und höchster Qualitätsanspruch sind in diesem stark wettbewerbsorientierten Markt unübersehbar.

Ein Symptom für das nahtlose Zusammenwachsen von Arbeit und Freizeit ist das Zusammenwachsen von Fernsehen und Computer in neuen multimedialen Anwendungen. Einen Schwerpunkt des prämierten Designs bieten daher Produkte dieser Zukunftsbranchen, die den Quantensprung zur Digitaltechnologie vollzogen haben. »Wir werden in Zukunft diesen Trend auf der »CeBIT home« zu einem modernen Messethema machen. Die »CeBIT home« trägt dem Zusammenwachsen der Fernsehtechnik, der »braunen Ware«, mit Computern Rechnung. Multimediaanwendungen ermöglichen den breiten Einsatz von Informationstechnik im Haushalt. Das umfaßt Homebanking ebenso wie Reisebuchungen bis hin zu sehr breiten Anwendungen sämtlicher Officetätigkeiten von zuhause aus«, so umschreibt Ernst Raue in seiner Doppelfunktion als iF-Vorsitzender und Bereichsleiter der Hannover Messe die sich verändernde Medienwelt, die die fließenden Grenzen zwischen Arbeit und Freizeit neu artikulieren wird. In der Zukunftsbranche Unterhaltungselektronik wurden nicht nur adäquat gestaltete neue Gerätefunktionen ausgezeichnet, sondern auch ein leicht recyclebares Fernsehgerät.

Generell fungiert Design in der Sparte Freizeit nach wie vor zur Erzeugung von Statussymbolen, wie die ausgezeichneten Sonnenbrillen, Reisegepäckstücke und Uhren zeigen.

"In the third millennium design will be an expression of total quality of life," forecasts Isao Hosoe, a Japanese designer resident in Italy who was a juror in the this year's iF competition. Despite the predominance of technology and rational scientific thought, the products were expected not to neglect human values, above all in order to redefine the issue of time in future within society. Isao Hosoe refers of course to the ever more fluid division between the world of work and leisure time. The Leisure category, like the Office category, was in quantitative terms already one of the largest sectors in the this year's selection. Given a likewise fluid border-line between professional and private uses, the standard of quality generated by the design played a leading role in the jury's work. Professionalization and the highest quality expectations are pronounced in this fiercely competitive market.

A symptom for the seamless convergence of work and leisure time is the combination of televisions and computers in new multimedia applications. One focal point of the award-winning designs was thus products for this future sector, products which have taken the quantum leap into digital technology. "We will in future be making this trend a modern trade fair theme at the 'CeBIT home'. The 'CeBIT home' takes into account the way TV technology, the 'brown boxes', is starting to blend with computers. Multimedia applications make possible the broad utilization of information technology in the home. This will include homebanking, travel reservations, right up to broad applications such as all the usual office work functions." This is how Ernst Raue, in his dual role as iF Chairman and Division Head of the Hannover Trade Fair describes the changing media world, which will lend a new expression to the fluid boundaries between work and leisure time. In the sector of the future, namely entertainment electronics, not only did suitably shaped new device functions pick up the awards, but also an easily recyclable TV set.

Generally speaking, design in the Leisure category continues to serve to engender status symbols, as the award-winning sunglasses, luggage items and clocks demonstrate.

Rucksack, Aktenmappe, Aktenmappe mit Überschlag, Collegemappe. *Backpack and assorted folders.*

HERSTELLER *MANUFACTURER* SPEZIA Fritz Lenk GmbH & Co., Dornhan, Germany
PRODUKT *PRODUCT* Rucksack/Aktenmappe/Collgemappe Backpack/portfolio/folder
DESIGN Mehnert, Wahrheit & Partner Industrie Design M. Wahrheit, Stuttgart, Germany

HERSTELLER MANUFACTURER Bang & Olufsen Technology A/S, Struer, Denmark
PRODUKT PRODUCT Beolab 2000 Lautsprecher Speaker
DESIGN Fitting Design Anders Hermansen, Copenhagen, Denmark
VERTRIEB DISTRIBUTION Bang & Olufsen Deutschland GmbH, Gilching, Germany

BEOLAB 2000, Stereo-Aktivlautsprecher, für Räume mit begrenztem Platzangebot. Der Anschluß an das Bang & Olufsen System im »Hauptraum« macht eine zusätzliche Stereoanlage überflüssig. Mit BeoLink-Technik Zugriff auf alle Audio-Funktionen des Hauptgeräts. Verbindet Funktionalität mit innovativem Design und Bedienungsfreundlichkeit: Die wichtigsten Funktionen lassen sich per Hand anwählen und steuern, die Fernbedienung kann auf ih-rem angestammten Platz im »Hauptraum« bleiben. Lautsprechertechnik für vollen Stereoklang im ganzen Raum.

The BEOLAB 2000 is an active loudspeaker special designed to provide full stereo sound in rooms with limited space. It is connected to the main Bang & Olufsen System; thus eliminating the need for additional stereo systems in other, smaller rooms. BeoLink technology affords access to all main system functions. The loudspeaker combines functionality with an innovative, user-friendly design. The most important functions can be adjusted either by hand or with the remote control unit.

AHS 4, elektrische Heckenschere. Ergonomisch optimierte, doppelte Griffposition: Die obere für senkrechtes, die untere für waagrechtes Heckentrimmen, auch bei Überkopfarbeit. Permanente Zweihandsicherung: sobald eine Hand den Griff losläßt, stoppt der Motor. Zusammen mit einem gegenläufigen Sicherheitsmesser ergibt dies ein Maximum an Sicherheit bei hoher Schnittleistung. Vibrationsarm. Kabelsicherung. Gehäuse aus cadmiumfreiem Kunststoff.

The AHS 4 electrical hedge trimmer features an ergonomically optimal grip with two positions, with the upper position intended for vertical trimming, the lower for horizontal trimming. (The same applies to overhead work.) It also boasts a two-hand safety feature: If the user lets go with one hand, the motor will stop. Together with a counter-rotating safety blade, it affords maximum safety and excellent low-vibration cutting performance. It comes with a cord protector and cadmium-free plastic housing.

HERSTELLER MANUFACTURER Robert Bosch GmbH Geschäftsbereich Elektrowerkzeuge, Leinfelden-Echterdingen, Germany
PRODUKT PRODUCT AHS 4 Heckenschere Hedge trimmer
DESIGN TEAMS - SLANY DESIGN, Esslingen, Germany

HERSTELLER MANUFACTURER Black & Decker Ltd., Spennymoor, Great Britain
PRODUKT PRODUCT links: GX 530 Luftkissenmäher Hoover mower rechts: GR 450 Sichelrasenmäher Sickle lawn mower
DESIGN Black & Decker Vince Cooper, Spennymoor, Great Britain
VERTRIEB DISTRIBUTION BLACK & DECKER GmbH, Idstein, Germany

links: GX 530, ein Luftkissenmäher, der auf einem Luftkissenpolster leicht und handlich über die Rasenfläche gleitet und auch an Hanglagen und in Winkeln wendig bleibt. Nach Rasenbeschaffenheit einstellbare Schnitthöhe des Messers (sechs Stufen). Ergonomisch geformter, frei beweglicher Handgriff, mit dem sich der Rasenmäher gut führen läßt. Das Schnittgut wird durch starken Sog, den ein Doppel-Lüfterrad-System erzeugt, in den Fangkorb transportiert. Schnittbreite 30 cm.

left: Riding on a cushion of air, the GX 530 Hoover mower virtually glides over the lawn, performing well even on slopes and over rough patches. The blade can be adjusted to various cutting heights (six settings), and has a cutting width of 30 cm. The ergonomically designed, mobile grip makes the mower easy to handle. The cut grass is drawn into the collection bag by the unique twin fan grass collection system.

rechts: GR 450, Sichelrasenmäher für große Flächen. Kraftvoller Motor, dennoch leise und nachbarschaftsfreundlich. Zum effektiven und schnellen Arbeiten tragen auch die guten Grasfangergebnisse durch entsprechende Gestaltung des Gehäuses und eine Schnittbreite von 42 cm bei. Dreifach höheneinstellbarer Lenkgriff zur komfortablen Anpassung des Geräts an die Körpergröße des Bedieners. In sieben Stufen einstellbare Schnitthöhe.

right: The GR 450 is a sickle lawn mower suitable for large areas. The powerful motor runs quietly and will not disturb the neighbors. The housing design and a cutting width of 42 cm affords excellent grass collection and gets the job done quickly. The handlebar can be set at three different positions to accommodate the height of the user. The cutting blade has seven height settings, and the grass collection bag can be emptied easily by simply lifting it off the frame.

GT 430, eine Heckenschere mit 400-Watt-Motor und besonders gehärtetem Getriebe. Daher keine Beschädigung des Motors, wenn das Messer blockiert. Komfortable Handhabung des Geräts aufgrund seines geringen Gewichts. Das 53cm lange, asymmetrische Messer arbeitet mit geringem Reibungsverlust und vibrationsarm. Bis zu 23mm starke Äste lassen sich exakt und sauber schneiden. Erhöhte Sicherheit und bessere Kontrolle beim Schneiden durch den rot markierten, auch in der Hecke gut sichtbaren Messerbalken und transparenten Handschutz. Kabelclip, der das Kabel vom Arbeitsbereich fernhält und es vor Beschädigungen schützt.

The lightweight GT 430 hedge trimmer boasts a 400-watt motor and an extremely durable drive unit that protects the motor from damage even if the blade becomes caught. The 53cm asymmetrical blade cuts with little frictional loss and almost no vibration. Branches of up to 23mm in diameter can be removed with a clean, exact cut. The transparent hand guard and the blade carrying rail, easily visible even inside the hedge due to its red markings, afford greater safety while improving cutting performance. A clip keeps the cord away from the work area.

HERSTELLER MANUFACTURER Black & Decker Ltd., Spennymoor, Great Britain
PRODUKT PRODUCT GT 430 Heckenschere Hedge trimmer
DESIGN Black & Decker Chris Murray Spennymoor, Great Britain
VERTRIEB DISTRIBUTION BLACK & DECKER GmbH, Idstein, Germany

HERSTELLER MANUFACTURER
PRODUKT PRODUCT
DESIGN

SABO-Maschinenfabrik GmbH, Gummersbach, Germany
32 EL Elektro Rasenmäher Electric mower
busse design ulm gmbh, Elchingen, Germany

32 EL, ein Elektrorasenmäher mit besonders leisem Motor. Gegen Spannungsüberschläge gesichertes Gehäuse, mehrfach isolierter Holm. Der breite Sicherheitsschaltbügel ermöglicht einhändiges Mähen. Wird das Gerät losgelassen, löst die Messerbremse einen Messerstop aus. Die Sicherheitskabelführung gewährleistet ein bequemes Führen und den Seitenwechsel des Kabels. Schnitthöhe sechsfach verstellbar.

The 32 EL is an electric mower with an especially quiet motor, featuring six different cutting heights. The motor housing is constructed to prevent electric shock, and the handle is also well-insulated. The wide safety switch lever affords one-handed mowing: If the user lets go of the mower, the blade brake will stop the blade. The safety cable guide allows the cable to be moved from one side to the other, making the mower easy to handle.

oben: WOLF HS 43 E, eine elektrische Heckenschere mit 43 cm Messerlänge für den fachgerechten Schnitt kleinerer Hecken. Neuartige ergonomische Grifform, handlich und leicht, Gewicht 3,0 kg. Messerstop mit Stillstandzeit von weniger als 0,02 Sekunden. Dabei bleiben Unter- und Obermesser exakt übereinander stehen, eine weitere Verminderung der Verletzungsgefahr. Mit einer Motorleistung von 500 Watt und einem Zahnabstand von 24 mm können auch stärkere Äste geschnitten werden.
top: The WOLF HS 43 E electric hedge trimmer weighs only 3 kg, and sports a 43 cm blade for cutting smaller hedges with precision. The novel, ergonomic handgrip is lightweight and thus easy to handle. The patented blade stop halts the blade in less than 0,02 seconds, whereby the upper blade always stops directly above the lower one – an added safety feature. A 500-watt motor and a distance of 24 mm between teeth also allow thicker branches to be cut.

rechts: WOLF RQ 745, Rasentrimmer mit einer Bodenrolle, die mit einer Gleitkufe kombiniert ist. Erleichtert das Trimmen, weil das Gerät nicht mehr getragen, sondern ähnlich wie ein Staubsauger an der Rasenkante entlanggeschoben wird. Breite Fußtaste für fünffache Winkelverstellung zur Anpassung an die Körpergröße des Anwenders. Ein zweiter Handgriff mit Schnellspannverschluß für die stufenlose Einstellung des Geräts, z.B. die Drehung um 180 Grad für den »Senkrechtschnitt« der Rasenkanten.
right: The WOLF RQ 745 lawn trimmer features a combination roller and runner which facilitates trimming, as the device can be pushed along like a vacuum cleaner. A wide footswitch adapts the angle of the trimmer to the height of the user, with five settings available. The unit can be smoothly adjusted to any position thanks to a second handgrip with a quick-action lock; it can thus be rotated 180° for trimming edges.

oben/above: WOLF HS 43 E Elektrische Heckenschere Hedge trimmer unten/below: WOLF RQ 745 Rasentrimmer Lawn trimmer HERSTELLER MANUFACTURER WOLF-Geräte GmbH Vertriebsgesellschaft KG, Betzdorf, Germany
PRODUKT PRODUCT
DESIGN WOLF-Geräte, Betzdorf, Germany

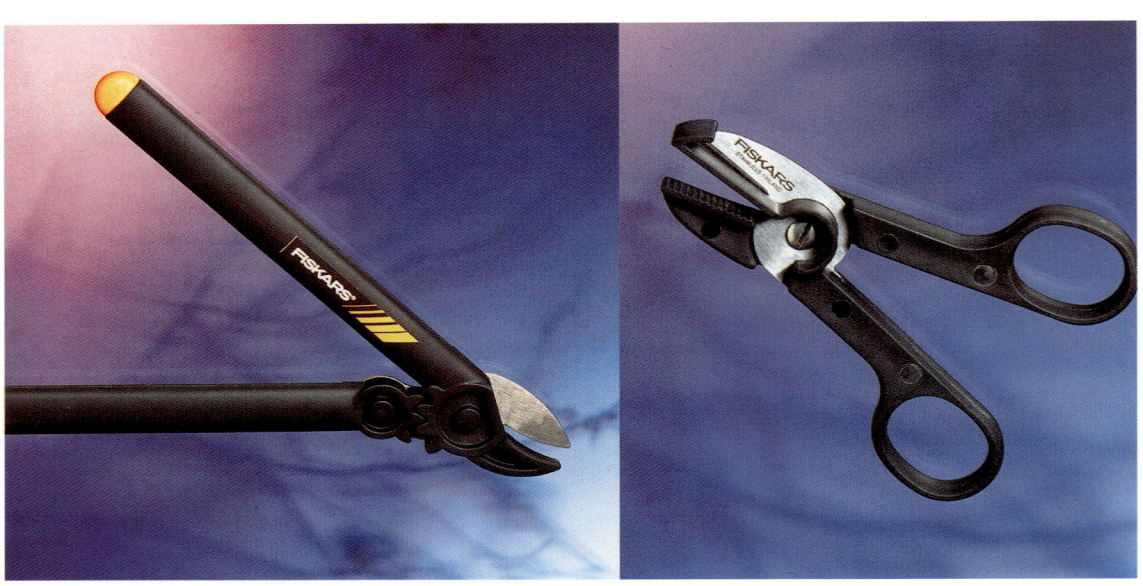

HERSTELLER MANUFACTURER
PRODUKT PRODUCT
DESIGN

Fiskars Consumer Oy Ab, Billnäs, Finland
links/left: Ästungsschere Pruner rechts/right:Blumenschere Flower cutters
Fiskars Consumer Oy Ab Olavi Lindén, Billnäs, Finland

links: ÄSTUNGSSCHERE mit neuen Eigenschaften und aus neuem Material. Durch Verwendung eines Planetenrades sind die Griffe nur etwa halb so lang wie bei herkömmlichen Modellen, dadurch Gewichtsersparnis und leichtere Handhabung. Auch als Gartenschere einzusetzen.
left: A PRUNER with novel features made from new materials: The use of planetary gears means the handles need only be about half as long as in other models, making the pruner lighter and thus easier to manage. It can also be used as garden shears.
rechts: BLUMENSCHERE aus Spritzguß. Robust und handlich, kann auch als leichte Gartenschere Verwendung finden.
right: These FLOWER CUTTERS were manufactured using injection molding. They are durable and easy to handle, and can also be used for light garden work.

FALTSPATEN für das Auto, für Camping und andere Freizeitaktivitäten. Kompakt und bruchsicher. Aus robustem glasfaserverstärktem Kunststoff gefertigt, darum zugleich leicht und handlich im Gebrauch. Kann auch als Hacke verwendet werden.

This compact, unbreakable FOLDING SPADE can be used for camping or leisure activities, and can even be stored in the car. Made of fiberglass-reinforced plastics, it is thus lightweight and easy to handle, and can also double as a hoe.

HERSTELLER MANUFACTURER Fiskars Consumer Oy Ab, Billnäs, Finland
PRODUKT PRODUCT Faltspaten Folding spade
DESIGN Fiskars Consumer Oy Ab Olavi Lindén, Svante Rönnholm, Veikko Mäkipelto, Billnäs, Finland

FREIZEIT *LEISURE* 267

HERSTELLER MANUFACTURER: rolly toys Franz Schneider GmbH & Co. KG, Neustadt bei Coburg, Germany
PRODUKT PRODUCT: Mega Trailer Drei-Seitenkipper 3-way tipping trailer
DESIGN: Dialogform, Ulrich Ewringmann, Taufkirchen, Germany

MEGA TRAILER, der erste voll funktionsfähige, zum Fahren an Kindertretfahrzeuge anhängbare Dreiseitenkipper dieser Größe. Materialbestimmtes Design (mit einem hohen Anteil an Kunststoffrecyclaten) mit technischer Anmutung: soll an »echte« Kippfahrzeuge erinnern. Material: vor allem PE, ein besonders umweltfreundlicher Kunststoff.

MEGA TRAILER is the first fully functional three-way dump truck toy of its size, for hooking up to children's pedal vehicles. The design takes into account the materials used (mainly recycled plastics), and its technical appearance is intended to evoke a »real« dump truck. Primary material is polyethylene, an environmentally-friendly plastic.

268 FREIZEIT LEISURE

HERSTELLER MANUFACTURER m design, Schwäbisch-Gmünd, Germany
PRODUKT PRODUCT mic.o.mic Design-Spielzeug Design toy
DESIGN TEAM MICKLITZ Klaus Micklitz, Schwäbisch Gmünd, Germany
VERTRIEB DISTRIBUTION WETNAUER TRADING COMPANY LTD., Basel, Switzerland

MIC.O.MIC., ein Design-Konstruktionsspielzeug im Bausatz. Schönheit, die man sieht und spürt: farbig, fröhlich und phantasieanregend. Übt das pädagogisch wichtige Zusammenspiel von Gefühl und Verstand (den Blick für Funktionen) ein. Die für die Herstellung verwendeten Kunststoffe sind nach den strengsten internationalen Normen ausgewählt.

The playful MIC.O.MIC. construction set sparks the imagination, creating beauty to be seen and touched. It helps users hone their sense of the interplay of feelings and reason. The plastics used were chosen in line with strict international standards.

HERSTELLER MANUFACTURER
Fenwick, Huntington Beach, USA
PRODUKT PRODUCT
Fenwick Casting Reel Wurfrolle Casting reel
DESIGN
ZIBA Design, Portland, USA

FENWICK-Wurfrolle, eine leichtgewichtige Rolle für das Wurfangeln. Wechsel vom Auswerfen zum Einholen des Köders durch einfaches Umschalten der Schnuraufwicklung. Abstufbare Geschwindigkeit beim Einholen des Köders zur Simulation eines lebenden Köders im Wasser. Am Ende der Rolle befindet sich ein Hebel für einen Umkehrsicherungsstop, wenn die Schnurspule frei drehen soll.

The FENWICK casting reel is a lightweight reel for spin fishing. Simply by switching a wire »bale«, the angler can change from casting to lure retrieval, whereby the lure is retrieved at varying speeds to simulate the movement of live bate in the water. The anti-reverse lever at the end of the reel allows the line spool to spin freely.

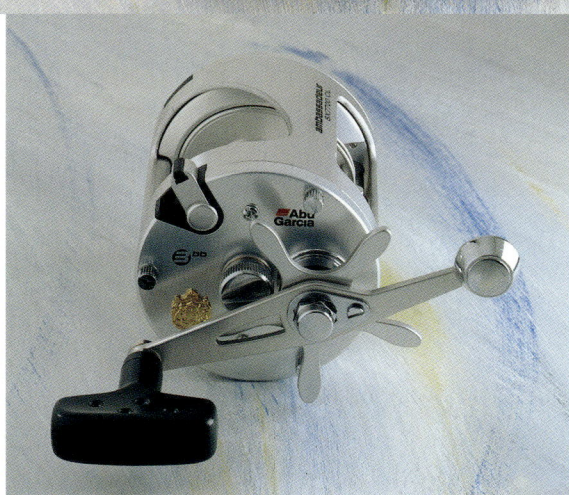

HERSTELLER MANUFACTURER Abu Garcia, Svängsta, Sweden
PRODUKT PRODUCT Ambassadeur SX 7700 CL Angelrolle Fishing reel
DESIGN Design A. Storz GmbH, Zell am See, Österreich

SX 7700 CL, eine neukonzipierte Wurfrolle. Das aus einem Stück gefräste Aluminiumstativ, die neu konstruierte MultiDisc Scheibenbremse mit Bremsscheiben aus einem Kohlefaserkomposit und ein neues Lagerungssystem der Spule erlauben Sportangeln auch unter härtesten Bedingungen. Kugelgelagerte, manuell feststellbare Spule für weichere und leisere Aufwicklung. Niedrig montierter, versenkter Rollenfuß, der Werfen und Aufspulen bequemer und leichter steuerbar macht – im Kampf mit einem großen Fisch ein echtes Plus.

SX 7700 CL is a fishing reel based on a novel concept. The one-piece extruded aluminum frame, the new MultiDisc drag system with friction washers made of composite carbon fiber, and an innovative spool mounting enable dedicated anglers to go fishing even under the worst conditions. The spool is mounted on ball bearings and can be manually adjusted, making retrieval smoother and quieter. The low-mounted, recessed reel base facilitates casting and retrieval – a real advantage when grappling with a large fish.

FREIZEIT LEISURE 271

HERSTELLER MANUFACTURER BREE Collection GmbH, Isenhagen, Germany
PRODUKT PRODUCT AIR TRANSFER 23 Boardcase hand baggage bag
DESIGN BREE collection GmbH, Wolf Peter Bree, Isenhagen, Germany

272 FREIZEIT *LEISURE*

HERSTELLER MANUFACTURER: BREE Collection GmbH, Isernhagen, Germany
PRODUKT PRODUCT: AIR TRANSFER 22 Reisetasche Travel bag
DESIGN: BREE collection GmbH, Wolf Peter Bree, Isernhagen, Germany

oben: AIR TRANSFER 22, eine Reisetasche aus reißfestem, wasserdichtem, dreifach veredeltem und extrem belastbarem Trylon. Luftdüsen sorgen für Belüftung des Tascheninnenraums, so bleibt die Wäsche frisch und knitterfrei. Besonders geeignet für Reisen zwischen verschiedenen Klimazonen. Aufteilung: eine große Hauptkammer mit Reißverschluß und zwei verschließbaren Schiebern, geräumige Reißverschlußtaschen sowie ein Reißverschlußfach an beiden Seiten. Geheimfach am Taschenboden (mit Reißverschluß). Zum Schleifschutz ist der Boden mit BREE-Schienen versehen.

top: AIR TRANSFER 22 is an extremely sturdy travel bag made out of tear-resistant, water proof Trylon. Air vents allow air to circulate inside the bag, keeping clothing fresh and wrinkle-free. The bag is especially suitable for traveling between different climates. It consists of a large compartment which can be locked with a small padlock, as well as generous outer pockets and a small compartment on either side, all of which sport zipper closures. There is also a zippered secret compartment in the bottom of the bag. The underside of the bag features BREE rails to prevent scuffing

links: AIR TRANSFER 23, ein Boardcase aus reißfestem, wasserdichtem, dreifach veredeltem Trylon, das extrem belastbar ist. Luftdüsen sorgen für Belüftung des Tascheninnenraumes, so bleibt die Wäsche, auch beim Wechsel der Klimazonen, frisch und knitterfrei. Drei Kammern, mit Doppelreißverschluß zu verschließen: in der ersten ein integrierter Kleidersack mit Befestigungshalterung; Mittelkammer ebenfalls für Kleidungstücke, hier sorgt eine elastische Kreuzhalterung für Ordnung; dritte Kammer mit drei Fächern für Geschäftsunterlagen.

left: AIR TRANSFER 23 is an extremely sturdy Hand-luggage bag made of tear-resistant, water proof Trylon. Air vents allow air to circulate inside of the bag, keeping clothing fresh and wrinkle-free even when traveling between different climate zones. All three compartments feature a double zipper closure that can be locked. The first contains an integrated garment bag with an adjustable strap to keep clothes in place; in the middle section, also for clothing, items are secured with an elastic cross-strap; the third compartment is for storing files and documents. The zippered left front pocket comes with integrated pen and credit card holders.

FREIZEIT LEISURE 273

HERSTELLER MANUFACTURER ADN SYSTEM SA, Echandens, Switzerland
PRODUKT PRODUCT 1995 ADN Armbanduhr Wrist watch
DESIGN Les Ateliers du Nord, Antoine Cahen, Lausanne, Switzerland
VERTRIEB DISTRIBUTION ADN SYSTEM SA, Echandens, Switzerland

1995 ADN WATCH, eine Armbanduhr, deren Gestaltung die Uhr nicht als beliebiges Modeobjekt, sondern als Instrument der Zeitmessung auffaßt. Darum die Verwendung einfacher, ästhetisch befriedigender Materialien, die zudem die Herstellungskosten niedrig halten. Quartzgesteuertes Uhrwerk in einem mikrokugelgestrahlten Gehäuse, gerändelte Krone, bombiertes Mineralglas und schwarzes geflochtenes Nylon-Armband. Wasserdicht bis in 30 m Tiefe.

The design of the 1995 ADN WATCH reflects the notion that a wristwatch is an instrument for measuring time rather than a frivolous fashion object. Simple materials were used to create an aesthetically pleasing design while keeping production costs low. The quartz clockwork is housed in a microballed case; other features include a milled crown, a convex crystal, and a black plaited nylon strap. Waterproof up to a depth of 30 m.

UNO von WATCHPEOPLE, die Einzeiger-Uhr, die sich dennoch minutengenau ablesen läßt: durch ein besonders gestaltetes Zifferblatt und Stundenzeiger. Ronda Quartzwerk. Messinggehäuse nickelfrei, wahlweise mattchrom oder schwarz. PCP-freies Lederband. Spezialverpackung aus Recyclingmaterial.

The novel UNO watch by WATCHPEOPLE has only one hand, but still displays the time accurately down to the minute thanks to a specially designed dial and hour hand. The watch features Ronda quartz movement, a PCP-free leather strap, and a nickel-free brass case, either in a matt chrome or matt black finish. It comes in a special box made of recycled paper.

HERSTELLER MANUFACTURER WATCHPEOPLE Schöll & Brassler GmbH, München, Germany
PRODUKT PRODUCT UNO Armbanduhr Wrist watch
DESIGN Designbüro Klaus Botta, Offenbach, Germany

HERSTELLER MANUFACTURER
KAI INTERNATIONAL CO., LTD., Tokyo, Japan
PRODUKT PRODUCT
KERSHAW LINER LOCK SERIES Taschenmesser Pocket knife
DESIGN
KAI INTERNATIONAL Katsumi Hasegawa, Tokyo, Japan

TASCHENMESSER, das leicht, mit einer einfachen Bewegung des Daumens, zu öffnen und zu schließen ist: die Klinge gleitet aus dem Schaft und rastet in einem Stellverschluß ein. Leichter Aluminium-Griff. Den Gesamteindruck bestimmt die rutschfeste Polymereinlage im Griff, die zugleich die Handhabbarkeit verbessert.

This HANDY POCKET KNIFE can be opened and closed with a simple flick of the thumb. The blade glides out of the shaft and locks into position. The lightweight aluminium handle rests comfortably in the hand and is extremely durable; the non-slip polymer inset makes the knife easier to handle and enhances its appearance.

LICHTMESSER in handgerechtem Design, eine praktische Kombination eines vielseitigen Taschenmessers mit einer kleinen Taschenlampe. Alles, was man am Schlüsselbund braucht: rostfreie Edelstahlklinge, rostfreie Schere, Nagelfeile mit Schraubendreher, Taschenlampe, dazu der Ring zum Befestigen am Schlüsselbund. Die Taschenlampe mit LED-Birne und Batterie.
The LIGHT KNIFE is a clever, practical design that combines a multipurpose pocket knife and a small flashlight, and includes a stainless steel blade and scissors, and a nail file with screwdriver, as well as a ring for attaching to a key-grip. The flashlight sports an LED bulb and replaceable battery.
STRUKTURA 5 Picknick, ein fünfteiliges Werkzeugmesser mit Picknickfunktion: durch Öffnen der Gabel läßt sich das Messer in zwei Teile zerlegen und dann als Messer und Gabel benutzen. Außerdem: Kapselheber-Schraubendreher-Kombination, Dosenöffner, Korkenzieher, Befestigungsring. Schalen aus hochwertigem Edelstahl mit gummiartiger Noppenstruktur sorgen für besondere Griffigkeit.
STRUKTURE 5 Picnic is a five-piece knife featuring a two-in-one knife and fork for picnicking. It also comes with a combination bottle-opener-screwdriver, can opener, corkscrew, and ring. The casing is made of high-grade steel, with a nubbed surface for easy gripping.

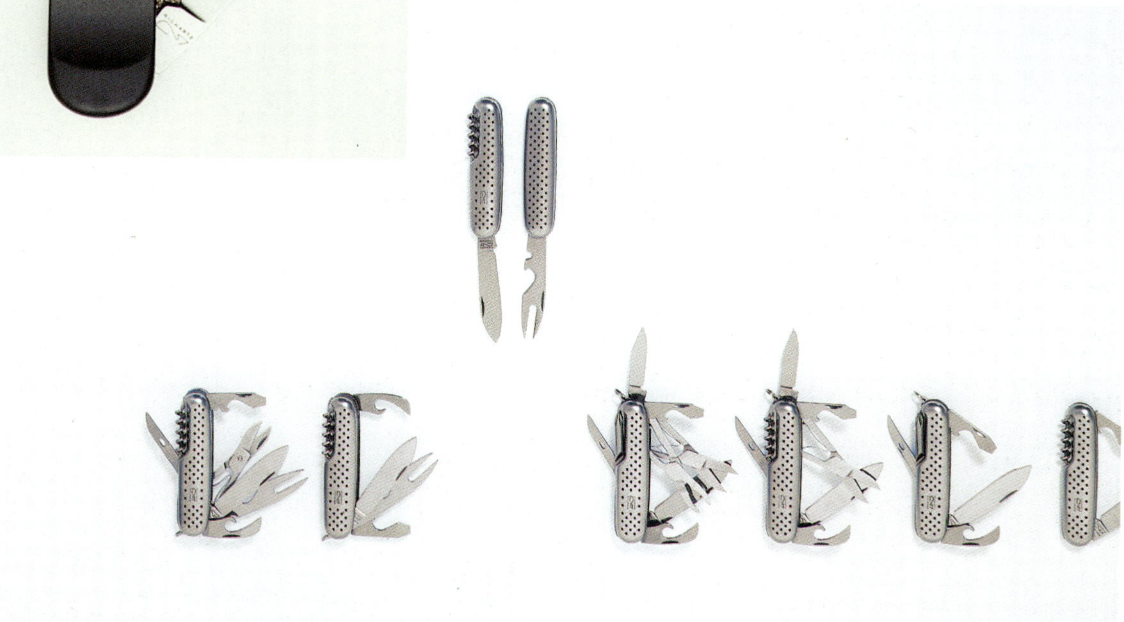

FREIZEIT *LEISURE* 277

HERSTELLER MANUFACTURER CARRERA International, Traun, Austria
PRODUKT PRODUCT F 0.9 Sportsonnenbrille Sport sunglasses
DESIGN Porsche design, Jörg Tragatschnig, Zell am See, Austria

278 FREIZEIT *LEISURE*

links: CARRERA F 0.9, eine Sportsonnenbrille für Kunden mit Markenbewußtsein und Sinn für funktionale Innovation.
left: CARRERA F 0.9 Sports Sunglasses are for discerning, brand-conscious customers with a taste for functional innovations.
rechts: AIR TITANIUM Case, ein Brillenetui passend zur AIR Titanium Brille und wie diese ein Produkt aus der dänisch-skandinavischen Design-Tradition, die Einfachheit, Funktionalität und minimalen Materialverbrauch bevorzugt. Material: gebürsteter rostfreier, Stahl. Ein Verschlußmechanismus ohne Scharniere, Schrauben oder Schweißstellen. Eine elegante Kombination aus gebürstetem Edelstahl, dem mattschwarzen Gummi der Einlage und dem mattschwarzen Kunststoff der Etuiseiten mit dem versenkten, diskreten AIR-Logo.
right: The AIR TITANIUM glasses case was designed to match the AIR Titanium eyeglass frames. Both case and frames are products of the Danish and Scandinavian design tradition, which values qualities such as simplicity, functionality, and minimal use of materials. The case is made of brushed stainless steel which creates an elegant combination with the black rubber lining and the matt-black plastic sides, on which the discreet AIR-Logo is engraved. Snaps shut without hinges, screws, or soldered joints.

HERSTELLER MANUFACTURER
Leica Camera GmbH, Solms, Germany

PRODUKT PRODUCT
Leica minilux Kamera Camera

DESIGN
Leica Camera, Manfred Meinzer, Solms, Germany

LEICA MINILUX, eine elegante und lichtstarke Sucherkamera mit kompaktem strapazierfähigem Titangehäuse und dem neu entwickelten Summarit 1:2,4/40mm, einem 6-Linsen-Objektiv, das auch bei schlechten Lichtverhältnissen noch lange ohne Blitz auskommt. Alle wesentlichen Funktionen wie Autofocus, Blitz, Programmautomatik für die richtige Belichtung (Blenden- oder Zeitvorwahl), Filmeinfädelung, Filmtransport und -rückspulung automatisch (abschaltbar für individuelle Bildgestaltung). Autofocus und Belichtungswert speicherbar. Vorblitz zur Minderung des »Rote-Augen-Effekts« bei Portraits. Serien Aufnahmen durch Festhalten des Auslöseknopfes.

The LEICA MINILUX is an elegant high-speed camera with a compact, durable titanium body and the newly developed Summarit 1:2.4/40mm, a six element lens which captures moods even in poor light without the flash. All essential functions are automatic, including autofocus, flash, automatic programs for correct exposure (aperture and exposure time settings), as well as film threading, advance and rewinding; however, these can also be switched off for creative photos. Autofocus und exposure values can be programmed for later use. The pre-flash reduces the red-eye effect when taking portrait photos. For serial photographs, just maintain pressure on the exposure release button.

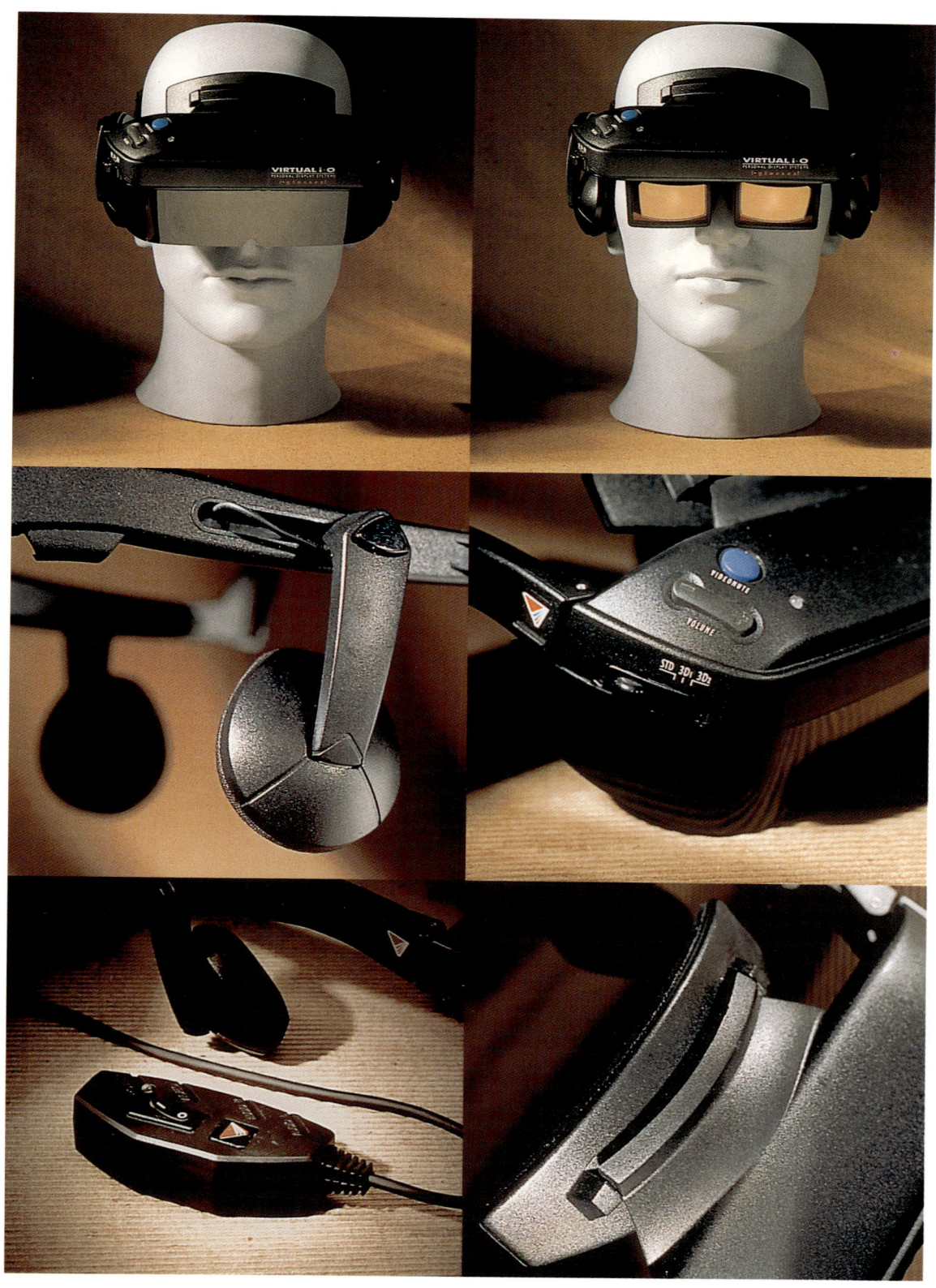

VIRTUAL i-O I-GLASSES! ist ein auf dem Kopf getragenes Personal Display System mit zwei Bildschirmen. Abnehmbares undurchsichtiges Visier, das Blendung von außen verhindert: für umfassende Immersionserfahrung der virtuellen Realität. Dennoch bleibt durch Optik und Design die äußere Umgebung im peripheren Blickfeld, darum keine Gleichgewichtsstörungen. i-glasses! produziert eine Bildfläche mit einer Diagonale von 203 cm in einer Entfernung von 3,3 m. Auch in einer Ausführung für Videos und elektronische Spiele sowie in einer PC-Version für Computerspiele und Anwendungen im Bereich der virtuellen Realität verfügbar.

VIRTUAL i-O I-GLASSES! is a binocular Personal Display System, or Head Mounted Display. The clip-on opaque visor blocks outside light to provide a more immersive virtual experience, while the optics and mechanical design allow users to maintain the external environment in their peripheral vision, critical for preventing motion sickness. i-glasses! produces an image area equivalent to an 80-inch (203 cm) screen viewed at 11ft (3.3 m). The device is also available in a video version for videos and electronic games and a PC version for computer games and virtual reality applications.

HERSTELLER MANUFACTURER Virtual i.-O INC, Seattle, USA
PRODUKT PRODUCT i-glasses! PDS Personal display system
DESIGN Virtual i.-O, Scott Mac Innes, Joe Park, Walter Webb, Chris Wiegel, Seattle, USA

FREIZEIT *LEISURE* 281

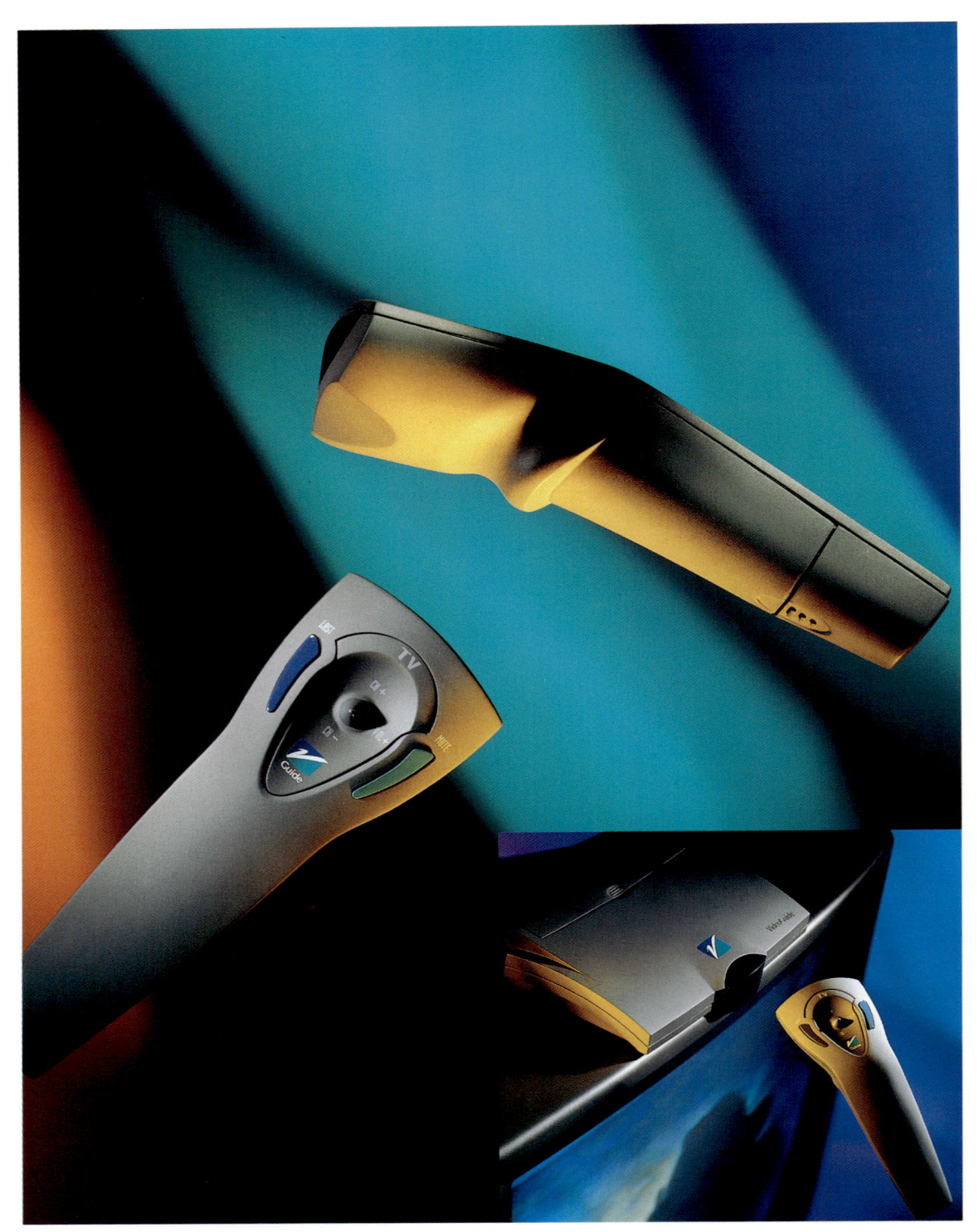

HERSTELLER MANUFACTURER VideoGuide, Bedford, USA
PRODUKT PRODUCT VideoGuide Fernbedienung Remote control
DESIGN IDEO, Scott Stropkay, Mark Nichols, David Privitera, Alan Vale, Tim Proulx, Otto DeRuntz, Lexington, USA

VIDEOGUIDE sind ein Fernsehempfänger und eine Universalfernbedienung zum Abrufen von Fernsehprogrammen, Nachrichten und Sportergebnissen. Ergonomisches Design für leichten Zugang zu allen üblichen TV-Funktionen (Ein/Aus, Lautstärke, Umschalten etc.). Bequeme Auswahl des Programms durch die ProgramGuide Software: kein Suchen des Kanals, eine Fernbedienung für TV-Gerät und Videorecorder. Auflistung von 7 Tagen TV-Programm auf dem Bildschirm. Vorausswahl für Aufnahmen durch den Videorecorder.

VIDEOGUIDE is a TV receiver and a universal remote control that instantly provides the viewer with show listings, news and sports scores. It is ergonomically designed and performs the most common TV functions (on/off, volume control, switching channels etc.). The ProgramGuide software makes it easy to select the desired program, and lists the entire week's shows on the screen. The remote also operates the video recorder, which can be programmed to record a show later in the week.

ANTENNE Bad Blankenburg Mobile Antennentechnik GmbH, Bad Blankenburg, Germany HERSTELLER MANUFACTURER
Mobilfunkantennen Autoantennen Car aerials PRODUKT PRODUCT
ANTENNE Bad Blankenburg Mobile Antennentechnik, Bad Blankenburg, Germany DESIGN

MOBILFUNKANTENNEN, die sich durch klare Linienführung und fließende Übergänge auszeichnen und sich angenehm mit modernem Fahrzeugdesign verbinden. Gleiche Gestaltungsbasis für verschiedene Antennentypen. Strahler sind samt Verbindung mit dem Anschlußkabel vor Umwelteinflüssen geschützt in einem Kunststoffgehäuse untergebracht. Trotz der filigranen Gestalt mechanisch sehr stabile Antennen, die auch extreme Fahrsituationen meistern und den Strahlungssmog im Fahrzeug deutlich reduzieren.
The clear, flowing shape of the new CAR AERIAL enables it to blend well with modern automobile designs. Various types of aerials are based on the same underlying design concept. A protective plastic housing keeps environmental influences away from the aerial and contacts with the connecting wires. Despite its slender shape, the aerial is highly stable, and can withstand extreme driving conditions while considerably reducing electrosmog inside the car.

FREIZEIT *LEISURE* 283

HERSTELLER MANUFACTURER SEGA Enterprises LTD., Tokyo, Japan
PRODUKT PRODUCT SATURN Computer Spielgerät Hand-held game controller
DESIGN IDEO Product Development, Jochen Backs, Matt Marsh, San Francisco, USA
VERTRIEB DISTRIBUTION SEGA OF AMERICA, INC., Redwood City, USA

SATURN GAME CONTROLLER, ein Computerspielgerät mit acht Tasten. Durch Betätigung von Tasten oder Tastenkombinationen werden den auf dem Bildschirm erzeugten Figuren Bewegungen und Aufgaben zugeordnet. Die Tasten sind in zwei Bereichen angeordnet: die Bewegung der Figuren erfolgt mit der rechten und die Richtungskontrolle mit der linken Hand. Das Gerät hat eine konkave Form, die auf die natürliche Haltung der Hand abgestimmt ist. Dadurch werden Verdrehungen von Handgelenk und des Unterarm vermieden.

The SATURN GAME CONTROLLER is an eight-button computer game device. Computer-generated characters are made to perform various tasks and actions by pressing individual or multiple buttons. Movement is controlled with the right hand, direction with the left. The device features a concave grip surface to accommodate the natural position of the hand, avoiding strain in the wrist and forearm.

Kasper & Richter GmbH, Ultenreuth, Germany HERSTELLER MANUFACTURER
BodyWatch Elektronik-Kilometerzähler Electronic pedometer PRODUKT PRODUCT
SCHMIDT-LACKNER-DESIGN, Heidelberg, Germany DESIGN

BODYWATCH ist ein elektronischer Kilometerzähler mit Laufstilerkennung für das Wandern und Joggen. Er zählt Gesamtstrecke oder Tageskilometer, die Schritte, mißt die Geschwindigkeit und den Kalorienverbrauch. Auch als Stopuhr zu verwenden. Energie durch Solar-Dualpower.

BODYWATCH is an electronic pedometer which can be programmed to your individual running or walking style. It measures total distance and shorter stretches, counts the number of steps taken, and monitors speed and calorie consumption. BodyWatch runs on solar power and can also double as a stopwatch.

FREIZEIT *LEISURE*

HERSTELLER MANUFACTURER
Sony Corporation, Tokyo, Japan
PRODUKT PRODUCT
RM-S 78T Fernbedienung Remote control
DESIGN
Sony Design Center, Tokyo, Japan
VERTRIEB DISTRIBUTION
SONY Deutschland GmbH, Köln, Germany

RM-S 78 T, eine völlig neu konzipierte Infrarot-Fernbedienung. Geformt wie ein Ei, steht sie dennoch aufrecht und ist praktisch, unkompliziert und sorgt für Unterhaltung. Für alle Fernsehgeräte, Videorecorder (VHS, 8mm und Beta) und Teletext von Sony geeignet.

The RM-S 78 T is a unique IR remote control unit. The device stands upright despite its egg-like shape; it is practical, easy to use, and entertaining. For use with all Sony television sets, video recorders (VHS, 8mm und Beta) and videotext.

286 FREIZEIT *LEISURE*

CUBIC SYSTEM Q3, MikroKompakt-HiFi-Anlage in CD-Größe. In drei Varianten: das Grundpaket aus CD-Tuner und Vorverstärker inklusive angesteuerten Monitor-Lautsprechern; Cubic-TC mit zusätzlichem Kassettendeck; Cubic-MD mit MiniDisc-Recorder. CD-Tuner mit 1 Bit DA-Wandler, 30 Radiostationsspeichern, Sleep Timer und Fernbedienung. Kassettendeck mit automatischer Bandwahl, Titelrücklauf, Dolby B und CD-Aufnahmesynchronisation. Das Mini Disc-Deck verfügt über einen optisch-digitalen Input, verschiedene Editierfunktionen sowie 25 Speicherplätze.

The CUBIC SYSTEM Q3 is a micro-compact Hi-Fi available in three versions: The basic package comes with a CD-tuner, pre-amp, and loudspeakers; the Cubic-TC includes a cassette deck; in the Cubic-MD a MiniDisc recorder replaces the cassette deck. The CD/tuner sports a 1-bit DA converter, 30 station pre-sets, an alarm clock and remote control. The cassette deck has automatic tape selection, title search, Dolby B" und CD recording synchronization; the MiniDisc deck features an optical digital input, various editing functions and 25 title memories.

Cubic System Q 3 Mikro-Kompakt-Anlage Micro-hifi-system   HERSTELLER MANUFACTURER
Sony Corporation, Tokyo, Japan   PRODUKT PRODUCT
Sony Design Center, Tokyo, Japan   DESIGN
SONY Deutschland GmbH, Köln, Germany   VERTRIEB DISTRIBUTION

FREIZEIT LEISURE 287

HERSTELLER MANUFACTURER Sony Corporation, Tokyo, Japan
PRODUKT PRODUCT CCD-TR 3000E Hi8 Camcorder
DESIGN Sony Design Center, Tokyo, Japan
VERTRIEB DISTRIBUTION SONY Deutschland GmbH, Köln, Germany

CCD-TR3000E, das HI8-HANDYCAM mit fortgeschrittenster Technik: optischer 16fach-Zoom, Antiverwackelsystem, hochauflösender LCD-Farbsucher. Sonnenfenster für die Verstärkung der Leuchtkraft des Sucherbildes. Automatische Aktivierung des Suchers, wenn sich das Auge nähert. »Still Picture«, die Funktion, die den Camcorder in einen Fotoapparat verwandelt. »Picture Effects« für ausdrucksstarke Verfremdungen des Bildes. Manual Gain, Shutter Speed und Weißabgleich für spezielle Aufnahmesituationen. 16:9 Aufnahmemodus für die zukünftigen Bildschirmformate. Lithium-Ionen-Akku. RC-Time Code und Data Code für nahezu bildgenauen Schnitt.

CCD-TR3000E is a HI8 HANDYCAM boasting state-of-the-art technology, such as a 16x zoom, super steady shot, and a high-resolution LCD color viewfinder. A sun window boosts the luminosity of the viewfinder, which is activated automatically as the user's eye draws near. The still picture function transforms the camcorder into a normal camera, while a range of picture effects yield creative photos. Special situations can be handled by functions such as manual gain, shutter speed and white balance. The camcorder's 16:9 format anticipates the screen format of the future. Additional features: a lithium ion battery, as well as a RC time code and data code for nearly single-frame precision.

288 FREIZEIT *LEISURE*

CPJ-100, ein leistungsstarker LCD Farbprojektor zur Projektion von Videos aus Camcorder oder Videorecorder, von Filmen von Laserdiscplayer oder TV-Set auf Wand oder Leinwand, mit einer Bilddiagonale von max. 1,50m. Integrierte Stereolautsprecher, doch ist auch der Anschluß an eine Dolby Surround-Stereoanlage möglich. Leichtgewicht (2,5 kg), mobil im Einsatz durch schwenkbare Linse (auch Deckenprojektion möglich), nach Anschluß an Netz und Zuspieler sofort einsatzbereit. Damit auch als professioneller Präsentationshelfer, für Schulungen oder Vorträge geeignet.

The CPJ-100 is a high-performance LCD color projector for projecting laser disc films and TV images as well as Camcorder or VCR video cassettes onto the wall or a screen. It features an integrated stereo loudspeaker, and can also be connected to a Dolby Surround stereo system. The lightweight unit (2.5kg) comes with a swiveling lens which enables projection on just about any wall surface (including the ceiling), and its simple, straightforward operation makes it suitable for use in training sessions or presentations.

HERSTELLER MANUFACTURER Sony Corporation, Tokyo, Japan
PRODUKT PRODUCT CPJ-100 LCD Farbprojektor LCDcolor projector
DESIGN Sony Design Center, Tokyo, Japan
VERTRIEB DISTRIBUTION SONY Deutschland GmbH, Köln, Germany

HERSTELLER MANUFACTURER
Blaupunkt-Werke GmbH, Hildesheim, Germany

PRODUKT PRODUCT
CX-Serie Autolautsprecher Car speakers

DESIGN
Blaupunkt-Werke, Wolfgang Strohmeier, Hildesheim, Germany

CX-LINE, ein Komponenten-Lautsprecher, deren modulare Konzeption einen freizügigen Einbau bei stets gutem Klang ermöglicht. Die Zwei-Wege-Lautsprecher, der Hochtöner auf einer Brücke über dem Tief-/Mitteltonchassis angebracht. Komfortabel einsetzbar wie ein Koax-System. Kommt in tiefen Einbauschächten der Hochtonanteil zu kurz, kann der Tweeter einfach herausgenommen und akustisch günstiger plaziert werden. Gute Integration in alle Kfz-Interieurs durch ein zurückhaltendes, auf wenige prägnante Stilmittel konzentriertes Design.

The modular conception of the CX-LINE two-way loudspeakers affords quality sound and flexible installation. The tweeter is located on a bridge above the bass/mid-range chassis, making the speakers as convenient to use as a coaxial system. If necessary, the tweeter can simply be removed and repositioned to yield a more favorable acoustic blend. The speaker fits in well with all car interiors thanks to its discreet design based on a few prominent stylistic elements.

Der BLAUPUNKT BREMEN RCM 127/NEW YORK RDM 127, Autoradio/Kassetten-Kombination. Die »aufgeräumte«, plastische Gestaltung der Bedienoberfläche ermöglicht dem Fahrer den direkten Zugriff auf die wesentlichen Funktionen. Bedienung der nachgeordneten Funktionen durch taktil zu erfassende »Soft Keys« zu beiden Seiten des Display. Öffnung und Schliessung des Kassettenschachts durch Anheben bzw. Absenken des Bedienpanels. Durch KeyCard-System gegen Diebstahl gesichert.

The BLAUPUNKT BREMEN RCM 127/NEW YORK RDM 127 is a combination car radio/cassette player. The control panel features a clear, three-dimensional design, with the most essential functions located closest to the driver. Soft keys on each side of the display possess special tactile qualities, and are used to operate the less important functions. The cassette deck is opened and closed by raising or lowering the control panel. The unit is protected against theft by the reliable, easy-to-use KeyCard system.

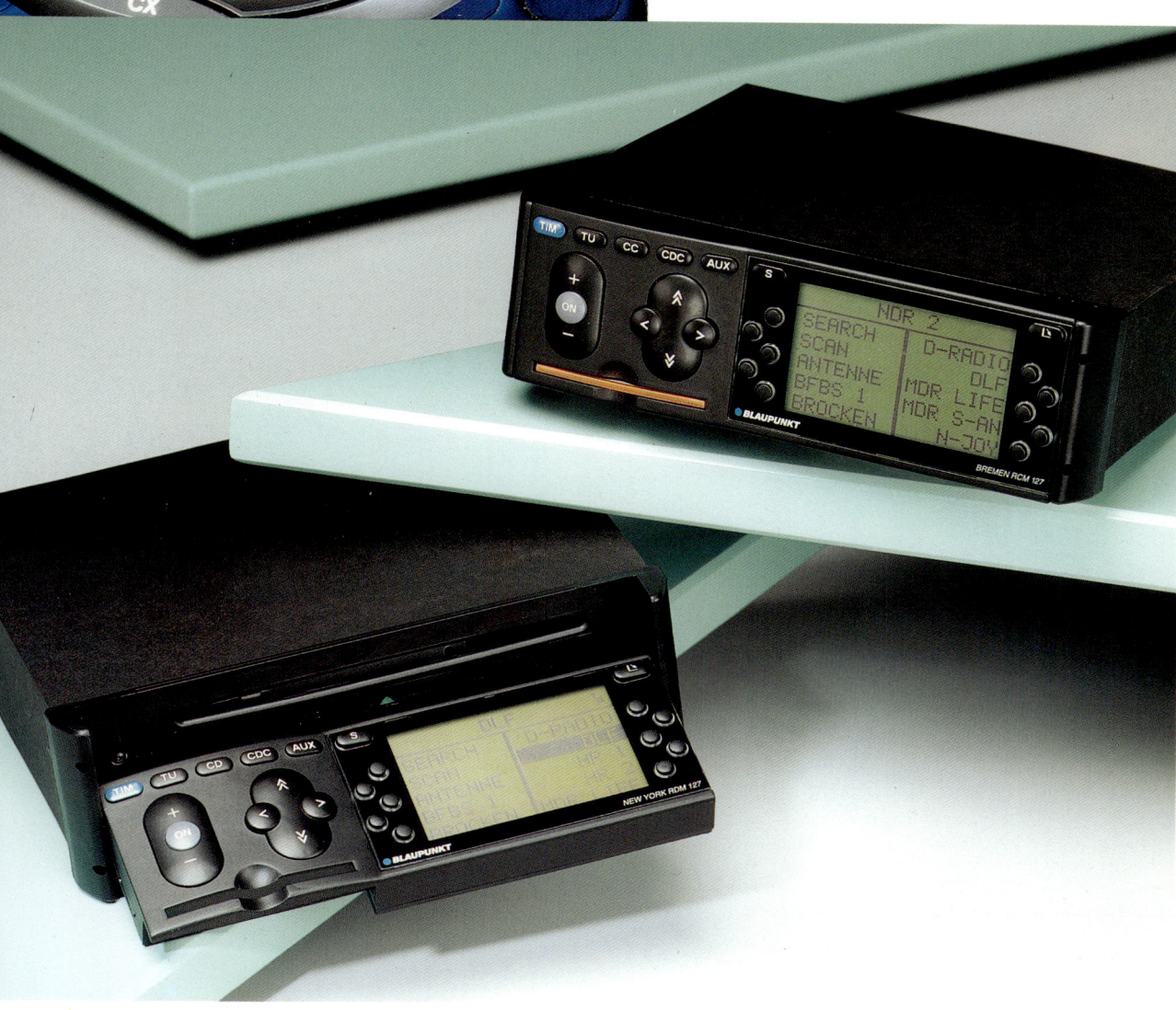

Blaupunkt-Werke GmbH, Hildesheim, Germany   HERSTELLER MANUFACTURER
Autoradio Carradio Bremen RCM 127, New York RDM 127   PRODUKT PRODUCT
Blaupunkt-Werke Wolfgang Strohmeier, Hildesheim, Germany   DESIGN

FREIZEIT *LEISURE*

HERSTELLER MANUFACTURER Blaupunkt-Werke GmbH, Hildesheim, Germany
PRODUKT PRODUCT RTV 255 EPC Videorecorder Video recorder
DESIGN Blaupunkt-Werke, Hildesheim, Germany

RTV 255, ein 2-Kopf-Mono-Videorecorder mit ShowView-Funktion. Bei Anschluß ans Stromnetz erfolgt eine vollautomatische Erstinstallation: die erreichbaren Sender werden eingestellt und in logischer Reihenfolge abgelegt, es werden Show View-Leitzahlen zugeordnet und die Uhr gestellt und später, wenn nötig, korrigiert. Alle Bedienschritte über Bildschirmmenue zu aktivieren, dadurch reduziertes Bedienfeld. Alle Laufwerkfunktionen mit Wippschalter zu regeln. In schwarz (RTV 255) oder silber (RTV 255 silver).

The RTV 255 is a two-head mono video recorder featuring Show View. Initial installation is fully automatic once the unit is plugged in: Available channels are preset and arranged in a logical order, ShowView numbers are assigned, the clock is set and later adjusted if necessary. All steps can be activated via the on-screen menu, so that only a few control elements are required on the recorder itself. Tape drive functions are operated via a rocker switch. The unit comes in black (RTV 255) or silver (RTV 255 silver)

Blaupunkt-Werke GmbH, Hildesheim, Germany   HERSTELLER MANUFACTURER
RTV 255 silber Videorecorder Video recorder   PRODUKT PRODUCT
Blaupunkt-Werke, Hildesheim, Germany   DESIGN

HERSTELLER MANUFACTURER
GRUNDIG AG, Fürth, Germany
5300 RDS Autoradio Car radio cassette player
PRODUKT PRODUCT
GRUNDIG PRODUKT DESIGN, Jürgen Schröder, Fürth, Germany
DESIGN

5300 RDS, ein komfortables Autoradio-Kassettenspieler mit CD-Wechslersteuerung. Die Gerätefront ist in drei Funktionsblöcke gegliedert: im linken, stark überwölbten Klangregelung und die Tonquellenwahl; ein Kassettenschacht und die dazugehörigen Tasten bilden den oberen Teil; als dritter Block ist das abnehmbare Bedienteil gestaltet, das Radiofunktionstasten, CD-Wechslersteuerung und Display zusammenfaßt. Ellipsoid und kugelförmig gewölbte Tasten, die damit taktile Prägnanz erhalten und blind bedient werden können.

The 5300 RDS is an easy-to-use car radio/cassette player with a CD auto changer. The front of the unit is divided into three functional areas: on the left, a strongly arched element houses the tone controls and mode selector; the cassette deck and its controls are located on top; and the third section is a detachable unit containing the radio controls, the CD auto changer and display. The ellipsoidal and spherical shapes of the control buttons make the controls easy to operate by touch alone.

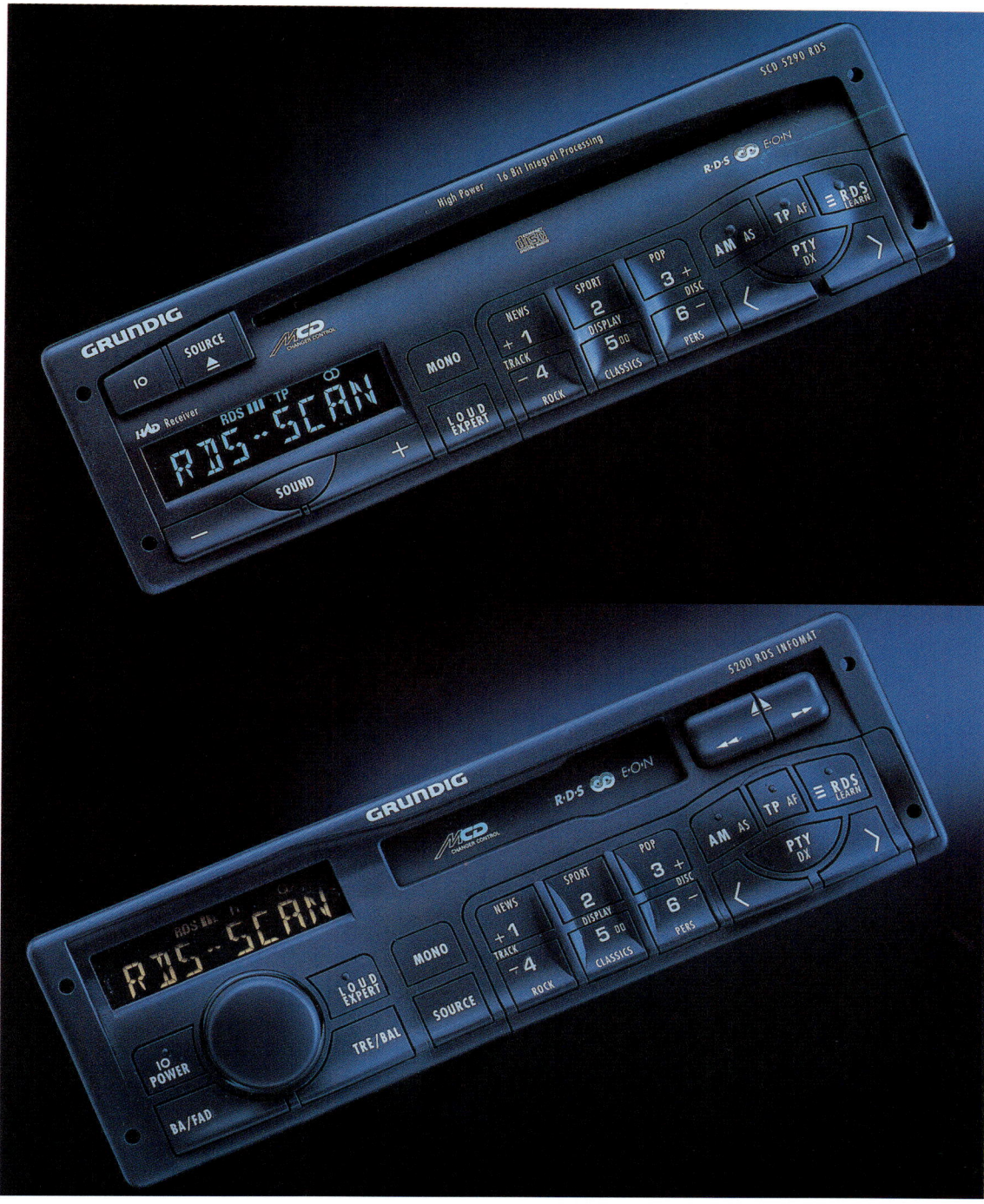

oben: SCD 5290 RDS, Autoradio/CD-Player, mit CD-Wechslersteuerung. Harmonisch vom CD-Schacht zum Tastenfeld gewölbte Oberfläche, eine taktile Landschaft, die der Fingerkuppe das Suchen erleichtert. Unmittelbar unter dem Display sind Volume-Wippe und Klangfunktionen untergebracht. Im Bereich des abnehmbaren Bedienteils führen ellipsoide Körper zu den Stationstasten, und ein Kugelabschnitt zu den Tunerfunktionen. Eine durchgehende Lippe erleichtert die Bedienung der unteren Tastenreihe.

above: The SCD 5290 RDS is a car radio/CD player with a CD auto changer. The attractive arched surface leading from the CD compartment to the control panel puts all the controls at your fingertips. The volume and other tone controls are located directly beneath the display. Ellipsoidal elements on the detachable operating unit lead your fingers to the pre-set station buttons, while a spherical element facilitates access to the tuner controls. A ridge spanning the length of the unit affords easy use of the bottom row of buttons.

unten: 5200 RDS, ein Autoradio-Kassettengerät mit CD-Wechslersteuerung. Die Gerätefront erleichtert als taktile Landschaft das Suchen der Fingerkuppen. Um den Lautstärkeregler sind die Klangfunktionen angeordnet. Im Bereich des abnehmbaren Bedienteils führen ellipsoide Körper zu den Stationstasten, ein Kugelabschnitt zu den Tunerfunktionen. Eine durchgehende Lippe erleichtert die Bedienung der unteren Tastenreihe.

below: The 5200 RDS is a car radio/cassette player with a CD auto-changer. The front sports a special tactile layout that puts the controls at your fingertips, with the volume surrounded by the other tone controls. Ellipsoidal elements on the detachable operating unit lead your fingers to the pre-set station buttons, while a spherical element facilitate access to the tuner controls. A ridge spanning the length of the unit affords easy use of the bottom row of buttons.

oben/above: SCD 5290 RDS Autoradio Car radio and cassette player unten/below: SCD 5200 RDS Autoradio-CD Gerät Car radio/CD-player
GRUNDIG PRODUKT DESIGN, Markus Müller, Fürth, Germany

HERSTELLER MANUFACTURER
GRUNDIG AG, Fürth, Germany
PRODUKT PRODUCT
DESIGN

HERSTELLER MANUFACTURER
NOKIA Unterhaltungselektronik GmbH, Düsseldorf, Germany
PRODUKT PRODUCT
NOKIA 8002 Twin Satelliten Receiver Satellite receiver
DESIGN
Nokia Design Center, Düsseldorf, Germany

NOKIA 8002 TWIN, ein Stereo Satellitenreceiver mit Twin-Funktion und ShowView. Bietet neben VPS als erster auf dem Markt Show-View-Programmierkomfort. Mit einem benutzerfreundlichen Bildschirmmenue sind bis zu 500 Speicherplätze programmierbar. Twin-Funktion für den Empfang zweier Programme gleichzeitig. ShowView- und VPS-Programmierung ist nur noch für den Receiver erforderlich, der Videorecorder wird über Infrarot automatisch mitgesteuert.

The NOKIA 8002 TWIN is a stereo satellite receiver featuring a twin function, and is the first on the market to offer Show View and VPS. Up to 500 channels can be programmed with a user-friendly on-screen menu. Twin function enables the simultaneous reception of two channels. ShowView and VPS need only be programmed on the receiver, as the video recorder is then automatically controlled using IR.

HERSTELLER MANUFACTURER NORDMENDE Thomson Technology, Hannover, Germany
PRODUKT PRODUCT Prestige 72 KPL TV-Gerät TV set
DESIGN THOMSON multimedia Design Center, Philippe Starck, Paris, France

PRESTIGE 72 KPL, Fernseher mit Dolby ProLogic Decoder, 4 Zusatzlautsprechern und dem neuartigen SENSAR-Bedienkonzept: durch die Rollkugel der Fernbedienung gesteuert, wandert der Cursor über den Bildschirm, und man blättert wie in einem virtuellen Buch. Menü zur Auswahl von Helligkeit, Farbsättigung, Bildschärfe, Klangbild oder Kontrast mit leichtverständlichen Symbolen: z. B. Sonne für Helligkeit, die ihren höchsten Wert erreicht, wenn das Symbol im Zenit steht. Die Formgebung aus Quadrat und Würfel entwickelt, mattschimmernde Oberflächen mit von Grau in Blau übergehendem Farbton.

The PRESTIGE 72 KPL television features a Dolby ProLogic Decoder, 4 external speakers and the novel SENSAR concept, whereby the trackball on the remote control moves the cursor across the screen and leafs through the menus. Brightness, color saturation, contrast, resolution or sound are adjusted with the help of easy-to-understand symbols: brightness is represented by a sun, which reaches its zenith when optimal brightness has been set. Square and cube forms are the basis for the design, and the matt-finished surfaces are an unobtrusive shade of gray fading into blue.

FREIZEIT LEISURE 297

HERSTELLER MANUFACTURER
LOEWE OPTA GmbH, Kronach, Germany
PRODUKT PRODUCT
Loewe ViewVision 6002 M Videorecorder
DESIGN
Phoenix Product Design, Stuttgart, Germany

LOEWE VIEWVISION 6002 M, ein Videorecorder, der einfache Bedienbarkeit mit hoch entwickelter Technik vereint. Verzicht auf überflüssige Einstellmöglichkeiten zeigt sich an der Gestaltung der Frontpartie mit nur vier Bedientasten. Dennoch umfangreiche Ausstattung: automatischer Sendersuchlauf mit Sortierung, automatische Uhreinstellung, Top-Speed-Laufwerk, ShowView. Alle Funktionen über Fernbedienung anwählbar. Sparsamer Verbrauch. Einfache Demontage und Materialkennzeichnung für die Trennung der recyclebaren Werkstoffe.

LOEWE VIEWVISION 6002 M is a video recorder which combines user-friendly operation with advanced technology. Superfluous programming functions have been eliminated, as is reflected in the front panel design with just four controls. Despite this simplicity, the video recorder offers a full range of features, including automatic channel search and sort, a self-adjusting clock, and a »Top Speed« tape drive. All functions can be operated via remote control. The unit consumes little energy, and its materials are clearly labeled for recycling purposes.

HERSTELLER MANUFACTURER LOEWE OPTA GmbH, Kronach, Germany
PRODUKT PRODUCT Loewe Modus Fernsehgerät TV set
DESIGN design studio hartmut s. engel, Ludwigsburg, Germany

LOEWE MODUS, ein Fernsehgerät mit zukunftweisender digitaler Technik. Zu einem Standgerät wird es mit einem interessanten Rack, in das auch der Videorecorder integrierbar ist. Sparsamer Verbrauch durch Verzicht auf überflüssige Funktionen, im Stand-By-Betrieb nur ca. 1 Watt Leistungsaufnahme. Automatische Lautstärkeanpassung, vollautomatisches Tuning und Sortieren der Sender. Sichere Bedienerführung auf dem Bildschirm. Einfache Demontage durch lösbare Verbindungen und Materialkennzeichnung für die sortenreine Trennung und Recycling der Werkstoffe.

The LOEWE MODUS is a television set featuring advanced digital technology; it saves energy by dispensing with superfluous functions, consuming only one watt in stand-by mode. This television boasts conveniences such as automatic volume control and fully automatic programming and sorting of channels. The user learns to operate it step-by-step with on-screen instruction menus. The set is easy to dismantle, and the materials are clearly labeled for sorting and recycling. An optional stand with a space for a VCR transforms the set into an attractive video entertainment center.

FREIZEIT LEISURE 299

HERSTELLER MANUFACTURER
LOEWE OPTA GmbH, Kronach, Germany

PRODUKT PRODUCT
Loewe systems Audio Video-System Audio video system

DESIGN
Phoenix Product Design, Stuttgart, Germany

LOEWE SYSTEMS, ein komplettes Audio-Video-System, bestehend aus HiFi-Anlage im High-End-Bereich, Fernsehgerät und Videorecorder. Durchgehende Gestaltungsmerkmale für alle Systemteile: etwa die Edelstahlplatte mit dem runden Auge für die Infrarotsignale, die die Bedienteile verdeckt. Kabelmanagement zur unsichtbaren Verkabelung der Komponenten, die neben- oder übereinander plaziert werden können. Fernsehgeräte im 16:9-Breitbildformat oder im 4:3-Format. Markante Lautsprecher unter der Bildröhre. Sparsamer Verbrauch (im Stand-By-Betrieb nur ca. 1 Watt). Leichte Bedienbarkeit durch reduzierte Bedienelemente an den Geräten. Einfache Demontage und Materialkennzeichnung für Trennung und Recycling der Werkstoffe.

LOEWE SYSTEMS is a complete audio video system comprising a high-end stereo system, a television set and a video recorder. The individual components have a consistent design, characterized by the high-grade steel panel with its round IR remote control sensor that conceals the controls. The cable management system ensures that all cables remain invisible regardless of whether the units are stacked or placed next to each other. The television comes in a 16:9 widescreen or 4:3 format, with its striking loudspeakers positioned just below the screen; it requires only one watt in stand-by mode. All system components can be operated with the same remote control unit. The components can be easily dismantled, and the materials are clearly identified for sorting and recycling.

HERSTELLER MANUFACTURER LOEWE OPTA GmbH, Kronach, Germany
PRODUKT PRODUCT Loewe CS 1 Fernsehgerät Videorecorder TV set
DESIGN LOEWE OPTA, Kronach, Germany

302 FREIZEIT *LEISURE*

LOEWE CS 1, ein Fernsehgerät aus neuen, recyclebaren Werkstoffen: Stahl für das Gehäuse, Keramik als Trägermaterial für die Elektronikkomponenten. Für das Recycling dieser Werkstoffe werden vorhandene Produktionswege genutzt. Dabei entstehen gleichwertige Rohstoffe und Schlacke, die umweltneutral wiederzuverwenden sind. 16:9 Breitbildformat. Leichte Bedienbarkeit über Bildschirmmenue, auf mechanischen Bedienteil wurde verzichtet. Gute zugängliche Anschlüsse für Kopfhörer, Camcorder etc. in seitlicher Anordnung. Sparsamer Verbrauch (weniger als 1 Watt im Stand-By-Betrieb). Automatische Programmierung und Sortierung der Sender.

The LOEWE CS 1 television set is manufactured using new, recyclable materials: steel for the cabinet, and ceramics as a base material for the electronics. These can be recycled using standard production methods, yielding equivalent raw materials and slag which can be reused without polluting the environment. The set features a 16:9 wide-screen format, with operating instructions available in on-screen menus. Easily accessible headphone and camcorder jacks are located on the side of the unit. Superfluous manual controls have been eliminated, and the television consumes little energy (less than one watt in stand-by mode). Channels are automatically programmed and sorted.

Ökologie/Design Auszeichnung Awarded for Ecology/Design: Vorbildlich durch die funktionsgerechten, weil unbrennbaren Werkstoffe Keramik und Stahl als Trägermaterial für die Elektronikkomponenten. Aufgrund des hohen Stahlanteils (auch Gehäuse) müssen nur wenige Teile zum Recycling demontiert werden. Exemplary use of the functionally-ideal non-combustible ceramic and steel as the bases for the electronic components. Given the high proportion of steel used (casing as well), only a few parts need to be removed for recycling.

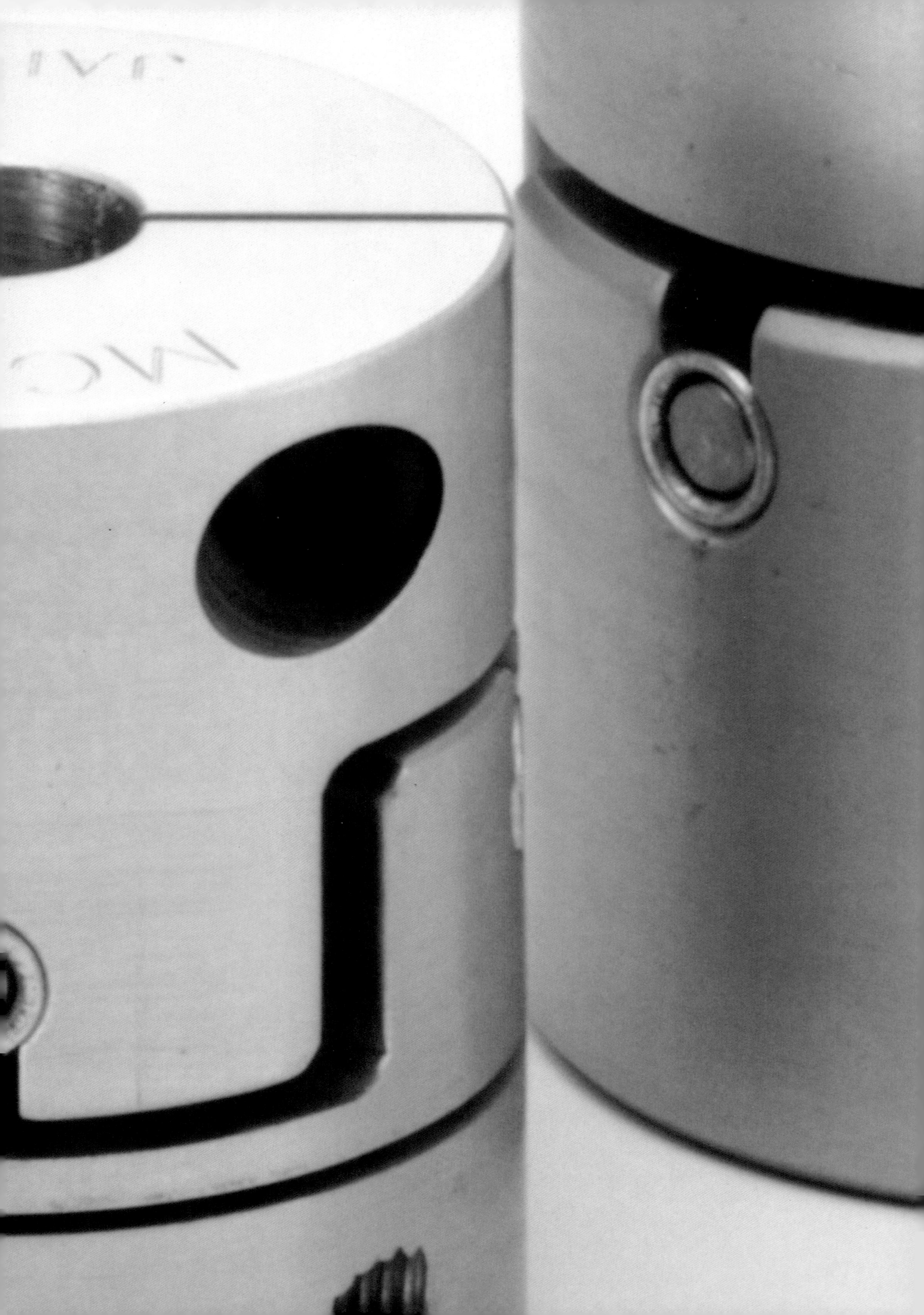

industrie
industry

INDUSTRIE *INDUSTRY*

Jury: Bob Blaich, Hartmut S. Engel, Andreas Haug, Hartmut Warkuß

Bei keinem anderen Design-Wettbewerb sind so viele Produkte aus diesem Sektor zur Beurteilung eingereicht. Das reicht von der Gestaltung einer feinmechanisch gefertigten Ventil-Insel bis zu Großanlagen. Geräte-Familien bekommen eine unverwechselbare Handschrift durch Design: reduzierte Formgebung, charakteristische Farbgebung, gute, durch übersichtliche Grafik gestaltete Bedienerflächen und Schalttafeln, und eine einheitliche, wiedererkennbare Linienführung. Design für Industriegüter ist ein traditionelles, mit der Hannover Messe, der größten Investitionsgütermesse der Welt, verwachsenes Thema und ein Sektor, auf dem sich momentan im Bereich Design erstaunlich viel bewegt.

Ernst Raue, in Personalunion erster Vorsitzender des Industrie Forum Design und Bereichsleiter der Hannover Messe: »Wir wollen in Zukunft noch mehr als bisher ein anregender Dienstleister für die großen Gebiete unserer Messen sein. Wir möchten damit auch deutlich machen, daß die Designinitiative Industrie Forum Design im Umfeld der weltgrößten Industriemesse stattfindet. Damit hat sie eine sehr breite Wirkung, denn an unseren Messen sind über 70 Länder und mehr als 20 000 Unternehmen beteiligt. Deshalb sehen wir hier die einmalige Chance, das Thema Design auch im Messekontext so professionell präsent zu machen, wie es auf der Welt besser nicht möglich wäre.«

Wie die Sonderauszeichnungen zeigen, beginnt sich die ökologische Komponente auf diesem Produktsektor durchzusetzen, und in der Industrie wird die Frage nach ökologischer Verträglichkeit immer mehr zum marktentscheidenden Faktor werden: Ernst Raue: »Dem müssen wir Rechnung tragen, weil in Zukunft ökologisch unverträgliche Produkte nicht mehr auf dem Markt sein werden. Leider gibt es noch viele Länder, wo Ökologie nicht so groß geschrieben wird, aber in den Industriegesellschaften wird es nicht mehr ohne Ökologiebewegung gehen, und auf lange Sicht wird industrielle Tätigkeit kaum denkbar sein, ohne den Materialkreislauf (Recycling) zu beachten. Der Designer muß diese Bedingungen bereits im frühen Vorfeld beachten.«

Designer- und Ingenieurleistung gehen im Bereich Industrie nahtlos ineinander über. Ein formschönes Industrieprodukt, ein modular aufgebautes Meßgerät, befindet sich sogar im Spitzenfeld der Preisträger unter den Top Ten.

In no other design competition were so many products from this sector submitted as entries. The range extended from the design of valve sets manufactured by the finest mechanical processes through to large-scale plant. Design often instills equipment lines with an unmistakable signature: a reduced shape, characteristic coloring, good user interfaces and switchboards featuring clear graphics, and a uniform, readily recognizable design. Design for capital goods is a traditional theme and sector that has evolved with the Hanover Trade Fair, the largest capital goods fair in the world. And at present much is happening in the sector in terms of design.

Ernst Raue, who doubles up as Chairman of Industrie Forum Design and Division head at the Hanover Trade Fair says: "We want in future to act to an even greater extent as a stimulating service provider for the main sectors represented at our fairs. In so doing, we wish to make clear that the Industrie Forum Design design initiative is active in those domains associated with the world's largest industrial trade fair. It thus has a very broad impact, for more than 70 countries and over 20,000 companies take part in our fairs. We therefore see this as a unique opportunity to give design as a theme a professional presence in the trade fair context, something which could not be achieved better anywhere else in the world."

As the special prizes show, the ecological component is beginning to win through in this product sector; and in industry the question of ecological compatibility is becoming an ever greater factor in beating competition: Ernst Raue reports: "We must take this into account, as in future ecologically incompatible products will simply have disappeared from the market. Unfortunately there are still many countries in which far less priority is attached to ecology, but in the industrialized nations the ecological movement is here to stay, and in the long run, industrial activity will hardly be conceivable if it fails to take the materials cycle into consideration, that is to say recycling. Designers must focus on these conditions from a very early stage onwards."

Design as well as engineering achievements merge almost unnoticeably in the Industry category. A beautifully shaped industrial product, namely a module-based measuring device, scored so high as to take its place among the other Top Ten prizewinners.

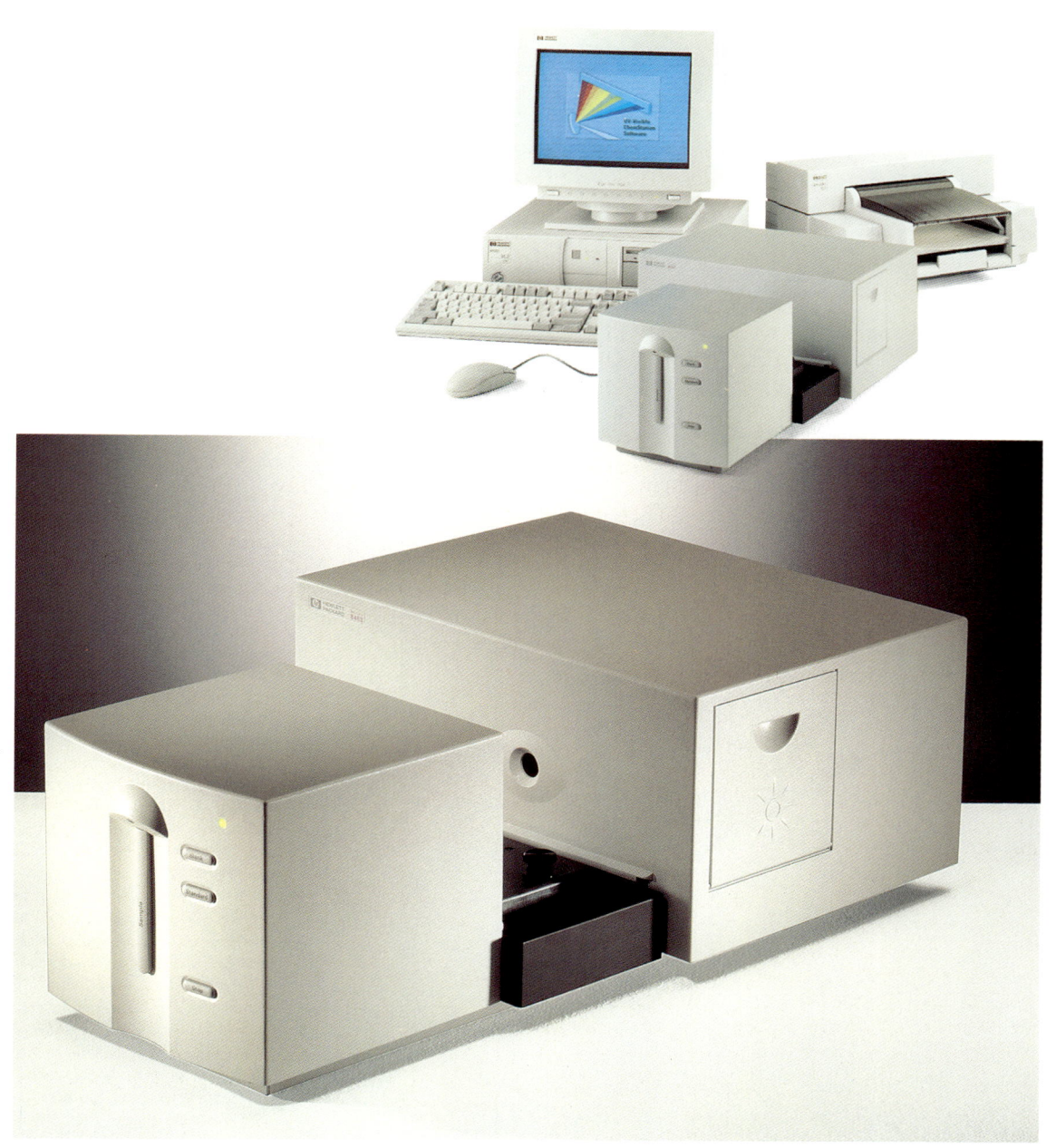

HP 8453, ein Spektralphotometer, in dessen Design Spitzentechnologie mit einer zukunftsweisenden Gehäusekonzeption verbunden wurde. Innen verwendeter EPP-Schaum schützt die Gerätekomponenten und reduziert dadurch den äußeren Verpackungsaufwand. Reparatur auf Baugruppenebene durch den Benutzer möglich. Einfache Bedienung mit deutlich symbolisierten Funktionen. Bildet mit dem Computer auch visuell ein System.

HP 8453 is a spectrophotometer with a design which perfectly combines leading-edge technology with a pioneering casing concept. The EPP foam used on the inside of the casing protects the components and therefore reduces the packaging inputs necessary. Repairs at the specific module level can be made by users themselves. The clear symbols for the functions enhance operational ease. The system blends together with the computer to form a visual unity.

Ökologie/Design Auszeichnung Awarded for Ecology/Design: Vorbildlich wegen eines neuartigen Recyclingkonzepts durch einfache Trennung aller Komponenten. *Exemplary for its new recycling concept and easy separation of all components.*

HERSTELLER MANUFACTURER Hewlett-Packard GmbH, Waldbronn, Germany
PRODUKT PRODUCT HP 8453 Spektralphotometer Spectrophotometer
DESIGN Raoul Dinter, Waldbronn, Germany, Consultant: Via 4 Design, Th. Gerlach

HERSTELLER MANUFACTURER
HYDAC International, Sulzbach, Germany

PRODUKT PRODUCT
SempaFilt Vario SFV Filtrationsgerät Filter

DESIGN
HYDAC International, Dipl. Ing. Designer Wolfgang Schabbach, Sulzbach, Germany

SEMPAFILT VARIO SFV, ein Gerät zur Ultra- und Mikrofiltration von Flüssigkeiten, für den Einsatz in der Lebensmittel-, der chemischen und pharmazeutischen Industrie. Die Filterelemente, sogenannte Kapillarmodule, verbrauchen sich nicht, dadurch geringere Umweltbelastung. Markante Form durch den Rahmen, der der Aufnahme aller Gerätekomponenten dient, die als modulare Bauteile ganz unterschiedlich zusammengesetzt werden können. Bedienelemente sind im drehbaren Bedienpanel angeordnet, das selbsterklärend konzipiert ist und sichere Überwachung ermöglicht. Kabel- und Schlauchträger rückseitig zusammengefaßt.

SEMPAFILT VARIO SFV is a filter system for ultra and microfiltration of liquids, specially designed for use in the food, chemical and pharmaceutical industries. The durable filter elements, so-called capillary modules, suffer no wear-and-tear, enhancing the environmental friendliness of the unit. The frame, on which all the system components are assembled, has been given a striking shape. The components themselves are module-based, allowing customized structuring of the equipment. The self-explanatory controls are laid out on a swivel panel and offer safe monitoring of all processes. The cable and hose ducts are gathered together at the rear of the unit.

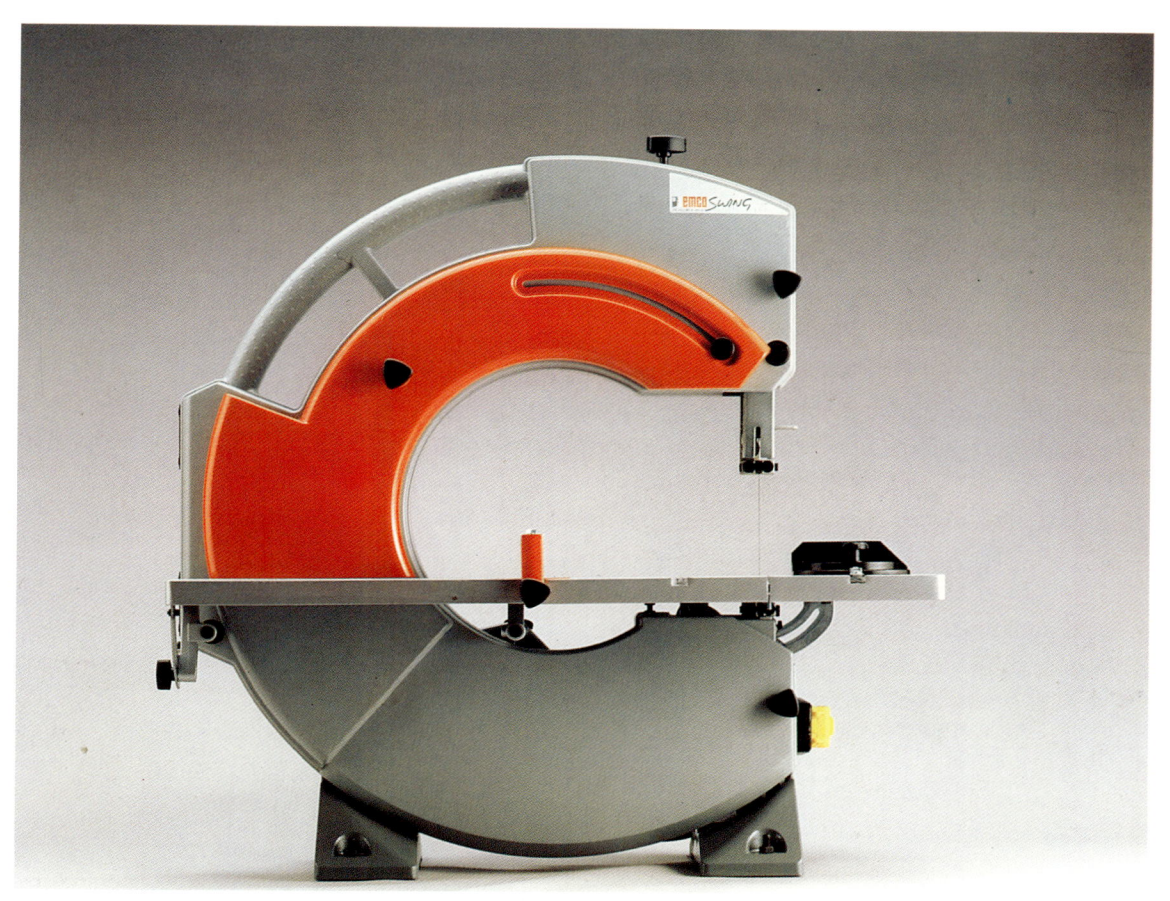

EMCO SWING, Bandsäge mit integrierter Teller- und Bandschleiffunktion. Für den Heimwerkermarkt. Das Design verbindet einfache Bedienbarkeit mit den CE- Sicherheitsanforderungen. Geringe Anzahl von Einzelkomponenten und damit einfache Fabrikmontage führten zu einem günstigen Preis. Vereinigt viele funktionelle Vorteile der Bandsäge: verlustarmer Direktantrieb der Bandsägerollen, einfacher Wechsel des Bandsägeblattes, integrierte Staubabsaugevorrichtung. Schneller Wechsel zwischen Säge- und Schleiffunktion, wobei der jeweils nicht genutzte Teil berührungssicher geschützt wird.

The EMCO SWING is a bandsaw with an integrated sanding disk and sanding belt for DIY use, with a design that affords straightforward operation while meeting safety specifications. As there are only a few individual components, the production is simple, allowing the unit to be offered at a favorable price. It combines a number of functional advantages, such as low-loss direct drive bandsaw rollers, an integrated sawdust collector, and an endless saw blade that is easy to replace. The user can switch rapidly between sawing and sanding, whereby the component not in use is protected against accidental contact.

HERSTELLER MANUFACTURER EMCO MAIER Ges.m.b.H., Hallein, Austria
PRODUKT PRODUCT EMCO SWING Bandsäge Band saw
DESIGN Industrial Design, Mag. Heinrich Krug, Hallein, Austria c/o EMCO Innovationscenter, Hallein, Austria
VERTRIEB DISTRIBUTION EMCO MAIER GmbH & Co. KG, Siegsdorf, Germany

HERSTELLER MANUFACTURER Hilti AG, Schaan, Principality of Liechtenstein
PRODUKT PRODUCT DC-SE 19 Schlitzgerät Slitting tool
DESIGN Scala Design, Böblingen, Germany
VERTRIEB DISTRIBUTION Hilti Deutschland GmbH, München, Germany

HILTI DC-SE 19, ein Schlitzgerät zur professionellen Ausführung von Elektrokanälen in allen gängigen Untergründen wie Beton, Mauerwerk, Kalksandstein und anderen. Gerätedesign im Kontext des Hilti Corporate Design: auch dieses neue Gerät des Programms hat die typischen Schürfrippen, Entlüftungselemente, Schriftfeld und Logo. Dominant sind die beiden Bügelgriffe, die in einer ergonomischen Grundstudie entwickelt wurden, in der auch viele Handhabungsdetails, wie z. B. die werkzeuglose Einstellung der Schlitztiefe, neu definiert wurden. Robuster Aufbau für den rauhen Einsatz, sichere Führung auch mit Arbeitshandschuhen. Bügelgriffe schützen zugleich beide Hände des Arbeitenden.

The HILTI DC-SE 19 is a professional slitting device used to cut channels for electrical conduits in concrete, masonry, sand-lime brick, and all other common materials. This new addition to the product line also reflects the principles of Hilti corporate design, and sports the typical ventilation slots, abrasion protection ribs, logo and lettering. Many operational details (such as adjusting the depth of cut without tools) were reworked in a basic study of ergonomic requirements, which also yielded the two large, striking hoop grips to protect the user's hands from both sides. The robust construction bears up under rugged conditions and the unit can also be handled safely with gloves.

310 INDUSTRIE INDUSTRY

HILTI TE 5 – DRS, der »kleinste Bohrhammer der Welt« mit neuentwickeltem Staubabsaugemodul. Entwicklung des Geräts im Kontext der Hilti Corporate Design (z. B. Farbdesign schwarz und rot) und des servicefreundlichen Baukastensystems. Kompakte Bauweise trotz des neuen Moduls durch diagonal gestellten Motor, eine Schrägwinkelbauweise, die das insgesamt dynamische Erscheinungsbild bewirkt. Ordnung der Formkomplexität durch bewußte, horizontale Linienführung und entsprechend geordnete Farbflächen mit volumenreduzierender Wirkung. Gekennzeichnete, entsorgbare Werkstoffe, Verbundteile nur beim Motor.

The HILTI TE 5 – DRS is the »smallest hammer drill in the world«, and sports a snap-on vacuum cleaner module. It was developed in keeping with aspects of Hilti corporate design (i.e., a black and red color scheme) and is easy to service thanks to its modular construction. The diagonal configuration lends the unit a dynamic and compact appearance, an effect enhanced by a deliberate, horizontal form and corresponding colors. The materials are labeled for easy recycling; the only compound component is the motor.

HILTI DX A 40, ein Bolzensetzgerät zum "Einschießen" von Bolzen in Beton oder Stahl. Im Gegensatz zu älteren Bolzensetzern repetiert die neue DX A 40 automatisch: eine enorme Entlastung des Anwenders. Dazu tragen auch ergonomische Gestaltung, schlagreduzierend wirkende Polster an den Handgriffen und die neue Gewichtsverteilung bei. Neu konzipiert wurde auch der integrierte Griffschutzbügel, der als Schalldämpfer ausgebildet ist und die Explosionsgase an einer sicheren Stelle nach außen leitet. Akzentfarbe "Schwarz" im Vordergrund der Farbgestaltung dieses Produktsegments. Sortenreine Entsorgung durch Konstruktion und Aufbau gesichert.

HILTI DX A 40 is an explosive-actuated tool used to 'shoot' bolts into concrete or steel. Unlike previous versions of this device, the new DX A 40 repeats automatically, facilitating the work tremendously. This advantage is enhanced by the ergonomic design, the shock-absorbing cushioning on the handgrips and a new weight distribution. The grip protector is an important design element. It serves as a muffler, and also guides the explosive gases safely into the open. The construction of the unit makes for simple, straightforward recycling.

HERSTELLER MANUFACTURER Hilti AG, Schaan, Principality of Liechtenstein
PRODUKT PRODUCT oben/above: TE5 -DRS Bohrhammer mit Staubsaugungsmodul unten/down: DX A 40 Bolzensetzgerät Power actuated tool
DESIGN oben/unten: ID&S. Industrie-Design Schindler, Wallenstädten, Germany

INDUSTRIE INDUSTRY 311

HERSTELLER MANUFACTURER Black & Decker Ltd., Spennymoor, Great Britain
PRODUKT PRODUCT links/left: KD 795 CRE 2-Gang-Schlagbohrmaschine 2-gear-drill rechts/right: KD 577 CRT Schlagbohrmaschine Drill
DESIGN Black & Decker Mark Stratford, Spennymoor, Great Britain
VERTRIEB DISTRIBUTION BLACK & DECKER GmbH, Idstein, Germany

links: KD 795 CRE, eine 2-Gang-Schlagbohrmaschine für härteste Anwendungen beim Bohren und Schrauben. Zwei mechanische Gänge bieten hohe Durchsetzungskraft und materialgerechte Drehzahlen. Sichere Handhabung, optimale Gerätekontrolle für präzise Arbeitsergebnisse. Power Sensor wählt beim Schrauben automatisch das optimale Drehmoment, stellt den Motor ab, wenn die Schraube bündig mit der Oberfläche abschließt. Spatengriffkonstruktion für optimalen Bohrfortschritt bei geringem Kraftaufwand. Großflächiger »Soft-Schalter«. Außerdem rautenförmig strukturierter Handgriff und Zweithandgriff für bequeme Handhabung und III Twistlok-Schnellspann-Bohrfutter für schnellen und einfachen Werkzeugwechsel. *left: The KD 595 CRE is a two-gear drill for managing even the most difficult drilling and screwdriving jobs. Two mechanical gears enable the efficient transmission of power from motor to drill bit, resulting in optimal torque and speed for the material at hand for improved control and accuracy. The Power-Sensor-function selects the required torque and stops the driving action once the screw is fully home. Maximum drilling force can be attained with less effort thanks to the drill's D-handle construction. The large soft-feel trigger is easy to operate, while the textured grip and secondary handle provided added comfort during use. Drill bits can be changed simply and quickly with the III Twistlok-keyless chucks.*
rechts: Drill KD 577 CRT, 1-Gang-Schlagbohrmaschine zum Schrauben und Bohren. 620 Watt-Motor, kraftvolles Schlagwerk für schnellen Bohrfortschritt, Power-Sensor für die automatische Präzision beim Schrauben, III Twistlok-Schnellspann-Bohrfutter, vibrationsdämpfende Softgriffe und einfach verstellbarer Zweithandgriff, Sanftanlauf für präzises Anbohren, Auto-Motorstop für mehr Sicherheit bei plötzlich verkantetem Bohrer, Sicherheitselektronik. *right: The KD 577 CRT is a single-gear drill ideal for screwdriving and drilling jobs. It features the following: a 620-watt motor and a powerful hammer action for fast drilling, a Power-Sensor control for screwdriving precision, III Twistlok keyless chucks, soft handgrips, an adjustable side handle, »soft start« to facilitate accurate drilling, an automatic power cut-off should the bit jam during use, and »no voltage release« electrical safety control.*

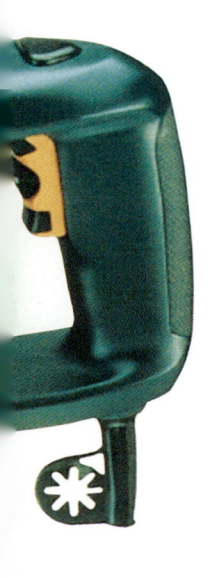

INDUSTRIE *INDUSTRY* 313

HERSTELLER MANUFACTURER I. kränzle GmbH, Bielefeld, Germany
PRODUKT PRODUCT kränzle Therm Hochdruckreiniger High pressure cleaner
DESIGN Günther Schulz, Remscheid, Germany

KRÄNZLE THERM, ein Heißwasser-Hochdruckreiniger für professionelle Anwendung.
KRÄNZLE THERM is a hot-water high-pressure cleaner for professional applications.

HERSTELLER MANUFACTURER ARCA Regler Gmbh, Tönisvorst, Germany
PRODUKT PRODUCT BIOVENT Hygiene Regelventil Hygenic control valve
DESIGN ARCA Regler, Heinz M. Nägel, Tönisvorst, Germany

ARCA BIOVENT, hygienisches Regelventil mit pneumatisch aktiviertem, vollkommen geschlossenem, spritzwassergeschütztem Mehrfeder-Membranantrieb aus massivem Chromnickel-Edelstahl. Ausschließlich wartungs- und schmiermittelfreie Konstruktionselemente. Baukastensystem, entwickelt als Komponente zum Einbau in Produktionsanlagen der chemischen und Lebensmittelindustrie, in denen besondere hygienische Anforderungen gelten. Optisch ansprechendes Design. Einfache, wirkungsvolle Reinigungsmöglichkeiten. Von der US-Gesundheitsbehörde für den Einsatz in der Lebensmittelproduktion freigegeben.

The ARCA BIOVENT is a hygienic control valve with a fully sealed pneumatic multi-spring diaphragm actuator made of solid chromium-nickel stainless steel. All components are non-lubricated and maintenance-free. The modular system was developed for use in production plants in the chemical and foodstuffs industry, where hygiene is especially crucial. The optically appealing unit is easy to clean, and has been approved by the US Food and Drug Administration.

HERSTELLER MANUFACTURER
Wilo GmbH & Co., Dortmund, Germany
PRODUKT PRODUCT
top-wilo Umwälzpumpen Pump for service water circulation
DESIGN
designpraxis diener ulm, Ulm, Germany

TOP-WILO, eine neu konzipierte Baureihe von Pumpen zur Brauchwasserumwälzung mit integriertem, elektronischen Motorvollschutz, Leistungsanzeige, Störmeldung und serienmäßiger Wärmedämmung durch Iso-Schalen. Nachrüstbar sind Betriebsdatenanzeige und eine digitale GLT-Schnittstelle. Hergestellt aus recyclefähigen Materialien und wasserlöslichen Lacken.
TOP-WILO is a new line of fully electronic pumps for service water circulation. An integrated motor protection plate, a malfunction indicator, and heat insulation are standard features throughout the series. A data display and digital interface are available as options. The pumps are made of recyclable materials and coated with water-soluble paints.

EEV ARGUS THERMAL IMAGING CAMERA, Rauchdurchsichtgerät für Rettungsdienste und Feuerwehr: zum schnellen Auffinden von Opfern im dichten Rauch, bei Dunkelheit und durch Mauern hindurch. Neues Design mit neuester elektronischer Bildverarbeitungstechnik. Nur ein einziger Funktionsknopf, Einhandbedienung, auch mit Handschuh und Atemgerät. Gehäuse besteht aus aluminosilicat beschichtetem Spritzguß und ist extrem hitzebeständig, spritzwasserdicht, stoßgeschützt.

The EEV ARGUS THERMAL IMAGING CAMERA is a rescue aid for locating people in dense smoke, darkness, and through walls. Its novel design incorporates the latest developments in electronics technology for one-handed operation at the touch of a single button. It can be used with or without gloves or a breathing mask. The injection-molded housing is coated with aluminosilicate to withstand high temperatures; it is also water and shock-resistant.

HERSTELLER MANUFACTURER EEV LTD, Chelmsford, Great Britain
PRODUKT PRODUCT EEV Argus Wärme-Bild Kamera Thermal-imaging camera
DESIGN Random Product Design, London, Great Britain

INDUSTRIE INDUSTRY 317

HERSTELLER MANUFACTURER J. Wagner GmbH, Markdorf, Germany
PRODUKT PRODUCT W 600 Feinsprühsystem Fine-spraying system
DESIGN Industrielle Produkte Hans Joachim Krietsch GmbH, München, Germany

318 INDUSTRIE *INDUSTRY*

WAGNER W 600, Feinsprühsystem, ein ganz neu konzipiertes Farbsprühsystem für den Heimwerkermarkt: mit deutlich verringerter Bildung von Farbnebeln in der Sprühumgebung. Dafür sorgt eine »Luftglocke«, die den Sprühstrahl umgibt, der seinerseits mit sehr niedrigem Druck aus der Düse austritt. Zur Verarbeitung auch von wasserverdünnbaren Lacken, Lasuren, Holzschutzmitteln. Im Innen- und Außenbereich universell einzusetzen, leicht zu bedienen (auch von Laien), schnell zu reinigen.

The WAGNER W 600 is a completely novel fine paint spraying system which considerably reduces the quantity of paint mist in the spraying area. The paint/air mixture emerges from the nozzle at very low pressure, and a mantle of air around the spray jet prevents the mist from spreading. It is suitable for paints, varnishes and wood preservatives, either water-based or containing organic solvents. It can be used both inside and outdoors, and is easy to operate and clean.

HERSTELLER MANUFACTURER
PRODUKT PRODUCT
DESIGN

SOUTHCO GmbH, Radolfzell, Germany
Flush-pull™ Schnappverschluß Flush-pull latch
SOUTHCO, Lynn B. Ziemer, Charles Scally, Paul Krape, Concordville, USA

FLUSH-PULL™, ein Schnappverschluß, bevorzugt zum Schliessen von Deckeln, Klappen, leichten Türen. Zum Öffnen läßt sich der Griff aus jeder Richtung zu einem max. Öffnungswinkel von 75° aus der Mulde ziehen. Zusätzlicher Griff ist nicht erforderlich. Falle aus Acetal mit besonderen Gleiteigenschaften, verschleißfrei: selbst nach 20.000 Schließzyklen völlig ohne Abnutzungsspuren. Mit integriertem Schloß lieferbar.

FLUSH-PULL™ is a latch specially designed for lids, covers or lightweight doors. To open, the handle can be pulled out to an angle of 75° in any direction. The catch bolt is made out of acetal resin, which has a natural lubricity, and will show no signs of wear and tear even after 20,000 times. It is available in a locking or non-locking version, and can be installed in panels of up to 22mm in thickness, requiring a single round hole.

LÖSBARE GESICHERTE MUTTER, die aus drei Teilen besteht: Kopf mit Außenrändel und innenliegendem Gewinde aus Aluminium, Einpreßhülse aus gehärtetem Stahl, und eine in dieser Hülse geführten Druckfeder aus rostfreiem Stahl. Diese Feder drückt den nicht verschraubten Kopf nach oben. Mit den unverlierbaren Muttern, die höheren Sicherheitsanforderungen als die meisten Flügelmuttern genügen, können die Inspektions- und Serviceklappen geschlossen werden. Metrische und Zollgrößen, die Oberfläche mattschwarz oder metallisch.

This RETRACTABLE CAPTIVE NUT made of aluminium and stainless steel features a concealed ejector spring, enabling it to disengage from the screw or bolt. It meets safety requirements more adequately than traditional wing nuts and prevents parts from being dropped, misplaced or lost. It can be used for service and inspection covers on machines and appliances. The nut is available in metric and imperial measurements and comes in a matt-black or metallic finish.

HERSTELLER MANUFACTURER SOUTHCO GmbH, Radolfzell, Germany
PRODUKT PRODUCT Lösbare, gesicherte Mutter Retractable captive nut
DESIGN SOUTHCO, Albert Frattarola, Kevin La Valley, Concordville, USA

INDUSTRIE *INDUSTRY* 321

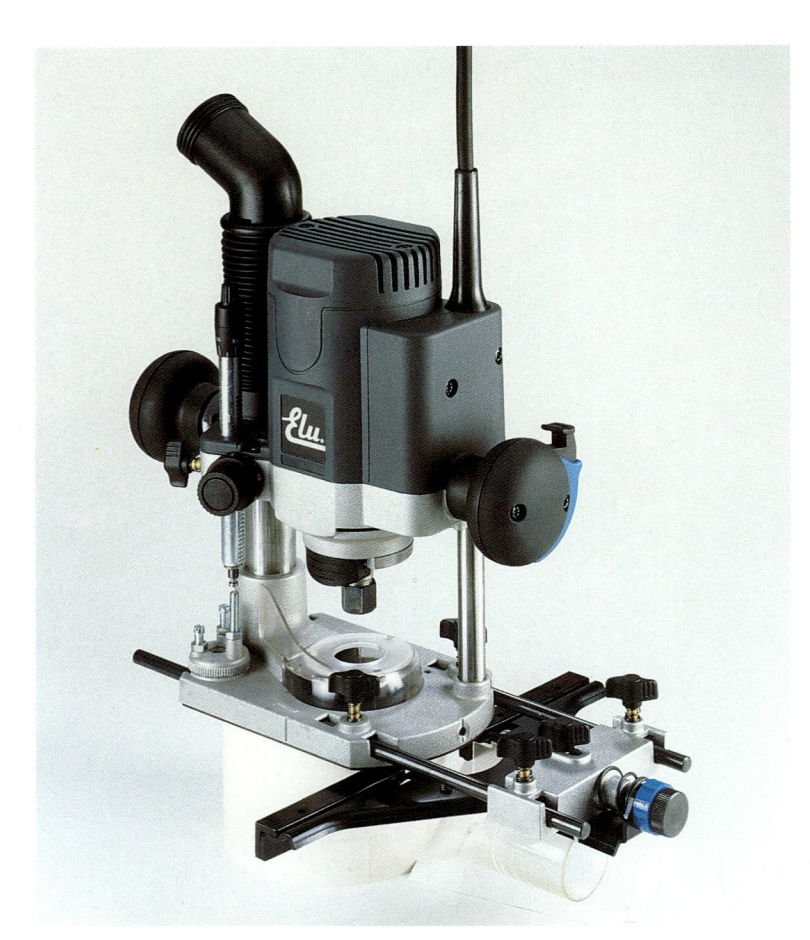

HERSTELLER MANUFACTURER	Elu S.p.A., Molteno, Italy
PRODUKT PRODUCT	OF 97 Oberfräse Router
DESIGN	ELU INTERNATIONAL, Michael Stirm, Idstein, Germany
VERTRIEB DISTRIBUTION	ELU INTERNATIONAL Black & Decker GmbH, Idstein, Germany

ELU OF 97, Oberfräse, ein Präzisionswerkzeug. Kritische und extrem belastete Bauteile werden aus speziellen Alu-Legierungen besonders exakt gefertigt. Präzisionstiefenanschlag (Toleranz 0,1 mm) Elektronische Drehzahlregelung, hochwirksames Staubabführungssystem, reduzierte Arbeitsgeräusche. ergonomisch perfekte Schalterkonstruktion.

The aluminium alloy components of the ELU OF 97 router are precision-engineered to afford accurate and efficient operation as well as reduce noise level. It features a precision bit gauge (tolerance of 0.1 mm), electronic speed control, an efficient sawdust collection system, and an ergonomic switch design.

AZ 17/AZM 170 ist eine Sicherheitsverriegelung, für die Sicherheit beim Arbeiten an Maschinen: Schalter und Verriegelung garantieren, daß Schutzgitter o.ä. geschlossen sind, bevor die Maschine anläuft. Besonders kompakt gebaut, für beengte Einbauräume. Mit seinem quadratischen Querschnitt ist der Schalter ohne Umbau in allen vier Richtungen zu montieren. Außerdem Schneid-Klemmtechnik zum schnellen Anschluß der Steuerkabel. Zum Schutz vor einem mißbräuchlichem Überbrücken der Sicherheitsschalter mit individuell codierten Schaltschlüsseln lieferbar.

The AZ 17 / AZM 170 is a safety switch/lock for machines. It guarantees that protective grids etc., are closed before the machine can be turned on. It is especially compact for use in tight spaces, and its square shape allows it to be mounted in four different directions without modification. The insulation displacement contacts make the control cables easy to connect. An individually coded switch key is also available to prevent unauthorized bypassing of the switch.

HERSTELLER MANUFACTURER K. A. Schmersal GmbH & Co. Industrieschaltgeräte, Wuppertal, Germany
PRODUKT PRODUCT AZ 17/AZM 170 Sicherheitsschaltuhr Safety switch
DESIGN Wings of Design, Walter Heidenfels, Danos Papadopoulos, Wuppertal, Germany

HERSTELLER MANUFACTURER
HYDAC International, Sulzbach, Germany

PRODUKT PRODUCT
SempaFilt Compact SFC Filtrationsgerät

DESIGN
HYDAC International, Dipl. Ing. Designer Wolfgang Schabbach, Sulzbach, Germany

SEMPAFILT COMPACT SFC, ein Gerät zur Ultra- und Mikrofiltration von Flüssigkeiten, für den Einsatz in der Lebensmittel-, der chemischen und pharmazeutischen Industrie. Mit Filterelementen, sogenannten Kapillarmodulen, die sich nicht verbrauchen, dadurch geringere Umweltbelastung. Bestimmend für die Formgebung ist der betonte Rahmen, der der Aufnahme aller Gerätekomponenten dient. Bedienelemente ergonomisch günstig an der Vorderseite zusammengefaßt. Rückseitig sind Kabel- und Schlauchträger in die Form integriert.

The SEMPAFILT COMPACT SFC is a device for the ultrafiltering and microfiltering of fluids in the chemical, pharmaceutical and foodstuffs industries. The filter elements, also called capillary modules, do not wear out or need replacement and thus help reduce waste products. The frame houses all other components and is the main design feature. The controls are conveniently located on the front of the unit, while the cable and hose supports are integrated into the back.

HYDAC PROCESSFILTER, LOW-PRESSURE PFL, zum Einbau in Rohrleitungen in der chemischen Industrie und der Verfahrenstechnik. Dient zum Abscheiden von Feststoffen aus Flüssigkeiten. Die Gestaltung wird von zwei Formelementen bestimmt: Der Zylinder durchläuft den Filter oben als optische Weiterführung der Rohrleitung horizontal und wird vom Filtergehäuse »umklammert«. So leitet er den Flüssigkeitsstrom »optisch« ins Filterelement. Die griffige Verschlußmutter ist werkzeuglos zu öffnen. Ihre dominante Farbgebung und das Logo ordnen den Filter in die Hydac-Produktfamilie ein.

The HYDAC LOWPRESSURE PFL PROCESS FILTER is for use in process technology and the chemical industry, and is installed in pipelines to separate particles from fluids. It features a unique design: The cylinder at the top of the filter is the optical horizontal continuation of the pipe. It is »clasped« by the filter housing and »optically« guides the fluid into the filter element. The gripping cap nut can be loosened without tools. The striking colors and logo characterize the filter as a member of the Hydac product range.

HYDAC International, Sulzbach, Germany HERSTELLER MANUFACTURER
ProcessFilter Lowpressure PFL Edelstahlfilter Stainless steel process filter PRODUKT PRODUCT
HYDAC International, Dipl. Ing. Designer Wolfgang Schabbach, Sulzbach, Germany DESIGN

INDUSTRIE *INDUSTRY* 325

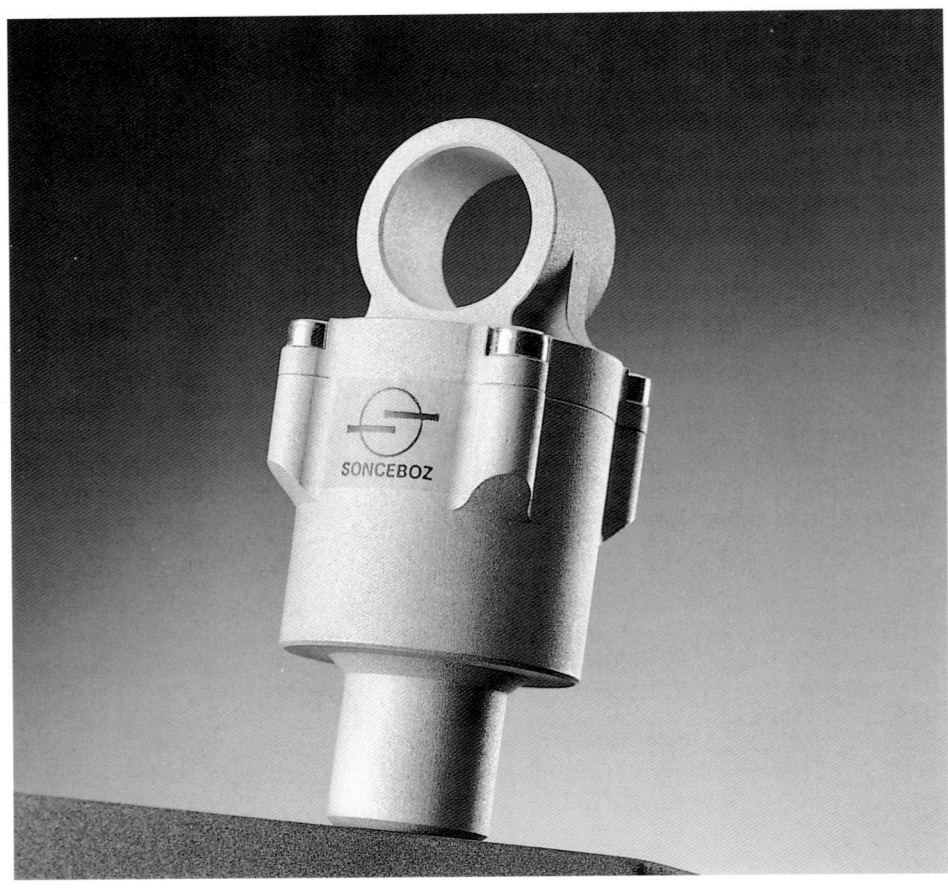

HERSTELLER MANUFACTURER SONCEBOZ SA, Sonceboz, Switzerland
PRODUKT PRODUCT Typ 7214 Linearantrieb Linear actuator
DESIGN SONCEBOZ SA, Sonceboz, Switzerland

LINEARANTRIEB TYP 7214, dessen Dauermagnetschrittmotor eine lineare Bewegung in 0,0125mm-Schritten ermöglicht. Geschwindigkeit motorabhängig, Kraft: 40 Newton bei 12 Volt. Die Spindelsteigung ist so gewählt, daß der Antrieb selbsthemmend ist und ein Zurückdrehen unter Last unmöglich wird. Lebensdauer 10 Jahre, Zyklenzahl: 6 Millionen Hübe; einsatzfähig bei Temperaturen zwischen –40° und +80° Celsius.

LINEAR ACTUATOR TYPE 7214 features is a permanent magnet stepping motor that permits linear motion at 0.0125mm per step. The speed depends on the motor rpm; the linear force is 40 newtons at 12 Volt. The spindle is constructed so as to prevent the motion from reversing under pressure. The unit has a service life of 10 years, or more than 6 million cycles, and can be operated at temperatures between –40° and 80° Celsius.

MINIATUR-KUPPLUNGEN mit hoher Verdrehungssteife und vorzüglichem Ansprechverhalten. Schlupf von Bolzen und Buchsen ermöglichen höchste Parallel- bzw. Winkelversetzungen und garantieren Minimal-Belastungen auf die Wellen. Durch den präzisen Sitz von Bolzen und Buchsen praktisch ohne Spiel.

This MINIATURE COUPLING features excellent torsion resistance and high responsiveness. The slipping action of the pin and bearing bush affords the greatest degree of parallel or angular displacement and guarantees minimal stress on the shafts. The exact fit between pin and bush means almost zero backlash.

NABEYA KOGYO Co., Ltd., Gifu, Japan   HERSTELLER MANUFACTURER
Miniatur Kupplungen Miniature coupling   PRODUKT PRODUCT
NABEYA KOGYO, Gifu, Japan   DESIGN

HERSTELLER MANUFACTURER Rohde & Sohn GmbH + Co. KG, Nörten-Hardenberg, Germany
PRODUKT PRODUCT WG-33 Winkelgriff Angled handle
DESIGN Rohde & Sohn, Dipl. Ing. Günter Rohde, Nörten-Hardenberg, Germany

WINKELGRIFF WG-33, als Bedienlement in beliebiger Länge für Schiebetüren und Auszüge von Maschinen und technischen Anlagen, auch als Kantenschutz geeignet. Mattglänzend in verschiedenen Farben.
WG-33 ANGLE HANDLES are available in any length for sliding doors and drawers in machinery and technical plants, and can also serve as edge protectors. They are epoxy-coated and sport a dull gloss finish in a choice of three colors.

HERSTELLER MANUFACTURER Klöckner-Moeller GmbH, Bonn, Germany
PRODUKT PRODUCT FAK Fuß- und Grobhandtaster Foot and palm switches
DESIGN busse design ulm gmbh, Elchingen, Germany

FAK Fuß- und Grobhandtaster, ein Befehlsgerät zum Schalten von elektrischen Kontakten, in rauhen Industrieumgebungen ebenso einsetzbar wie zum Beispiel in Fernsehstudios. Auffälliger Not/Aus-Taster in den Signalfarben Rot/Gelb. Ob mit flacher Hand, Faust, Knie oder Fuß, mit Handschuhen oder ohne, die als Kugelkappe ausgebildete Betätigungsfläche ist von allen Seiten sicher zu bedienen. Die seitlich heruntergezogene Trennebene zwischen Ober- und Unterteil erleichtert die Verdrahtung der Kontaktelemente, vier ausbrechbare Kabeleinführöffnungen zur optimalen Positionierung des Schalters.

FAK foot and palm switches are for controlling electrical contacts, with applications ranging from harsh industrial environments to television studios. They feature a conspicuous red and yellow Emergency/Stop switch. The domed actuating surface can be operated from all sides with an open palm, fist, knee or foot, with or without gloves. The division between cover and base has been extended down the sides of the device, thus facilitating the wiring of contact elements. Four punch-out cable entry points enable optimal placement of the switch.

HERSTELLER MANUFACTURER	item Industrietechnik und Maschinenbau GmbH, Solingen, Germany
PRODUKT PRODUCT	Abdeckprofil System Cover Profile System
DESIGN	item, Solingen, Germany
VERTRIEB DISTRIBUTION	item Industrietechnik und Maschinenbau GmbH, Solingen, Germany

ABDECKPROFIL SYSTEM. Konstruktionen aus Profilstäben sind oft durch eine Vielzahl von sichtbaren Nuten und Hinterschnitten gekennzeichnet. Diese Hinterschnitte sind bei der Erstellung der Konstruktion zur Verbindung der Profilstäbe untereinander und zur Befestigung verschiedener anderer Komponenten funktionell notwendig. Nach der Erstellung der Konstruktion beeinträchtigen die Hinterschnitte die leichte Reinigung und besonders eine sachliche und eigenständige optische Erscheinung. Das item Abdeckprofil System ermöglicht die staubdichte Abdeckung der Hinterschnitte und eine individuelle Gestaltung der Konstruktion. Der Anwender wird durch die Wahl der Geometrie, der Farbe und des Oberflächenmaterials der Abdeckprofile zum Gestalter. Dazu können die Abdeckprofile nachträglich und ohne mechanische Bearbeitung von Hand befestigt und ohne Beschädigung wieder demontiert werden.

COVER PROFILE SYSTEM. Frames bult from profile sections often feature large numbers of visible grooves which are necessary for making connections between profiles and for securing various other components. These machine features impair the easy cleaning of the assembled frame and detract from its visual integrity and aesthetic appearance. The cover profile system from Item provides a dusttight seal for the grooves and lends the construction a more individual and professional appearance. Item cover profiles are available in various geometries, colours and surface materials and thus offers the user a whole range of design options. They can be fitted by hand without any need for additional machining and can be used with existing frames. The profiles can also be removed easily without any risk of damage.

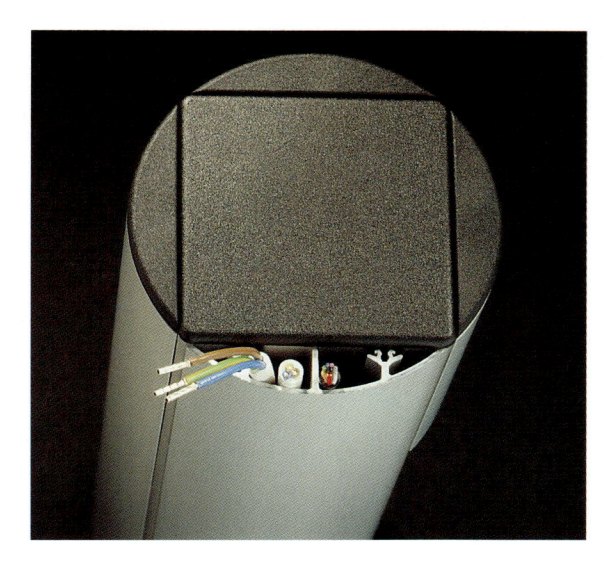

HERSTELLER MANUFACTURER
Odenwälder Kunststoffwerke GmbH & Co. Gehäusesysteme KG, Buchen, Germany
PRODUKT PRODUCT
TOP-KNOBS Dreh- und Schalterknöpfe Tuning and controlling knobs
DESIGN
polyform Industrie Design, Martin Nußberger, Ludwig Segenschmid, München, Germany

TOP-KNOBS, außergewöhnliche Serie von Dreh- und Schalterknöpfen. Seitliche Befestigung durch Innensechskantschraube auf zylindrische Achsen. Schlichter, leicht bombierter Knopfkorpus mit stets gleicher Aussparung am Umfang für einsteckbare Markierungselemente in Form von »Stift«, »Kugel«, »Scheibe« »Fahne«, die die Schalterstellung auf markante Weise kennzeichnen. Fünf Größen für zwei Achsdurchmesser. Sensible und trotzdem kontrastreiche Farbgebung durch NC-Schema. Polyamid mit matter Oberfläche.

TOP-KNOBS are a extraordinary series of tuning and controlling knobs which spin on a cylindrical axis with a hexagon socket. The simple, lightly dished knobs all feature a recess into which various elements in the shape of a peg, a sphere, a disk or a flag can be inserted. Each of these shapes indicates the set position of the knob in a unique way. The knobs are made out of polyamide with a matt surface. They come in five sizes and two different axis diameters, with a color scheme that is tasteful yet rich in contrast.

INDUSTRIE *INDUSTRY* 333

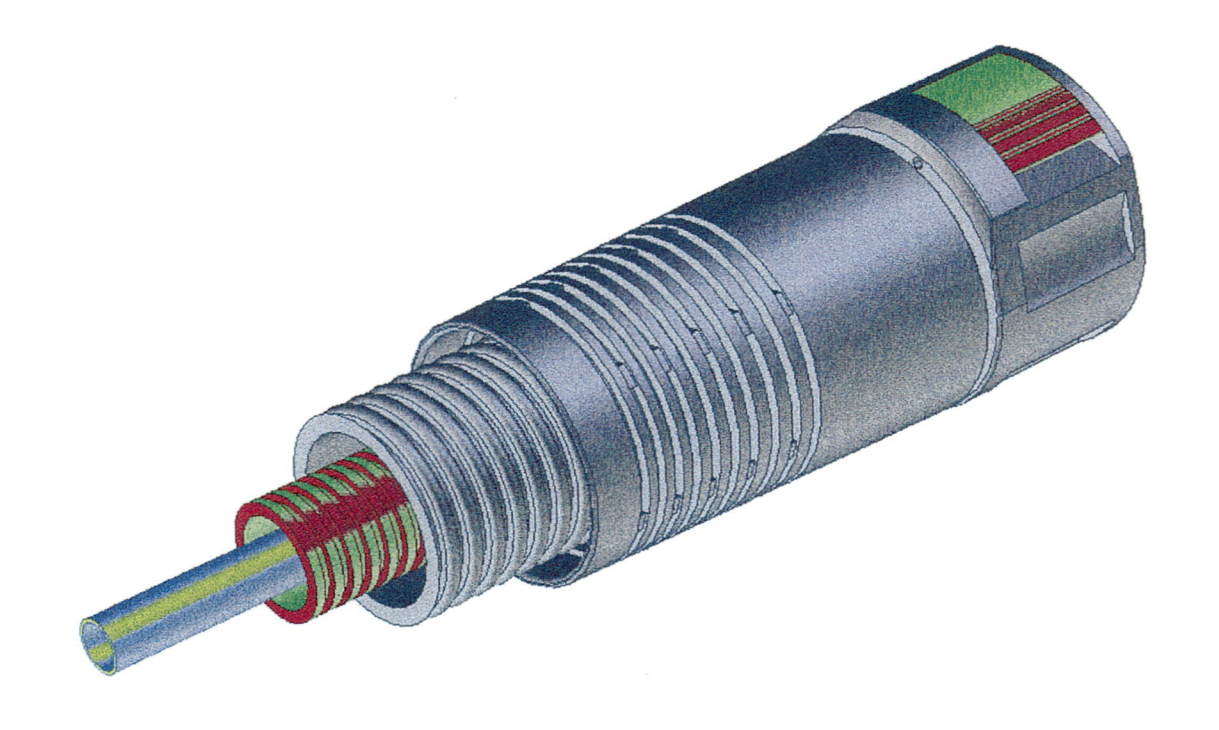

HERSTELLER MANUFACTURER FESTO Tooltechnic KG, Esslingen, Germany
PRODUKT PRODUCT IAS 2 Schlauchsystem Hose system
DESIGN STUDIOWERK-DESIGN, Kern . Schirrmacher, Inning, Germany

IAS 2, ein Schlauchsystem zum Betrieb von Druckluftwerkzeugen. Drei Funktionen, drei konzentrische Schläuche: Zuführung der Druckluft; Abführen der entspannten Druckluft (damit werden Ölnebel vermieden); Absaugen des Schleifstaubes (für staubarmes, effektives Arbeiten). Schnellkupplung mit einem Drehelement, das ein Gegeneinander-Drehen von Druckluftwerkzeug und Schlauchsystem gestattet und damit die Handhabung des Werzeuges wesentlich erleichtert. Klares technisches Design des Kupplungsstückes, macht die Funktion der Bajonettkupplung selbsterklärend.
The IAS 2 is a hose system for operating pneumatic tools. Its three concentric hoses supply compressed air, remove unstressed compressed air to prevent oil mist, and collect sawdust for more effective work. The system is connected to the tool via a quick-action coupling, which enables it to be twisted to the angle that best facilitates use. The function of the bayonet coupling is self-explanatory thanks to its clear, technical design.

CLASSIC TIGER, Steuerventil für Aktoren in allen Industriebereichen. Kompakte Bauweise mit hoher Durchflußrate, schnelle Reaktionszeiten. Umweltfreundlich mit ölfreier Druckluft zu betreiben. Metallteile recyclingfähig. Modulares Verpackungssystem.

CLASSIC TIGER is a control valve for actuators in all areas of industry. Its compact design affords a high rate of flow and fast reaction times. The valve is highly environmentally friendly: It operates using compressed air and thus requires no lubrication; metal parts recyclable. It features a modular packaging system.

FESTO KG, Esslingen, Germany — HERSTELLER MANUFACTURER
Classic Tiger Steuerventil Control valve — PRODUKT PRODUCT
FESTO Entwicklungsabteilung, Esslingen, Germany — DESIGN

HERSTELLER MANUFACTURER
FESTO KG, Esslingen, Germany
PRODUKT PRODUCT
CPE-10, CPE-14 Muffenventil In-line valve
DESIGN
FESTO, Esslingen, Germany

336 INDUSTRIE *INDUSTRY*

oben: CPE-10 und CPE-14, Compact Muffenventile mit hoher Durchflußleistung bei minimaler Ventilbaubreite. Geringer Einbauraum erforderlich, niedriges Gewicht. Umfangreiche Ventilfunktionen als Baukastensystem. Geringe Leistungsaufnahme, Magnetspulen formal integriert, mit und ohne Handhilfsbetätigung.
top: The CPE-10 and CPE-14 are light-weight compact socket valves allowing high flow rates at minimal valve width. A comprehensive range of valve functions is available as part of a modular system. Features include low power consumption, an integrated solenoid, and optional manual override.

CPV-10, ein Ventilinsel-Baukasten mit geringen Abmessungen ermöglicht den Einbau direkt im Arbeitsraum der Maschine. Multifunktionale Anwendungsmöglichkeiten durch umfangreiche Ventilfunktionen. Wählbare elektrische Ansteuerungen: Einzel-, Multipol-, Feldbus-, ASI-Anschluß, auswechselbare Verkettungsplatten, modulare, platzsparende und einfache Ventilmontage im 2er Raster.
The CPV-10 is a compact Terminal valve system that can be easily installed directly within the working area of the machine. It features an extensive range of valves for multifunctional applications. Single, multipole, field bus or ASI electrical connections can be used to power the valves, and the sub-bases are interchangeable.

HERSTELLER MANUFACTURER
FESTO KG, Esslingen, Germany
PRODUKT PRODUCT
CPV-10 Ventilinsel Terminal valve
DESIGN
FESTO, Esslingen, Germany

INDUSTRIE *INDUSTRY* 337

HERSTELLER MANUFACTURER FESTO Tooltechnic KG, Esslingen, Germany
PRODUKT PRODUCT CDD 12 ES + MC 15 CDD Akku-Bohrschrauber und Ladegerät Cordless drill screwdriver and quick charger unit
DESIGN STUDIOWERK-DESIGN Kern. Schirrmacher, Inning, Germany

CDD 12 ES Akku-Bohrschrauber mit besonders kompakter, geschlossener Bauweise. Eigenständiges Design: die kurze Bauweise sorgt für Vorteile im Hinblick auf Ergonomie, Handhabbarkeit und Funktionalität. Die Gestaltung des Griffes läßt mehrere Griffpositionen zu, Fingermulden seitlich und vor dem Rechts-/Linksschalter ermöglichen präzises Führen und Halten des Schraubers. Leistungsstark durch hochwertigen Motor, 2-Gang-Planetengetriebe und die elektronische Drehzahlregelung mit Auslaufbremse. Das dazugehörige Ladegerät MC 15 CDD lädt den Hochleistungsakku in 15 Minuten auf.

The unique, compact design of the CDD 12 ES cordless drill/screwdriver offers advantages in terms of ergonomics, functionality and handling. The shape of the handle permits it to be held in various ways, while the finger grips on the side and in front of the directional switch allow the unit to be guided with precision. The CDD 12 ES also boasts a powerful motor, 2-speed planetary gear and electronic speed control with a run-down brake. The accompanying MC 15 CDD quick charger recharges the battery in just 15 minutes.

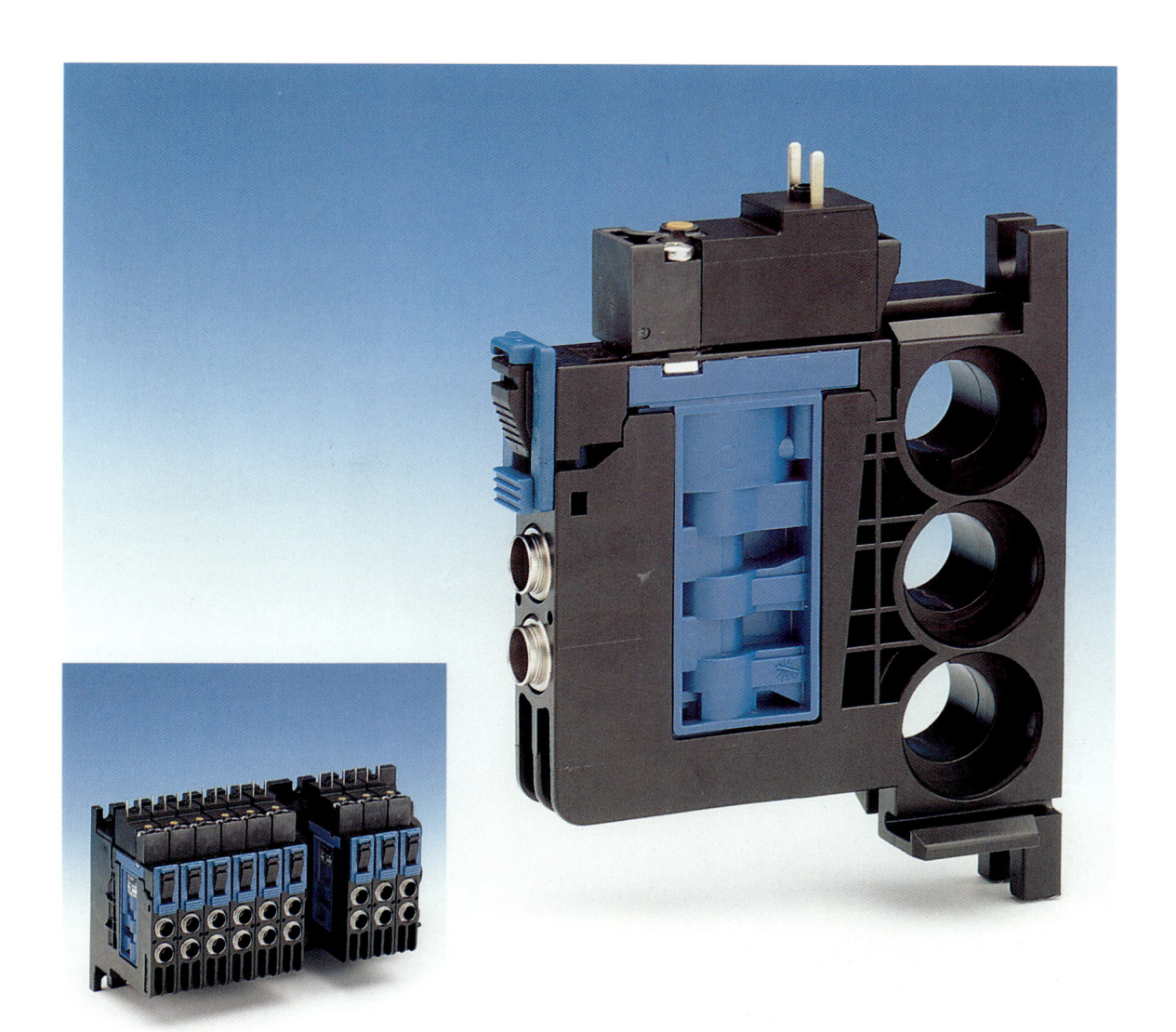

Mannesmann Rexroth Pneumatik GmbH, Hannover, Germany — HERSTELLER MANUFACTURER
Compact 15 Magnetventil Solenoid valve — PRODUKT PRODUCT
Mannesman Rexroth Pneumatik, Hannover, GmbH — DESIGN

Das COMPACT 15 VENTIL bietet den Vorteil eines klassischen Grundplattenventils mit den Vorteilen eines In-Line-Ventils. Die völlig andersartige Gestaltung der Grundplatte ermöglicht eine verlustarme Strömungsführung vonn 700 l/min. bei einer Ventilbreite von 15 mm. Grundplatten und Ventile können ohne Werkzeug zusammengeklippt werden.

VALVE TYPE COMPACT 15 offers the advantage of the classic subpiate valve with the advantages of an in-line valve. The completely different construction of the subplate allows a low-loss flow of 700 l/min. by a valve width of 15 mm. Subplates and valves have to be clipped without using tools.

INDUSTRIE INDUSTRY 339

HERSTELLER MANUFACTURER
Siemen + Hinsch mbH, Itzehoe, Germany
PRODUKT PRODUCT
SIHI dry Schraubenspindel Vakuumpumpe Screw-spindle vacuum pump
DESIGN
3D factory Jens Storm, Martin Langkau, Kiel, Germany

SIHI^{DRY}, Schraubenspindel-Vakuumpumpe. Neuartige Konzeption als »trockenlaufende Vakuumpumpe«: die isochor arbeitende Verdrängermaschine wird mit einem berührungslos schnellrotierenden Schraubenspindelpaar in vertikaler Bauweise betrieben. Die elektronische Motorpaar-Synchronisation sorgt dafür, daß die Pumpe vollständig ölfrei (»trocken«) läuft. Zuverlässig durch elektronisch geregelten Rotoreinzelantrieb und Selbstüberwachung. Drehzahlvariation und neuartige Kühlsysteme erweitern das Einsatzspektrum. Anwendungsbezogene Werkstoffe und eine verschleißfreie Konstruktion garantieren eine lange Standzeit.

The novel SIHI ^{DRY} vacuum pump is an isochoric displacement machine driven by two non-contact rapidly rotating screw-spindles. Electronic synchronization of the dual motor means the pump operates completely oil-free (»dry operation«). and is highly dependable thanks to an electronically controlled single rotor drive and self-diagnosis system. Its variable speed function and a new cooling system make it useful for a wide range of applications. Suitable materials and elimination of wearing parts guarantee a long service life.

Hersteller Manufacturer: Luther & Maelzer GmbH, Wunstorf, Germany
Produkt Product: ALS 11 Adapterladesystem Adapter loading system
Design: Design Drei, Jan-Michael von Lewinski, Hannover, Germany

ALS 11, ein Adapterladesystem, das bei der Einrichtung von Leiterplattenprüfmaschinen benötigt wird. Aus einem mit ca. 20.000 Nadeln gefüllten Magazin füllt es die Testadapter mit Prüfnadeln. Damit die Nadeln die gewünschte Position erreichen und nicht »danebengehen«, wurde großer Wert auf einfache und sichere Handhabung gelegt: Das schwenkbare Mittelteil des Ladesystems rastet in bestimmten Positionen automatisch ein. Klare, nachvollziehbare Gliederung der Elemente. Gerät benötigt wenig Stellfläche.

The ALS 11 is a compact adapter loading device for loading PCB (printed circuit board) testing machines. It fills the test adapter from a magazine containing 20,000 needles. Controlled, straightforward operation is necessary to ensure that the needles are positioned correctly. The rotating mid-section of the loading device automatically locks into pre-set positions. The functional elements are arranged in a way that is clear and easy to understand.

Hartmann & Braun AG, Frankfurt, Germany HERSTELLER MANUFACTURER
Contrans I Interface Baugruppen Interface units PRODUKT PRODUCT
Uwe Lichtenvort, Essen, Germany DESIGN

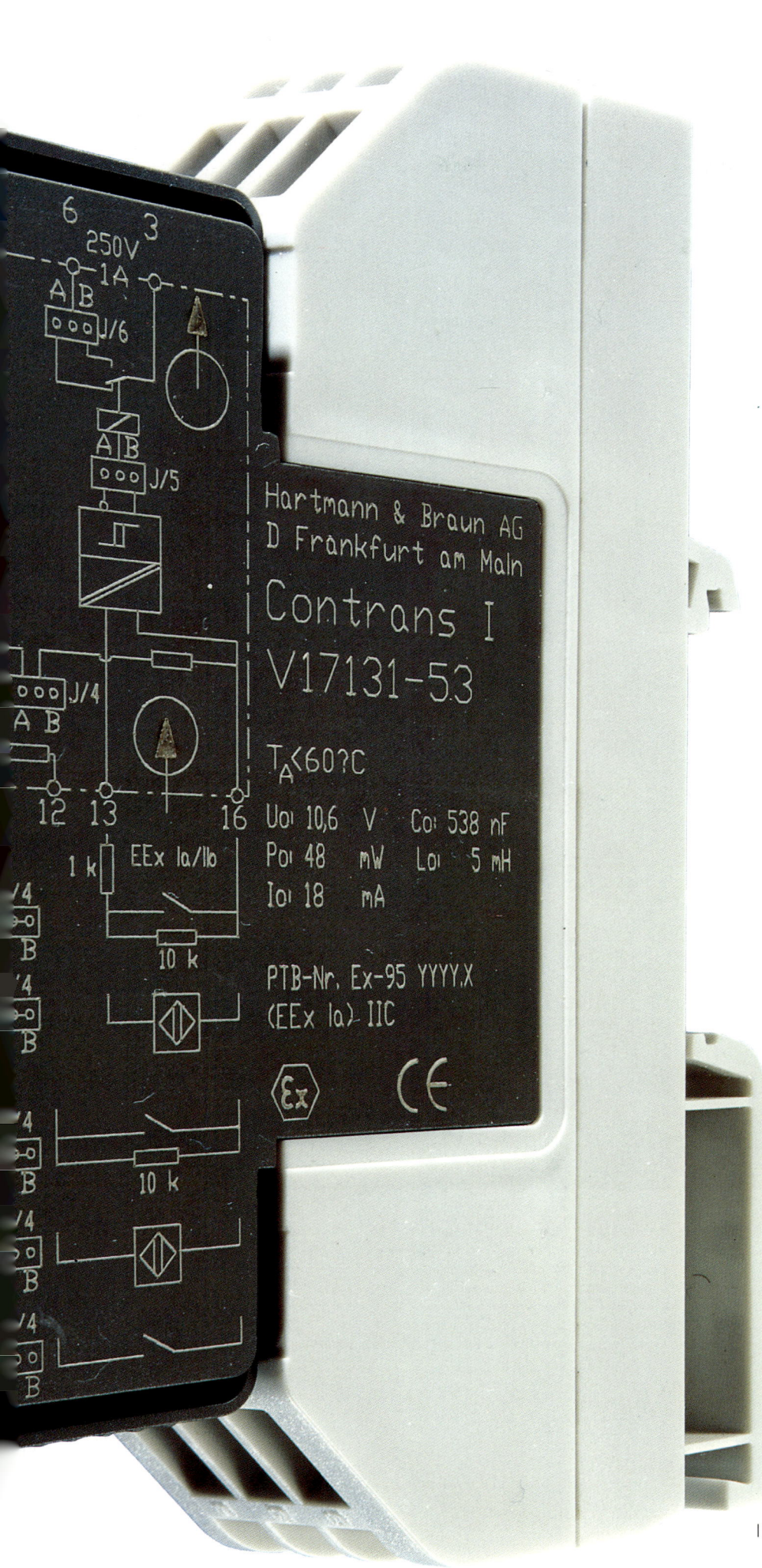

CONTRANS I, Interfacebaugruppen, die den Funktionsumfang von Steuerungen und Automatisierungssystemen erweitern. Werden eingesetzt, um elektrische Signale aus explosionsgefährdeten Bereichen sicher zu erfassen. Gesamte Anschlußtechnik in einem Sockel, der auf Hutschiene oder Montagewand aufgeschnappt wird. Bedienungsanleitung mit international verständlicher Darstellung unverlierbar auf den Modulseiten angebracht. Ökologischer Aspekt: Schutz vor elektromagnetischen Störfeldern ohne zusätzliche Metallbeschichtung der Kunststoffteile, Laserbeschriftung statt Aufdruck, sortenreines Zerlegen der gekennzeichneten Kunststoffteile.

CONTRANS I interface units enhance the range of functions performed by control and automation systems. They are used to receive electrical signals safely in areas where the danger of explosion exists. All connections are situated on one base which is snapped onto a top hat rail or mounting rail. The international operating instructions are attached to the module to prevent loss. Environmental considerations: The plastic elements are protected from electrical magnetic interference without additional metal coating, and numbered to facilitate dismantling and sorting according to grade; laser inscription is used instead of imprinting.

HERSTELLER MANUFACTURER
Parsytec Computer GmbH, Aachen, Germany

PRODUKT PRODUCT
Parsytec CC Hochleistungscomputer Cognitive computer

DESIGN
Via 4 Design GmbH, Nagold, Germany

PARSYTEC CC, Hochleistungs-RISC-Personal Computer, der speziell für die Mustererkennung in der Investitionsgüterindustrie entwickelt wurde. Das jeweils benötigte System wird aus leistungsfähigen Kameras und Scannern in Verbindung mit intelligenten und schnellen Auswerteverfahren aufgebaut. Solche kognitiven Maschinen lesen im Serieneinsatz handgeschriebene Belege und Formulare, finden Krebszellen in Tomografiebildern, sortieren Briefe oder erkennen Falschgeld.

The PARSYTEC CC is a high-performance PC featuring RISC technology, and was developed for pattern recognition applications in the capital goods industry. The required pattern recognition system is created using powerful cameras and scanners in combination with swift, smart evaluation processes. These »cognitive machines« are used to read handwritten forms, find cancer cells in tomographic images, recognize counterfeit currency, and sort mail, among other things.

344 INDUSTRIE *INDUSTRY*

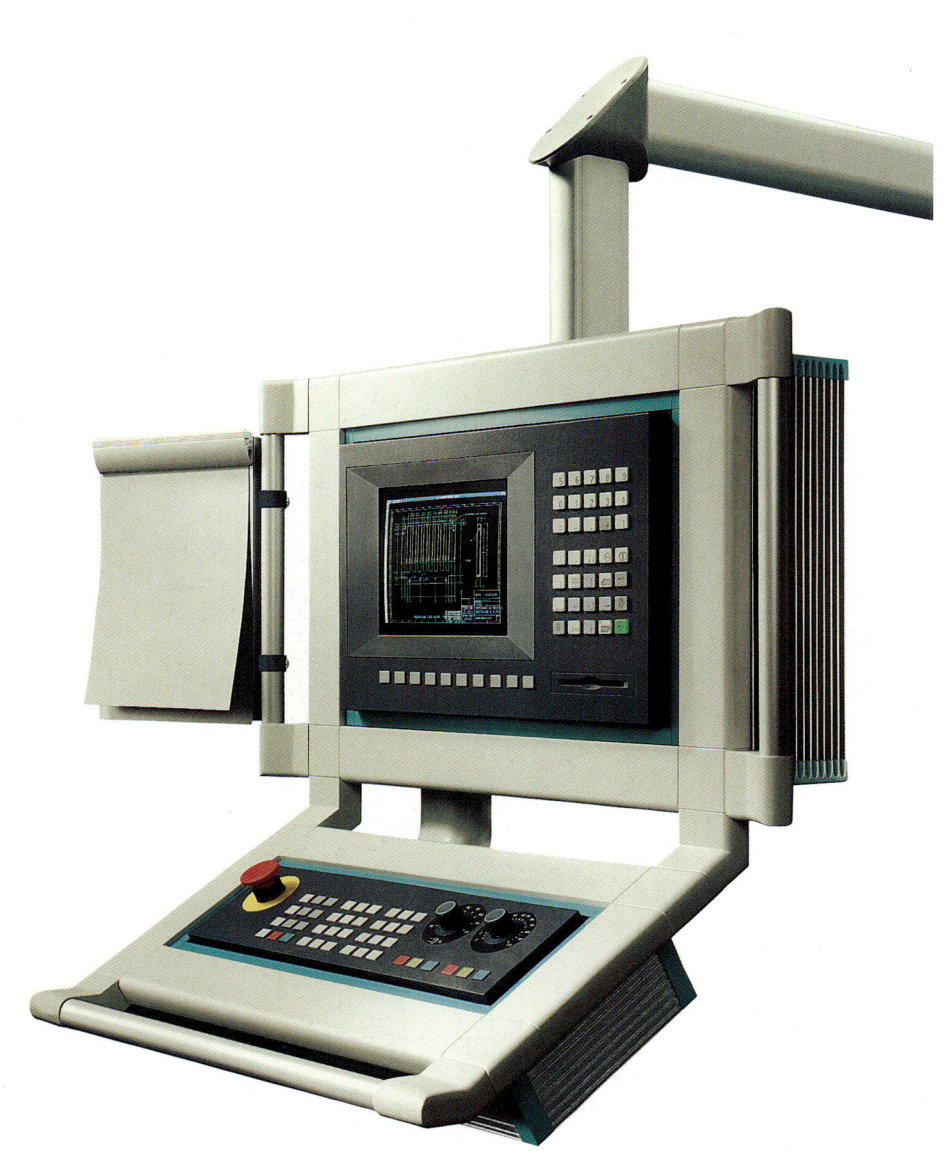

COMMAND-PANEL VIP 6000, ein Flachbediengehäuse, modular und kompakt aufgebaut, mit unbegrenzter Anwendungsvielfalt. Wahlweise mit Tastaturgehäuse oder -wanne. Sechs Grundmodelle und Bauformen, individuelle Anpassung der Gehäuseabmessung möglich. Mit umlaufenden anprofilierten Schraubkanälen im 25mm-Raster ist ein individueller Innenausbau möglich. Von der Rückseite frei zugängliche, variable Befestigung. Farbige Kederprofile zur Abdekkung der Befestigungsschrauben und individueller Designgestaltung. Gehäuseoberfläche mit und ohne Kühlrippen lieferbar.

The COMMAND-PANEL VIP 6000 is a compact, modular control panel/keyboard housing with virtually unlimited applications. It comes with either a keyboard housing or a keyboard tray, and is available in six basic sizes for a custom fit with other components. Continuous interior grooves at intervals of 25mm allow individual components to be mounted with screws. The unit can be accessed from the back, and clip-on mounting elements allow adaptation to nearly all control panels. Colored piping conceals mounting screws and gives the unit an individual appearance. The housing surface is available with or without cooling ribs.

HERSTELLER MANUFACTURER Rittal-Werk Rudolf Loh GmbH & Co. KG, Herborn, Germany
PRODUKT PRODUCT COMMAND-PANEL VIP 6000 Modulares Flachbediengehäuse Flat control panel housing
DESIGN Witte Design, Kay-Uwe Witte, Tony Douglas, Offenbach, Germany

INDUSTRIE INDUSTRY 345

HERSTELLER MANUFACTURER
AEG Aktiengesellschaft, Warstein-Belecke, Germany
PRODUKT PRODUCT
Thyrosoft 3 DC Sanftanlaufgerät Soft starter
DESIGN
Van Dijk/Eger/Associates Münster, Germany Zeist, The Netherlands

THYROSOFT 3DC dient dem »sanften Anlauf« von Drehstrommotoren auf die Nenndrehzahl. Die integrierte Funktion des Sanftauslaufs ist bei Bedarf aktivierbar. Die elektrische Auslegung entspricht einem Einsatzbereich für Motoren von 5,5 kW bis 450 kW in der 400V-Ausführung und 7,5 kW bis 630 kW in der 500V-Ausführung. *The THYROSOFT 3DC brings three-phase current motors smoothly up to nominal speed, and the integrated soft-start function can be activated as required. It is designed for use with 400V motors ranging from 5.5 kW to 450 kW, and 500V motors from 7.5 kW to 630 kW.*

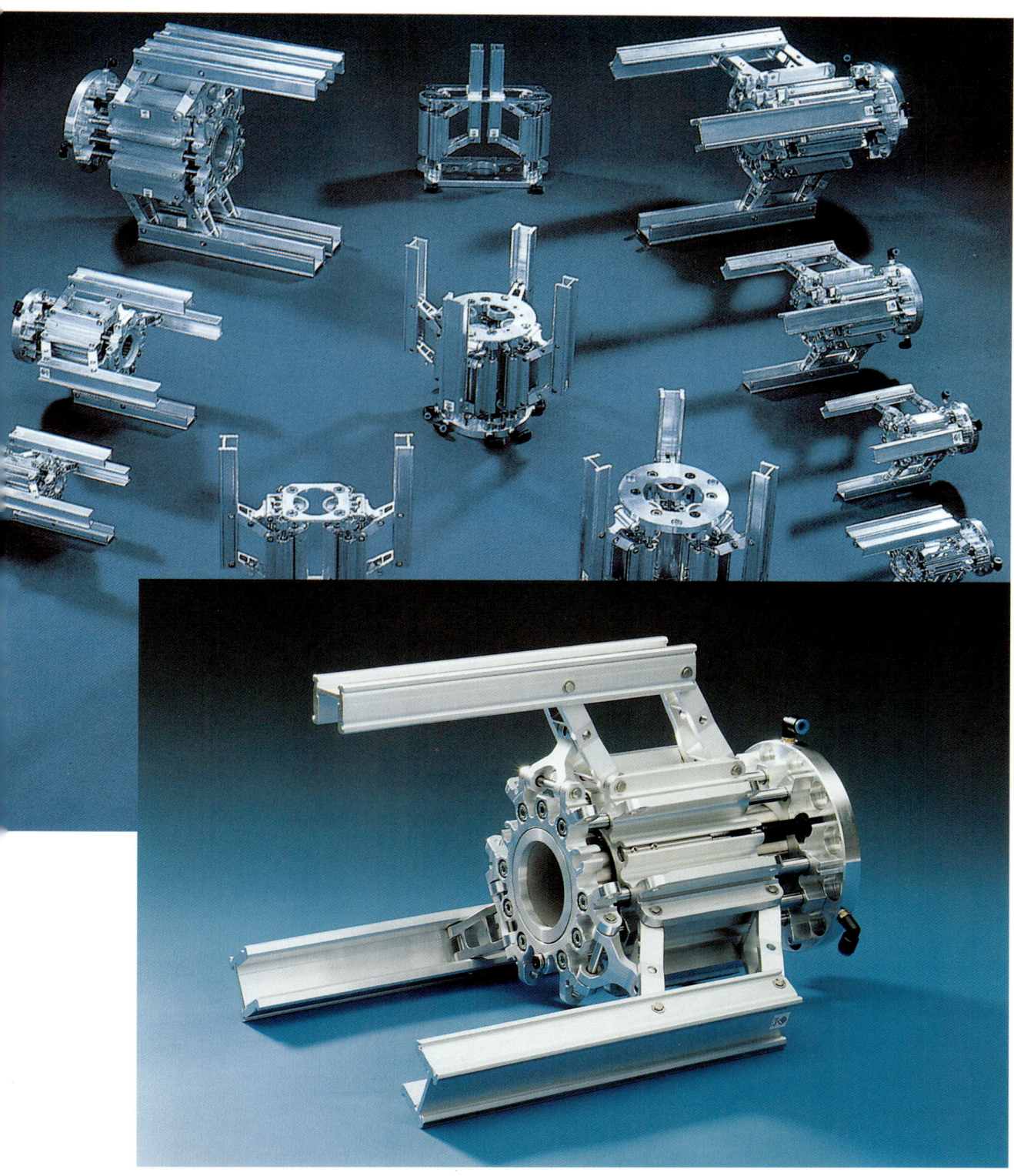

HERSTELLER MANUFACTURER GMG - Gesellschaft für modulare Greifersysteme m.b.H., Soest, Germany
PRODUKT PRODUCT Greifer für Roboter Robot gripper
DESIGN GMG Prof. Dr. M. Mohsen Saadat, Dipl.-Ing. Joachim Gokorsch, Soest, Germany

GREIFER C110 für Industrieroboter und Handhabungsgeräte. Arbeitet nach einem neuartigen, weltweit patentierten kinematischen Prinzip, mit pneumatischem Antrieb und schmierungsfreien Drehgelenken für bis zu 6 Greiffinger. Großer Greiferhub, exakt parallele und schwenkende Fingerbewegung. Geringes Eigengewicht bei hohen Leistungsdaten. Sechs verschiedene Basiselemente: Grundplatte, Kopfplatte, Schieber, Lenker, Kurbel, Finger, alle aus Strangpreßprofilen. Material- und Gewichteinsparung, geringer Energie- und Fertigungsaufwand, Einzelteile sind wiederverwendbar. Wartungs- und schmierungsfrei, dadurch sehr umweltfreundlich.

The C110 GRIPPER is for industrial robots and handling devices, and functions according to a novel kinematic principle that has been patented worldwide. Up to six gripper fingers are operated via pneumatic actuation and lubrication-free swivel joints. The gripper has a large stroke, and the fingers can swivel as well as move perfectly parallel to one another. Manufacturing the six basic elements out of extruded aluminium profiles results in a lightweight product and reduces material and energy consumption. This environmentally-friendly gripper is maintenance-free, and the individual components can be recycled.

INDUSTRIE *INDUSTRY* 347

HERSTELLER MANUFACTURER
PSION PLC London, Great Britain
PRODUKT PRODUCT
PSION Workabout Mobiler Computer Hand-held computer
DESIGN
Frazer Design Consultants, London, Great Britain
VERTRIEB DISTRIBUTION
PSION GmbH, Bad Homburg, Germany

PSION WORKABOUT, ein Computer zur mobilen Datenverarbeitung. Funktionen auf das praktisch Notwendige konzentriert, dadurch sehr günstiges Preis/Leistungsverhältnis. Für alle Unternehmen in den Bereichen Handel, Vertrieb, Dienstleistung und Fertigung.
The PSION WORKABOUT is a hand-held computer which dispenses with superfluous functions. Those employed in commerce and industry can now enjoy the benefits of a high quality portable computer at a hitherto unheard-of low price.

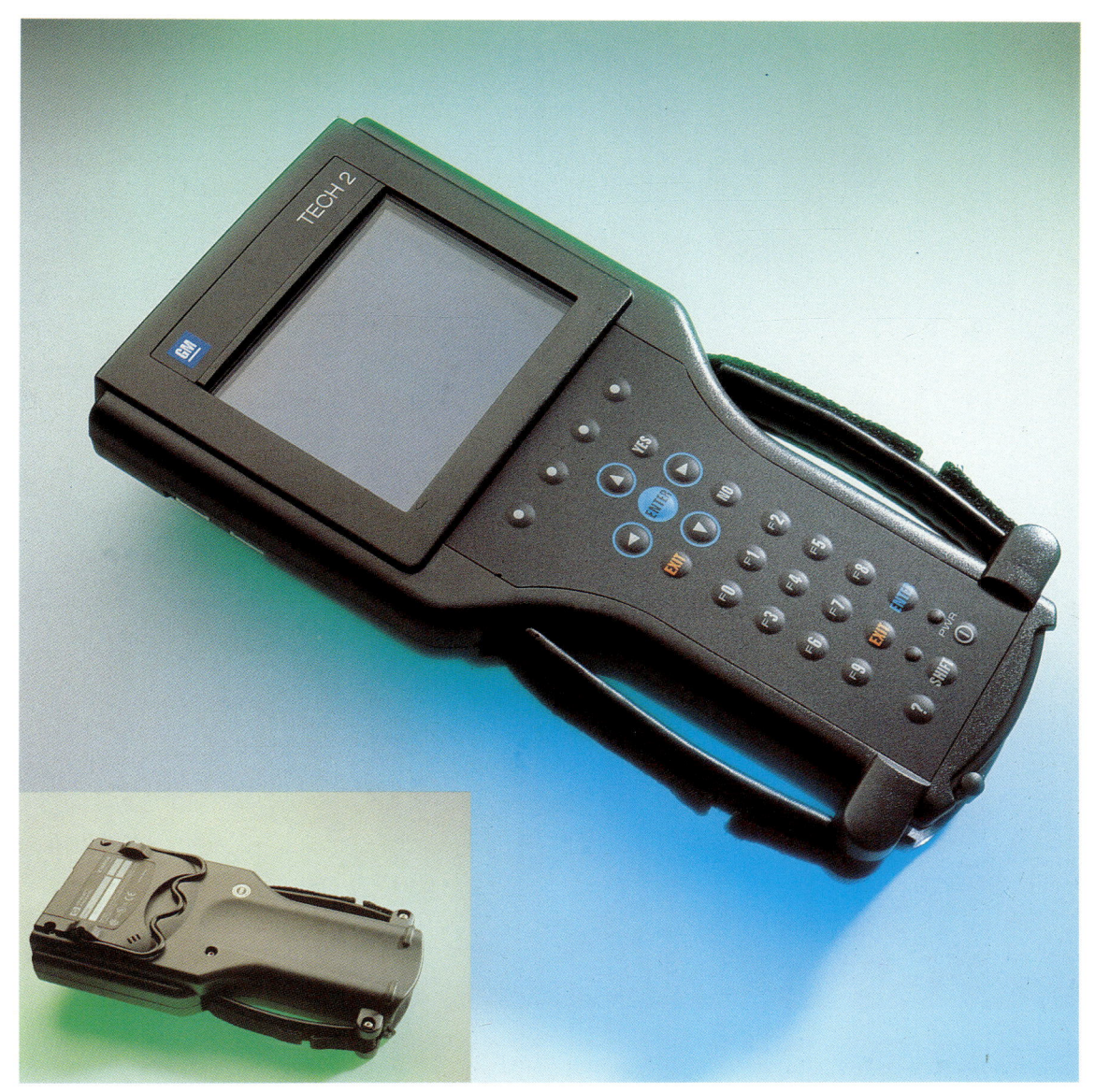

TECH 2, ein weltweit eingesetztes Diagnose-Gerät für alle Modelle von General Motors. Es ist für den Einhandbetrieb entwickelt, für Rechts- oder Linkshänder. Kommunikation mit dem Kraftfahrzeug durch das austauschbare und upgrade-fähige VCI-Modul (vehicle communications interface).

TECH 2 is used worldwide for electronic diagnosis of General Motors vehicles. It is designed for one-handed use in either hand, and communicates with the vehicle through a VCI (vehicle communications interface) module, which can be exchanged and upgraded.

HERSTELLER MANUFACTURER Hewlett-Packard Company Integrated Systems Division, Sunnyvale, California, USA
PRODUKT PRODUCT Tech 2 Automobil-Diagnosegerät Automotive Diagnostic tool
DESIGN Dave Skinner, Redwood Shores, California, USA

INDUSTRIE *INDUSTRY* 349

oben/above: FLUKE 40/41 Power Harmonics Analyse Gerät Power harmonics analyzer unten/below: FLUKE 865/867 Grafische Multimeter Graphical multimeter
HERSTELLER MANUFACTURER FLUKE CORPORATION, Everett, USA
PRODUKT PRODUCT
DESIGN FLUKE CORPORATE DESIGN, Indie King + Stratos Product Development Group, Everett, USA unten/below: FLUKE CORPORATE DESIGN + ENGINEERING TEAM Steve Fisher, Everett, USA

oben: FLUKE 40/41, Power Harmonics Analyser, ist ein Testgerät für Stromverteilungssysteme, zur täglichen Störfallbehebung, Korrektur und Optimierung. Das Produkt wurde für extreme Umgebungen entwickelt und kann mit Schutzhandschuhen bedient werden. »Semantische« Formgebung erleichtert die Bedienung. Bedienelemente besser geschützt in Vertiefungen. Das Gehäuse ist völlig abgedichtet gegen Wasser und Schmutz und bietet einen sicheren Griff.

top: The FLUKE 40/41 Power Harmonics Analyser is an analyzer for troubleshooting, correcting, and optimizing the performance of power distribution systems. It was developed for use in rugged environments, and thus can also be operated wearing a glove. It bears a »semantic« design that facilitates operation, and the controls are recessed for greater protection. The housing is completely gasket-sealed to protect against water and dirt and provide a secure grip.

unten: FLUKE 865/867, grafische Multimeter, sind spezielle Testgeräte für die tägliche Störfallbehebung in Stromverteilungssystemen. Kompakte und handliche Bauweise, einfach zu bedienen. Seitliche Rundungen zeigen, wo das Gerät anzufassen ist. Am Design der Bedienelemente wirkten potentielle Anwender mit, so wurde eine einfache, übersichtliche Gestaltung des Bedienfelds erreicht.

below: The FLUKE 865/867 grafical multimeter are special testing devices for trouble-shooting in power distribution systems. It is compact and easy to use, with curved sides that facilitate gripping and allow the unit to be rested against the body for added support. Potential users helped design the straightforward, clearly organized control panel.

SIMATIC S7-400 Speicherprogrammierbare Steuerung zum Einsatz in Montagehallen (Auto-, Schwerindustrie), komplette Gerätefamilie in gekapselter Blockbauform. Einfache Variantenbildung durch modularen Aufbau. Einfache Montage/Demontage. Material: sortenreiner Kunststoff mit Kennzeichnung durch Recyclingzeichen. Laserbeschriftung statt Klebeschilder. Außenverpackung aus recyclefähiger Pappe.
The SIMATIC S7-400 programable control device was designed for use in assembly plants in the automobile and heavy industries, and comprises a complete set of encased, block-shaped devices. This modular design is the basis for a variety of combinations that are easy to assemble and dismantle. Units are made of pure-grade plastic labeled for recycling and packaged in recyclable cardboard. Laser inscription was used instead of adhesive labeling.

HERSTELLER MANUFACTURER Siemens Aktiengesellschaft, Berlin - München, Germany
PRODUKT PRODUCT SIMATIC S7-400 Speicherprogrammierte Steuerung Programable controller
DESIGN Siemens Design, Thomas Blümel, München, Germany

HERSTELLER MANUFACTURER Siemens Aktiengesellschaft, Berlin - München, München, Germany
PRODUKT PRODUCT SIMAS JOB COMPACT 200 Kommissionierungsanlage für Druckjobs in Rechenzentren Order-commissioning module for print jobs in computer centres
DESIGN Siemens Design, Andreas Preussner, München, Germany

SIMAS JOB COMPACT 200, Kommissionieranlage für Druck-Jobs (Papierstapel aus Einzelblättern oder eine gestapelte Endlosliste) in Rechenzentren. Gestaltung in architekturorientierter Leichtbauweise. Visuelle Kontrolle der Arbeitsabläufe durch transparenten Plexiglasaufbau. Farbe: anthrazit-matt. Kompakte Bauweise mit großer Lagerkapazität. Bedienfreundlicher, sekundenschneller Zugriff. Kommissionierzelle im Störfall begehbar. Recyclebare Materialien.

The SIMAS JOB COMPACT 200 is a user-friendly Order–commissioning module for printing jobs (either single sheets or continuous paper) in computer centers, and features an architecturally inspired lightweight construction. The work processes can be visually monitored through a sheet of transparent acrylic glass. The compact unit has a large storage capacity, and can be serviced in the event of a malfunction. It is made of recyclable materials and comes in matt charcoal-gray.

INDUSTRIE *INDUSTRY* 353

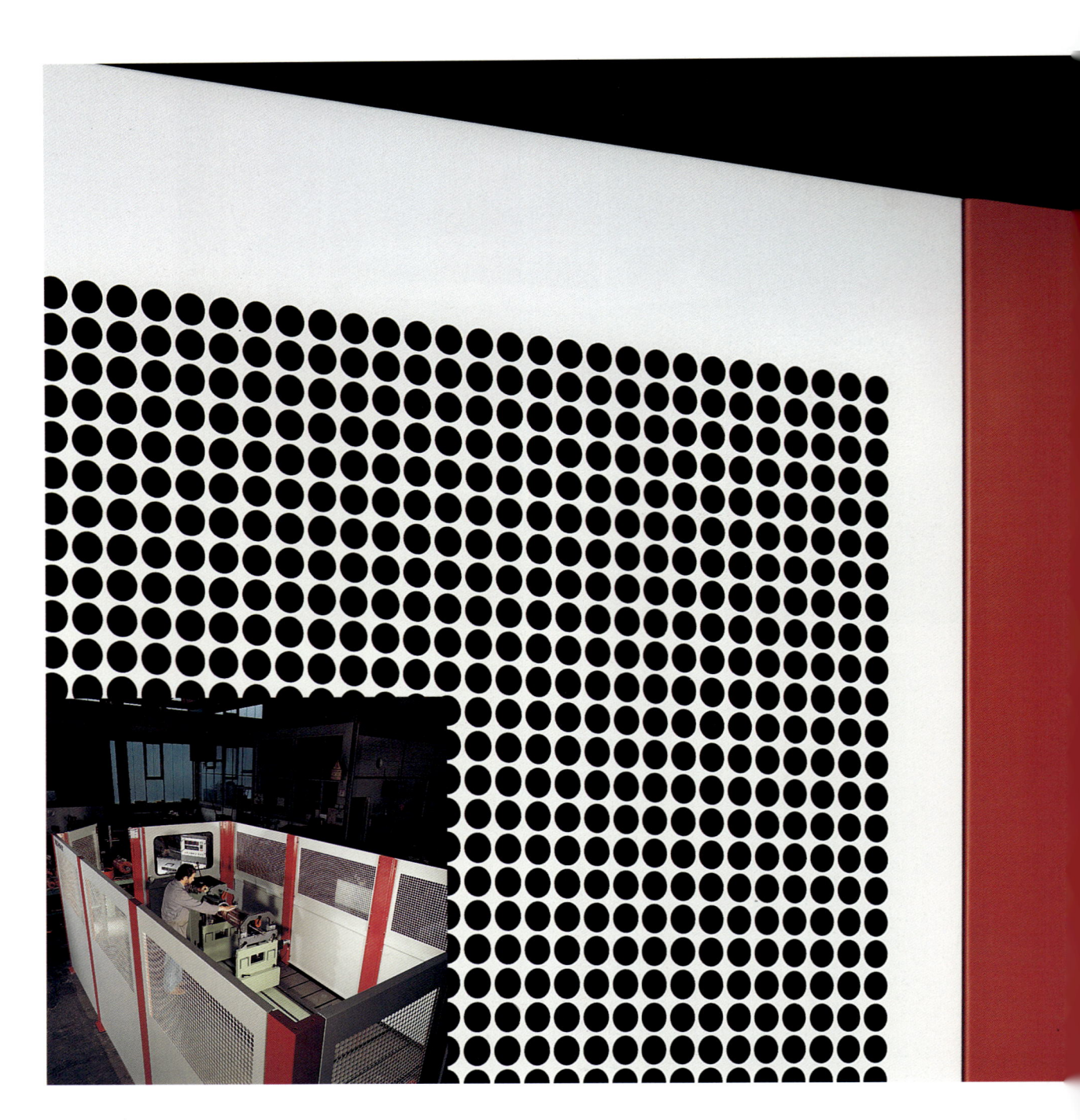

HERSTELLER MANUFACTURER ALVO Metalltechnik GmbH, Winterbach, Germany
PRODUKT PRODUCT Schutzzaun-Baukasten Protection barrier system
DESIGN desko Ingenieurbüro für design und konstruktion, Schwäbisch Hall, Germany

354 INDUSTRIE *INDUSTRY*

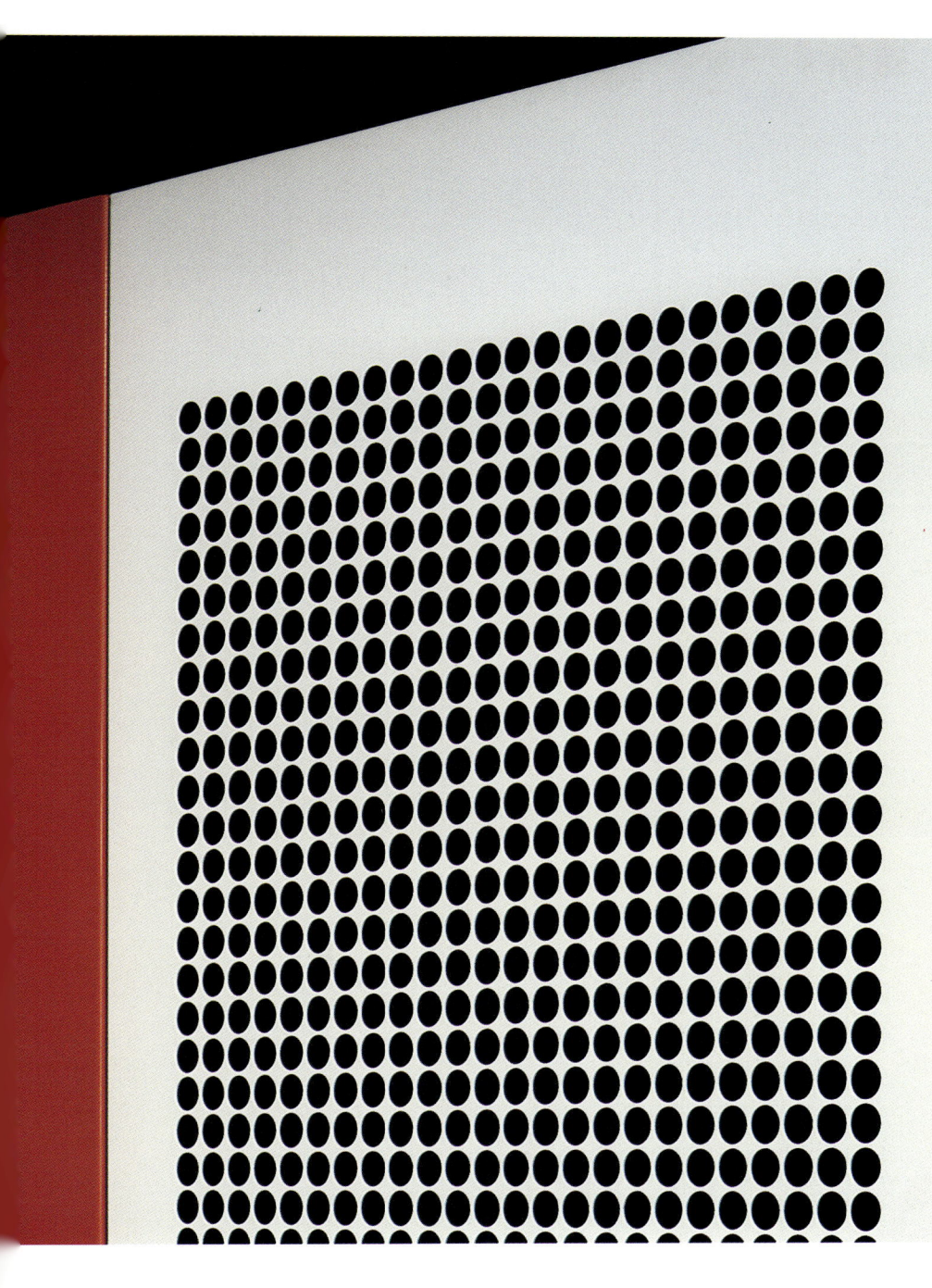

SCHUTZZAUN als vielseitig variables Baukastensystem zur sicheren und ansprechenden Umzäunung von Anlagen und Maschinen (entspricht den Sicherungsanforderungen nach ISO 7475 Klasse B). Auf den Boden geschraubte Pfosten tragen Flächenteile, Schiebe- und Schwenktüren, die vollflächig, gelocht oder mit Sichtfenstern versehen geliefert werden. Alle Teile aus pulverbeschichtetem Stahlblech.

The PROTECTION BARRIER is a flexible modular system for protecting the area around machinery while simultaneously enhancing its appearance. It meets ISO 7475 Class B safety requirements. Posts are secured to the floor, providing a stable surface to mount panels and sliding or hinged doors. The panels are available in solid, perforated or windowed versions. All components are made of epoxy-coated sheet metal.

HERSTELLER MANUFACTURER
EHT Werkzeugmaschinen GmBH, Teningen, Germany
PRODUKT PRODUCT
ECOPRESS 125 Doppelzylinder Abkantpresse Double-cylinder folding press
DESIGN
Baum Design, Kirchzarten, Germany

ECOPRESS 125, Doppelzylinder Abkantpresse. Konstruktiv und im Design überarbeitete Doppelzylinder-Gesenkbiegepresse. Klare und geradlinige Formgebung unter Berücksichtigung ergonomischer, sicherheits- und herstellungstechnischer Aspekte: als Basis für eine daraus resultierende Maschinenreihe für unterschiedliche Anforderungen. Einfach verständliche Bauform im Longlife-Design. Verzicht auf unnötige oder selten gewünschte Funktionen, die als Optionen zugefügt werden können. Wartungs- und reparaturfreundlich.

The ECOPRESS 125 is a double-cylinder folding press with a clear, linear form that incorporates ergonomic considerations as well as safety and manufacturing regulations, and provides the basis for a whole range of machines created to meet various requirements. Its straightforward design dispenses with unnecessary seldom-used functions; these may be added as an option. The sturdy construction affords a long service life, and is easy to service and repair.

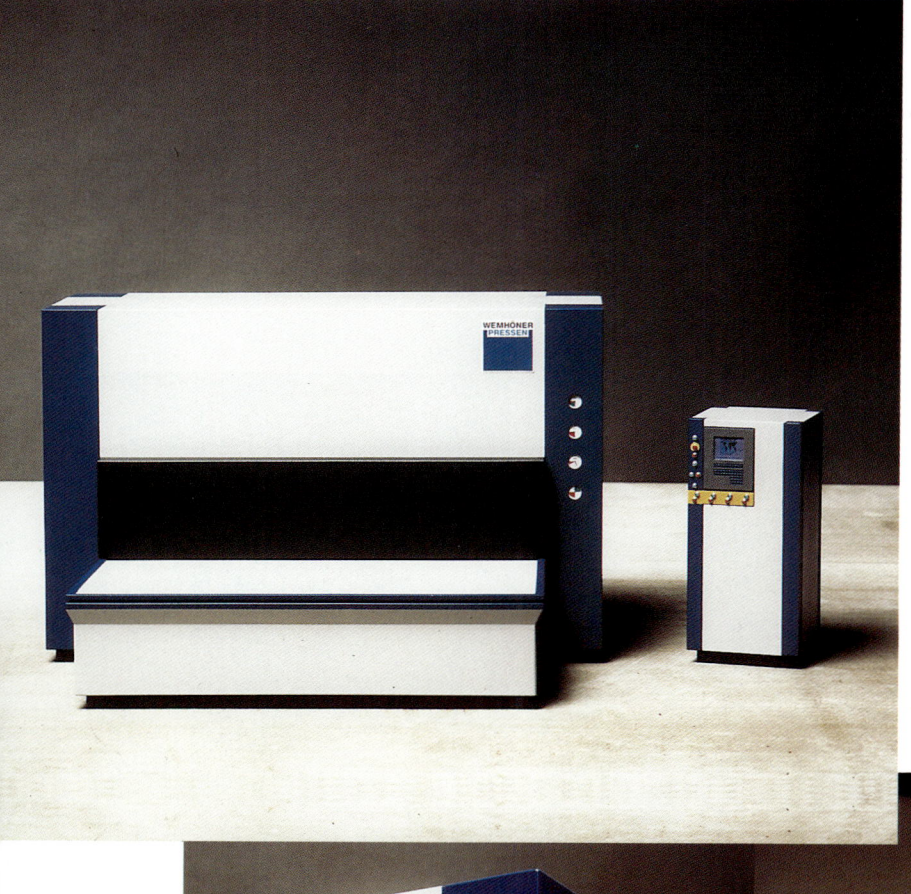

HERSTELLER MANUFACTURER Heinrich Wemhöner GmbH & Co. KG Maschinenfabrik, Herford, Germany
PRODUKT PRODUCT VARIO PRESS Formteilpresse Molding press
DESIGN Könekamp & Bross, Braunschweig, Germany

VARIO-PRESS, eine konsequente Weiterentwicklung der Membran-Form-Pressen des Herstellers: ermöglicht nun das Beschichten von unterschiedlich profilierten Trägerplatten ohne Membran, also ohne das Teil mit dem größten Verschleiß. Damit wird eine verbesserte Umweltverträglichkeit und ein verringerter Energieverbrauch bei erweiterten Einsatzmöglichkeiten erzielt. Außerdem verkürzte Preßzeiten, die zu höherer Wirtschaftlichkeit führen. Neu ist auch die rechner-, bildschirmgestützte Benutzerführung, mit der nach ergonomischen Gesichtspunkten entwickelter Software. Komplett zu demontieren, zum großen Teil aus wiederverwertbaren Materialien.

VARIO-PRESS. Wemhöner has taken its original Membrane-Press one step further. It laminates complicated structures, such as supporting panels with varying profiles, without a membrane -the component that suffers the greatest wear. The press is thus gentler on the environment and consumes less energy; at the same time, it is more versatile and efficient, as pressing time is reduced. On-screen controls and software facilitate ergonomic operation. It can be completely dismantled, and consists primarily of recyclable materials.

HERSTELLER MANUFACTURER Heidelberger Druckmaschinen AG, Heidelberg, Germany
PRODUKT PRODUCT Speedmaster 52 Druckmaschine Printing press
DESIGN Heidelberger Druckmaschinen, Heidelberg, Germany

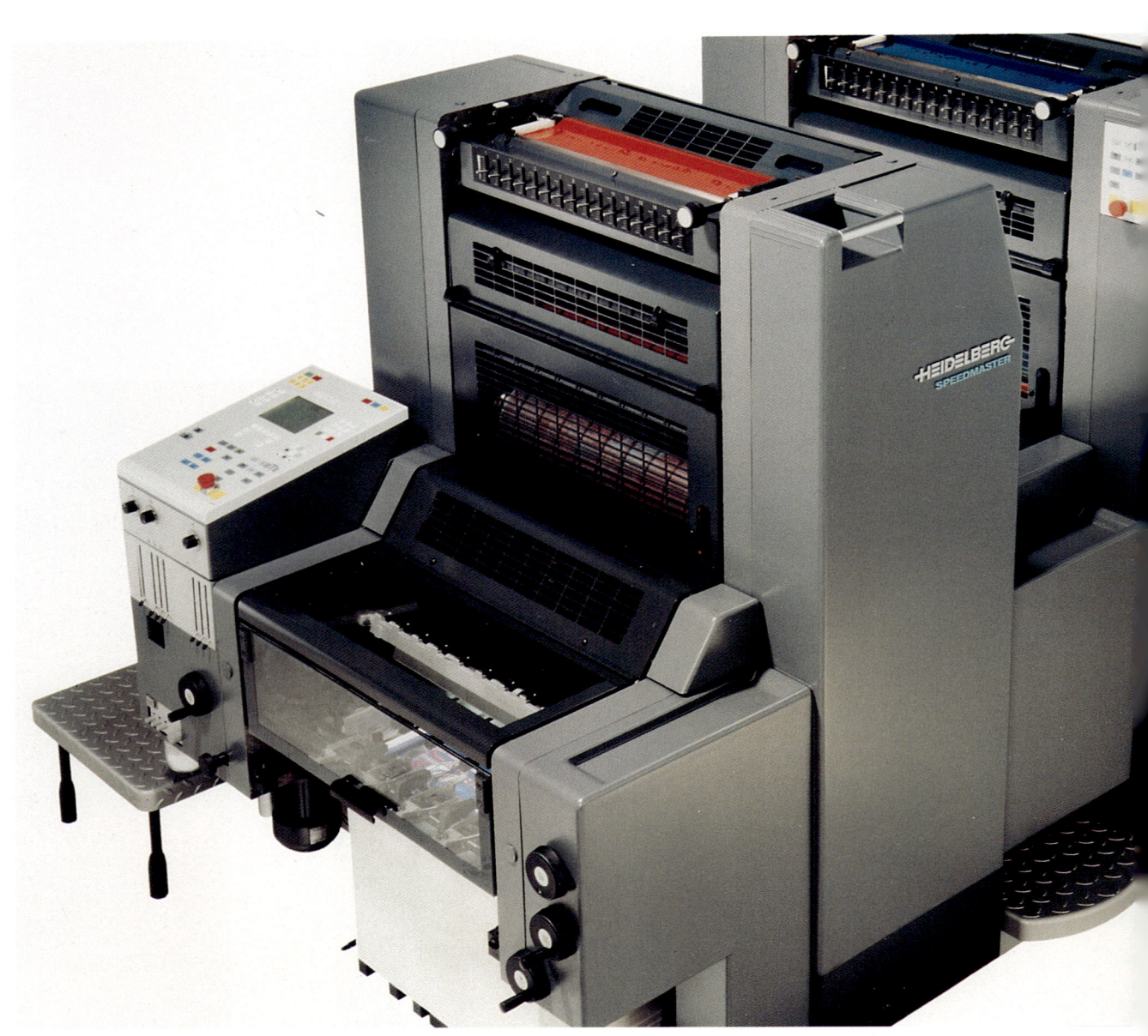

SPEEDMASTER 52, Druckmaschine, für das Format 37 x 52. Spitzenqualität bei häufigem Auftragswechsel, Tempo beim Einrichten und im Fortdruck. Sicherer Bogenlauf. Einfache Bedienung durch viele ergonomisch durchdachte Details und technische Merkmale. Alle wesentlichen Arbeitsgänge beim Einrichten, Fortdruck und Reinigen laufen CPTronic gesteuert automatisch und präzise ab.

The SPEEDMASTER 52, a printing press in the 37 x 52cm format. Its ergonomic design reflects the careful consideration given to details and technical aspects, and affords easy operation. All essential processes are controlled smoothly and automatically by the CPTronic system. Initialization and run-on take place swiftly and safely, and excellent quality is maintained even when handling a number of different printing jobs.

358 INDUSTRIE *INDUSTRY*

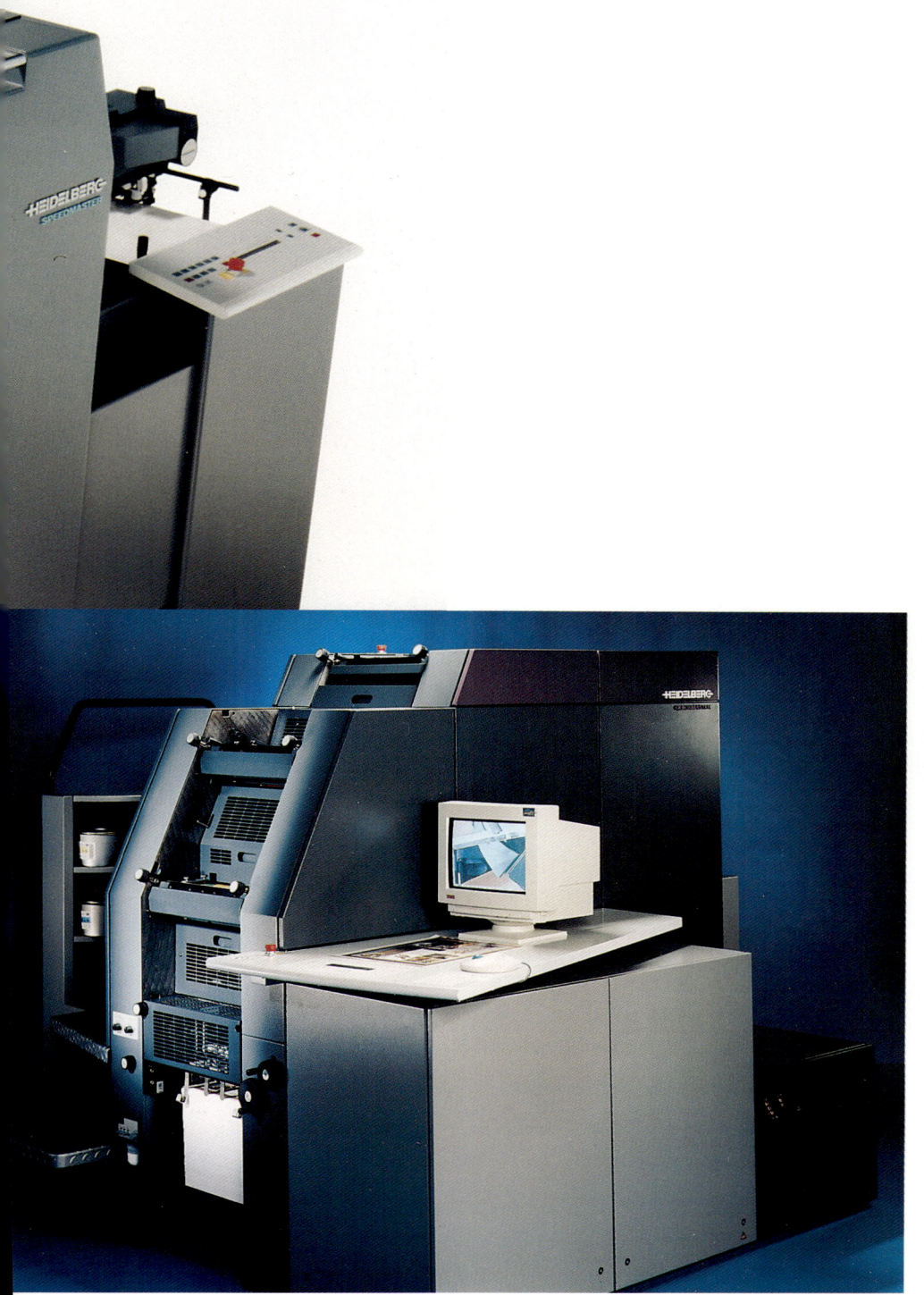

QUICKMASTER DI 46-4, Systemlösung für »Computer-to-Press«-Aufträge. Modernste Lasertechnologie bildet die Grundlage für Direct Imaging. Digital vorliegende Dokumente werden mit nur einer Ethernet-Verbindung der Druckvorstufe direkt an die Quickmaster DI geschickt. Damit direkter Druck von PostScript-Dokumenten bei kürzesten Rüstzeiten und hohe Fortdruckgeschwindigkeiten. In der Lernphase wird der Bediener von einer Bedienerführung unterstützt, die später ausgeschaltet werden kann.

The QUICKMASTER DI 46-4 is the perfect solution for »computer-to-press« projects. State-of-the-art laser technology creates the basis for direct imaging, and digitally stored documents in the pre-printing stage are sent directly to the Quickmaster via an Ethernet connection. This enables PostScript documents to be printed with the shortest possible set-up time and rapid run-on speeds. The user is initially aided by operating instructions that can be later shut off.

HERSTELLER MANUFACTURER
Heidelberger Druckmaschinen AG, Heidelberg, Germany
PRODUKT PRODUCT
Quickmaster DI 46-4 Computer-to-Press Anlage Computer-to-press processor
DESIGN
Heidelberger Druckmaschinen, Heidelberg, Germany

HERSTELLER MANUFACTURER Buser AG, Wiler, Switzerland
PRODUKT PRODUCT Rota..ac 5 Rotationsdruckmaschine Rotaryscreen printing machine
DESIGN iDesign AG, Michael Koch, Biberist, Switzerland
VERTRIEB DISTRIBUTION Buser AG, Wiler, Switzerland

ROTAMAC 5, Rotationsdruckmaschine für höchste Druckqualität durch perfekten Farbauftrag. Optimale Betriebs- und Bedienungssicherheit, farblich markante, übersichtliche Bedienungselemente, ergonomische Bauweise. Druckgut zur Qualitätskontrolle sichtbar. Ökologische Aspekte: geringe Restfarbmengen, minimaler Frischwasserverbrauch für die Reinigung, alle Materialien nach Ablauf der Lebensdauer (auf 20 Jahre angelegt) ohne Sondermüll zu entsorgen. Eigenständiges Erscheinungsbild, der »Fluß« des bedruckten Stoffs bestimmt die Gestaltung von Druckwerk und Bewegungsabläufen.

The ROTAMAC 5 rotary screen printing machine achieves maximum print quality through superlative color application processes. It possesses optimal safety features, clearly arranged controls in bold colors, and an ergonomic construction. The material between the printing groups is easily visible, enabling quality control. Environmental considerations include a low quantity of color residue and minimal water consumption required for cleaning; all materials can be easily disposed of at the end of the service life (estimated at 20 years). The machine's unique design reflects its mechanical movements as well the »flow« of the printed fabric.

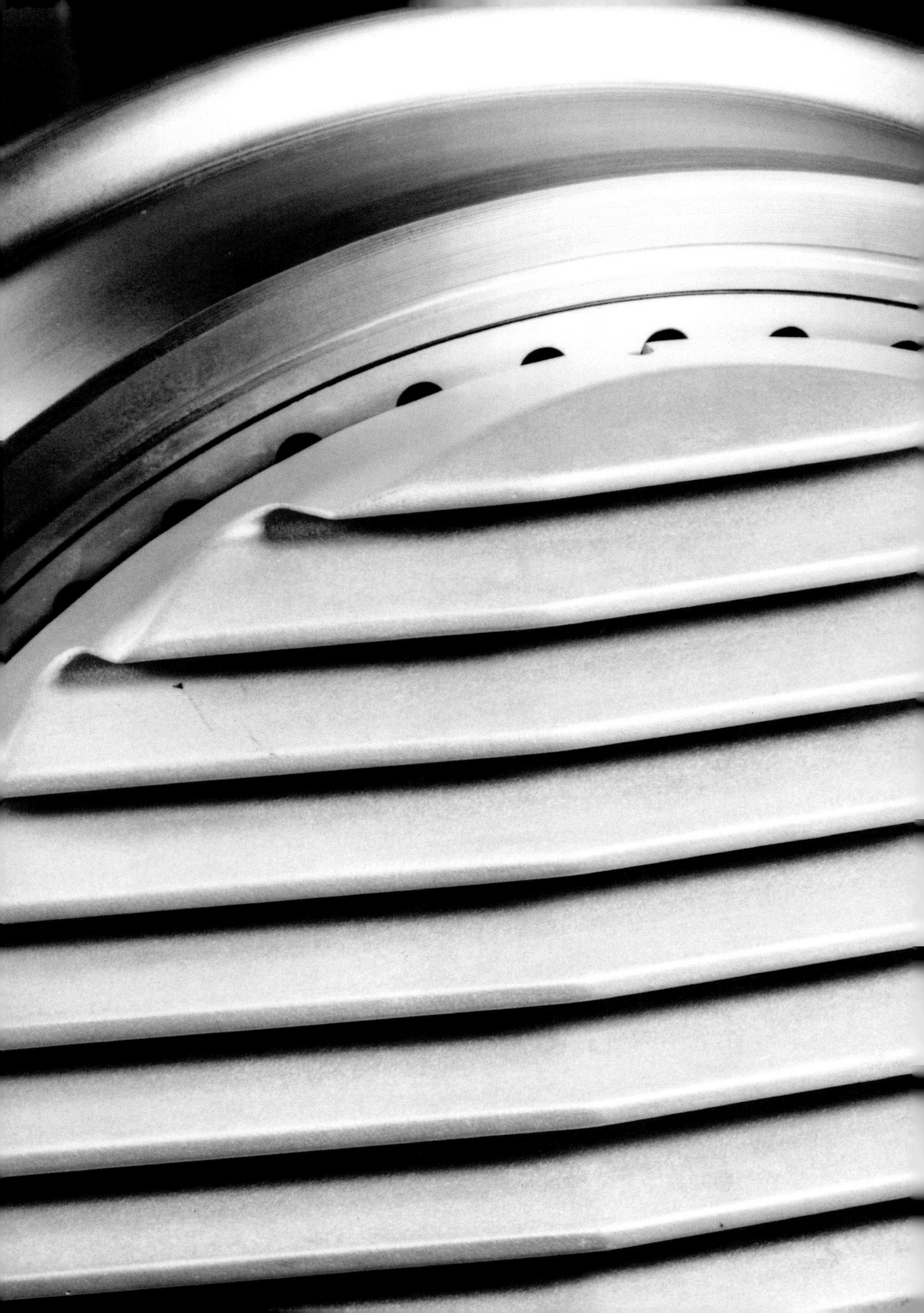

transport +verkehr
transportation

TRANSPORT+VERKEHR TRANSPORTATION
Jury: Bob Blaich, Harrtmut S. Engel, Andreas Haug, Hartmut Warkuß

Höchster Designstandard drückt sich im raffinierten Detail aus, z. B. in der Gestaltung eines Türgriffs. »Normalerweise erwartet man eine symmetrische Lösung. Der Trick ist die konsequente Asymmetrie, die den Türgriff noch abstrakter wirken läßt und zunächst garnicht an ein Auto erinnert. Wenn man etwas kaum beachtet, wie ich Autos, und man plötzlich über ein solches Detail Leidenschaft entdeckt, bedeutet das, daß hier etwas ganz besonderes entstanden ist«, so beurteilt Andrée Putman die Wirkung der neuen 5er Serie von BMW. Sie verkörpert die Gruppe der Befürworter eines kultivierten Automobildesigns.

Die Diskussion um die vorgestellten Automobile verlief erwartungsgemäß auch unter den Juroren denkbar konträr. Kritisiert wurden hauptsächlich Designergebnisse, die sich viel zu stark vom Marketing anstatt von unabhängigen Designanalysen leiten ließen. Automobildesign begäbe sich, geführt vom Marketing und nicht von Ingenieuren, in einen gefährlichen Kreislauf, weil sogar die Modelle, die bislang wegen ihrer konsequent durchgehaltenen Einfachheit und Stringenz im Design ausgezeichnet wurden, immer mehr durch marktorientierte Extra-Features überladen würden. Solche Auswirkungen des Marketings führten das Automobil in eine Identitätskrise, war von Skeptikern unter den Juroren zu hören. Nutzfahrzeuge für den öffentlichen Sektor sind durch solche Identitätskrisen in ihrer Formgebung und Konzeption nicht gefährdet. Hier läuft die Evolution auf praktische Verbesserungen hinaus wie beispielsweise die Erzielung einer Bodenhöhe von nur 17 cm bei einer Straßenbahn oder die ergonomische Durchgestaltung eines Hubfahrzeuges. Eine Innovation im Bereich der Schienenfahrzeuge wurde besonders beachtet und bestaunt: eine Rad- und Bremseinheit für Drehgestelle, entwickelt von einem Hochschulteam, das in seiner Rippenstruktur sowohl formschön wie nützlich ist. Geringe Masse, kleines Bauvolumen, Schallabschirmung und gute Aerodynamik erzielen Einsparungen und damit einen idealen Gebrauchswert. Mit diesem Verkehrsprodukt waren sogar die Ökologen in der Jury einverstanden und haben eine Auszeichnung verliehen.

The highest design standard is expressed by the most refined details, for example in the design of a door handle. »Normally you expect a symmetrical solution. The trick is consistent asymmetry, which makes the door handle appear even more abstract and initially does not even bring a car to mind at all. If you hardly notice something, and in my case that something is cars, and you suddenly discover a passion via such a detail, then this means that you have come across something really extra special.« This was Andrée Putman's assessment of the effect of the new BMW 5 Series. It is representative for those who believe automobile design should be a cultured affair.

The jury's discussion on the automobiles presented proceeded as expected - it was quite fiery with great controversies. On the whole, designs were criticized which focused far too strongly on marketing instead of independent design analyses. The feeling was that automobile design, informed by marketing and not by engineering, was caught in a dangerous spiral, because even the models which had won prizes to date for their consistently straightforward and stringent designs, were tending to be weighed down by an ever greater number of market-oriented extras. Skeptics among the jury members even believed that the consequences of marketing's influence was leaving automobiles in an identity crisis. Utility vehicles for the public sector are not endangered by such identity crises in terms of design and conception. Here, advancements concentrate on practical improvements: for instance ensuring that a streetcar's ground clearance is a mere 17 centimeters or that a lifting vehicle boasts an ergonomic design through and through. An innovation in the area of rail-bound vehicles was considered exceptional and greatly admired: an integrated wheel and brakeset for bogies, developed by a university team. The ribbed structure of the set is both beautiful and useful, for the low mass, small volume, noise insulation and superiative aerodynamics make real savings and therefore offer an ideal utility value. Even the ecologists among the jury members were happy with this transportation product, and gave it an award.

GPC 2000, deichselgeführter Niederhubkommissionierer mit einer Tragfähigkeit von 2,0 t. Die kompakte Antriebseinheit mit niedriger Linienführung bietet gute Rundumsicht und Manövrierfähigkeit. Ein großzügig gestalteter Fahrerplatz, nach modernsten ergonomischen Gesichtspunkten konstruierte Rückenlehne für sicheres und ermüdungsfreies Fahren. Rundum geschützte, sowohl nach oben wie nach beiden Seiten entnehmbare Batterie. Auswahl der Werkstoffe unter dem Aspekt der Wiederverwendbarkeit.

The GPC 2000 is a low-level order picker with a two-ton capacity. The low design of this compact power unit affords excellent visibility and maneuverability. The spacious driver's seat features a backrest which incorporates the latest ergonomic principles to prevent fatigue. The battery is protected on all sides and can be removed from above as well as from both sides for replacement. Materials were chosen keeping environmental considerations in mind.

Crown Lift Trucks Ltd., Workingham, Great Britain HERSTELLER MANUFACTURER
SC 3000 3-Rad Gegengewichtstapler, 3-Wheel counterbalanced rider truck PRODUKT PRODUCT
Crown Equipment Corporation, Mike Gallagher, New Bremen, USA DESIGN

HERSTELLER MANUFACTURER Stadtwerke Frankfurt/Main, DÜWAG, Siemens AG
PRODUKT PRODUCT Niederflurstraßenbahn, Low-Floor Tramcar
DESIGN Lindinger & Partner, Hannover

366 TRANSPORT+VERKEHR *TRANSPORTATION* BESTE DER BRANCHE *BEST OF GROUP*

NIEDERFLUR-STRASSENBAHN-ZUG, der durch seine neuartige Konstruktion mit zur Renaissance der Straßenbahn beigetragen hat. Kompakte Laufwerke mit Radnabenmotoren ermöglichen einen zwischen den Rädern durchlaufenden Fußboden, damit eine niedrige, auch für Behinderte oder Fahrgäste mit Kinderwagen bequeme Einstiegshöhe. Zum Fahrgastkomfort tragen auch ergonomisch ausgefeilte Sitzprofile bei. Neuartige Fahrerrückwand mit integriertem Schrank. Vorne aufklappbare Front zur besseren Wartung von Scheinwerfern und Wischern, leicht zugängliche Anordnung der Aggregate auf dem Dach. Ökologische Aspekte: verringerte Geräuschemission, Rückspeisung der Bremsenergie, das Recycling erleichternde Konstruktion.

The novel construction of this LOW-FLOOR VEHICLE has contributed to the come-back of the street car. Its compact running gears sport wheel-housed traction motors that enable the floor to be mounted between the wheels the entire length of the car, resulting in easier access for the disabled or those with baby carriages. The ergonomic shape of the seats further enhances passenger comfort. The new bulkheads feature an integrated storage cupboard, and the front can be opened out to facilitate maintenance of headlights and screen wipers. The roof equipment is also easily accessible. Ecological considerations include lower noise and exhaust emission, recuperation of the braking energy, and the recycling-friendly construction.

Ökologie/Design Auszeichnung Awarded for Ecology/Design: Vorbildlich durch langlebige Produktgestaltung. *Exemplary for its timeless and durable design.*

HERSTELLER MANUFACTURER
Volkswagen AG, Wolfsburg, Germany
PRODUKT PRODUCT
Polo
DESIGN
Volkswagen, Wolfsburg, Germany

VW-POLO, in neuem glattflächigen Design mit großen Überwölbungen, ist kürzer, aber breiter und höher als sein Vorgänger, hat einen längeren Radstand und wirkt kompakt und handlich. Die ansteigende Seitenfensterlinie stützt stilistisch das abfallende Dach und vermittelt im Zusammenspiel mit der stärker geneigten Windschutzscheibe und der steilen C-Säule ein Gefühl von Dynamik. Höhere Fahrleistung bei niedrigerem Kraftstoffverbauch durch aerodynamisch günstige Form. Das Motorenprogramm erfüllt die strengen amerikanischen und die kommenden europäischen Abgasgrenzwerte. Größtmöglicher Innenraum auf kleiner Verkehrsfläche, das großzügige Raumgefühl wird auch durch Ausstattungsdetails und Farbgebung vermittelt. Einsatz von umweltfreundlichen Materialien, d. h. ohne Asbest, FCKW und Cadmium.

The VW-POLO sports a new, sleek design with gently rounded contours. Wider, with more headroom and a shorter overall length than its forerunner, it is still compact and manageable thanks to a longer wheel base. A more slanted windscreen and the upward sweep of the side window profile, which stylistically underscores the slight downward slope of the roof, make the Polo a highly dynamic vehicle. It affords greater driving performance while consuming less fuel, and offers the greatest possible interior space over a small area. This impression of space is enhanced by the interior furnishings and color scheme. The range of engines meets strict US emission requirements as well as future European limits. The car is manufactured using environmentally-friendly materials without asbestos, CFCs or cadmium.

HERSTELLER MANUFACTURER Mercedes-Benz AG, Stuttgart, Germany
PRODUKT PRODUCT E-Klasse Limousine
DESIGN Mercedes-Benz Design, Sindelfingen, Germany

Die neue E-KLASSE von Mercedes-Benz ist ein Spitzenprodukt in Technik und Design. Ziel des Designkonzepts war es, im Rahmen der mercedestypischen Charakteristik eine Form zu schaffen, die die E-Klasse als individuelle Baureihe aus der Produktfamilie des Unternehmens heraustreten läßt. Die neue Front stellt ein spannungsreiches Wechselspiel aus Tradition und Innovation dar. Neue Stilelemente gehen mit markenspezifischen Gestaltungsmerkmalen, wie z.B. der Kühlermaske, eine Symbiose ein und machen die E-Klasse unverkennbar zu einem Mercedes.

The new E-CLASS from Mercedes-Benz is a top-class product, both in engineering and design, and was intended to exhibit typical Mercedes characteristics while standing out as a distinctive model within the Mercedes product line. It is a vibrant blend of tradition and innovation: New stylistic elements harmonize with typical Mercedes design features, such as the radiator grille, making the E-class unmistakably a Mercedes-Benz.

TRANSPORT+VERKEHR *TRANSPORTATION* 371

HERSTELLER MANUFACTURER Mannesmann Demag Fördertechnik AG, Geschäftsbereich Systemtechnik, Offenbach, Germany
PRODUKT PRODUCT Cardesor Parksystem Parking system
DESIGN TEAMS - SLANY DESIGN, Esslingen, Germany

Parksystem CARDESOR, ein automatisches Parkhaus zur computergesteuerten Ein- und Auslagerung von PKWs. Der Benutzer übergibt bzw. übernimmt sein Fahrzeug an einer Check-Kabine. Es wird über fördertechnische Einrichtungen automatisch und vor fremdem Zugriff sicher wie in einem Tresor geparkt. Das Parksystem bietet großen Bedienkomfort, schnelle Fahrzeugbereitstellung sowie hohe Sicherheit für Benutzer und Fahrzeug.

Parksystem CARDESOR is an automatic parking system featuring computer-controlled car parking and retrieval. The car is dropped off at a check booth, where it is automatically parked using materials handling equipment. Vehicles are well-protected from unauthorized access. The parking system offers convenient, swift handling of vehicles as well as added safety for both driver and vehicle.

372 TRANSPORT+VERKEHR *TRANSPORTATION*

Türöffnertaste der BAUREIHE 56, für den Außeneinsatz in öffentlichen Verkehrsmitteln konzipiert. Sie zeichnet sich aus durch ein erstklassiges taktiles Schaltgefühl. Bei vorspringender Einbauweise werden die Befestigungsschrauben durch den Rahmen abgedeckt. Auch frontbündiger Einbau von der Rückseite her möglich, in diesem Fall entfällt der Rahmen.

The SERIES 56 is an external push-button door opener for public transportation, and features an outstanding tactile design. The screws are concealed by the frame if the unit is surface mounted; if it is flush-mounted, the frame is omitted.

HERSTELLER MANUFACTURER EAO Elektro-Apparatebau Olten AG, Olten, Switzerland
PRODUKT PRODUCT Baureihe 56 Türöffnertaste für öffentliche Verkehrsmittel Pushbutton for use in public transportation
DESIGN EAO, Olten, Switzerland

TRANSPORT+VERKEHR *TRANSPORTATION* 373

HERSTELLER MANUFACTURER Skidata Computer GmbH, Gartenau, Austria
PRODUKT PRODUCT links/left: APT 450 Codiergerät Coding unit, rechts/right: APT 450 Parkschranke Barrier
DESIGN links: KISKA Industrial Design Bernd Tomasini, Anif, Austria rechts/right: KISKA Industrial Design Tom Meissner-Braun, Anif, Austria

APT 450, Kodiergerät zur Auswertung, Kodierung und Beschriftung von Tickets aus unterschiedlichen Materialien und mit Techniken (Barcode, Magnetcode, Chipkarten und Berührungslos) sowie der automatischen Quittungserstellung. Um Bedienerfehler auszuschließen, werden alle Kartentypen über ein einziges Kartenmaul zugeführt und verarbeitet. Nach der Kartenausgabe erfolgt die automatische Quittungsausgabe an gleicher Stelle. Trotz erhöhter Funktionalität gegenüber den Vorgängermodellen reduzierte Abmessungen.

The APT 450 is a coding unit for evaluating, encoding and printing tickets of various materials. It is compatible with a wide range of coding systems (bar code, magnetic code, smart card and contactless), and generates receipts automatically. In order to eliminate errors, there is only one slot for all ticket types; after the ticket has been issued, the customer receives the receipt via the same slot. This coding unit is more compact than previous models, and also features a wider range of functions.

APT 450, Parkschranke in neuartiger Bauweise: Standfuß und Motorgehäuse sind aus einem einzigen Edelstahlrohr, das Getriebe ist in einem aufgesetzten Aluminiumgußteil montiert, das die Bewegung der Schranke durch seine Formgebung symbolisiert. Durch diese Bauweise konnten Außenabmessungen und auch die Herstellungskosten deutlich verringert werden. Der Schrankenbaum ist zum Schutz vor Verletzungen und aus Gewichtsgründen aus GFK gefertigt und von innen beleuchtet, damit auch bei Nacht gut sichtbar.

The APT 450 parking barrier features a novel design in which the tubular steel stand doubles as a casing for the motor, with the gears housed in a cast aluminum casing at the top. The shape of the casing is analogous to the movement of the barrier. This type of construction also makes the unit more compact and considerably lowers production costs. The barrier boom is made of glass fiber reinforced plastic to minimize weight and reduce the risk of injury, and illuminated to ensure good visibility at night.

BMW AG, München, Germany
R 1100 RT Motorrad Motorbike
BMW Design Team, München, Germany

BMW R 1100 RT, sportlich konzipiertes Tourenmotorrad. Design im Windkanal entwickelt, wirksamer Schutz vor Wind und Wetter ohne ausladende Verkleidungen. Ausgelegt auf hohe Fahrsicherheit und -stabilität, auch bei voller Zuladung von 208 kg. High-Tech-Bremsanlage mit serienmäßigem ABS. Zweizylinder-Boxermotor mit Motor-Elektronik und 3-Wege-Katalysator. Die Neigung des Windschilds kann per Tastendruck reguliert werden. Individuell regulierbare Warmluftführung für die Hände des Fahrers. Serienmäßiger Koffer mit 66 l Stauraum. Neue Farben: glaciergrün, sinusblau, sienarot-metallic.

The sporty BMW R 1100 RT was developed in a wind tunnel and as a result offers excellent protection from wind and weather without heavy protective covering. The motorbike affords a high degree of driving safety and stability, even when bearing its maximum load of 208 kg. It features state-of-the-art brakes with a standard anti-locking system. The flat twin electronic engine comes with a three-way catalytic converter. The tilt of the windshield can be adjusted at the touch of a button, and a hot air heater can be individually regulated to keep the driver's hands warm. All models in the series feature a compartment with 66 liters of storage space.

BERNDS Faltrad, ein Tourenrad für einfaches »Park and Ride«: keine verschmutzten Kleidungsstücke, kein Werkzeug mehr, um das Rad zu falten. Wartungsfreier Zahnriemenantrieb mit 4- bzw. 7-Gang-Nabenschaltung. Hochwertige Pulverlackbeschichtung.
The BERNDS folding bike: a touring bike designed for those who »Park and Ride«. It eliminates the problem of soiled clothes, as no tools are required to fold the bicycle. It features a maintenance-free toothed belt drive with 4 or 7 gears and a hub gearshift, and comes in a high-quality powder paint finish.

BERNDS, Detmold, Germany HERSTELLER MANUFACTURER
BERNDS Faltfahrrad Folding Bike PRODUKT PRODUCT
BERNDS/HAUPT, Detmold, Germany DESIGN

Ökologie/Design Auszeichnung Awarded for Ecology/Design: Vorbildlich durch Funktionsgerechtheit. Exemplary given its functional design.

TRANSPORT+VERKEHR *TRANSPORTATION* 377

HERSTELLER MANUFACTURER Wiha Werkzeuge, Willi Hahn GmbH & Co. KG, Schonach, Germany
PRODUKT PRODUCT Klapp-Halter für Stiftschlüssel, Allen key Grip ClapStar
DESIGN Baum-Design, Kirchzarten, Germany

KLAPP-HALTER mit 6-teiligem und 3-teiligem Einsatz. Die durch Klemmelemente festgehaltenen Schlüssel können einzeln entnommen werden. Durch 3 Rastungen beim Auf- und Zuklappen arretierbar. Die Werkzeug-Größen sind im Halter markiert. Umweltgerechte Produktion: Verwendete Materialien schwermetallfrei und voll recyclebar.
The GRIP comes with a six-piece or three-piece inset, and can be locked into three different positions during opening or closing. The Allen keys are held in place with clips for individual insertion or removal, and their sizes are indicated on the holder. This environmentally-friendly product is made of fully recyclable materials that are free of heavy metals.

Busch & Müller KG Fahrzeugteilefabrik, Meinerzhagen, Germany HERSTELLER MANUFACTURER
DToplight plus Fahrrad-Rücklicht, Bicycle rearlight PRODUKT PRODUCT
Fritz Niggemann-Tolxdorff, Essen, Germany DESIGN

D.TOPLIGHT PLUS, Dioden-Rücklicht, am Fahrradgepäckträger zu montieren. Dynamobetrieb mit elektronischer Standlichtfunktion. Ausgestattet mit neuartigen, superhellen Leuchtdioden. Die Lebensdauer der LEDs beträgt ca. 100.000 Stunden, kein Lampenwechsel erforderlich. Die Standlichtautomatik auf Kondensatorbasis (ohne Akku und ohne Batterie) wurde wegen Umweltfreundlichkeit ausgezeichnet. Aus recyclebarem Kunststoff, bruchsicher und korrosionsbeständig.

D.TOPLIGHT PLUS is a diode rear lamp for bicycles, to be mounted onto the luggage carrier. It is powered by a dynamo and sports new, superbright diodes with a service life of around 100,000 hours, making bulb replacement superfluous. The condenser-based technology (no batteries required) was awarded a prize for environmental friendliness. The unbreakable diode is made of corrosion-resistant recyclable plastic.

Ökologie/Design Auszeichnung Awarded for Ecology/Design: Vorbildlich durch Standlichtfunktion ohne Batterie, funktionsgerechte, langlebige Gestaltung. Exemplary for its ability to provide battery-free light while stationary, functionally ideal and durable design.

TRANSPORT+VERKEHR TRANSPORTATION

HERSTELLER MANUFACTURER Pfaff-silberblau Hebezeugfabrik GmbH, Friedberg, Germany
PRODUKT PRODUCT LB Wandseilwinde Wall-mounted winch
DESIGN Hartmann & Selic Industriedesign, Augsburg, Germany

Wandseilwinde LB (Leichtbau), zum Heben und Senken von Lasten bis 1000 kg. Leichte Bedienung durch eine klare und eindeutige Formensprache und die Verwendung von Piktogrammen. Mit Ausnahme der gesteckten Abdeckungen und des Griffs ist das Gerät eine verzinkte Ganzstahlkonstruktion. Die Wandbefestigung ist gleichzeitig Gehäuse, dadurch entfällt ein zusätzliches Kunststoffgehäuse. Bauteile sind leicht trennbar, daher hohe Servicefreundlichkeit und Demontage.

This LB light-weight wall-mounted WINCH was designed to hoist and lower loads of up to 1,000 kg. Clear, unambiguous symbols and pictograms facilitate operation. The entire winch, apart from the push-fit covers and handle, is made of galvanized steel: The wall mounting also serves as the housing, eliminating the need for an additional plastic housing. The components are easy to dismantle for straightforward servicing.

Ökologie/Design Auszeichnung Awarded for Ecology/Design: Vorbildlich durch einfache und funktionserklärende Gestaltung und sparsamen Materialeinsatz. *Exemplary for the sparing use of materials, timeless design and durability.*

380 TRANSPORT+VERKEHR *TRANSPORTATION*

Jungheinrich Aktiengesellschaft, Norderstedt bei Hamburg, Germany HERSTELLER MANUFACTURER
ETX-Kombi Hochregal- und Kommissionierstapler High Rack Stacker/Order Picker PRODUKT PRODUCT
Michael Niebuhr, Bargteheide, Germany DESIGN

ETX-KOMBI, batteriegetriebenes Gerät zum Stapeln und Kommissionieren für Hochregallager. Hubhöhe max. 11m, Tragfähigkeit 1.250 kg. Bedienstand fährt mit Lastaufnahmemittel nach oben. Zentrales Bedienpult mit vollelektrischer Ansteuerung aller Funktionen. Klappbarer Stuhl und neigbares Bedienpult, Bedienung im Stehen und im Sitzen möglich.
The ETX-KOMBI is a battery-operated vehicle for stacking and order picking in high-bay warehouses, with a maximum height of 11 m and a load capacity of 1,250 kg. The loading platform is raised using the load handling device. The vehicle features a central control panel from which all functions are electrically actuated. The fold-away seat and tilting control panel enable operation both while seated and standing.

HERSTELLER MANUFACTURER Crown Gabelstapler GmbH, Roding, Germany
PRODUKT PRODUCT GPC 2000 Niederhubkommissionierer Low-level order picker
DESIGN Crown Equipment Corporation Mike Gallagher, New Bremen, USA

GPC 2000, ein deichselgeführter Niederhubkommissionierer mit einer Tragfähigkeit von 2,0 t. Die kompakte Antriebseinheit mit niedriger Linienführung bietet gute Rundumsicht und Manövrierfähigkeit. Großzügig gestalteter Fahrerplatz, nach modernsten ergonomischen Gesichtspunkten konstruierte Rückenlehne für sicheres und ermüdungsfreies Fahren. Rundum geschützte, sowohl nach oben wie nach beiden Seiten entnehmbare Batterie. Auswahl der Werkstoffe unter dem Aspekt der Wiederverwendbarkeit.

The GPC 2000 is a low-level order picker with a two-ton capacity. The low design of this compact power unit affords excellent visibility and maneuverability. The spacious driver's seat features a backrest which incorporates the latest ergonomic principles to prevent fatigue. The battery is protected on all sides and can be removed from above as well as from both sides for replacement. Materials were chosen bearing environmental considerations in mind.

MA180C, ein Elektro-Gabelhubwagen mit kleinem Wendekreis und einer Tragfähigkeit von 1,8 t. Unaufdringliches Design durch klassische Linienführung und Rundungen. Die seitlichen Stützräder sind innerhalb der geschlossenen Kontur untergebracht. Batterieabdeckhaube aus Spezialkunststoff, daher leichter als herkömmliche Stahlabdeckungen und dennoch bruchfest und stoßabsorbierend, das Material geht nach einem Stoß in seine ursprüngliche Form zurück. Leichte Bauweise, darum geringer Energieverbrauch und längere Einsatzdauer. Hohe Servicefreundlichkeit.

The A180C is an electric pallet truck with a short turning circle and a capacity of 1.8 metric tons. Its discreet design features classic elements and curves, with the side support wheels tucked away into the closed housing of the vehicle. The battery cover consists of black »Mastershock« plastic, making it lighter than typical steel covers. This material is also unbreakable and highly shock proof, and resumes its original shape following a collision. The lightweight construction of the vehicle affords longer action time and reduced energy consumption. The internal components are arranged so as to permit straightforward servicing.

HERSTELLER MANUFACTURER MIC S.A., Argentan Cédex, France
PRODUKT PRODUCT A 180 C Elektro-Gabelhubwagen Electric pallet truck
DESIGN MIC, Argentan Cédex, France
VERTRIEB DISTRIBUTION MIC Vertriebs-GmbH, Hamburg, Germany

HERSTELLER MANUFACTURER VSG Verkehrstechnik GmbH, Bochum, Germany, BSI Bergische Stahl-Industrie GmbH, Remscheid, Germany
PRODUKT PRODUCT Integral Rad/Brems-Einheit Wheel/brake-unit
DESIGN Prof. Dr.-Ing. Fritz Frederich, Aachen, Germany
RWTH Rheinisch Westfälische Technische Hochschule Aachen, Institut für Fördertechnik und Schienenfahrzeuge

INTEGRAL vereinigt Rad, Lagerung und Bremse in einer Baugruppe und ersetzt damit den Radsatz konventioneller Schienenfahrzeuge. Das Rad besteht aus Nabe, zwei dünnen Stegen und dem Reifen. Die Teile sind miteinander verklebt. Am Rad befestigte Ronden aus Sintermetall und feststehende Rippenplatten bilden die Bremse. Die Baueinheit ist in klaren geometrischen Formen gestaltet. Das System hat eine geringe Masse, kleines Bauvolumen, gute Aerodynamik und gute Schallabschirmung. Einfache Montage und Zerlegbarkeit.

INTEGRAL combines the wheel, bearings and brake in one unit, replacing the wheelset of conventional rail vehicles. The wheel consists of a hub, two slender webs and the rim, all of which are glued together. The brakes are formed by stationary ribbed aluminium plates and sintered metal discs that are attached to the wheel. The compact, aerodynamic assembly features a clear, geometric design, a low mass, and good noise absorption. It is easy to install and dismantle.

Ökologie/Design Auszeichnung Awarded for Ecology/Design: Vorbildlich durch extrem sparsamen Materialeinsatz. Exemplary for its extremely sparing use of materials.

HERSTELLER MANUFACTURER ABB Henschel AG, Alcatel-SEL, LHB, BPR design für die DB AG
PRODUKT PRODUCT Interregio Steuerkopf Power car
DESIGN BPR design Jens Peters, Frank Schuster, Stuttgart, Germany
VERTRIEB ABB Henschel AG, AHE/FZ

Der INTERREGIO-Steuerkopf wurde für die Deutsche Bahn AG entwickelt. Für den Einsatz am Anfang und am Ende des Zuges, so daß nun auch beim »Interregio« ein Umkoppeln der Lok überflüssig wird. Die aerodynamische Linie des Steuerkopfes mit der schräg gestellten Frontscheibe verleiht dem Zug ein markantes Aussehen. Abdeckung von Kupplung und Druckluftanschlüssen durch automatisch zu öffnende Verkleidung. Transparente Raumteilung zwischen Führerstand und Fahrgastraum. Dadurch wird nicht nur die Attraktivität des Arbeitsplatzes für den Fahrer erhöht, sondern auch dem Fahrgast ein Blick auf Strecke und Führerstand ermöglicht.

The IR power car was developed for Deutsche Bahn (the German Railroad Company). Interregio trains can now be controlled from both the driver's cab and the rear of the train, enabling operations to be reversed without having to uncouple the locomotive. The aerodynamic shape and sloping windscreen lend the power car a distinctive appearance. The coupling and compressed air supply are concealed behind a panel which is opened automatically. A transparent divider separates the driver's cab from the passenger area, providing the driver with a more attractive working environment and affording passengers a clear view ahead.

TRANSPORT+VERKEHR *TRANSPORTATION* 385

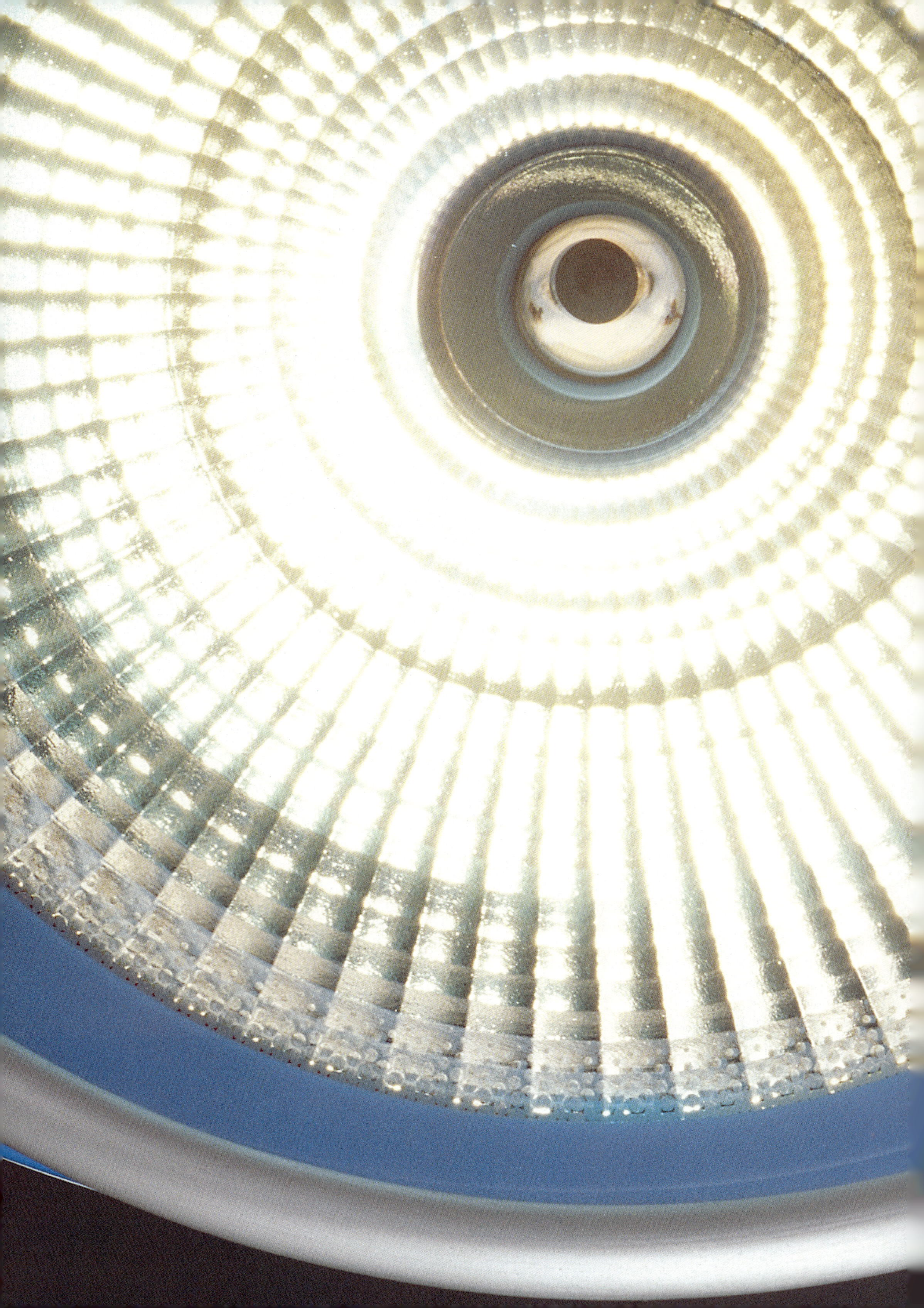

medizin
medical

MEDIZIN *MEDICAL*
Jury: Bob Blaich, Hartmut S. Engel, Andreas Haug, Hartmut Warkuß

»Man erlebt medizinische Geräte mit ganz anderen Emotionen als beispielsweise ein Auto. Das Gefühl einem Auto gegenüber kann Spaß, Sport, Glück und Freiheit bedeuten. Hospital-Gegenstände sind genau mit dem Gegenteil verbunden: Sie müssen an die Zuverlässigkeit der Wissenschaft erinnern, müssen beruhigen, nicht aufregen. Sie müssen einem die Gewißheit geben, daß alles sorgfältig bedacht worden ist«, so umreißt die Jurorin Andrée Putman die Designaufgabe im Bereich Medizin. Tatsächlich ist Medizin seit einem Jahrzehnt ein Sektor, wo Designqualität geradezu als unverzichtbarer Standard für Hersteller und Nutzer gesehen wird. Der Anreiz für den Designer besteht darin, im Bereich Medizin folgende drei Aspekte zu berücksichtigen: Erstens auf die Sicht des Patienten bezogen, zweitens auf die Sicht des bedienenden Personals und drittens auf die Sicht des Arztes, der die Ergebnisse zu interpretieren hat. Die Benutzerfreundlichkeit dieser Geräte definiert sich so: praktisch in der Handhabung und weniger bedrohlich im Aussehen.

»Heutzutage sind, speziell im Bereich der Medizin, hard rules durch soft rules mit großem Erfolg ersetzt worden«, meint der Corporate Design-Spezialist Bob Blaich, Jury-Leiter dieser Kategorie, zu den neuesten Trends und Erfolgen der Großanbieter Siemens und Philips. Die Harmonisierung der Designleistungen ist das Erfolgsrezept der Großanbieter. Beim modernen Design-Management steht nicht die eng gefaßte Regel, sondern das »große Bild« im Vordergrund. »Diese Produkte sind für einen weltweiten einheitlichen Markt bestimmt und sollten sowohl technisch als auch ästhetisch eine kompatible Einheit darstellen«.

Doch wie die Zahl der ausgezeichneten Produkte zeigt, sind auch kleine Design-Studios mit Individuallösungen sehr erfolgreich. In dieser Auswahl findet man gutes Design bei Produkten mit starken sozialen Komponenten: Unterstützungsgeräte für die Krankenpflege, Gehhilfen und ein Spezialbett, das sich mit wenigen Handgriffen demontieren läßt.

Das Resumé des Jury-Vorsitzenden: »Die Medizintechnik fand ich persönlich am interessantesten, weil hier innerhalb der letzten Jahre eine unerhörte Verbesserung des Designs stattgefunden hat. Was hier geschah, ist vergleichbar mit der Entwicklung im Computer-Design. Wer kein gutes Design anbot, war weg vom Fenster«.

»We experience medical instruments with completely different emotions than we have when, for example, we look at a car. The feelings associated with a car may be fun, sports, happiness and freedom. Hospital objects are linked in our minds with quite the opposite: They have to remind us of the reliability of science, must calm us and not excite us. They must give us the assurance that everything has been very carefully considered,« says jury member Andrée Putman when commenting on the brief facing designers of medical instruments. In fact, for over a decade medicine has been a sector where design quality is quite clearly regarded as an indispensable standard for manufacturers and users alike. The challenge for the designer is to tackle the following three aspects in the area of medicine: in the first place, the viewpoint of the patient has to be taken into account, secondly the viewpoint of the serving personnel, and thirdly, that of the doctor who has to interpret the results. User-friendliness among such instruments is therefore defined as follows: they must be practical to handle and less threatening in appearance.

»Today, specifically in the area of medicine, hard rules have been replaced with soft rules with great success,« avers corporate design specialist Bob Blaich, jury chairman in this category, when commenting on the latest trends and successes by major manufacturers Siemens and Philips. The harmonization of services provided is the recipe the big players have for success. Modern design management does not stress narrowly grasped rules, but instead foregrounds the »big picture«. »These products are intended for a uniform global market and are meant to present a technically as well as aesthetically compatible unit.«

However, the number of award-winning products shows that even small design studios have been successful with individual solutions. In the selection, good design is also to be encountered among products with a strong social thrust: equipment offering support in nursing care, walking frames and a special bed which can be disassembled with only a few twists and turns.

The jury chairman summarizes: »I personally found the medical technology section the most interesting, because here an unprecedented improvement in design has taken place over the last few years. What has happened here is comparable with developments in computer design. Anyone who does not offer good design has no chance at all.«

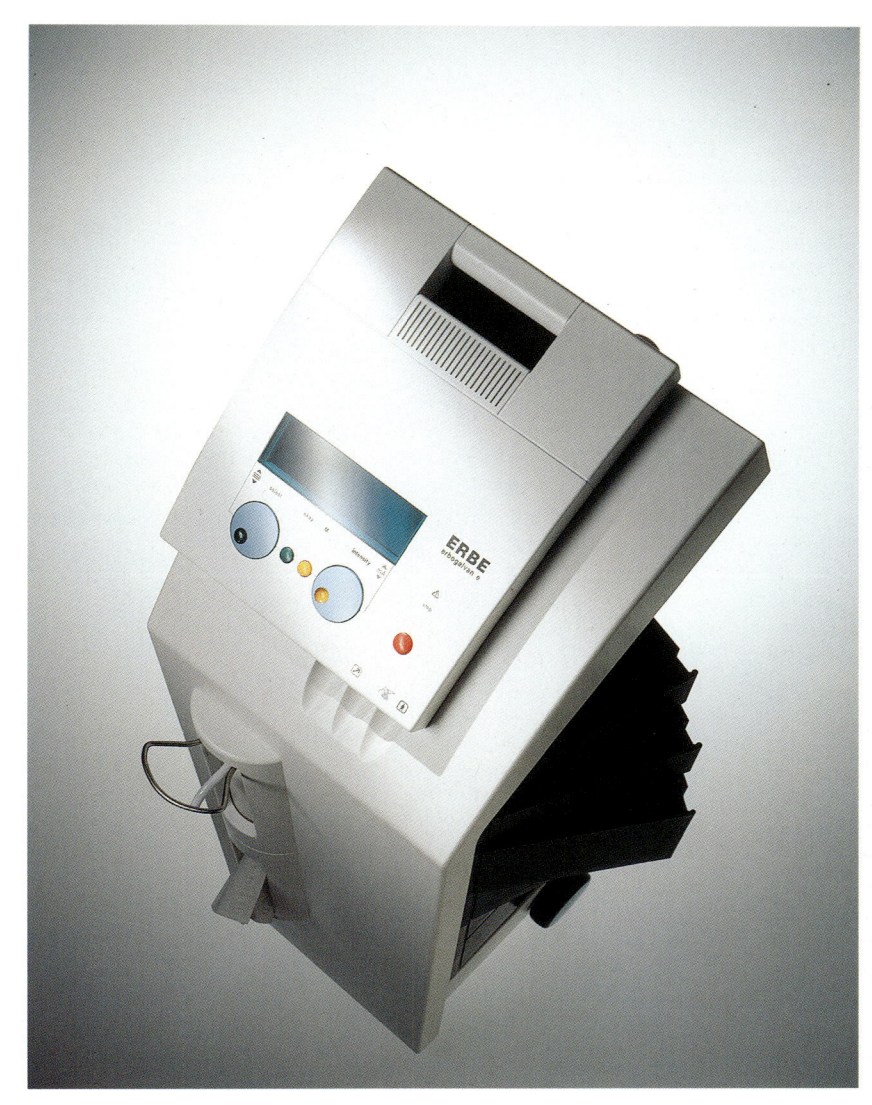

Erbe Elektromedizin GmbH, Tübingen, Germany HERSTELLER MANUFACTURER
Erbogalvan E Elektrotherapiegerät Electric therapy unit PRODUKT PRODUCT
Design Tech Jürgen R. Schmid, Ammerbuch, Germany DESIGN

ERBOGALVAN E, ein mobiles Elektrotherapiegerät, flexibel im Einsatz und leicht zu bedienen. Durchdachte Detaillösungen wie die »Schwenkfächer« fassen das gesamte Zubehör für die Reizstrombehandlung. Der Drehpunkt der seitlich herausschwenkbaren Fächer ist so gewählt, daß sich alle Utensilien in Reichweite befinden. Die elektrischen Anschlüsse sind übersichtlich angeordnet, Fehlbedienungen damit ausgeschlossen. Bei Standardbehandlungen muß nur das diagnostizierte Krankheitsbild eingegeben werden. Das Gerät schlägt daraufhin die geeignete Stromtherapie vor. Konstruktion aus leicht zu trennenden und recyclebaren Materialien.

The ERBOGALVAN E is a mobile electrotherapy unit that affords straightforward use for a variety of applications. Carefully thought-out details such as the »swivel compartments« provide enough space to store all therapy accessories, and are constructed so as to put these items within easy reach of the therapist. The electrical connections are clearly arranged, virtually eliminating operating errors. For standard treatment, the user need only enter the medical diagnosis; the machine selects the appropriate settings. The materials used can be easily sorted and recycled.

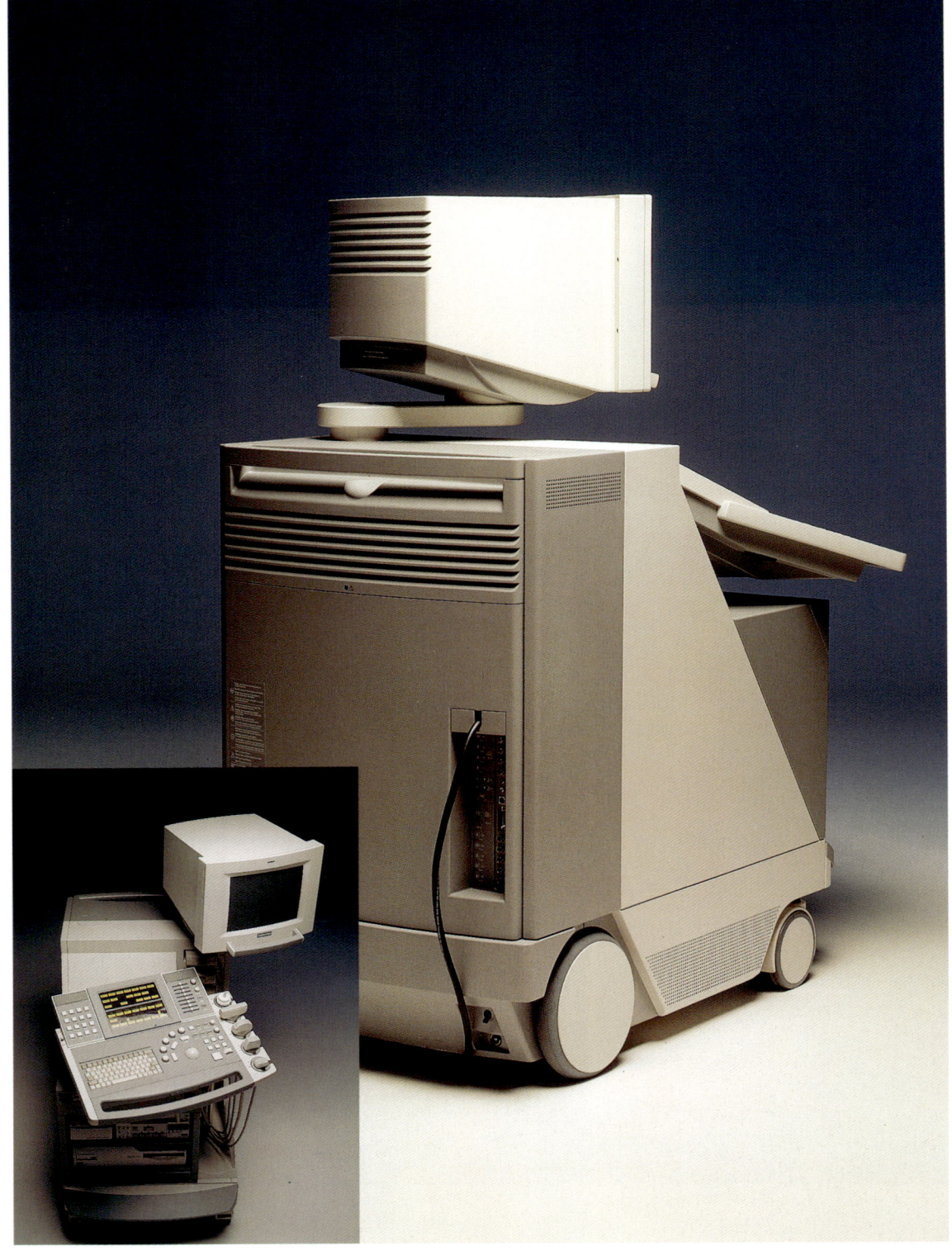

HERSTELLER MANUFACTURER Siemens Medical Systems, Inc. Ultrasound Group, Issaquah, USA
PRODUKT PRODUCT SONOLINE Elegra Medizinisches Ultraschallgerät Medical ultrasound system
DESIGN Siemens Medical Systems, Inc. Ultrasound Group, Stephen Hooper, Anthony Grasso, Dean J. Bidwell, Matthew Willkens, Patrick Flood, Peter Wung, Issaquah, USA
Siemens Design, Ruth J. Soénius, Helmut Jochum, München, Germany

SIEMENS Q 4000, ein medizinisches Ultraschallgerät mit leistungsstarker Bildgebung. Um eine einfache Bedienbarkeit zu gewährleisten, konzentriert sich das Design auf die Bedienoberfläche. Traditionelle Bedienelemente kombiniert mit multifunktionellem Touch Screen, dessen Bedienfunktionen eingeblendet werden, so daß der Benutzer mit der einen Hand das Gerät bedienen und mit der anderen die Untersuchung durchführen kann. Die Augen bleiben dabei stets auf den Monitor gerichtet. Die ausziehbare und drehbare Bedientastatur kann nach oben und unten verstellt werden. Ausdrucksstarkes Design setzt die Funktionsbereiche farblich voneinander ab.

The SIEMENS Q 4000 is a medical ultrasound system providing top performance imaging capability. The design focused primarily on the user interface to ensure ease of use. Traditional controls are coupled with a multifunction touch screen that includes a heads-up display to the monitor, allowing the user to keep one hand on the control panel and the other on the patient without having to look away from the monitor. The control panel can slide in and out, rotate left and right, and move up and down. The design utilizes graphic color fields to denote the various functional areas.

390 MEDIZIN *MEDICAL* BESTE DER BRANCHE *BEST OF GROUP*

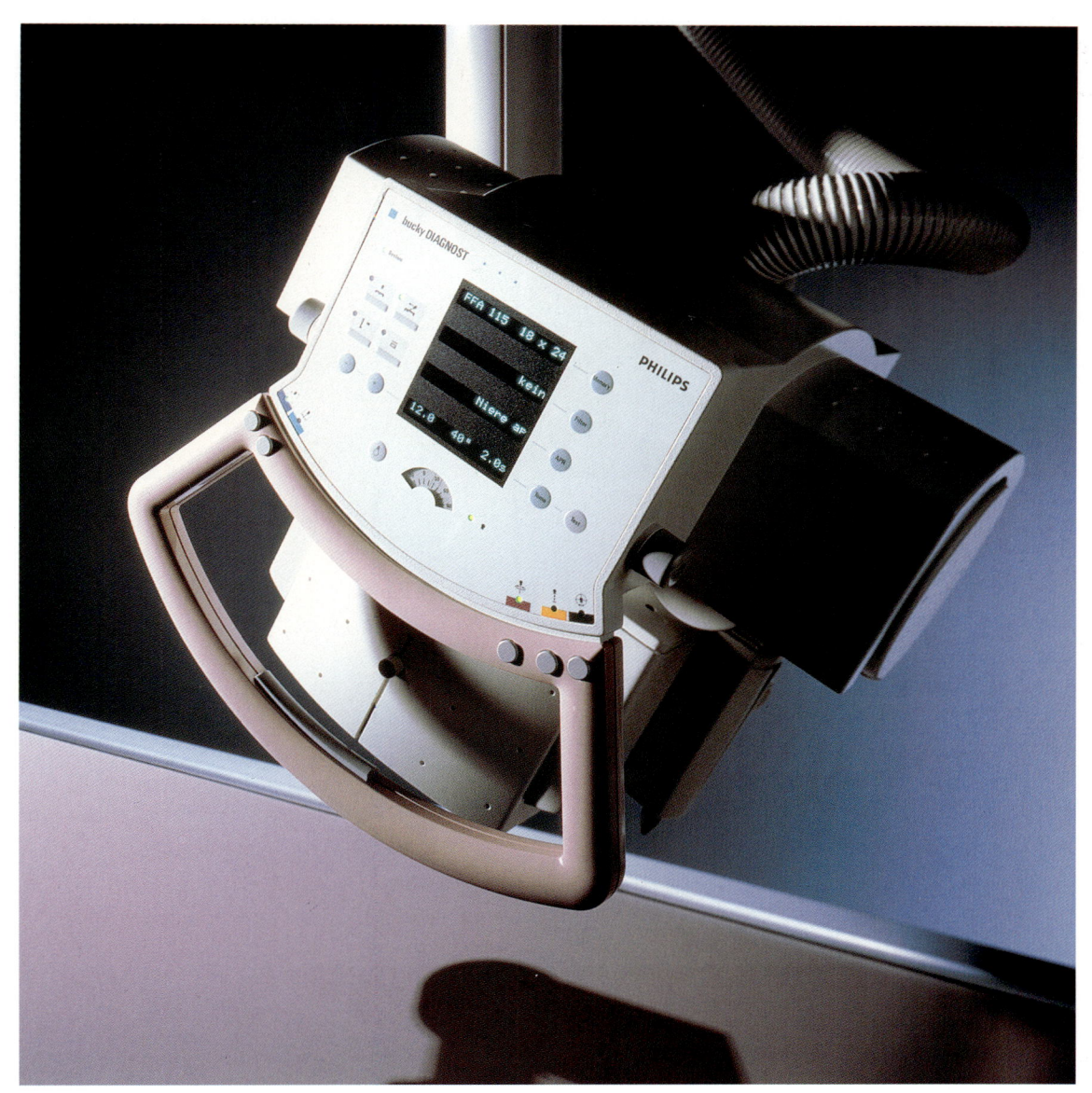

BUCKY DIAGNOST, »low end« Universal-Röntgensystem, das einfach und leicht zu gebrauchen, bedienungsfreundlich und kosteneffektiv ist. Designentwicklung nach Benutzerumfragen und nach Krankenhausbesuchen. Durchgängige Designsprache für alle Systemkomponenten: Deckenaufhängungseinheit, Tisch und Generatorkonsole. Höhere Funktionalität in dem mit der Röntgenstrahlröhre verbundenen Kontrollbereich, dadurch besserer Kontakt zwischen Arzt und Patient. Keine unnötigen Wege mehr zur und von der Generatorkonsole. Verbesserte ergonomische Umsetzung und semantische Hinweise an Bedienerkonsole und Kontrollgriff.

The BUCKY DIAGNOST is a »low end« all-purpose X-ray system that is simple and easy to use, as well as cost-effective. The design was based on findings yielded by user surveys and visits to hospitals. The system sports a consistent design throughout, linking the ceiling suspension unit, the table and the generator console. The connection between the X-ray tube and the control area enhances functionality, affording better doctor-patient contact and eliminating unnecessary trips to and from the generator console. The user panel and the control handle feature optimal ergonomics and unique semantics.

HERSTELLER MANUFACTURER Philips Medizin Systeme, Hamburg, Germany
PRODUKT PRODUCT Allgemeines Röntgensystem für Diagnostik All purpose X-ray diagnostic system
DESIGN Philips Corporate Design, Eindhoven, The Netherlands

HERSTELLER MANUFACTURER
Otto Bock Orthopädische Industrie, Duderstadt, Germany
PRODUKT PRODUCT
Dyna Ankle Dynamische Sprunggelenkorthese Dynamik ankle orthosis
DESIGN
megaform Designstudio Stockburger, Braunschweig, Germany

DYNA ANKLE, eine dynamische Sprunggelenk-Orthese für die funktionelle Behandlung der Außenbandverletzung. Sie stabilisiert das Knöchelgelenk und erlaubt die kontrollierte Bewegung im Knöchelbereich. Nutzbar als Liegeschale direkt nach der Verletzung bis zur sicheren Ausheilung, auch z.B. beim Gehen. Aufgrund ihres filigranen Designs im normalen Schuh zu tragen. Als Spritzgießteil mit austauschbaren Verschlußteilen gefertigt und nicht – wie allgemein üblich – als Tiefziehprodukt. Dadurch entfallen die sonst erforderliche Nachbearbeitung und zusätzlicher Verschnitt.

The DYNA ANKLE is a dynamic ankle orthosis for treating sprains and ruptures of the deltoid ligament. It stabilizes the ankle joint and permits controlled movement of the ankle, and can be worn directly after injury has occurred up until the ankle is fully healed. The orthosis is suitable for use with normal shoes. It consists of an injected molded form featuring removable closures. Dispensing with the usual deep-drawing production method eliminates the need for subsequent processing and cuts down on waste products.

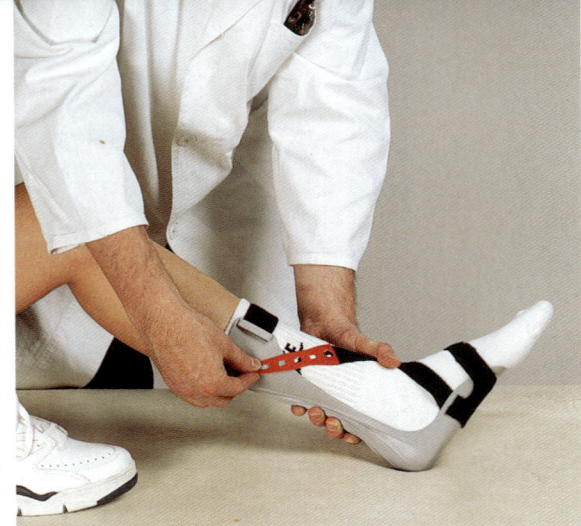

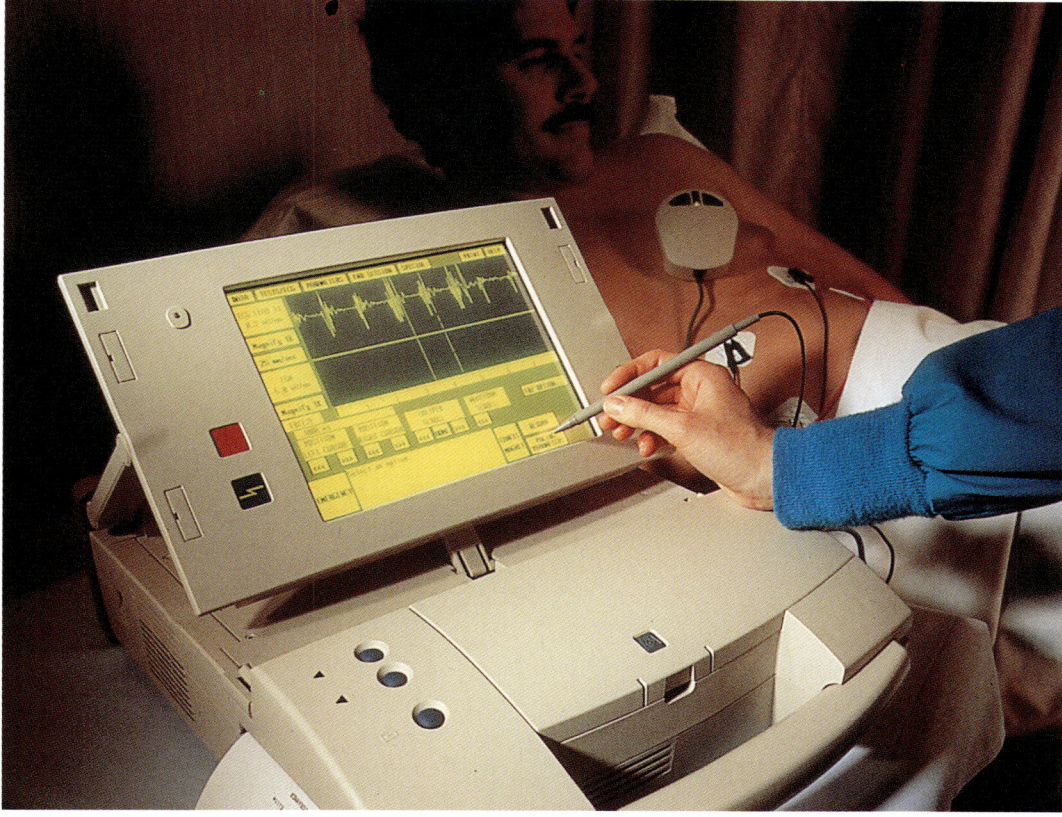

MEDTRONIC 9790 ist ein tragbarer Programmierer für Herzschrittmacher zur Überprüfung und Veränderung der Parameter von eingesetzten Herzschrittmachern. Stellt als Programmier-Eingabegerät die Verbindung zum Herzschrittmacher her: Signale des Schrittmachers werden abgerufen und/oder neue eingegeben, indem der Arzt das Eingabegerät auf der Brust des Patienten über den Herzschrittmacher hält. Das Programmiergerät hat einen Flachbildschirm mit "Stylus"-Eingabegerät, um die abgerufenen Informationen einzustellen.

The MEDTRONIC 9790 is a portable pacemaker programmer for monitoring and adjusting the parameters of implanted pacemakers in patients. It communicates with the implanted pacemaker via a radio frequency (RF) unit. The doctor places the RF unit on the patient's chest so that it may send (program) and receive (interrogate) signals emitted by the pacemaker. The programmer features a screen with a stylus input, which is used to adjust the information displayed.

Tragbarer Programmierer für Herzschrittmacher Portable pacemaker programmer
Medtronic Inc., Minneapolis, USA Hersteller manufacturer
IDEO Product Development, Jochen Backs, Jane Fulton Suri, Sean Corcorran, Palo Alto, USA Produkt product
Design

MEDIZIN MEDICAL 393

HERSTELLER MANUFACTURER Stair Assist Corporation, Portland, USA
PRODUKT PRODUCT Stair Assist Power Bar Gehhilfe für Treppen Walker for stairs
DESIGN ZIBA Design, Portland, USA

STAIR ASSIST ist eine motorisierte »Gehhilfe« für Treppen. Ohne die komplizierte Mechanik und teure Installation, die bei einem herkömmlichen Treppenlift anfallen, dadurch auch preiswert, gibt der Stair Assist Menschen, die sonst auf fremde Hilfe angewiesen wären, Bewegungsfreiheit.

STAIR ASSIST is a motorized »walker« for stairs available at an affordable price. By avoiding the mechanical complexity and costly installation of a chair lift, Stair Assist makes independent living a reality for thousands of people who would otherwise require assistance climbing the stairs.

394 MEDIZIN MEDICAL

Scandinavian Mobility EC - Hong A/S, Hong, Denmark HERSTELLER MANUFACTURER
Scan Bed 500 Pflegebett für häusliche Pflege Home care-bed PRODUKT PRODUCT
Christina Halskov, Hanne Dalsgaard, Copenhagen, Denmark DESIGN
Scandinavian Mobility GmbH, Hannover, Germany VERTRIEB DISTRIBUTION

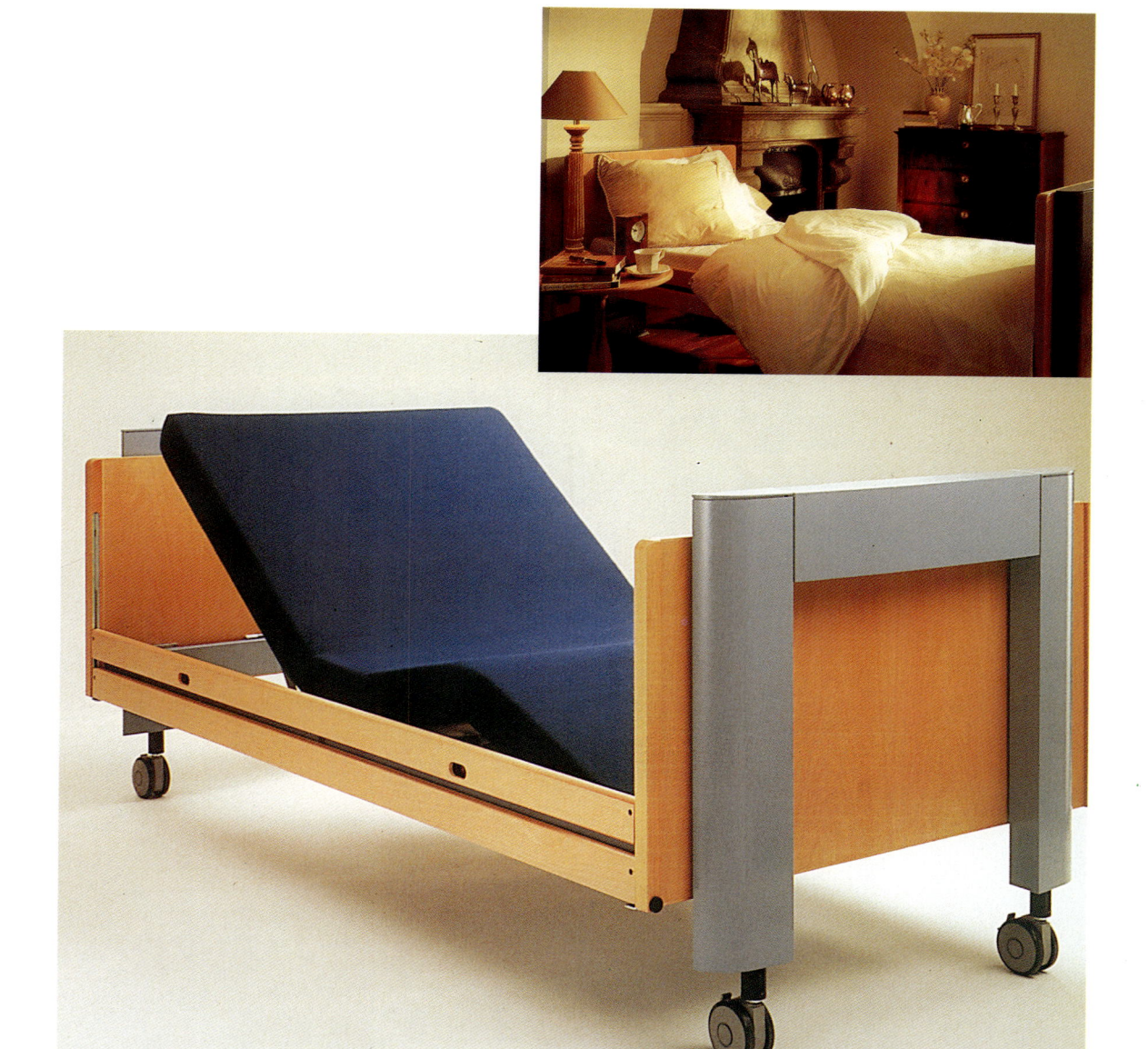

SCAN BED 500, ein Pflegebett für die häusliche Pflege, das in Formgebung und Technik neue Wege geht. Es wirkt trotz aufwendiger Technik nicht klinisch, bietet Mobilität, Unabhängigkeit und Wohlbefinden. Viergeteilte, teilbare Liegefläche aus Aluminium, die durch einen leicht zu bedienenden Handschalter stufenlos eingestellt werden kann. Die nach ergonomischen Gesichtspunkten arbeitende Technik verhindert automatisch, daß es in dem Winkel zwischen Rücken- und Beinteil zu Zwangshaltungen kommt. Leicht zu reinigen, von einer Person mühelos zu transportieren und ohne Werkzeug zu zerlegen und zu montieren.

The SCAN BED 500 is innovative both in design and technology, and avoids a clinical appearance despite sophisticated equipment. It offers patients mobility, independence and a sense of well-being. The aluminium mattress support is divided into four sections; it can be smoothly adjusted with an easy-to-use handswitch. The ergonomic technology prevents undesirable angles between the back and leg sections. The bed is easy to clean, and can easily be transported by one person. No tools are required for assembly and dismantling.

MEDIZIN MEDICAL 395

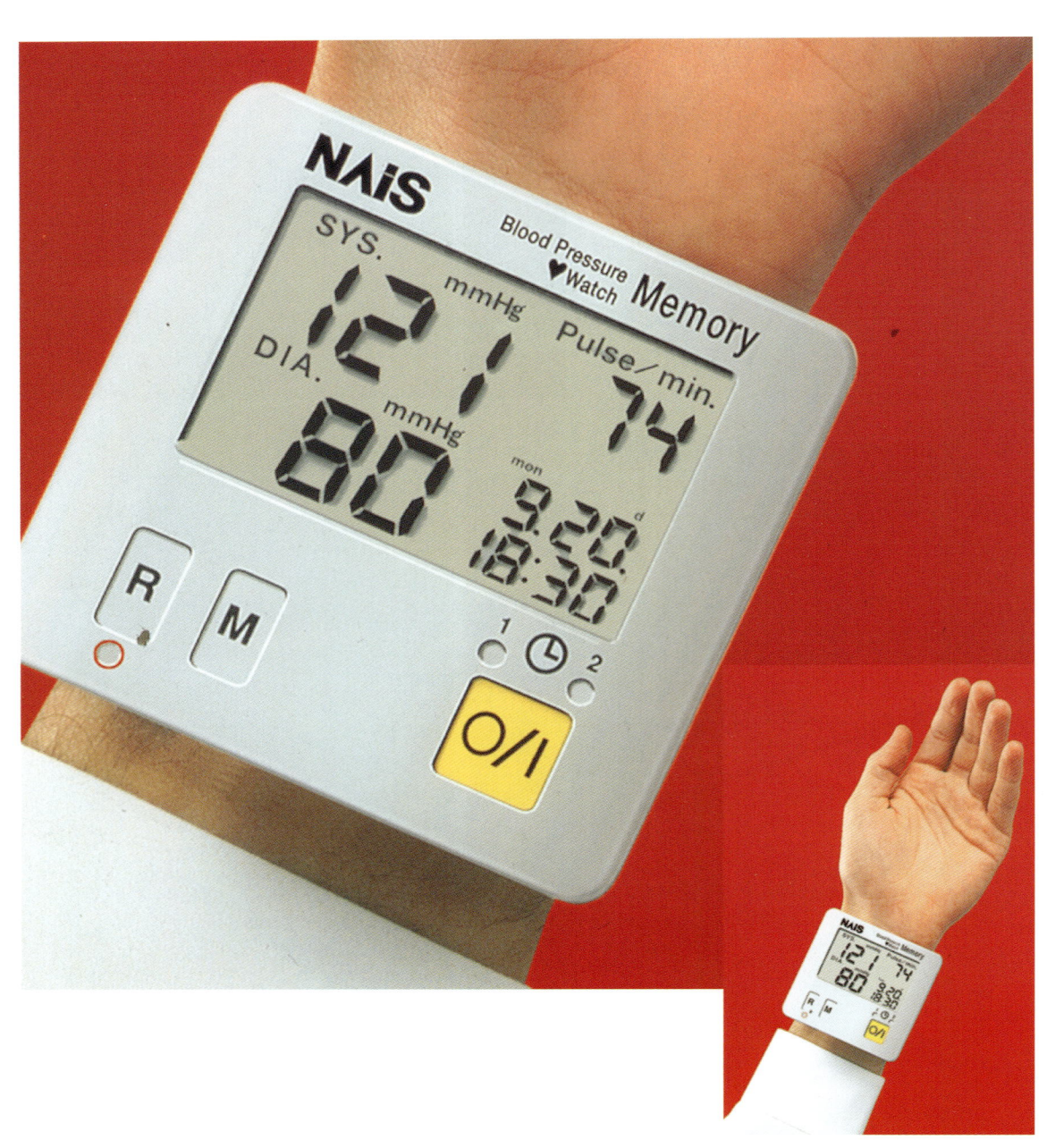

HERSTELLER MANUFACTURER
Matsushita Electric Works, Ltd., Osaka, Japan

PRODUKT PRODUCT
Single Unit Wrist Sphygomanometer EW 274 Sphygomanometer

DESIGN
Matsushita Electric Works Ltd., Home Appliance A&I Design Office, Osaka, Japan, Prof. Florian Seiffert, Wiesbaden, Germany

SPHYGMOMANOMETER EW 274 zum Messen des Blutdrucks am Armgelenk, so daß der Patient oder Benutzer den Ärmel nicht hochrollen muß. Riemen und Gehäuse bilden zur Erleichterung des Anlegens eine Einheit. Großes LCD-Display zeigt Blutdruck, Puls, Datum und Uhrzeit gleichzeitig an. Bis zu 30 Messungen können gespeichert werden und sind jederzeit auf Knopfdruck im Display ablesbar. Daher entfällt das Aufschreiben der Werte für die Vorlage beim Arzt. Das Gerät ist kompakt und leicht überallhin mitzunehmen.

SPHYGMOMANOMETER EW 274 measures blood pressure at the wrist so that the user no longer has to roll up his sleeve. The belt and body are integrated into one compact, portable unit, making the device easier to use. A large LCD display shows blood pressure, pulse, date and time simultaneously. Up to 30 readings can be stored and called up at the touch of a button, enabling the user to show the readings to the doctor without having to write them down first.

396 MEDIZIN MEDICAL

HERSTELLER MANUFACTURER HITACHI MEDICAL CORPORATION, Chiba-ken, Japan
PRODUKT PRODUCT AIRIS Magnetisches Resonanzbildsystem Magnetic resonance imaging system
DESIGN Design Centre Hitachi, Tokyo, Japan

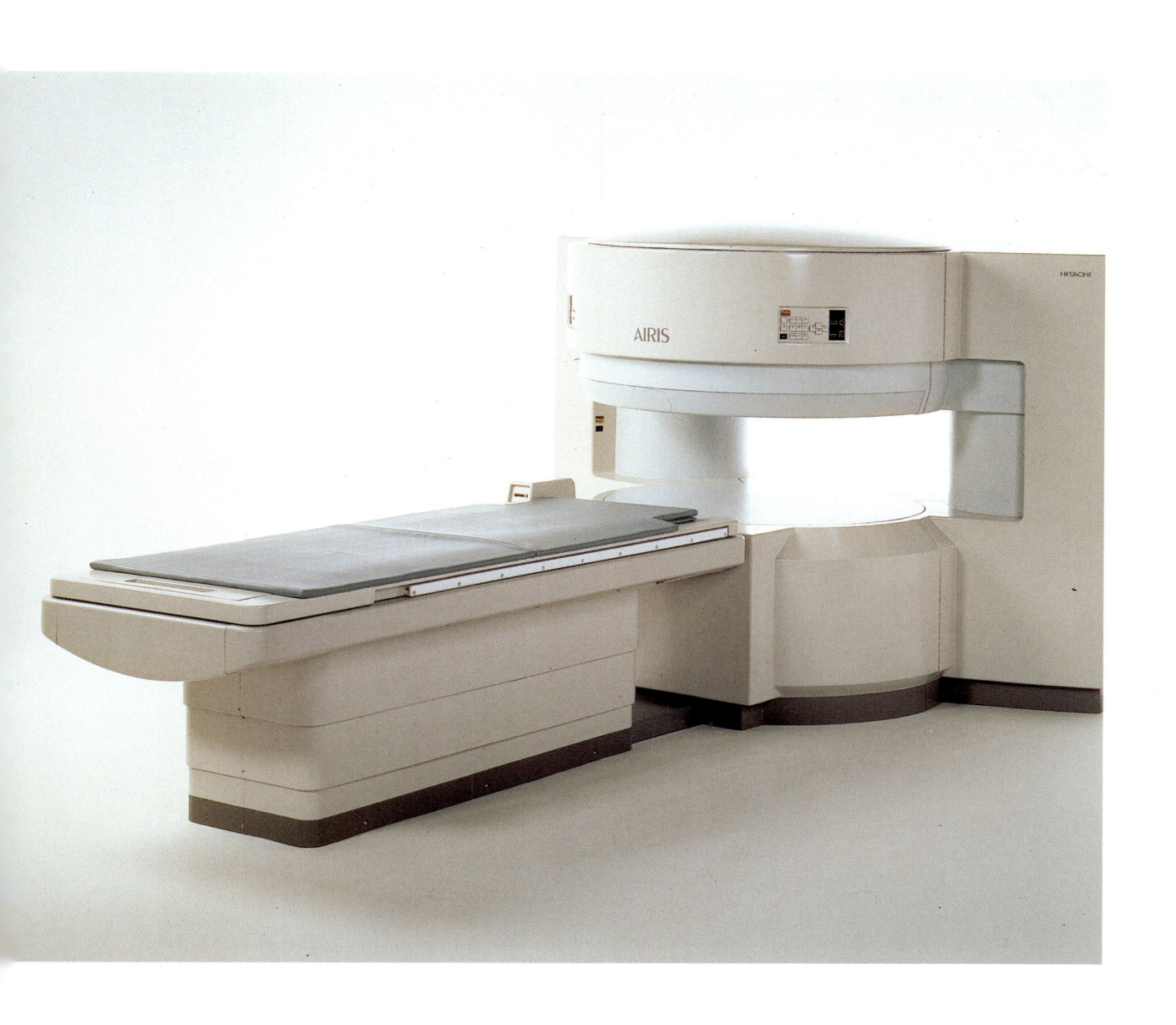

AIRIS ist ein magnetisches Resonanzbild-System vom Typ 0.3T. Das offene Gestell hat eine vordere Öffnung von 210 Grad und ist auch von den Seiten zugänglich, die Rückseite ist frei in einem 70°-Bereich, so daß bei Patienten weit weniger klaustrophobische Ängste auftreten. Stark verbesserte Bedienbarkeit. Durch die großzügige frontale und rückwärtige Öffnungskapazität des Gestells steht den Patienten und für das untersuchende Personal viel Platz zur Verfügung. Weiterentwickelte Bildfunktionen und hohe Bildqualität.

AIRIS is a Type 0.3T magnetic resonance imaging system. The gantry features a front opening of 210° that is also accessible from the sides, and a rear opening of 70°, significantly reducing symptoms of claustrophobia in patients. These generous proportions also ensure that both patient and operator will have sufficient space. The system is easy to operate, and offers high image quality as well as advanced imaging functions.

MEDIZIN MEDICAL 397

HERSTELLER MANUFACTURER CHEMUNEX, U.K.LTD., Derby, Great Britain
PRODUKT PRODUCT ULTRA SENSITIVE MICROBIAL ANALYSER Microbial analyser chemscan
DESIGN Weaver Associates, Philip Gray, Martin Riley, London, Great Britain

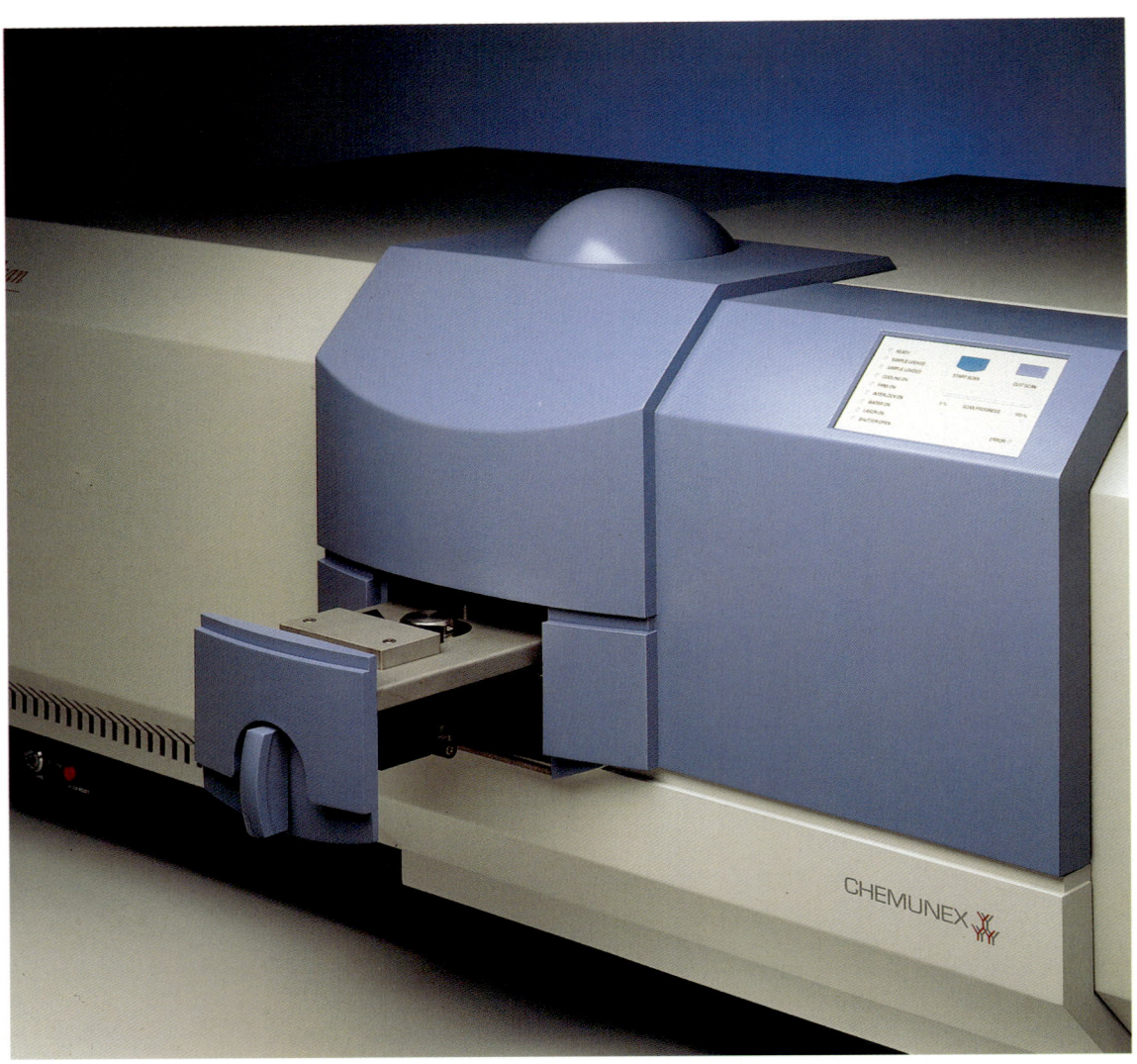

CHEMSCAN®, ein hochempfindliches mikrobielles Analysesystem. Zur Untersuchung der Keimfreiheit von Flüssigkeiten in der pharmazeutischen Industrie, für Lebensmittel- und Getränkehersteller, für die Wasserwirtschaft und industrielle Anwender im Umweltschutz. Die neue Technologie erlaubt den zuverlässigen Nachweis einer einzelnen Zelle ohne Inkubation. Damit wird die typische Nachweisdauer von 3 bis 14 Tagen auf 15 bis 30 Minuten reduziert. Die Probe wird mit einfachen Handgriffen geladen, und nach nur einem Tastendruck läuft die analytische Prüfung ab.

CHEMSCAN® an ultra-sensitive microbial analysis system for testing the sterility of liquids in the pharmaceutical, food, water, and environmental protection industries. New technology allows highly accurate single cell detection without an incubation phase, reducing the typical 3–14 day test cycle to 15–30 minutes. After loading the test sample, a single keystroke initiates the analytical sampling process.

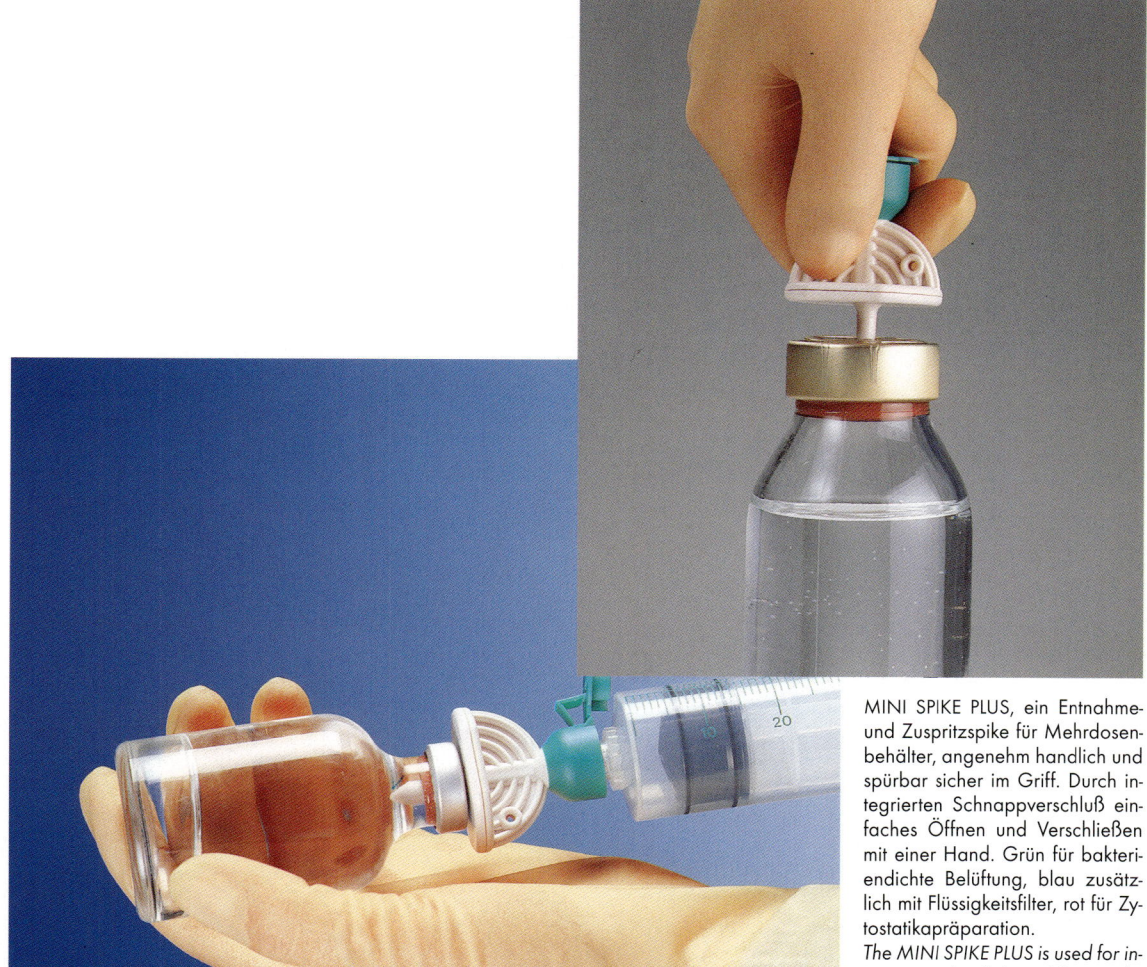

B. Braun Melsungen AG, Sparte Medical, Melsungen, Germany HERSTELLER MANUFACTURER
Mini-Spike Plus Injection and withdrawal System Entnahme- und Zuspritzspike PRODUKT PRODUCT
CONTEC DESIGN GBR, Burgdorf, Germany DESIGN

MINI SPIKE PLUS, ein Entnahme- und Zuspritzspike für Mehrdosenbehälter, angenehm handlich und spürbar sicher im Griff. Durch integrierten Schnappverschluß einfaches Öffnen und Verschließen mit einer Hand. Grün für bakteriendichte Belüftung, blau zusätzlich mit Flüssigkeitsfilter, rot für Zytostatikapräparation.

The MINI SPIKE PLUS is used for injection and withdrawal from multidose vials. It is easy to use and affords an especially secure grip. The integrated snap cap makes it simple to open and close with one hand. It comes in three colors: green is a bacteria-proof air filter, blue is an additional fluid filter, and red is for cytostatic solutions.

MEDIZIN MEDICAL 399

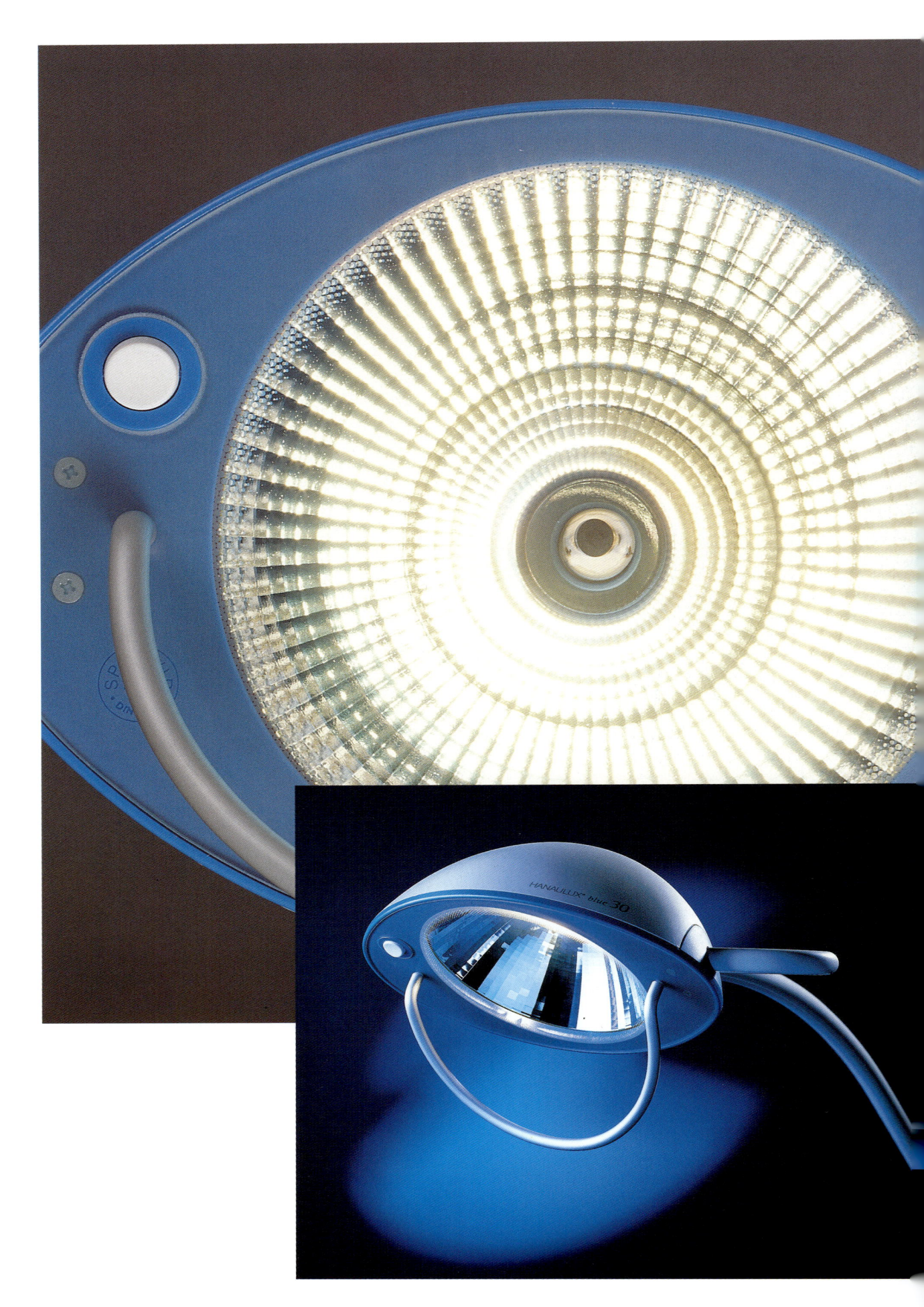

HERSTELLER MANUFACTURER Heraeus MED GmbH, Hanau, Germany
PRODUKT PRODUCT HANAULUX blue 30 Untersuchungsleuchte Examination light
DESIGN Eckart + Barski, Frankfurt, Germany

400 MEDIZIN *MEDICAL*

HANAULUX BLUE 30, eine medizinische Untersuchungsleuchte für den mobilen Einsatz in Krankenhaus und Arztpraxis. Basisleuchte für ein Produktprogramm in Stativ-, Wand- und Deckenausführung.

The HANAULUX BLUE 30 is a portable examination light for use in hospitals and doctors' offices. It is the basic model for a line of products comprising a floor lamp as well as a wall-mounted and ceiling-mounted version.

Ökologie/Design Auszeichnung Awarded for Ecology/Design: Vorbildlich durch Einfachheit und Konzentration auf die Hauptfunktion. Exemplary for its simplicity and the focus only on main functions.

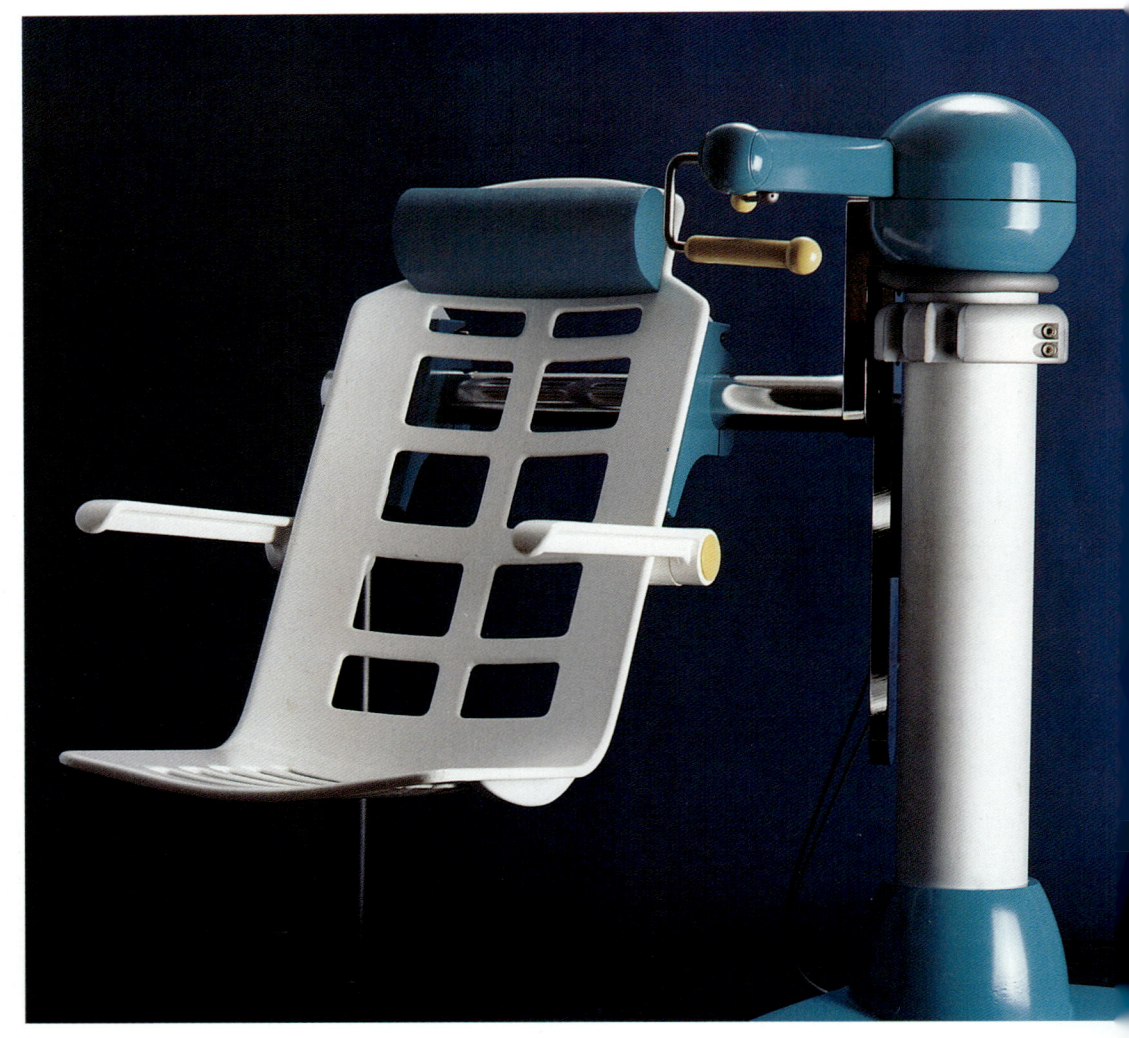

HERSTELLER MANUFACTURER
FeinwerkTechnik GmbH Geising, Geising, Germany
PRODUKT PRODUCT
Badlift Bath lift
DESIGN
Designprojekt GmbH Dresden, Eberhard Marx, Dresden, Germany
VERTRIEB DISTRIBUTION
Fumelli-Vertriebs-GmbH, München, Germany

BADLIFT für Körperbehinderte, die mit diesem Gerät ohne fremde Hilfe ein Vollbad nehmen können. Alle Funktionen sind rein mechanisch realisiert. Der Hub wird hydraulisch mit dem anliegenden Wasserdruck des Leitungsnetzes betrieben. Damit entfallen aufwendige elektrische Schutzvorkehrungen. Die Funktionselemente wurden gestalterisch so optimiert, daß eine Bedienung für Menschen mit unterschiedlichsten Behinderungsarten leicht möglich ist. Der Badlift hebt sich in technischer Lösung, Design und Farbgebung von den allzuoft rein technisch anmutenden Hilfen für körperbehinderte Menschen ab.

The BATH LIFT was designed to enable the physically disabled to have a proper bath without help from others. All functions are completely mechanical, and the lift is powered by the hydraulic pressure available in the water supply system. This eliminates the need for costly electrical safety measures. The functional elements were optimized to allow persons with various disabilities to operate them with ease. The appealing design and color of the bath lift distinguish it from other aids for the disabled, which all too often have a cold, technical appearance.

Ökologie/Design Auszeichnung Awarded for Ecology/Design: Vorbildlich durch einfachen Wasserantrieb und funktionserklärende Gestaltung. Exemplary, water powering and a self-explanatory design.

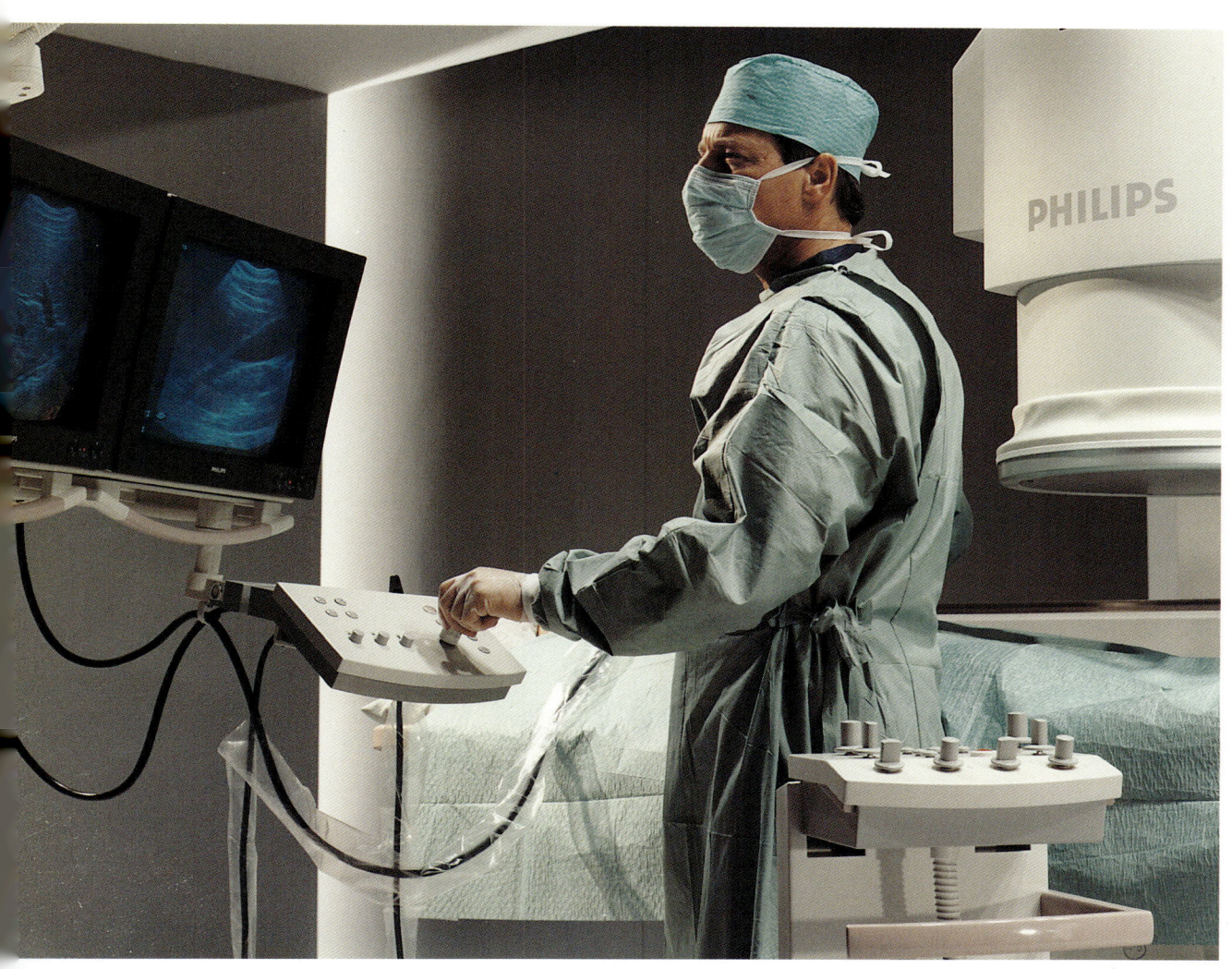

PHILIPS SCANNER 200X, integriertes Ultraschallsystem, weltweit eines der ersten Systeme, das mehrere bilddiagnostische Verfahren vereint. Wahlmöglichkeit zwischen Ultraschall und Röntgenaufnahme bei gleichzeitiger Nutzung der Vorteile beider Verfahren. Der Radiologe kontrolliert nur die funktionalen Vorgänge bei der Organidentifizierung und der Nadelführung. Keine möglicherweise schädlichen Röntgenstrahlen bei diesen Funktionen. Dieses »verdichtete« Ultraschallsystem bietet gegenüber Geräten mit großem Anwendungsbereich Kostenvorteile, ist zugleich einfacher zu bedienen und greift nicht in die stattfindenden Röntgenaufnahmeprozesse ein. Minimales Design, selbsterklärendes Layout des Bedienpaneels, geringe Standfläche.

The PHILIPS SCANNER 200X is an integrated ultrasound system, one of the first in the world to offer multi-modality imaging. It is used to switch between ultrasound and x-ray modalities. The radiologist controls only the functions required for organ identification and needle guidance without needing to use any harmful x-rays for these procedures. This »condensed« ultrasound system is less expensive than multi-application systems, is easier to operate and does not interfere with the x-ray procedure taking place. The straightforward design includes a self-explanatory control layout and uses minimal floor space.

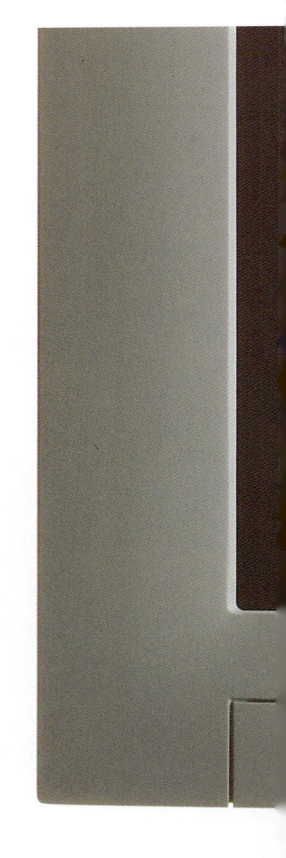

HERSTELLER MANUFACTURER: evosoft Softwarevertriebs GmbH, Nürnberg, Germany
PRODUKT PRODUCT: SICARE Sprachfernsteuergerät für Behinderte Voice remote control system for the handicapped
DESIGN: Siemens Design, Anke Osthues, München, Germany

SICARE, ein Fernsteuerungssystem mit Spracherkennung für motorisch behinderte Personen. Objekte wie Telefon, Rollstuhl, Bett, Fahrstuhl, Türen, Computer, Fernseh-, Rundfunk- und HiFi-Geräte können mit Sprachbefehlen über Infrarot/Funk gesteuert werden. Durch den eigenständigen Zugriff auf die Umgebung über Sprachbefehle gewinnen behinderte Personen Selbständigkeit und Privatsphäre zurück. Verwendung im privaten Bereich wie in Kliniken. 100%-ige Zuverlässigkeit der Spracherkennung bei richtiger Durchführung der Sprachlernphase. Das Handgerät besteht aus Ober- und Unterschale. Material: Kunststoff. Ein Köcher nimmt das Gerät auf und stellt die Verbindung zur Stromversorgung her. Die zurückhaltende Farbgebung mit den frischen Akzenten gibt dem Gerät eine positive Ausstrahlung.

SICARE is a remote control system featuring speech recognition for the physically disabled. It enables users to operate devices such as telephones, wheelchairs, beds, lifts, doors, computers, televisions, radios and stereos by means of verbal commands, thus helping them to lead more private, independent lives. It is intended both for private use and in clinics. Speech recognition is 100% reliable if the device is properly trained. It is housed in a special casing which connects it to the power supply, and its convenient shape makes it easy for caretaking personnel to manage. The discreet color scheme with its fresh accents gives the system an attractive appearance.

HYGIENE-CENTER, ein Gerät für Reinigung, Desinfektion, Sterilisation und Pflege (Ölen) von Dentalinstrumenten. Korpus aus hochglanzlackiertem Stahlblech. Front aus glänzendem Kunststoff, in drei Funktionsbereiche gegliedert. Bündig eingelegte Bedienfolie. Einfache Handhabung durch Tastendruck. Automatisierter Funktionsablauf.

The HYGIENE CENTER is a device for cleaning, disinfecting, sterilizing and maintaining (oiling) dental instruments. The body is made of sheet steel with a high-gloss paint finish; the front is made of glossy plastic and divided into three functional areas. A control foil has been flush-mounted on the device, sporting push-buttons for easy operation. It features automatic functional sequencing.

HERSTELLER MANUFACTURER Siemens Aktiengesellschaft Berlin - München, München, Germany
PRODUKT PRODUCT HYGIENE CENTER System für Dental-Instrumentenhygiene Hygiene center for instrument hygiene
DESIGN Siemens Design, Tilman Phleps, München, Germany

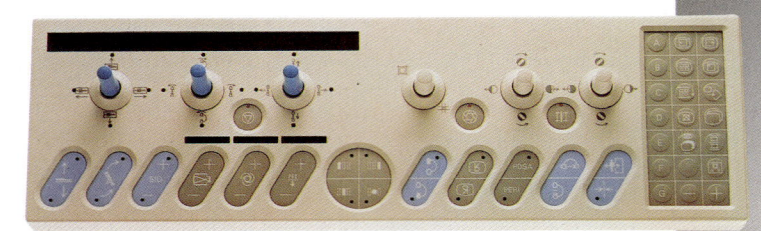

HERSTELLER MANUFACTURER
Siemens Aktiengesellschaft Berlin - München, München, Germany
PRODUKT PRODUCT
POLYSTAR Steuereinheit Control panel
DESIGN
Siemens Design, Gerd Helmreich, München, Germany

POLYSTAR Bedienkonsole zur Steuerung medizinischer Großgeräte und der Bildbearbeitung. Flache Bedienkonsole mit Bedienerführung durch Joysticks und Tastmulden aus weichem Material. Beleuchtete Bedienoberfläche ermöglicht Steuerung im abgedunkeltem Raum (»Nacht-Design«).
The POLYSTAR control panel was designed for large-scale medical appliances and image editing. The flat console is operated using joysticks and soft touch-buttons, providing the user with context-sensitive help. The illuminated operator interface enables use in darkened rooms (»Night Design«).

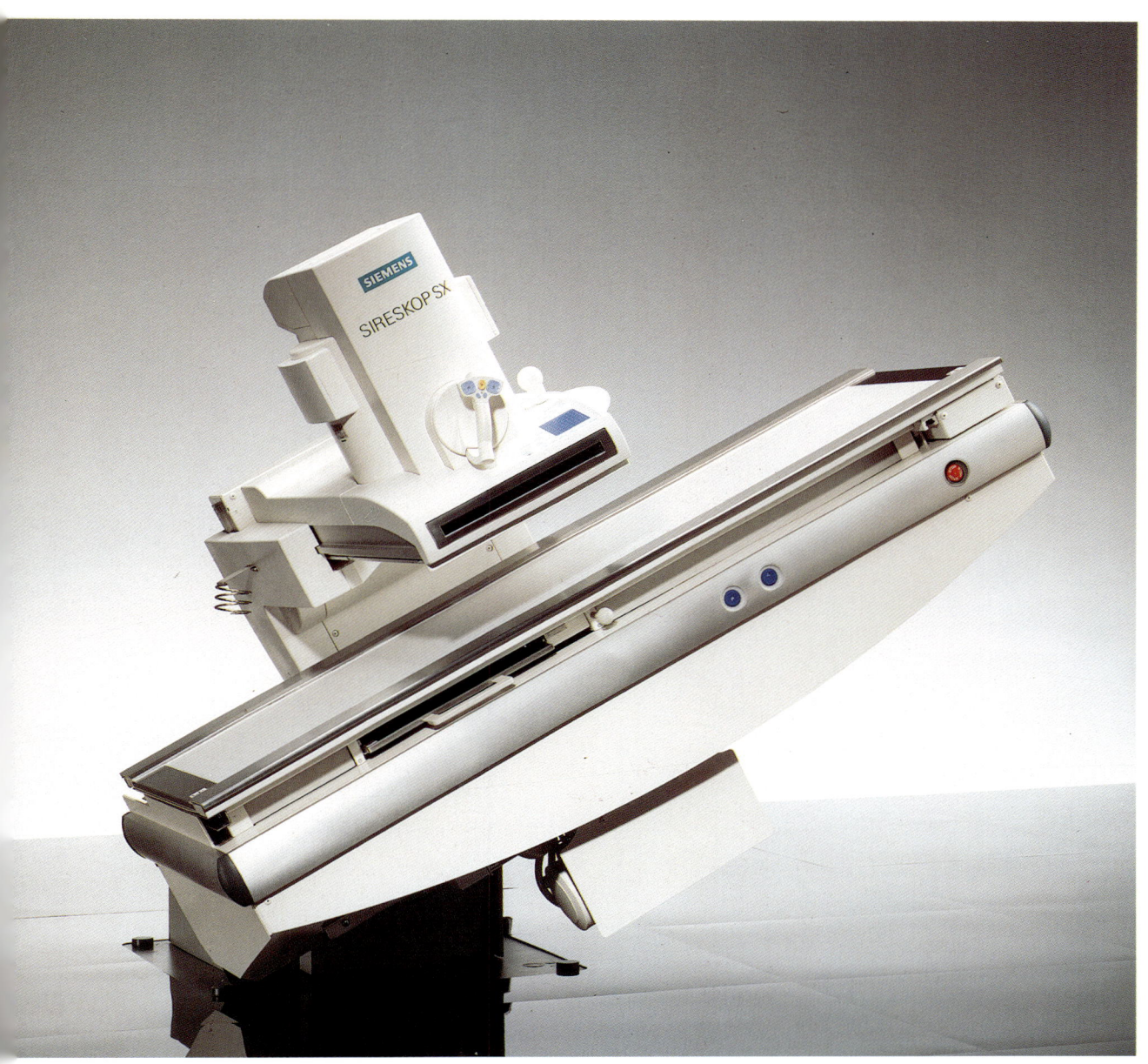

SIRESKOP SX, Untertischröntgengerät für Kliniken und radiologische Praxen. Überwölbungen und Strukturierung der Gerätefront durch unterschiedliche Materialien lassen das Gerät schlank erscheinen. Neuartige, ergonomisch optimierte Steuerung. Technisch neu: der kardanisch aufgehängte Steuergriff und die Fingermaus-Steuerung.

The SIRESKOP SX is an X-ray unit built to fit under a table, and is intended for use in clinics and radiological surgeries. The curved front is constructed using various materials, and lends the device a slender appearance. It sports a new, ergonomically optimal operating mechanism as well as a universal control handle and finger-mouse control – a technical innovation.

HERSTELLER MANUFACTURER Siemens Aktiengesellschaft Berlin · München, München, Germany
PRODUKT PRODUCT SIRESKOP SX Untertischröntgengerät X-ray unit
DESIGN Siemens Design, Gerd Helmreich, München, Germany

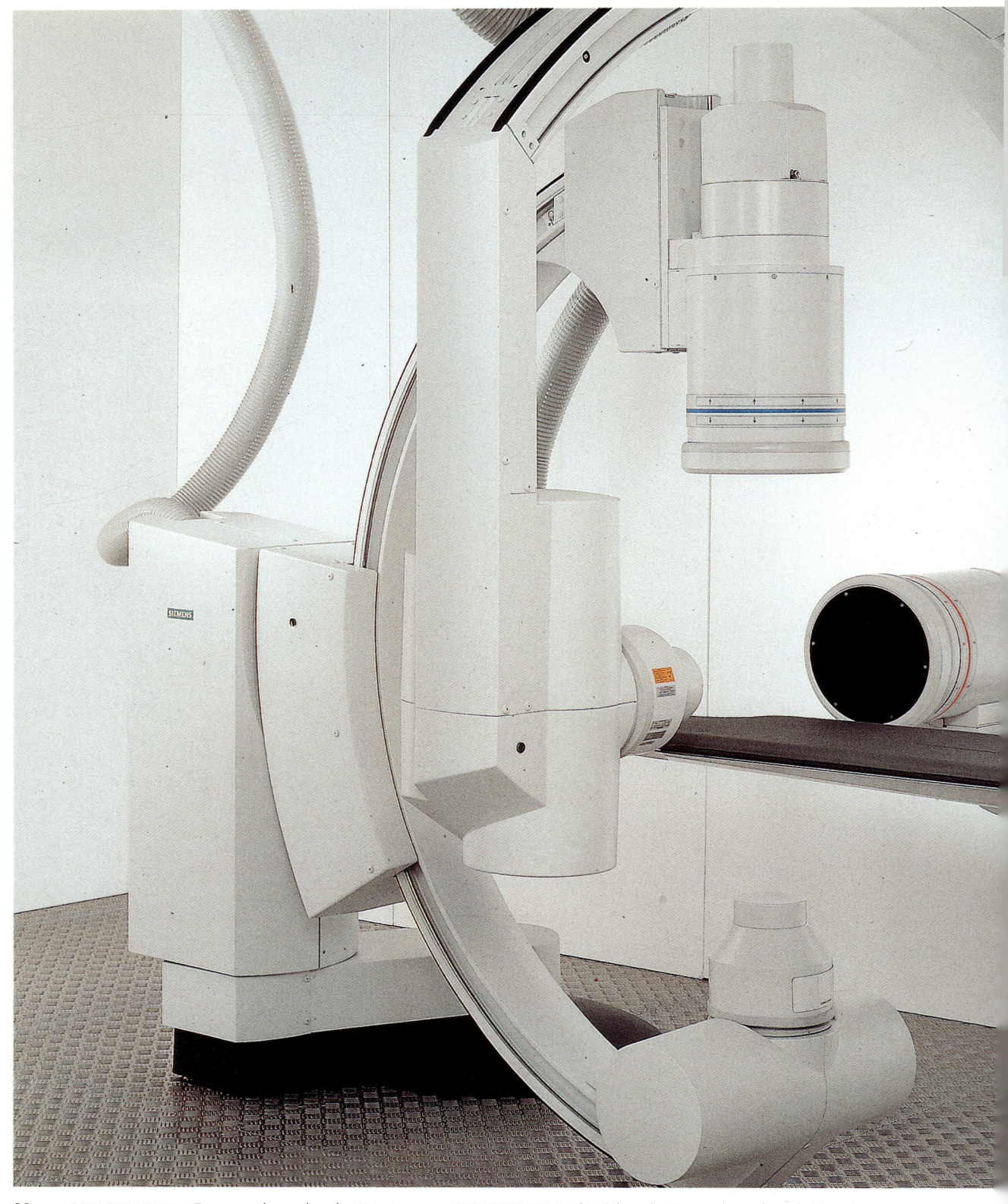

HERSTELLER MANUFACTURER Siemens Aktiengesellschaft Berlin - München, München, Germany
PRODUKT PRODUCT COROSKOP T.O.P. Einebenen-Herzkatheter-Labor Single plane heart catheter lab.
DESIGN Siemens Design, Jens Pattberg, München, Germany

C-Bogen COROSKOP T.O.P. - Einebenen-Herzkatheter-Labor für die Angiokardiographie und die Intervention am Herzen. Die extrem schlanke Bauweise ermöglicht einen optimalen Zugang zum Patienten. Durch den Boden-Drehpunkt kann man eine Ganzkörperuntersuchung vornehmen ohne den Patienten umzulagern. Einfache Bedienung mit Multifunktions-Joystick. Hohes »UpTime« macht Reparaturen überflüssig. Lebendauer des Gerätes etwa 10 Jahre. Danach ist das Gerät völlig recyclebar.

COROSKOP T.O.P. This C-shaped frame Single plane heart catheter lab is for angiocardiography and medical intervention involving the heart. The extremely slender construction enables optimal access to the patient. As the pivot point is on the ground, head-to-toe examinations can be performed without having to shift the patient. The device is simple to operate using a multifunctional joystick, and provides a service life of about 10 years, after which it can be fully recycled.

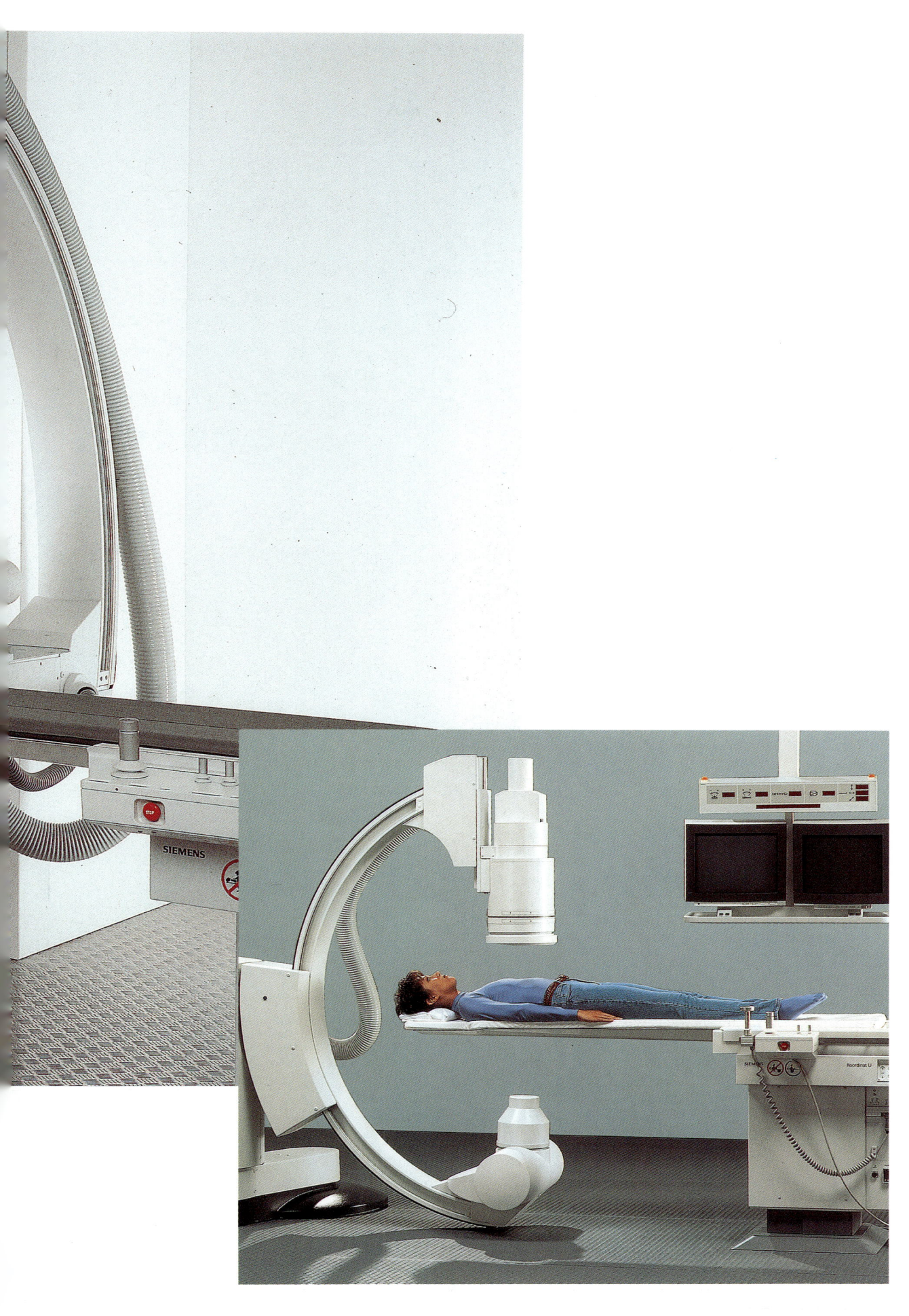

MEDIZIN *MEDICAL* 409

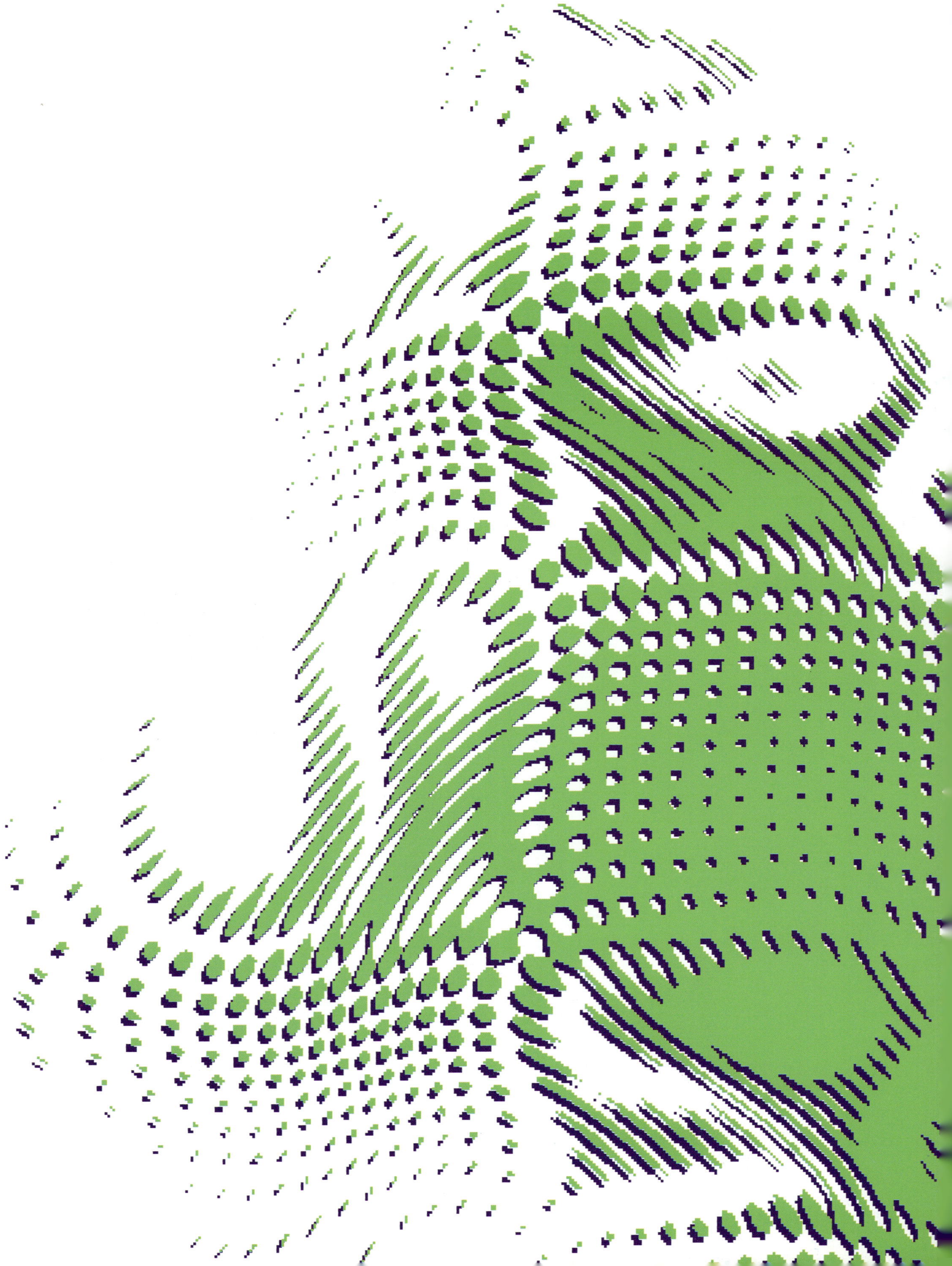

inter face

INTERFACE

Jury: Prof. Burghardt Schmitz, Joannes Vandermeulen, Frank Zebner

»Die Benutzer interaktiver Produkte werden zeitweilig von einer anderen Welt absorbiert. Sind sie deshalb verunsichert und haben Angst, sich zu verlieren? Würden sie jemanden heiraten, der zwei Dörfer weiter entfernt wohnt?« beschreibt mit skurillem Humor der belgische Interface-Experte Joannes Vandermeulen die noch immer ungewohnte Virtualität des neuen Mediums.

Neben der Ökologie stellt Interface, die gestaltete Schnittstelle zwischen Mensch und Maschine, den zweiten »Crossover«-Aspekt« des Wettbewerbs dar. Erwartungsgemäß gab es zu diesem Thema viele Fragen an die Experten, auch von anderen Jurymitgliedern, die wissen wollten, ob Gestaltung und Konzeption jener »Schnittstellen« an Geräten, die Verständnis und Bedienung ermöglichen, gut oder schlecht gelöst seien.

Der Begriff »Interface« geht nach Auffassung der Juroren weit über den traditionellen Begriff der Benutzeroberfläche, bestehend aus Produktgrafik und Tastatur, hinaus, vergleichbar mit dem »Sprung in eine neue Technologiewelt«, denn man hat es mit Virtualität zu tun und nicht mit der physischen Präsenz eines Gegenstandes, den man manuell bedient. Im Interface, im virtuellen Teil, wird auf die Hardware verwiesen. Dieselben Bedienungsknöpfe sollten deshalb, so fordert die Jury, wieder im Display in Ablaufdiagrammen auftauchen. Ausgezeichnet wurden nur wenige der eingereichten Lösungen: Im Bereich des digitalen Fernsehens ein Mudtimediagerät zur Dekodierung digitaler Programme, im Bereich Telekommunikation ein sich selbst erklärendes Display für ein Telefaxgerät, aus dem Kopierbereich - ausgezeichnet als Top Ten - ein interaktives Bedienungsfeld, das es ermöglicht, eine komplizierte Maschine ohne Studium der Gebrauchsanweisung zu bedienen, im Bereich der Haustechnik eine Steuerung, die per Fernbedienung Troubleshooting im Energierversorgungsbereich korrigiert, ohne in das Leitungssystem zunächst physisch einzugreifen. Als vorbildliche Lösung beurteilte die kritische Jury ein Kommunikationskonzept für innerbetriebliche Marketing-Kommunikation von IBM und ein öffentliches Forum, eine Web site im Internet, um die Idee einer geplanten Weltausstellung international zu kommunizieren.

The users of interactive products are occasionally absorbed by another world. Are they therefore uncertain of themselves and are frightened of getting lost? Would they marry somebody who lives only two villages away? This is the witty way in which Belgian interface expert Joannes Vandermeulen describes the still unaccustomed virtuality of the new medium.

Alongside ecology, interface -the designed link between person and machine - was the second »crossover aspect« in this year's competition. As expected, for this category many had questions in store for the specialists, and this included other members of the jury: many were eager to know whether the design and conceptualization of »interfaces« for devices, which make it possible to understand and use them, were good or bad.

In the opinion of the jurors, the concept of »Interface« goes well beyond the traditional idea of a user interface, composed of product graphics and a keyboard, comparable with a »leap into a new technological world«, for here you come up against virtuality and not with the physical presence of an object, which one handles manually. In the interface, the virtual part, you are referred to the hardware. The same user controls should, or so the jury demanded, therefore reappear in the display in the flow charts. Only a few of the solutions entered won awards: In the area of digital television, a Multimedia device for decoding digital programs, in the area of telecommunications a self-explanatory display for a fax machine, in the area of copiers, and this won a Top ten award, an interactive control panel which makes it possible to use a complicated machine without studying the instructions, in the area of house technology a control system which undertakes remote controlled troubleshooting for a heating system, without any physical intervention in the control system initially being necessary. The critical jury judged a IBM's communications concept for internal marketing communications and a public forum, an Internet Web site, to be an ideal solution to communicating the idea of a planned world fair internationally.

HERSTELLER MANUFACTURER Telekom, Bonn, Germany
PRODUKT PRODUCT AF 385 D Telefaxgerät Fax machine
DESIGN Design Drei, Wolfgang Wagner, Hannover, Germany

AF 385 D, ein Faxgerät für Normalpapier. Die wesentlichen Funktionen wie Papiereinlegen, Service, das Beheben von Papierstaus, sind benutzerfreundlich direkt von vorne möglich. Gesendete Vorlagen werden platzsparend direkt hinter dem Papiereinzug gesammelt, fliegen also nicht auf dem Tisch herum. Das TonerJet Direktdruckverfahren ist eine Weltneuheit: das bedeutet keine Wegwerfbauteile und geringere Verbrauchs- und Wartungskosten, darum umweltfreundlicher und weniger aufwendiger Betrieb als beim Laserdruckverfahren. Zudem erleichtern vielfältige Funktionen, durchdachte Benutzerführung über Display und Trackwheel, Ok- und Stoptaste den Einsatz des Geräts.

AF 385 D is a fax machine using normal paper. The main functions such as paper tray, service, and paper jam are easily accessible from the front. Sent documents are collected in a space-saving tray directly behind the paper feed and thus don't lie around the table. The direct TonerJet printer is a first worldwide: no more throwaway components and lower operation and maintenance costs, for more ecological use than with laser printers. Moreover, the wide range of functions, carefully thought-out controls via the display and trackwheel, OK and Stop buttons make the fax simple to use.

INTERFACE 413

EXPO 2000 Hannover GmbH, Hannover, Germany   HERSTELLER MANUFACTURER
»VIRTUAL EXPO« Bildschrimoberfläche EXPO 2000 for Internet   PRODUKT PRODUCT
Medienlabor, München, Germany   DESIGN

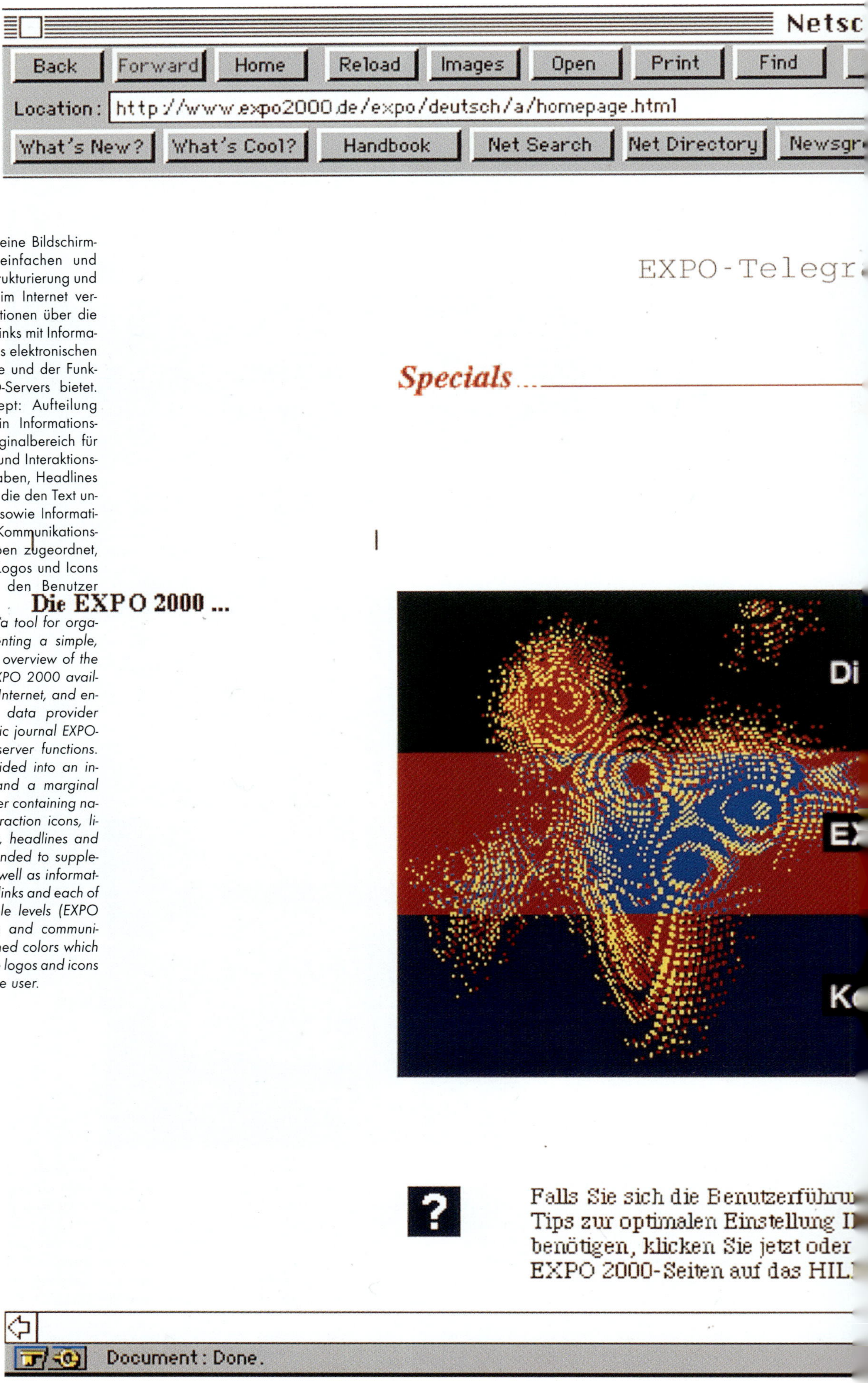

VIRTUAL EXPO, eine Bildschirmoberfläche zur einfachen und übersichtlichen Strukturierung und Präsentation der im Internet verfügbaren Informationen über die EXPO 2000, der Links mit Informationsanbietern, des elektronischen Journals EXPOzine und der Funktionen des EXPO-Servers bietet. Gestaltungskonzept: Aufteilung des Bildschirms in Informationsbereich und Marginalbereich für die Navigations- und Interaktions-Icons, Inhaltsangaben, Headlines und kleine Bilder, die den Text unterstützen sollen, sowie Informationsgrafik. Den Kommunikationsebenen sind Farben zugeordnet, die auch in den Logos und Icons auftauchen und den Benutzer führen.

VIRTUAL EXPO is 'a tool for organizing and presenting a simple, clearly structured overview of the information on EXPO 2000 available through the Internet, and enables access to data provider links, the electronic journal EXPOzine and EXPO server functions. The screen is divided into an information area and a marginal area, with the latter containing navigation and interaction icons, listings of contents, headlines and small images intended to supplement the text, as well as information graphics. The links and each of the three available levels (EXPO 2000, EXPOzine and communication) are assigned colors which also appear in the logos and icons to further assist the user.

EXPO2000

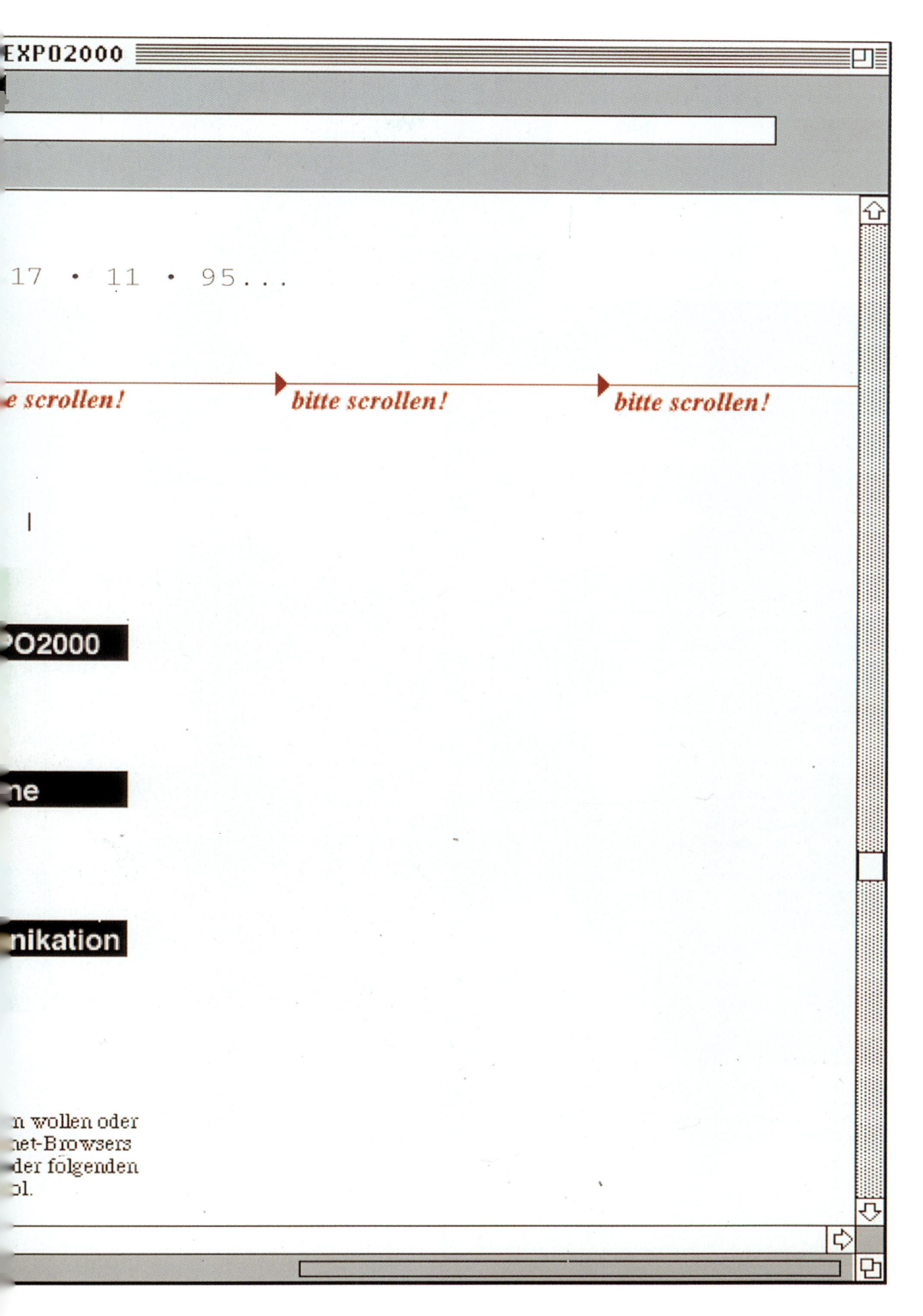

17 • 11 • 95...

e scrollen!   ▶ bitte scrollen!   ▶ bitte scrollen!

|

O2000

ne

nikation

n wollen oder
net-Browsers
der folgenden
ol.

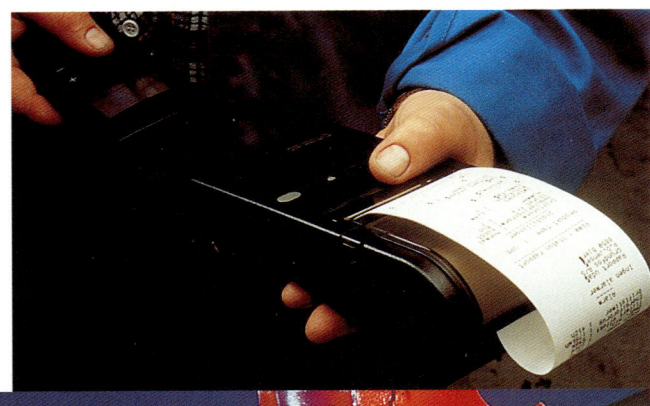

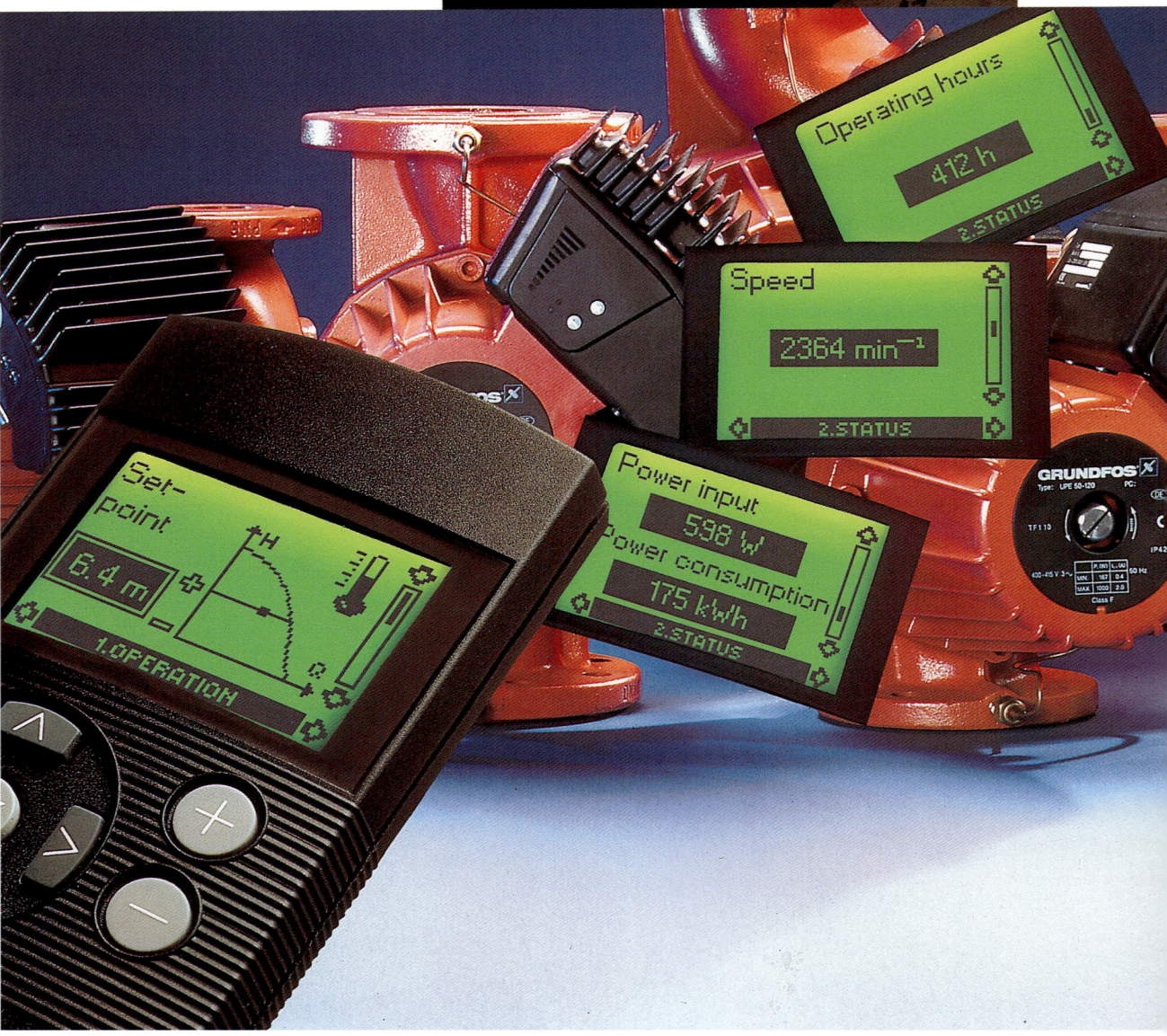

HERSTELLER MANUFACTURER
GRUNDFOS A/S, Bjerringbro, Denmark
PRODUKT PRODUCT
R 100 Kommunikationseinheit Communications unit
DESIGN
GRUNDFOS, Bjerringbro, Denmark

GRUNDFOS R100 Controller, ein Gerät zur drahtlosen Zwei-Wege-Kommunikation mit der Heizungsanlage. Verbindet per Fernbedienung intelligente Pumpen, Kreiselpumpen, Normmotoren etc. des Grundfos-Systems.

The GRUNDFOS R 100 communications unit provides cordless two-way communication between the remote control and the heating system. It can be used with smart pumps, Grundfos standard motors, centrifugal pumps etc.

416 INTERFACE

FLUKE 865 GMM, grafisches Multimeter, ein spezielles Testgerät für die tägliche Störfallbehebung in Stromverteilungssystemen. Kompakte, handliche Bauweise, einfach zu bedienen. Seitliche Rundungen zeigen, wo das Gerät anzufassen ist. Auch ein Abstützen des Gerätes am Körper wird durch Rundungen komfortabel gemacht. Am Design der Bedienelemente wirkten potentielle Anwender mit, so wurde eine einfache, übersichtliche Gestaltung des Bedienfelds erreicht.

The FLUKE 865 GMM graphic multimeter is a special graphic multimeter for power distribution systems. It is compact and easy to use, with curved sides that facilitate gripping and allow the unit to be rested against the body for added support. Potential users helped design the straightforward, clearly organized control panel.

FLUKE CORPORATION, Everett, USA   HERSTELLER MANUFACTURER
FLUKE 865 GMM Grafisches Multimeter Graphic multimeter   PRODUKT PRODUCT
FLUKE Corporate user interface design + Engineering Team, Steve Fisher, Everett, USA   DESIGN

INTERFACE 417

Virtual i.-O INC., Seattle, USA HERSTELLER MANUFACTURER
i-glasses! PDS-personal display system PRODUKT PRODUCT
Virtual i.-O, Scott Mac Innes, Jae Park, Walter Webb, Chris, Wiegel, Seattle, USA DESIGN

VIRTUAL i-Oi-GLASSES! ist ein Personal Display System (das kleinste Head Mounted Display mit 2 Bildschirmen) zur raumunabhängigen Projektion von Bild und Stereoton. Durchsichtige Optik mit abnehmbaren undurchsichtigen Visier. Ohne Visier kann sich der Benutzer auf den äußeren Rahmen beziehen, was unerläßlich ist, um Gleichgewichtsstörungen vorzubeugen. Die Bildfläche simuliert einen Bildschirm mit einer Diagonale von 203cm, der aus 3,3m Entfernung betrachtet wird. So entsteht ein unmittelbares, einem Privattheater ähnliches Unterhaltungsumfeld. Das Gerät ist wie eine Brille zusammenzuklappen.

VIRTUAL i-O i-GLASSES! is a binocular Personal Display System, or Head Mounted Display. The clip-on opaque visor blocks out outside light to provide a more immersive virtual experience, while the optics and mechanical design allow users to maintain the external environment in their peripheral vision, critical for preventing motion sickness. i-glasses! produces an image area equivalent to an 80-inch (203cm) screen viewed at 11 ft (3.3m). The device is also available in a video version for videos and electronic games and a PC version for computer games and virtual reality applications.

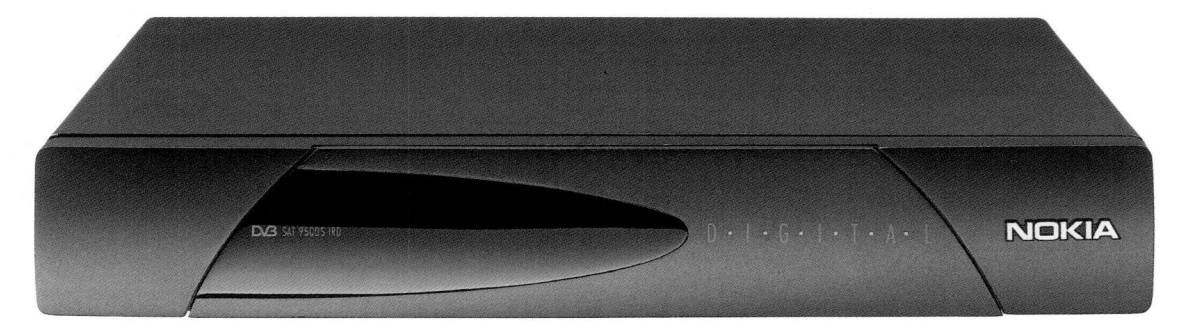

HERSTELLER MANUFACTURER NOKIA Unterhaltungselektronik GmbH, Düsseldorf, Germany
PRODUKT PRODUCT DVB 9500 S Multimedia Terminal Multimedia terminal
DESIGN NOKIA Design Center, Düsseldorf, Germany

NOKIA DVB 9500 S, ein digitales Multimedia-Terminal für den Empfang interactiver Dienste und Programme. Einfachste Bedienung über das klar gegliederte, elektronische Programmverzeichnis. Empfang digitaler Satelliten-Programme, Multimedia-Terminal für PC, Drucker, CD-ROM-Laufwerk, etc. Zugang zum Telefonnetz (Modem), Fax, E-mail und Zugriff auf Internet, Anschlußmöglichkeit für analoges TV, Radio, HiFi-Anlage und Videorecorder. Programmverzeichnis und Software können durch »Downloading« auf den neuesten Stand gebracht werden. Dem neuartigen Produkt entspricht das markante Design.

The NOKIA DVB 9500 S is a digital multimedia terminal for interactive services and programs. Operation is made simple with clearly structured electronic program directories. The unit receives digital satellite programs, functions as a multimedia terminal for PCs, printers, CD-ROM drives, etc., and via a modem enables access to the telephone network, fax, e-mail and the Internet. It can also be used to hook up analog TV sets, radios, stereo systems and video recorders. The program directories and software can be upgraded to include the latest developments through downloading. The striking design reflects the innovative nature of the product.

INTERFACE 419

IBM Corporation, Armonk, USA
IBM worldwide sales promotion design guide
Lippincott & Margulies

HERSTELLER MANUFACTURER
PRODUKT PRODUCT
DESIGN

Formats menu

Promotional
- Cover elements
- Inside spreads
- Back covers
- Things not to do
- More examples

- Developing family looks

- Locating templates and type specifications

Application briefs
- Front page elements
- Inside spreads
- Back pages

Spec sheets
- Front pages
- Inside spreads
- Back pages
- More examples

Formats: Promotional: **Cover elements**

A headline provides the greatest opportunity to state the key benefit of the offering to our customers. It gives the reader a reason to turn the page and find out more. Good headlines are brief and easy to understand. And they connect conceptually with the accompanying imagery. Headlines are set in Bodoni Antiqua Italic.

Generally, initial caps should only be used for offering names, however requirements of native languages may take precedence.

Overview

Why worldwide design standards?
Worldwide standards for the design and production of printed sales promotion materials are one of the key efforts underway to strengthen the IBM brand image and identity.

Consistent, high-quality sales promotion materials reflect the quality and reliability of our products and services. They help customers, and potential customers, quickly recognize IBM as the source of the offering.

By working from a single system of design standards worldwide, we can focus creative efforts on developing exceptional content, rather than on recreating basic grids each time we produce a new brochure or specification sheet. This will enable us to produce sales promotion materials faster and at lower cost.

| Quit | Overview | Formats | Elements | Templates | Contacts | Main |

420 INTERFACE

Ein DESIGN-LEITFADEN zur Erstellung von Werbemitteln, Broschüren usw., mit dem sich IBM einen weltweit einheitlichen Auftritt verschafft. Der für IBM-Mitarbeiter und Vertragshändler entwickelte, in Arbeitsschritte gegliederte Leitfaden präsentiert als interaktives Medium (CD-ROM) mit Handbuch die Grundelemente Typografie und Bildbearbeitung sowie Formatvorlagen für DOS- und Macintosh-Betriebssysteme, nutzt entsprechende Grafikprogramme und ermöglicht so die menügeführte Erstellung kompletter Broschüren in allen international gängigen Formaten. Um diesem Werkzeug breite Einsatzmöglichkeiten zu verschaffen, wurden die Systemanforderungen an den PC bewußt niedrig gehalten.

The DESIGN GUIDE is a functional tool that consolidates IBM's multiple design formats, allowing a cohesive IBM image and identity to be implemented on a worldwide basis. The step-by-step-guide was developed both as an interactive and printed manual, and takes users through basic elements of the system such as typography, image development and formats. Accompanying templates are available for PC and Macintosh platforms, and allow for a brochure designed in standard US and ISO sizes. The templates and interactive manual are distributed on a CD-ROM, which is aimed at internal IBM design staff and outside vendors who produce sales promotion materials for IBM on a worldwide basis.

iF DESIGNWETTBEWERB 1996 *iF DESIGN COMPETITON 1996*

ANDRÉE PUTMAN
Frankreich/France

Geboren in Paris. Arbeitete mehrere Jahre als Designerin für PRISUNIC und als Journalistin bei »Les cahiers de ELLE«. 1978 Gründung von Ecart International, spezialisiert auf Neu-Editionen von Möbeln von Eileen Gray, Robert Mallet-Stevens, Mariano Fortuny u. a. Karriere als Innenarchitektin. Größere Projekte: Villen und Hotels wie Morgans in New York, Im Wasserturm in Köln; Ladenausstattungen für Bally und Ebel (weltweit); Kunstmuseen in Rouen und Bordeaux; zuletzt Innenausstattung der Concorde für Air France; Mitarbeit an einem Film von Peter Greenaway.

Andrée Putman was born in Paris. She worked as a journalist at »Les Cahiers de ELLE, continued for the chain store PRISUNIC designing house-wear. Remarkable publicity generated by residence projects. In 1978 she founded Ecart International, specializing in new editions of furniture pieces of Eileen Gray, Robert Mallet-Stevens, Mariano Fortuny, among others. Some of her major projects include hotels such as Morgans New York, Im Wasserturm Cologne, stores for Bally and Ebel (world-wide), art museums in Rouen and Bordeaux. She redesigned the interior of Concorde airplane for Air France and worked on the set of Peter Greenaway's latest film.

PROF. HERBERT LINDINGER
Deutschland/Germany

Studium in Linz und an der HfG Ulm. 1962-1968 Dozent an der HfG Ulm. Gastprofessor an der Ohio State University und am National Institute of Design, Ahmedabad. Seit 1971 Professor und Direktor des Institutes für Industrial Design an der Universität Hannover. Gestaltung von U-Bahnen, Fahrzeugen, Helikoptern, Ausstellungen, Plätzen. Zahlreiche Preise für Architektur und Design. Vorstandsmitglied iF Industrie Forum Design Hannover.

Herbert Lindinger studied in Linz and at the College of Design in Ulm, where he was also a lecturer from 1962-68. He has served as a visiting professor at Ohio State University and the National Institute of Design in Ahmedabad. Since 1971, he has held a post as professor and director of the Institute for Industrial Design at Hannover University. His works include designs for subways, automobiles, helicopters, exhibition and public spaces, and he has received numerous awards in architecture and design. He is member of the board of iF Hannover.

ROBERT BLAICH
USA

Geboren und aufgewachsen in den USA. Ehrendoktor der schönen Künste, Universität Syracuse. Seit fast 40 Jahren in diversen Funktionen im industriellen Designmanagement und in der Unternehmenskommunikation tätig. War elf Jahre als geschäftsführender Direktor »Corporate Industrial Design« bei Philips Electronics, Niederlande. Danach Gründung von Blaich Associates in den USA. Vorstand des ICSID, Mitglied in vielen Arbeitsgruppen, Vortragstätigkeit, Buchautor, veröffentlichte u. a.: »Product Design and Corporate Strategy« und »New and Notable Product Design«.

Robert Blaich was born and educated in the US, and holds an honorary Doctor's Degree in Fine Arts from Syracuse University. His career encompasses the diverse activities of industrial design management and corporate communications. He served as Managing Director of Philips Corporate Industrial Design in The Netherlands for 11 years, and subsequently founded Blaich Associates in the US. In addition to his position as president of the ICSID, he is also chairman or member of a number of interdisciplinary task forces and committees. He has lectured at various professional conferences and is the author of »Product Design and Corporate Strategy« and »New and Notable Product Design«.

HORST DIENER
Deutschland/Germany

Studium an der HfG Ulm, zehn Jahre als Designverantwortlich in ehemaliger Gugelot-Design GmbH, 1974 Gründung der designpraxis diener Ulm. Heute mit 20 Teammitgliedern in allen designrelevanten Gebieten tätig, Corporate Design und Beratung im Designmanagement, für Unternehmenskultur und bei Marketingstrategien. Die Entwicklungsschwerpunkte: ganzheitliches Systemdesign für Investitions- und Konsumgüter von Konzeption, Konstruktion, Modellbau, Prototypenbau, Betreuung bis zur Markteinführung. Verschiedene Lehrtätigkeiten, Vorstand des Club off Ulm e.V., Mitglied im HfG-Stiftungsbeirats. Zahlreiche Auszeichnungen und Preise.

Studied at the HfG Ulm. Ten years in charge of design at Gugelot-Design GmbH. In 1974, he founded designpraxis diener Ulm, his own design studio. Together with 20 team members, he handles corporate design, design management consultancy, corporate culture and marketing strategies with a focus on holistic system design for capital and consumer goods, from the conception stage up through to the market launch. He is the chairman of Club off Ulm e.V. as well as a member of the Board of Trustees of the HfG. Guest lecturer at various schools. Numerous awards.

NORBERT HAUGG
Deutschland/Germany

Geboren 1935. Maschinenbaustudium an der TU München, Abschluß als Diplomingenieur. Nach diversen Aufgaben als Projektingenieur in der Industrie wurde er 1967 Prüfer im Deutschen Patentamt, dort als Referatsleiter bzw. Leiter der Abteilung Organisation und Planung. 1983-1986 Richter am Bundespatentgericht. 1986-1988 Hauptabteilungsleiter im Deutschen Patentamt. 1988-1991 Vorsitzender Richter am Bundespatentgericht. 1991-1995 Vizepräsident des Bundespatentgerichts. Seit August 1995 Präsident des Deutschen Patentamts.

Norbert Haugg was born in 1935 and received a degree in mechanical engineering from the Technical University in Munich. After working as an industrial project engineer, he was hired as an inspector for the German Patent Office in 1967, where he was later made head of the organization and planning department. Between 1983 and 1986 he served as a judge in the German Federal Patent Court, and then as presiding judge, at the German Patent Office. After holding the vice-presidency of German Federal Patent Court from 1991-1995, he became president of the German Patent Office in August 1995.

ERNST RAUE
Deutschland/Germany

Geboren 1954. Betriebswirt mit den Schwerpunkten Vertrieb und Marketing. Arbeitete in mittelständischen und Konzernbetrieben der Zuliefer- und Bürotechnikindustrie. Beteiligt am Auf- und Ausbau von Fachmessen der Hannover Messe und der CeBIT. Geschäftsbereichsleiter und Mitglied der Unternehmensleitung der Deutschen Messe AG. 1. Vorsitzender des iF Industrie Forum Design Hannover.

Ernst Raue was born in 1954 and studied in business economics with a focus on sales and marketing. He has worked for smaller companies as well as corporate groups in the office technology and component supplying industries, and has participated in erecting and expanding trade fairs at Hannover Messe and CeBIT. He is head of his business division and a member of corporate management at Deutsche Messe AG, and is also chairman of iF Industrie Forum Design Hannover.

IF DESIGNWETTBEWERB 1996 *IF DESIGN COMPETITON 1996*

CHRISTOPH T. BÖNINGER
Deutschland/Germany

Studium Industrial Design FH München und Environmental Design Art Center, Pasadena. 1983-1987 bei Schlagheck & Schultes Design, München. Leitete von 1987 bis 1990 Siemens Corporate Design, USA, und ist seit 1990 verantwortlich für das Investitionsgüterdesign bei Siemens Design, München und Erlangen. Diverse Auszeichnungen. Lehrauftrag Industrial Design an der FH München.

Christoph Böninger studied industrial design at the Technical College in Munich and environmental design at the Art Center in Pasadena. 1983-1987, he worked with Schlagheck & Schultes Design in Munich. 1987-1990 he worked as manager of Siemens corporate industrial design in the US, and since 1990 has been in charge of capital goods design at Siemens in Munich and Erlangen. He has received a number of awards, and holds a teaching position in industrial design at the Munich Technical College.

JENS CLAUSEN
Deutschland/Germany

Maschinenbaustudium. Abschluß als Diplomingenieur. 1984-1991 Mitarbeiter der Abteilung Forschung und Entwicklung der Continental AG, Hannover. Seit 1991 Mitarbeiter am Institut für Ökologische Wirtschaftsforschung (IÖW), Berlin, Forschungsfeld: ökologische Unternehmerpolitik. Arbeitsschwerpunkte: Umweltmanagement, Ökodesign und Umweltberichterstattung.

Jens Clausen, Germany, was trained in mechanical engineering, and worked in R&D at Continental AG in Hanover from 1984-1991. Since 1991 he has been employed at the Institute for Ecological Economic Research (IÖW) in Berlin. His main field of research is ecologically oriented economic policy, with a focus on environmental management, ecological design and reporting on environmental issues.

HARTMUT S. ENGEL
Deutschland/Germany

Studium Elektrotechnik und Industrial Design in Stuttgart, Darmstadt und Pforzheim. 1968 Gründung eines eigenen Design-Büros in Ludwigsburg. Berät und entwickelt technisches Design für Kunden mit dem Anspruch, Design als »Unternehmenskonzept« zu realisieren. Mitglied in VDID und im Werkbund, Gastdozent. Internationale Auszeichnungen und Preise.

Hartmut S. Engel, Germany, studied electrical engineering and industrial design in Stuttgart, Darmstadt and Pforzheim, and founded his own design studio in Ludwigsburg in 1968. He works as a consultant and develops technical designs for clients who wish to implement design as a corporate concept. He is member of VDID and Werkbund, as well as a guest lecturer, and has received international prizes and awards.

ANDREAS HAUG
Deutschland/Germany

Design-Studium an der Staatlichen Akademie der Bildenden Künste, Stuttgart. 1975-1982 zusammen mit Hartmut Esslinger und Georg Spreng geschäftsführender Gesellschafter von Esslinger Design. 1982-1984 Partner von Hartmut Esslinger, Mitinhaber von frog design. 1984-1987 Design-Consultant und Vice-President of Design von frog design, Altensteig. Zusammen mit Tom Schönherr Gründer und Mitinhaber von Phoenix Product Design. Internationale Designerfahrung, zahlreiche Auszeichnungen.

Studied design at the State Academy for the Plastic Arts in Stuttgart. 1975-1982: Managing Partner of Esslinger Design, together with Hartmut Esslinger and Georg Spreng. 1982-1984: Worked in partnership with Hartmut Esslinger as co-owner of frog design. 1984-1987: Design consultant and Vice-President of Design at frog design, Altensteig, Germany. 1987: Founder and co-owner of Phoenix Product Design, in partnership with Tom Schönherr. International design experience and awards.

CAROLIEN G. VAN HEMEL
Niederlande/The Netherlands

Studium an der Technischen Universität Delft. Danach Designerin von Bewegungshilfen und Spielzeug für körperlich behinderte Kinder, in Indien und den Niederlanden. Forschungsprojekt und Dissertation über Environment-Design (DFE) Mitarbeit im EcoDesign Programm des Innovations Centra Network Nederland (ICNN) als Supervisorin und Trainerin der 20 ICNN-Consultants. Verfasserin von Artikeln, Vortragstätigkeit. Neubearbeitung von PROMISE, eines Handbuchs für Design.

After graduating from the Technical University in Delft, Carolien van Hemel worked as industrial design engineer of mobility aids and toys for physically disabled children in India and the Netherlands. She started a PhD research on Design for Environment (DFE) involved in the EcoDesign program at the Innovation Centra Network Nederland (ICNN), where she supervises and trains 20 ICNN consultants. She has published magazine articles, and is currently revising PROMISE, an environmental design manual.

ISAO HOSOE
Italien/Italy

Geboren 1942 in Tokio. Studium Flugzeugbau, 1965 Abschluß als Bachelor of Science, 1967 Master of Science an der Nihon University, Tokio. Professuren für Design an der Domus Akademie, Mailand, am Politecnico Milano, an der I.S.I.A., Florenz, und an der Universität von Siena. Mitautor der Publikation »Playoffice« (Tokio 1991). Zahlreiche internationale Ausstellungen wie »Work Encounter: Domesticity in the office« auf der Triennale Mailand, Ankäufe u. a. vom Victoria and Albert Museum London, Centre Georges Pompidou Paris und Chicago Atheneum.

Isao Hosoe was born in Tokyo in 1942. He studied aerospace engineering at the Nihon University in Tokyo, 1965 Bachelor of Science, 1967 Master of Science. He is currently a professor of design at the Domus Academy in Milan, the Politecnico Milano, the I.S.I.A. in Florence, and the University of Siena. He is co-author of »Playoffice« (Tokio 1991), and has participated in numerous solo and collective exhibitions like »Work Encounter: Domesticity in the office« held at Triennale Milan. Some of his works have been selected for permanent collections at places such as the Victoria and Albert Museum London, Centre Georges Pompidou Paris and Chicago Atheneum.

MARTIN ISELI
Schweiz/Switzerland

Geboren 1952. Studium der Elektrotechnik und des Industrial Design. Arbeitete zunächst als freischaffender Designer in Bern. Seit 1989 Leiter des Fachbereichs Ascom Corporate Industrial Design, Schweiz. In dieser Funktion arbeitet er mit seinem Team im Bereich Telekommunikation für Ascom und Bang & Olufson. 1989-1991 Vorstandsmitglied des SID. Gastdozent HTL Horw/Bern, Veröffentlichungen in diversen Publikationen.

Martin Iseli was born in 1952. After completing studies in electrical engineering and industrial design, he started his career as a freelance designer in Bern. Since 1989 he has been in charge of corporate industrial design at Ascom in Switzerland, where he and his team focus on telecommunications for Ascom and Bang & Olufson. He was a board member of SID (association of Swiss designers) from 1989-1991. He is also a guest lecturer at HTL Horw/Bern and the author of a number of publications.

CARL AUGUST SAUTIER
Deutschland/Germany

Geboren 1947. Kaufmännische und betriebswirtschaftliche Ausbildung. Leitende Tätigkeiten in Vertrieb und Marketing. Seit 1987 bei Wilkhahn verantwortlich für das Designmanagement, zum dem auch das ökologische Management gehört. Federführend beteiligt an der Einführung eines ökologischen Controlling, aus dem die Grundlagen für Konzept und operative Steuerungselemente zum umfassenden ökologischen Umbau von Wilkhahn entwickelt werden. Fachbeirat bei iF Industrie Forum Design Hannover.

Carl August Sautier was born in 1947. He studied business and business management, and has held management positions in sales and marketing. Since 1987, he has been in charge of design management at Wilkhahn, where his duties also extend to ecological management. He was responsible for the introduction of an ecological audit which ultimately led to the comprehensive ecological restructuring at Wilkhahn.

IF DESIGNWETTBEWERB 1996 *IF DESIGN COMPETITON 1996*

PROF. BURKHARDT SCHMITZ
Deutschland/Germany

Geboren 1957. Studium Industrial Design in Berlin. Seit 1983 Mitarbeit in der Produktentwicklung Roericht, Ulm. Diverse Lehraufträge. Professor im Studiengang Visuelle Kommunikation, FH Schwäbisch Gmünd. Mitbegründer der Gestaltungsgruppe 7.5, Berlin. Seit 1992 Professor an der HdK Berlin, Fachbereich Design. Gründung der Fachgruppe ID 5 »Neue Medien«. Gegenwärtiger Arbeitsschwerpunkt sind spatiale Ordnungssysteme.

Professor Burkhard Schmitz was born in 1957 and studied industrial design in Berlin. In 1983, he began work in Produktentwicklung Roericht in Ulm. He has held various teaching positions, including the chair of visual communication at the Schwäbisch Gmünd Technical College. In 1991 he co-founded the design group 7.5 in Berlin. Since 1992 he has been a professor of design at the Berlin School of the Arts. He also established ID 5 «New Media, which is currently focusing on spatial ordering systems.

JOANNES VANDERMEULEN
Belgien/Belgium

Studium der Archäologie und Linguistik. Ein beruflich bedingter USA-Aufenthalt führte ihn zum Interaction Design. Gründung von »Using It«, eines eigenen Büros mit derzeit 12 Mitarbeitern, Beratung und Entwicklung interaktiver Produkte. Besondere Erfahrungen im Design graphischer Benutzeroberflächen für Client/Server-Systeme. Lehrauftrag an der Universität Leuwen, regelmäßige Vortragstätigkeit.

Educated as an archaeologist and a linguist Joannes Vandermeulen became interested in interaction design after a job-related stay in the USA. His 12-person company »Using It« assists developers of interactive products in focusing on the user. He is highly experienced in designing graphic user interfaces for client/server systems, and teaches seminars at the University of Leuwen in addition to speaking regularly at conferences.

HARTMUT WARKUSS
Deutschland/Germany

Geboren 1940 in Breslau. Begann 1964 als Designer bei Mercedes-Benz und wechselte 1966 zu Ford, 1968 zu Audi. Entwurf des ersten Audi 80. 1976 Verantwortung für das Audi-Design. Mit dem Audi 100, Modell 83, realisierte das Team unter seiner Leitung die konsequente Umsetzung aerodynamischer Erkenntnisse. Das Modell prägte entscheidend die Audi-Linie. Er leitet seit 1993 Volkswagen-Design und das »Center of Excellence Design« des Volkswagen-Konzerns.

Hartmut Warkuß was born in Breslau in 1940 and started his career in 1964 as a designer for Mercedes-Benz. In 1966 he was hired by Ford, and in 1968 by Audi, where he designed his first Audi 80. He was put in charge of design at Audi in 1976, and under his management, the Audi design team succeeded in incorporating new aerodynamic findings in the design of the Audi 100. This Model 83 model had a decisive impact on Audi style. Since 1993, he has been responsible for design at Volkswagen, as well as the »Center of Excellence Design« of the Volkswagen Group.

FRANK ZEBNER
Deutschland/Germany

Geboren 1962. Studium Produktgestaltung in Schwäbisch Gmünd und Offenbach am Main. Seit 1990 im Siemens Design Center, als Referent für Interface Design. Lehrauftrag an der Staatlichen Akademie der Bildenden Künste, Stuttgart. Vortragstätigkeit. Designberater für die EXPO 2000 Hannover.

Frank Zebner was born in 1962, and studied product design in Schwäbisch Gmünd and Offenbach. He has been in charge of interface design at Siemens Design Center since 1990, and teaches at the State Academy of Fine Arts in Stuttgart, in addition to giving lectures. He is also a design consultant for EXPO 2000 in Hanover.

Außergewöhnliche Technik.
Ausgezeichnetes Design.

HERSTELLER INDEX *INDEX OF MANUFACTURERS*

ABB Henschel AG
Neustadter Straße 62
D-68309 Mannheim
Seite/page 385

Abu Garcia
S-37681 Svängsta
Phone +46-456-8300
Fax +46-456-23662
Seite/page 271

ADN SYSTEM SA
Rte de la Chocolatière 23
CH-1026 Echandens
Phone +41-21-7024292
Seite/page 274

AEG
Aktiengesellschaft
Fachbereich
Industriekomponenten
Emil-Siepmann-Straße 32
D-59581 Warstein-Belecke
Phone +49-2902-763-720
Fax +49-2902-763-617
Seite/page 346

AEG
Hausgeräte GmbH
Muggenhoferstraße 135
D-90429 Nürnberg
Phone +49-911-323-1173
Fax +49-911-323-2283
Seite/page 197

AEG
Lichttechnik GmbH
Absatzförderung
Rathenaustraße 2-6
D-31832 Springe
Phone +49-5041-75-241
Fax +49-5041-75-441
Seite/page 230

Alcatel Mobile Phones
32, avenue Kléber
F-92707 Colombes Cedex
Phone +33-1-46521913
Fax +33-1-46528024
Seite/page 100

Alcatel Mobile Phones
Holderäckerstraße 10
D70499 Stuttgart

ALVO
Metalltechnik GmbH
Talstraße 4-6
D-73650 Winterbach
Seite/page 354

ANTENNE
Bad Blankenburg
Mobile Antennen-
technik GmbH
Bahnhofstraße 44
D-07422 Bad Blankenburg
Phone +49-36741-369-0
Fax +49-36741-36963
Seite/page 283

Aqua Butzke-Werke AG
Postfach 610340
D-10925 Berlin
Seite/page 155

Aquis GmbH
Wasser-Luft-Systeme Lindau
Balgacherstraße 17
CH-9445 Rebstein
Seite/page 154

Arbonia AG
Industriestraße 23
CH-9320 Arbon
Phone +41-71-474722
Fax +41-71-474847
Seite/page 244

ARCA
Regler GmbH
Kempener Straße 18
D-47918 Tönisvorst
Phone +49-2156-7709-9
Fax +49-2156-7709-55
Seite/page 315

arco meubelfabrik bv
Parallelweg 2 III
NL-7100 AA Winterswijk
Phone +31-5430-124-05
Fax +31-5430-12395
Seite/page 144

arCom Gesellschaft für Zu-
gangssicherungs-
systeme mbH
Spechtweg 1
D-38108 Braunschweig
Phone +49-531-2156-0
Fax +49-531-2156-222
Seite/page 235

ART-LINE
Wohndecor GmbH
Am Gewerbehof 1 Nr. 7-9
D-50170 Kerpen
Phone +49-2273-909522
Fax +49-2273-909512
Seite/page 148

Artemide S.p.A.
Via Bergamo 18
I-20010 Pregnana Milanese
Fax +39-2-93290362
Seite/page 224

Artemide GmbH
Itterpark 5
D-40724 Hilden
Phone +49-2103-2000-0
Fax +49-2103-2000-11

Ascom Business
Systems AG
Ziegelmattstraße 1
CH-4503 Solothurn
Phone +41-65-243128
Fax +41-65-242382
Seite/page 102

ASKO Furniture Ltd.
Askonkato 3
FIN-15101 Lahti
Seite/page 115

AUTHENTICS
artipresent GmbH
Max Eyth Straße 30
D-71088 Holzgerlingen
Phone +49-7031-6805-0
Fax +49-7031-6805-99
Seite/page 177

Bang & Olufsen A/S
Telephone Division
Peter Bangsvej 15
DK-76+ Struer
Seite/page 103

Bang & Olufsen
Technology A/S
Peter Bangs Vej 15
DK-7600 Struer
Phone +45-97-851122
Fax +45-97-850060
Seite/page 42, 260

Bang & Olufsen
Deutschland GmbH
Rudolf-Diesel-Straße 8
D-82205 Gilching
Phone +49-8105-389-0
Fax +49-8105-389-280

BAUFA-WERKE
GMBH
Baufastraße
D-58708 Menden
Phone +49-2373-957-0
Fax +49-2373-957-296
Seite/page 242

BEGA
Gantenbrink-Leuchten
GmbH & Co. KG
Hennenbusch 1
D-58708 Menden
Phone +49-2373-966-0
Fax +49-2373-966-460
Seite/page 203, 204, 206

BERNDS
Wittekindstraße 16
D-32758 Detmold
Phone +49-5231-17777
Fax +49-5231-17778
Seite/page 377

Black & Decker Ltd.
Green Lane Ind. Estate
GB-Spennymoor
Co. Durham DL16 6JG
Seite/page 262, 263, 312, 313

Black & Decker GmbH
Black & Decker-Straße 40
D-65510 Idstein
Phone +49-6126-21-0
Fax +49-6126-21-2753

Blaupunkt-Werke GmbH
Robert-Bosch-Straße 200
D-31132 Hildesheim
Phone +49-5121-49-4731
Fax +49-5121-49-2590
Seite/page 291-294,

BMW AG
BMW-Haus Petuelring 130
D-80788 München
Phone +49-89-38245448
Fax +49-89-38243696
Seite /page 46, 376

Otto Bock
Orthopädische Industrie
Postfach 1260
D-37105 Duderstadt
Seite/page 392

Robert Bosch GmbH
Geschäftsbereich
Elektrowerkzeuge
Max-Lang-Straße 40-46
D-70771 Leinfelden-
Echterdingen
Phone +49-711-758-2753
Fax +49-711-758-2811
Seite/page 261

Braun AG
Frankfurter Straße 145
D-61476 Kronberg
Phone +49-6173-30-2543
Fax +49-6173-30-2440
Seite/page 190, 191

B. Braun Melsungen AG
Sparte Medical
Schwarzenberger Weg 73-79
D-34212 Melsungen
Phone +49-5661-71-4671
Fax +49-5661-71-3813
Seite/page 399

BREE
Collection GmbH
Gerberstraße 3
D-30916 Isernhagen-Kirchhorst
Phone 05136-8976-12
Fax 05136-8976-80
Seite/page 272

Bruck Lichtsysteme
GmbH & Co. KG
Industriestraße 22a
D-44628 Herne
Phone +49-2323-591-0
Fax +49-2323-591-105
Seite/page 202

BSI Bergische
Stahlindustrie GmbH
Papenberger Straße 38
D-42859 Remscheid
Seite/page 362, 363, 384

BTicino S.p.A.
Corso Porta Vittoria 9
I-20122 Mailand
Seite/page 238

BÜRO CONCEPT
Weidendamm 28
D-30167 Hannover
Seite/page 153

BULO
Kantoormeubelen N.V.
Industriezono Noord II
B-2800 Mechelen
Phone +32-15-282828
Fax +32-15-282829
Seite/page 114

Busch & Müller KG
Fahrzeugteilefabrik
Auf dem Bamberg 1
D-58540 Meinerzhagen
Phone +49-2354-9156
Fax +49-2354-915700
Seite/page 379

Buser AG
Bahnhofstraße
CH-3428 Wiler
Fax +41-65-453224
Seite/page 360

Canon Giessen GmbH
Canonstraße 1
D-35394 Giessen
Seite/page 81

Caradon
M. K. Electric
Arnold Centre
Paycock Road
GB-Basildon
Essex SS14 3EA
Phone +44-1268-56300
Fax +44-1268-563538
Seite/page 254

428 HERSTELLER *MANUFACTURER*

MagnaDur® für ultimative Schärfe.
Mit TWINSTAR eröffnet ZWILLING ein neues Kapitel in der Schneidtechnik. Jahrelange Forschung und Produktentwicklung haben uns ans Ziel gebracht. MagnaDur®: Die ultimative Schneide von TWINSTAR ist spezialbeschichtet, hart wie technische Keramik und diamantgeschliffen.

Alles im Griff.
Auf der Grundlage umfangreicher Design-Studien des Fraunhofer Instituts hat ZWILLING eine besonders handliche Grifform entwickelt. Die Griffgrößen leiten sich ab von der menschlichen Hand und nicht von der Klingenlänge. Für jeden Schneidvorgang ist der Griff optimal proportioniert. TWINSTAR Messer liegen komfortabel in der Hand und sorgen somit für unbeschwertes Arbeiten und noch mehr Sicherheit in der Küche.

Perfekt in Form.
TWINSTAR steht für vollendetes Design vom Griff bis zur Spitze. Die Kochmesser-Kollektion wird höchsten ästhetischen und funktionalen Ansprüchen gerecht. Ob Profi- oder Hobbykoch, TWINSTAR bietet alle wichtigen Messertypen für ein besonderes Schneid- und Kochvergnügen.

Technik mit Scharfsinn.
Untersuchungen eines unabhängigen Labors haben bewiesen, daß TWINSTAR mit der innovativen MagnaDur® Schneide mehr als 1000mal länger scharf bleibt als herkömmliche Messer mit glatter Schneide. Das Geheimnis: eine bei ca. 2000° C aufgebrachte Spezialbeschichtung, die der Schneide zu ihrer außergewöhnlichen Leistung verhilft.

Handfeste Argumente.
TWINSTAR Messer von ZWILLING zeichnen sich aus durch absolute Qualität, funktionales Design und Sicherheit. Die neue Kochmesser-Kollektion ist auf jeden Bedarf zugeschnitten und sorgt für noch mehr Spaß beim Schneiden und Kochen.

Weitere Informationen über unsere Produkte erhalten Sie bei:

ZWILLING J.A. HENCKELS AG
Grünewalder Str. 14-22
42657 Solingen
Telefon (0212) 882-0
Telefax (0212) 882-300

TWINSTAR® SCHNEIDEN VON MORGEN IST HEUTE!

ZWILLING J.A.HENCKELS

HERSTELLER INDEX INDEX OF MANUFACTURERS

CARRERA
International
Holzbauernstr. 20
A-4050 Traun
Phone +43-7229-770-221
Fax +43-7229-63865
Seite/page 278

CENTRA-BÜRKLE
GmbH
Böblinger Straße 17
D-71101 Schönaich
Phone +49-7031-673-476
Fax +49-7031-673-244
Seite/page 248

CHEMUNEX
UK. Ltd
18-22 St. Peters Church Yard
GB-Derby
Derbyshire DD4 48Z
Phone +44-1332-299010
Seite/page 398

Crown
Gabelstapler GmbH
Chamer Steig 10
D-93426 Roding
Seite/page 382

Crown Lift Trucks Ltd.
Fishing Road
GB-Workingham
Berkshire RG 11 2 JT
Seite/page 365

Eisenwerke
Fried. Wilh. Düker
Würzburger Straße 10
D-97753 Karlstadt
Phone +49-9353-791-260
Fax +49-9353-791-198
Seite/page 162

D + S
Sanitärprodukte GmbH
Industriestraße
D-69198 Schriesheim
Phone +49-6203-102393
Fax +49-6203-102394
Seite/page 158, 159

Duscholux AG
Postfach 49
CH-3602 Thun
Seite/page 158, 159

Duscholux GmbH
L-6930 Mensdorf
Seite/page 158, 159

DZ LICHT
Innenleuchten GmbH
Hans-Böckler-Straße 2
D-58730 Frödenberg
Phone +49-2373-975-101
Fax +49-2373-975-109
Seite/page 208

EAO Elektro-
Apparatebau
Olten AG
Tannwaldstraße 88
CH-4601 Olten
Seite/page 373

EEV LTD
Waper House Lane
GB-Chelmsford
Essex CMI 2QU
Seite/page 317

EHT
Werkzeugmaschinen GmbH
Emmendinger Str. 21
D-79331 Teningen
Phone +49-7641-4 60 90
Fax +49-7641-10 78
Seite 356

ELBIT CTV
Migdal Haemek
ISRAEL
Seite/page 239

Elu S.p.A.
Via G. Verdi 13
I-22047 Molteno, Como
Seite/page 322

Elu International
Black & Decker GmbH
Richard-Klinger-Straße
D-65510/65502 Idstein
Phone +49-6126-2786
Fax +49-6126-2753

EMCO MAIER
Ges.mbH
Fabrik für Spezialmaschinen
Friedmann-Maier-Straße 9
A-5400 Hallein
Phone +43-6245-891-291
Fax +43-6245-89665
Seite/page 309

EMCO MAIER
GmbH & Co. KG
Sudetenstraße 10
D-83313 Siegsdorf
Phone +49-8662-666-22
Fax +49-8662-12168

Erbe Elektromedizin GmbH
Waldhörnlestraße 17
D-72072 Tübingen
Seite/page 389

van Esch bv
Edisonstraat 5
NL-5051 DS Goirle
Phone +31-13-5348738
Fax +31-13-5348760
Seite/page 110

Exhibitgroup/Giltspur Inc.
201 Mill Road
Edison, New Jersey 08817
USA
Phone +1-908-248-3484
Fax +1-908-287-3663
Seite/page 108

EXPO 2000
Hannover GmbH
Thurnitistraße 2
D-30519 Hannover
Phone +49-511-8404-154
Fax +49-511-8404-140
Seite/page 414

FAGERHULT AB
S-56680 Habo
Phone +46-46-108-500
Fax +46-46-108-770
Seite/page 216

Fast Security AG
Kaiser-Wilhelm-Platz 5
D-80336 München
Seite/page 92

FeinwerkTechnik GmbH
Dresdener Straße 16
D-01778 Geising
Seite/page 402

Fenwick
5242 Argosy Avenue
Huntington Beach
CA 92648, USA
Seite/page 270

FESTO KG
Ruiter Straße 82
D-73734 Esslingen
Phone +49-711-347-2600
Fax +49-711-347-2163

FESTO
Tooltechnic KG
Ulmer Straße 48
D-73728 Esslingen
Phone +49-711-3107-632
Fax +49-711-3107-727
Seite/page 334-338

Fiskars Consumer Oy Ab
P.O. Box
FIN-10330 Billnäs
Phone +358-11-377721
Fax +358-11-36350
Seite/page 266, 267

Fissler GmbH
Im Wörth
D-55743 Idar Oberstein
Phone 06781-403-0
Fax 06781-403-321
Seite/page 182

FLOS SpA
Via Angeolo Faini 2
I-25073 Bovezzo (Brescia)
Phone +39-30-2712161
Fax +39-30-2711578
Seite/page 201, 219

FLOS GmbH
Am Probsthof 94
D-53121 Bonn
Phone +49-228-97964-0
Fax +49-228-613653

FLUKE CORPORATION
P.O. BOX 9090
USA-Everett, WA 98206-90
USA
Seite/page 350, 417

FORON Hausgeräte GmbH
Arnsfelder Straße 4
D-09518 Niederschmiedeberg
Phone +49-3735-605-202
Fax +49-3735-605-251
Seite/page 174

Friatec AG
Steinzeugstraße 50
D-68229 Mannheim
Phone +49-621-486-690
Fax +49-621-486-1598
Seite/page 164

Fröscher GmbH & Co. KG
Bahnhofstraße 13
D-71711 Steinheim
Phone +49-7144-204-0
Fax +49-7144-204-114
Seite/page 122

Fumelli-Vertriebs-GmbH
Scharfenbergstraße 8

D-81825 München
Gaggenau-Werke
Haus- und
Lufttechnik GmbH
Eisenwerkstraße 11
D-76571 Gaggenau
Phone +49-7225-65-353
Fax +49-7225-65-105
Seite/page 181

Garny
Sicherheitstechnik GmbH
Dreieichstraße 12-16
D-64546 Mörfelden
Seite/page 76

GLASHÜTTE LIMBURG
Gantenbrink GmbH & Co.
Postfach 14 63
D-65534 Limburg
Phone +49-6431-204-123
Fax +49-6431-204-103
Seite/page 205, 207

GLORIA-Werke
H. Schulte-Frankenfeld
GmbH & Co.
Postfach 11 60
D-59321 Wadersloh
Phone +49-2523-77-159
Fax +49-2523-77-120
Seite/page 237

GMG-Gesellschaft
für modulare Greifersysteme
Am Vreithof 5
D-59494 Soest
Phone +49-2921-4062
Fax +49-2921-4042
Seite/page 347

Grass AG
Möbelbeschläge
Bundesstraße 10
A-6973 Höchst
Phone +43-5578-2211-58
Fax +43-5578-2211-59
Seite/page 150

Hans Grohe
GmbH & Co. KG
Auestraße 5-9
D-77761 Schiltach
Phone +49-7836-51-1297
Fax +49-7836-51-1170
Seite/page 156

Grundfos
Management A/S
P.D. Jensensvej 7
DK-8850 Bjerringbro
Phone +45-8668-1400
Fax +45-8668-14245
Seite/page 252, 253, 416

GRUNDIG AG
Kurgartenstraße 37
D-90762 Fürth
Phone +49-911-703-7253
Fax +49-911-708736
Seite/page 107, 294, 295

Wilhelm Grundmann (WG)
Rohrbacher
Schlosserwarenfabrik
Grundmannstraße 24
A-3163 Rohrbach/Gölsen
Phone +43-2764-2202-0
Fax +43-2764-2202-60
Seite/page 149

Modus von Wilkhahn, Postfach 2070, 31844 Bad Münder, Tel. (0 50 42) 999-0

Wilkhahn

HERSTELLER INDEX INDEX OF MANUFACTURERS

Hagenuk
Telecom GmbH
Produktmarketing MP
Westring 431
D-24118 Kiel
Phone +49-431-8818-4502
Fax +49-431-8818-331
Seite/page 61

Hartmann & Braun AG
Gräfstraße 97
D-60484 Frankfurt am Main
Phone +49-69-799-3332
Fax +49-69-799-2220
Seite/page 342

Heidelberger
Druckmaschinen AG
Kurfürstenanlage 52-60
D-69115 Heidelberg
Phone +49-6221-92-7342
Fax +49-6221-92-7329
Seite/page 359

HERAEUS
MED GmbH
Postfach 1563
D-63405 Hanau
Phone +49-6181-35-5827
Fax +49-6181-35-5934
Seite/page 400

HESS
FORM + LICHT
Schlachthausstraße 19-19/3
D-78050 Villingen-
Schwenningen
Phone +49-7721-920-0
Fax +49-7721-920-250
Seite/page 227

Hewlett-Packard Company
7+ 71st Avenue
USA-Greeley, CO 80634
Phone +1-970-350-4220
Fax +1-970-350-4675
Seite/page 74

Hewlett Packard Company
8+0 Foothills Blvd.
USA-Roseville
CA 95747-5596
Phone +1-916-785-5352
Fax +1-916-785-3096
Seite/page 75

Hewlett-Packard Company
5301 Stevens Creek Blvd.
USA-Santa Clara
California 95052
Phone +1-408-553-2965
Fax +1-408-553-2918
Seite/page 72

Hewlett Packard GmbH
Analytische Meßtechnik
Hewlett-Packard-Straße 8
D-76337 Waldbronn
Phone +49-7243-602-339
Fax +49-7243-602-414
Seite/page 50, 307

Hewlett-Packard
Fort Collins Division
3404 East Harmony Road
Fort Collins
CO 80525, USA
Seite/page 73

Hewlett-Packard Company
Integrated Systems Division
1266 Kifer Road, MS 1021
Sunnyvale, CA 94086, USA
Phone +1-408-746-5585
Fax +1-408-746-5571
Seite/page 349

Hilti AG Befestigungstechnik
Postfach
FL-9494 Schaan
Phone +41-75-236-3026
Fax +41-75-236-2971
Seite/page 310, 311

Hilti Deutschland GmbH
Eisenheimer Straße 31
D-80687 München
Phone +49-89-57001-0

Hitachi Medical Corporation
2-1 Sintoyofuta
Kashiwa-shi
Chiba-ken 27, Japan
Phone +81-471-31-3221
Fax +81-471-31-1170
Seite/page 397

HOESCH
Metall + Kunststoff
GmbH & Co.
Postfach 10 04 24
D-52304 Düren
Phone 02422-54-312
Fax 02422-54-276
Seite/page 161

HÜPPE GmbH & Co.
Industriestraße 3
D-26160 Bad Zwischenahn
Phone +49-4403-67-370
Fax +49-4403-67-106
Seite/page 163

Hüppe Form GmbH
Sonnenschutz-
und Raumsysteme
Postfach 25 23
D-26015 Oldenburg
Phone +49-441-402-282
Fax +49-441-402-454
Seite/page 240

HYDAC Filtertechnik GmbH
Industriegebiet Werk 6
D-66280 Sulzbach
Phone +49-6897-509-01
Fax +49-6897-509-676
Seite/page 308, 324, 325

IBICO Portuguesa
Importacao et Exportacao Lda
Zona Industrial / Apartado 98
4970 Arcos de Valdevez
Portugal
Seite/page 130

IBICO Deutschland GmbH
Industriestraße 36
D-79807 Lottstetten
Phone +49-7745-610-0
Fax +49-7745-610-200

IBM Corporation
Old Orchard Road
Maildrop 139
Armonk, NY 10504, USA
Phone +1-914-765-7367
Fax +1-914-765-6015
Seite/page 22, 64, 65, 420

IBM Corporation
3039 Cornwallis
Reasearch Triangle Park
NC 27709, USA
Phone +1-919-254-8688
Fax +1-919-254-8588
Seite/page 66, 88

IDL-Industrie und Design
Licht GmbH
Chemnitzer Straße 19
D-09212 Limbach-Oberfrohna
Phone +49-3722-92345
Fax +49-3722-93057
Seite/page 218

iGuzzini Illuminazione
Deutschland GmbH
Bunsenstraße 5
D-82152 Planegg/München
Phone +49-89-856988-0
Fax +49-89-856988-33
Seite/page 222

IMPEX ELECTRONIC
Handelsgesellschaft m.b.H.
Am Metternicher Bahnhof 11
D-56072 Koblenz
Phone +49-261-2704-57
Fax +49-261-28050
Seite/page 128

Interflex
Datensysteme GmbH
Zettachring 16
D-70567 Stuttgart
Phone +49-7464-382-338
Fax +49-7464-382-118
Seite/page 62

item
Industrietechnik
und Maschinenbau GmbH
Postfach 12 01 04
D-42676 Solingen
Phone +49-212-6580-183
Fax +49-212-62049
Seite/page 330

K. E. Jensen
Grussau 59 B
D-22359 Hamburg
Phone +49-172-4101315
Fax +49-40-6033425
Seite/page 116

Jungheinrich
Aktiengesellschaft
Friedrich-Ebert-Damm 129
D-22047 Hamburg
Phone +49-40-6948-3314
Fax +49-40-6948-3586
Seite/page 381

Justus GmbH
Weidenhauser Straße 1-7
D-35075 Gladenbach
Phone +49-6462-923-303
Fax +49-6462-6811
Seite/page 241

KAI International Co., Ltd.
3-9-7 Iwamato-cho
Chiyoda-Ku
Tokyo 101, Japan
Phone +81-3-3866-3741
Fax +81-3-3864-1439
Seite/page 276

Franz Kaldewei
GmbH & Co.
Beckumer Straße 33-35
D-59229 Ahlen
Phone +49-2382-785-209
Fax +49-2382-785-255
Seite/page 166, 168

Kasper & Richter GmbH
Erlanger Straße 14
D-91080 Uttenreuth
Seite/page 285

Klöckner-Moeller GmbH
Hein-Moeller-Straße 7-11
D-53115 Bonn
Phone +49-228-602-539
Fax +49-228-602-1617
Seite/page 329

Kontron Elektronik GmbH
Oskar-v.-Miller-Straße 1
D-85386 Elching
Phone +49-8165-77-719
Fax +49-8165-77-503
Seite/page 71

KORALLE
Sanitärprodukte GmbH
Industriegebiet Hollwiesen
D-32602 Vlotho
Phone +49-5733-14-313
Fax +49-5733-14-295
Seite/page 157

Kotzolt Leuchten
L. & G. Kotzolt GmbH & Co.
Lagesche Straße 72-76a
D-32657 Lemgo
Phone +49-5261-219-280
Fax +49-5261-219-436
Seite/page 213

I. kränzle GmbH
Elpke 97
D-33605 Bielefeld
Phone +49-521-200083
Fax +49-521-200089
Seite/page 314

Kratzert & Schrem GmbH
Fabrik für Büroartikel
Hesselbühl 5
D-88630 Pfullendorf
Phone +49-7552-2609-0
Fax +49-7552-2609-10
Seite/page 131

Kyushu Matsushita Electric Co.,
Design Center
1-62, 4-Chome Minoshima
Hakata-Ku
Fukuoka-City 812, Japan
Phone +81-92-477-1373
Fax +81-92-477-1370
Seite/page 80

LaCie, Ltd.
87+ SW Creekside Place
USA-Beaverton, OR 97005
Seite/page 89

LC-Banktechnik GmbH
Heinrich-Rieger-Straße 1
D-73430 Aalen
Phone +49-7361-9481-0
Fax +49-7361-9481-18
Seite/page 117

Leica Camera GmbH
Oskar-Barnack-Straße 11
D-35606 Solms
Phone +49-6442-208-327
Fax +49-6442-208-360
Seite/page 280

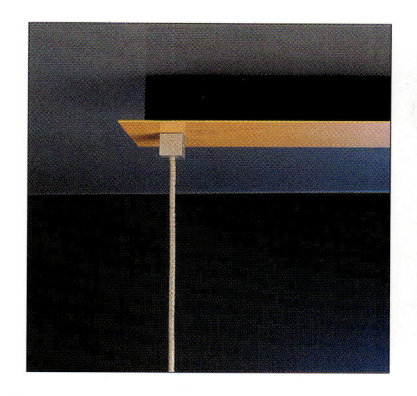

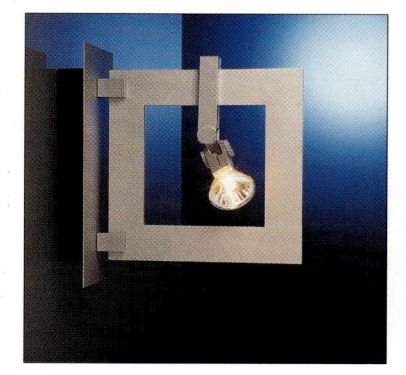

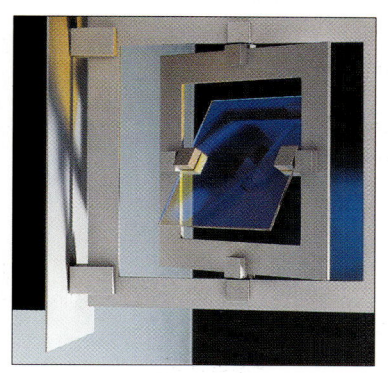

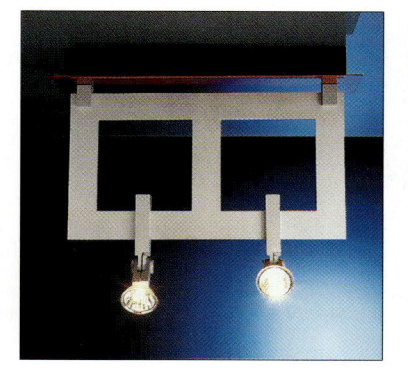

Alulite ceiling & wall · Alulite mirror

iF
Industrie
Forum
Design
Hannover

idl

idl   GmbH
Am Neuen Weg 3
82041 Oberhaching
fon   089-6131075
fax   089-6133700

HERSTELLER INDEX INDEX OF MANUFACTURERS

Leifheit AG
Leifheitstraße
D-56377 Nassau
Phone +49-2624-977255
Fax +49-2624-977402
Seite/page 171, 176

Louis Leitz Produktion GmbH-
Siemensstraße 64
D-70469 Stuttgart
Phone +49-711-8103-420
Fax +49-711-8103-486
Seite/page 132

Lindberg Optic Design A/S
Frichsparken 40
DK-8230 Åbyhøj
Phone +45-86-752911
Fax +45-86-752933
Seite/page 279

Linotype-Hell AG
Mergenthaler Allee 55-75
D-65760 Eschborn
Phone +49-6196-98-2006
Fax +49-6196-98-2194
Seite/page 79

LOEWE OPTA GmbH
Industriestraße 11
D-96317 Kronach
Phone +49-9261-99-272
Fax +49-9261-99-635
Seite/page 298, 303

Loewe Binatone GmbH
Robert-Bosch-Straße 5
D-63225 Langen
Phone +49-6103-7501-18
Fax +49-6103-7501-39
Seite/page 106

LOGITECH International SA
Moulin du Choc 1
CH-1122 Romanel/Morges
Phone +41-21-863-5078
Fax +41-21-869-9717
Seite/page 90

LTS
Licht- und Leuchten GmbH
Waldesch 24
D-88069 Tettnang
Phone +49-7542-9307-0
Fax +49-7542-53340
Seite/page 210

LUCEPLAN SPA
Via Ernesto Teodoro
Moneta 44/46
I-20161 Milano
Phone +39-2-66203411
Fax +39-2-66203400
Seite/page 217, 223

Lüderitz Licht GmbH
Rote Mühle 58
D32312 Lübbecke
Phone +49-5741-336-110
Fax +49-5741-336-112
Seite/page 214

LUNOS-Lüftung
GmbH & Co.
Ventilatoren KG
Wilhelmstraße 31-34
D-13593 Berlin
Phone +49-30-362+1-17
Fax +49-30-362+1-89
Seite/page 251

Luther & Maelzer GmbH
Hagenburger Straße 554
D-31515 Wunstorf
Phone +49-5031-174-0
Fax +49-5031-174-109
Seite/page 341

Magic Helvetia
CH-1093 La Conversion
Seite/page 192

MAGNUS OLESEN A/S
Agertoft 2, Durup
DK-7870 Roslev
Phone +45-97-592411
Fax +45-97-592922
Seite/page 116

Mannesmann Demag
Fördertechnik AG
Geschäftsbereich
Systemtechnik
Carl-Legien-Straße 15
D-63073 Offenbach
Phone +49-69-8903-468
Fax +49-69-8903-695
Seite/page 372

Mannesmann Rexroth
Pneumatik GmbH
Bartweg 13
D-30453 Hannover
Phone +49-511-2136-274
Fax +49-511-2136-429
Seite/page 339

Matsushita
Electric Works, Ltd.
International Marketing Sales
1048, Kadoma
Kadoma-shi
Osaka 571, Japan
Phone+81-6-906-4582
Fax +81-6-906-4579
Seite/page 193, 396

Mayr Schulmöbel
Gesellschaft mbH
Mühldorf 2
A-4644 Scharnstein
Phone +43-7615-2641-0
Fax +43-7615-7879
Seite/page 152

Medtronic Inc.
Product Manager Nancy
Perrypool
7000 Central Ave
Minneapolis
MN 55432, USA
Seite/page 393

MEONIC
Entwicklung und Gerätebau
Mainzerhofplatz 13/7
D-99084 Erfurt
Phone +49-361-6649310
Fax +49-361-6431782
Seite/page 87

Mercedes-Benz AG
D-70322 Stuttgart
Phone +49-7031-909816
Fax +49-7031-909771
Seite/page 370

Messmer Pen GmbH
Schützenstraße 3
D-79312 Emmendingen
Phone +49-7641-9202-0
Fax +49-7641-9202-22

Seite/page 136

MIC S.A.
1, rue de l'industrie
F-61208 Argentan
Cédex
Seite/page 383

MIC Vertriebs-GmbH
Usedomstraße 1-5
D-22047 Hamburg
Seite/page 383

mic design
Produktion GmbH
Königsturmstraße 21
D-73525 Schwäbisch-Gmünd
Seite/page 269

Microsoft Corporation
One Microsoft Way
Redmond
WA 98052-6399, USA
Phone +1-206-882-8080
Fax +1-206-936-7329
Seite/page 60

Miele & Cie
GmbH & Co.
Carl-Miele-Straße 29
D-33332 Gütersloh
Phone +49-5241-89-4141
Fax +49-5241-89-4140
Seite/page 178, 179

Mono-Metallwarenfabrik
Seibel GmbH
Industriestr. 5
D-40822 Mettmann
Phone +49-2104-9198-0
Fax +49-2104-9198-19
Seite/page 184

mor'log Produkte
Mainzer Straße 118
D-64293 Darmstadt
Phone +49-6151-898197
Fax +49-6151-898297
Seite/page 151

NABEYA KOGYO Co., Ltd.
Kurachi Mukaiyama
Seki-City
Gifu 501-32, Japan
Phone +81-575-23-1121
Fax +81-575-23-1129
Seite/page 327

NEC Technologies, Inc.
Business Unit
Vice President-Graphics
1255 Michael Dr.
Wood Dale
Illinois 60191, USA
Phone +1-708-238-7806
Fax +1-708-860-8697
Seite/page 85

NEC Corporation
Headquarter NEC Building
7-1, Shiba 5-chome, Minato-Ku
Tokyo 108-01, Japan
Phone +81-3-3798-6613
Fax +81-3-3798-6619
Seite/page 94

Nisko ARDAN GROUP
8 Timna Street
Holon Industrial Zone
Israel
Seite/page 249

NOKIA GmbH
Opitzstraße 12
D-40470 Düsseldorf
Phone +49-211-90895-464
Fax +49-211-90895-457
Seite/page 296, 419

NORDMENDE
Thomson Technology
Göttinger Chaussee 76
D-30453 Hannover
Phone +49-511-418-4301
Fax +49-511-418-4305
Seite/page 297

NRG Enterprises
7801 89th Place SE
USA-Mercer Island
WA 98040
Seite/page 246

Océ Nederland B.V.
P.O. Box 101
NL-5900 MA Venlo
Phone +31-77-359-2821
Fax +31-77-359-5471
Seite/page 54

Odenwälder
Kunststoffwerke GmbH & Co.
Gehäusesysteme KG
Friedrich-List-Straße 3
D-74722 Buchen
Phone +49-6281-404-150
Fax +49-6281-404-170
Seite/page 332

Österr. Philips
Industrie GmbH
Elektronikfabrik Wien,
Gutheil-Schoder-Gasse 10
A-1102 Wien
Seite/page 96, 403

Olivetti S.p.A.
Via Jervis, 77
I-10015 Ivrea (To)
Phone +39-125-523720
Fax +39-125-522983
Seite/page 86

Olympus Optical Co., Ltd.
Shinjuku San-Ei Building
22-2, Nishi Shinjuku
1-chome, Shinjuku-ku
Tokyo 105, Japan
Seite/page 104

Olympus Optical Co.
Europa GmbH
Wendenstraße 14-16
D-20097 Hamburg
Phone +49-40-23773-673
Fax +49-40-23773-272
Seite/page 95, 104

OMK Design Ltd.
30 Stephen Street
GB-London W1P 1PN
Phone +44-171-631-1335
Fax +44-171-631-3227
Seite/page 124

F. W. Oventrop KG
Paul-Oventrop-Straße 1
D-59939 Olsberg
Phone +49-2962-82239
Fax +49-2962-82239
Seite/page 245

...Erfolgreiche Schnittmenge...

Als Externe das Interne zu konzipieren, hat uns herausgefordert und - es hat viel Spaß gemacht! Wir freuen uns, daß unser E-PAC-Gehäusekonzept zu diesem Erfolg beigetragen hat. Herzlichen Glückwunsch unseren Partnern Hewlett Packard und Parsytec zur IF-Auszeichnung!

via 4 Design

DMT GmbH
Feinwerktechnische Komplettlösungen
Innovative Konzepte, Entwicklung, Konstruktion,
Rapid Prototyping, Beschaffungsstrategien,
Serieneinführung von elektronischen Geräten.
Schlotterbeckstraße 20, D-71034 Böblingen
Telefon 49-(0)7031-7160-0, Telefax -20

DMT

HERSTELLER INDEX INDEX OF MANUFACTURERS

Panasonic
Deutschland GmbH
Winsbergring 15
D-22525 Hamburg
Phone +49-40-8549-0
Fax +49-8549-2043
Seite/page 80

Parsytec
Computer GmbH
Jülicher Straße 338
D-52070 Aachen
Seite/page 344

Ums-Pastoe bv
Rotsoord 3
NL-3523 CL Utrecht
Seite/page 59

PERTO S.A.
BR 290, KM 75
Distrito Industrial
520 Gravataí- RS
BR-94060
Phone +55-51-489-1333
Fax +55-51-489-1503
Seite/page 88

Pfaff-silberblau
Hebezeugfabrik GmbH
Äußere Industriestraße 18
D-86316 Friedberg/Derching
Phone +49-821-7801-0
Fax +49-821-7801-299
Seite/page 380

Philips
Dictation Systems
Gutheilschodergasse 12
A-1101 Wien
Seite/page 96

Philips
International B.V.
Domestic Appliance &
Personal Care
Europaweg 8
NL-9700 AE Groningen
Phone +31-50-192318
Fax +31-50-189822
Seite/page 171, 194, 195

Philips Lighting B.V.
Centre Industrial de Miribel
Rue de Brotteaux
F-01702 Miribel
Seite/page 229

Philips Medizin Systeme
Röntgenstraße 24
D-22335 Hamburg
Phone +49-40-50782756
Fax +49-40-50782908
Seite/page 391

Pohlschröder
GmbH & Co. KG
Steinbrinkstraße 61
D-44319 Dortmund
Phone +49-231-9214-634
Fax +49-231-9214-609
Seite/page 125

Polaroid Corporation
565 Technology Square
Cambridge, MA 02139, USA
Seite/page 70

Port Incorporated
66 Fort Point Street
Norwalk, CT 06855, USA
Seite/page 129

Psion PLC
85, Frampton Street
GB-London NW8 8NQ
Seite/page 348

Psion GmbH
Saalburgerstraße 157
D-61350 Bad Homburg
Phone +49-6172-965420
Fax +49- 6172-965440

Randstad
Uitzendbureau bv
Diemermere 25
NL-1112 TC Diemen-Zuid
Seite/page 131

Ress + Sohn
Möbelfabrik
Ottelmannshäuser Straße 1
D-97631 Bad Königshofen
Seite/page 146

RIBAG Licht AG
Kesslerstraße 1
CH-5037 Muhen
Phone +41-62-73790-10
Fax +41-62-73790-18
Seite/page 212

Gebr. Richartz & Söhne
Vereinigte Stahlwarenfabriken
Merscheiderstraße 94
D-42699 Solingen
Phone +49-212-330041
Fax +49-212-330045
Seite/page 277

Rittal-Werk
Rudolf Loh
GmbH & Co. KG
Postfach 16 62
D-35726 Herborn
Phone +49-2772-505-0
Fax +49-2772-505-319
Seite/page 345

Rohde & Sohn
Industriestraße 9
D-37176 Nörten-Hardenberg
Phone +49-5503-104-1
Fax +49-5503-8318
Seite/page 328

rolly toys
Franz Schneider
GmbH & Co. KG
Siemensstraße 13-19
D-96465 Neustadt
bei Coburg
Seite/page 268

Rosenthal AG
Wittelsbacher Straße 43
D-95100 Selb
Phone +49-9287-72-566
Fax +49-9287-72-573
Seite/page 188

ROSSI DI ALBIZZATE SPA
Via Mazzini 1
I-21041 Albizzate/Varese
Seite/page 109

Rowenta Werke GmbH
Waldstraße 232
D-63071 Offenbach am Main
Phone +49-69-8504-332
Fax +49-69-8504-305
Seite/page 196

SABO
Maschinenfabrik GmbH
Auf dem Höchsten 22
D-51645 Gummersbach
Phone +49-2261-704-9
Fax +49-2261-704-104
Seite/page 264

Sahm
GmbH & Co. KG
Westerwaldstraße 13
D-56203 Höhr-Grenzhausen
Phone +49-2624-188-48
Fax +49-2624-188-60
Seite/page 189

Samsung Electronics Co., Ltd.
416, Maetan-3Dong
Paldal-Gu
Kyungki-Do 441-742
Suwon City, Korea
Seite/page 78

Samsung Electronics
Holding GmbH
Samsung House
D65843 Sulzbach
Phone +49-6196-582-0
Fax +49-6196-582-192

Scandinavian Mobility
EC-Høng A/S
Saebyvej 48
DK-4270 Høng
Seite/page 395

Scandinavian Mobility GmbH
Lohweg 2
D-30559 Hannover
Phone +49-511-95882-0
Fax +49-511-592654

K. A. Schmersal GmbH & Co.
Industrieschaltgeräte
Postfach 24 02 63
D-42279 Wuppertal
Phone +49-202-6474-861
Fax +49-202-6474-100
Seite/page 323

Schneider GmbH & Co
Produktions- und
Vertriebs KG
Martin-Heinrich-
Klaproth-Straße 28
D-38855 Wernigerode
Phone +49-3943-561-204
Fax +49-3943-561-200
Seite/page 139

Schönbuch Collection
Möbelmarketing GmbH
Benzstraße 17
D-71101 Schönaich
Phone +49-7031-7598-0
Fax +49-7031-7598-44
Seite/page 111

Schwan-STABILO
Schwanhäußer GmbH & Co.
Schwanweg 1
D-90562 Heroldsberg
Phone +49-911-567-1370
Fax +49-911-567-4444
Seite/page 137

Sedus Stoll AG
Brückenstraße 15
D-79761 Waldshut-Tiengen
Phone +49-7751-84-348
Fax +49-7751-84-360
Seite/page 112

SEGA Enterprises LTD.
23-15, 3-Chome,
Ohmori Minami, Ohta-Ku
Tokyo 143, Japan
Seite/page 284

Sega of America, Inc.
255 Shoreline Drive,
Suite 200
Redwood City, 94065 CA.
USA

Seko/LT BTicino
Einsteinstraße 1
D-79108 Freiburg
Phone +49-761-51435-12
Fax +49-761-51435-50
Seite/page 238

SHARP Corporation
22-22 Nagaike-cho,
Abeno-ku
Osaka, 545, Japan
Phone +81-6-6211221
Seite/page 97

SHARP Electronics
(Europe) GmbH
Sonninstraße 3
D-20097 Hamburg
Phone +49-40-2376-2271
Fax +49-40-2376-2300

Siemen + Hinsch mbH
Lindenstraße 170
D-25524 Itzehoe
Phone +49-4821-77101
Fax +49-4821-771130
Seite/page 340

Siemens AG
Berlin-München
Wittelsbacherplatz 2
D-80333 München
Seite/page 101, 236, 351,
352, 366, 404-407

Siemens AG
Beleuchtungstechnik
Ohmstraße 50
D-83301 Traunreut
Phone +49-8669-33-535
Fax +49-8669-33-443
Seite 228

Siemens
Medical Systems Inc.
Ultrasound Group
22010 S.E. 51st Street
Issaquah, WA 98029, USA
Phone +1-206-557-1649
Fax +1-206-557-1779
Seite/page 390

Silit-Werke GmbH & Co. KG
Postfach 13 52
D-88493 Riedlingen
Phone +49-7371-189-229
Fax +49-7371-13360
Seite/page 180

SIRRAH SRL Gruppo iGuzzini
Via Molino Rosso, 8
I-40026 Imola (Bologna)
Seite/page 222

Skidata Computer GmbH
Untersbergstraße 40
A-5083 Gartenau
Phone +43-6246-888-0
Fax +43-6246-888-7
Seite/page 374, 375

Spitzentechnik, die Maßstäbe setzt.

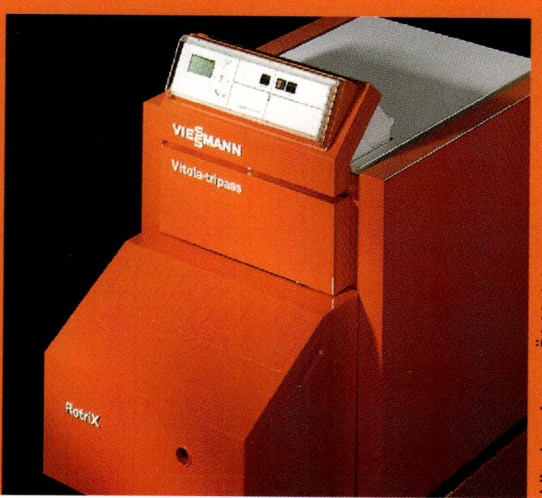

Vitola-tripass Öl-Heizkessel 18 bis 27 kW

Was heute als Spitzentechnik gelten will, muß sich vor allem an einem messen lassen: der Umweltverträglichkeit. Das heißt weniger Verbrauch an fossilen Rohstoffen und weniger Schadstoffemissionen. Lassen wir Zahlen sprechen: 60 mg NO_x/kWh und 5 mg CO/kWh (nach DIN) sind Werte, die sogar die weltweit strengsten Anforderungen des Hamburger Förderprogramms erfüllen. Erreicht werden sie von unserem Öl-Heizkessel Vitola-tripass mit RotriX-Brenner. Was auch den „Bundespreis für herausragende innovatorische Leistungen für das Handwerk 1995" wert war. Nur ein Jahr zuvor hatte der MatriX-Gasbrenner sowohl einen deutschen (BDI '94) und europäischen (EBEAFI '94) Umweltschutzpreis erhalten.

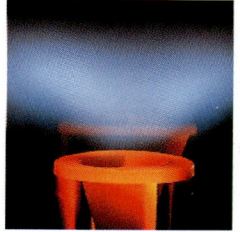

RotriX-Ölbrenner

Mit dem HighTech-, Comfort- und Basis-Programm können wir für jeden Bedarf den passenden Heizkessel bieten. Qualität ist damit keine Frage des Preises mehr.

VIESSMANN
Heiztechnik

Viessmann Werke · 35107 Allendorf (Eder)
V. 1169/2

HERSTELLER INDEX / INDEX OF MANUFACTURERS

SONCEBOZ SA
Rue Rosselet-Challandes
CH-2605 Sonceboz
Phone +41-32-981111
Fax +41-32-981100
Seite/page 326

Sony Corporation
6-7-35 Kitashinagawa
Shinagawa-ku
Tokyo 141, Japan
Phone +81-3-448-3220
Seite/page 286-289

Sony Deutschland
GmbH
Hugo-Eckener-Straße 20
D-50829 Köln
Phone +49-221-5966-0
Fax +49-221-5966-4999

Southco GmbH
Herrenlandstraße 58
D-78315 Radolfzell/Bodensee
Phone +49-7732-56091
Fax +49-7732-53039
Seite/page 320, 321

SPEZIA
Fritz Lenk GmbH Co.
Wagnerplatz 10
D-72175 Dornhan
Phone +49-7455-938912
Fax +49-7455-2290
Seite/page 259

STAEDLER MARS
Moosäckerstraße 3
D-90427 Nürnberg
Phone +49-911-9365-721
Fax +49-911-9365-400
Seite/page 138

STAFF GmbH & Co. KG
Grevenmarschstraße 74-78
D-32657 Lemgo
Phone +49-5261-212-330
Fax +49-5261-212-234
Seite/page 34, 220, 221

Stair Assist Corporation
PO Box 8157
USA-Portland, OR 97207
Seite/page 394

STENG Licht Stuttgart GmbH
Blumenstraße 36
D-70182 Stuttgart
Phone +49-711-23880-0
Fax +49-711-23880-88
Seite/page 226

Stollmann
Entwicklungs- und
Vertriebs-GmbH
Mendelsohnstraße 15D
D-22761 Hamburg
Phone +49-40-8988-288
Fax +49-40-8988-444
Seite/page 93

Supercomputing
Systems AG
Technopark 1
CH-8005 Zürich
Seite/page 82

Supercomputing
Systems B.V.
NL-3016 BG Rotterdam

Targetti Sankey Spa
Via Pratese 164-C.P. 6273
I-50145 Firenze
Phone +39-55-3791-1
Fax +39-55-3791-266
Seite/page 225

Targetti
Licht Vertriebs-GmbH
Zum Eisenhammer 7/a
D-46049 Oberhausen
Phone +49-208-26031
Fax +49-208-26037

Deutsche Telekom
Postfach 2000
D-53105 Bonn
Phone +49-228-181-9428
Fax +49-228-181-9480
Seite/page 98, 99, 413

Telia AB
Magnusladulåsgatan 2
S-118 81 Stockholm
Phone +46-8-455-2956
Fax +46-8-455-2988
Seite/page 105

Gebrüder Thonet GmbH
Michael-Thonet-Straße 1
D-35066 Frankenberg
Phone +49-6451-508-160
Fax +49-6451-508-168
Seite/page 143

Tombow Pencil Co, Ltd
6-10-12 Toshima, Kita-ku
Tokyo 114, Japan
Seite/page 135

Tombow Pen & Pencil GmbH
Urbacher Straße 12-13
D-53842 Troisdorf
Phone +49-2241-43041
Fax +49-2241-405147

TRION Präzisionselektronik
GmbH & Co. KG
Voltastraße 5
D-13355 Berlin
Seite/page 18

Umax Data System, Inc.
No. 1-1, R&D II Road
Hsinchu, Taiwan
Seite/page 84

Unifor Spa
Via Isonzo 1
I-22078 Turate (Como)
Phone +39-2-967191
Fax +39-2-96750859
Seite/page 118, 145

Unifor Vertrieb
Deutschland
Christian Robert GmbH
Barerstraße 32
D-80333 München
Phone +49-89-282248
Fax +49-89-281520

VideoGuide
209 Burlington Road
Bedford, MA 01730, USA
Seite/page 282

Viessmann Werke
GmbH Co.
Industriestraße 5
D-35107 Allendorf/Eder

Phone +49-6452-70-2331
Fax +49-6452-70-2145
Seite/page 38

Villeroy & Boch AG
Postfach 11 20
D-66688 Mettlach
Phone +49-6864-81-2652
Fax +49-6864-81-2287
Seite/page 160

Virtual i-O INC
1000 Lenora Street
Suite 600
eattle WA 98121, USA
Phone +1-206-382-7412
Fax +1-206-382-8810
Seite/page 281, 418

VOKO Vertriebsstiftung
Büroeinrichtungen KG
Am Pfahlgraben 4-10
D-35415 Pohlheim
Phone +49-6404-929-594
Fax +49-6404-929-615
Seite/page 120

Volkswagen AG
D-38436 Wolfsburg
Phone +49-5361-92-+68
Fax +49-5361-92-0466
Seite/page 368

VSG Verkehrstechnik GmbH
Alleestraße 70
D-44789 Bochum
Seite/page 384

J. Wagner GmbH
Postfach 1120
D-88677 Markdorf
Seite/page 318

Wallace & Tiernan GmbH
Auf der Weide 10
D-89305 Günzburg
Phone +49-8221-9040
Fax +49-8221-904121
Seite/page 250

WATCHPEOPLE
Schöll & Brassler GmbH
Pfingstrosenstr. 29a
D-81377 München
Phone +49-89-7192033
Fax +49-89-7195499
Seite/page 275

Max Weishaupt GmbH
D-88475 Schwendi
Phone +49-7353-83-244
Fax +49-7353-83-358
Seite/page 247

Weitnauer
Trading Company Ltd.
Petersgasse 36-38
CH-4001 Basel

Wemhöner GmbH & Co. KG
Maschinenfabrik
Lehmkuhlenweg 30
D-32052 Herford
Phone +49-5221-7702-0
Fax +49-5221-7702-39
Seite/page 357

Wiesner Hager
Möbel GmbH
Linzer Straße 22
A-4950 Altheim

Phone +43-7723-2431-411
Fax +43-7723-2431-471
Seite/page 123

Wiesner Hager Möbel GmbH
Goethestrasse 1
D-97072 Würzburg

Wiha Werkzeuge
Willi Hahn GmbH & Co. KG
Obertalstraße 3-7
D-78136 Schonach
Phone +49-7722-959-0
Fax +49-7722-959-159
Seite/page 378

WILA Leuchten GmbH
Vödeweg 9-11
D-58638 Iserlohn
Phone +49-2371-823-172
Fax +49-2371-823-200
Seite/page 211

Wilhelmi-Werke
GmbH & Co KG
Dr. Hans-Wilhelmi-Weg 1
D-35633 Lahnau

Wilkhahn
Wilkening + Hahne
Postfach 2070
D-31844 Bad Münder
Phone +49-5042-999-217
Fax +49-5042-999-497
Seite/page 30

Wilo GmbH & Co.
Nortkirchenstraße 100
D-44263 Dortmund
Phone +49-231-4102-570
Fax +49-231-4102-575
Seite/page 316

WINI Büromöbel GmbH & Co.
Postfach 11 60
D-31861 Coppenbrügge
Phone +49-5156-979-302
Fax +49-5156-979-300
Seite/page 126

WK Wohnen
Einrichtungs-GmbH
Manufact
Karin Staude
Heilbronner Straße 4
D-70771 Leinfelden-
Echterdingen
Phone +49-711-79096-0
Fax 049-79096-225

WMF AG
Eberhardstraße
D-73312 Geislingen
Phone +49-7331-25-8816
Fax +49-7331-258997
Seite/page 186, 187

WOLF-Geräte GmbH
Vertriebsgesellschaft KG
D-57517 Betzdorf
Phone +49-2741-281-235
Fax +49-2741-281-312
Seite/page 265

Zwillingswerke
J.A. HENCKELS AG
Grünwalder Str. 14-22
D-42657 Solingen
Phone +49-212-882-367
Fax +49-212-882-400
Seite/page 185

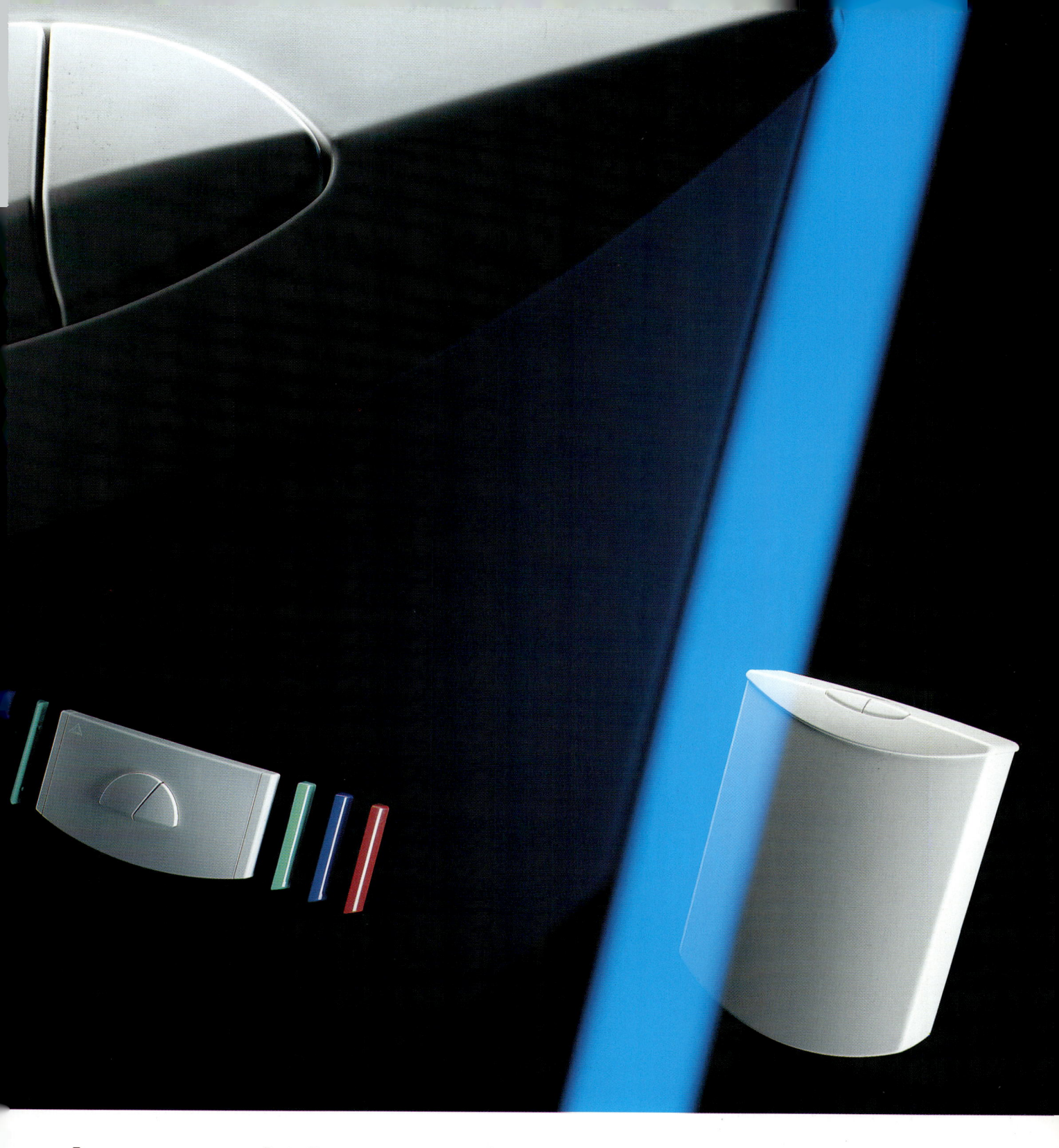

Elegant und ökonomisch

Der FRIATEC Spülkasten 4000 besticht durch eine optimale Synthese aus Ästhetik und Funktionalität: zeitlos schönes Design mit einer völlig neuen umweltschonenden 2-Mengen-Spültechnik. Die Betätigungsplatte der Unterputzspülkästen ermöglicht durch austauschbare Dekorleisten in unterschiedlichen Farben und Formen die Anpassung an eine individuelle Badgestaltung.

FRIATEC AG · Sanitair Division · Postfach 71 02 61 · D-68222 Mannheim

UNSERE PHILOSOPHIE IST EIGENTLICH RECHT EINFACH: OHNE DESIGN KEIN PREIS.*

*Abb.1: **Staff Strahlerprogramm Dancer**
1993 mit dem IF Siegel des Industrie Design Hannover als einer der „zehn Besten des Jahres" ausgezeichnet Design: Hartmut S. Engel

*Abb.2: **Staff Lichtleitsystem Wega**
1995 ausgezeichnet mit dem IF Siegel des Industrie Design Hannover. Das Prädikat „Bester der Branche 95" gilt einem individuell einsetzbarem Lichtsystem.

*Abb.3: **Zumtobel Optos**
Zahlreiche Design-Auszeichnungen bestätigen die Harmonie von elegantem Design und Variabilität. Mit unterschiedlichen Optiken bietet dieses Lichtsystem einen großen Freiraum für kreative Spielräume.

*Abb.4: **Zumtobel „Mildes Licht" RCA-Anbauleuchte**
1995 ausgezeichnet mit dem österreichischen Staatspreis für Design. Ein Leuchtensystem mit hohem Anspruch an Design und Technik. Eingesetzt in Bereichen, in denen Nutzungsvielfalt und Flexibilität gefragt sind Design: Karin Pesau

ZUMTOBEL **STAFF**
DAS LICHT ®

1

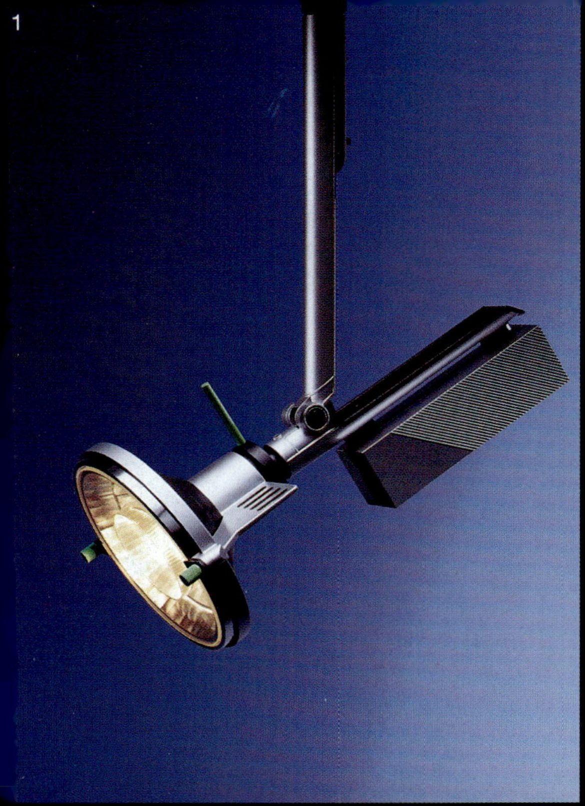

2

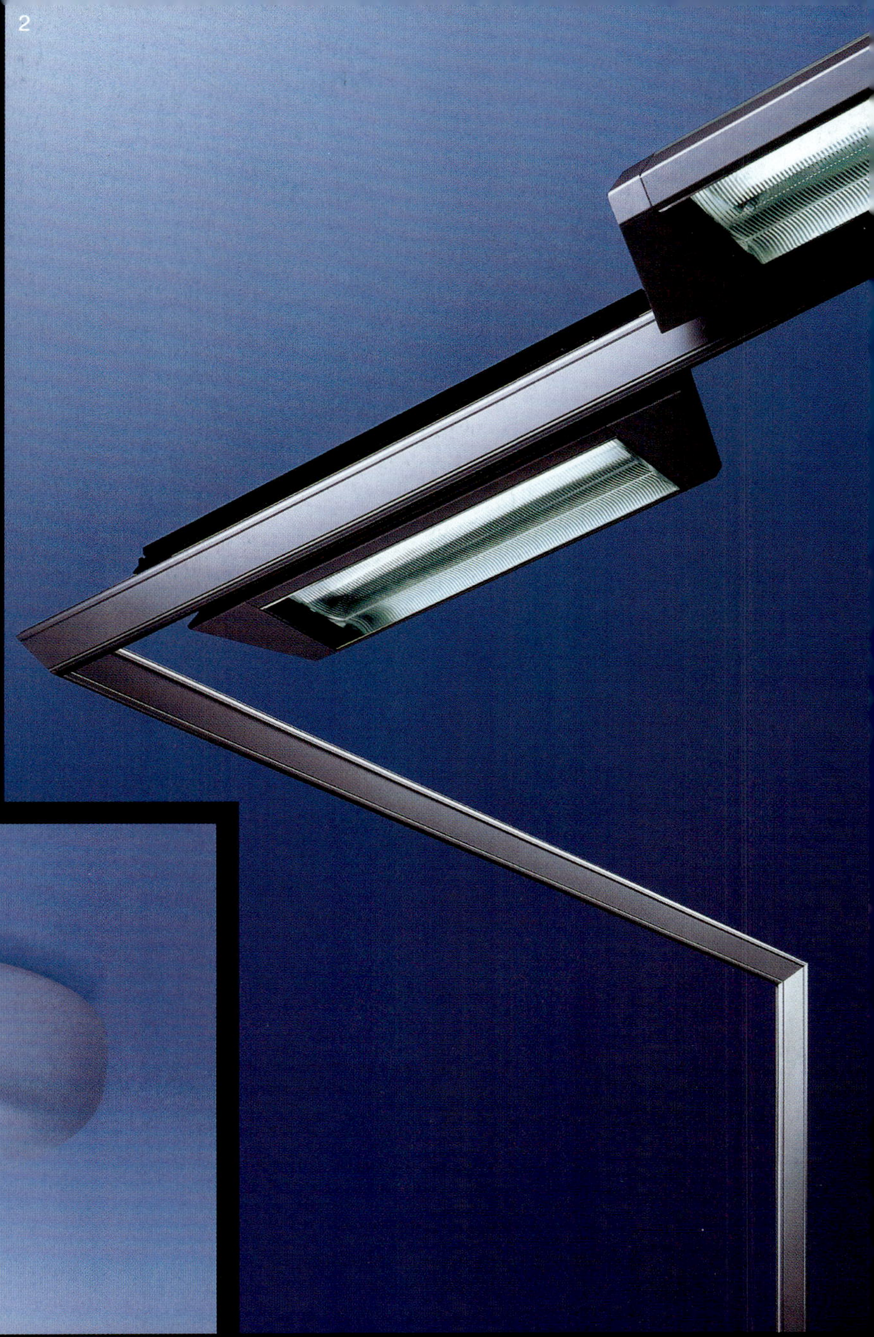

3

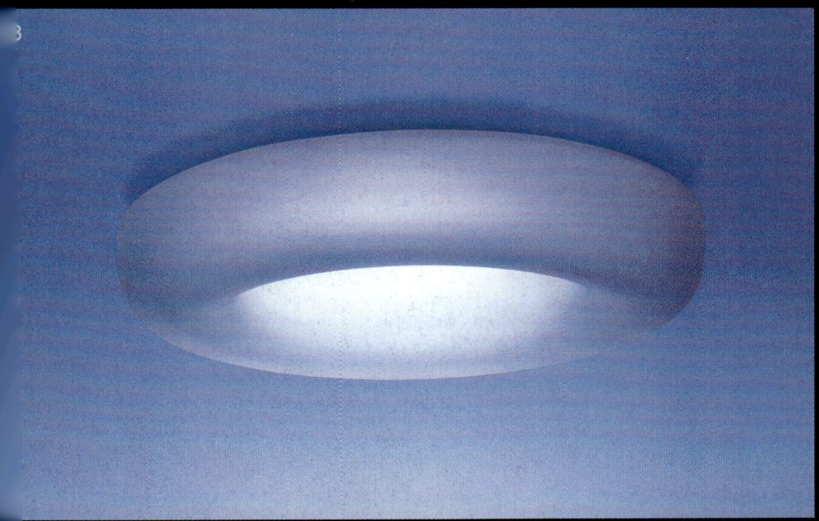

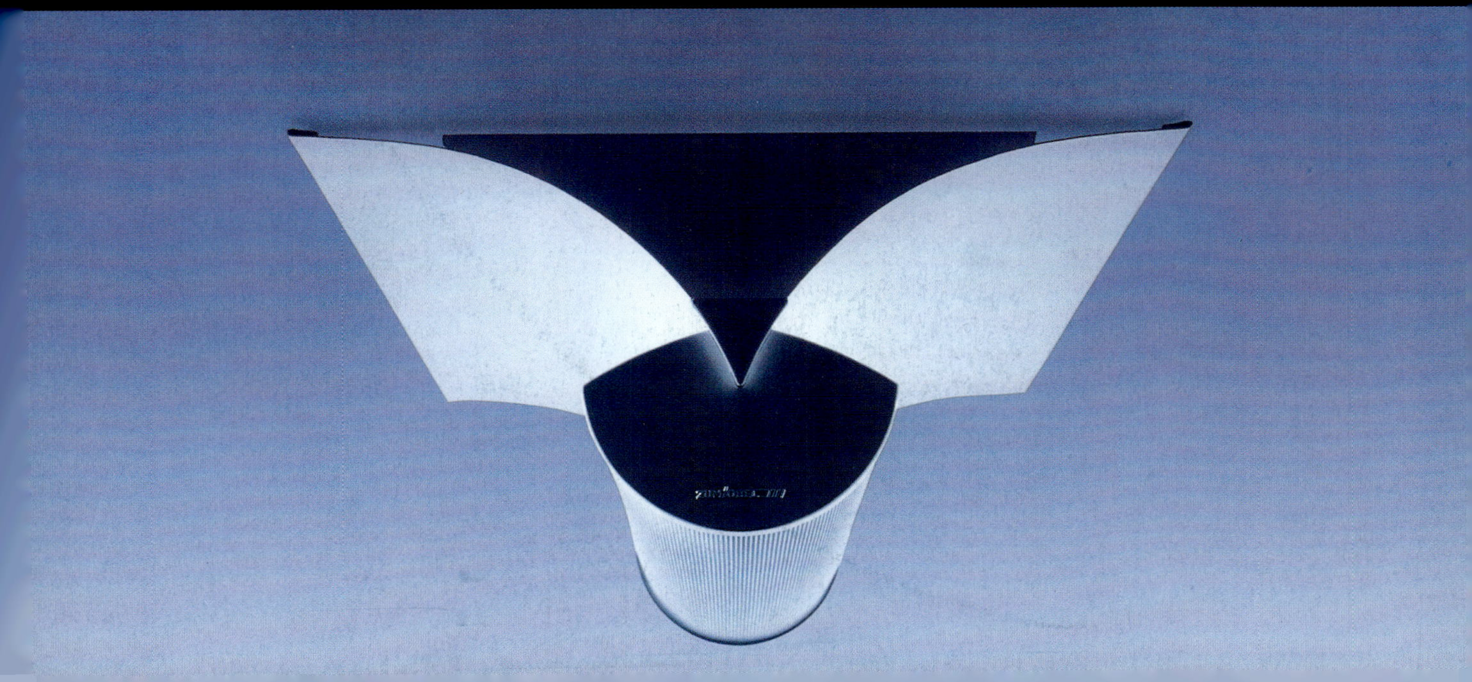

DESIGNER INDEX *INDEX OF DESIGNERS*

Thomas Althaus
Kaiser-Wilhelm-Ring 24
D-40545 Düsseldorf
Seite/page 146

Karl Axel Andersson
Ringgatan 1
S-21212 Malmö
Seite/page 177

APEX PRODUCT DESIGN
215 Vauxhall Bridge Road
GB-London SW1V 1EJ
Phone +44-171-6306070
Fax +44-171-6309938
Seite/page 254

Artefakt, Fiegl/Pohl
Alte Fabrik
Liebigstraße 50-52
D-64293 Darmstadt
Phone +49-6151-20749
Fax +49-6151-20759
Seite/page 162

Artemide S.p.A.
Designdepartment
Via Bergamo 18
I-20010 Pregnana Milanes
Fax +39-2-93290362
Seite/page 224

Ascom Corporate
Ziegelmattstraße 1
CH-4503 Solothurn
Phone +41-65-243128
Fax +41-65-242382
Seite/page 103

Atelier für Gestaltung
Andreas Papenfuss
Rothäuserbergweg 9
D-99425 Weimar

Axis Design Europe
2 Cosser Street
GB-London SE1 7BU
Phone +44-71-633 9911
Fax +44-71-620 0238
Seite/page 110

Babel Design
Burgplatz 4
D-74199 Untergruppen-
bach-Vorhof
Phone 07130-6886
Fax 07130-1657
Seite/page 161

Design Ballendat
Linzer Straße 22
A-4950 Altheim
Phone +43-7723-4421
Fax +43-7723-4422
Seite/page 152

Claire Bataille & Paul Ibens
Venusstraat 14
B-2+0 Antwerpen 1
Seite/page 114

Baum-Design
Entwicklung von
Industrieprodukten
Am Hohrain 1
D-79199 Kirchzarten
Phone +49-7861-6969
Fax +49-7661-61781

Seite/page 356, 378

Klaus Begasse
Arminstraße 3
D-70178 Stuttgart
Seite/page 227

BERNDS
Wittekindstraße 16
D-32758 Detmold
Phone +49-5231-17777
Fax +49-5231-17778
Seite/page 377

BEST. Büro für
Produktgestaltung
Am Brögel 19
D-42283 Wuppertal
Phone +49-202-88595
Fax +49-202-899355
Seite/page 237

Prof. Bitsch & Partner
Kaiser Wilhelm Ring 23
D-40545 Düsseldorf
Seite/page 235

BMW Design
BMW-Haus
Petuelring 130
D-80788 München
Phone +49-89-38245448
Fax +49-89-38243696
Seite 46, 377

Prof. Ulrich Böhme
Plauckstraße 78
D-70184 Stuttgart
Seite/page 122

Klaus Botta Designbüro
Lammertstraße 15-19
D-63075 Offenbach
Phone +49-69-868816
Fax +49-69-864824
Seite/page 130, 275

BPR design
Florianstraße 18
D-70188 Stuttgart
Phone +49-711-16650-0
Fax +49-711-16650-21
Seite/page 385

Achim Bredin
Alte Bahnhofstr. 198-200
D-44892 Bochum
Seite/page 202

Wolf Peter Bree
Gerberstraße 3
D-30916 Isernhagen-
Kirchhorst
Phone +49-5136-8976-12
Fax +49-5136-8976-80
Seite/page 272, 273

BTicino S.p.A.
Corso Porta Vittoria 9
I-20122 Mailand
Seite/page 238

Büchin DesignGmbH & Co.
Betriebs-KG
Colditzstraße 30
D-12099 Berlin
Phone +49-30-7515080
Fax +49-30-7513085

Seite/page 155

busse design ulm gmbh
institut für produktplanung
und produktentwicklung
Nersinger Straße 18
D-89275 Elchingen
Phone +49-7308-2043
Fax +49-7308-818-99
Seite/page 264, 329

Canon Deutschland GmbH
Europark Fichtenhain A10
D-47807 Krefeld
Phone +49-2151-345-330
Fax +49-2151-345-333
Seite/page 81

Achille Castiglioni
Piazza Castello 27
I-20121 Milano
Seite/page 219

C. D. B
The Agency C. D. G.
Prof. Luigi Colani
Schmidhofweg 1
D-50769 Köln
Seite/page 245

Leo Christmann
Äußerer Möhnhof 4
D-73566 Bartholomä
Seite/page 117

cognito
Kommunikation und Design
Sofienstraße 21
D-68794 Oberhausen-
Rheinhausen
Phone +49-7254-75732
Fax +49-7254-72772

CONTEC DESIGN GBR
Wollenweberstraße 22
31303 Burgdorf
Seite/page 399

Crown Equipment Corporation
14 West Monroe St.
New Bremen, Ohio 45869
USA
Seite/page 365, 381

Design Drei
Kaiser-Wilhelm-Straße 13
D-30559 Hannover
Phone +49-511-513123
Fax +49-511-513133
Seite/page 98, 99, 341, 413

Design Partners
Fassaroe House
Bray, Ireland
Seite/page 90

Design Planet
Hausener Straße 2
D-63165 Mühlheim
Phone +49-6108-71915
Fax +49-6108-72447
Seite/page 93

designpraxis diener ulm
Irisweg 3
D-89079 Ulm
Phone +49-7305-964814
Fax +49-7305-964830

Seite/page 38, 241, 316

Designprojekt GmbH
Dresden
Semperstraße 15
D-01069 Dresden
Phone +49-351-4715061
Fax +49-351-4715066
Seite/page 402

Design Tech
Jürgen R. Schmid
Zeppelinstraße 53
D-72119 Ammerbuch
Phone +49-7073-9189-0
Fax +49-7073-9189-17
Seite/page 389

Designworks USA
2201 Corporate Center Drive
CA 91320 Newbury Park
USA
Phone +1-805-4999590
Fax +1-805-4999650

desko Ingenieurbüro
für design und konstruktion
Krebenweg 19
D-74523 Schwäbisch Hall
Phone +49-791-59110
Fax +49-791-59368
Seite/page 354

Dialogform
Wallbergstraße 3
D-82024 Taufkirchen
Phone +49-89-6128251
Fax +49-89-6128253
Seite/page 268

Dietz
Design Management GmbH
Oskar-von-Miller-Straße 54
D-60314 Frankfurt/Main
Phone +49-69-405705-0
Fax +49-69-442530
Seite/page 148

Van Dijk/Eger/Associates
Huis ter Heideweg 56
NL-3705 LZ-Zeist
Seite/page 346

Van Dijk, Eger
Associates GmbH
Nottulner Landweg 90
D-48161 Münster
Phone +49-2534-800160
Fax +49-2534-800161
Seite/page 346

3 D factory
Wulfsbrook 40
D-24133 Kiel
Seite/page 340

Eckart + Barski
Corporate Industrial Design
Deutschherrnufer 32
D-60594 Frankfurt am Main
Phone +49-69-626977
Fax +49-69-629695
Seite/page 400

Erwin Egli
Pfeffergässlein 43
CH-4051 Basel
Seite/page 212

Gesundes Sitzen
kann so gut aussehen.

PORTO

Ob klassisch-elegant oder farbig-modern, in dezentem Leder oder mit frischen Dessins. PORTO garantiert gesundes, dynamisches Sitzen. Vom Sekretariat bis zum Chefbüro.

Sedus®

Prospekte und
Händlernachweis:

Sedus Stoll AG
Brückenstraße 15
D-79761 Waldshut
Tel. (07751) 84-247
Fax (07751) 84-245

DESIGNER INDEX *INDEX OF DESIGNERS*

ELU INTERNATIONAL
Black & Decker GmbH
Richard-Klinger-Straße
D-65510 Idstein
Phone +49-6126-21-2786
Fax +49-6126-21-2753
Seite/page 262, 263

design studio
hartmut s. engel
Monrepos-Straße 7
71634 Ludwigsburg
Phone +49-7141-2345-0
Fax +49-7141-2345-20
Seite/page 34, 214, 299

Exhibitgroup
Giltspur Inc.
201 Mill Road
Edison, New Jersey
NJ 08817, USA
Phone +1-908-248-3484
Fax +1-908-287-3663
Seite/page 108

Wulf Fiedler
Auf dem Grat 7
D-14195 Berlin
Seite/page 217

Fitting Design
Abenra 31
DK-1624 Kopenhagen K
Seite/page 260

FLUKE CORPORATION
P.O. Box 9090
Everett
WA 98206-9090, USA
Seite/page 350

Fraunhofer Institut
für Arbeitswissenschaft
und Organisation
Nobelstraße 12
D-70569 Stuttgart
Phone +49-711-970-2173
Fax +49-711-970-2299
Seite/page 185

Frazer
Design Consultants Ltd.
6 Hampstead West
224 Iverson Road
GB-London NW6 2HL
Phone +44-71-624-6011
Fax +44-71-328-6085
Seite/page 348

frog design
4600 Bohannon Drive,
Suite 101
Menlo Park, CA 9402, USA
Phone +1-415-328-3764
Fax +1-415-328-3766
Seite/page 90

frog design inc.
1327 Chesapeake Terrace
Sunnyvale, CA 94089
USA

Konstantin Grcic
Erhardtstraße 10
D-80469 München
Phone +49-89-2011926
Fax +49-89-2011944
Seite/page 177

Grundig Produkt Design
Kurgartenstraße 37
D-90762 Fürth
Phone +49-911-703-7253
Fax +49-911-708736
Seite/page 107, 294, 295

Christina Halskov
Havehuset Bregade 76 A
DK-1260 Kopenhagen
Seite/page 395

Hampf
Industrial Design AB
P.O. Box 2032
S-42911 Särö
Phone +46-31-937130
Fax +46-31-936891
Seite/page 105

Hartmann & Selic
Industriedesign
Riedingerstraße 24/F16
D-86153 Augsburg
Phone +49-821-422098
Fax +49-821-422099
Seite/page 380

Heidelberger
Druckmaschinen AG
Konstruktionsbüro III/F + E
Kurfürstenanlage 52-60
D-69115 Heidelberg
Phone 06221-92-7342
Fax 06221-92-7329
Seite/page 258, 259

Hitachi, Ltd.
Design Centre
1-280 Higashi-koigakubo
Kokubunji-shi
Tokyo 185, Japan
Phone +81-423-26-7149
Fax +81-423-27-7797
Seite/page 397

Hervé Houplain
87, Av. Denfert Rochereau
F-75014 Paris
Seite/page 128

Hood Association
Marrion Place
Dublin 2, Ireland
Seite/page 92

i Design AG
Poststraße 10
CH-4562 Biberist
Phone +41-65-322812
Fax +41-65-324812
Seite/page 360

ID&S
Industrie-Design Schindler
Alte Straße 9
D-64521 Wallerstädten
Phone +49-6152-54936
Fax +49-6152-53031
Seite/page 391

IDEO
81 Hartwell Avenue
USA-Lexington,
MA 02173
Phone +1-617-863-0022
Fax +1-617-863-0022
Seite/page 70, 282

IDEO Product Developement
1527 Stockton Street
USA-94133 San Francisco, CA
Phone +1-415-6172310
Seite/page 85, 284

IDEO Product Development
660 High Street
Palo Alto, CA 94301, USA
Phone +1-415-617-2310
Fax +1-415-323-9183
Seite/page 393

Industrielle Produkte
Hans Joachim Krietsch GmbH
Ingolstädter Straße 60
D-80939 München
Phone +49-89-3119941
Fax +49-89-3116061
Seite/page 318

Jacob Jensen Design
Hejlskovvej 104
DK-7840 Hoejslev
Seite/page 181

King-Miranda Associati
Via Forcella 3
I-20144 Milano
Phone +39-2-8394963
Fax +39-2-8360735
Seite/page 222

KISKA Industrial Design
Niederalm 297
A-5081 Anif
Phone +43-6246-3488
Fax +43-6246-3488-18
Seite/page 374, 375

Martin Kliesch
Hünefeldstraße 75
D-42285 Wuppertal
Seite/page 244

Könekamp & Bross
Wilhelm Raabe Straße 7
D-39014 Braunschweig
Phone +49-531-790404
Fax +49-531-795443
Seite/page 357

Industrial Design, H. Krug
c/o EMCO
Innovationscenter Salzachtal
Bundesstraße Nord
A-5400 Hallein
Phone +43-6245-892-0
Fax +43-6245-892-728
Seite/page 309

Kubus produkt design
Langer Wall 18
D-37574 Einbeck
Phone +49-5561-72969
Seite/page 150

Dorian Kurz & Partner
Engelsberg 44
D-42697 Solingen
Phone +49-212-336983
Fax +49-212-337198
Seite/page 163

Lammel und Kratz
Victoriastraße 24
D-52066 Aachen
Seite/page 158

Lang
Produkt Design
Alwinenstraße 12
D-65189 Wiesbaden
Phone +49-611-376345
Fax +49-611-371991
Seite/page 115

Jürgen Lange Design
und Partner
In der Stegmühle
D-71120 Grafenau
Phone +49-7033-44113
Fax +49-7033-42886
Seite/page 111

Frank Lenz
Reinickendorfer Straße 73
D-13347 Berlin
Phone +49-30-4555415
Fax +49-30-4554198
Seite/page 18

Les Ateliers du Nord
Antoine Cahen &
Claude Frossard
Place du Nord 2
CH-1005 Lausanne
Phone +41-21-320-5807
Fax +41-21-320-5843
Seite/page 192, 274

David Lewis
Store Kongensgade 110 c
DK-1264 Copenhagen
Seite/page 42

Lichtenvort Design
Bützgenweg 2
D-45239 Essen
Phone +49-201-407096
Fax +49-201-402267
Seite/page 342

Lindinger & Partner
Brahmsstraße 3
D-30177 Hannover
Phone +49-511-623088
Fax +49-511-392884
Seite/page 366

Studio
De Lucchi
Via Pallavicino, 31
I-20145 Milano
Phone +39-2-430082-300
Fax +39-2-43008244
Seite/page 86, 224

LUNAR Design
537 Hamilton Avenue
Palo Alto, CA 94301, USA
Phone +1-415-326-7788
Seite/page 72

MA Design
Steinstraße 6
D-24118 Kiel
Phone +49-431-800-02-11
Fax +49-431-800-02-12
Seite/page 79, 95

PeterMaly
Design und
Innenarchitektur
Oberstraße 46
D-20144 Hamburg
Seite/page 143

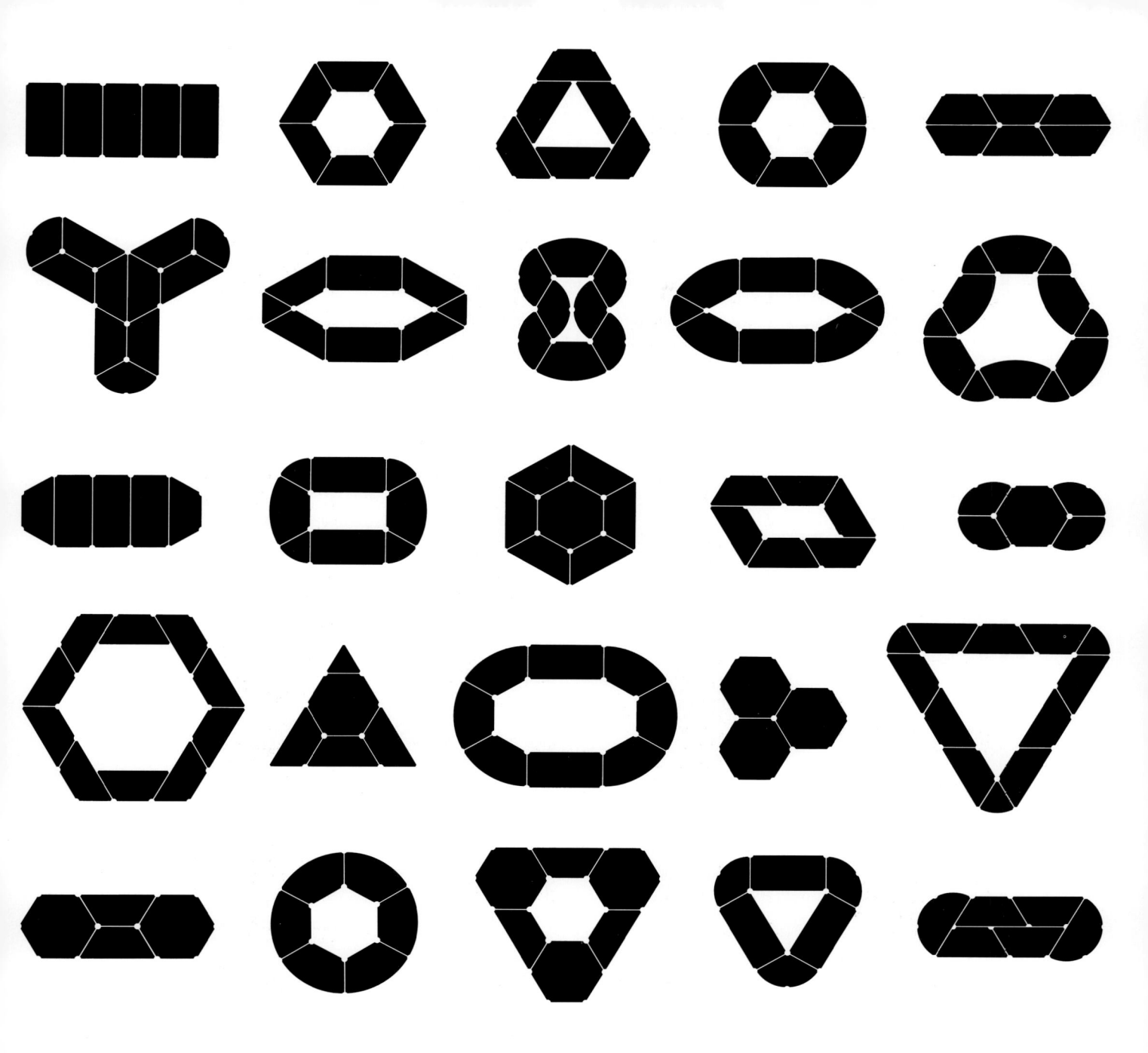

Zeichen der Zeit: Radius, das flexible Konferenztisch-Programm. Mit nahezu unbegrenzten Möglichkeiten. Und mit einer Auszeichnung vom Industrie Forum Design Hannover. Mehr Informationen unter Telefon: 02 31/92 14-421. Oder per Fax: 02 31/92 14-609.

INDUSTRIE FORUM DESIGN HANNOVER

Mehr Ideen pro m². **Pohlschröder**
Ein Steelcase Strafor-Unternehmen

DESIGNER INDEX *INDEX OF DESIGNERS*

Silvia Mantowski
Krämerbrücke 33
D-99084 Erfurt
Seite/page 87

Charles Marks
Oude Braak 19
NL-1012 PS Amsterdam
Phone +31-20-240706
Fax +31-20-240706
Seite/page 144

Matsushita Electric Works Ltd
A & I Design Office
1048 Kadoma, Kadoma-shi
Osaka 571, Japan
Phone +81-6-908-6819
Fax +81-6-906-4579
Seite/page 193

Design Mattis
Karlstraße 96
D-64285 Darmstadt
Phone +49-6151-65001
Fax +49-6151-65002
Seite/page 182

Medienlabor München
Lothringer Straße 13
D-81667 München
Seite/page 414

megaform
Designstudio Stockburger
Petzvalstraße 50
D-38104 Braunschweig
Phone +49-531-374689
Fax +49-531-375955
Seite/page 392

Mehnert, Wahrheit & Partner
Flurstraße 13
D-70372 Stuttgart
Phone +49-711-5590575
Fax +49-711-5590574
Seite/page 259

Mercedes-Benz Design
D-71059 Sindelfingen
Phone +49-7031-90-9816
Fax +49-7031-90-9771
Seite/page 370

Meyer-Hayoz AG
Brühlbergstraße 89
CH-8400 Winterthur
Phone +41-52-20901-02
Fax +41-52-20901-09
Seite/page 82

MHO Design
Oswaldo Mellone
Rua Iraci, 272
BR-01457-000 Sao Paulo-SP
Seite/page 88

MIC S.A.
1, rue de l'industrie
F-61208 Argentan Cédex
Seite/page 383

moll design
reiner moll & partner
Turmgasse 7
D-73525 Schwäbisch Gmünd
Phone +49-7171-67542
Fax +49-7171-5754
Seite/page 160

Montgomery Pfeifer
461 Bush Street
San Francisco, CA 94108
USA
Seite/page 91

Jasper Morrison
92 Newark Street
GB-London E1 2ES
Phone +44-71-2470123
Fax +44-71-2471030
Seite/page 148

NABEYA KOGYO
Co Ltd
Kurachi Mukaiyama
Seki-City
Gifu 501-32, Japan
Phone +81-575-23-1121
Fax +81-575-23-1129
Seite/page 327

NEC Design Ltd
20-36, 2-chome
Takanawa
Minato-Ku
Tokyo 108, Japan

Neumeister Design
Industrial Design Team
Von-Goebel-Platz 8
D-80638 München
Phone +49-89-171774
Fax +49-89-1784792
Seite/page 62, 71, 106

Michael Niebuhr
Lohe 1 b
D-22941 Bargteheide
Seite/page 381

Fritz Niggemann-Tolxdorff
Urbachstraße 40
D-45239 Essen
Seite/page 379

ninaber/peters/krouwel
industrial design
de witte port
Noordeinde 2d
NL-2311 CD Leiden
Phone +31-71-5141341
Fax +31-71-5130410
Seite/page 59, 134, 211

NOKIA
Design Center
Opitzstraße 12
D-40470 Düsseldorf
Phone +49-211-90895-464
Fax +49-211-90895-457
Seite/page 296, 419

Océ Nederland B.V.
Industrial Design Department
P.O. Box 101
NL-5900 MA Venlo
Phone +31-77-359-2821
Fax +31-77-359-5471
Seite/page 54

Olympus Optical Co., Ltd.
Shinjuku San-Ei Building
22-2, Nishi Shinjuku
1-chome
Shinjuku-ku
Tokyo 105, Japan
Seite/page 104

OMK Design Ltd.
30 Stephen Street
GB-London W1P 1PN
Phone +44-171-631-1335
Fax +44-171-631-3227
Seite/page 124

Ottenwälder & Ottenwälder
Sebaldplatz 6
D-73525 Schwäbisch Gmünd
Phone +49-7171-69624
Fax +49-7171- 69675
Seite/page 230

Luciano Pagani
Via Daniele Crespi 15
I-20123 Milano
Seite/page 118

Ole Palsby
Strandvejen 203
DK-29+ Hellerup
Seite/page 187

Andreas Papenfuss
Rothäuserbergweg 9
D-99425 Weimar
Seite/page 139

Patzak Design
Beckstraße 25
D-64287 Darmstadt
Phone +49-6151-424851
Fax +49-6151-424852
Seite/page 76

Philips Corporate Design
Building OAN, P.O. Box 218
NL-56+ MD Eindhoven
Phone +31-40-732179
Fax +31-40-732325
Seite/page 96, 171, 194, 195, 229, 391, 403

Phoenix Product Design
Kölner Straße 16
D-70376 Stuttgart
Phone +49-711-9559760
Fax +49-711-559392
Seite/page 61, 156, 168, 298, 300

polyform
Pappenheimstraße 9
D-80335 München
Phone +49-89-596181
Fax +49-89-5504494
Seite/page 332

Porsche Design
Flugplatzstraße 21
A-5700 Zell am See
Phone +43-6542-7227-0
Fax +43-6542-7227-22
Seite/page 278

Michael Post
Rabenstraße 71
D-88471 Laupheim
Seite/page 174

pro Industria
Büro für Industrial Design
Merscheider Straße 94
D-42699 Solingen
Phone +49-212-320581
Fax +49-212-338613
Seite/page 277

PULS Design
Mainzer Straße 118
D-64293 Darmstadt
Phone +49-6151-898302
Fax +49-6151-898297
Seite/page 151

Random Product Design Ltd
29 Grand Union Centre
West Row
GB-London W10 5AS
Phone +44-1252-794099
Fax +44-1252-794959
Seite/page 317

Raved Designs
57 Wingate Street
Herzliya Pituach 46752, Israel
Phone +972-9-572182
Fax +972-9-572128
Seite/page 239, 249

Aldo Rossi
Via Santa Maria alla Porta 9
I-20123 Milano
Phone +39-2-7201+46
Seite/page 188

RWTH
Rheinisch Westfälische
Technische Hochschule Aachen
Institut für Fördertechnik
und Schienenfahrzeuge
Seffenter Weg 8
D-52074 Aachen
Phone +49-241-80-5563
Fax +49-241-8888-145
Seite/page 384

Marc Sadler Design
Via dei Torreti 5
I-31011 Asolo (Treviso)
Seite/page 219

Samsung Electronics Co., LTD.
Design Center/Planning Group
21st Fl., Yonsei Jaedan
Servance Bldg., 84-11. 5-Ga
Namdaemoon-Ro, Chung-Ku,
Seoul 100-095, Korea
Seite/page 78

Richard Sapper
Via Beretta 3
I-20121 Milano
Phone +39-2-867266
Seite/page 78

Scala Design
Technische
Produktentwicklung GmbH
Wolf-Hirth-Straße 23
D-71034 Böblingen
Phone +49-7031-226908
Fax +49-7031-227809
Seite/page 310

Schaefer Design
Einwanggasse 23
A-1140 Wien
Seite/page 149

Schlagheck Design
Tegernseer Landstraße 161
D-81539 München
Phone +49-89-651089-01
Fax +49-89-651089-90
Seite/page 210

Finding new ways

FESTO

Festo KG

Postfach
D-73726 Esslingen
Telefon 07 11 / 91 99 21-15
Telefax 07 11 / 91 99 21-2
Limburgstraße 31
D-73734 Esslingen

DESIGNER INDEX *INDEX OF DESIGNERS*

Schmidt-Lackner-Design
Römerstraße 45
D-69115 Heidelberg
Phone +49-6221-163280
Fax +49-6221-163783
Seite/page 285

Michael Schneider
Körnerstraße 12
D-50823 Köln
Seite/page 184

Scholpp
Produktgestaltung
Untere Gasse 13
D-71739 Oberriexingen
Phone +49-7042-98242
Fax +49-7042-98281
Seite/page 164

schroerdesign
Ludwig-Marum-Straße 38
D-76185 Karlsruhe
Phone +49-721-591303
Fax +49-721-555571
Seite/page 248

Günther Schulz
Ringelstraße 22
D-42897 Remscheid
Seite/page 314

Siebeneinhalb
Biggel + Schmitz
Nithackstraße 7
D-10585 Berlin
Phone +49-30-3417034
Fax +49-30-3427063
Seite/page 125

Siemens Design
St.-Martin-Straße 76
D-81541 München
Phone +49-89-4133-3411
Fax +49-89-4133-1753
Seite/page 26, 101, 228, 236, 351, 352, 390, 404-407

Dave Skinner
Design
43 Pelican Lane
Redwood Shores
CA 94065
USA
Seite/page 349

Johnny Soerensen
Architekt M.A.A.
Groennegade 3
DK-1107 Copenhagen
Phone +45-33-325030
Fax +45-33-324272
Seite/page 116

Sony Design Center
6-7-35 Kitashinagawa
Shinagawa-ku
Tokyo 141, Japan
Phone +81-3-3448-2111
Seite/page 286-289

Sottsass Associati Srl
Via Melone 2
I-20121 Milano
Phone +39-2-864441
Fax +39-2-809596
Seite/page 166

SOUTHCO, Inc.
210 N. Brinton Lake Road
Concordville
PA 19331, USA
Phone +1-215-358-6346
Fax +1-215-358-6312
Seite/page 320, 321

Uwe Spannagel
Mauritius Wall 80
D-50676 Köln
Phone +49-2175-2515
Fax +49-2175-2515
Seite/page 92

Philippe Starck
27 Rue Pierre Poli
F-92130 Issy
Les Moulineaux
Phone +33-1-41088282
Fax +33-1-41089665
Seite/page 201

Andreas Störiko
Milano, Italy
Seite/page 32

Design A. Storz GmbH
Wiesenweg 18
A-5700 Zell am See
Seite/page 271

STUDIOWERK-Design
Kern. Schirrmacher
Forellenstraße 11
D-82266 Inning
Phone +49-8143-1869
Fax +49-8143-8711
Seite/page 334

SYN
Product Design
Oeltzenstraße 10
D-30169 Hannover
Phone +49-511-131122
Fax +49-511-131122
Seite/page 153

TEAM MICKLITZ
Königsturmstraße 21
D-73525 Schwäbisch-Gmünd
Phone +49-7171-62195
Fax +49-7171-38521
Seite/page 269

TEAMS
Slany Design GmbH
Heilbronner Straße 50
D-73728 Esslingen
Phone +49-711-312079
Fax +49-711-312040
Seite/page 132, 171, 176, 180, 247, 261, 372

TEUFEL DESIGN
Stergweg 44
D-89079 Ulm
Seite/page 250

THOMSON
multimedia
Design Center
Philippe Starck
F-92050 Paris
La Défense 5
Seite/page 297

Studio Thun
9, Via Appiani
I-20121 Mailand
Phone +39-22900-0270
Seite/page 189

Rud Thygesen
Oestergade 26 C
DK-1100 Kopenhagen
Phone +45-33-123242
Fax +45-33-322780
Seite/page 116

Universität Essen
Gesamthochschule Essen
Lehrstuhl für
Industrial Design
Universitätsstraße 12
D-45141 Essen
Phone +49-201-183-3355
Fax +49-201-183-2787
Seite/page 112

Hans Vetter
Geroksstaffel 1
D-70180 Stuttgart
Seite/page 226

Via 4
Design GmbH
Inselstraße 1
D-72202 Nagold
Phone +49-7452-8399-12
Fax +49-7452-8399-12
Seite/page 50, 154, 307, 344

Virtual i.-O INC
1000 Lenora Street
Suite 600
Seattle WA 98121
USA
Phone +1-206-382-7412
Fax +1-206-382-8810
Seite/page 281, 418

VOKO Vertriebsstiftung
Büroeinrichtungen KG
Am Pfahlgraben 4-10
D-35415 Pohlheim
Phone 06404-929-594
Fax 06404-929-615
Seite/page 121, 122

Volkswagen AG
1701/0 E/Design
D-38436 Wolfsburg
Phone 05361-92-0068
Fax 05361-92-0466
Seite/page 368, 369

Weaver Associates
2a Westbourne
Grove Mews
GB-London W11 2RU
Phone +30-71-2214420
Fax +30-71-7271880
Seite/page 398

wiege, wilkhahn
entwicklungs gesellschaft
Postfach 20 70
D-31844 Bad Münder
Phone +49-5042-999-900
Fax +49-5042-999-901
Seite/page 30

Wings of Design
Atelier für
Produktgestaltung
Berliner Straße 39 a
D-42275 Wuppertal
Phone +49-202-645028
Fax +49-202-649818
Seite/page 323

Witte Design
Kleines Gäßchen 15
D-63075 Offenbach
Phone +49-69-868855
Fax +49-69-868051
Seite/page 345

Peter Zegers
Josef-Jenne-Weg 7
D-58708 Menden
Seite/page 208

Zender
Design Studio
Friesenstraße 8
D-32760 Detmold
Phone 05231-58274
Seite/page 213

ZIBA Design Inc.
305 Northwest
21st Avenue
Portland
Oregon 97209, USA
Phone +1-503-223-9606
Fax +1-503-223-9785
Seite/page 60, 73, 89, 246, 270, 394